THE OXFORD HISTORY
OF ENGLAND

Edited by SIR GEORGE CLARK

THE OXFORD HISTORY OF ENGLAND

Edited by SIR GEORGE CLARK

THE
LATER STUARTS
1660–1714

BY

SIR GEORGE CLARK
Sometime Provost of Oriel College, Oxford

SECOND EDITION

OXFORD
AT THE CLARENDON PRESS

Oxford University Press, Walton Street, Oxford OX2 6DP

Oxford New York Toronto
Delhi Bombay Calcutta Madras Karachi
Petaling Jaya Singapore Hong Kong Tokyo
Nairobi Dar es Salaam Cape Town
Melbourne Auckland

and associated companies in
Berlin Ibadan

Oxford is a trade mark of Oxford University Press

Published in the United States by
Oxford University Press, New York

ISBN 0-19-821702-1

First published 1934
Second edition 1956
Reprinted (with corrections) 1961, 1965, 1972, 1976
Reprinted 1979, 1985 (three times), 1987, 1988, 1991

Printed in Great Britain by
Butler and Tanner Ltd, Frome, Somerset

PREFACE TO THE SECOND EDITION

IT is now twenty-one years since the first edition of this volume was published. Even during the war, which interrupted historical studies less gravely in other countries than in Great Britain, research on this period was active. It has added so much to our knowledge that many of the details and some even of the more important conclusions of the book needed revision. In successive reprints corrections were made within the limits of what could be done without disturbing the paging, but it has at last become necessary to reset the entire text. While I was engaged in the work my friend Mr. Godfrey Davies very kindly read the whole book and gave me much valuable information and advice. My thanks are due not only to him but also to the Rockefeller Foundation and to the Trustees of the Henry E. Huntington Library, whose generosity enabled me to work undisturbed in the wonderful environment of that seat of learning.

G. N. C.

OXFORD
15 *April* 1955

PREFACE TO THE FIRST EDITION

THE footnotes in this volume are not intended to show what authorities have been followed, except in passages where, for one reason or another, a reference seems to be specially needed. My acknowledgements of obligations to printed books are thus given jointly by the footnotes and by the Bibliography at the end. Amongst more personal debts I must first mention that which I owe to the fourteen other writers whose books, along with this, are intended to form a complete History of England. Our discussions have taught me much that could not have been learnt in any other way. I have also, for a good many years past, had frequent conversations with three historians who know this period as if they had lived in it: Sir Charles Firth, Dr. Keith Feiling, and Professor Geyl. It would be impossible to name all the others who have answered my questions, corrected my mistakes, and freely shared their knowledge with me: I can only express my deep sense of gratitude. It has been my good fortune that the book has been read in proof by Mr. E. S. de Beer. His expert knowledge of the period and his literary judgement have been of equal value. In preparing the book for the press I have received generous and skilful help from Mrs. O. S. Franks. In many parts of the work, from the drudgery upwards, I have owed most to my wife.

G. N. C.

OXFORD
15 *April* 1934

NOTE TO THE REPRINT OF 1940

IN the present reprint a number of corrections have been made, for some of which I have to thank reviewers and other scholars.

G. N. C.

OXFORD
1 *September* 1939

CONTENTS

CONTENTS

LIST OF MAPS

At end

INTRODUCTION

THIS volume deals with English history under the later
Stuarts, that is from 1660 to 1714. It begins with the
Restoration of King Charles II. His father Charles I had
been defeated in civil war, and put to death in 1649. Attempts
had then been made to govern England as a puritan republic,
but they had ended in failure. Many of those who had joined in
them came to recognize that only a king could unite the English
nation in a healthy political life. They therefore combined with
those who had always remained loyal to the house of Stuart,
and together they brought back Charles II. The nation has
never repented of this decision of 1660 in favour of monarchy.

Charles lived until 1685. His reign was troubled by disputes
about religion and about the limits of the royal power, but the
mass of Englishmen had learnt their lesson, and there was no
new civil war. Charles was succeeded by his Roman catholic
brother James II, formerly duke of York, in whose short reign
the troubles came to a head. In 1688 James lost his throne, but
even the revolution was bloodless. It did more than bring in
a new king, William III, who reigned jointly with his wife,
Mary II, until 1694, and as a widower alone until 1702. It also
registered another decision from which the nation has never
gone back, that the monarchy should be a constitutional or
limited, not an absolute, monarchy, that England should be
a country governed by law. William III was succeeded by
Mary's sister, Queen Anne, in whose reign, which lasted until
1714, the unity of England under its constitutional monarchy
was consolidated in the face of great dangers, and broadened
by the union with Scotland. During the four reigns the governing class became accustomed to a rudimentary kind of party
government.

Looked at from another point of view, the period is divided
into five intervals of peace and four wars. There were two wars
against the Dutch in the reign of Charles II (1665–7 and 1672–4)
and afterwards two against the French, the Nine Years War
under William III (1689–97) and the War of the Spanish
Succession (1702–13). In all these wars the navy played a great
part, and in the French wars the British army was much larger

and more important than it had ever been before. The size and expense of the fighting services brought about a transformation of public finance, and reacted in many ways on the constitution. Partly because of the wars, and partly in spite of them, there was a great growth of commerce and of overseas possessions, while industry adjusted itself to these new conditions. Its changes were aided by a great scientific and intellectual movement, which made itself felt, and more powerfully, in other directions. It affected literature, and even the arts, of which architecture and music were the most vigorous. Its rationalism contributed to the establishment of religious toleration, though without full civil rights for dissenting minorities. Religion and religious institutions lost their pre-eminence in politics and thought.

The whole period, though it decided so much, lasted only fifty-four years, less than one full human life. There were old men living at the end of it who could remember it all—Gilbert Burnet, bishop of Salisbury, its historian; the duke of Marlborough, the greatest of all English soldiers; Sir Isaac Newton, the greatest mathematician of his age; Sir Christopher Wren, the best English architect; and William Penn, the founder of Pennsylvania. As they looked back upon it, each of them must have seen it in the light of his own experience, and in the experience of each there was something which was unfamiliar, perhaps even unintelligible, to some or all of the others. The modern historian, who tries to see the history of England in their time as a whole, has to reckon with the experience not only of these five representative men, different as they were, but with all the innumerable others at home and abroad by whom English history was made. Some, like the statesmen and artists, were articulate. Now and again some surviving record enables us to see into the mind of a country parson or a shopkeeper or a labouring man; but the great majority can be known only obscurely and in the mass, from what others have said about them. Yet England lived in all of them, and English history cannot be known as a whole except by giving his due to each. Only in this way can we seek the connexions between the different aspects of the national life, political, religious, artistic, or whatever they may be. No one man can have knowledge or sympathy wide enough to do justice to all; the historian can only make his contribution to a common stock. It will be useful in proportion to its fairness; and this book is intended to give an impartial account of English history under the later Stuarts.

NOTE ON DATES

DURING this period two calendars were in use. The Julian or Old Style used in England was several days behind the Gregorian or New Style used in most continental countries, ten days in the seventeenth century, eleven in the eighteenth. Thus William III sailed from Holland on 11 November 1688, but when he landed in England four days later it was the anniversary of the Gunpowder Plot. There was another difference between the two calendars. On the Continent the year began on 1 January. Sometimes that reckoning was used in England, but for most purposes the year began on Lady Day, 25 March. Thus William and Mary were proclaimed king and queen on 13 February 1688 by the English reckoning, but on 23 February 1689 by the New Style. In order to avoid the inconvenience of giving dates in the form $\frac{13}{23}$ February 168$\frac{8}{9}$ or $\frac{24 \text{ March } 1708}{4 \text{ April } 1709}$, in this volume all dates in the text are given simply in New Style. Dates which occur in references to books in the footnotes are given as they are in the books. It should be noted that Ireland used the Old Style and Scotland retained the Old Style but dated the beginning of the year from 1 January.

I

THE RESTORATION

THE Restoration of King Charles II released the English
people from the fears and repressions of nearly twenty
years. All over the country the maypoles were set up again,
loyal toasts were drunk immoderately, puritanism was repudiated and derided. The rejoicings were greatest along the
line of road where the king made his way with pageantry and
ceremonial from Dover harbour to his palace of Whitehall.
Noblemen and gentlemen attended on horseback, mayors and
aldermen in their gowns, country-folk were morris-dancing on
the greens; children strewed flowers and sweet herbs before the
cavalcade. For the principal actors, however, the merry-making
and display were the background to important and sometimes
even anxious business. They, especially the king himself and his
chancellor, Sir Edward Hyde, as they rode along, were picking
up the threads of government, making decisions, getting to know
the men with or against whom they would now have to work,
well aware that the success they were enjoying needed to be consolidated by sound policy and could easily be jeopardized by an
error of temper or judgement.

It was on the personal character of the king more than on any
other single factor that success or failure depended, and he had
many of the gifts that were needed. He reached the age of
thirty on the day when he entered London, a good figure of a
man and in vigorous health. His individuality was impressed
on the world in general by his appearance and habits. Every one
knew his spaniels and his long stride as he walked in St. James's
Park. He was easy of access, unassuming, and friendly. He was
an interminable talker, but his talk was shrewd and witty. In
his roving and adventurous life he had learnt to know men and
women. That he had many mistresses was not, at least in
the national mood of the moment, or according to the common
standards of the period, a serious disadvantage. Experience was
to show that, for all his courage and good nature, he was not the
man to make any heroic stand for principle, unless indeed it
were the one principle to which he seemed to owe his throne,

that of hereditary right. For the present this was hidden in the future. His facile professions of goodwill convinced those who appealed for his aid. Nor did it seem to be a serious matter that, although he was capable of strenuous work in an emergency, in ordinary times he lacked application.[1] In this respect his qualities seemed to be admirably supplemented by those of the chancellor. Edward Hyde, still only of middle age, was a lawyer-statesman of the right English line, a good speaker, good on paper, diligent, firm, and sincere. He had conferred on the country one imperishable service: he had worked continuously and successfully to identify the royal cause with the cause of legality, and the Restoration therefore stood, as he stood, not for absolutism and arbitrary power, but for the common law, for the historic institutions of the country, including parliament, for regularity and precedent and good order.

It did indeed stand also, in the nature of things, for the victory of a party or a group of parties in the nation over those who had been in office and in power during the protectorate. In their first task, therefore, that of manning the administration, Charles and Hyde were faced in a fairly acute form by a difficulty which always awaits a restored régime. An important part of the nation, including many of those who had recently been at the centre of affairs, could not be employed. Among those who could, there were some men whose services in the past deserved reward but who were unlikely to be equally valuable in the different conditions of the new era, while, in the distribution of offices care had to be taken to keep a balance between the cavaliers and the presbyterians, whose alliance had brought them back to power. This work was well done. Hyde was the dominant figure of the government,[2] while Sir Edward Nicholas, one of the secretaries of state, and Ormonde, who became a duke and lord steward,

---

[1] Some modern historians have chosen to deny this accepted view; but the grounds they advance, besides being insufficient in themselves, cannot stand against the express statements of six men who knew Charles well and, in their different ways, were all good judges of character, Clarendon (to Ormonde, 19 September 1662, in Lister, *Life of Clarendon*, iii. 222), Cominges (to Louis XIV, 4 February 1664, in J. J. Jusserand, *A French Ambassador at the Court of Charles II*, p. 87), Burnet (*History*, ed. Airy, ii. 468), Pepys (*Diary*, 15 May 1663), Halifax (*Character of King Charles II*), Evelyn (*Diary*, 4 February 1685).

[2] He was raised to the peerage as Lord Hyde in November 1660 and created earl of Clarendon in 1661. Born in 1609, he had helped to prepare the impeachment of Strafford, but from 1641 had been an adviser of Charles I. He went into exile in 1646 and became titular lord chancellor in 1658; dismissed in 1667, he died in France in 1674.

had served like him on Charles's council in his exile. The office of lord treasurer went to the earl of Southampton, the most influential of the royalists who had remained in England, a former councillor of Charles I. On the other hand, the new royalists were not slighted. George Monck, the strongest man in England, was content with the Garter, a dukedom (with the title of Albemarle), an estate, a small pension, the non-resident lord-lieutenancy of Ireland, which he resigned after less than two years, and a seat at the council board.[1] Edward Mountagu, who had brought over the navy to Charles, had performed an easier task than the man who had brought over the army, but he too received the Garter, with an earldom and offices in the household and in the navy.[2] Monck's kinsman, William Morice, became the second secretary of state, and another member of the privy council was Sir Anthony Ashley Cooper, a young man, 'sagacious, bold, and turbulent of wit', who had changed sides once already before becoming one of the links between Charles and the presbyterians. His career was to take a direction which none foresaw in the first days of the new régime.[3]

For the time being the king and his ministers could do little or nothing by themselves except fill up offices and carry on the daily work of administration. To settle the larger outstanding questions and to lay down the main lines of the necessary settlement they needed a parliament. The skill and wisdom of Clarendon had made the Restoration unconditional, but in the Declaration of Breda Charles had promised four things. There was to be a free and general pardon, excepting only such persons as should thereafter be excepted by parliament. There was to be a liberty to tender consciences; no man was to be disquieted or called in question for differences of opinion in matter of religion, and the king would be ready to consent to such act of parliament as should be offered to him for the full granting of that indulgence. All things relating to the recent grants, sales, and pur-

[1] Born 1608; served at Cadiz 1625, then in the Dutch army, in Scotland 1640, in Ireland and in the royalist army in England; taken prisoner by Fairfax 1644; served in Ireland, under parliament and, after vicissitudes, commanded army in Scotland, with one interval, from 1651; died 1670.

[2] Born 1625; distinguished himself on the parliamentary side in the civil war and from 1656 served at sea; blown up in his ship at the battle of Solebay 1672.

[3] Born 1621, he inherited large estates, served first under Charles I and then in the parliamentary army; created Lord Ashley 1661, earl of Shaftesbury and lord chancellor 1672, dismissed 1673; president of the council 1679 but dismissed in the same year; charged with high treason 1681; fled to Holland 1682, died 1683.

chases of land were to be determined in parliament. The king would be ready to consent to any act or acts of parliament for the payment of arrears of pay due to Monck's army. The men were to be received into the royal service upon as good pay and conditions as they then enjoyed. It was therefore upon parliament that the responsibility was to fall of working out in practice the four great principles upon which the Restoration was grounded.

The convention parliament which had resolved that Charles should be king was an irregular assembly and it was not adequate for this task. The house of commons, in which there was a strong presbyterian element,[1] had been elected in the usual way; but the elections had been held without the king's writ. For the time being it seemed best to avoid a general election, and so the convention was kept in existence until 9 December, its status being defined by an act declaring it to be a legal parliament, though to make assurance doubly sure, its proceedings were subsequently confirmed by its successor. In its seven months of work the convention disposed of three large and difficult pieces of business. The divergence of views within it between the revengeful extremists and the more moderate men who had some degree of sympathy with the late régime led to a good deal of delay, and this sometimes irritated the king and his ministers, who naturally wanted to allay as quickly as possible both the clamourings of their friends for justice, and the fears of their reconciled opponents that they might be exposed to persecution. What was done was, on the whole, moderate and wise, and reached a degree of clemency unusual in that cruel age. An Act of Indemnity was passed pardoning all those who had taken part in the rebellion or the subsequent republican governments except some fifty named individuals. The process by which these names were selected involved some ugly bargaining and some concessions to influence, but in the end those condemned to death included only two men not prominently concerned in the trial and execution of Charles I, and of these only one was executed. That was the younger Sir Harry Vane, an extremist who had opposed both Charles I and Cromwell. He died because

[1] Miss L. F. Brown, in *Eng. Hist. Rev.* xxii. 51, gives evidence against the formerly accepted view that there was a presbyterian majority. In the circumstances of the moment it was, however, misleading to divide members simply into those who were presbyterians and those who were not, and the proportions of the different groups cannot be stated numerically.

the new government feared him, and in spite of the king's promise to spare his life.

Closely involved with the indemnity was the land problem. The confiscation or compulsory sale of the estates of the church and of the royalists had been one of the methods by which the revolutionary governments had crushed opposition and raised funds; but it was impossible simply to hand back all such landed property to its former owners or their heirs. Some of it had been taken away from them years before and had changed hands in the interval, so that it was now held by persons who had paid good money. The new owners were not unrepresented in the convention, and, in any case, while the government could not afford to buy them out, it would not do anything so unjust and so unpopular as to evict them without compensation. Whatever was done, someone must be injured; but a course was taken which did as little harm as was well possible. Lands previously belonging to the king or queen or to the church were restored, as were those directly confiscated from their owners. Even here, however, some of the intruders were able to buy their estates again, since they could provide cash which the rightful owners needed more than their land. Royalist individuals, however, who had parted with property by their own acts, even though compelled to do so in order to pay the sums exacted from them, were not reinstated except in the few cases where they could prove in a court of law irregularities not condoned by the Act of Indemnity. This was the first serious example of Charles's ingratitude. Like most other restored monarchs, he had to reckon with the dangers of going to extremes in rewarding his faithful friends.

In all this both king and convention showed that, as Englishmen have often done before and since, they could behave like unimaginative men of business, although there were strong passions alive, both base and noble, which might easily have wrecked this golden chance of national co-operation.[1] In their third large piece of reconstruction, that of the national finances, their work was not in the event so satisfactory, though at the time of the initial arrangement they cannot justly be charged with anything worse than a lack of foresight and skill. The financial problem had several different sides. The fundamental point was that much of the constitutional quarrel between the earlier

---

[1] How far the resentment of the dispossessed passed into the party opposition of later years is a complicated question which needs further research.

Stuarts and their subjects had been due to finance: the nation had been unwilling to give the kings as much money as they asked, or indeed as much as they needed, and the system of raising a revenue had been such as to give rise to collisions and shortages of money whenever parliament was out of harmony with the Crown. Part of the revenue, that from Crown lands and feudal dues, was the ancient hereditary possession of the Crown, but this, fell far short of the needs of government and had to be supplemented by parliamentary grants. These had been paid for by taxes as antiquated as some of the feudal items of hereditary revenue, and a reform was needed in the whole machinery of taxation and of public finance in general. The experience of the interregnum, when very large sums had been needed to pay for military and naval expenditure, had gone some way to show what could be done by more modern methods; but for the moment the need for money was so pressing that no general reorganization could be expected.

Money was wanted for three purposes. First, the ordinary daily outlay of government must be provided for. Secondly, the army must be paid off. Monck had persuaded and manœuvred it into withdrawing from its old habit of interfering with politics; but so long as it remained on foot, uncertain whether its extensive arrears of pay would ever be forthcoming, it was a menace to order. Thirdly, there were some abnormal expenses to be met, especially debts contracted by Charles I in the last seven years of his life and others owing by Charles II on account of services rendered to him in his exile. No question was raised of paying the debts of the government of the protectorate: its creditors had backed a losing cause and had to bear the consequences. The convention, after a good deal of pressure from the king, made a provision which was intended to be adequate and which his advisers accepted in the first instance as being so. Special provisions were made for paying off the army partly by assessments, that is, by taxes of a type much used during the troubles, a direct tax or rate on real and personal property, in which each locality had to raise a named sum and itself assess the contribution of each individual taxpayer. No special provision was made for the floating debt of half a million on the navy or for the royal debts: what was assigned to these had to come from the revenue available for current expenditure. The method adopted for providing this revenue marked a slight advance towards more modern methods. The king surrendered his feudal dues from wardships, tenures *in capite*, knight service, and the other survivals from the medieval system in which the monarchy was financed by its position at the head of the land-holding system. He was granted instead by parliament for life certain sources of income from taxation which, together with the remaining hereditary revenues of the Crown, were calculated to yield a fixed yearly income of £1,200,000.

Unfortunately this sum was not adequate for a reasonable scale of expenditure. The financial system was indeed so badly organized that it was impossible to foresee how much money would be needed. There was no unified system of national accounts. The treasury had no control over the administrative or departmental finance; this was exercised by the king in his privy council, but only parliamentary committees drew up statements of the debts of the various branches of the administration. To make matters worse, the calculations on which the new taxes were fixed turned out to be wrong. During the first years of Charles's reign they never yielded as much as they were intended and expected to yield. This was due partly to the lack of the information necessary for correctly forecasting the yield of taxes; partly to the depressed condition of trade and economic life generally, an unforeseen factor, which diminished the yield of every tax. For some years the commons did all that was 'humanly possible' to keep their promise to Charles: they increased the excise and in 1662 imposed a very unpopular hearth-tax; but the task was beyond their powers. Nor was the administration able to tide over those difficulties which were temporary by a sound and economical method of borrowing. The lord treasurer, Southampton, was disinterested and a hard worker, but neither he nor his subordinates had much skill in finance. 'It took Charles's servants seven years to grope their way to anything like a proper system of raising credit on the revenue. During these seven years the treasury tried every conceivable and clumsy method of anticipating the revenue receipts by means of credit,'[1] especially the farming of taxes and the pledging of taxes to the city of London or to private bankers. In farming the customs the treasury dealt with sound and reliable men, but, in the various local farms into which the excise had to be cut up,

---

[1] W. A. Shaw, *Calendar of Treasury Books and Papers*, i. xxxvii. From 1671 the customs were not farmed but controlled by commissioners appointed by the Crown.

there was much trouble with dishonest or defaulting farmers and with over-estimates of yield. Justices of the peace did not back up the farmers against the resisting populace.

If parliament and the treasury were, from the start, unequal to coping with the financial problem, the king did what little he could to help them. He paid the cash portion of his wife's dowry, £180,000, into the exchequer, as also the purchase money for Dunkirk. He mortgaged and finally sold Crown lands to the value of some hundreds of thousands of pounds, paying the money into the exchequer. It is indeed impossible to trace fully the history of such parts of his expenditure as did not pass through the exchequer, and it was here that he provided for his mistresses. It has been argued that these ladies really cost the country very little; but it was indisputably unfortunate that they should have cost a penny.[1] Southampton, like Ormonde and Clarendon, objected to them in the first place on grounds of morality and decorum, but it was a secondary complaint not lacking foundation that, at a time of need, they caused wasteful expenditure. Clearly the financial situation was one which, in the event of any unusual strain, would create a need for more revenue, with a corresponding reluctance and suspicion on the side of parliament. Until this new and heavier strain was felt, however, it was not intolerable. Debt was piling up, but not unmanageably. The deficit with which Charles began his first Dutch war was over a million; but if it had not been for the war, history would have forgotten it. It was a deficit of somewhere near one year's parliamentary revenue, less than one year's revenue from all sources. To have such a handicap at the beginning of a war was, however, a serious matter, and thus it came about that one of the wedges which split the cohesion of the Restoration settlement was that of financial shortage.

From the technical point of view of the lawyer there was no necessity for a new settlement of the constitution. Nothing that had taken place since the outbreak of the Civil War needed to be undone because none of it had been done in such a way as to have any legal effect. The decisions of the courts of law in the cases

[1] The worst instance belongs to a period of comparatively sound finance. It is the perpetual grant of the 'Richmond shilling' on coal made in 1677 to Charles's French mistress, the duchess of Portsmouth, on behalf of her son the duke of Richmond: at the time of the grant the proceeds of the tax already approached £10,000 a year. See J. U. Nef, *Rise of the British Coal Industry* (1932), ii. 306.

that had come before them were confirmed by a special act. Charles II had been in theory king since the moment of his father's execution in 1649, and none of the acts done since that time which would normally have required the participation of the king could be regarded as having been validly done. On the other hand, all those measures of the Long Parliament which had received the assent of Charles I were valid. The abolition of the prerogative courts held good. From Clarendon's point of view the restored monarchy was none the worse for being without these prerogative courts, the star chamber and high commission, the council of the North and the council of the Marches of Wales. They had been more than instruments of an unpopular policy; they had been rivals of the ordinary courts of law. All that was done, therefore, to define the legal nature and effect of the Restoration was to pass a short act of parliament, the first act of the first regular parliament of the reign, which not only affirmed the nullity of all the proceedings of the usurping governments, but prescribed the penalties of praemunire—loss of all property and imprisonment for life—for all who should maintain in writing or speech that any of them had been valid. The act also repudiated the opinion that any of the obligations entered into during the revolutionary period, for instance by the Solemn League and Covenant, still were or ever had been binding.

There were few prosecutions under this act. Its main purpose was fulfilled by the declaratory clauses. In the eyes of the law the Restoration meant merely the terminating of illegalities, not the setting up of something new. The simplicity of the legal position did not, however, correspond with the social realities. A constitution is the machinery, the system of legal and customary forms, by which social forces are enabled to express themselves in acts of state; and, whatever might be the theory of the matter, it was impossible that the same constitutional system could be adequate or could even come into operation again after so many years of upheaval. There were, of course, some institutions so toughly rooted that they survived this, as they survived other revolutions. Although the organization of the legal profession altered considerably, no substantial change took place in the law courts. The attempt to substitute the English language for French and Latin in law-books and legal proceedings was abandoned. Nor was there any marked change in the local administration by justices of the peace, though, as we shall see, there were changes in municipal corporations. The attempts of the law reformers of the first two Stuart reigns to introduce ideas and methods from Roman law and other sources extraneous to the common law of England were not resumed, the more so since the institutions specially favourable to these attempts, the prerogative courts, were not revived. Where the changes came about was in the apparatus of central control and in the parliamentary machine which kept such contact as there was between central control and public opinion.

The parliamentary machine was restored to its old state. The house of lords had ceased to exist during the revolutionary period, but it began coming back to life when the Restoration was being prepared. First there assembled the few peers who had fought against Charles I, then the new peers who had succeeded their fathers since his time, afterwards the loyal peers, so that soon after Charles's return the house was with one exception complete. The exception was that of the bishops, who were excluded by an act, which had duly received the assent of Charles I, disabling all ecclesiastics from exercising civil authority. There was much to justify such a law, and in the first phase of the Restoration, when the bishops carried themselves high and the presbyterians were strong in the convention, they were still left out of parliament, but they were so much a part of the old order that their return was bound to come, as it did in 1662. The old house of lords was thus reconstituted, and Charles kept it pretty much as it had been. At his return there were 142 peers and, although he created a number of peerages then and at other times, especially when he had to reward his supporters in party strife, at the end of his long reign there were only 145.[1] He did not at first expect the house to play so important a part as it did in politics; it gave a lead in much of the keenest party strife of the reign, and it engaged in a series of disputes with the house of commons.

Disputes between the two houses have arisen in times of acute party difference, especially when the social authority of the peerage is changing or ill-defined. This second condition was now present. The three subjects of dispute between the two houses each show its effect. The first was that of the commons' claim to control finance. Financial control had been one of the

---

[1] The increase of numbers down to 1714 was noticeable but not important: at that date there were 26 spiritual and 187 temporal peers, including the 16 Scottish representative peers who had sat since 1708, a total of 213.

major issues in the time of Charles I, and, as we have seen, it was to be so again. In the interregnum, finance had been managed by parliamentary committees, and the commons now showed in several ways that they intended to keep some degree of control. They made a new claim that money bills not only must be first introduced in their house but must not be amended in the other. In a series of disputes over minor taxes in 1661 and 1671 they made this claim good. The second series of disputes ended mainly in favour of the lords; they were concerned with the judicial powers of the upper house. In the leading case of *Skinner* v. *The East India Company* they did indeed fail to establish their right to act as a civil court of first instance. In *Shirley* v. *Fagg* in 1675, however, they acquired the new judicial function of hearing appeals from the court of chancery. They held fast to their right to try members of their own body indicted for treason or felony. In the third class of disputes, those arising from impeachments, they further strengthened their position as against the commons. Impeachment is a process in which the commons act as accusers and the lords as judges. It was frequently resorted to in the time of Charles II, and against offenders of two kinds. The less important were those who were rightly or wrongly accused of crimes committed in their personal and private capacity; the more important were ministers who were impeached because the commons objected to their policy, and of these not one was in the end condemned. To use impeachment in such cases was, in fact, straining the law. Some were saved by the peers, others by the intervention of the king; but the upshot of much discussion of principles and details on these occasions was to strengthen the position of the lords as controlling the operation of the system.

The commons had strengthened their hold on finance, and they carried over from the revolutionary period a method of working which was later to provide the means by which they gradually increased their influence over the administration. This was the system of committees, the foundation of all development in procedure. The composition of the house of commons was the result of a long historical growth, and to a great extent it was founded on conditions which had long passed away. Constituencies were unequal, electoral qualifications were various and almost all irrational, with the result that some parts of the country were unrepresented and, where there was representation, it was haphazard. The short-lived written constitutions of the protectorate had shown that greater regularity could be introduced without difficulty. Clarendon himself recognized that it would be desirable to renew the attempt, though he thought it must be postponed to some more convenient season.[1] A man who was in some ways typical of the prevailing tendencies of thought, Sir William Petty, also saw the absurdity of the existing anomalies,[2] but the favourable opportunity of the restoration was not taken, and so it happened that first one thing and then another postponed the step, so that in the end it was never taken until 1832.

The first obstacle was the revival of opposition to the Crown. It became part of the policy of the restored government to exclude its opponents from the municipal corporations which returned four-fifths of the members of the house of commons. From the time of the remodelling of municipal charters in the interregnum to the Occasional Conformity Act in Queen Anne's time, the moves and counter-moves in this matter were far more important than mere questions of anomalies, and by the latter date a new obstacle to reform had, as we shall see, appeared. The Corporation Act of 1661 set up commissioners who, during the following three years, cleared up the uncertainties regarding the validity of the charters under which the municipal corporations were acting. The house of commons did not allow the Crown to make as thorough a revision of municipal liberties as it had hoped, but the general tendency was to restrict parliamentary elections to Anglican common councils. The same policy was pursued when occasion offered by judicial intervention in municipal disputes.[3] In the redistribution of parliamentary seats no more was done than to grant two members each to the city and county of Durham, which had hitherto been unrepresented because they formed the palatinate or ecclesiastical principality. A step important for the distant future was, however, taken by the commons in 1673–8 when they made such objections to the granting of representation to the borough of Newark by the king that this prerogative was never again exercised, and the reform of parliament was left to parliament itself.

More crucial for the present than the questions about the

[1] *Great Rebellion*, ed. W. D. Macray, v. 299.
[2] *Petty Papers*, ed. Lord Lansdowne (1927), i. 7–8, 14–21.
[3] See J. H. Sacret in *Eng. Hist. Rev.* xlv. 232.

structure of parliament was the question of how the central administrative machine should be organized. Clarendon stood for the old system of the Tudors and the early Stuarts, under which the king in his privy council had been the guiding and driving power. The work of government was, however, already so varied that this simple machinery had developed in two ways. A number of committees of council, some permanent, others temporary, were needed to deal with special matters, and certain ministers had acquired a special importance as links between the council and the various executive officers or bodies with whom it corresponded. Historians have disputed much about the exact stages of development and the relations between the elements here involved. The future was to decide that a committee of council, the cabinet, was to become supreme over the administration; that it was to consist mainly of the heads of departments, and that it was to be responsible to parliament and unanimous in support of a prime minister. As yet no one knew that these four principles would grow together into a well-knit whole. The cabinet, whether under that name or under some such other designation as 'the committee for foreign affairs', emerged definitely in the early years of Charles II, and had indeed been anticipated before the civil war. But there was no prime minister in the modern sense. The king himself took part in cabinet meetings, and Clarendon's overwhelming influence was personal and not due to any office or recognized position.

The chief co-ordinating ministers were the two secretaries of state. Their offices, as in the administrations of Spain, France, and the Spanish Netherlands, were roughly divided into geographical spheres, in this case the northern and the southern departments; but one or other of them was always the more important and the more important generally dealt with home affairs as well as his share of foreign affairs. They had, besides their own executive work, extensive functions in setting the other departments of state in motion. These bore little resemblance to modern government offices. In particular most of them were not under individual heads. More and more it became the custom for the department to be managed not by a man but by a board. This type of organization, which survives in the older English universities, is typical of the seventeenth century. It was to be found in or soon after this period in Sweden, Denmark, Holland, France, and elsewhere. Without controversy and for reasons which are partly unexplored it spread·in the English constitution in this period. The rule of committees in the interregnum, when individuals liked to share their grave responsibilities, prepared the way for it. The distrust of kings for their politicians assisted it. At bottom, however, it was the expression of the fact that the country was governed by men who were neither merely the king's servants nor merely men of position in the country, but some of them more the one and others more the other, all of them something of both, members, in fact, of a composite but powerful governing class. That the monarchy worked with and through this class was shown by the coexistence of these boards with the unifying and expediting work of the secretaries. Without them the system would have been too cumbrous to move. As it was the work of government was somehow done by the lords commissioners of the treasury, the navy board, the board of ordnance, the successive committees and boards of trade and plantations, the commissioners of customs, the boards which dealt with the other branches of taxation, and the minor boards which swarmed about them. After the time of Clarendon, instead of committees of council, boards independent of the privy council, actuated and linked by the secretaries of state, became the rule. This was the foundation on which the cabinet system grew up. How it did so was to be dictated partly by the course of the party struggles which were to follow the fall of Clarendon. What might already have been predicted, however, was that the power which would ultimately prove successful in controlling· this curious administrative machine would itself be a committee, not an individual, and would be in some close relation to parliament which was itself connected by innumerable ties with the governing class.

The commons indeed, though less homogeneous than they seem to have become in the eighteenth century, were mostly landed proprietors or their relatives. The enactment of Queen Anne's reign by which membership was confined to those having a landed estate of not less than £300 per annum was easily evaded and did not in itself signify the exclusion of a real wave of landless men who were pressing to get in.[1] It was, however, an interesting

[1] Bills for the same purpose had been introduced earlier in the period: one failed to obtain the royal assent in 1696 and another in 1702. The ostensible purpose of the act was to exclude men whose lack of property would make them amenable to corruption, and for some of its supporters this was a genuine argument. See below, p. 239.

symbol of the character the commons liked to sustain. Even in
the Restoration period those of them who had risen as merchants
or attorneys or party pamphleteers all assumed the dress and
manners of the gentry. That class, the class in which men wore
wigs and swords, was entering on its classical period. There were
several other indications, besides the landed qualification for
parliament, that it was consolidating its social power. The corn
laws and the progress of large estates showed this on one side. On
another there were the game laws, which were built up in this
period, and were clearly examples of legislation for the benefit
of the governing class.[1]

The work of local administration and petty justice was falling
more completely into the hands of the justices of the peace; some
other authorities, such as those connected with the old division
of counties into hundreds, faded into insignificance about this
time. The gentry gained a varied experience of public work in
direct contact with the people, and this helped to make them a
good reservoir of parliament-men. They had that many-sided
local power and consequence which belonged to their class from
its rise in the middle ages to its decline in our own time. In most
of the villages of England the manor house was the centre. It had
servants and horses, gun-dogs and hounds; it was a home of
sport and hospitality, bustling and, no doubt, for the villager
sometimes bountiful and sometimes dictatorial. It had more or
less of the comforts and conveniences in which the standards of
London, which more of the squires were getting to know, were
quickly rising; it might even have elegances and treasures of art.
If its owner had made the grand tour or mixed in London society,
it might diffuse something of enlightenment.

As yet, however, this last was an uncommon side of country
life. The first earl of Anglesey, who died in 1686, is said to have
been the first English nobleman to collect a great library,[2] and
collecting generally had hardly yet become an occupation of
country gentlemen. Indeed we must beware of drawing a
rounded picture of this class at this time as a homogeneous body
combining authority and cultivation. It was not a hereditary

[1] See below, pp. 38, 407. Perhaps it is as well to explain that wigs did not come
into general use until a few years after 1660.
[2] This seems to be confirmed by the list of English libraries in Evelyn's letter to
Pepys in 1689 (*Memoirs*, ed. Bray, iv. 296 ff.), from which it is at least clear that
almost all the really valuable private collections of books and manuscripts belonged
to ecclesiastics.

class in any strict sense; already its social strength was partly derived from the fact that it easily absorbed the newly rich. The Tudors with their Heralds' College had tried to give formality to English class distinctions,[1] but the social conditions were too fluid for this to mean rigidity. The gentry were not a caste, and, again, they did not carry out the whole of the work of local administration. The work of tax-collecting was in the hands of professional servants either of the Crown or of the tax-farmers. All the executive work of the sheriffs was done by paid officers. The boroughs had their own affairs in their own hands, and, though they were deferential to the neighbouring magnates, the small employers who became mayors and councillors were often enough independent. The period from the Restoration to the end of the century was indeed one in which, for reasons not yet fully understood, the gentry showed no great enthusiasm for the work of local government. Whether from lack of leisure or lack of energy and public spirit, only about half of those nominated to the commission of the peace took the simple legal steps which were necessary to qualify them to act. That there was a change in this respect is a sign that in the eighteenth century the class became more settled and more uniform.

Even then they were not quite so dominant as is sometimes supposed.[2] Most of the better literature of the period was written for them, and so we see their England through their eyes; but there were many villagers who saw little of them. Where the land was owned by a college or a dean and chapter, or in the outlying manors of a great nobleman, there was no resident squire. From such villages the overseers of the poor made an occasional journey to have their acts authorized, or the constable to be sworn in by a justice of the peace, but the great man's influence was distant and occasional. In the home counties there were coming to be residents of a middle station between the farmers and the lord of the manor, men retired from business or the professions, who were not bound by the old, simple, social ties. We shall see that the squire's ally or dependant, the parson, had in many places to reckon with a nonconformist element among his parishioners, and in secular matters as in ecclesiastical the English countryside was also not without leaders who

---

[1] For the decline in this period of the marshal's jurisdiction in matters of heraldry see Holdsworth, *Hist. of English Law*, i, 3rd ed. (1922), 578–9.

[2] For their numbers see note A at the end of this chapter, p. 25.

belonged to divergent social types. In hundreds of villages the men who were looked up to were not gentlemen by blood and coat armour, but farmers or millers or maltsters. In this, as in so much else, there was a rich variety.

Looking back over the constitutional machinery as a whole, we may say that there were prospects of conflicts over some things; but that there was also going on a steady growth of the organs needed by the state to carry on its work. Behind all this there still loomed, however, the graver problems of religious organization which had split the nation and diverted what might have been forces of constitutional progress into the paths of armed opposition. These could not be left to solve themselves. The immediate confusion was such that king and parliament must give a lead in disentangling them, and the chances of an easy solution were from the first very slight. The life of the established church had undergone a breach of continuity. Its property, as we have seen, had been partly confiscated; that part had been taken which supported the higher clergy. It was not a difficult matter to set this right. The tithes of the parish clergy had been threatened, but they were still due. Difficulties began with the problem of *personnel*. Of the nine thousand and odd benefices more than two thousand were held by presbyterians, men who were opposed to the rule of bishops, partly because they disapproved of the worldly splendour of prelatical power, but mainly because they wished for stricter moral and spiritual supervision by assemblies of ministers and elders organized on the Calvinistic model. In addition to these, nearly four hundred congregationalist ministers held benefices of the church of England. These intruders had been leaders of the movement which upset the old régime. Most of them, though inevitably distrusted, were not political enemies of the new; but something had to be done to absorb them into it or to render them harmless. The clergy who came back from the hardships of exile or from straitened living in hiding-places among the faithful in England would have been more than human if they had not wanted reinstatement and something more.

Nor was it merely a question of places and livings. The desire to find shelter and emotional stability in a dignified and well-regulated community, a church, is no less an authentic form of religion than the passion to be saved as an individual and to rescue fellow individuals. Ecclesiastical loyalty is as real as

sectarian conviction. All those who believed in decency and
order in religion had been shocked and alarmed by the extrava-
gances of the last years, and the reaction now came as it was
bound to come. 'Fanatic' became a common term of aversion.[1]
Samuel Butler's burlesque *Hudibras* (1663–78), ill-made, small-
minded, and monotonous as it is, delighted every enemy of puritanism from the king downwards, and gave us a dozen proverbial
expressions which are still in use. But the strong and deep
religious movement of the sects was still alive. It was not to
be stopped by bargains between political parties and it was
unaffected by a change of mind in the governing class, for its
roots were among the shopkeepers and artisans and yeomen,
obscure but tenacious people. John Bunyan was thirty-two at
the time of the Restoration and had twenty-eight years of
ministry before him. The quakers were active in the countryside
and no less than seven hundred of them were soon to be released
from an imprisonment which could not now be regarded as
legal. There were perhaps forty thousand of them altogether,
men, women, and children, the most inspired and the most unmanageable among a body of sectaries which numbered altogether at most a tenth of the population.[2] It was necessary
that something should be laid down as to whether this un-
regulated religious life should go on, and how.

Among the churchmen there were some whose views of
liturgy and church order earned them, a few years after this
time, the name of 'high churchmen'. Rather less accurately they
are sometimes called Laudians. Although they were royalists
and disciplinarians, they were more apt than Archbishop Laud
to seek for some degree of ecclesiastical independence from the
state. For a variety of reasons they were now more influential
in the church of England than Laud and his followers had ever
been. They had gained ground both among the royalists who
were exiles in France and among those who remained in
England. They were opposed to relaxing the regulations which
offended the dissenters, and they were equally opposed to tolerat-
ing sects outside the established church. They had no distinctive
theology of their own. Among them there were Calvinists, like
Morley, the bishop of Winchester. At the other extreme among
them were some who still thought it possible to find common

[1] A. Wood, *Life and Times*, i. 303.
[2] See note B at the end of this chapter, p. 26.

ground with the Roman catholics, or at least with the Gallicans.
Both in England and in France 'la cabale des accommodeurs',
active during the Stuart exile, still lingered on until the sixteen-
seventies. The high church position, however, had never been
accepted by the whole nation even in the time of Elizabeth;
still less under James I and Charles I, and now it was impracticable. Some concessions from it could meet with a response from
the dissidents. The baptists and quakers, indeed, were opposed
to any kind of state church; but the independents and presbyterians, in their different ways, accepted the idea of an established church. The presbyterians hoped for concessions which
would enable them to come in, and, once in, they would not
tolerate dissent. The other sects hoped for toleration. Some
Anglicans advocated the universal toleration of all who called
themselves Christians, supposing that the protestant dissenters
would balance the Roman catholics. Others, of the wing
furthest removed from the high churchmen, wanted comprehension for the presbyterians. If this were achieved they could
a lso afford to tolerate the sectaries, since nonconformity would
be reduced to a remnant. This aspect of comprehension did not
escape the notice of those who asked to be tolerated.

The decisions of the king and parliament on these points were
of the utmost importance in determining some of the main lines
not only of ecclesiastical policy but of social and political life for
more than two hundred and fifty years to come. We are still in
many ways living under their influence. They were not reached
quickly. Personal and temporary complications delayed them,
and after Charles's return there was a period of hesitation and
fumbling which lasted for almost a year. The king himself was
the son and heir of one who was regarded as a martyr for the
church of England, but he seldom or never showed much feeling
for that church. He was without serious personal religion, and
his theological opinions, so far as he had any, were those of the
deism which was common by this time among unprejudiced men
of position. He was therefore inclined to be tolerant of differences of belief, and he was disposed to be particularly indulgent
to the Roman catholics, that body among his subjects who were
the most generally feared and ill-treated. He owed his safety in
flight from Worcester to the loyalty of Roman catholic subjects.
On his travels he had learnt that the faith of his mother and of
his powerful cousin the king of France was at least as comfortable

a companion for monarchy as any other. He had promised the pope and the catholic powers that he would work for the repeal of the penal laws, and he meant to keep his promises.

His minister Clarendon had come over to the royal cause from the opposition twenty years before because it was the cause of the Anglican church, but he was not indisposed to make politic offers which might confuse and divide the dissidents. So long as the convention parliament sat there seemed a chance of a general toleration. 'Of this you may be assured,' the king said to a deputation of quakers, 'that you shall none of you suffer for your opinions or religion, so long as you live peaceably, and you have the word of a king for it.'[1] The number of people who desired real and general toleration was, however, so small that in the sorting-out of forces, it was certain that there would be a bargain between some to the disadvantage of others. At first it looked as if the Anglicans and the presbyterians would be reconciled. The presbyterian leaders were prepared to accept a modified form of episcopacy on the lines traced out by James Ussher, archbishop of Armagh, before the Civil War, in which the bishops should have synods associated with them. Charles issued on 4 November 1660 a declaration in favour of this arrangement. High preferments were offered to some of the chief presbyterians. A conference met at the bishop of London's lodgings in the Savoy to work out the forms of worship and belief. This Savoy Conference failed completely. The men who met in it were not equal to their task. The bishops offered some real concessions, which are embodied in the Prayer Book of 1662, but they were too limited to bring any response. The foremost of the presbyterians, Richard Baxter, had wonderful and commanding qualities, faith and leadership, learning and intellectual subtlety; but he tragically lacked the qualities which were needed now. He had no sense of humour. He had never had training or experience in negotiating, or in getting business through assemblies. Not a statesman, he was also not more charitable than the opponents he now met. He did not wish Roman catholic worship to be permitted, and he would have excluded the 'intolerable heresies' of the sectaries from the comprehension which he, not they, desired. Against the hardening resistance of the Anglicans he could do nothing. Before the conference ended the Cavalier parliament met,[2] and its great decisions were taken in the spirit

[1] R. Hubberthorn, *Works* (1663), p. 271. [2] See below, p. 55.

of narrow exclusiveness, which the progress of events quickly converted into persecution.

A bill was introduced in the convention to give effect to the declaration of 4 November, but the influence of the court was exerted against it and it failed to pass. Clarendon, against his better judgement, allowed himself to be carried along by the ecclesiastics and the squires in a series of acts which has long been known as the Clarendon Code.[1] It is not unusual now for these to be described as essentially the work of political authority, not of the church itself, and it is true that they were largely dictated by the fear that nonconformity might again play a political part like that of puritanism in the time of Charles I. The church and churchmen did not, however, protest against even the most rigorous of these laws. The ideal of comprehension was abandoned, and except for one or two brief appearances, did not reawaken until 1689. There was already in force an act of Queen Elizabeth which imposed severe penalties on all who obstinately refused to hear divine service or attended conventicles or encouraged others to do so. In 1661 the jurisdiction of the ecclesiastical courts was revived; not, as it turned out, an important revival. For some time after the Restoration the names of laymen who committed ecclesiastical offences appear in the records of these courts, but they never again exercised the power over laymen which had been so unpopular in former times. The Corporation Act excluded from municipal corporations all those who refused to take the sacrament according to the rites of the church of England. What those rites were to be was defined in the next year under the Act of Uniformity. This authorized anew the Prayer Book and the various formularies of belief and restricted the holding of benefices to episcopally ordained clergy.[2] A bill in the lords to permit the king to excuse individuals from the necessity of complying with it was rejected.

The Clarendon Code was modelled on the persecuting laws made against the church of England by the Puritans during

[1] Dr. Keith Feiling proved from a minute study of contemporary correspondence that Clarendon's attitude was less consistently Anglican and depended more on personal factors and political exigencies than he and his apologists afterwards claimed (*Eng. Hist. Rev.* xliv. 290; see also ibid. xlii. 407). R. S. Bosher, *The Making of the Restoration Settlement, the Influence of the Laudians* (1951) corrects all previous accounts.
[2] The house of commons asserted but did not exercise its right to revise the Prayer Book, which it authorized as amended by convocation.

their period of rule. This severity must have contributed to the nervous and violent state of public opinion which lasted all through Charles's reign. It was not deliberately planned, but resulted from events. From 1662 until 1672 it had a dramatic unity and the quakers bore the brunt of it. In January 1661 a crack-brained enthusiast named Thomas Venner, a wine-bottler by trade, led a band of fifty men in a senseless attempt to set up in London the monarchy of King Jesus. He was easily captured and hanged; but the regiments which had not yet been disbanded were retained in service and the frightened justices of the peace up and down the country imprisoned quakers to the almost incredible number of more than four thousand.[1] An act of the next year, the Quakers' Act, inflicted severe penalties on their meetings for worship, that for a third offence being transportation. In 1663 there were ominous comings and goings among the discontented nonconformists and old Cromwellian officers. Some conspirators were arrested in the county of Durham in the spring. In October two hundred men collected under arms at Farnley Wood near Leeds. They collected only to scatter again. There were arrests all over the country. Twenty-one plotters were executed in Yorkshire.[2] This was the excuse for the Conventicle Act which imposed penalties for attendance at worship not in Anglican forms, and applied to all nonconformists. It was nominally in force until 1669, but for some time before that little was done to apply it. The way in which it was ignored, especially in London during the great plague and after the fire, led, however, to a second Conventicle Act in 1670. In 1665 the Five Mile Act forbade any noncon-formist minister to live or visit within five miles of any corporate town or any place where he had acted as minister, unless he took an oath to which few could submit. Much was done under all these acts to harry the nonconformists; principally no doubt because it was feared, though needlessly, that their meetings would be seed-beds for new seditions and rebellions. The prob-able effect of all this was to check their growth and spirit, not to encourage it, though in some outlying places the Five Mile Act spread their influence. How many the sufferers were is not exactly known except for the quakers, who kept the best records.

---

[1] Braithwaite, *Second Period of Quakerism* (1919), pp. 9, 114.
[2] See H. Gee in *Royal Hist. Soc. Trans.*, 3rd ser., xi. 125, and J. Walker in *Yorkshire Archaeol. Soc. Journal*, xxxi. 348.

Of these there were about 1,300 in prison in 1662 after the Quakers' Act, and about 500 in 1672 when the Declaration of Indulgence gave them relief. Many had died of their sufferings.

The main importance of the Clarendon Code lies, however, not in the persecution but in the great social change brought about especially by the first two acts, the Corporation Act and the Act of Uniformity. They assumed that in religion England was now to be divided. The church of England was to be purged of fanatics and heretics by oaths and subscriptions. In fact on St. Bartholomew's Day 1662 nearly a thousand incumbents who were unwilling to accept the liturgy or doctrines vacated their livings.[1] That so many should make so great a sacrifice for principle was an ominous fact for the church they left. That church indeed was to hold not only the church buildings and glebe farms, the tithes and lands, but also the keys of power. Its opponents were not to choose burgesses for parliament. To it were reserved all the teaching places and emoluments of the universities, and no one without a licence from a bishop was to act as a schoolmaster or to instruct or teach youth in any private house or family. It has been pleasantly written that the Act of Uniformity 'gave a standing to Dissent which it had never possessed before'. That is true.[2] Dissent was now recognized for the first time as lawful; but it was depressed to a position of disadvantage. Those who adhered to it were excluded from power, and this led perhaps to a general diminution of numbers and certainly to a falling-off of those who cared for social status or entertained social ambitions. The English presbyterians, who had been the nearest rivals of the church of England, were for this reason the hardest hit. During the eighteenth century many of their remnant became unitarians, and their original tradition virtually came to an end.[3] Nonconformity lived on mainly

[1] A. G. Matthews, *Calamy Revised* (1933), pp. xiii, lxi, reaches the figure of 936 in addition to 760 already ejected in 1660 and 1662. Of these at least 420 were in full Anglican orders before the Civil War and 45 more after the Restoration.

[2] C. J. Abbey and J. H. Overton, *English Church in the Eighteenth Century*, i. 384. This implication was not, however, understood by parliament, cf. the objection of the commons to Lord Roberts's bill for empowering the Crown to give licences for protestant nonconformist worship: 'It will establish schism by a law.' (*Commons' Journals*, 5 March 1662/3.)

[3] The 'three persuasions' co-operated for political purposes. The presbyterians did not set up their own form of church government, but were virtually independents. The so-called 'happy union' between them and the congregationalists agreed upon in 1690 soon broke down partly through the stricter Calvinism of the latter: see R. W. Dale, *Hist. of English Congregationalism* (1907), pp. 475–84, 506–14.

among the humble people. It shared in the general decline of religious fervour. Its one positive new contribution to religious life in this period was hymn-writing: Isaac Watts in the reign of Queen Anne transcended sectarian boundaries. Nonconformity, however, was strong enough to continue as a permanent element in English life, an element which in less than a century was to receive new accessions of numbers from the methodist movement.

It was not until 1871, with the opening of the universities of Oxford and Cambridge to protestant nonconformists, that they received full equality of civil rights; and in the whole of the long period in which they gradually emerged from their disabilities, they formed a separate body of interests and opinions. In education they did not weakly acquiesce in all that was intended for them, but, even before the law allowed it, they built up schools and academies of their own.[1] As the universities were closed to them, they did not need to follow the prevailing classical curriculum and they used their freedom to experiment, naturally not always wisely, but on the whole with fruitful results. The men who benefited from this were to come to the fore in the eighteenth century, but already in Queen Anne's time one of the leading politicians, Robert Harley, earl of Oxford, and one of the leading literary men, Daniel Defoe, came from these schools;[2] and it is not fanciful to see in both of them traces of the characteristic nonconformist outlook, a scepticism about some accepted standards, and a seriousness about some matters which most men take comparatively lightly. The expression 'the nonconformist conscience', used in a later age, illustrates the fact that the two parts of the nation found it difficult to understand one another. It results from the existence of a partly independent nonconformist morality and culture.

From the rise of this culture in the days of the Clarendon Code dates the division of English social life between 'church' and 'chapel' which persisted down to the Victorian days. It became one of the dividing lines in party politics, in the press, and in everything else, even in economic life. It is well known that all over the western world in that age, a great share in economic development was taken by exiles. In England, as in other protes-

---

[1] Several quaker schools of Charles II's time are mentioned by W. C. Braithwaite, *Second Period of Quakerism* (1919), pp. 525 ff.

[2] So did Bolingbroke, but he was also at Eton.

tant countries, there had long been families of huguenot refugees who had become great capitalists, devoting to that work the energy and the force of character which could not find scope in the public life of an alien country. The effect of the Clarendon Code was to put the protestant nonconformists in a similar position, and from this time we read of quakers and other sectaries who were manufacturers or merchants or bankers. There was something more behind this. The sobriety and industry which puritanism fostered were favourable to business success. It would, however, be too simple to say merely that by an inherent fitness the puritans gravitated to the counting-house and the counter. The law gave them no choice. Nor did puritans as such contribute more than their religious opponents to the decline of ecclesiastical control over business life, and to the individualism which was developing in economic theory.[1] Even the English Roman catholics, who had been settled for generations in a dignified segregation, made their contribution to this movement of thought. As we shall see, 'political arithmetic', or statistical science, began in our period, and it was altogether alien to the medieval state of mind in which ethical considerations governed economics. Of its two founders one, John Graunt, became a Roman catholic. The other, Sir William Petty, had part of his education at Leyden, but another part with the Jesuits at Caen. Religious differences were overridden by the tendencies of business life and economic thought.

TWO STATISTICAL NOTES

A. Social Divisions (see above, p. 16).

The best estimate we have of the numbers and average incomes of different classes in England is that of Gregory King for 1696 (printed in George Chalmers's edition of King's *Observations* (1804) and in other books, such as Charles Davenant's *Works*, ed. Whitworth, ii. 184). Here most of the totals are reached by multiplying the number of households ('families') by the presumed number of heads per family: the latter number is arbitrary, and perhaps in

[1] See H. M. Robertson, *Aspects of the Rise of Economic Individualism* (1933), and R. D. Richards, *Early Hist. of English Banking* (1929), pp. 220–2. These two authors criticize the views expressed in R. H. Tawney, *Religion and the Rise of Capitalism* (1926). Of the numerous books and essays written in England on this subject since it was reopened by Max Weber in 1904, in my opinion none has got nearer the truth than H. G. Wood, 'The Influence of the Reformation on Ideas concerning Property' in *Property, its Duties and Rights* (1913).

some cases too small. The whole has at least this authority, that it was generally accepted at the time as reasonable. The column of incomes gives the best indication we have of how far money went. It is impossible to say how many of our pounds are equivalent to one pound sterling then; but this table indicates roughly what a given income would buy.

Number of Families	Ranks, Degrees, Titles, and Qualifications	Heads per Family	Number of Persons	Yearly Income per Family
				£
160	Temporal lords	40	6,400	3,200
26	Spiritual lords	20	520	1,300
800	Baronets	16	12,800	880
600	Knights	13	7,800	650
3,000	Esquires	10	30,000	450
12,000	Gentlemen	8	96,000	280
5,000	Persons in greater offices and places	8	40,000	240
5,000	Persons in lesser offices and places	6	30,000	120
2,000	Eminent merchants and traders by sea	8	16,000	400
8,000	Lesser merchants and traders by sea	6	48,000	198
10,000	Persons in the law	7	70,000	154
2,000	Eminent clergymen	6	12,000	72
8,000	Lesser clergymen	5	40,000	50
40,000	Freeholders of the better sort	7	280,000	91
120,000	Freeholders of the lesser sort	5½	660,000	55
150,000	Farmers	5	750,000	42 10s.
15,000	Persons in liberal arts and sciences	5	75,000	60
50,000	Shopkeepers and tradesmen	4½	225,000	45
60,000	Artisans and handicrafts	4	240,000	38
5,000	Naval officers	4	20,000	80
4,000	Military officers	4	16,000	60
50,000	Common seamen	3	150,000	20
364,000	Labouring people and out-servants	3½	1,275,000	15
400,000	Cottagers and paupers	3¼	1,300,000	6 10s.
35,000	Common soldiers	2	70,000	14
	Vagrants, as gipsies, thieves, beggars, &c.		30,000	
	Total		5,500,520	

For our present purpose the small variations between the printed versions of this table may be disregarded. A valuable, though to some extent provisional, account of King's procedure is given by Dr. D. V. Glass in *Eugenics Review*, January 1946, pp. 170 ff.

B. Religion (see above, p. 18).

It appears to be impossible to make a good estimate of the numbers of adherents of the different churches at any time during the period. There is the standing difficulty that every church has a more definite body of members, surrounded by a fluctuating and less definite body of their relations and sympathizers. In addition, in this period, the persecutions and civil disabilities led many people at times to conceal their sympathies. In 1680

Algernon Sidney wrote of the protestant nonconformists as 'above a million of men' (*Savile Correspondence*, p. 168), but this is absurd. The modern estimate of 30–40,000 men, women, and children for the quakers in 1661 (W. C. Braithwaite, *Beginnings of Quakerism*, p. 512) is perhaps the best figure available. In 1676 Archbishop Sheldon collected figures which have been used as the basis of various attempts to deal with the whole question. The fullest publication of them is in G. Lyon Turner, *Original Records of Early Nonconformity*, 3 vols., 1911–14. Their final result is to give the proportion of conformists to protestant nonconformists as about twenty-two to one, and to papists as about 178 to one. They are, however, very incomplete and they were put together in the different dioceses in various quite different ways. Worse still, it was known that Sheldon's purpose was to prepare for new repression by proving how few the dissenters were. In many places there are rolls of baptist members which exceed the numbers given by the incumbents for all denominations. Dr. Thomas Richards, in a careful study with special reference to Wales in *Trans. of the Soc. of Cymmrodorion* (1925–6), Supplement, discredits the returns generally, and shows that they under-estimate the number of dissenters. Mr. S. A. Peyton in *Eng. Hist. Rev.* xlvii. 99 attempts to vindicate the returns by comparison with certain records of quarter sessions and archdeacons' courts; but this is to prove *obscurum per obscurius*. The general conclusion of E. D. Bebb, *Nonconformity and Social and Religious Life, 1660–1680* (1935), p. 45, is that from 1660 to 1700 the number was about 150,000 to 250,000.

It does not seem possible to judge whether the numbers of nonconformists increased or declined during our period, but it may well have risen from 1672 to the end of the century. Early in the reign of George I Daniel Neal estimated the number of dissenting congregations in England as 1,107, besides 43 in Wales. In England 247 were baptist and 860 presbyterian or independent, the presbyterians being perhaps more than double the independents. Under William III 1,000 or more permanent meeting-houses were built (see R. W. Dale, *Hist. of English Congregationalism* (1907), pp. 475–84, 506–14). In 1693 there was another religious census in the province of Canterbury, of which the fullest account is in *Calendar of State Papers, Domestic, 1693*, pp. 448–9.

The number of Roman catholic priests is hard to fix. The 'Particulars of Priests in England and Wales, 1692' in *Catholic Record Soc. Miscellanea*, vii (1911), gives, without touching Cornwall, on the authority of a single observer, the names of about a hundred. For full statistics of the Jesuits see H. Foley, *Records of the English Province of the Society of Jesus*, vol. vii, pt. 1 (1882), pp. xc ff. In 1660 there were 150. The Popish Plot reduced their numbers for a few years below 100, but it will be noted that no such result followed the penal enactment 11 Wm. III, c. 4. The English religious houses and colleges on the Continent, though not on English soil, belong to English history. Even those, like the nunneries, which were only occasionally in contact with England by correspondence or by personal coming and going, helped to keep catholicism alive in the times of persecution.

II

INTELLECTUAL AND ECONOMIC
TENDENCIES

RELIGIOUS persecution more severe than that of the Clarendon Code was still to occur in more than one quarter of Europe including enlightened France, but the English system of repression belonged to a world of ideas which was rapidly becoming archaic. The Act of Uniformity was accompanied by a Licensing Act which put the old Stuart system of the censorship of the press on the basis of parliamentary authority, but kept its narrowly ecclesiastical spirit. The number of master-printers in England was to be allowed to dwindle to twenty, after which none was to be admitted except with the approval of the archbishop of Canterbury and the bishop of London. Control was, however, not exercised merely through the Stationers' Company. No book was to be published without a licence from a censor appointed, according to the subject, by the appropriate civil or ecclesiastical authority. There were to be no printing-presses except in London, Oxford, and Cambridge. The act was made originally for two years, but successive renewals carried it down to 1679 and it was renewed in 1685 to last until 1693. A number of men were brave enough to print pamphlets which the censor would never have passed, and one of them, John Twyn, in 1664 even suffered the penalties of treason. Whether the censorship succeeded in restraining dissident thought can scarcely be judged; but the system was rigid and it was enforced by frequent prosecutions.[1] When William III landed in England his secretary noted that in Exeter, the capital of the west, there was not a press on which he could print a manifesto.[2]

Yet this was an age of intellectual activity. In the seventeenth century many of the germinal discoveries were made in mathematics, physics, and other branches of natural science. It was

---

[1] The system broke down in the disturbed conditions of 1678. For some details of the enforcement see J. Walker in *History* (New Series), xxiv (1950), 219 ff.

[2] Constantijn Huygens, *Journaalen*, i (1876), p. 19.

then that the special activity which we call scientific began to be a leading element in European thought. That activity is one of unbiased inquiry, shrinking from no conclusion merely because it is unorthodox. It is also positive and experimental: it tests its conclusions not only by reasoning but also by observation. It has never been altogether absent from the world, but at this time it was spreading and flourishing. In England, though the ground had been prepared for it by a series of workers for a century and more, it seemed suddenly to break into flower just at the time with which we are concerned. Groups of scientists had been quietly investigating during the recent civil strife, and one of these groups, which had come together in London and Oxford, was the direct forerunner of a famous society, the great Royal Society, which still exists and which has permanently associated the name of King Charles II with the scientific movement.

Charles was not a scientist, though he liked to watch experiments and talk about them, nor, when he became the patron of the Society in 1662, was he doing anything more than taking up a movement which had already established its position. He had the merit of being four years ahead of his cousin Louis XIV in this, but Louis does not appear to have been merely following Charles's example. Science was fashionable in the highest circles. In England Prince Rupert experimented in mezzotint engraving, though he did not invent it, and devised some improvements in firearms and gunpowder. Even the dullest of all the relations of the Stuarts, Queen Anne's consort, Prince George of Denmark, was interested in mathematics and mechanics.[1] But it was not from royal and distinguished patronage that the movement derived its strength; nor did the Royal Society do more than afford opportunities for scientists to compare ideas, to plan a rudimentary co-operation, and to crystallize the specific aims of science from the rather confused and general curiosity with which they started. Fortunately among its early members there were several men of great intellectual gifts, and they were engaged on problems of much importance. If we ask why it was at this time and not earlier or later that England took a place among the leading countries in scientific work, perhaps even

---

[1] See the dedication to J. Harris, *Lexicon Technicum*, i (1704). Prince George supported the publication of Flamsteed's and Tycho Brahé's works. His work at the admiralty no doubt kept alive his interest in navigation. See also below, p. 382.

somewhat ahead of France and Holland, it is difficult to give a precise answer. If it had not been for the civil disturbances, it would probably have come earlier; in the time of Charles I there had been intercourse with the leading continental thinkers, and that would have had its effect. During the interregnum the preparatory work went on. Robert Boyle was in England learning chemistry from the year of Marston Moor; John Wilkins, who married Oliver Cromwell's sister and became the first secretary of the Royal Society, was the centre of the group in Oxford. This included Boyle. With them were John Wallis and Christopher Wren, excellent mathematicians and the immediate precursors of Newton. There was William Petty, a versatile pathfinder who ranged from anatomy to economics, and there were also some undergraduates of promise, one of whom was John Locke.

What happened at the Restoration therefore was simply that the scientific movement came out into the open daylight of fashion and favour, and this was primarily due to the real and striking advances that it was making. But the men of fashion and business were no doubt attracted to it because its discoveries had obvious practical applications. It led at once to greater exactness and wider possibilities in a number of practical pursuits, not only in agriculture, manufactures, medicine, and surgery, but in those arts which specially concerned the state, navigation, naval architecture, gunnery, and engineering.

Most of the scientists of the time were men who ranged widely over the still little-developed branches of scientific study, but there was something of an interruption in the co-ordination of their results into a general synthesis or philosophy. Thomas Hobbes, who had undertaken this in the previous generation, was now an old man—he had been born in the year of the Spanish Armada—and, although his sceptical and materialistic spirit did much to clear the way for the scientists, he was himself no scientist and little of a mathematician, and his scornful unorthodoxy was distasteful to the England of the restoration. The next Englishman to make a philosophy, himself also not strong in science and mathematics, was Locke, whose publications of this kind came a generation later. In the interval therefore the theologians still held together the main threads of English thought, and the relation of theology to the scientific tendency was of vital importance.

It looked as if the two might form an effective union. By several different if frequently connected paths they came into contact; indeed the contact was so close that we may say it resulted from the general atmosphere of thought, from the exchanges of conversation and the separate thinking of hundreds of individuals, rather than from the influence of a few great books. There was a decline of patristic studies, the examination of the Greek and Latin fathers, who showed exactly what had been the authoritative practices of the early church. They went on, but in a subdued way, and for the most part among rather isolated groups like the non-jurors of the next generation. The fathers were already studied not only as the vehicles of tradition, but as historical authorities in a more ordinary sense. A great French catholic scholar, Richard Simon, published his *Critical History of the Old Testament* (translated in 1682), which revealed these books too as historical documents, embodying the accidents of time, not the expression of changeless divine revelation; and Simon's readers were driven farther on this road than he went himself.[1]

It would be hard to say whether much direct influence was exerted in England by the incomparable *Tractatus Theologico-Politicus* of Spinoza, which was published in Latin in Holland in 1670 and translated in 1689. It has been truly said that this book contains all the ideas of the English rationalistic writers; but Spinoza was a marked man, a reputed atheist, in an age when the reputation of atheism was still socially unpleasant if no longer physically dangerous; moreover there were, as we have said, many other ways by which these ideas may have worked through to English minds. There was a subterranean English tradition of deism, a belief in an impersonal single deity, already a century old; and, before Spinoza wrote, the important change was already coming about by which English writers tried to justify orthodox Christianity itself not on the ground that it was divinely revealed but on the ground that it was reasonable.[2] This insistence on reason was characteristic of English theology from the time of Locke to that of Joseph Butler in the middle of the eighteenth century, of the orthodox as well as of the deists, and it was

[1] For instance, John Hampden the younger. The original French edition of Simon's book (1678) was suppressed.

[2] Sir Charles Wolseley, for instance, published in 1669 *The Unreasonableness of Atheism made Manifest*, and in 1672 *The Reasonableness of Scripture Belief*, which latter alarmed his orthodox friends.

developed by the thinkers of the restoration period who came to be known as latitudinarians or latitude-men.

These names, like most such labels, are used differently by different writers, and they are also applied to the great political ecclesiastics, tolerant and undogmatic, of the time of William III and Queen Anne; but they first came into vogue as applied to a more original and less powerful school in the early years of Charles II. In 1662 a tract gave *Account of the New Sect of Latitude-Men*.[1] In the next year Gilbert Burnet paid a visit to Cambridge, met and admired and noted these men,[2] and two years later Richard Baxter gave an account of them.[3] They were the men best known in our time as the Cambridge Platonists. They were university men and they wrote in an academic manner that was soon to become old-fashioned, with frequent citations of authorities and little order or arrangement. They had specially close links with Emmanuel College and its puritan tradition; but they had other ancestries besides. They innovated among English theologians in that they took the ground of philosophy, not merely dealing with church government and expounding revelation, but considering religion and reason as universally valid. Their favourite text, since the early days of Benjamin Whichcote in Charles I's time, had been that from Proverbs xx. 27: *Mens hominis lucerna Domini*; 'the spirit of man is the candle of the Lord', though some of them translated it 'the understanding of man'. In the midst of theological controversy they insisted that the essentials of religion were very few. Some contemporaries unfairly blamed them for reducing religion to ethics, and some of them were enthusiasts for natural science and admirers of Descartes, the great master of the systematic tendency of seventeenth-century science. Their leader Henry More, however, ceased to be an admirer of Descartes, and others of them wrote polemically against him. They represented, in fact, an opposition to the materialism of Descartes and Hobbes. Some of them strangely combined enthusiasm for science with credulity about the occult. In More, Cudworth, and in an Oxford writer, Joseph Glanvill, the tendency to mysticism has some of its roots in the old Neoplatonism which has given the school the name of Platonists; but it includes less healthy elements

---

[1] By S. P., who is now thought to be not Simon Patrick, but Samuel Parker, the translator of Grotius, *De Veritate*.

[2] *Own Times*, ed. Airy, i. 334.

[3] *Reliquiae Baxterianae*, pt. ii, c. 6.

of cabbalistic and spiritualist lore, stories of ghosts and magic. These are not unnatural developments of a sceptical and undogmatic faith. They might have run to dangerous lengths if the school had not consisted of disciplined and truly religious men.

That they are valued today is indeed partly a result of new conditions. In their own time some of them rose to high preferment, and as a body they had some influence on the course of thought; but they remained exceptional almost to the point of ineffectiveness. They were outside the main stream of Anglican theology, and that stream flowed strongly. The later Caroline divines, the writers of the time of Charles II, were admired in their own time and also during the ecclesiastical revival of the nineteenth century when their voluminous works were reprinted, and even read. Indeed a few are sometimes read even now. Their interminable arguments against the papal supremacy are now unreadable, though they seemed very important then, with popery spreading on the Continent, and they made the papacy as dreadful to educated opinion as *The Pilgrim's Progress* and Foxe's *Book of Martyrs* made it to the unintellectual reader.[1] On the side of political ideas they worked out the theory of the restored monarchy. That it would be a submissive theory was inevitable. A many-sided experiment in liberty had been tried and failed. Submission and adulation of the Crown were to be expected, and, if the clerics sometimes went very far, it must be remembered that exaggeration in all complimentary and ceremonial language was a universal habit of the age. Few can have read with much enthusiasm the bitter words in which, eleven years after the restoration, John Milton taunted the victors:

> But what more oft, in nations grown corrupt,
> And by their vices brought to servitude,
> Than to love bondage more than liberty—
> Bondage with ease than strenuous liberty—
> And to despise, or envy, or suspect
> Whom God hath of His special favour raised
> As their deliverer?

A theory was required, not of bondage, but of authority, and there were theories of authority in the field which were not

[1] For the question how much of the fear of popery was due to anxiety among the possessors of former church property, see the note at the end of this chapter, p. 54, below.

acceptable. That which Hobbes had constructed on the basis of his materialistic philosophy was definitely alarming both to good Christians and to all who felt any apprehensions about arbitrary power. The doctrine of non-resistance was not open to the same objections. Intended primarily to condemn the opposition to Charles I, it was in essence simply that kings ruled by a divine right and that to resist them was therefore a crime against God. Those who stated this doctrine were not drawing up a programme for their own action. So far as they provided for the case of royal commands not in accordance with the subject's conception of the divine will, they did so by the special doctrine of passive obedience. This was not peculiar to the Anglicans. It was also held by the quakers.[1] It is closely related to the teaching: 'Resist not evil.' It is the doctrine of what in modern times has been called passive resistance, the doctrine that it is a duty if unlawfully commanded to do a thing, not to do it but passively to undergo the punishment inflicted for disobedience. For the time being, however, there seemed no likelihood that churchmen would need it to guide them in their own conduct.

If its political theory was uninteresting and if its prevalent theology was out of touch with the vital principles of contemporary thought, the church of England had its best side in the unpretending piety of laymen and of the parochial clergy.[2] Some of its unofficial literature from this period has a lasting fragrance. The little volume of lives of churchmen by Izaak Walton, the author of the *Compleat Angler*, is formless and a little tame, but very attractive. The churchmen of the restoration restored the dignity of the traditional worship and at their best retained the gravity of puritanism without its inhumanity. Some of the best men of the new reign derived, in their different ways, strength and wisdom from their church. John Evelyn, the diarist, is a type of the Christian gentleman, and for such characters some of the credit is owing to the institutions under which they grow.

[1] See a definition of 1661 by Edward Burrough quoted in Braithwaite, *Second Period*, p. 17.
[2] There has been much discussion of a passage in Macaulay's *History* (ed. Firth, i. 318) describing in exaggerated terms the poverty and low social status of the clergy. There were many lamentable instances, especially among the curates who did the work of absent incumbents, and among the domestic chaplains of great houses. On the other hand, there were among the clergy men of rank and many others who kept a position of dignity and independence. See the Rev. C. H. Mayo in *Eng. Hist. Rev.* xxxvii. 258.

When all this is said, it remains true that the church of England, like the sects outside it, pursued its own intellectual course with only a limited response to the great movements of the time, and expressed too often in controversy the spirit of exclusiveness and censure. In the later years of the period with which this volume deals, many educated Englishmen both in that church and outside it found a new agreement in the liberal philosophy of John Locke, but that philosophy and the acceptance which it obtained can only be understood in the light of the intervening history, and we must therefore defer any notice of them until much later.[1]

It was inevitable that the continuance for generation after generation of religious controversy and the strife of ecclesiastical parties should lead to a secularizing tendency, a tendency to regard material values as more real than those which were less tangible. Such a tendency may be seen in the frequency of the argument for toleration on economic grounds. To those who most surely believe in it, toleration is more than a support for religion; it is even of the essence of religion itself, and there were some who understood it so, but even some of these, and still more the mass of moderate and fair-minded men, were apt to argue for it on the mundane ground that it was good for trade. Dutch trade had benefited by it, as the numerous writers on the Dutch republic pointed out. The report of a parliamentary committee on the decay of trade in 1669 advised that 'some ease and relaxation in ecclesiastical matters' would be 'a means of improving the trade of this Kingdom'. The economists, the liberal philosophers, the quakers, and the Stuart kings all echoed the argument.

There were indeed some who were not convinced. 'Men may amuse themselves', wrote one, 'with the instance of the United Provinces; which they say flourish in trade and riches by maintaining all religions. But the question is one of religion not of trade nor riches. . . . Religion and trade cannot be both at once at the height.'[2] Right or wrong this writer was behind the times. Trade was not a thing to look down upon. A generation later another ecclesiastic, a great man in his way, had enough breadth

---

[1] See below, p. 385.

[2] H. Thorndike, *Of the Forbearance or Penalties which a Due Reformation Requires* (1670), reprinted in *Works*, v (1854), 480-1. He cites Ecclus. xxvi. 29 and xxvii. 2.

of mind to write of 'the men of trade' as 'generally speaking the best body in the nation, generous, sober and charitable'.[1] The social structure and habits of mind of the English were decidedly setting into those of a business nation. Not a step was retraced of the rapid movement in this direction which had come about under the protectorate. The resettlement of the Jews was not disturbed: in 1662 they openly established their first synagogue in London,[2] and a number of Jewish families in England at the present day proudly trace their descent from its earliest members. Until about 1690 the Jews were from time to time subjected to attacks on their freedom to engage in certain kinds of business, or to do so on equal terms; and even after that they were shut out from full civil rights and from some privileged commercial occupations. But they established themselves firmly as valuable members of the community, above all in finance and overseas commerce. Again, while there are only a handful of businesses now existing which trace back some sort of continuity to any earlier period, the number increases steadily from the time of Charles II. Among these are a number of banks, some manufacturing concerns, some public utility services, and, from the time of Queen Anne the oldest of the insurance companies. Other elements of the business structure of the country go back to this period; the financial and commerical press may be said to trace its history from 1692, and the first of the long series of London directories of addresses dates from 1677.

It was not that commerce and industry were ousting the landowning and agricultural classes from their commanding position. A supposed opposition between the landed and the moneyed interests became increasingly one of the commonplaces of political pamphleteers, who wished to win the support of one by arousing its suspicions of the other. But this conflict of interests was almost fictitious. The more carefully society is analysed, the more clearly it appears that there was constant association and interchange between the two. There were ancient landed estates

---

[1] Burnet, *Own Time*, Conclusion.

[2] The first synagogue belonged to the Sephardim or Jews of Spanish and Portuguese descent: it was outgrown and reconstructed in 1674; a third, still used, was consecrated in 1701. The Ashkenazim, or Jews of the German rite, seem to have had a place of meeting in 1660, but their continuous history in England begins in 1690, after which they came in considerable numbers. By 1700 there were Jewish colonies in most of the seaport towns. The city of London did not admit professing Jews to its freedom, and they were excluded from political life by their inability to take Christian oaths.

which would furnish a surplus for investment in commerce and industry, and new ones could be built up by wealth acquired in the army, the navy, politics, the law, and even the church, but it is not an exaggeration to say that it was a normal process, almost the normal process, for the successful merchant and even the exceptionally successful manufacturer to buy a landed estate and establish a line of country squires or baronets or even peers.

Research has not detected, though it may yet do so, any general relation between the investment of commercial capital in land and the agricultural progress which was undoubtedly a feature of this time. There were improving landlords, and improvements needed money; but it cannot be said that the men from the towns as a body were more given to improvement than other landlords. Nor is it easy to say how much headway was made in applying new methods to agriculture. The steady output of new books and the reprinting of older books advocating new methods must have made some impression, and the new scientific botany was being applied, not always with equal wisdom, to the problems of cultivation. Unhappily, however, we have so few records of estates or farms that we cannot say much about the dissemination of the new methods.[1] Not only new methods of cultivation, but other factors also contributed to an increase of production. Inclosure of common fields continued on a large scale, and after the outbreak of the Civil War no attempt was made by any government to check inclosure. It was, however, unpopular, and nothing came of a number of attempts to facilitate it by general legislation. Its spread cannot yet be indicated by statistics, nor can we say much about its social effects at this time. That it involved injustice to the poor we may safely assert.[2] Whether it led to so much building up of larger estates by laying farm to farm as substantially to diminish the number of small landowners we do not know. In some parts of the country we do know that the tendency, assisted by inclosure from the waste, was the other way.

The restoration, or the period within which it fell, saw a great

[1] See the valuable articles by Mr. T. H. Marshall on 'Jethro Tull and the New Husbandry' in *Economic Hist. Rev.* ii. 1, and by Mr. R. V. Lennard on 'English Agriculture under Charles II: the Evidence of the Royal Society's Enquiries', ibid. iv. 23.

[2] Whether for this or for other reasons there was agrarian disorder in or before 1670–1, the date of the Acts 22 and 23 Car. II, c. 7, against rick-firing and cattle-maiming.

change in the public policy regulating the corn trade. The main
concern of that policy now ceased to be the interest of the con-
sumer, who wanted a plentiful and cheap supply; it became a
producer's, or perhaps rather a producer's and trader's policy.
Since the beginning of the seventeenth century the need of the
growing population of London for corn had been a cause of
agricultural progress and of changing trade organization; by
1660–89 these improvements had outrun the needs of London's
own consumption and there was consequently concentrated
there a corn surplus which became available for export. From
about this time London ceased to import corn from abroad.
The navigation laws and other enactments ousted the foreigner,
that is the Dutchman, from the corn trade. The granaries of
London were relinquished to private enterprise. In 1663 came
the last of the series of laws which laid it down that corn might
be exported so long as a certain price was not exceeded. In this
there was the novel provision of high import duties when prices
were low. From 1670 there was no general rule against the
export of corn, however high the price, but the export was
frequently prohibited. The protection against imported corn
was increased in various acts, and bounties came to be paid on
exports. This policy became stereotyped in 1689 when the
protection of agriculture became the counterpart of the high
land-tax with which William III financed his war. The
machinery for administering this law was, however, defective:
there was no proper method of ascertaining prices. The period
of William III and Queen Anne was marked by a number of
bad harvests, including two years of real famine, 1698 and 1709,
so that the prices of corn were high and exports were low. This
corn law policy did not yet exercise its full influence; but it is
important as an expression of the social forces at work, the more
so because the export bounties had scarcely any parallels on the
Continent.

Such prosperity and progress as agriculture showed in spite of
bad years was a part of a general economic consolidation which
outlasted repeated vicissitudes. We may take various criteria of
economic welfare. As to population we have only indirect and
dubious arguments. It is held by some that from 1630 to 1750
the population of England and Wales increased from 5,600,000
to 6,517,000,[1] but there is no certainty whether our period saw

[1] J. Brownlee in *Public Health*, xxix (1916), 237. Dr. Brownlee says that, on the

an upward or a downward movement. General appearances
indicate that the population increased.

Another criterion of prosperity is that of price levels. The
great revolution caused by the rise in prices seems to have run
its course in England by or somewhat before the middle of the
century, and until the last quarter of the eighteenth century
there seems to have been no very great change, though what
change there was ran in an upward direction and was therefore
favourable to increasing production. The evidence about the
standard of living is scanty. There are some grounds for thinking
that the conditions of the poorest class grew worse in the latter
part of the seventeenth century.[1] The theory that the rise in
wages in the time of Charles II outran the rise in prices may or
may not be true; it does not at any rate seem to have been
proved.[2]

We have no statistics for production and we have to infer its
course from general impressions. In agriculture, apart from
disturbances like the run of bad harvests in the 1690s, we may
fairly say that it was a time of increasing output. The same in-
ference from the effect of inventions in mining, and in the various
manufactures, together with what we know of the spread of large
scale organization (though the effect of this last on output must
remain very uncertain) justify a similar conclusion about industrial production. In neither case, however, can we assign even
the roughest figures. For foreign trade, at any rate after 1696, we
have figures which show an increase in the last years of the
period. We have no reason to doubt the belief which was generally held at the time that the period from 1660 to 1688 saw a
great increase in shipping and foreign trade. The previous
depression had been so prolonged that this gives our period,
apart from the wars and some other special circumstances, the
character of a period of rising prosperity, an impression which
is confirmed by what we know of colonial expansion, the East
India trade, and the development of financial technique in
banking and insurance. These and similar changes made it so
much easier for the state to attract money from the country that
the great increase in the public revenue may have been due

basis of these figures, the population was 'nearly constant'; but from the economic
point of view they represent a considerable change.

[1] S. and B. Webb, *English Poor Law History*, pt. i, *The Old Poor Law*, pp. 152–3.

[2] Thorold Rogers, *Hist. of Agriculture and Prices*, v. 12, is the place where the
theory was formulated.

rather to the increased accessibility of wealth than to an increase in its amount; but when this and all other deductions are made, the evidence still seems to show that, apart from fluctuations, England was much richer at the end of the period than at the beginning.

The fluctuations were serious, and they have been examined with some care in the discussion of business cycles. No exact periodicity can be traced in them, and the main deciding factors seem to have been political, wars and expectations of war or of revolution. The European peace of 1678 was soon followed by great activity, and the depression which came in 1682–6 seems to have had the character of the collapse of a boom. It was the only bad depression in peace-time, while, on the other hand, the only really prosperous period of war-time fell in the later years of the war of the Spanish Succession. This seems to have resulted from the ripening in this period of all the various forces of expansion and productivity which we have already noticed. The wars, of course, even when they depressed and interrupted trade, stimulated the production of war-materials. The payment of subsidies, by which the English obtained allies abroad, meant not merely that valuable paper was exported but that these continental powers used their credit in England to supply their needs.

One of the most striking features of the economic organization of England in this period was the dominance of London. In the city proper and its suburbs there were hundreds of thousands of people, perhaps a tenth of the population of the whole country,[1] while the next largest town was Bristol with less than thirty thousand souls. London, indeed, was probably the most populous city in Europe. It was the greatest English port, but it also had congregated in it all the life of the king's court, the government departments, the law-courts, and the greatest part of the miscellaneous population which lived by the arts and the professions or by fashion and pleasure. The metropolitan corn-market

[1] Most modern historians adopt the estimate of three-quarters of a million, or about one-seventh of the population of England and Wales. This is ultimately derived from the *Observations on the Bills of Mortality* (1662–74) by Graunt and Petty; but their primitive statistical methods cannot be trusted. The best figure available for the seventeenth century is an estimate of 1631, made in connexion with the corn-supply, which gives 130,280 men, women, and children under the jurisdiction of the lord mayor including Southwark (W. H. and H. G. Overall, *Analytical Index to the Remembrancia of the City of London* (1878), pp. 345, 389). At a guess this represents 230,000 for the city and suburbs together. Growth went on until and throughout our period, but it cannot be accurately gauged.

which we have noticed already was one among a number of such markets. London drew provisions and necessaries from all over the country, coals by sea from Newcastle, cheeses from Cheshire, droves of geese and turkeys waddling by road from Norfolk, timber from Sussex and Hampshire, cider from Devonshire, bacon from Gloucestershire, black cattle from Wales, fresh salmon from the Severn and Trent and even from the Tweed. The wealth of London commanded amenities which could not be found elsewhere, and the amenities attracted new residents who added again to its wealth. Thus the concentration of capital in London, constantly growing, gave the opportunities for the developments in finance which were turning the English into a nation of business men. Only in the light of these facts do we see the immense historical importance of the situation of the capital, the seat of government, in London and Westminster, the focus of all this economic power.

One way in which the progress of the period may be described is by saying that the English overtook much of the lead which the Dutch had established in economic matters. Dutch managers or artisans were imported in this and the previous period for a con‑siderable number of kinds of work, draining and diking, metal-work including type-founding, textiles, glass-blowing, earthen-ware, brick-making, ship-building, and its subsidiary trades like rope-making. In a number of matters of business method and organization, such as insurance, Dutch examples were followed, and pamphlets urged the imitation of the Dutch as the way to prosperity. Among the men prominent in one way or another in the economic history of the time, it is surprising how many had personal contact with them. It was, indeed, not only from Holland that the English were learning. New inventions were coming in from other countries as well, from France, for instance, where fountain-pens had been sold for a few years before Samuel Pepys began to use one in 1663. England was coming more closely into contact with the outside world. The first English calico-printing works, using Indian methods, were set up in the time of Charles II. In the same reign a type of chain-pump was introduced from China, and in the last quarter of the century England shared in the general European intercourse with China. Tea came into use, as did the coffee of the nearer East. They were drunk not from pewter but from porcelain, which had been a curiosity seen only in palaces.

Horizons were widening not only geographically but also, as we have seen, intellectually. It is a question of great interest how far the scientific movement affected economic life, how far, to put it more precisely, there was any anticipation of that marriage of science and industry which is one of the main characteristics of the life of our own time. There was a strong interest among the leading thinkers of the time in the practical applications of their discoveries. The great Huygens had done much for the perfecting of clocks and watches, a field in which Robert Hooke was also at work. Newton worked at optical glasses and, as we shall see, on the art of striking coin. Among the early fellows of the Royal Society a distinct group, John Evelyn, Houghton, the economic journalist, Petty, John Beale, Joseph Moxon, John Collins, investigated industrial and agricultural processes and machinery. John Locke wrote about the 'large field for knowledge' in labour-saving and economic inventions.[1] It was a period of inventive activity. An economic writer who corresponded with Locke enumerated devices by which processes were made quicker and cheaper in sugar-refining, distilling, the making of glass bottles, tobacco-cutting, smelting, and textile manufactures.[2] He might have added the bolting-engine (used in flour-mills for sifting), machinery used in watch-making, improvements in the stocking frame.

These did not indeed all spring directly from scientific studies. Some of them were the work of mere practical men, even if some of the artisans were themselves scientists like Robert Anderson, a writer on ballistics who, though 'peculiarly skilful . . . in the application of mathematicks to this matter' was by trade a weaver.[3] It has indeed been pointed out that in England only 169 patents for new inventions were issued in the whole period and that of these many were for quite impracticable proposals. Not all the new inventions were patented, but their number and their economic effect ought not to be exaggerated. The significance of the period is that science, though it did not yet exert its full influence on industry, was taking up the position from which it was soon to do so. The crowning proof of it, the turning-point, was the invention of the steam-engine by Newcomen. New-

---

[1] Lord King, *Life and Letters of Locke* (1829), p. 88; *Human Understanding*, Bk. IV, c. xii. 12.

[2] J. Cary, *Essay on Trade* (1695), pp. 145–7.

[3] Harris, *Lexicon Technicum*, i (1704), s.v. 'Ordnance'.

comen, a baptist ironmonger, was a simple craftsman, but the process by which this invention came to perfection cannot be explained except by tracing it back to the scientists. Newcomen was in contact with Savery, who knew the Dutch language and translated from it one of Coehoorn's books on military engineering. From Savery's invention it is necessary to go back through Hooke and Papin, a Frenchman employed by the Royal Society, to the mighty brains of Boyle and Huygens, further still through Pascal and Torricelli to Galileo Galilei himself. The history of the invention of the steam-engine is nothing less than the history of the scientific movement as a whole.[1] King Charles II afforded one of the greatest examples of the blindness of the amateur when in 1664 he 'mightily laughed' at the Royal Society 'for spending time only in weighing of ayre, and doing nothing else since they sat'.[2] What they were doing was to investigate atmospheric pressure, and it was a short step to the pressure of steam. The experimenters themselves did not foresee that the motive power which came into practical use as a result of their work, and which before the death of Queen Anne was raising water from a mine in Staffordshire, was to become after two more generations one of the governing forces of the world.

Neither the scientists nor the men of business appeared to contemporaries to be the real leaders of economic life. Governments paid continuous attention to matters of trade and used all the resources of the state to further it. A series of committees and councils collected economic information and advised the government on programmes of development and legislation. In 1660 a council for foreign plantations and a council for trade were set up side by side, bodies advisory to the privy council and composed partly of important privy councillors, including the secretaries of state, partly of colonial officers and business men. Some of the members sat on both. By 1665, however, these councils ceased to meet, and the privy council had to rely on temporary or standing committees of its own until 1668, when a new council of trade was established, followed in 1670 by a council for the colonies, which in 1672 became a council for trade and plantations. This was smaller in numbers, and its members were paid. It had as its secretary after 1673 no less a person than John Locke, and altogether, in spite of being 'strengthened' by the

---

[1] It is well described in R. L. Galloway, *The Steam-Engine and its Inventors* (1881).
[2] Pepys, *Diary*, 1 February 1663/4.

addition of some eminent politicians, it carried out a good deal of useful work in collecting information and advising the privy council how to co-ordinate policy. In 1675, however, the same thing happened as had happened before, the advisory body was dropped, and the privy council again fell back on an executive committee of its own. So things continued until 1696. In that year the house of commons, dissatisfied with the defence of commerce in the war, made a move towards the establishment of a parliamentary committee for trade with executive powers, and, in order to prevent such an invasion of his prerogative, the king set up a board of trade which lasted for more than a century. This was a board of the usual pattern with eight paid, and well-paid, members, besides the great officers of state who nominally belonged to it, and a staff who were in fact a government department.

The board of trade kept closely in touch with the merchants, and there is ample evidence that merchants were officially and privately consulted by other departments in such a way as to exert a steady and growing influence on policy. The effect of this was seen in an elaborate and rigid system of trade regulation. In the earlier seventeenth century deep-seated causes, such as the great fall in the value of money and the increased power of the territorial states, had led to a growth of protectionist opinion and policy in Europe generally, and this now became more intense. The English Navigation Act of 1651 came almost at the beginning of the new phase. It met with retaliation abroad, but England continued to lead the way in protectionist measures.

The resulting system of commercial policy, which grew less systematic with time through the heaping up of incoherent regulations, was that afterwards discussed by Adam Smith under the name of 'the mercantile system'. It aimed at encouraging English trade both negatively, by duties and prohibitions, and positively, by bounties and relatively lighter duties, in order to increase manufactures, to bring about a mutually profitable relation with the colonies and to obtain a 'favourable' balance of trade. Its first element was the tariff. This was meant to protect the home market and to assist the traders who wished to sell in foreign markets. There were restraints on the importing from foreign countries of such goods as could be produced at home. Agriculture had not only the corn laws, but also restrictions on the

importing of live cattle and dairy-produce. The wool manufacture was protected by the prohibition both of the importing
of foreign manufactured goods and of the exporting of raw wool.
Merchants, though shut out from these branches of trade, were
favoured in other directions, in particular by drawbacks or
repayments of all or part of the duties on certain exports and on
foreign goods re-exported. A number of commercial treaties
were made, of which the purpose was to facilitate trade with
particular countries, and some of these will be noted later; but
none were made in the seventeenth century by which any important mitigations were introduced into the English tariff.

The commercial system was a system of imperial and not
merely of English commerce. The navigation laws were the
main factor in relations with the colonies, but they had also the
purpose of encouraging manufactures, shipping, and ship-building. They were meant to promote the economic welfare of both
parties, the colonies as well as the mother country, but on the
basis of a crude division of functions between the old country
and the new. The carriage of goods to or from the colonies was
prohibited except in British-built ships owned by Englishmen,
and having Englishmen to the proportion of not less than three-
quarters of their crews. No colonial produce from any part of
the world was to be imported into England except in such ships.
But the term 'Englishmen' included the colonists, who were
thus able to share in the monopoly, so that both ship-building
and commerce flourished along the sea-board of North America.
Exports from the colonies were controlled; certain 'enumerated
commodities' were to be shipped only to England. The list of
1660 included sugar, tobacco, raw cotton, indigo, ginger, and
dye-woods; in Queen Anne's time rice and naval stores were
added. Among these the greater part were products of the
Caribbean region: only tobacco and naval stores came in important quantities from the North American mainland. The
colonists could take their other products where they liked. They
were not, however, free to go where they pleased for imports.
All commodities of the growth, production, or manufacture of
Europe were to be laden in England.[1] This was intended to
build up a staple-trade in England. Stocks of goods produced
at home and imported, were to be accumulated in the ware-

[1] There were certain exceptions, such as Portuguese salt and wines and Irish and
Scottish provisions and horses.

houses of English ports in such quantities that the English merchants could control their markets. The shipping provisions also laid it down, in order to exclude the Dutch, that none of these goods were to come to England except in English ships or those of their country of origin. Lastly, England began to restrict the freedom of the colonies to engage in manufactures: in 1699 their woollen manufactures were restrained.

Policy in commercial matters can operate only within the limits set by the policy of other countries and by geography. England needed imports, and she needed therefore to keep on terms with the countries which had them to sell. For some of them there was indeed a choice between alternative sources of supply, as for the textile raw materials, wool, silk, flax, and cotton, or for saltpetre, sulphur, and wines. For one great group of products which were classed together under the heading of naval stores—timber, pitch and tar, hemp—we were dependent on the Norway and Baltic trades. Only at the end of the period was a serious beginning made in developing the supplies from our own North American colonies, so that down to the end of the war of the Spanish Succession our naval needs made it a necessity for British policy to keep open the trade with the Swedish and Danish ports and Danzig. England depended on the world-market established in Amsterdam for spices, the products of the Malay archipelago. Spices were more important in those days than they are now. The scarcity of fresh meat in the winter led to their being much used in preserving meat, besides which there was a fashion for highly seasoned food.[1] The hope of setting up a market for spices independent of the Dutch East India Company died out, but the plans for a staple-trade were carried on for the products of hither India, where spices were not grown, but which sent rich cargoes of calicoes, raw silk, indigo, and saltpetre.

The period is extremely important in the history of the British East India trade, and the expansion of that trade the most important single change in English economy. The East India Company was the greatest British commercial institution; we shall gain a measure of its greatness when we come to deal with

[1] In 1674 Anthony Wood (*Life and Times*, ed. Clark, ii. 300) wrote: ' 'Tis to be wondered at our ancestors who were given so much to eat spices. Wee now, since the pox came up, eat none and will suffer none to be in meat. That trade fails.' But the trade did not fail, and the change in fashion, if real, was commercially unimportant.

two incidents of striking political importance, those of the Darien Company and the South Sea Company.[1] The other trading companies were far less important. The Merchant Adventurers, the old monopolists in the export of English cloth to Germany, were now in decline. Their method of limiting the volume of their trade and keeping up prices was obsolete; the interlopers were right when they claimed that the way to capture the market was to sell cheap. From the restoration to the revolution the policy of parliament vacillated between throwing the trade open and sustaining the company's monopoly, but in 1689 the monopoly was abolished and the company merely lingered on, steadily becoming less influential until, when it is last heard of in the nineteenth century, it was nothing more than a dining club in Hamburg. The Levant Company, which traded with Turkey, was a rival to the East India Company and to the decadent Russia Company. At the time of the Restoration it was losing ground to the Dutch and from the early eighteenth century to the French. It escaped having its trade thrown open in 1689, but the commons had already prevented it in 1674 from narrowly restricting its membership. The Eastland Company, which handled the Baltic trade, suffered not only from foreign competition but also from the shortage of British tonnage in the time of the Navigation laws. It had no real importance after 1673.

Protectionism in its newer forms operated through tariffs and other forms of royal and parliamentary control. It was becoming unfavourable to privileged companies for foreign trade. The American trade, which already included the famous triangular trade in which British exports were exchanged for slaves in Africa and slaves for American products, was in the hands of private firms, and the grandiose plans of various African companies made little impression on the real economic history except in the brief period 1674–87.[2] The important trade with Portugal and its colonies was also an affair of private firms. It underwent a considerable change during the period, for Portugal's principal export to England at the beginning was sugar and at the end was wine. In exchange the Portuguese took mainly cloth, and at the death of Queen Anne Portugal and its colonies provided the principal market for English cloth after those of Holland and Turkey.

[1] See below, pp. 281, 249.   [2] See below, p. 331,

Imports made the country to a certain extent dependent on the foreigner, but exports did not provide a simple form of payment with which the foreigner could be induced to bring his goods. They did not make each selling nation reciprocally dependent on us. This was because we had to import things we could not produce, but the exports in which we had anything like a natural monopoly were few, and for the most part we exported manufactured goods which competitors on the Continent could also make. Our exports of corn, as we have seen, did not amount to much. Coal went in increasing but still unimportant quantities to Holland.[1] The output of the mines increased in spite of difficulties with water, against which new kinds of pumps, culminating in the steam-pump, gave aid, and in spite of the new difficulties of explosions at the lower levels which were now being mined; but the greater part of this increase was absorbed at home. Here the use of coal fuel in industry and in the domestic hearths of London and other towns accessible by water provided a substitute for wood-fuel, which was becoming scarce and dear; and the growing numbers employed in the mining and transport of coal were an important element in the general industrial advance. Another product of extractive industry, fuller's earth, was a prohibited export, but it found its way to our textile competitors. All these articles, however, together with the fish, cattle products, malt, tin, and lead which we exported, were far less in value than our textile exports.

Of these woollens were, as of old, by far the most important. Technical improvements were being made in their production; dyeing, spinning, and warping all improved in the period, and improvements in the loom began. The organization of the industry was far from uniform throughout the country, but it mainly belonged to the type for which the best name is 'the putting-out system'. Under this system, roughly speaking, the worker owns the machinery and the capitalist owns the material, which he puts out to the worker. Within this definition there are included many degrees of dependence or independence of the workers, for instance many forms of indebtedness to the capitalist

---

[1] Nef. i. 79, 84, estimates the annual exports of British coal in 1661–70 at 109,000 tons and in 1681–90 at 150,000, the total annual production for the latter period at 1,280,000 as compared with 51,400, of which 12,000 was exported, in 1541–50. For the meaning of these figures see T. S. Willan, *The English Coasting Trade, 1600–1750* (1930), App. 3.

putter-out; and the system may exist with various degrees of specialization of functions on the side both of worker and putter-out. In this period the great west of England woollen industry, which exported cloth of high quality to western and central Europe, and the newly introduced West Riding worsted industry were more definitely capitalistic than the Yorkshire woollen industry, with its more difficult work and less expensive materials. Some of the capitalists gave out work to large numbers of people, and the industry, perhaps especially under the pressure of military demands, was capable of developing great productive power. Its organization tended to become correspondingly complex, and as new types of middlemen grew up the older, less specialized, trades invoked the help of parliament and, after long agitation, got a futile act of parliament in 1697, which was meant to bind the industry down to its existing stage of growth.

The minor textile industries are interesting less for their share in the bulk of British trade than for the indications they give of expansive forces and political support. Calico-printing began in the time of Charles II, and in 1700, after a long controversy, it was protected by an import-prohibition against Indian printed calicoes. Cotton was growing in importance and was becoming localized in Lancashire. Silk was almost wholly an industry of the French refugees who had come in during the religious wars of the sixteenth century and were followed by a fresh wave when Louis XIV persecuted the huguenots. Having a clean sheet to work on, it started with a comparatively advanced capitalistic organization. In Canterbury, which was one of its centres, though far less important than Spitalfields, the chief of them, there was in the last years of the seventeenth century a workshop with twenty looms under one roof. The silk-workers, especially from 1692 when the Royal Lutestring Company was established for the making of *taffetas lustrés* and other expensive fabrics, received high protection by various acts of parliament; but in its formidable task of capturing foreign markets from the French it made only modest progress.

Linen also, in spite of great efforts by projectors and the legislature, failed to become more than a subsidiary British manufacture. Here again the huguenots supplied skilled workmanship, and numbers of plans, half commercial and half philanthropic, were formed for the spinning of flax in workhouses and similar institutions. The industry was entirely exempted from the control of guilds and corporations; but the new companies which were set up soon resigned any attempt at large-scale centralization. In 1698 England virtually dropped out of the protectionistic competition with Holland and other linen-producing countries, but the industry took root in Scotland and Ireland.[1]

The metal industries were also going forward. The old Sussex iron industry was beginning to decline, perhaps mainly because of its poor communications with London, when Spanish competition was growing less, but Swedish continually greater.[2] In Staffordshire and Shropshire, however, especially under the leadership of Abraham Darby, the founder of a quaker dynasty of iron-masters, much progress was made in the manufacture of iron pots and utensils of various kinds. In Queen Anne's reign Darby was using a new process at Coalbrookdale, smelting with coke fuel, which was to solve in the future a problem caused by the inadequacy of supplies of charcoal. It was only one among a number of inventions new to England or altogether new which he used in the iron industry and that of copper which had been his earlier sphere. He had visited Holland and brought Dutch brassfounders to Bristol: the main upshot of his work was that he supplied the home market with a variety of goods formerly imported from abroad. Among the other iron-masters of the time the most remarkable was Sir Ambrose Crowley, a magnate who married two of his daughters into the aristocracy. He too imported foreign workmen, Liégeois. He was an alderman of London, but his works were in Durham and Northumberland near the coal and easily connected with London by the coasting trade. He not only worked up English ironmongery towards the continental standard, but he was a model employer of the benevolent autocratic type, and under his capitalistic auspices were established disablement, superannuation, and medical benefits for his work-people.

If protectionism was the external expression of the rise of the business economy in England, at home it was expressed in the relaxation of state control over industry and trade. The guilds and corporations which in every locality had once controlled the recruiting, conditions of work, output and remuneration of every

[1] See below, p 319.
[2] See Rhys Jenkins in *Newcomen Soc. Trans.* i. 31–33.

industry were by this time on the road of decline. The state had, in fact, no policy for industry except that of protecting it by regulating trade.

The tendency to improvement, the combination of wealth and enterprise, is seen also in internal transport. One of the advantages of England as a business country was the excellence of its internal communications. Amongst these must be reckoned the coastwise routes of navigation. The frequent harbours, natural and artificial, and the many navigable rivers made it an accessible country. Not much, however, had been done towards a real modernization of the routes. The beginning of a movement which was to become vastly important belongs to the Restoration period. Already a few short pieces of waterway had been rendered navigable, and pamphleteers, some of them with knowledge of the Low Countries, had proposed attempts on this or that river. After the Restoration the improvement of rivers began in earnest, and by the end of the first quarter of the eighteenth century there was scarcely a place in England, except in the hills of the west and north, which was distant by more than a long day's haul from navigable water.

To the same time belong the unobtrusive beginnings of the great remaking of the road-system which the eighteenth century completed. One or two of the main post-roads were taken in hand. The old system by which each parish was liable for the upkeep of its roads was clearly insufficient, and parliament began to authorize the levying of tolls from traffic. For the present, however, the traffic seems to have developed more rapidly than the road-system. In 1675 there was published John Ogilby's *Britannia*, the first road-book based on an actual survey of the roads, a fine piece of work undertaken at the express desire of King Charles II. This was a sign of the greater attention now paid to questions of transport. The improvements in the public services of vehicles were very notable. The old stage-wagons survived as cheaper and slower conveyances, but stage-coach services quickly developed from the time of the Restoration. The usual fare in the middle of Charles II's reign was a shilling for every five miles, and the distance covered between forty and fifty miles a day. Oxford could be reached from London in twelve hours: the last stage-coaches on the improved roads of the nineteenth century took half that time and the fastest railway trains of the nineteen-thirties seventy minutes. The quality of the roads varied much from one part of the country to another: in the Midlands they were for the most part very bad, but the era of improvement began.

With few and unimportant exceptions[1] the legislature tried to promote the welfare of the poorest only by amending the poor-law. The old system of wage-assessment was still in force, and justices from time to time drew up rates of wages; but it is doubt-ful how far this administrative activity controlled the wages actually paid. Instead of revising the rates, justices often merely re-enacted the old lists and the whole system was growing more lax. In the poor-law several different currents of ideas were at work. Each of them led to innovations, but these were not co-ordinated, and some of the new methods were adopted only locally, so that the poor-law system became more confused and more incalculable in its effects. The first, and perhaps the most important, change was in the law of settlement. A pauper was entitled to poor-relief in the place of his birth. The poor-law authorities of London and Westminster were apt to be burdened with charges for the poor who drifted into the metropolis from all parts of the country. They promoted an act in 1662 which established the power of removing to their places of 'legal settle-ment' persons who might become chargeable. It was a general act, not confined to London and Westminster, and therefore its result was, to put it in the simplest form, to give the local authori-ties an interest and a duty in seeing that the labourers did not wander from their native places. It hampered the mobility of labour and it drastically limited the freedom of the poor. There were always certain exceptions, and before the end of William III's reign no less then five explanatory and amending statutes were necessary; but in the end the law was very severe against any working man who could not get work for a full year or other-wise approve himself above the poverty-line. The disciplinary element in the poor-law was much to the fore in this period. John Locke wrote a report on pauperism for the board of trade in which his individualistic liberalism appears at its worst: he emphasized the vice and idleness of the poor. In the same spirit the law for punishing vagrants was strengthened under William

---

[1] Such as the prohibiting of the truck-system in the woollen, linen, cotton, and iron manufactures by 1 Anne, st. 2, c. 23, an act of which other clauses were of a disciplinary nature. Provisions against truck began in the reign of Elizabeth I and protests against it even earlier.

III and codified under Queen Anne. But Locke was a charitable man, and he may be partly excused because he did not understand that the other causes of unemployment were trifles beside lack of demand. No one grasped the relevance of this fact to the poor-law, and the result is seen in the second characteristic change of the period, the rise of new types of workhouses.

Here the disciplinary motive played a part. The worst workhouses, or houses of correction and bridewells, were prisons under another name. But there was also genuine philanthropy at work. The quakers, for instance, set up workhouses of their own, at Bristol in 1696 and at Clerkenwell in 1701. Benevolence was by no means absent from the administration of the law now that it was left to the churchwardens and overseers, with some supervision from justices of the peace and none at all from the central executive. It was sometimes interested and sometimes indistinguishable from corruption. The farmer who was an overseer might save his own pocket by generous doles of weekly out-relief to his labourers. Under William III attempts were made to check these abuses, partly because it was believed that the poor-rates cost too much. For England and Wales they amounted to a sum probably not much lower than half a million pounds a year, and they were probably growing.[1] But, although there were some who wanted economy even at the cost of oppression, the prevailing opinion, in which Locke shared, was that with better organization, philanthropy could not merely be economical, but could even be made to pay. So parish poorhouses were converted into spinning-schools. Private acts of parliament were passed combining the parishes of the greater towns so that they set up large union workhouses, where paupers of every kind were set to unskilled manufactory work.[2] Not only London but Bristol, Hull, Exeter, Crediton, Liverpool, Colchester, and King's Lynn had them before the end of William's reign, and Worcester, Plymouth, Norwich, and other places in Queen Anne's. The hope that they would be profitable was delusive. It was impossible for long together to find men and women with character and education enough to acquit them-

[1] The Report of the board of trade, 23 December 1697, in C.O. 389/14, on the the basis of returns from 4,415 parishes computes the total very roughly at £400,000. In Queen Anne's time the total may have been about a million (Eden, *State of the Poor* (1797), i. 229, 314).

[2] Until about the beginning of this period 'workhouse' (see *Oxford Eng. Dict.*) meant simply a factory.

selves decently in the responsibility of managing these institutions. Before long the 'union' became a new evil worse than the old; yet it was created by an honest if short-sighted hope of combining benevolence with better social organization.

NOTE ON THE FEAR OF A RESUMPTION OF CHURCH LANDS

(See p. 33 above and p. 125 below)

From the Treaty of Dover in 1672 to the Revolution of 1688 the return of papal authority in England was, or seemed to be, in the region of practical possibilities. Some people said that it would involve the resumption by the church or the religious orders of the lands confiscated from them in the sixteenth century. Two questions may be asked about these statements: were they sincere, and were they well-founded. Major M. V. Hay, in *The Jesuits and the Popish Plot* (1934), gives three instances, from 1676 to 1689, in which opponents of Rome expressed their fears, and one in which William, Lord Russell disclaimed it as a motive. Lord Stafford, after his condemnation in 1680 told the peers that some had wanted to restore these lands, but he had told the duke of York that they were in so many hands that it could not be done. In 1685 the papal nuncio Adda wrote of this fear 'whether real or pretended' as a motive of Halifax and others rich in church property for opposing 'whatever can advantage religion': Foxcroft, *Halifax* (1896), i. 460. Richard Baxter at the age of 76 thought that the church lands would be restored if Roman powers prevailed: *Last Treatise*, ed. F. J. Powicke (1926), p. 20. John Dryden published *The Hind and the Panther* in 1687 as a work of Roman catholic persuasion. He wrote:

> That pious Joseph in the church behold
> To feed your famine, and refuse your gold—

adding a reference to 'The renunciation of the Benedictines to the Abbey lands'. This renunciation was known to the contemporary public from *A Sermon preach'd before the King on November the 13. 1686* by Dom Philip Ellis, published by His Majesty's command, 1686, where the authorities for it are cited on p. 28.

III

FOREIGN AND DOMESTIC POLICY,
1661–8

THE Restoration settlement in England was, as we have seen, an attempt to create a sufficient degree of harmony for the purposes of government by reverting to the parliamentary and royal constitution and the Anglican establishment. At best this could not be more than the harmony of the privileged and the unprivileged, a harmony in which one part of the nation made only the negative contribution of submissiveness; but that in itself need not have led to a new discord. The new strife which broke down the settlement was not simply a renewal of the old, but a product of the changing course of events, and it differed from the old divisions of the civil war not only in being fought over different issues, but also in assuming the new form of a contest between organized political parties. The questions at issue were generically the same, religion, constitutional or arbitrary government, and taxation; but they arose in new cases. In religion, for instance, the quarrel was not about episcopacy but about toleration. And it is a sign of the growing political sense of the nation that, although when opposition arose against Charles II, it had some personal and intellectual continuity with the opposition to Charles I, and although its leaders often thought and acted in terms of conspiracy and rebellion, its final achievement was the creation of the historic whig party.

The regular parliamentary history of the reign began with the general election of 1661. This election has not yet been studied in detail. We do not know how far its result was due to a spontaneous expression of public opinion and how far to pressure exerted by the court and its friends, but, however it was achieved, the result was definite. The parliament was not dissolved until 3 February 1679: it is therefore sometimes called the long parliament of the Restoration. The cavalier parliament, as it was also called, had a powerful majority of royalist Anglicans. It contained less than sixty presbyterians, and the city of London in returning two presbyterians and two independents was

exceptional. We have seen how the temper of the house of commons sharpened the legislation against nonconformists. Half the
members of the convention were returned again, and there were
a hundred members who had sat in the Long Parliament of
Charles I. The commons throughout this long period were learning to work together and consciously to claim a large part in
affairs, and although the intermittent sessions occupied only
sixty months in the eighteen years, this continuity was an important factor in re-establishing parliamentary authority. When
the parliament ended only two hundred of its original five
hundred members remained, and the new members who came
in at by-elections largely reflected the growing discontent of
the country with the royal policy.[1] Clarendon, although he had
the great wisdom to see that co-operation with parliament was the
best basis for the monarchy, wished parliament to take a more
modest place than would satisfy it even in 1661. Nor did he pay
enough attention to the vital links which might have made co-
operation with parliament really successful. None of the leading
ministers of Charles II sat, after reaching their height, in the
house of commons. Of the secretaries of state Sir William
Morice, unimportant in his office, is said to have justified his
long tenure by his handiness in parliament; but Sir Henry
Bennet, who soon became a peer, was no parliamentarian, and
if Henry Coventry did pretty well, Sir Joseph Williamson and
Sir Leoline Jenkins were definitely unpopular with the house.[2]
The king was never so well represented in the commons as he
should have been.

An enactment was made in 1664 which laid open another
matter for contest between king and parliament. In the long
controversy of the seventeenth century one of the disputed points
about the power of parliaments was that of their duration. The
more continuous they were, the greater their power: the ideal
of the presbyterian oligarchy of the interregnum had been an
assembly like the Dutch states-general which met every day of
the week and all the year round. Oliver Cromwell had stuck to

[1] W. C. Abbott in *Eng. Hist. Rev.* xxi. 21, 254 gives an excellent general account
of the parliament, but his inferences from the figures of seats, bills passed, and
divisions should be controlled by comparison at each point with the fluctuating
conditions which determined them.
[2] For the dates between which they held office see below, p. 461. Henry Bennet,
born 1618; secretary of state 1662–74; created Lord Arlington 1663; earl of
Arlington 1672; lord chamberlain 1674; died 1685.

the English tradition according to which the council was permanent and the parliament assembled for a few weeks in the year to vote taxes and to redress grievances, but did not continuously supervise the government. This was the accepted view of parliament throughout our period: it is the view of Locke in his *Civil Government*. This tradition had been defined by the Triennial Act of 1641, which laid it down that there was to be no interval of more than three years between parliaments, and prescribed an elaborate machinery by which, if the king failed to summon a parliament when the time came, each of the subordinate functionaries who took part in its summoning was to act even without the usual orders. The position now arose that some discontented persons tried to read into this act the quite different principle, which was not in it and formed no part of the law until 1694, that a parliament was not to last more than three years, but at the end of that time must be dissolved so that a new general election should bring the opinion of the constituencies to bear on the government. This gave an opportunity for amending the existing law, which in any case had an antimonarchical flavour, and the amendment took the form of re-enacting it without the safeguarding machinery for carrying it out. In due time Charles II took advantage of this; he ruled without a parliament from March 1681 until his death in February 1685.

The effective opposition to Charles began among those who had welcomed the Restoration. It was not merely that there were no republicans in the cavalier parliament. In the country at large, in spite of the repressive religious code, republicanism was prostrate. When every allowance is made for the secrecy of the channels in which it had to work, it remains true that the plots and risings were small and foolish, with no real chance of success and not supported by any considerable body even among the Puritan fanatics. The impression they made was exaggerated by the romancing of secret agents and by the general nervousness of the public. It was not until the Rye House Plot of 1683 that middle-aged or elderly survivors of the New Model Army were able to get together into something like a diminutive revival of the Good Old Cause. Among the cavaliers in the house of commons there were, however, discontented groups which were bound to combine. The loyal majority was too large for the government to be able to satisfy every claimant for reward.

The many-sided personal unpopularity of Clarendon made matters worse. In the religious debates, in which he tried not very skilfully to steer between the severity of the bishops and the king's laxity, the commons showed for the first time how obstinate they could be. In December 1662, within five months of the exodus of the nonconformist incumbents, Charles was emboldened by Bennet and his friends to take a step to soften the asperity of the new laws. He issued a document, often called the first Declaration of Indulgence, announcing that he intended to ask parliament to pass a measure to 'enable him to exercise with a more universal satisfaction that power of dispensing which he conceived to be inherent in him'. The commons were furious. The bill to allow the king to dispense with[1] the Act of Uniformity and all other laws relating to oaths, subscriptions, and religious conformity never reached them from the lords; but they raged against the Declaration, and demanded the expulsion of Jesuits and Roman catholic priests from the kingdom. Clarendon, by failing to stand out against this, fatally weakened his position at court, but it was financial mismanagement and the Dutch war which brought him down. His essential failure lay in foreign policy.

Charles II had come back without the help of foreign arms or foreign money. He was under no serious obligations to foreign powers, and to that extent he was able to begin his foreign policy with a clean sheet. Such limitations as lay upon his freedom of action came from the side of his subjects. More than one powerful group among them had a vested interest in one or other article of foreign policy, and it was impossible that there could be a complete breach of continuity here. Charles and his entourage had lived in foreign countries and had been in touch with foreign courts; but they had been rather suppliants than negotiators, and not one of them had a statesman's knowledge of European affairs. At the modest price of sparing the life of John Thurloe, the foreign minister of the protectorate, they were able to start from a series of able memoranda in which he explained the existing situation. After that they learnt mainly by trial and error: the organization of the secretaries' office and the training of the diplomatists were built up as they went along.

The existing situation was confused, but the confusion arose

[1] That is not to do away with them, but to exempt individuals from their effects.

from certain adventurous liabilities of the protectorate which were easily liquidated. The country was at war with Spain. No active military or naval operations were in progress; there was no prospect that any could be started to advantage, and no money to start them with, so, without considering whether the war had served any useful purpose, the government had to make a peace for which the Spaniards were willing and anxious. By this they did not relinquish their claim to Jamaica, though the English remained in occupation there,[1] but they gave up Dunkirk. To a policy like that of Cromwell, which contemplated intervention in continental wars as a means of making England safe by making her dangerous, the possession of a permanent landing-place between France and the Spanish Netherlands was of incalculable advantage. Dunkirk might have become what Calais had been. Charles, however, was not in a position to carry on such a policy. Their recent experiences had given his people a distrust of armies, and, when he cut down his military establishment to about five thousand men, he began a phase of policy which lasted for a generation, in which Great Britain neither did nor could send any effective armed force abroad. Although it seemed humiliating it was therefore not surprising that in 1662 Dunkirk, the garrison of which was costing more than £100,000 a year, was sold to France for some £400,000. Clarendon did not foresee that the corsairs of Dunkirk would inflict losses of millions of pounds on English merchant shipping in every French war of that century and the next.[2]

That Dunkirk went to France and not back to Spain was a result of Charles's having adhered to Cromwell's choice of the French side in the great contest of the European powers. The hostility of France and Spain, already centuries old, arose from causes with which Great Britain had nothing to do. It was one

[1] See below, p. 325. British sovereignty over Jamaica was recognized in the Treaty of Madrid, 1670.
[2] For details of the transaction see C. L. Grose, 'England and Dunkirk' in *American Hist. Rev.* xxxix (1933), 1, and 'The Dunkirk Money' in *Journal of Modern Hist.* v (1933), 1. Dr. Grose did not consider how difficult it would have been to defend Dunkirk against French attack: the histories of Calais, Ostend, and Gibraltar suggest that it would have been almost impossible. In the text, as throughout this volume, I have converted French livres into pounds sterling by the rough and ready method of dividing by twelve and taking the nearest round figure. This was often done during the period. The par of exchange was altered more than once. From 1676 to 1701 it stood at £3 to 40 livres or 13 livres 6 sous 8 deniers to the pound, but the exchange was usually against the livre.

of the data from which British policy had to be constructed. In an aggressive phase of British aims it provided a choice of allies and a choice of gains: by its means Cromwell had gained Jamaica and Dunkirk. Even in a phase of comparative abstention, such as that which now began, it was difficult to keep away from its centripetal power. For a few months its force had been mitigated by the Peace of the Pyrenees of 1659 which had ended a Franco-Spanish war of twenty-four years. By this Louis XIV gained frontier-provinces in both north and south, and a Spanish wife whose marriage opened a prospect of dynastic union in the future. Nevertheless he continued in an indirect way to wear down the strength of his neighbour. Portugal, once a free country but eighty years before subjected to Spain, had been waging a war of independence since 1640. Count Schomberg, a marshal of France but by birth a German protestant prince with an English mother, took command of the Portuguese army, the same man who thirty years later was killed at the battle of the Boyne. His appointment, approved by Louis, was negotiated in London, and Charles gave him an English peerage.

Portuguese diplomacy won another and a greater success in London. Charles was a bachelor, and in the interests of dynastic security it was necessary that he should marry. His council considered a variety of possible brides and showed almost as little skill in angling for them as had been shown over the marriage of Charles I. Any choice implied friendship with one power and enmity with others, but these considerations were imperfectly appreciated. When the strong-minded queen-regent of Portugal offered her daughter, Catherine of Braganza, what made the greatest impression in London was that the offer included the richest dowry any bride had ever brought to England, more than £800,000 in cash, with Bombay and Tangier. The offer was accepted. Our oldest ally had an excellent bargain. By sacrificing two possessions which she could not hope to hold much longer, she saved the rest of her crumbling empire. Bombay was of so little visible use to Charles that he soon thought of evacuating it and was glad to hand it over to the East India Company in 1668. Tangier might have become as important an English base for the Mediterranean as Gibraltar and Minorca were to be in the eighteenth century. It might have become a rich trading entrepôt. A great mole was built there, the most ambitious work that English engineers had ever undertaken. But England was

not yet ready to maintain such an outpost. To hold it a garrison
of three thousand men was needed. It proved to be more expensive than Dunkirk, and, as Charles's domestic and financial
difficulties increased, the attacks of the Moors became harder to
repel. In 1683 the garrison was withdrawn and English political
power in the Mediterranean was interrupted until the end of the
policy of military abstention from European affairs. Not even
the first of the benefits expected from the Portuguese match was
to materialize: Charles never begot a lawful heir.

Disappointing as they proved, these benefits were the only
solid inducements held out by the policy of friendship with
France. That policy was not, however, simply due to the allure-
ments of French diplomacy. Nor did it spring only from the
natural preference of Charles and his friends for the country of
his dazzling cousin Louis XIV, the country which had already
become the leader of the world's fashions and manners. These
played their part, especially in making the English forget that
they did not need alliances except for their own defence or to
further their own plans; but the French policy was also connected
with the most realistic element in British policy, that which dealt
with the Dutch. The old rivalry with the Dutch in the East
Indies, in North America, on the west coast of Africa, the old
friction in Europe over maritime law and the mercantilist policy
had continued after the peace of 1654. There had been successful
settlements of particular disputes, but the broad conflict of
interest was still one of the leading facts of England's international position. The renewal and strengthening of the Act of
Navigation in 1660 showed that the English meant to persist in
the policy of using the power of the state against Dutch commercial wealth. Not only did the merchants interested in these
measures retain their influence over the government: the tradition of economic policy established in the interregnum actually
became stronger after the Restoration. The newly revived factor
in English policy, the court, joined in it with the City. Princes,
ministers, and the members of their high circles took shares in
the great joint-stock companies and saw to it that these got at
least such naval and military help as could be conveniently
spared. The duke of York, lord high admiral, was the first
governor of the Royal African Company. He bought £3,000
worth of East India stock in 1684. He succeeded Prince Rupert as
governor of the Hudson's Bay Company, and when he became king

he was succeeded in his turn by John Churchill, afterwards duke of Marlborough. Thus the leading naval and military adminis- trators were personally interested in commercial and colonial expansion, and soon after the Restoration they hoped to hasten that expansion by disputing the power of the Dutch. The econo- mists held up the Dutch as examples for imitation. Some of them pointed out 'how to outdo the Dutch without fighting',[1] but to the men in power this seemed a roundabout method. The Dutch had not built up their trade and empire without fighting. Oliver Cromwell's wars had aroused the spirit of Drake and Hawkins not only against the Spaniards but also against the Dutch.

When the Restoration came about the Dutch hoped to con- clude a triple alliance with France and England; but the prospects of this were slight from the first. Two possible obstacles were indeed surmounted, the Portuguese question and the dynastic question, in spite of the fact that Charles, in the shortage of trained diplomatists, had to make use of the old Cromwellian resident at The Hague. Sir George Downing, although he served well afterwards at the treasury, showed himself in this employment both a muddler and a bully. The Dutch were at war with Portugal: it was they who were breaking up the Portuguese colonial empire. They had, however, no real prospect of advantage from continuing this war, and the English wished to stop it both as rivals of the Dutch and as friends of the Portuguese. A peace was therefore made in 1661 which admitted the Dutch to the valuable Portuguese trade but without depriv- ing the English of the commercial concessions of the marriage treaty. The dynastic difficulty lay in the fact that Charles, as the uncle of the boy William III of Orange, might be expected to work against the exclusion of that prince from the offices held by his ancestors, an exclusion equally dear to Cromwell and to the ruling party in the Dutch republic. Charles and Clarendon, however, did not show the least disposition to raise the question. A treaty was therefore made in 1662 which continued the agree- ments made by Cromwell after the first Dutch war. It provided for the settlement of disputes by arbitration, but it did nothing about new questions which had arisen since the former treaty, and Charles's attempts to borrow money in Holland had failed. Their hope of a triple alliance having come to nothing, the

[1] This is part of the title of Andrew Yarranton's *England's Improvement by Sea and Land* (1677).

Dutch had to content themselves with a treaty of commerce and defensive alliance (27 April 1662) with France. France was thus the friend of England and the ally of the Dutch, but Anglo-Dutch rivalry remained.

It took three years for this rivalry to boil up into acknowledged war, though it was less than two years before acts of hostility began. This second Anglo-Dutch war is the clearest case in our history of a purely commercial war. It was a war of which the purpose was simply to take by force material places and things, especially ships; for once the question hardly arises whether the military means accorded well with the political aims.[1]

The fighting began when Captain Robert Holmes reached the West coast of Africa in the winter of 1663–4 with a small squadron to support the Royal African Company against the encroachment of the Dutch. He took the island of Goree, north of the Gambia river, and Cape Coast Castle on the Gulf of Guinea. Before the Dutch had matured their preparations for a counter-stroke, another blow fell in America: Colonel Nicolls with three ships seized the New Netherlands. Before the end of 1664 the great de Ruyter with twelve ships recaptured the African possessions; a battle-fleet under the duke of York and Prince Rupert was making prize of Dutch ships in the Channel, and Mr. Pepys, the ablest official of the navy board, wrote in his diary: 'War is begun.' It had been undertaken very light-heartedly. The idea of fighting the Dutch again was generally popular; and it was assumed that the naval feats of the Commonwealth could be repeated or bettered. The diplomatic position was indeed uncomfortable. Charles, in private correspondence with his sister Henrietta, who was married to 'Monsieur', the only brother of Louis XIV, was trying to get an alliance with France, but some of his ministers had better hopes of an alliance with Spain, especially Lord Arlington, the ablest opponent of Clarendon, who had a better knowledge of Europe than the others, if no better judgement. In reality there was nothing to hope from either side. Spain was weak and France was too ambitious to make enemies gratuitously; neither of them had any quarrel with the Dutch that was worth a war, and the English made neither any offer that was worth considering. France stood to gain if the English and Dutch weakened one another, and she used her influence to keep Spain neutral. Thus, in spite of much

[1] For the colonial aspects of this war and of the peace see below, pp. 327–49.

diplomatic coming and going, the alliances remained exactly as they had been, and the English prepared yet another predatory swoop. In December 1664 Admiral Thomas Allin was ordered to attack the Dutch merchant fleet homeward bound from Smyrna. He fell upon them in the latitude of Cadiz, but nearly all their ships got clear. The prelude had been disappointing; but in March England declared war.

This war lasted until the summer of 1667, two years and a half. The English on the whole had the better of the fighting, but in the general upshot it was the least successful of our Dutch wars. It was not quite so much a simple naval duel between the English and the Dutch as the first war, but from the English point of view the part played by allies was unimportant. The English accepted an offer of help in return for subsidies from Bernhard von Galen, bishop of Münster, a vexatious neighbour of the Dutch on their eastern frontier. He overran the province of Overyssel with his troops but, with help from some of the princes of western Germany, these were easily ejected.[1] The French, in tardy fulfilment of their treaty, declared war on the Dutch side in January 1666 and took a small share in the land war. Their fleet from Toulon, with a strength of forty-five sail, even made a leisurely voyage in 1667 with a view to a junction with the Dutch; but, although it reached Dieppe, it turned back on the approach of the English and, with the loss of one ship, took refuge in Brest. The junction was never effected. The real war was the Anglo-Dutch war at sea. In tactics and organization this war shows almost completed the general type of naval warfare as it lasted until Nelson's time. The close-hauled line was the normal battle formation: the ships in a line fore and aft fired broadsides at one another. More use was made of fire-ships, the torpedoes of that age, than in later wars. There were other transitional features, such as the controversy on both sides as to whether commands should be given to 'tarpaulins' or to gentlemen like the soldiers Albemarle and Opdam who had not been bred to the sea. But in the main the new type of naval warfare was full grown. The English ships were heavier and more weatherly, the Dutch flatter-bottomed and so able to manœuvre in shallower water. The English discipline was perhaps better; but the decision lay with numbers and skill rather than in any great difference of equipment or methods. At the beginning of the war the English

[1] See C. Brinkmann in *Eng. Hist. Rev.* xxi. 686.

had about 160 ships with 5,000 guns and more than 25,000 men; the Dutch, counting the same classes of ships, had fewer of them and they were smaller, but they carried rather more guns and men.

In the campaign of 1665 the Dutch admiral Opdam put out with positive orders to fight. Off Lowestoft he lost his life in a smashing defeat: 16 of his ships were sunk and 9 more captured, with the loss of 2,000 lives. Two months later, however, the Dutch fleet was at sea again, and in the meantime there had been an ignominious British failure in the north. The great de Ruyter was convoying home a rich merchant fleet from the East, taking the route 'north about' round Scotland. The neutral king of Denmark agreed for a share of the spoil to let the English attack this fleet in his harbour of Bergen in Norway, but there were misunderstandings and the plans went wrong. The British ships were met by the fire of Danish forts and beaten off with the loss of 6 captains killed and 400 men killed and wounded. Denmark got out of the entanglement by becoming an ally of the Dutch, and England declared war (though it was only a nominal war) on the Danes.

Next year came the Four Days' Battle in the Channel, the bloodiest naval engagement of the age. The English had an initial disadvantage, for Prince Rupert with twenty ships had been detached against the French, who never came into action. It was an English defeat, but to the surprise of the Dutch the English did what they themselves had done in the previous year and were at sea again within two months. Now the English won a victory off the North Foreland and for a time had command of the sea. Holmes burnt two warships and 140 merchantmen in the Vlie, and even landed a few troops who sacked the humble villages of the island of Terschelling.

Both sides by now were feeling the strain of the war. The Dutch had raised enormous sums of money in loans, and were nearing the end of their great financial resources. The English were contending against more terrible forces than any human enemy. From the spring of 1665 to the end of 1666 the Great Plague raged.[1] It was the last and worst of the epidemics of

[1] The best medical authority is C. Creighton, *History of Epidemics in Britain*, i (1893), c. xii; but Creighton's belief in telluric and climatic causes for epidemics and ignoring of bacterial infection caused him to draw false conclusions from his valuable collection of facts. W. G. Bell, *The Great Plague in London* (1924), is the fullest account. There were sporadic occurrences of plague until 1679.

bubonic plague which had afflicted England at intervals since the Black Death of 1348. London was its chief, though not its only scene, and at the climax it caused close on seven thousand deaths in the London bills of mortality in one week. The panic and misery of the plague have left a ghastly mark on the literature and correspondence of the period. The methods used for coping with it were either futile superstitions, or measures that made it actually worse. The court retired to Hampton Court and then to Salisbury, leaving tough old Albemarle to represent the government in London. Not a few of the clergy deserted their flocks, and no one could invoke the law against the venturesome nonconformist ministers who came to risk their lives in filling the gaps.

The plague was waning and its worst was a year behind when the second visitation came, which seemed to the nerve-racked and credulous populace an evidence of the wrath of God. In the first week of September 1666, after a long dry spell, an easterly wind took hold of an accidental fire near London Bridge and drove it through the city. In four days more than 13,000 houses were destroyed, together with the churches and public buildings which stood among them. The value of the property lost was estimated at from seven to ten million pounds, not a penny of which was covered by insurance, since effective fire insurance was yet to come. Very few deaths resulted from the flames, though there were a few murders. One was the judicial murder of a miserable Frenchman who persisted, though the judges and jury and every one else knew he was innocent, in an insane confession that he had started the fire as part of a Roman catholic plot. His madness was one case of the instability from which thousands suffered in their several ways, and the wonder is that the people stood the disaster as they did. The king worked well and bravely in quelling the fire and calming the refugees who camped in the outlying fields. Albemarle, who could keep men steady, was summoned from the fleet. London made shift once more among the ruins; but for a nation at war this nervous stress at home was a heavy disability.[1]

In the winter of 1666-7 there were riots in many parts of the

---

[1] That no adequate precautions were taken for some time yet, or indeed could have been taken until London was rebuilt, is shown by the fire at Wapping on 19 November 1682 which destroyed the houses of 1,500 families, doing damage of £35,446 to houses and £20,948 to goods (Steel and Crawford, *Tudor and Stuart Proclamations*, no. 3739).

country, provoked by unemployment and high taxation. The fire was a blow to commerce and consequently to the public revenue and credit. Even without it the financial situation was grave. The expectations of rich booty from Dutch shipping had come to very little, and the provision made by parliament for the war had in any case been nowhere near enough. When the war began the commons granted the unprecedented sum of two and a half millions, to be spread over three years, though with 102 opposition votes against 172. In 1665 they heard, in a session held in Oxford because of the plague, that this had all gone in one year; yet they voted a further million and a quarter. Sir George Downing, now teller of the exchequer, moved in conjunction with this vote an appropriation clause: the money was to be for the purposes of the war alone. Clarendon and Southampton did not like this, but it was harmless and, if the Crown was really to co-operate with parliament, it might have been even helpful to the Crown. It formed a precedent which was followed in some but not in all other cases in Charles's time. It was dropped under James II, but after the Revolution the principle became permanently fixed. It was, however, dangerous to a government which managed its finances badly, and in this war the finances not only went wrong, but directly led to disaster.

Before the last campaigning season of the war, that of 1667, the government took two momentous decisions. The first was to enter upon negotiations for peace. The success of these was rendered more likely by the fact that Louis XIV was about to begin an invasion of the Spanish Netherlands. He was about to make a direct advance towards his great ambitions, and therefore he wished to disembarrass himself of his nominal war against England. The Dutch were apprehensive as to where his ambitions might lead him, and they too were therefore anxious for peace. There seemed to be a case for the second decision of the British government, though Albemarle opposed it, the decision to economize by sending no battle-fleet to sea, but to engage only in commerce-destroying and to rely on fortifications for coast-defence. In June 1667 the folly of this decision was signally proved. The negotiations were dragging and the Dutch decided to hasten them by carrying out plans long and carefully matured for a raid up the estuary of the Thames. They broke the boom which guarded Chatham harbour, burnt four ships of the line, towed away the *Royal Charles*, of 80 guns, once named *Naseby*, and the largest vessel of the fleet. With this trophy they sailed coolly home undamaged. Other shots were fired in the next two months, and further Dutch attempts on the Thames were unsuccessful; but this startling and humiliating reverse in effect decided the peace.

The treaty signed at Breda on 31 July 1667 brought England one substantial gain, the New Netherlands. This acquisition closed the gap in the English possessions along the American coast-line and gave us the command of the trade-route from the Great Lakes through the Hudson–Mohawk gap to a seaport appointed by geography to become one of the world's great cities, New Amsterdam, now called New York. New York was already, as it has always been, a cosmopolitan town, and, although the Dutch language lingered in the Hudson valley until the nineteenth century, the little republic could never have had the men or the power to keep control over Manhattan Island as it fulfilled its destiny. From that point of view it might as well go early as late, and the English got nothing else of moment. They gave up Surinam in northern South America. A claim to Polaroon or Pulo-Run (the island of Run) was also given up: this spice island naturally went with the other Dutch conquests from the Portuguese in the Malay Archipelago. The English also accepted the Dutch interpretation of the navigation laws according to which the Dutch had the right to import as though they had been their own all commodities produced or manufactured in Germany or the Spanish Netherlands and carried through Holland by water or land. On the symbolic question of the right of the British flag to a salute in the British seas, a phrase was used ('the Channel or British Sea') which much restricted the area in which this honour was to be accorded.

In some respects this treaty marks the turning-point in the history of Anglo-Dutch relations. The most acute phase of colonial and economic rivalry was now over. In America and West Africa the main problems were settled; elsewhere they were well on the way to settlement. The ensuing period laid the foundations of a community of interest which ultimately found expression in alliance. This alliance was from 1689 one of the principles to which British policy, except for one interruption, remained constant for more than two generations. It would have been impossible if the rivalry of the two nations had not been softened; but this softening was partly due to the recognition of common dangers and only partly to the growing contentment of each nation with what it had kept for itself in the old struggles. It is significant that the elder Sir Philip Meadows, although he drafted a pamphlet in favour of co-operation with the Dutch[1] in 1672 did not venture to publish it until 1689. Of the outstanding questions some were not touched by the settlement of Breda. The squabbles on the west coast of Africa broke out again a few years later.[2] The chance of English aggression in the Malay Archipelago lasted until their factory at Bantam was broken up by native allies of the Dutch in 1682. The Breda treaty helped the two peoples to keep out of each other's way; but if other circumstances had set them on opposite sides of European quarrels more lastingly than they did in the war of 1672–4, their economic rivalry, instead of fading away, might have been fought out to a finish.

Already, as it was, the aspect of the greater European quarrels had facilitated the Anglo-Dutch agreement. The French aggression against the Spanish Netherlands overshadowed everything else, and this shadow, shifting in area and intensity but never more than momentarily lifting, was to hang heavy throughout the whole of the period with which we are occupied. The future of the Spanish empire was a matter of universal concern. It was the largest of the European empires: nothing had been lost since the great days of Philip II except the revolted provinces which formed the Dutch republic, the border provinces conquered by France, Jamaica and Dunkirk. In North and South America, and in Italy Spain was still the greatest territorial power; her other scattered possessions, from the Philippines to the Netherlands, would themselves have been enough to make a respectable state. But war and misgovernment had disorganized and impoverished this empire in every part. It was a fundamental weakness that Spain could not supply her empire with manufactured goods, but had to buy them, principally from France, England, and Holland. Such, however, was her protectionist policy that they could only come in by smuggling either to Old Spain or to the colonies. The commercial treaty with England in 1667 removed some of the impediments to this trade. Portugal and France, as might be expected of neighbours, were Spain's

---

[1] *Observations concerning the Dominion and Sovereignty of the Seas*; see T. W. Fulton, *The Sovereignty of the Seas* (1911), p. 524.
[2] See below, p. 332.

old enemies. England for the time being was friendly with France
and in alliance with Portugal and thus, though for no very
strong reason, not available as an ally. The enmity of the Dutch,
now that their independence was an established fact, was no
more than a tradition; but the Dutch too were allies of the
French. The historic ally was the Austrian branch of the Habsburg family of which the other branch ruled in Spain, and the
prospect was already becoming clear that the emperors, the
rulers of Austria who were also the heads of the loose federation
of Germany, would be driven to extremes in resisting the efforts
of Louis to build up a party of dependants among the German
princes. The great question was what sacrifices Spain would have
to make to grasping enemies and, like Portugal, to scarcely less
grasping friends. It was uncertain which character any of the
other powers would assume, and for the English and Dutch it
was uncertain whether they would in the long run side with the
French or against them.

On the death of his father-in-law, Philip IV of Spain, Louis
had made an open alliance with Portugal and had invaded the
Netherlands, claiming them, on a ground which cannot have
convinced even its inventors, for his wife. His military success
was immediate, and the Dutch saw that a danger had come
close of which they had long been apprehensive, that of a complete French conquest of the Spanish provinces. This would
abolish the convenient buffer-state, making the strongest power
in Europe their next neighbour and the owner of the once great
port of Antwerp which they had been able virtually to close.
Now that they were at peace with England the French advance
was their greatest problem. They had to decide whether to
resist or to bargain for a share of the spoil which would serve as
a guarantee against the worst dangers. It was a problem which
concerned the English too, for since the time of Elizabeth they
had always held, rightly or wrongly, that it was better to see the
opposite coast-line in weak hands than in strong and better to
see it ruled by three powers than by two.

After the outbreak of war the emperor tried to build up an
alliance to help Spain, but Spain would not or could not pay the
necessary price in troops or subsidies, and the emperor was
crippled by the French influence in Germany, so he gave up the
attempt and chose the alternative method of a settlement by
agreement with France. On 19 January 1668 he made a secret

treaty in which it was laid down how much territory in the
Netherlands France was to take in the present war. She agreed
to promote peace between Spain and Portugal and the great
ultimate issue was faced in a plan for the partition of the whole
Spanish empire, should the new king Charles II die, as seemed
certain and even imminent, without issue. The frontier laid
down in this treaty was one which the Dutch had already shown
themselves willing to accept, but in effect the treaty left France
practically unopposed. It was high time for the Dutch and
English to sink their differences. The emperor's action in making
friends with the aggressor had, however, made France much
more independent of their good opinion. Neither of them had
much inducement to cling to the idea, which both had entertained, of agreeing with Louis for a share of his conquests in
Flanders.

During the Dutch war political changes in England had contributed to loosen the English dependence on France to which
Clarendon had become increasingly attached. Clarendon's solid
virtues were not of the sort to make him popular. His didactic
pomposity was unwelcome in the cheerful court of Charles II,
and his choice of the narrow Anglican settlement had alienated
the tolerant. The first open attempt to oust him was a move for
his impeachment made by the Roman catholic earl of Bristol
in 1662. There were no plausible grounds for an impeachment;
those put forward by Bristol were ruled by the judges not to
amount to treason, and in any case one peer could not impeach
another, so this incident strengthened the minister instead of
weakening him. He really was weakened, however, when in
October 1662 Sir Henry Bennet, afterwards earl of Arlington,
was made secretary of state. Arlington was antipathetic to him
in every way. He did not scruple to advance himself by means of
Charles's mistresses. His relations with popery were ambiguous.
He had been resident in Spain, and he was afterwards to marry a
Dutch wife: his personal tendencies, even if he had no more serious
political designs, were towards these two powers and away from
France. He was, it is true, one of the promoters of the Dutch war,
but Clarendon, who was dragged into that war without ever
really wanting it, got all the blame, and became the scapegoat
for the confusion and depression in which it ended. Charles
knew that Clarendon could not achieve that co-operation with
parliament which was necessary for the smooth working of

government. Before the summer of 1667 was over the old man
was dismissed. In the stage which constitutional government had
then reached, a fallen minister was a dangerous man. Clarendon's enemies had the more reason to dread his return because
his daughter Anne had, though to his great anger, become first
the mistress and then the wife of the king's brother James, duke
of York, the heir-presumptive to the throne. They therefore
impeached him, and after an alarming crisis in which the king
showed him no sympathy, he withdrew into exile, never to
return.

In December 1667 a parliamentary committee of nine persons
was appointed to examine the accounts. There followed a pro-
tracted constitutional dispute. In the end the commons made
good their right to inquire, but the body they appointed for the
purpose consisted of members of neither house. It revealed gross
incompetence and malversation, but no one was punished and
there was no reform of the system. The experience of this war
made the commons justifiably unwilling to trust the government
with money.

For the moment Arlington had charge of foreign policy, and
the drift away from France was hastened. Sir William Temple
was sent to Holland to invite the Dutch to join in pressing and if
necessary forcing Louis to make peace with Spain. The two
powers agreed in a few days (on 28 January 1668) to put before
the belligerents as their terms of mediation a frontier-line in
Flanders which had already been agreed upon by the French
and the Dutch. When they made this proposal, the two powers
were still suspicious of one another. The English feared that the
Dutch might still divide the Spanish Netherlands with France.
The Dutch feared that the English would drive the French into
open disagreement and then leave them alone to face the brunt
of war. If they had known of the agreement in which Louis's
negotiations with the emperor had ended, they would not have
entertained these fears, but, on the other hand, they would not
have taken the credit for the happy issue of the main negotiations. France was willing for peace, and it was concluded, first
between Spain and Portugal (13 February 1668), then between
Spain and France (2 May). France returned the detached
province of Franche-Comté but kept her conquests in Flanders:
Charleroi, Ath, Binch, Douai, Tournai, Oudenarde, Lille,
Armentières, Courtrai, Bergues, Furnes. It is evident from the

map that this was not a frontier with which she would be permanently content. It was inconvenient in every respect but one: it provided an excellent take-off for a further advance. Yet in spite of the unsatisfactoriness of its results, and the fact that it did not really cause even these results, and that it was an imperfect and unstable understanding, the Dutch alliance of Temple was long regarded as a master-stroke of diplomacy. This was not merely because Temple, one of the best living writers of English prose, took many opportunities of writing in his own praise. It was mainly because his alliance anticipated the successful combination of the Dutch and English against France in 1689. That combination was successful, at least in the sense that it lasted for many years. It was applauded because it put an end to the vacillating and undignified dependence on France and abstention from Europe. But, when Temple's famous treaty was signed, these were soon to be resumed.

His achievement is usually called the Triple Alliance: there was a third ally, Sweden. The appearance of Sweden in this combination was, however, due to a temporary departure from the normal Swedish policy. Sweden had no concern in the disputes of the French and Spaniards; her business was with the Baltic and northern Germany. Her standing rivalry with Denmark had long been a matter of interest to the Dutch, who were sure of one party as an ally if the other put obstacles in the way of the Baltic trade. England too was concerned in this, and immediately before the Restoration England and Holland had carried out a joint mediation in the north which had in some respects served as a model for their greater mediation between France and Spain. This settlement had followed the death of the conqueror Charles Gustavus of Sweden, and Sweden was now in a period of comparative weakness and ineffectiveness. Normally she had been one of the ring of states—Sweden, Poland, Transylvania, Turkey—by means of which the French kept up pressure on Germany and on Austria from the flanks and rear; but recently economic and political affairs in the Baltic region had estranged her from France. The French had entered into agreements with the Danes and the Dutch; the Swedes in 1665 had made a commercial treaty with England. On the occasion of a vacancy in the elective throne of Poland, the neighbour of Sweden's possessions across that sea, France had not supported the same candidate as the Swedes and the emperor. This difficulty was temporary because France changed sides and in the end a native nobleman, not favoured by any of the foreign powers, was chosen. But France was acting in other matters with Sweden's rival Brandenburg. Another circumstance of the moment which may have furthered Sweden's action was the predilection of Count Dohna, the Swedish representative at The Hague and a relation of the house of Orange. Before many months were over, however, Sweden gravitated back to her accustomed position. England was soon to do the same.

IV

FOREIGN AND DOMESTIC POLICY,
1668-78

Up to this point British foreign policy had been unskilful, but except in the imperialistic rivalry with the Dutch, it had only partially stirred up the greatest questions both at home and abroad. Now there came a change. For the remainder of Charles's reign foreign relations were carried on in an atmosphere of passion and danger, of conspiracy and crusade, in which foreign policy became involved in party strife at home. This was the first result in England of the great power which France had now acquired on the Continent. Louis XIV, with the aid of the best diplomatic service in the world, built up a party of his supporters in every country in Europe. In England his party consisted of King Charles II and his more devoted adherents. Very soon after the formation of the Triple Alliance, Temple began to notice an unfriendly tenacity in the way in which Arlington insisted on the ever-recurring commercial disputes with the Dutch. Charles, even during Temple's negotiation, assured his sister Henrietta in their private correspondence that none of his existing engagements stood in the way of a close understanding with France, for which nothing need be conceded except a commercial agreement. When the French treaty was made, however, it contained no commercial agreement and no promise of commercial advantages except such as might be won from a resumption, with France as an ally, of the struggle against the Dutch. For the view Louis in the end took of the situation created by the Triple Alliance was, that to compass his ends in relation to Spain, he must not merely neutralize the Dutch or work on them through his supporters there, but break their power by war. He isolated them by a diplomatic preparation which was a model of completeness. Spain agreed to help the Dutch, but only with auxiliary troops, not as a belligerent state. The emperor and the German princes all showed themselves content to let Louis go on. Sweden, the warlike bishop of Münster, and the elector of Cologne even promised in return for money to join in the war. Charles, as we have seen, in doing likewise was merely reverting to his former policy. Yet his demeanour was that of a conspirator, not a patriot king. The treaty, the celebrated Treaty of Dover of 1 June 1670, was concluded not through the regular channels of diplomacy but in a secret personal negotiation between Charles and Henrietta. Only an intimate group of the ministers knew of its terms, and the others were hoodwinked with a sham treaty from which the more startling clauses were omitted. These embodied the supreme act of Charles's life, his personal policy, of which the fulfilment and failure and exposure and reversal run through the history of the next forty years.

The camouflage treaty provided for a new Dutch war. The other provided that Charles, who declared himself convinced of the truth of the Roman catholic religion, was to announce his conversion when the affairs of his kingdom permitted. Although he had every reason, so the treaty declared, to expect that his subjects would obediently accept this, at the same time it was stipulated that the king of France should demonstrate his friendship by money payments amounting to about £166,000 and by lending 6,000 French troops, should they be needed to carry out the plan. The accepting of French subsidies was a way out of Charles's financial difficulties, undignified but intelligible in view of the perpetual inadequacy of parliamentary grants. He was not the first to think of such an expedient. Richard Cromwell, immediately after his father's death, applied unsuccessfully to Mazarin for a loan of £50,000.[1] Once Charles had resorted to it, it remained as a habit for the next few years: under this and four subsequent agreements down to 1678 Charles received a total of £741,985, or on an average £123,664 a year. On each occasion, however, Louis got something in return, and the money price he paid was on each occasion remarkably small. It is astonishing that Charles should have risked the obviously terrible dangers which he must now run with public opinion at home. He had already had ample proofs of the force of religious intolerance and the dread of Rome among his people. The revelation of his secret plan, which might be made and in due time was made as soon as it suited Louis, would expose him to the full strength of that fierce antipathy. Even if he mastered it, the

[1] Bordeaux to Mazarin, 15 September 1658, in Guizot, *Richard Cromwell* (1856), i. 233-4, Eng. tr. i. 231-2.

struggle was bound to divide his realms so as to render them impotent in European affairs; he had chosen to join Louis in such a way as to surrender all power of controlling his action. For this great miscalculation his own easy good nature, his tolerance and his French leanings, must bear the chief blame. Among his ministers Arlington changed to this side apparently only out of compliance with the king's humour. The only one who was out-and-out in favour of the new policy was the extremist Sir Thomas Clifford.[1] Among the bamboozled were Ashley, a dangerous man to deceive, and the rich, ungovernable duke of Buckingham.[2] These four, with the earl of Lauderdale, the powerful Scottish secretary, were the dominant group for the next three years. By a coincidence their initials formed the name, by which they have ever since been remembered, of the Cabal.

The foreign policy to which the Cabal were now committed was a gamble on the issue of a Dutch war. The French alliance seemed, indeed, to make victory certain; but the weak point of the policy was that the understanding with France was from the first imperfect. In the treaty Charles had scored a point by keeping in his own hands the decision as to when war should begin: Louis was to fix the date, but only after Charles's announcement of his conversion. In the event, however, that announcement was never made, and war was declared in March 1672 when Louis's preparations were complete. The negotiations with the Dutch which preceded it were so insincere that no more need be said about them than to quote the utterance of Arlington himself: 'Our business is to break with them and yet to lay the breache at their door.'[3] The always available commercial and maritime disputes were fomented. An insult to the British flag was deliberately provoked when the yacht *Merlin*, bringing home the wife of the conciliatory and now superseded ambassador Temple, sailed through the Dutch fleet and demanded a salute which it knew would be denied. Before the declaration of war Sir Robert Holmes attempted a stroke against merchant shipping like those of the previous war. He attacked

---

[1] Although it is not known whether Clifford actually was a Roman catholic, his political conduct was such as to make many believe him so.

[2] Born 1628, son of the favourite of Charles I; fought on the royalist side at intervals, 1642–51; returned from a quarrelsome exile and married the daughter of Fairfax, 1657; held various offices 1669–74; something of an author; died 1687.

[3] Violet Barbour, *Arlington*, p. 182.

the Dutch Smyrna fleet in the Channel. The attack, however, was a failure. Holmes came away with two prizes, and the declaration followed five days later somewhat lamely.

The third Dutch war was in its general character entirely unlike the other two.[1] England was not the chief opponent of the Dutch, and from the Dutch point of view the naval operations were not the main part of the war. For them it was primarily a land war, the most dangerous land war they ever had: the French invasion of their country came very near to destroying their independence. One of the English objectives was to join in this land war. The Treaty of Dover had promised them a part of the Dutch seaboard. They were to have the island of Walcheren on which Flushing stands, and with it Sluys and Kadzand, commanding the other side of the mouth of the Scheldt; but these they were to take for themselves by landing troops and thus making a diversion in the rear while Louis advanced from the east. This diversion was never made; for the Dutch, mainly through the genius of de Ruyter, had the better of the fighting at sea.

The Dutch were numerically inferior to their opponents. At the outbreak of war they had about 130 ships with 4,500 guns and 26,000 men, while the English and French together had 172 ships, 5,000 guns, and about the same number of men. When hostilities began in 1672 contrary winds and the slowness of their fleet in getting ready for sea made the Dutch fail in an attempt to forestall the union of the French and English squadrons. The first serious encounter was therefore the battle of Southwold Bay, where on 7 June de Ruyter with 91 ships of the line, after a feint retreat to his own coast, surprised the English and French, to the number of 101, as they lay inshore. The fight was not decisive, but it postponed for a month the sailing of the British fleet and troopships. Lack of money and the necessities of the land war compelled the Dutch to unrig a third of their ships and use the men as soldiers: henceforth they were on the defensive. De Ruyter followed a system of postponing battle until conditions were favourable by making use of the shoals and islands of the Dutch coast. He seems to have thought it enough to contain the French squadrons, concentrating his attack on the English. Naval authorities regard his operations as amongst the classical examples of strategy. For the remainder of that year, however,

---

[1] For its colonial aspects see below, pp. 328–49.

it was the weather which checked the plans of both sides, impartially preventing an attempt of the allies to land on the island of Texel and a Dutch raid on the French fleet wintering in Brest.

It might have been expected that a new Dutch war would do more than anything else to unite the king and the nation. When Clarendon fell there had indeed been a chance of a fresh start; but the mutual suspicions about money and religion had not been removed and now the course of events made them many times worse. The terms of the secret Treaty of Dover were not actually published until 1682,[1] but before the Dutch war had lasted long the secret was half-guessed. Parliament did not meet from April 1671 to January 1673, and the new policy was sufficiently disclosed in the overt events of that time. Two days before the formal opening of war against the Dutch a Declaration of Indulgence was issued. This was not, like the Declaration of 1662, a tentative announcement, to be followed by an appeal for parliamentary authority. Charles now acted on his prerogative, and threw himself on his people. By virtue of his 'supreme power in ecclesiastical matters' he suspended all penal laws against 'whatsoever sort of nonconformists or recusants', that is against protestants and Roman catholics alike. Places were to be licensed for the public worship of protestant dissenters under approved 'teachers', and Roman catholics were to be allowed to exercise their worship in private houses. This was in essentials the policy which the nation, after many tribulations, accepted in 1689, the policy which permitted religious hatred to subside into the national unity of the eighteenth century. It came as a deliverance to the suffering nonconformists, and it came well at the moment when the new war required a united people.[2] Yet the moment and the manner were ill-judged and the Declaration was a renewal of domestic strife.

From about this time for many years to come it was one of the constant factors in English history that a solid body of Englishmen, who disagreed about many other things, were agreed in fearing three things which they believed to be closely allied—popery, France, and arbitrary power. The alliance was stronger in their imaginations than in reality, but it was their convictions, not the facts, which made our history. They saw clearly an

[1] See E. S. de Beer in *Eng. Hist. Rev.* xxxix. 86.

[2] See F. Bate, *The Declaration of Indulgence, 1672* (1908) and the Introduction by [Sir] Charles Firth for its permanent effect in strengthening nonconformity.

advance of popery in high places in England. The duchess of
York, Clarendon's own daughter, had lately died a convert, and
it was hardly a secret that her widower, the heir to the throne
and head of the navy, was of the same faith. Of the ministers
Clifford acted with the papists and Arlington had joined them.
The king never committed himself until he lay on his death-bed,
but his sympathies were not concealed. All this seemed to have
some connexion with the French alliance, and there was something about the French alliance which its authors wished to
hide. 'The public articles are ill enough, what are then the
private articles?' was a question asked in the house of commons
by 'iron Strangways', a Dorset squire who hated dissent but
equally hated France and stood in the old ways of the constitution.[1] The war came suddenly, not, like the last, as the climax
of a long, ascending wrangle. It came when parliament was not
sitting, and it was no wonder that when the new session began
the commons were not amenable to persuasion.

They voted money for the war—£1,200,000 to be spread over
three years—but this time they drove a hard bargain. They did
not definitely vote supply until the king, after vainly trying to
put them off, had cancelled the indulgence and allowed the seal
of the Declaration to be broken. More than this, they passed
the Test Act. By this every holder of any office, civil or military,
was to take the sacrament of the Lord's Supper according to the
usage of the church of England, and to take the oaths of supremacy and allegiance, together with such a declaration against
transubstantiation as all Roman catholics were bound to refuse.
A religious ceremony was made into a test of fitness for holding
secular office, an insidious degradation to which the Anglican
church in its alarm submitted, and from which it was not reluctantly delivered until the nineteenth century was well on its
course.[2] The immediate political effects of the measure were
severe. The duke of York, despite his service at Southwold Bay,
had to resign the admiralty. Clifford, whose fiery opposition had
ruined the chance of compromise, went too, and before the
summer was out he died, perhaps by his own hand.

In 1673 the Dutch fleet was again raised to 130. The main

---

[1] K. G. Feiling, *Hist. of the Tory Party*, pp. 145, 148, n. 4.
[2] There were partial precedents, for instance in the communion service at St.
Margaret's, Westminster, on 27 April 1614, when the commons attended together,
partly in order to detect recusants; see C. Smyth, *Church and Parish* (1955), pp. 6-19.

force under de Ruyter seems gradually to have increased from about 50 to 75 ships of the line, that of the allies from about 80 to about 90, of which a third were French. The Dutch, though not fully concentrated, were first at sea. They began with a raid towards the Thames, intending to sink block-ships and impede the concentration of the allies; but this attempt was frustrated by a squadron under Prince Rupert and by the arrival of the French in the Channel. In June the allied fleet came out and, at the Schooneveld banks at the mouth of the Scheldt, de Ruyter attacked and compelled it to withdraw. A week later, after another engagement at the same place, the English returned to their own coast. In August far away in America the Dutch admiral Evertsen with three and twenty ships easily recaptured New York. Before the end of the month came the great battle of the Texel (21 August). The allies came out with troops for landing, and the Dutch decided to give battle because their rich East India fleet was approaching, and its cargoes were needed to pay for the war. There was confusion between the English and the French, but both fleets suffered heavily. The importance of the battle lies less in the losses of one side or the other than in the fact that it ended the possibility of an English invasion and opened the blockaded Dutch ports. After that nothing of moment happened in the war at sea. Before the spring England and Holland made a separate peace.

Parliament had been prorogued when the Test Act received the royal assent in March, but the excitement was not over when it met again in the autumn. The prince of Orange employed agents to invigorate the opposition. One of them, Pierre du Moulin, published a pamphlet, also in March 1673, which did more than anything else to make the danger of popery seem bound up with the French alliance.[1] The duke of York married the Roman catholic princess Mary d'Este, a sister of the duke of Modena, and in spite of his rising unpopularity he still had much influence with the king. It was partly through this influence that the final stage in the collapse of the Cabal came in November with the dismissal of lord chancellor Shaftesbury. Shaftesbury, by origin a presbyterian, had been an enthusiast for the indulgence and his zeal for the Dutch war had been of a piece with his former career, for he had long been in close touch at the board of trade and elsewhere with commercial imperialism.

[1] See K. H. D. Haley, *William III and the Whig Opposition* (1953).

As a man he was ambitious and factious, indeed unscrupulous. It cannot be pretended that his life was consistently spent in the service of principle, and when he supported the Test Act he may well have been moved by resentment at the king's deceit over the Treaty of Dover. But for all this his dismissal and his work as an opposition leader from the beginning of 1674 mark a turning-point in party history. While the Cabal was in office the 'country party' in opposition had been in many ways the heirs of the policy of Clarendon; but when Charles II was driven back to Clarendon's policy at home and an anti-French policy abroad, there was an irreconcilable body in parliament and the country which still feared arbitrary power by itself as much as it had feared it in conjunction with popery and France. The events from the Treaty of Dover to the Test Act had brought constitutional questions to the front, and the significance of Shaftesbury is that, although his own constitutional record in office was not blameless, he now led this new opposition. It was an opposition with a doctrine behind it. Close to Shaftesbury stood his physician and confidential servant, the great John Locke, and Locke had already in his mind a reasoned system of civil and religious liberty, that is of toleration and constitutional government. Years afterwards he was to set it out in a book which reigned as a manual of orthodoxy for generations. At present it was still a revolutionary doctrine, but, as it spread through pamphlets and parliamentary speeches, it gathered to it a growing body of Anglican and nonconformist opinion. It superseded the Biblical and antiquarian arguments for mixed monarchy or fundamental law which had been inherited in various forms from the Puritan revolution.[1] In its simplest terms it was the doctrine that governments must rule with the consent of their subjects. Those who held it were not, however, democrats. As against the radicals of the commonwealth-time they insisted on the sacredness of property. Taxation without parliamentary authority, the worst offence of the Stuarts, attacked both property and consent, so the theory that governments exist to preserve property worked conveniently into their doctrine. In the complex terms of actual politics it was clipped by the selfishness of vested interests and interwoven with the bargains of parliamentary management.

[1] See Catherine B. A. Behrens, 'The Whig Theory of the Constitution in the Reign of Charles II' in *Cambridge Historical Journal*, vii (1941), 42 ff.

The treaty of Westminster of 19 February 1674 which ended the Dutch war contained an acknowledgement, scarcely better than the Dutch had already given, of the honours due to the English flag; and it bound the Dutch to pay a modest indemnity of about £180,000. Except for these points and a favourable stipulation on the law of neutrality at sea, England was virtually content with a return to the position existing before the war. That was all Charles II had gained by his gamble, by a war expenditure of six millions, and by the sacrifice of thousands of lives. It was not, however, the naval fighting which had led to this result. It is to be accounted for by the effect of two things on the unstable unity of the British nations, the moral and economic strain of war and the progress of events on the Continent.

Here we must follow the European developments down to the general peace, which was not made until the treaty of Nymwegen in 1678. From the first the course of the war was unforeseen. By all reasonable calculations the French armies, overwhelming in numbers and led by Condé and Turenne, the most celebrated generals of the time, ought to have been irresistible. The party which had been in power in Holland for twenty years had had confidence in France as one of its principles; the Dutch military preparations had been neglected, and at the last minute little could be done to make ready. An inevitable revulsion of national opinion hurried on the step which the dominant party had so long been obstructing inch by inch: William III of Orange, now twenty-one years of age, was called to the offices of his house. As captain-general he took command of the army which was to hold the defensive inundations. A few days after the French crossed the frontier he became stadholder and so acquired the chief influence over the cumbrous machinery of administration. It was a rare stroke of destiny by which these offices fell to a youth who was to make himself in a few months the second most important man in Europe. In person he was almost a dwarf, with a slight deformity of the back, and he suffered much from asthma. Physically brave and energetic, he was a hard disciplinarian and a stern master. In a narrow and unimaginative way he lived for his duty, and his duty was that of a soldier and a statesman. He had read little and travelled less, but he was a judge of character, and he had the prestige of an heroic name. In business he was quick to apprehend and slow to decide, a contemner of forms but unswerving in his hold of principle.

In his first year he was learning by trial and error both in the field and in diplomacy. His first instinct was to use his dynastic position as the nephew of Charles II to divide his enemies by seeking a separate peace with England. This would have been far less of a surrender than to go on with the negotiations with the French which the Dutch states-general had begun, but in which Louis demanded political and religious conditions of the most crushing severity. There was enough chance of a separate English peace in 1672 for Louis to be on his guard against it, and William would have been content with far worse terms than were obtained in 1674. English diplomatists, including Arlington himself and Buckingham, whose policy was consistent neither with Arlington's nor for long with itself, travelled over to the Continent to carry on confused negotiations which led to nothing. The French attack was resisted. Amsterdam stood firm, and the great Condé settled down in Utrecht to winter quarters. William turned to the policy which was to be his throughout the remainder of his life, that of building up a coalition against the French. He already had an auxiliary force from the governor of the Spanish Netherlands. In the spring of 1672 Brandenburg, whose outlying possessions touched the Dutch frontier on the Rhine, had made an alliance with the Dutch, to be followed in the autumn by the emperor. In the next year the Brandenburgers withdrew, but Denmark, Lorraine, Spain, Trier, and Mainz more than filled up the void. William took the offensive against the French communications on the Rhine, and the Dutch soil was freed of French troops before the year was out. In the next year the Dutch were joined by the elector palatine, by Brunswick-Lüneburg (which we know by the name of its capital Hanover), and by the empire in its federal capacity. Like the English, Münster and Cologne made peace in that year, and the remaining allies of the French, the Swedes, were set upon by Brandenburg and Denmark. The Dutch were thus the centre of a great European coalition which was able to hold its own.

The public finance of the Cabal was disastrous. During the years 1669-72 parliament voted additional grants to the extent of £660,000, but this sum was not enough to cover the deficit in the ordinary revenue, let alone provide for the war. By 1672 the government was in debt to the extent of over two millions:

it owed about a million to the bankers and had anticipated one year's revenue. In January 1672 the crude expedient of the Stop of the Exchequer was suddenly resolved upon. The government stopped paying interest on part of its debt to the bankers, and thus was able to spend the revenue as it came in on the war services instead of on the interest on debt. In due time interest on the money thus withheld was paid at the rate of 6 per cent., but the government had destroyed the confidence of the financiers, and even seriously damaged their business. Five considerable bankruptcies in the city resulted sooner or later from the Stop. Charles now began to raise money by selling fee-farm rents, that is by living on capital.

It was fortunate that Clifford, who had become lord treasurer in 1672, had to leave office in consequence of the Test Act and that his successor was Sir Thomas Osborne, better known as the earl of Danby.[1] For the third time, in the ministry of Danby, Charles II seemed to have an opportunity of carrying on his government without provoking new disorders. Danby had no French leanings. In European affairs, which he did not profess to understand, he relied on the advice and adopted the principles of Sir William Temple. The Dutch war being over, England was neutral while the European fighting continued. Her trade was profiting from neutrality with the wide definition of neutral rights conceded when she made peace. Trade revival, accompanied by something equally unfamiliar, good management at the Treasury, at last put public finance on a sound footing. The yield of the old taxes rose so that for the first time the estimates of 1660 were exceeded. Danby worked in well with the City. He also paid much attention to the management of parliament. By providing places for aspiring members and cash bribes for the merely grasping, he secured regular attendance and some degree of discipline. Comparisons in this matter are difficult, and it is doubtful whether his ministry marked a stage in the rise of parliamentary corruption.[2] It did mark a step towards the party

---

[1] He changed his name six times: born 1631, succeeded to baronetcy 1647, created Viscount Osborne of Dunblane in the peerage of Scotland 1673, Viscount Latimer later in the year, earl of Danby 1674, marquis of Carmarthen 1689, duke of Leeds 1694. He was lord treasurer 1673–9, and lord president of the council 1690–9; died 1712.

[2] Temple in *Works*, ii. 249, gives Clifford the blame usually assigned to Danby, and Mr. W. C. Abbott in *Eng. Hist. Rev.* xxi. 45 ff. has shown that corruption was growing during the period of the Cabal.

system. Danby tried to consolidate a body of supporters of the government by these means. It was the natural remedy for such troubles as had been caused by the defections of the previous period; but it naturally did not pass unchallenged. In 1675 there was a place-bill, an unsuccessful attempt to restrict the Crown's right of multiplying place-holders in parliament. Before long there was to come the counter-move of closer organization by the government's opponents.

Danby remained in office until 1679. He carried no legislation of any importance, and his only project worth mentioning was very much like an attempt to exclude all parties except his own from any effective share in government. This was a bill to impose as a fresh test on all office-holders a declaration that resistance to the king was unlawful, and with it the same oath that had been imposed on nonconformist ministers by the Five Mile Act, to abstain from all endeavours to alter the government in church and state. In spite of the oratorical efforts of Shaftesbury, Buckingham, and Halifax, this bill would probably have been carried if it had not been for the outbreak of the quarrel between the two houses over the case of *Shirley* v. *Fagg*.[1] The interest of the period lies not in legislation or in attempts at it, but in an interaction of foreign policy and parliamentary politics which makes it quite unlike any other period in our history. England did not depart from her neutrality and she did not take any decisive part in continental affairs; but the belligerent powers were continuously active in trying to influence her policy. For Louis XIV the advent of an anti-French minister was the less alarming because Charles II continued to pursue a personal policy of his own, and Danby, in spite of his convictions, several times consented to be an instrument of it. Charles, however, was inconstant, and Louis, having gracefully submitted to the loss of England as an ally, aimed at preventing her from becoming an enemy by keeping her in tow as a would-be mediator of a general peace. For this he relied primarily on his old method of paying cash; and even before Danby failed in his attempt to work up a zealous Anglican reaction and to obtain money grants for a really anti-French policy, the effectiveness of this method was increased by the possibility of using it to alienate Charles from his parliament. Thus the first of the secret agreements which Charles and Louis made in this

[1] See above, p. 11.

period stipulated that if parliament were to make the vote of supply dependent on war with France, then Charles was to dissolve it and to receive £100,000 a year from Louis.

This was in 1675. As it happened the opposition wanted nothing more than a dissolution, for a general election, as at any time since the first Dutch war, bade fair to reduce the number of the government's supporters. They did not press for war against France, but they demanded the recall of the English troops which were serving as auxiliaries in the French army, much as other English regiments of older standing were serving against them with the Dutch. In the circumstances Charles did not dissolve parliament, but merely prorogued it from 22 November 1675 to 15 February 1677. None the less, he got his money.

During the prorogation Charles went much farther by an exchange of personal letters with Louis in which each king undertook to conclude no treaty of alliance with a foreign power except with the other's consent. When parliament met again, the opposition peers committed a tactical blunder by urging an unsound antiquarian argument that the parliament, in virtue of an unrepealed but obsolete statute of Edward III, had been illegal ever since the end of its first year of existence. The exasperated house of lords demanded an apology and, when they refused it, committed them to the Tower, where Shaftesbury remained until February 1678. For the moment Danby was in a strong position, and, as the continued success of the French was strengthening the popular sympathy for Holland, he got a vote of nearly £600,000 for building thirty ships of war. But the opposition was more anti-French than Danby: the commons addressed the king in favour of active measures against France. Now, however, the inconsistency of their position became clear. The king had been coping for seventeen years with financial difficulties in which they had never given him adequate support, and each of his two wars had made these difficulties worse. He replied that if he were to intervene he must be given the necessary funds. The commons told him plainly that they did not trust him with money, and demanded that the alliance should be concluded first. Charles roundly refused to give up the fundamental right of the Crown to make peace and war.

This argument was appropriately followed by a third secret agreement: parliament was not to meet again until May 1678, and in the meantime Louis was to pay £166,000. Immediately after this there came, however, a momentary aberration of Charles which had enormous consequences for the future. For all his weakness Charles really did desire an end of the European war: as long as it lasted public feeling at home must continue to be excitable and it might become impossible to carry on the government without plunging in on one side or the other. The peace congress which had been sitting for many months was making no headway, and Danby now prevailed on Charles to press matters on by reviving the policy of Temple's Dutch alliance, in a new form. For some years there had been talk at intervals of a marriage between Mary, the elder daughter of the duke of York, and William of Orange. William was the only nephew of the duke and the king. As a man he was well fitted to maintain any inheritance that might come to him. The marriage would be a consolidation of the Stuart family interest. It might serve to detach William from any possible opposition and as he was an acknowledged protestant champion it would soften the unpopularity of James as a Roman catholic. The marriage was rapidly arranged. It was celebrated on 17 November 1677, and it was accompanied by discussions of the terms of mediation which England should press upon France. As it turned out these discussions had no influence on the course of events. The results of the marriage belong to the period of the peace and of the next and greater war.

When the marriage occurred Louis stopped his payments to Charles, and Charles broke his agreement by summoning parliament for 7 February 1678. Charles refused an offer of money for a further prorogation, and when parliament met in a warlike mood his speech from the throne was all that it could wish. He said that, having failed to save the Spanish Netherlands by friendly means, he must do so by force of arms, and he asked the money for an army of thirty to forty thousand men and for ninety warships. On 10 January 1678 Laurence Hyde, a younger son of Clarendon,[1] had in fact already signed a treaty of defensive alliance with the Dutch; but, in spite of all these appearances, England did not join in the war and Louis made the peace of Nymwegen in the summer on his own terms by his own method of coming to a separate understanding with the republican party

---

[1] Born 1641; first lord of treasury 1679; earl of Rochester 1681; lord treasurer 1685-7; lord-lieutenant of Ireland 1700-3; president of the Council 1710-11; died 1711.

in Holland. The steps by which he effected this and isolated the prince of Orange belong to European history. Here we are concerned only with the means by which he held England at arm's length. This he did by blowing some of the mines that his tunnellers had been laying for twenty years.

When Charles asked for money, parliament by a majority of over forty authorized him to raise 30,000 men and equip ninety ships. Some soldiers were actually landed at Ostend, and, with strict provisions for appropriation, money enough was voted for active measures. But by this time the opposition was again displaying its old reluctance to trust the king with money or troops. There were grounds for this. Laurence Hyde's treaty was never ratified by the Dutch, though on 3 March a treaty was concluded at Westminster which was acted upon when the real alliance of the English and the Dutch began eleven years later. Until then it slept quietly in the office of the secretaries of state. On 25 March Charles had again secretly approached Louis, offering his help in bringing Spain and Holland to terms in exchange for about £500,000 a year for three years. This time, however, Louis refused. He did not need to spend the money. He had seen to it that Charles should be kept out of the way by his own subjects. His ambassador, assisted by the protestant Ruvigny,[1] had had conversations with most of the opposition leaders. They had agreed that Charles should not have a generous grant of money or an army, which might be employed against English liberties. The whig fears of arbitrary government had risen to such a height that the more consistent of these men feared now and later to see the government strengthened by any alliance abroad. Some of them knew the danger of French hegemony in Europe, but feared it less than the Stuart interest consolidated with that of Orange. Among these was Algernon Sidney, afterwards famous as a martyr for liberty,[2] who, like Buckingham and others, even accepted money from Louis. He spent it not on himself but on his cause, which no doubt means that he spent it in bribery; but the mere fact that he accepted it came as a shock to the historian who discovered it a century

---

[1] Henri de Massue, marquis de Ruvigny, born 1648, was the son of a former French ambassador in London and first cousin of Rachel, wife of William, Lord Russell. Retiring to England in consequence of the persecution of the huguenots, he served in the wars of William III and Anne, became a peer in 1692 and earl of Galway 1697; died 1720.

[2] See p. 105 below.

later.[1] By that time the claim of patriotism was regarded as paramount, but in Sidney's time it was not yet so. Most of the political idealism of that age was setting in the direction of national resistance to political domination; but this was not the only political ideal. There were causes in which honourable men accepted foreign aid against their fellow countrymen. Charles II did so for the cause of monarchy. Protestantism too was still international: Ruvigny lived to serve in the field against Louis XIV and to become a British general and ambassador. Civil liberty also had for some men the highest of all claims, and if Sidney was wrong, it was through a misplaced loyalty, not delinquency.

The idealists of both colours for the moment did not matter. In the spring of 1678 the commons lost patience with the king and attacked his ministers, vainly demanding the removal of Lauderdale. Charles adjourned them to 23 May, and before they reassembled Louis relented and made his fourth subsidy agreement: in return for about £500,000—the amount he had named before—Charles was to mediate in the French interest, and if he failed, then to recall his troops from Holland, and to prorogue parliament for another four months. This money he never earned. When parliament met on 23 May the king announced that peace was imminent, and the commons hastened to vote £200,000 for paying off all troops raised since the previous autumn. Louis, however, delayed the peace by insisting on the restitution of the territories taken from his ally Sweden; the chance of war seemed to come near again. The disbandment was postponed; reinforcements were sent to Flanders, and on 15 July parliament was prorogued before it could change its mind. Sir William Temple himself was again in Holland as ambassador, and on 26 July he concluded a treaty of alliance which, he ingenuously wrote, put Charles 'once more at the head of Christendom'. A fortnight after it was signed Louis made peace with the Dutch, on the harsh terms which William and Danby and the duke of York had hoped to avert. It was the highest point his power had yet reached; but his opponents, though they had failed, had shown that it might still be checked.

---

[1] Sir John Dalrymple (*Memoirs of Great Britain and Ireland*, vol. i, 1771, Preface): 'When I found in the French dispatches Lord Russel intriguing with the court of Versailles, and Algernon Sidney taking money from it, I felt very near the same shock as if I had seen a son turn his back in the day of battle.'

One result of the hardening of party formations always is that all great issues tend to become party issues. This was exemplified in Danby's time by the development of an economic cleavage between the whigs and their opponents. The cause of civil and religious liberty began to have links with that of protectionism. There were several points of contact. One, which came later, was the co-operation of the tories with the East India Company, but the most important was the growing economic jealousy of France. Even before the personal government of Louis XIV began, his minister Foucquet had joined in the contest of navigation laws by imposing a duty of 50 sous per ton on foreign shipping in French ports. After his time Colbert had enforced an all-round system of protection, and the war of 1672–8 had been preceded by a regular tariff war with Holland, in which some of the French measures had hit the English as well as the Dutch. Colbert had also built a powerful navy, and after de Ruyter was killed in 1676 a good deal of the English feeling against the Dutch began to be diverted against France. In English parliamentary circles the dread of French domination was, at least to a considerable extent, a dread of French commercial progress. The conquests of Louis XIV included some of the manufacturing towns of the Spanish Netherlands, and threatened to extend not only to the others but also to the once-great port of Antwerp. According to the current doctrine regarding the balance of trade, British trade with France, while it benefited the French, was actually detrimental to English prosperity. It had an adverse balance, and it consisted largely in the importing of luxuries like wine. In 1678 therefore, when the commons voted the supplies for a French war, they forced on the government by a species of tacking one of the classical measures of the old mercantile system, a prohibition of all imports from France. This prohibition lasted until 1685, when the Parliament of James II substituted for it a heavy, though not prohibitive tariff; but trade with France continued to cause parliamentary disputes until after the Treaty of Utrecht.

V

CRISIS AND REACTION[1]

IF all sorts of questions were becoming party matters, there were still none which could compare with religious questions in their power of generating violent feeling, and it was over religion that England, almost simultaneously with the peace of Nymwegen, was flung into a crisis that was almost a revolution. Crises come when nations are ready for them. The tenor of English life since all except old men could remember had been violent and dangerous. The tension and suspicions of the last few years had done their work on the overwrought nerves of the people. Little was needed to let loose a panic, and that little was done when two of the vilest liars in the world concocted the story of the Popish Plot.

Although the plot was fictitious, it is necessary to say briefly what it was alleged to be. At first it was a plot by the Jesuits to assassinate Charles II and massacre protestants, in order to bring about the succession of his Roman catholic brother James, duke of York. From the beginning this central lie was surrounded with a mass of confused allegations, which at times bordered on half-truths, about intrigues of the papists with foreign princes or with discontented elements like the Scottish presbyterians. That they should have been in some sort of touch with their friends was neither surprising nor reprehensible, and in the Danby era their correspondence, of which a good deal survives, had the asperity which was common to all partisanship in that age. The duchess of York's secretary, Edward Coleman, had taken part in this dangerous but not treasonable or wicked correspondence, and he was one of the persons accused. Later, when success and acclamation had emboldened the accusers, they went on to invent charges against the duke himself and even against Queen Catherine, who could not have been suspected except by such as believed that every Roman

[1] The word 'reaction' is used throughout this volume not as a term of disapprobation but primarily to describe the policy of restricting constitutional liberties. In Europe generally at the time this autocratic tendency was regarded as making for efficiency and in some places it was a reforming tendency.

catholic was a blood-thirsty fanatic. The two main inventors of all this were Titus Oates and Israel Tonge.

Titus Oates was a man of bad character and supreme effrontery. A well-grounded indictment of perjury had almost ruined his career in 1675, but he had escaped from Dover Castle. He had been expelled from school, from a naval chaplaincy, and from a Jesuit college. When he became a public figure he was still in authentic Anglican orders, to which he added a bogus degree as D.D. of Salamanca, his studies at Cambridge not having borne any fruit of that kind. His collaborator Israel Tonge was an older man and had on paper better qualifications. He really was a D.D. of Oxford, where he had been put in as a fellow of University College during the Commonwealth, and he had at one time been a successful schoolmaster. He was now a beneficed clergyman, but he was poor and was a professional writer against the papists. His guilt may be palliated by the theory that he is more likely than Oates to have believed what he said and wrote, but both of them, and half a dozen other informers who sprang up to corroborate and supplement their charges, were men whose testimony ought never to have been accepted. As it was, when with some difficulty Oates succeeded in getting a hearing before the privy council, the king, no bad judge of men, saw through him and asked questions which plainly showed that he had, for instance, never seen certain people whose conversation he professed to report. There must have been numbers of others who saw equally clearly that the charges were fictitious; but the revengeful panic of the public frightened them into silence. Once a false charge is made uncritical people will always find circumstances which seem to point to its truth. They will do so the more readily if it is a charge against those whom they already hate and fear.

In this instance a genuine black mystery was suddenly added to the imaginary nightmare. Oates had made his first formal depositions before a Westminster justice of the peace, Sir Edmund Berry Godfrey. Godfrey was a man of family and education: more than one economic historian has lately been interested in the means, not altogether creditable, by which he had prospered in the trade of a wood-monger.[1] Knighted for his services during the great plague, he was now highly esteemed as

---

[1] See Ellen A. MacArthur in *Eng. Hist. Rev.* xliii. 78; E. Lipson, *Economic Hist. of England*, ii. 147; J. U. Nef, *Rise of the British Coal Industry*, i. 397 n., ii. 104.

a public-spirited and charitable protestant; he was a friend of Pepys and Gilbert Burnet and an acquaintance of lord-treasurer Danby. Oates appeared before him twice but the matter passed out of his hands to the privy council, which heard the informer on 6 October 1678. On 22 October, which was a Saturday, Godfrey was about his business during the day but did not come home at night. Nothing was heard of him until the Thursday evening, when his dead body was found in a ditch below Primrose Hill, lying face downwards and transfixed with his own sword. How it came there no one knows. Medical evidence at the inquest seems to have proved that the sword was run through it after death. The coroner's jury found an open verdict of wilful murder. It is not impossible that Godfrey died a natural death, but that those who were with him when he died, whether papists or not, tried to clear themselves of suspicion by staging a sham suicide.[1] Suspicion turned, as was inevitable, furiously against the papists. Shaftesbury and his allies, whom some regarded as contrivers of the whole crisis, at any rate took advantage of it and fanned the popular excitement. A Roman catholic silversmith named Miles Prance was arrested and maltreated and confessed to complicity. He retracted and then reaffirmed his confession, and on his evidence three innocent men were hanged. Theirs was not the first blood, for the nation had gone mad as soon as Godfrey was found dead. On 21 November 1678 Lord Chief Justice Scroggs condemned a banker, William Staley, to death for treasonable words, and before the end of the year Edward Coleman and three others had followed him. The same cruel judge sentenced twenty-one men to death during this reign of terror, seven Jesuits among them. In the whole country the victims numbered about thirty-five.

The name of Scroggs is infamous for his brutality to his victims, but when in some of the later trials before him he exposed the falsity of the evidence and obtained acquittals, he was himself set upon by the accusers and even impeached by the house of commons. All popish recusants were ordered to depart ten miles from London. Oates was maintained at the public expense, and lorded it in London like a saviour of his country. The wildest stories were believed. One day there was a false alarm that the French had landed in the Isle of Purbeck. Five

---

[1] I am indebted to Professor J. W. Williams for this ingenious, and I believe new, suggestion.

weeks later there was a fire in the Temple, and Oates told the privy council that he suspected it was a papist contrivance. The houses of lords and commons joined in the hunt, examining witnesses, ordering arrests, adding to the confusion. Not until 1681 did the judicial murders cease. The last day of 1680 saw the execution of William Howard, Viscount Stafford, who was condemned by his peers. In the new year there perished Edward Fitzharris and a greater victim, Oliver Plunket, the Roman catholic archbishop of Armagh and primate of Ireland. The charges against Plunket of conspiracy to bring a French army to Ireland were as foolish as they were false. The earl of Essex, who was himself to die miserably after two more years, had known well enough when he was lord-lieutenant of Ireland what sort of man Plunket was, and he told the king that the archbishop was innocent. 'Then, my lord', the king answered, 'be his blood on your own conscience. You might have saved him if you would. I cannot pardon him because I dare not.'

By this time the nation was returning to its senses. Oates was beginning to lose his credit and to disgust his supporters. Even the court ventured to moderate the persecution: Scroggs was relieved of his office in the spring and retired, richly pensioned, to edit a remunerative edition of his thirteen state trials. But neither the court nor the nation could shake off the consequences of their frenzy and their timidities. The episode of the plot had given a new turn to policy in all its aspects. When it began the positions of the leading figures were unusual and to that extent unstable. Charles and his brother were estranged from Louis XIV and working in some degree of harmony with Danby and William of Orange, two inveterate opponents of Louis, while Louis was supporting the parliamentary opposition to their attempts at strengthening the executive. Few in England were much interested in the continental war, and, though the treaties of peace were not all signed until 5 February 1679, there was no real question of English intervention from the time of Oates's disclosures. The first result of these was to make the succession question the central interest of the next ten years and one of the leading interests of the next forty and more. Those for whom the fear of popery was genuine and those who played upon that fear were equally interested in preventing James from following his brother on the throne. At the beginning of November 1678 Shaftesbury in the lords and Lord Russell, the earl of

Bedford's heir, in the commons demanded his removal from the king's councils. The king persuaded his brother to refrain from attending the meetings of the privy council and assured the two houses that 'he was ready to join with them in all the ways and means that might establish a firm security for the Protestant religion'.[1] He was understood to mean that he would consent to limit James's powers if he should succeed. He gave his assent to an act to exclude from both houses members who refused to take an oath even stricter than that applied by the Test Act of 1673 to the holders of offices under the Crown; but the lords by an amendment had excluded the duke of York from the operation of this act. With that unpopular exception it came into force immediately, and no Roman catholics sat in either house of parliament until 1829. The other question which most occupied the minds of the opposition was the disbandment of the ten thousand troops raised for the war abroad. Charles not unnaturally wanted to keep them on foot for his own protection. The opposition were determined they should be dismissed, and made a proposal, which the king rejected, that some sixty thousand of the militia should be put under arms and maintained so for six weeks. The French ambassador pressed on both king and opposition the desirability of disbanding the force which might yet be inconvenient to his master, and the commons in December voted money for the disbandment. This time they made sure that the money should not be used to keep the forces on foot. Instead of paying the money into the treasury they resolved that it should pass through the chamber, or treasury, of the city of London.[2]

In the discussions of this matter ominous words had been said about Danby. Danby had shown his disbelief in Oates and he had now few friends. The king disliked him for the recent concessions which he had advised; the opposition for his lukewarmness over the plot and for his complicity in the maintenance of the troops. He was vulnerable in more directions than one, but the attack came in a way which shows well how confused political relations had become. In spite of his hostility to France he had on more than one occasion allowed himself, as the king's servant, to be over-persuaded into becoming the instrument of Charles's financial dealings with Louis. His share in them was

---

[1] *Lords' Journals*, xiii. 345.
[2] This device had been suggested in 1675: Grey, *Debates*, iii. 360.

plainly shown in some letters to Ralph Montagu, once the British ambassador in Paris, now disappointed of promotion and his personal enemy, who dramatically revealed the secret in the house of commons. Danby was impeached. There was a long list of charges covering his financial and general administration. Some of them were justified[1] but on the most serious he could have defended himself, if he had stooped to do so, by pleading the king's express orders. There was little hope that the lords would long resist the rage of the commons; but the king knew better than to stand by and let his minister suffer. He had before him the warning of what had ensued when his father had given way to the accusers of Strafford. Only one other course was possible: on 3 February 1679 the Long Parliament of the Restoration was dissolved. In the height of the panic and for the first time in eighteen years, there was a general election.

Charles appears to have hoped to carry on his anti-French policy with a more manageable house of commons than the last, but such hopes were wildly miscalculated. The result of the election reflected the state of the country: whereas in the old parliament there had been some 150 votes on which the king could count in urgent cases, in the new there were not more than twenty-five or thirty.[2] Before it met, Charles wrote to advise James to leave the country, and James went into exile in Flanders. A beginning was at last made with disbanding the troops, and it was announced that Danby would cease to be lord treasurer as soon as he had wound up the current business of his office. It was of no avail. The proceedings against him were at once resumed. A bill of attainder was rushed through its stages in the commons; Danby surrendered and was committed to the Tower. A pardon granted him by the king was declared by the commons to be illegal, but the lords managed to protract the proceedings so that they were never concluded. Danby, however, remained in the Tower for five years and out of office for five more; but he lived to be again a minister, to be impeached again, to become a duke, and to pass the age of eighty.

After Danby's fall Charles tried to overcome his difficulties by a reconstruction of the ministry which was also intended,

[1] See Doris M. Gill in her useful article on 'The Relationship between the Treasury and the Excise and Customs Commissioners' in *Cambridge Historical Journal*, iv (1932), 97.

[2] The proceedings in this and the two following elections are analysed by Mr. E. Lipson in *Eng. Hist. Rev.* xxviii. 59 ff., 416 and Mrs. George, ibid. xlv. 552 ff.

perhaps not seriously, to inaugurate a new constitutional system.[1] It was undertaken partly or mainly on the advice of Sir William Temple, and he was probably the inventor of its curiously doctrinaire constitutional arrangement. The privy council had grown too large. It was dismissed and a new council set up, which was to have some thirty members arranged in categories. Half were to be ministers and half without office. There were to be two ecclesiastics, two dukes, two earls, and so on. This body, the king announced, was to transact all business, and there was in future to be no hole-and-corner cabinet. On its political side this was an attempt to combine both parties in the king's service: Shaftesbury was made president of the council. But no constitutional conjuring trick could alter the disposition of forces and reconcile their conflicts. The new council soon proved in its turn too large, and the main business was settled in private meetings of ministers which resembled cabinets though they were not so called. The king, instead of accepting the advice of the majority of the council, preferred that of the ministers who were on the side of prerogative, such as Sunderland and Laurence Hyde, later earl of Rochester, and first lord of the treasury. He did not win over the opposition leaders, and the resistance of parliament went angrily on. The commons resolved that 'if His Majesty shall come by any violent death, it shall be revenged to the utmost upon all Papists'. Then a bill was introduced for the exclusion of the duke of York from the imperial Crown of England. The issue of the succession was thus challenged directly. The bill passed its second reading, and this has been called the culminating point of the authority of Shaftesbury.[2] The strength of the exclusionist cause was easier to see than its weaknesses. It was evident that there were still many obstacles before such a project could become law. With strict economy Charles might be able to carry on the finances without parliamentary grants. Trade was very active. The yield of the customs was good. Rather than surrender to Shaftesbury, Charles therefore gave up the new scheme of government. In spite of the advice of the majority of the council, the new parliament was prorogued after it had sat for less than three months, and before it could meet again it was dissolved. Shaftesbury was dismissed.

This session left behind it one permanent monument, the

---

[1] See E. R. Turner in *Eng. Hist. Rev.* xxx. 251.
[2] Ranke, *Hist. of England*, iv. 83.

Habeas Corpus Amendment Act. The writ of habeas corpus was an instrument by which the courts of law could order any one who was wrongfully imprisoned or otherwise detained to be brought before them in person so that his case could be examined. It could be used against private persons, but it could equally be used against the king's officers, so that it afforded a valuable safeguard to the opponents of the Crown if these officers should ever exceed their duty or go beyond the law. It had been used in this way under Charles I, but since then a number of devices had been found by which political prisoners could be deprived of its benefits. The new act, which had been prepared in the previous parliament, declared these illegal, and it has ever since been looked upon as a mainstay of individual liberty. It has indeed been suspended in times of war and domestic unrest in 1689, 1696, and 1708, and at various times after the close of our period; but at least it has made it impossible for the Crown to detain a prisoner in defiance of both parliament and the courts. In few if any of the other countries of western Europe was the executive subjected to such a restriction at this time: the contrast with the irresistible force of the French *lettres de cachet* was sharp. It is hard to be sure why Charles gave it his assent, especially as it passed the lords by a very narrow majority. James II, when he came to the throne, desired its repeal; but in 1679 constitutional reaction had not fairly begun, and the act might one day be useful to friends of the king's, like Danby and the popish lords who were at that time in the Tower. It seems indeed that the first two men to apply for its benefits were Samuel Pepys and Sir Anthony Deane, the ship-builder, both of whom were arrested in the time of the Popish Plot.[1]

Charles met two more parliaments, his third in 1680 and his fourth in 1681; but the first of these passed only two unimportant acts and the second none at all. They had no effect except to hurry on the crisis to abortive revolution. The second general election of 1679 was on the whole a repetition of the last. The antagonisms were even sharpened by a brief but dangerous illness of the king. For James to have stayed abroad would have been to risk throwing away the succession; with the king's approval he came quickly and secretly to Windsor. When he arrived, the king had recovered, but it was too much to expect that James would quietly go back to take the same risk again.

[1] A. Bryant, *Samuel Pepys*, ii (1935), 271.

This time he merely went to Brussels to bring his family, and with them he took up his residence in Edinburgh, where he found work to do and was near at hand.[1] By now, however, the exclusion question had developed so that James was no longer the only man whose presence or absence affected it. Shaftesbury and his followers had chosen among the various alternative successors, and, as it turned out, they had made the worst possible choice. If James were set aside, and if he had no son or if his sons too were set aside as papists, the Crown would pass in the natural course of things to one or other of his daughters Mary and Anne. The law had never decided that the eldest daughter should precede the younger in the succession, but of these two staunch protestant princesses, the grand-daughters of Clarendon, the elder had obviously the greater attractions, since she was the wife of William of Orange, while Anne was still unmarried. William was a great man and an acknowledged champion of protestantism; he was also the only nephew of Charles II, and in his own right the next heir after Mary and Anne. Yet by a fateful error of judgement Shaftesbury did not pin his hopes on William. To have done so would indeed have meant that the policy of exclusion would be worked out in a moderate spirit. William never in his life desired to see the rights of the English Crown subordinated to those of parliament: he wished for no diminished inheritance. Moreover his life-work was resistance to France, and Shaftesbury, who had been the most anti-Dutch of the Cabal, was the leader of a party in French pay. These things and his own ambition turned Shaftesbury to another choice.

Nine weeks after his royal father's execution there had been born to Charles II in Rotterdam, or so he believed, a natural son who was now known as James, duke of Monmouth and Buccleuch. At the age of thirty he was handsome and charming, a success with women, an athlete and the husband of one of the richest heiresses in Britain, Anne Scott, in her own right countess of Buccleuch. He had seen service on land and sea, and in 1679 commanded the army at Bothwell Bridge.[2] The king doted on him, and indulged him at every turn, an indulgence which was often called for, since Monmouth was brainless, ungovernable, vain, and ambitious. Ever since his boyhood there had been rumours that Charles intended to have this son

[1] See below, p. 272.   [2] See below, p. 271.

legitimized; there were growing rumours that he had been
legitimate all along, and that the king had married his mother
Lucy Walter. As the question of exclusion had come to the fore-
front, Monmouth's relations with the protestant party had become close. Shaftesbury had been blind enought to support all
his pretensions, and the time had now come when Monmouth,
equally with James, was a cardinal figure in the drama. When,
therefore, James retired to Scotland, it was necessary that some
decision should be taken about Monmouth. In the last resort
the one principle which Charles never abandoned was the
principle to which he believed himself to owe his crown, that of
hereditary succession. He stood by it now, and not only deprived Monmouth of his commission as general but ordered him
to leave the kingdom. He withdrew to protestant Holland.

These measures against Monmouth were not the only visible
signs that Charles had abandoned the policy of concession,
though he was still estranged from Louis and still had no policy
of constitutional reaction. The dismissal of Shaftesbury marks
another step in the formation of parties. The struggle was no
longer a division among the king's advisers but between the
ministers and a parliamentary and popular opposition. It is no
mere coincidence that the two party names whig and tory became current about this time. Both were originally terms of
abuse: whigs were Scots presbyterian rebels and tories Irish
catholic bandits. The parties to which they were applied were
on the one hand the exclusionists, who wanted parliamentary
limitation of the Crown and toleration for protestants only, on
the other hand the supporters of hereditary succession and the
prerogative. They disagreed about these principles, and they
were competitors for office and power, so that their principles
were then and always subject to the constant transforming pressure of personal and tactical interests. In relation to some questions they were still imperfectly defined: the parties were not yet
irrevocably ranged against one another on foreign or economic
issues, but during the period of the struggle over the succession
these came gradually forward until all were interlocked and
a decision over one often carried with it the decision of the rest.

During the years 1679, 1680, and 1681 this shifting of the issue
was scarcely visible in the excitement of the contest for power.
Shaftesbury organized his party throughout the country.[1] In

[1] Although instructions in identical form were given by various constituencies to

London there were clubs which had emissaries all over the provinces, and the machine was such that it might turn to revolution or even to rebellion. At the same time pressure was exerted directly on the king. Before 1679 was out Monmouth came back to London without leave. He was deprived of his chief remaining offices, but he remained in England and toured the west country to arouse the enthusiasm of his supporters. James too came back to court, but before the parliament met, the king made him return to Scotland. The parliament assembled, after various postponements, on 1 November 1680. Charles appealed to it in vain to grant money to save Tangier. He seems still to have hoped that he could revive a national policy with grants from this parliament; but it proved even more violent than the last. The commons passed a new exclusion bill and rejected a proposal to name James's daughters as next in the succession; but already the opponents of Monmouth were gathering strength. In the lords his cause was resisted by George Savile, earl of Halifax, a man of subtle wit and intellect, rich and inscrutable, who never chose his side before it was necessary to choose and never did himself permanent harm by his choice.[1] To him went the credit for the rejection of the bill, but he was for a limitation and immediately went on to advise the temporary banishment of James. The lords resolved to form an association for the protection of the king like that which had been formed in 1585 to defend Queen Elizabeth. The commons passed a series of defiant resolutions, demanding the restoration of Monmouth's offices.

Charles was thus driven back to dependence on France. The estrangement between him and Louis since 1678 had been real and mutual. In 1680 Louis wrote of him to his ambassador Barillon, 'Whatever he may promise me he will break everything to get a regular income from his parliament,' and 'He only treats with me to derive an advantage in his future negotiations with his subjects.'[2] His ministers were at that time making

their members in the election to the convention of 1660 (Anglicanism and freer trade being the main points), the general election of 1681 seems to have been the first in which there was a widespread circulation of a form of instruction by party agents. See the documents and a lucid analysis of the whole subject in C. S. Emden, *The People and the Constitution* (2nd ed. 1956).

[1] Born 1633, head of a great Yorkshire family and first cousin of the politicians Henry and Sir William Coventry; created Viscount Halifax 1668, privy councillor 1672; opposed Test Acts; earl 1679, and marquis 1682; lord privy seal 1682–5, and 1689–90; d. 1695.   [2] Ranke, *Hist. of England*, iv. 103.

approaches to Holland, the emperor, and Spain. On 10 June
Charles even made a treaty with Spain by which he undertook
to summon parliament for the date when it actually did assemble,
and undertook to maintain the settlement of Nymwegen. But
the parliament which the Dutch and Spaniards had openly
recommended frustrated this policy. Charles renewed his applications to Louis and, although no agreement had been reached,
he was hopeful that they would succeed. This was his frame of
mind when his third parliament was dissolved on 20 January
1681.

That he summoned yet another shows how slowly he recognized the logic of his position, for this fourth parliament was
even noisier and more futile than the third. It met in Oxford,
away from the London aldermen and the London mob, and the
whigs carried themselves as if they were ready for extremities.
The London members came with ribbons in their hats with the
motto woven in them 'No Popery, No Slavery'. The sittings
lasted for one week. The council offered as a last expedient a
plan of regency by which James was to have the royal dignity
without its exercise, all his powers being entrusted first to Mary
and then to Anne. It was an ingenious offer, and perhaps it was
made in good faith; but to men who had already gone so far it
looked like a trap. James would have been a poor creature if he
could not have broken through such restraints. The commons,
crowded into the uncomfortable little convocation house, rejected the plan and resolved to bring in another bill for plain
exclusion. That was on Saturday. On Monday, 7 April, Charles's
last parliament was dissolved. On 8 April came the first payment under an agreement made by word of mouth between
Barillon and Rochester, by which Charles was to have £400,000
in the next three years.

Charles had been driven back to his dependence on France;
his opponents next gave him the opportunity of beginning at
last a reaction in which he attacked the strongholds of their
power by vigorous and well-planned constitutional changes.
The moment of the dissolution of the Oxford parliament was the
last chance for a whig revolution. In the nature of the case it is
impossible to guess and unprofitable to speculate what would
have happened if the opposition leaders had tried to keep the
parliament in being and raise the country against the king. There
is no evidence that either their preparations or the state of public

opinion were so favourable to action of that kind as they had been in the time of Charles I or as they were to become in the time of James II. And it is certain that once the Oxford parliament dispersed they lost their nerve and their cohesion, the best among them letting unwise extremists take matters into their own hands. Three months after the dissolution Shaftesbury was arrested, and he perhaps expected to be condemned for treason. While he lay in the Tower one of his minor followers, Stephen College, 'the protestant joiner', was convicted and executed in Oxford on evidence much like that which could be brought against the earl. London, however, was still a whig stronghold, and the grand jury, selected by whig sheriffs, found no true bill, so that Shaftesbury was once more released. But there was no fight left in him: he was over sixty and his health was gone. He advised his friends to take extreme courses; it was only a question of time when he would be arrested again, and at the end of 1682 he fled to Holland. His term of exile was ended a few weeks later by death.

Monmouth in the meantime had been showing a demonstrative but almost aimless activity which exasperated the government without strengthening his own cause. Deprived of his remaining offices he had undertaken another and longer provincial progress, which ended with his arrest at Stafford as a disturber of the peace. After his release on bail, a few weeks before Shaftesbury's flight, he was scheming irresolutely with the remaining whig leaders, and also more and more with an underworld of needy lawyers and excitable old Cromwellian officers. He hesitated between two kinds of treason, open insurrection and mere murder, and when the crazy underlings chose the latter, both he and his friends had been near enough to their plans to be implicated in their guilt. Richard Rumbold, who had been one of the guards about the scaffold at the execution of Charles I, had married the widow of a maltster and was settled in her home, the Rye House at Hoddesdon in Hertfordshire. Near by, the narrow road to Newmarket ran between high banks, where the king often passed on his way to the race-meetings or home. To block the road and seize the king's person seemed feasible enough: the plan was made. But swords would have to be drawn; some of them feared what they might have to do if the king resisted. According to the official narrative an accidental fire at Newmarket burnt down half the town: the king and his brother came away before their time and the plot was frustrated. Ten weeks later one of the conspirators sold the secret to the government. Several of the small fry were condemned and executed, but their fate was overshadowed by that of the magnates who were implicated in the confessions and revelations. Monmouth lay in hiding. Lord Grey of Werke escaped to Holland. Lord Howard of Escrick turned to give evidence against his associates, but three great men were taken to the Tower. The earl of Essex was the son of one of the most conspicuous of those who had died for the cause of Charles I. He himself had served well as lord-lieutenant of Ireland and as first commissioner of the treasury for a few months after the fall of Danby. Since then, however, he had gone deep into the exclusionist plans, and he forestalled the executioner by cutting his throat with a razor. The two who remained to stand their trial were Lord Russell and Algernon Sidney. Both belonged to noble families which had played an illustrious part in the history of two centuries. Both were men of character and principle, and neither had been active in the murder-plot. Russell, however, refused even after his sentence to renounce the position that there are cases in which it is justifiable to resist the powers that be. Sidney was convicted only of having elaborated this doctrine in a manuscript treatise which lay unpublished in his desk.[1] They were the last English aristocrats to die for those opinions, and their death made a deep and lasting impression among their class. Far as that oligarchy was from the customs and institutions of feudal chivalry, it still retained something of the feeling that resistance by its own members was no vulgar insubordination but had an affinity to lawful war. By making martyrs of two such adversaries, the Stuarts incurred a resentment which stiffened aristocratic resistance until the time of their children's grandchildren.

For the moment, indeed, it seemed that the king was victorious over all his enemies. The reaction which had been gathering force now ran unchecked. On the day when Russell was beheaded the university of Oxford solemnly condemned a long series of the opinions of the whig thinkers and those akin to them.

---

[1] His *Discourses concerning Government* were first printed in 1698. Historians sometimes speak of them as having influenced Locke. Locke may have heard of their contents, and their ideas were in the air, but in his tract of 1703 *Some Thoughts concerning Reading and Study for a Gentleman*, he says he has not read the book (*Works*, iii. 296). His autograph library catalogue shows that he possessed it.

Cambridge a little later undid an indiscretion. Monmouth, who had been chancellor of that university, was deposed by the king. The university had his portraits burnt and expunged his name from its records. The horrors of the Popish Plot had already worked themselves out. The day before the execution of Stephen College the detestable Oates had been turned out of his lodgings at court and forbidden the council chamber. His credit sank towards its true level, and in 1684 he was fined the impossible sum of £100,000 for calling the duke of York a traitor. Unable to pay he lay in irons in the King's Bench prison, awaiting worse things that were in store for him. Another sign of the same changed state of the country was the release on bail of Danby and the Roman catholic lords. The centre of the reaction, however, lay in a methodical attempt to root out the constitutional growths that had enabled the whigs to build up their enterprise. Without a parliament, indeed, it was impossible to make legislative changes, and there was no chance of a parliament that would join in a reactionary policy. There still remained members of the privy council who wanted a new parliament: Halifax advised it after the Rye House Plot, and again in the spring of 1684, when the period had gone by during which, according to the Triennial Act, it was permissible for no parliament to meet. The other ministers, however, held that the right to summon parliaments or not to summon them was essential to the prerogative: they even discussed whether to assert this argument in a proclamation. From that defiance, however, they shrank; and they busied themselves with such measures as needed no parliamentary sanction.

The balance of forces in the country could be materially altered by the spirit in which the existing laws were enforced, or rather by the choice which was made between those that were enforced and those that were allowed to sleep. A number of Roman catholics who had been imprisoned were now released in various parts of the country, but country justices were allowed to treat the protestant dissenters as severely as in the first months of Charles's reign. The Rye House Plot roused all the dormant fears that dissent was the prime cause of sedition, and all over the country ministers and teachers were rounded up and punished for breaches of the Clarendon Code. The bench was ready to take part in repression. For a few years after the Restoration the judges had held their offices not during the good pleasure of the Crown but, in the terms of their patents, during good behaviour. After the fall of Clarendon, however, Charles II had found it increasingly difficult to rely on the decisions of judges who rose by the ordinary course of professional success. The majority of the able common lawyers throughout his reign were against the pretensions of the Crown. When critical cases affecting the prerogative came before the courts, the king made sure, so far as he could, of the results. Whether to remove them from his path or merely to make way for men more likely to be pliable, he frequently dismissed his judges, and in this his example was followed by James II. There were enough dependable men of ability in Charles's time to fill up the vacant places, and the reaction was largely the work of a subservient bench.[1]

All over Europe in the sixteenth and seventeenth centuries the tendency towards absolute monarchy encountered two main kinds of resistance, that of aristocracies and that of privileged corporations. In England the latter was ultimately to prove the more important of the two, and one of the distinctive characteristics of English life in later centuries is that the vigorous self-direction of a large number of half-private associations was able to resist the state-control which on the Continent resulted equally from revolution and from monarchist reaction. Down to this time, indeed, the toughness of the English corporations had not been tested, because only one group of them had given serious trouble to the government. The East India Company, the greatest commercial society, had backed the usurping government, but it and the other trading companies which had done the same had come quietly to heel at the Restoration. The universities had given no trouble worth mentioning and now were leading the current movement of opinion. The Inns of Court had not been involved in politics.[2] The church of England had been brought under control long before and showed no sign of self-will. Most of the dissenters were not yet formed into regular national bodies. The one exception to the rule that subordinate social groups were submissive was that of the municipal corporations. In many of these whiggism had an entrenched *point d'appui*. In spite of the exclusion of dissenters,

---

[1] See Sir W. Holdsworth, *Hist. of English Law*, vi. 500–11, 523–30.

[2] Their liberties were, however, encroached upon by the judicial decision of 1668 that a king's counsel had the right to be called to the bench of his inn. This was not formally reversed until 1845.

which indeed had often been evaded, they had obstructed the policy of successive governments in a variety of ways, but especially through their control of parliamentary elections and by their direct and indirect judicial functions. The most conspicuous example was the London city corporation. The popularly elected sheriffs had chosen juries which had struck great blows for liberty. In 1671, after long delays, the judgement of Chief Justice Vaughan, no friend to nonconformity, in Bushell's case, which had resulted from the virtual acquittal of William Penn and another quaker on a charge of riot, had established the rights of juries as they still remain. Jurors could no longer be punished for their verdicts. The freeing of Shaftesbury by the grand jury had been the culmination of a long series of such checks to the Crown.

The position of the corporations had one great weakness. Their liberties had been granted by charter, and charters could be revoked, at least if they were legally proved to have been overstepped, by the same royal authority from which they came. It is an almost invariable rule that any body that transacts business not of the very simplest kind must from time to time by inadvertence or in pardonable error do something which is technically beyond its powers. Usually this does not matter: if no one is injured no question is raised. But there are openings for a vigilant adversary, and the Crown lawyers now turned their ingenuity to discovering lapses which might render the municipal charters forfeit, in order that there might be substituted others more strictly drawn. This, it will be remembered, was no more than the more energetic resumption of a policy which had been carried out in the early years of the reign and to some small extent in the interval. The judges made short work of the charters. There were some preliminary victims like Evesham and Norwich, then in 1683 down went London. After that it was useless for the smaller towns to do anything but surrender, and they handed in their charters to the judges by the dozen. In London the government got control even before the forfeiture of the charter: by pressing the neglected legal rights of the lord mayor they succeeded in getting first one tory sheriff, then two, and, in short, in counteracting the whole power of the whigs. This was perhaps the most striking illustration of what has been called the triumph of Charles.

If we look before and after we shall be little disposed to call it an unqualified triumph. Opposition was silenced, but the king had not won over the dissatisfied subjects. His victory over the City was too easy: it tempted men to think that a little firmness would scatter all the forces of liberty. But the conditions were already ceasing to be altogether favourable. In the autumn of 1682 there had been some bank failures, but the crisis had been brief; in 1684, however, a real depression began which lasted, spreading and deepening, through the next three years. At first it did not much affect foreign trade, but the peaceful state of Europe was breaking up, and soon international relations became a matter of concern for English business men.

The reaction in England, like so many other movements which seem to require no explanation beyond the local facts, was only a phase of a reaction in Europe. In France the 1680s saw the gradual intensification of measures against the huguenots. Even before toleration was finally withdrawn from them by the Revocation of the Edict of Nantes in 1685 this was unsettling French industry and driving one family after another into exile, perhaps in England. Louis XIV felt himself master in France, because he felt himself master in Europe. During the period of Oates his old minister Pomponne had written a trenchant summary of French interests in England: 'This perpetually agitated state of England is that which suits us best. So long as she is divided within herself she will be little equal to making herself considerable abroad and to holding that balance which seems to lie naturally in her hands among the contentions of Europe.'[1] Once Charles became his pensioner again, Louis proceeded on this assumption, the more so since James also became detached from William of Orange and threw himself whole-heartedly on the French and catholic side. Louis was able, without English interference, to make a number of encroachments at the expense of Germany and the Spanish Netherlands, and the diplomacy of Charles's last years consisted of a series of evasions and refusals when the victims and their friends appealed for his help, not knowing how far he was committed to France and not being able to express their suspicions openly. No direct and immediate British interest was touched by Louis's advance, and the traditional argument that it was contrary to British interests to allow the French to absorb the Spanish Netherlands was a hypothetical and contingent argument, relating to what would be the

[1] *Mémoires: État de l' Europe* (1868), p. 548.

ultimate effect on British interests of a change in the strategic geography of Europe. By now, however, this view was held by a growing number of the whigs, and the whigs were also jealous of the rising French exporting manufactures. On Charles's side it may be urged that he was trying to perpetuate the prosperity of the recent years by keeping out of European entanglements, and that by so doing he took at least one of the possible ways of preventing the European quarrels from coming to a head.

In his time none of them did come to a head, but he was not in a position to influence the course of European events. In this critical period the navy fell into a state of weakness and disorganization. The crisis of the Popish Plot deprived it of its two ablest administrators. The duke of York was the first, and the second Samuel Pepys, who was thrown into the Tower and driven from office in 1679. It seems to have been largely through this personal accident that the services concerned with the maintenance and building of ships became corrupt and inefficient. The sums of money voted by parliament and actually paid over for naval purposes were adequate, but they were misspent. After the warlike preparations of 1678 the number of ships in sea-pay was reduced, but the whole fleet was in good condition, and the thirty new ships[1] were building. The admiralty board appointed in the next year so far neglected its duties that by the end of the reign there were only twenty-four ships of all sorts at sea, the remainder were in disrepair, especially the new ships, not one of which had ever been out of harbour. Great expenditure would have been necessary to make the fleet ready for service. Worst of all was 'the unconcernment wherewith his then Majesty was said to suffer his being familiarly entertain'd on that subject'. Only in May 1684, after the return of James, did the king come to a sudden determination to deal with the navy. He revoked the admiralty commission and took the business into his own hands with the assistance of James. Pepys was recalled and drew up a plan of reform, but its execution, though successful, was not completed until 1688.[2] During the last phase of Charles's reign the British navy as a factor in European politics counted for nothing. British foreign policy therefore was unable to influence the course of events abroad.

[1] See above, p. 87.
[2] Naval administration from 1678 to 1688 is admirably treated by Pepys in his *Memoirs relating to the State of the Royal Navy* (1690).

The main effort of Louis's policy in these years was the 're-unions'. In 1679 he began to work out juridical claims to certain towns and pieces of territory which had been in one way or another feudally connected with the lands he had recently annexed. In a different medium the process was fundamentally akin to the *quo warranto* proceedings against the English boroughs. As each claim was completed it was followed by the occupation of the place: the ruthless Louvois, who in 1679 succeeded Pomponne in controlling foreign policy, exploited the divisions of the defeated enemies of the last war. He paid little attention to the possibility that at last even they might stand and fight. The system of alliances, never quite stable, became on the whole somewhat more favourable to France. Sweden, whose pride was wounded by her obvious dependence on French patronage at Nymwegen, and whose king had grievances of his own against the French in Germany, drifted away from co-operation with France and Denmark. Brandenburg, on the other hand, Sweden's opponent in Germany, went right over to the French side and made a subsidy-treaty by which she joined the growing group of princes who were willing to stand aside or co-operate while Louis aimed at the headship of the empire itself for himself or a protégé. A year after the peace there began a new Hungarian revolt against the emperor, and Louis succeeded in averting a league of the east European powers against the Turks.

It was thus without serious anxieties about interference from outside that Louis's officials, from the autumn of 1679 to that of 1681, proceeded methodically with the absorption of fiefs and liberties in the bishoprics of Metz, Toul, and Verdun, and in Alsace. The great imperial free town of Strasbourg, the strategic capital of Alsace, capitulated to a French army. On the same day the duke of Mantua in exchange for money admitted French troops to the citadel of Casale on the Po, a position equally threatening to the duke of Savoy in Turin, to the Spaniards in Milan, and to the republic of Genoa. Worst of all were the encroachments on the Spanish Netherlands: after some minor advances, the great fortress of Luxemburg, the strong left flank of the Spanish and Dutch defences, was surrounded by French troops. Spain was too weak to defend Luxemburg; the Dutch were ready to fight for it, and this might well involve England. English opinion might easily become so excited that

Charles would have to choose between revolution and a new war-parliament which would renew all his domestic troubles.

By this time there were protests from Germany and stirrings of opposition elsewhere. On 10 October 1681 Sweden and Holland made a treaty which was the nucleus of a new coalition against France; but now there came a danger of a Turkish war and this favoured Louis's attempts to get the reunions recognized by the princes whom he had robbed. While he was negotiating for this end in Germany, he suddenly announced that, because of the Turkish danger to Christendom, he would raise the siege of Luxemburg and leave his differences with Spain to the adjudication of King Charles of England. The spontaneous joy of Charles and his brother, when in March the French ambassador told them of this at Newmarket, is proof enough that they for the moment were relieved from a dilemma. There seemed to be a chance of bringing about the acquiescence of Spain in something short of mere surrender, such, for instance, as the demolition of the fortress. At any rate the crisis was postponed, and there followed such diplomatic delays and obstructions from the side of Spain and her Dutch allies that Charles never had to arbitrate.

The rest of Europe was convulsed by great events in the year 1683, but England stood aside, though even her own dissensions did not altogether exorcize her sympathies and fears. While the emperor was piecing together alliances among the German princes, and taking advantage of an estrangement between France and her ally the king of Poland, the Turk was making ready to march. The imperial commander, the duke of Lorraine, fell back on Vienna, and in July there began the eight weeks' siege of Vienna in which for the last time Islam knocked at the closed gate of the west. In the glory and pride of its relief Louis XIV had no share. When the rations were running short in Vienna he moved 35,000 troops into the Spanish Netherlands, and while the imperialists were following their victories down the Danube he took advantage of their inability to wage war on two fronts. Spain showed an unexpected resistance, but gained nothing by it. Courtrai and Dixmude fell. In December the Spaniards at last were goaded to a declaration of war. They had two allies, but Charles of England had long since departed from his policy of 1680, and without English help the Dutch were not willing to fight. Prudence made them avail themselves of the fact that the war, though in fact forced by Louis, had been technically declared by Spain: the *casus foederis* under their treaty of 1673 had not arisen, and they remained neutral. They were uneasy about dangers in their rear: Brandenburg, Denmark, and Cologne were keeping the friendly German princes on the alert and might well do more. Spain was isolated. It seemed that nothing could stand against Louis. He had an unsettled quarrel with the republic of Genoa. That port, by which Spain had access to her north Italian lands, more vital to her than all the Netherlands, was bombarded and laid in ruins. Luxemburg fell. On every side defence seemed only to spell disaster, and in the summer of 1684 Spain and the empire acquiesced in the re-unions. At Ratisbon a twenty years' truce was signed, which left Strasbourg and Luxemburg to the French.

England had stood aside, but these events were events in English history. To stand aside was to give help to Louis, and that was to alienate William of Orange, to divide the Stuart interest, and to cause one Englishman after another to turn his eyes towards the possibility of linking the cause of 'civil and re-ligious liberty' with that of Christendom against the Turk, the Low Countries against the French, trade against armed competi-tion. After the Rye House Plot William sent his most intimate friend, Hans Willem Bentinck, to congratulate the king and the duke of York on their escape, and the duke, although in a friendly way, insisted that William should show his solidarity with them in European as he did in domestic affairs. It was not a difficult task for the French diplomatists to foster little misunderstandings in the shadow of this great divergence. When Monmouth went to The Hague, or when a rumour started that William intended to visit London, his uncles were easily put out of humour. Yet, in spite of the experience of so many years, Charles II never came to believe that it was best to choose one side without reserve. Even before the truce of Ratisbon was concluded he promised the emperor's ambassador that he would guarantee the German parts of the truce of Ratisbon against any breach and would even call a parliament to support this guarantee. Louis agreed by treaty with the Dutch that Charles should give his guarantee to the Spanish clauses; but it was contrary to his plans that the English should guarantee the German clauses. He had further ambitions in Germany, and, near as he had come to provoking a general war, he still hoped, before the twenty years of the truce were up, to go forward on that side. His aim was to leave the Spanish Netherlands as they were, and, thus contenting the English and the Dutch, to separate the German and Italian questions from the rest. The imperial ambassador asked for something more definite than an oral promise. There were delays about the answer, evasions, and Charles broke his word. It has been said from a German point of view that this was the fatal moment of the house of Stuart.[1] If this decision contributed substantially to that which Louis made four years later when he began a new war in Germany, then it was so. If Louis made war in Germany because he trusted that England's abstention separated the German question from Europe, he misunderstood the diplomatic position; but in any case, as we shall see, he misunderstood the state of England.

In the winter after the truce of Ratisbon, Charles II was more free from immediately pressing anxieties than at any other time in his twenty-five years' reign. Except for the Turkish war, which was far enough away, Europe was at peace again. At home there was no opposition, and there was no reason to anticipate that anything serious would result from the rivalry between Halifax, the one minister unfavourable to France and the duke of York, and Rochester, whose financial management was criticized with damaging effect. Rochester, indeed, in Halifax's famous phrase was 'kicked upstairs'. He had to move to a position of higher dignity but less actual power as lord president of the council, and he accepted the reversion of the lord-lieutenancy of Ireland. At the treasury the capable Sidney, Lord Godolphin,[2] now had the chief place. Halifax may have had high hopes; he may have thought of bringing Monmouth back. The friends of Danby had their eyes on the chances that he might come back to office on 'a national foundation'.[3] But outwardly there was quiet. Monmouth was abroad, and every one knew him for a worthless featherweight. The few unmanageable pedants and fanatics who were living impecuniously in Dutch lodging-houses, John Locke and his like, were better out of the way. There was nothing to fear from dispirited whig aldermen or discarded ministers in their distant country houses. A business nation could be governed satisfactorily, it seemed, without the medieval

[1] Klopp, *Der Fall des Hauses Stuart*, ii (1875), 442.

[2] Born 1645 and inherited estates in Cornwall; sat in parliament from 1668; a lord of the treasury 1679; secretary of state and Baron Godolphin 1684; again at the treasury 1687, 1690–6, 1700–1; lord treasurer 1702–10; died 1712.

[3] Reresby, *Memoirs*, $\frac{12}{22}$ February 1683/4, $\frac{19}{29}$ April 1684.

machinery of parliament. So, when Charles went down with a stroke in February 1685, it looked as if he was dying when at last he could be spared. The duke of York locked the door of the royal bedchamber. Old Father Huddleston, who had risked his life long before to help his king on the escape from Worcester, came quietly in by the backstairs and gave him the *viaticum* for a longer journey.

VI

JAMES II

IF tragedy is the story of a man of high worldly rank whose sufferings are due to his virtues as well as to his vices, then the reign of James II was tragic, and it is not surprising that historians whether favourable to him or not, should take his personal share in them as the guiding thread through the events. The change from the precarious peace in the last years of Charles to the hastening catastrophe which followed is involved with the change from the easy, clever temporizer to his inadaptable, indeed obstinate, successor. But kings are symbols, and James's history is the history of that which he symbolized. In the last phase of his brother's reign he was already so much at the centre of power that his accession meant little change in policy. What James as king set out to do was, in fact, to revive the Stuart policy of 1672 after the failure of the opposition to it. His position in England was strong, and in Scotland even stronger. The reaction became a little more open and straightforward, but it also became more popular, and what followed was merely the working-out of the contradictions which lay half-hidden in the existing situation. The constitution was in unstable equilibrium, and the revolution which ruined the Stuart dynasty was a shifting of the conditions on which the British peoples were to co-operate in their political life.

The extemporary words in which James addressed the privy council on his accession delighted both those who heard them and many of those who afterwards read them as a public proclamation. He disclaimed any desire for arbitrary power and took his stand on the existing laws. He said, 'I have often heretofore ventured my life in defence of this nation; and I shall go as far as any man in preserving it in all its just rights and liberties.' There was a distribution of honours, but no change in the personnel of the government. The new king's brother-in-law, Rochester, indeed, became full lord treasurer; but Halifax succeeded to his place as lord president. Parliament was summoned in order that authority might be obtained for raising the taxes which had been voted for the lifetime of the late king. In the same proclamation the king took the technically illegal but perfectly reasonable step of ordering the collectors of customs to carry on their duties as before.

In religious matters nothing happened at first which can have been quite unexpected by the Anglicans who had rejected the Exclusion Bill. James did not indeed continue to treat his religion as a purely private matter. Hitherto, although every one knew he belonged to the Roman catholic church, he had never publicly taken part in its rites. On the second Sunday of his reign he heard mass with open doors in the chapel of the palace at Whitehall. He desired, as he told the French ambassador, full freedom of worship for his co-religionists, and also the removal of their civil disabilities, especially those imposed by the Test Acts. He ordered the release of all those, of whatever persuasion, who had been imprisoned on religious grounds during the last few years; but he had no wish to champion the cause of protestant nonconformity. The attempts of Charles II to bring in general toleration had shown that nothing was more likely to divide the nation. James believed that the loyal Anglicans and the loyal Romanists had much in common, that the protestant nonconformists were republicans at heart and were their common enemies. Some observers knew that the Roman catholics were not all equally prepared to run the risks of an attempt to relieve their disabilities. The king and his immediate supporters, amongst whom several of the most vehement were recent converts, seemed to English Roman catholics who were not politicians and even to the statesmen of Rome, to be rash and to be endangering all toleration by a policy which might well revive the fears of the protestants. The high churchmen were still less united on the question; but the king was confident and proud of taking risks. His understanding with the bishops was sufficient for the present; though from the outset the menace of disunion lay near the surface. He made it clear to the archbishop of Canterbury and the bishop of London that the professions of his first speech had a negative as well as a positive side. If they failed in their duty, for instance by permitting the lower clergy to inveigh too freely, as they were already doing, against the dangers of popery, they must not expect his protection. 'I shall readily find means of attaining my ends without your help.' Sancroft, the archbishop, was a peaceable old man; but the diocesan of London, a younger son of the great royalist family of Compton, was a protestant to the bone and a man whom it was not wise to threaten.

The general election was quite unlike the three which had led on to the confusion of Charles's last parliaments.[1] In a number of boroughs the new charters ensured a result favourable to the court, and although other boroughs were still awaiting their charters, the executive had various means of exerting pressure both there and in the counties, which it used to the full. There were grumblings from the opposite party, but we do not know whether these methods were carried farther than in the past. The new parliament was more favourable to the Crown than any that had met since 1661. Before it assembled an act was done which, if it were not for the cruelty characteristic of that age, we should have to call an act of justice. Titus Oates, convicted of two of his many perjuries, was sentenced to be unfrocked, heavily fined, imprisoned for life, unmercifully flogged, and annually exhibited in the pillory. This was a sample of the severity which now characterized the reaction as long as it lasted, and helped to create sympathy even for its most worthless victims.

The revolutionary elements of the opposition had no longer the power to influence elections or to raise disturbances in London. They had no case to put before the governing class and no leaders in England. Those who had been their leaders, and those whose acts had already made them irreconcilable enemies of the new king, were in exile. They were led astray by that ignorance of their real position which is common among political exiles. Monmouth himself was requested at the beginning of the new reign to quit the Spanish Netherlands, and betook himself to Holland. Here William of Orange gave him the advice which was best in all ways, that he should take service under the emperor against the Turks. He paid heed instead to a knot of desperate men. The magistrates of Amsterdam, in spite of the stadholder's warnings and interventions, allowed him and his friends to buy munitions and to charter ships. In May the earl of Argyle slipped across to his own country in the western highlands in a hopeless attempt to raise a revolt,[2] and three weeks later Monmouth with about 150 followers landed at Lyme Regis. In a windy manifesto he denounced King James as a usurper and as the murderer of Essex and even of Charles II; he declared

---

[1] See R. H. George in *Trans. Royal Hist. Soc.*, 4th ser., xiv (1935), 167 ff.
[2] See below, p. 274.

himself the legitimate son of Charles and announced that he would submit his claim to the throne to a free parliament, which was to take the place of the unlawful assembly then in session.

It was less than a month from the time when Monmouth landed until he was taken by the king's troops, who found him disguised and sleeping in a ditch after the rout of his deluded followers. In the first few days the government felt some alarm. The Devonshire militia retreated before the rebels who gathered as Monmouth marched from the coast. But there never was any military danger. Perhaps 4,000 foot and 500 horse collected round the duke, but the weapons and armour which he had brought from Holland were never distributed, there was no organization and there were hardly any officers. Not only did they lack trained officers: there were very few gentry among them and very few men trained to arms. After its first wavering the militia stiffened, and the regular troops which came down from London alone outnumbered the rebels. They included the seasoned garrison of Tangier and were easily superior in artillery. Bristol, against which Monmouth moved, was more than ready to resist. Reinforcements were available in plenty. In Oxford the undergraduates and the more spirited dons were enrolled as volunteer militia. William of Orange promptly sent over the three veteran Scots regiments which had been for generations in the service of the states-general of the United Netherlands. The royal army was under the command of the elderly and torpid earl of Feversham, a Frenchman and a nephew of the great Turenne, who had held offices in England for a number of years, but his second in command was the best of all British officers, Lord Churchill. They had nothing to do except to make methodical movements until the rebels were cornered. Shut up in the town of Bridgwater, Monmouth tried to break free by a night-attack across the drained marshes of Sedgemoor, but his army blundered in disorder against the well-posted royal troops, who cut them to pieces.[1]

The real interest of the rebellion is neither military nor picturesque but social. It was the last popular rising in the old England. Monmouth landed in the west country, where he had already fostered the enthusiasm of the people by his progresses. It was a region where nonconformity was strong, and perhaps one

[1] See M. Page, *The Battle of Sedgemoor*, 2nd ed. (1932).

reason for this was that there was a considerable number of small freeholders. But the most important social fact about Somerset, Devon, and Wiltshire, from which his army was drawn, was that this was one of the great industrial regions of England. Most of the towns where his army quartered, Axminster, Taunton, Shepton Mallet, Frome, were clothing towns. The last three lay close to the mines of Mendip, and Bridgwater was a trading port. Historians have done little to examine the composition of the rebel force, and the records of these humble people are obscure; but it cannot be irrelevant to notice that times were far from good in the mines[1] and that the English woollen industry was sinking into a depression with which the parliament was occupied during these very days. Poverty and unemployment among the wage-earners were Monmouth's recruiting agents.[2]

Argyle had been captured after failing to collect more than a few hundred adherents. He and Rumbold the maltster of the Rye House died in Edinburgh, Monmouth on Tower Hill. Their followers in the west were treated with needless harshness. The soldiery summarily hanged a good number of fugitives and after them came the lord chief justice, Lord Jeffreys, holding his bloody assize round the western circuit. There has been some dispute about the exact number of executions, but the best opinion seems to be that about 150 persons suffered death and 800 were transported to the hard servitude of the West Indies.[3] In any case it is certain that Jeffreys bore himself so brutally as to raise a lasting resentment. Another unsavoury part of the government's vengeance was the granting to individual courtiers of the rebels who were to be sent as slaves to the plantations.

The rebellions increased the loyalty which the parliament had already shown before the news came of Monmouth's landing. James repeated in his opening speech the words of his welcome declaration to the privy council. At the same time he demanded as a right the continuance for his life of the revenue enjoyed for life by Charles II, and this was granted without difficulty. There were indeed grumblings from some influential

---

[1] See J. W. Gough, *Mines of Mendip* (1930), pp. 164–8, 215.

[2] In a list of 275 names of persons absent from their homes in Taunton in June 1685 made by the constable of the hundred, the occupations of 213 are specified. Of these at least 120 were textile workers. (See *Somerset Archaeological Society: Proceedings* (1892), p. 152.) See also Evelyn, *Diary*, 8 July 1685.

[3] See p. 344 below and Sir Charles Firth, *Commentary on Macaulay's History* (1938), p. 286.

members about the late constitutional proceedings and about the conduct of the general election. A committee of the commons even proposed that the king should be asked to publish a proclamation for putting the laws in execution against all dissenters; but this came to nothing. The house rejected the committee's recommendation and declared itself wholly satisfied with the king's gracious word. Then came the rebellion in the west. By enabling him to enlist new troops it played into James's hands, and the support of parliament promised him an opportunity of removing the most irksome of the weaknesses of the Stuart monarchy. When the second session of the parliament met on 19 November he announced in his downright way that the national militia was ineffective against attacks of this kind, which was evidently true, and 'that a well-disciplined standing force was indispensable to guard against all disturbances from without and from within'. He owned that there were officers in this army who had not taken the tests, and he said that, in view of their past services and of possible future needs, he intended to keep them.

Thus the great question was raised in parliament, and although the actual point under discussion was less than the whole issue, there was no doubt that the system of Anglican exclusiveness was to be challenged. Halifax, the one firm opponent of France in high office, had been dismissed in October, and it was known that the reason was his refusal to take part in an attempt to repeal the tests and the Habeas Corpus Act. By a menacing coincidence Louis XIV in the same month revoked the Edict of Nantes, and it required neither secret information nor alarmist suspicions to convince thousands of Englishmen that this had a bearing on the intentions of their king. The debates in both houses revealed a deep current of opposition. The commons indeed imprisoned one zealous member who used the language of defiance; but Halifax and Bishop Compton had a weight of parliamentary opinion behind them when they stated their position. The commons were willing to make a large grant, no less than £700,000, but not unconditionally. They wanted a reform of the militia as an alternative to a standing army. They wanted to be satisfied on the point of religion, but it seemed probable that they would accept the compromise of allowing certain exemptions from the tests by statute. But that was not enough for the king. He wanted freedom to give any office civil or military to a Roman catholic. Rather than accept less he

decided to do without the grant, and by a sudden stroke like
those of his father and his brother he prorogued the parliament
on 30 November 1685. Although dissolution did not come until
12 July 1687, it never met again.

Without a parliament James could still pursue his policy, and
his discontented subjects had to watch helplessly the occupation
of one powerful position after another by his adherents. What
impressed London most was the new army. In 1685 a considerable part of it, numbering about 16,000, was concentrated in a
summer training-camp on Hounslow Heath, which was repeated in each of the three following years. In Ireland, which
had a separate military establishment, many of the protestant
officers and soldiers were dismissed, and drafts of catholic recruits
were sent over to England. These changes in the army would
have caused anxiety even if they had not been in close connexion with a policy of repression. As it was, Hounslow was so
near London that it seemed to have been chosen for the purpose
of keeping the capital in awe, though in the outcome the soldiers
showed an unforeseen sympathy with the opinions of the Lon-
doners. The army was not merely a force at the disposal of the
government: it took on something of the character of an army
led by Roman catholics. There was no law against the enlist-
ment of popish soldiers, and a chapel-tent was provided for their
use. A famous constitutional leading case in the law-courts even
established the right of papists to hold commissions as officers.
Sir Edward Hales was made governor of Dover, the nearest port
to France, and his servant Godden brought a collusive action
against him, suing him for not taking the sacrament and the
oaths according to the Test Act. The king had exercised in
Hales's favour his power of dispensing with the law. It was un-
questionable that there was such a thing as the dispensing
power: dispensations from some of the laws, such as those which
prohibited corporations from owning landed property, were
frequent and universally recognized as valid. In this case ten of
the twelve judges at once held that the dispensation was lawful,
the eleventh hesitated and then agreed, only one stood out.
Hales kept his commission and next year he was made governor
of the Tower of London and master of the ordnance. Already
Richard Talbot, earl of Tyrconnel, another papist, had the chief
command of the forces in Ireland, and the fear of massacre by
Irish soldiers was added to the growing alarms of the protestant

English. In 1686 Tyrconnel became lord-lieutenant of Ireland in the place of the king's brother-in-law Clarendon. A few weeks later Vice-Admiral Herbert was turned out of all his offices, and succeeded in command of the fleet by a Roman catholic, Sir Roger Strickland.

A policy of innovation, especially when it involves the displacement of office-holders, carries within itself a tendency to go to extremes. The new men in office are likely to be less experienced than the old, and so less careful of public opinion. They will do all they can to abolish the old institutions from which their predecessors drew support. Those of them who are new recruits to the cause, or whose record of loyalty is doubtful, will be forward to prove their zeal. So it was now. The lord chancellor was Jeffreys. Among the five commissioners who discharged the lord treasurer's office the clock-work Godolphin and two other able financiers carried on their work from the last reign; but with them were the Roman catholic lords Bellasyse and Dover. The privy seal was held by another Romanist, Lord Arundell of Wardour. The admiralty was in the experienced hands of the lord high admiral, the king himself. The less important of the two secretaries of state was the earl of Middleton, who, since he refused to change his religion, was allowed little say in anything. The more important was Robert Spencer, earl of Sunderland, who also succeeded Halifax as lord president of the council. This vigorous man made no scruple about conversion, and urged the king forward so rashly that some have thought he was deliberately planning his ruin. Of the ministers he alone was in the inmost circle of the advisers. Its other members were two privy councillors, Nicholas Butler another convert, and, strangest of all to English eyes, the Jesuit Edward Petre, who seems to have had little to recommend him except zeal and noble blood.

Under these auspices the ruling policy became not merely one of advancing Romanist individuals. That went on, and there was a steady trickle of conversions among peers and lawyers, justices of the peace, mayors, place-holders of every kind. Popish institutions also were established, a chapel in the City, a Jesuit school at the Savoy, a girl's school in St. Martin's Lane, a Franciscan friary in Lincoln's Inn Fields, one for the Dominicans near by, a Benedictine house in Clerkenwell. A papal nuncio was publicly received at court. Steps were taken to revive a Roman catholic hierarchy by the consecration of bishops. Pressure was put on corporations of various kinds, such as the Inns of Court, to admit papists to their numbers. But no great results could be obtained without an attack on the church of England itself and on those corporations which were most closely bound to it. The king, as a Romanist, did not wish to exercise the royal supremacy. In 1686 he therefore erected a body of commissioners for ecclesiastical causes, which was to carry on the government of the church, with large powers of suspending, depriving, and excommunicating clergymen. As it was at first constituted the archbishop of Canterbury was at its head and with him were two other bishops, three great officers of state, and one of the two chief justices. In itself this might have been harmless and even useful, but from the start the commission was under suspicion. The occasion for setting it up arose from Compton's refusal to exercise his disciplinary powers in the way desired by the king: he was suspended from his office. Archbishop Sancroft excused himself from serving on grounds of health, and later another bishop resigned. Both in name and in its powers the body bore an alarming resemblance to the high commission court which the Long Parliament had abolished in 1641. The Act had forbidden the establishment of any new authority with like powers, and the new commission was therefore deemed illegal.[1]

The commissioners acted as the king's instrument in some proceedings relating to the universities of Oxford and Cambridge. Here, as in the municipalities and the city companies, he set himself to override the spirit of corporations, and it was here that he encountered the most obstinate resistance. In Cambridge the vice-chancellor refused to admit a Benedictine monk to a degree and was deprived of his office. In Oxford the bishop, Samuel Parker, who was also archdeacon of Canterbury, worked for the Romanists. The master of University College, Obadiah Walker, a writer of some note on liberal education,[2] became a convert and the mass was celebrated in his college in addition to the Anglican service in the college chapel. When the president of Magdalen died in 1687, the fellows received a royal mandate to elect a convert who was technically ineligible. They behaved

---

[1] The argument of Lingard, *Hist. of England* (1849), x. 212, that the act was repealed by 13 Car. II, c. 12, does not appear to be sound.

[2] See his book *Of Education, especially of Young Gentlemen* (1673), which ran into ix editions.

with courage, with correctness, and with that resourceful obstinacy which is characteristic of university politics. The king
dropped his first candidate. His second was the pluralist bishop.
The fellows persisted in electing their own man, and the king
came down in person to bully them. In the end he got his way:
the recalcitrant fellows to the number of twenty-five were turned
out. When the bishop died Bonaventura Giffard, one of four
new vicars apostolic, became head, and for a few months under
his rule Magdalen became almost altogether Roman catholic.

Having alienated the church of England by these high-handed
proceedings James was driven back to the policy of 1672, that of
all-round toleration. He renewed the attempts to relieve the
protestant nonconformists and so to gain their support and that
of the more liberal element in the established church. On 14
April 1687 he issued a new declaration of indulgence, more
thorough-going than his brother's. This granted full liberty of
worship in public only and a general suspension of the tests. It
generalized the dispensing power into a suspending power. But
it contained phrases which showed that the lesson of 1673 was
not altogether forgotten: it repeated the king's promise to maintain the established church, and declared that he had no intention of disturbing the holders of monastic and church lands
secularized in the Tudor times. It declared that the king did not
doubt the concurrence of parliament, when it should meet, in
this declaration. He knew well enough that the prorogued parliament would not be so compliant, so he dissolved it, and took
more systematic steps than had ever been taken before to prepare
for a parliament of the complexion he wanted. The personal
and constitutional remodelling of corporations was pressed forward. A new and difficult undertaking was a general attempt
to mould the representation of the counties. Here there were no
charters to revise: everything turned on the good will of the
administrative officers. These were all nominees of the Crown,
and a beginning was made with the lord-lieutenants, of whom
the majority were displaced as unwilling to carry out the work.
After this the lord-lieutenants presented to their deputies and
to all the justices of the peace three questions. Would they, if
elected to parliament, vote for the repeal of the penal laws and
the tests? Would they support candidates who were willing to
do so? Would they support the king's Declaration by living
friendly with those of all persuasions? The result of this inquiry

was highly unsatisfactory to James.[1] It revealed so much opposition that he had to drop the plan of holding a parliament that year. He persisted, however, in the policy of toleration, and though there were clear signs that it was making less impression than his attacks on Anglicanism, he persisted in such a way that he still further incensed the Anglicans without even gaining over a majority of the protestant nonconformists.

On 7 May 1688 he issued his second Declaration of Indulgence. This repeated the substance of the last and added a promise that parliament should meet in November at the latest. It was followed a week later by an order in council under which the bishops were to distribute the declaration throughout their dioceses and it was to be read on two successive Sundays in every church in the kingdom. The public excitement had already reached a dangerous pitch, and it was no time to press the opposition into a corner. Sancroft and six of the other bishops took the moderate course of presenting a petition to the king requesting him to withdraw the order, but on the ground that the dispensing power appeared to them illegal. The petition was printed and circulated. There were only seven churches in the whole of London where the declaration was read and only six dioceses where it was dispersed. The king had put himself in a position where retreat would be ignominious, but advance might lead to revolution. Angry and still self-confident, he ordered the prosecution of the bishops for publishing a seditious libel against his majesty and his government. The question whether they had infringed the letter of the law did not weigh with the public. The sight of seven such men imprisoned in the Tower and standing in the dock was a symbol of a deeper issue. The judges were divided. At first the jury disagreed. There was a night of suspense. The verdict came like a trumpet call between the two camps of the divided nation: not guilty.

The king would not have been so blind, and the people would not have been so moved, if it had not been for another event, awaited with hope and fear, which happened two days after the bishops were sent to the Tower. All through the earlier months of the reign the friends of the existing order had one consolation which made them patient. The king had no heir. He had been married to his second wife Mary of Modena for fifteen years.

[1] The returns were printed by Sir George Duckett with the title *Penal Laws and Test Act, 1687–8*, 2 vols. (1882–3).

They had had children, but only to see them die in infancy, and it was believed that they would have no more. The heir presumptive, if not in law at least for all practical purposes, was no less a person than William of Orange. True, he also was childless; but he was much younger than his uncle, and no one expected then that James would live as he did in the end to be sixty-eight and that his nephew would only survive him by six months. There seemed, then, to be a prospect that the course of events would bring relief to the English church by mere lapse of time, but this reserve of hope was dissipated when in the winter of 1687–8 the queen was again with child. In the seventeenth century people would believe anything. The catholics thought it was a miracle and the whigs said it was an imposture. It was neither. On 20 June 1688 the queen was delivered of a son.

William of Orange had kept close touch with English affairs throughout James's reign. He looked at them from a point of view which was not identical with that of any Englishman. By birth and marriage he was on the side of the monarchy. By his nationality, his official position in the Dutch republic and the whole work of his life, he was bound to consider England not as an isolated state but as a part of Europe. His relations with James followed a course dictated partly by English events and partly by European, but step by step these two series of events converged. The discontented English seemed to have nothing to hope for except from him, and his own purposes seemed to require him to become their champion. Louis XIV had not been able to fulfil his programme of turning the truce of Ratisbon into a permanent peace, to leave him in possession of his gains. That would only have been possible if the Turkish danger had continued to immobilize the empire and if his system of alliances had hung together, but neither of these conditions had held good. The Turkish war on the Danube continued to be the chief concern of the emperor and of the eastern powers, and some of these, notably Poland, obtained no successes; but the Venetians made reconquests in the Adriatic and Aegean regions, while the imperialists pressed on victoriously down the Danube year after year. The storming of Ofen or Buda, the capital of Hungary, in 1686, after 145 years of Turkish rule, was followed in the next year by another brilliant campaign which led to a palace revolution in Turkey and to the recovery of the rest of Hungary by the

Habsburgs. The eastern ring of client-states was no longer of any use to Louis. It is indeed true that the emperor, to gain these advantages, had to allow Louis to make new encroachments and prepare for new claims on the western frontier of Germany: he deliberately chose to neglect or subordinate his interests there for the time being. But the emperor's indifference was also partly due to a weakening of the support on which Louis could reckon in Germany itself. Three or four questions had arisen which had made him new enemies there.

One of the more important states of western Germany was the Electoral Palatinate. It lay astride of the Rhine between Strasbourg and Mainz. Its princely house came to an end in 1685 with the death of the elector Charles, the grandson of Elizabeth, queen of Bohemia, the hapless daughter of James I of England. By former treaties part of the inheritance went to a distant German cousin, and part to the dead elector's sister Elizabeth Charlotte. This lively woman was the second wife of Louis's brother Monsieur, once the husband of Henrietta of England. Louis, as usual, made the most of this French claim, though not so much as it was feared he might. He offered, in view of the Turkish war, to submit the matter to papal arbitration; but this ostensibly magnanimous offer displeased the 'Great' Elector of Brandenburg, who was already disappointed by his failure to gain anything from his French alliance and indignant at the oppression of the huguenots. The Great Elector in 1686 veered over towards the emperor. A subsidy treaty by which he was to send 7,000 troops to the Danube was followed, after dexterous and deceptive Austrian concessions to him, by a twenty-years' alliance directed against French aggression.

This was a much more important event than the league made in the same year 1686 at Augsburg, which French ministers and historians afterwards represented as a move of hostility to France. To this the parties were the emperor, Spain, Sweden, Bavaria, and a number of the minor unarmed states of south Germany. Its purpose was indeed to guard against France in that quarter, but it did not include provisions for effectively arming; it was never ratified by all the participants and no action was taken under it. It was, no doubt, a sign of growing alarm and of a tendency towards co-operation; but there were still petty quarrels to hold the German states apart. A Danish threat to Hamburg revived the old ill-feeling between Brandenburg and Hanover.

Bavaria, like Austria, was tied by the Turkish war. Louis felt safe to continue his threats and advances. Disregarding the treaties he built three forts at wide intervals in the territory of minor princes in alliance with him on the German side of the frontier.

The emperor acquiesced, though refusing to make a definitive treaty. By this time Saxony, Bavaria, the Palatine, and Trier were all alienated, and when another major territorial question was raised, the German situation became unfavourable to Louis. On the left bank of the lower Rhine, marching with the Spanish Netherlands and uncomfortably near the Dutch, lay the ecclesiastical principality of Cologne with which the same prelate now held Liége and Münster. The old prince-bishop was an ally of Louis, still more so was the dean of his cathedral, William cardinal von Fürstenberg, bishop of Strasbourg. To complete his arrangements for making use of the electorate in time of war, Louis induced the cathedral chapter in January 1688 to elect Fürstenberg coadjutor to the bishop with the right of succession. This made French domination in Germany a direct threat to the Dutch. It brought the prospect of a general war visibly nearer.[1]

In more than one of the quarrels which seemed to be leading up to war there was a religious element. In France and England the protestants were being oppressed; still more so in Savoy, where also France was instigating the persecution. The Habsburgs were restricting religious liberty in Hungary. The new elector was restoring catholicism in the Palatinate. Protestants all over Europe had a sense of common danger and common interests, and they looked across the frontiers for allies and leaders. But two great facts made it certain that if the general war came the dividing line between the two sides would not be religious. First was the opposition between France and the emperor. Second was the attitude of the Holy See. This must be attributed partly to the personal decisions of the disinterested and saintly Innocent XI, who was pope from 1676 to 1689. Innocent had been at odds with Louis early in his pontificate over the relations of church and state in France. He had regarded the

---

[1] The archbishop died on 8 June. In the election neither Fürstenberg nor his opponent, a brother of the elector of Bavaria, obtained the requisite number of votes, so that the decision fell to the pope, who gave it in favour of the Bavarian; but Fürstenberg maintained his claim by arms.

persecution of the huguenots with misgivings, not only because he wished to unite all Europe against the Turks, but also because he wished to prevent the revival of religious strife.[1] When James II of England had sent the earl of Castlemaine as his ambassador to Rome, Innocent had received him coldly and had not granted the request for a cardinal's hat for Petre. Consistently with all this the pope had been willing to arbitrate or mediate in the affairs of the Palatinate, but unwilling to promote a definitive peace between Louis and the emperor. He had in fact tried to dissuade both James II and Louis from the steps which in the end led to conflict. In 1687 Louis chose to begin a serious quarrel with Innocent over the question of the immunities of ambassadors in Rome. Here Louis was refusing to surrender a right to petty local misgovernment because it was against his principles to surrender anything whatever. The pope was not to be intimidated, and their relations at this critical moment were worse than strained.

These were the other factors which William of Orange had to watch as he picked his way among the conflicting opinions about English affairs. He did not know, nor indeed did any one except the parties immediately concerned, how closely James was linked with Louis at his accession. There is indeed something almost inexplicable in the fact that James on his accession, without offering anything definite in return, made an immediate application to Louis for money.[2] It is hard to understand not only because at that time in public James was all for parliamentary grants and a national policy, but also because he did not in fact prove a faithful servant of Louis. At first, desiring peace, he tried to restrain Louis from provocative action about the Palatinate. There is no real reason to doubt the sincerity of his own subsequent professions that he never intended to subordinate British to French interests, and that, even when the general war came in sight, he thought he could keep out of it and allow England as a neutral to grow rich by trade as she had done in the last war. He saw no incompatibility between this and friendship with France. His correspondence with William maintained an amicable tone until the spring of 1687 or later. In some things

[1] For his attitude see J. Orcibal, *Louis XIV et les protestants* (1951), especially pp. 139–47.

[2] For the sums actually paid during the reign see R. H. George in *Journal of Modern Hist.* iii (1931), 392.

William was more than obliging, as in sending over the troops at the time of Monmouth's rebellion, in others less, as in refusing to appoint an English catholic to the command of his English regiments. James had sense enough to express his dissatisfaction in moderate if frank and simple language, and if he made rather more of it in conversation with the French ambassador, that is not necessarily more than another example of the duplicity which was fashionable in diplomacy. Some people went much farther in the game of being on both sides at once, and James, by renewing the defensive treaty of 1678 with the Dutch, showed openly that he regarded himself as being committed to neither side. These manœuvrings for position are less important than the geography of the ground on which they took place. It was becoming steadily clearer that there was a solid community of interest between William, the anti-popish party in England, the Dutch republic, and the emperor.

This community of interest was drawn closer when in 1687 James sounded William, as he was sounding every other person of influence in English affairs, on the repeal of the tests. William had other correspondents in England besides the king. Some of them, as he well knew, were merely anxious to be on both sides; but the others included a growing number of responsible and trustworthy politicians. He was even in personal contact with some of these. The king's inquiry cannot have come as a surprise, nor by that time can William's answer. He took the same position which Halifax expressed in masterly and influential pamphlets. He said that he was entirely for toleration, but he could not do anything against the interests of protestantism: in other words, he was against the penal laws but in favour of retaining the tests. James did not press the point or express any annoyance. He had still no reason for forcing a breach with William; but this incident dispelled some of the uncertainties on which hopes might still be founded. By means of a pamphlet from the pen of his friend the pensionary Fagel, the attitude of William and his wife was soon made known to the whole country.

The idea was, however, already present to the minds of many politicians both in England and abroad that William might become an active leader against James. There is no evidence that William, as has been suspected, had already used this possibility as a lever in his diplomacy of the previous year; but it was certainly in the air from the time when Everard van Weede, lord of Dykveld, was in England as ambassador extraordinary of the Dutch, between February and May 1687. He came for the ostensible purpose of removing the anxieties of his masters about James's armaments and intentions. He entered into close and confidential relations with the king's opponents. Nearly a year elapsed, however, before a question arose on which William's policy came into open contradiction with that of his father-in-law. In January 1688 James, intent on building up an army which would be equally useful at home and abroad, decided to call home the six regiments of his subjects, three English and three Scottish, which were under William's command in the service of the states-general. The states gave leave to the officers to return but not to the soldiers.

For William the problem of intervention in England was first a continental problem, military and political. He had to make sure that it would not arouse suspicion or hostility among the anti-French powers. Of these the hardest to manage were the Dutch. They had to think first of their own defence in a general war, and the party was still strong which held that by friendship with France they might keep out of a war over German questions. James's demand for their regiments looked, indeed, like an attempt to weaken them. Louis alarmed and irritated the Dutch still further in the spring of 1688 by a series of commercial measures which began a tariff war. He did not indeed intend to provoke them to fight. His measures against their shipping, fisheries, textile industries, and agricultural exports were taken partly for reasons of economic policy; they were incidents in the long-standing three-cornered rivalry of England, Holland, and France. If they had a political motive it was to give the Dutch a taste of the bad results of French hostility so as to frighten them out of war, not to goad them into it. But mutual suspicion was now at such a height that anything except the most conciliatory conduct increased the chances of a rupture. The French ambassador at The Hague suspected that the new strictness in collecting the customs, which had been let out to farm at William's instance, might be due to a desire to raise money for armaments. Bevil Skelton, the English ambassador in Paris, got a snub from James for suggesting that his freedom from a definite alliance with France might be a contributory cause of the insolence of the Dutch. In May there was obvious activity in the English naval dockyards.[1] In June Louis warned James of his danger from the Dutch preparations. By that time William was discussing the question of intervention in the plainest terms with his English correspondents. There were various forms which intervention might take, but one thing he would not do was to repeat the mistakes of Monmouth. He made it known that he would not come at all unless he received a written invitation from a number of responsible men. The document he wanted was agreed on the day when the bishops were acquitted and in July it was brought over by Arthur Herbert, lately vice-admiral of England.

This invitation is remarkable not only for its results but equally for its manner. It is cool, business-like, and unemotional, as carefully drafted as a lawyer's conveyance. After a survey of the situation, the signatories promise 'if the circumstances stand so with your Highness, that you believe you can get here time enough, in a condition to give assistance this year sufficient for a relief under these circumstances which have been now represented, we, who subscribe this, will not fail to attend your Highness upon your landing'. The announcement of a rebellion could not be more formal or less demonstrative. The line of cipher at the end which conveyed the names was worthy of the gravity of the document. All the history of the last ten years was in those names. There was Danby, the old half-forgotten minister who had planned the marriage of William and Mary. Side by side were a Russell, the sailor cousin of the Lord Russell who had been beheaded, and Algernon Sidney's brother Henry, lately minister in Holland and commander of the English regiments there. There was the suspended bishop of London. Three peers signed with them. One was Lumley, whose troop of horse had captured Monmouth, but who had at an uncertain date become a convert to protestantism. Shrewsbury, the next, had taken the same step. The other was Devonshire, whose son had married Lord Russell's daughter. These seven names combined political experience with wealth, popularity, and territorial influence. True, some were wanting. The great Halifax had been too circumspect to accept the chance of joining. The earl of Nottingham, faithful as he was to the church of England interest, would not engage against his king.[2] But there were yet others

---

[1] See J. R. Tanner, 'Naval Preparations of James II' in *Eng. Hist. Rev.* viii (1893). The activity resulted from orders given in February.

[2] Daniel Finch, born 1647, succeeded as second earl 1682; first lord of the

who could not be asked to adhere openly but were known to be sympathetic enough to join the movement if it had a chance to succeed. Lord Churchill was not only James's best military officer. His wife was the close friend of the Princess Anne, and the three were openly and honourably committed to suffer any extremity rather than give up their protestant religion. Strangest of all, the reckless Sunderland, the hottest of the reactionaries, lost his nerve and was dismissed from office. The whole military and political machine was ready to break to pieces under James's hand.

William's great decision was taken as soon as the invitation arrived: this was all he wanted. He would go now if he could, and he lost no time in clearing the way. Amsterdam had been at odds with him in recent years, but the patricians of Amsterdam received the secret well. Hans Willem Bentinck spent July and August in North Germany arranging to hire troops on behalf of the stadholder: here too all went well. The Great Elector's son, who had lately succeeded him, was in the secret now, together with the Landgrave of Hesse-Cassel and the heads of three of the four branches of the house of Brunswick, though not of the fourth and most important, Hanover.[1] The mere fact that troops were hired did not prove in what direction it was intended to use them. These agreements were made by William as a sovereign prince without the authority of his masters the states-general, but it was clearly time for James and Louis to look to their own forces. James in August was asking for French ships to be handy at Brest: if they were available to join his own there would not be much to fear at sea. His ambassador in Paris, who knew more than his master told him and did not like what he knew, was a party to a step of Louis which was meant to help, but only exasperated, James. This was a protest to the states-general against their armament, with a declaration by the French ambassador there, the skilful Count d'Avaux, that Louis would treat any attack on England as directed against himself.

This time Skelton earned more than a snub from Sunderland: he was recalled and thrown into the Tower. James resented the public patronage of France and still clung to his shred of

admiralty 1681–4; secretary of state 1688–93 and 1702–4; president of the council 1714–16; died 1730. Though its literary form makes it somewhat difficult to use, *The Conduct of the Earl of Nottingham*, ed. W. A. Aiken (1941) is a valuable collection of materials for his public life.

[1] None of these princes belonged to the League of Augsburg.

independence. Nor, to tell the truth, was Louis in a position to give him effective help. He might have made a military demonstration against the Dutch frontier, but that would have been to bring in the Dutch against him in the German war which he was preparing. Even as it was the *démarche* at The Hague roused Dutch feeling on William's side. And Louis as late as the second week of September hoped that the Dutch would attempt nothing against England that year. If they did, it might be awkward for James, but for Louis it might have advantages; England would be neutralized once again by internal divisions, and with James clinging to his freedom of action in spite of everything, perhaps it was better so. But why did not Louis, at the time of d'Avaux's declaration, get ready his ships? The answer is simple, though it appears to have been unknown to James. The ships were not there. At Brest there were not the necessary forces. The naval strategy of France has always been complicated by the fact that she has two sea-coasts, the Atlantic and the Mediterranean. At Toulon the necessary ships were in existence, but they were not ready for sea. It would be impossible to get them ready that year.[1] Louis, in short, had no weapon to use against the Dutch except bluff. He had already decided on war in Germany in the second half of August, and he tried in one breath to frighten the Dutch out of attacking England and to frighten them out of intervening in Germany: Fürstenberg in Cologne was included with James in the same declaration as under French protection. It was a risky way of keeping the Dutch out of both countries, but it came very near to keeping them out of England. William was in painful anxiety. He wrote that he had never felt greater need of the help of God. He watched every point of this baffling situation. A brave man, Jacob van Leeuwen, Bentinck's secretary, slipped across to England in September to talk to Russell, Lumley, and the rest. One by one the Dutch authorities came into line, and late in September the states took into their service the forces William had raised. Suddenly an overt act of Louis's cleared up all the uncertainties. He marched his army against Philippsburg far away on the upper Rhine. For that campaigning season the Dutch were safe. The states of Holland agreed to the English plan. After them William appealed to the states-general 'now or never', and they joined in the venture.

[1] This is clear from the letters printed in P. Clément, *L'Italie en 1671* (1867), pp. 336 ff.

While his chance of European support was melting away, James had seen signs enough that his English machine was jamming and breaking, and side by side with his last belated efforts to keep up the policy of the free hand in relation to France, there ran a last attempt to reconstruct the good understanding between the monarchy, the church of England, and a parliament. At the end of August it was announced that parliament was to meet in November. Then there came a declaration that when it met, the king would only endeavour a universal liberty of conscience, that he would secure the church of England, and that Roman catholics should remain incapable of sitting in the house of commons. Sir Roger Strickland was superseded in command of the fleet by a protestant officer, a friend of the king's, Lord Dartmouth. But by that time the danger from overseas was immediate and overshadowed everything. It was impossible to face the confusion of a general election and the writs for the parliament were recalled. Only executive action could be taken to conciliate the people. The suspension of the bishop of London was removed. The city of London was given back its charter and ancient privileges as before the *quo warranto*. All the municipal charters granted since 1679 were annulled. A general pardon, with very few exceptions, was proclaimed. Some of the popish lord-lieutenants were turned out. The fellows of Magdalen were restored. The ecclesiastical commission was abolished. But the concessions were too obviously inspired by fear. The Dutch had stopped the ports, but rumour said that the prince was on board his fleet and only awaiting a fair wind. People were saying that all these benefits were only the work of the invader.

King James had written on 8 October that he expected William to be ready to embark a week later and then to come across with the first easterly wind.[1] This forecast was only slightly premature; the fleet put out on the twenty-ninth but it made a false start. A storm scattered it, causing the loss of one vessel and some horses, and damage which took a few days to repair. On Thursday, 11 November, a new start was made, and on the Saturday morning crowds of watchers on both the French and English coasts saw the fleet running before a fresh easterly wind through the Straits of Dover into the Channel. The troop-

---

[1] To the Duchess Sophia of Hanover, in *Memoirs of Mary, Queen of England*, ed. Doebner, pp. 71–72; French translation in *Lettres et mémoires de Marie*, ed. Bentinck, pp. 2–3, misdated 28 September 1687.

transports, numbering about two hundred, were arranged in nine divisions, and an escort of forty-nine warships was disposed around and among them, with light vessels on the flanks, in the van, in the rear, and in attendance. It was a cumbrous but a very imposing force. The warships outnumbered the thirty-two sail which James had collected at the Gunfleet off the Essex coast, and were probably their equals in equipment and personnel.

Nevertheless as a naval operation William's expedition was a gamble. It was not decided on the morning of 11 November whether the objective was to be the west country where Monmouth had landed or the north, which was equally disaffected and equally far from the home counties, where James's army was concentrated. That decision depended solely on the wind, and it was made either later on that day or on the next when the fleet was already at sea.[1] The west was chosen, but in either event the plan was to race for a landing, leaving the unbeaten English fleet behind on the flank of the communications with Holland. We have no direct information about the way in which this plan was formed: we do not know whether any of the naval men spoke up for the orthodox strategy by which the hostile fleet should first have been engaged and the road laid open, so that there need be no further anxiety about communication with the base. In any such discussion much must have been said about the state of opinion in the English fleet. It was not, strictly speaking, a hostile fleet. The sailors, only a few days before, had as good as mutinied against the introduction of catholic chaplains. Many of the officers were in communication with William of Orange and his friends. The commander-in-chief of their opponents was their old mess-mate Herbert. Everything had been done by propaganda to make the most of all this; but William and his officers knew well that an encounter must be avoided if it could be avoided by any means. The least touch might wake the ancient hatreds of the Dutch and the English seamen. One broadside might make them forget their religion and their politics and the interests of Europe, to remember only the Medway and the Four Days' battle. So the plan was to slip by and land, leaving to chance what might happen

---

[1] Here A. B. Powley, *The English Navy in the Revolution of 1688* (1928), pp. 79–80, is supplemented by *Correspondentie van Willem III en Bentinck*, ii (1928), 610 ff., especially pp. 623–4.

if the fleets met after the landing. Any battle would be better than one with scores of transports wallowing among the combatants.

Fortune favoured this gamble so signally that men talked for generations of the protestant wind. The wind which blew the invaders down the Channel prevented Dartmouth from getting away from his badly chosen anchorage, but when he did come clear it dropped, and he lay helplessly becalmed for two days in sight of Beachy Head. When at last he was able to move in pursuit he was met by a south-westerly gale which compelled him to take shelter in Portsmouth. The navy, on which King James had spent his best energies and pinned all his hopes, never came into action. The disembarkation of William's troops was effected without the smallest hitch or interruption on the shores of Torbay. On 5/15 November, the anniversary of the frustrated Gunpowder Plot, in the hundredth year after the Spanish Armada, the great grandson of William the Silent and of King James I, slept among his soldiers on English soil.

From the first whispered suggestion that his destiny might lead him thither, William had never lost sight of the fact that, whatever else it might be, this was a professional military problem. He had about him now the largest disciplined force that had ever landed in England. The nucleus was formed by the three English and three Scots regiments from Holland, mustering some four thousand men. With them were Swedes, Brandenburgers, Dutch guards, cavalry from Würtemberg, mercenary Swiss, and French huguenot volunteers. In all there were some 11,000 foot and 4,000 horse. The veteran Schomberg, once a marshal of France, famous long since in Portugal, was second in command.

Little need be said about the military part of the expedition. It was indeed essentially a military operation, not a popular insurrection. Arrangements had been made for the formation of a certain number of infantry and cavalry units from the Englishmen who should join the prince, and this was done, though the numbers who came in were disappointing. The lack of numbers did not, however, inconvenience the invading force. Having made sure that Plymouth, the arsenal of the west, was friendly, it moved forward deliberately and methodically, and its list of quarters from Exeter to Knightsbridge is as orderly as if it had been on a training march. There were one or two encounters of outposts. At Wincanton and in the town of Reading there were a few casualties; but there was no effective opposition. On one night William slept badly with thinking about the widely scattered billets of his troops, but the soldiers had nothing to complain of except rain and mud, and the real anxieties of their leaders were political. Of these the first resolved itself reasonably quickly, the doubt about the reception they would have from the country. In the west, so soon after the Bloody Assize, it was to be expected that the gentry and the populace generally would be cautious; but after a very few days they began to come in, and within a fortnight of the landing William had about him the earls of Macclesfield, Abingdon, and Wiltshire, Lord Colchester, Lord Cornbury, the son and heir of the king's brother-in-law Clarendon, and Sir Edward Seymour, the proudest of the western grandees.[1] Lord Lovelace had been arrested in an attempt to get through, and others were hanging back, but every day brought news of fresh adherents. Danby and his friends were masters of York. Delamere was raising troops in Cheshire. Devonshire declared himself at Nottingham.

Best of all were the desertions from the king's own court and army. Cornbury's flight had been startling, but there was worse to follow. On 29 November the king took up his headquarters at Salisbury, where three roads to Exeter diverge. His officers were divided as to the wisdom of advancing and forcing an engagement. If the morale of the army was sound, a battle would have been the best way of putting the invaders in the wrong. However careful they were to put their English troops foremost, and however careless James might be in allowing his Irish to take the leading part, bloodshed would make the nation rally to the king. But the morale of the troops was uncertain, and there was the defence of London to think of. Churchill urged an advance, and with him the soldierly duke of Grafton, a natural son of Charles II and the son-in-law of Arlington. They were playing for their lives, and when the decision had been taken to retreat, they rode off by night to join the enemy. The royal troops began their withdrawal, and next night there went Lord Drumlanrig, the young duke of Ormonde, and even Prince George of Denmark, the husband of the Princess Anne.

[1] Born 1633; fourth baronet; sat in parliament from 1661; speaker and treasurer of the navy under Charles II; opposed Exclusion Bill; in office 1692-4 and 1702-4; died 1708.

Twenty-four hours later the princess herself, the one remaining
member of the house of Stuart who was loyal, escaped in disguise
from Whitehall under the escort of the bishop of London, to
begin a roundabout journey to the revolted counties.

While the leaderless army fell back before him William played
with faultless skill a game in which his chief weapon was silence.
His problem, not unlike that of General Monck, was ten times
more difficult. Every one knew why he had come, and no one
knew exactly what he would do. His banner bore the words,
with the 'Je maintiendrai' of his illustrious house, 'the Liberties
of England and the Protestant Religion'. He had, however,
assured the emperor and the states of Holland that he had no
intention of injuring the king or of appropriating the crown to
himself, and that he would attempt to secure a repeal of the
penal laws against catholics. In the declaration which preceded
his coming he promised to refer to a free parliament the redress
of grievances, the succession generally, and the legitimacy of
the prince of Wales. How could he carry out this programme,
which must involve the irreconcilable enmity of James, still
lawfully king, without either a permanent danger of counter-
revolution, or measures which would divide his supporters? The
English tories who were now on his side, Bishop Compton,
Seymour, Danby, were no friends to the dissenters. The emperor
was sensitive to the claims of the catholics and of monarchy.
The Dutch wanted their army for home defence—France
declared war against them on 26 November—and had no wish
to see their stadholder become a king elsewhere, or be drawn
into the endless domestic strife of England. The exiles from
Holland wanted no compromise with James. They distrusted
their new allies and did not understand the unanimity of the
country to which they had come back: at first they did not
believe that even as a deserter Churchill would dare to come
back to the western counties where he had been the most active
of the generals who broke up Monmouth's men. Yet these exiles
were the most deeply committed to William's cause. It would be
hard to satisfy both them and the new friends. Once William
broke his silence it might seem that he must lose his commanding
position. He might lose more than that; he might still lose
everything.

In his haste to make concessions James had been checked by
military necessity: the intended parliament had been dropped

because an election would have turned everything into confusion. Neither the concessions nor direct advances to the bishops and other aggrieved persons did anything to win back support for the king; and immediately before his departure for Salisbury a considerable number of peers, headed by Sancroft and including Rochester, Clarendon, and Grafton, had petitioned him to summon a parliament and at the same time to negotiate with the prince of Orange. That was almost to accept the prince's terms, since a free parliament was his chief demand: it showed that there was scarcely any one outside the catholic inner circle who was whole-heartedly against the prince; but it equally implied what James ignored when he scornfully refused to negotiate, that much or all of the prince's declared programme might be fulfilled without sacrificing the king or the essentials of the monarchy. He promised a parliament only when William should have left the island. He was a brave man, but he was the son of Charles I and he was beginning to think of his own safety, and that of his wife and son. He was beginning to think that safety was only to be found in the friendship of France, to which he had always been so reluctant to commit himself finally. Barillon was the only foreign diplomatist who accompanied him to Salisbury. On the day when they left London, the baby prince of Wales was sent down to Portsmouth, where he was waited upon by Lord Dartmouth, who now came ashore for the first time since he took command of the fleet.

After the return from Salisbury the desertions had made it clear that James's position was untenable. He called a meeting of between forty and fifty peers, spiritual and temporal, who were in or about London, to discuss the summoning of a parliament. He had to concede not only that writs should be issued the next day but also that an amnesty should be granted to William's supporters for what they had already done, and that there should be a negotiation with William to ensure that the elections should not be vitiated by military pressure on one side or the other. Three commissioners were chosen to go to the prince, and they were well chosen. They were all clear-headed, able, and moderate men, and although two of them had been in correspondence with William, they had not joined him and so they were not in any false position in trying to effect a compromise. These two were Halifax and Nottingham. The third, Godolphin, was still in office at the treasury; Nottingham was like him a tory, and only Halifax had been removed from the privy council.

The three commissioners met William on 18 December at a roadside inn, the 'Bear' at Hungerford on the Bath road, only sixty-four miles from London. He and they knew how much depended on their negotiations, and the answer they took back was so evidently fair and so exactly consonant with all William's former professions that neither side could be sure of having gained an inch. William agreed to remain more than forty miles from London if James would withdraw his troops the like distance on the other side, and if precautions were taken against the introduction of any French troops during the elections, and if the existing law as to the exclusion of catholics from office were in the meantime obeyed. To the whigs it appeared as if William was weakening, as if he would be too easily satisfied. Certainly he had gone to the utmost limit of correctness, and he cannot have known how the mind of James was playing into his hands. For behind the screen of negotiation and of parliamentary writs, James had other plans. The first to discover it was Dartmouth, who received orders to have the prince of Wales conveyed to France. The loyal admiral replied that though he would risk his life in defence of the throne, he would be no party to handing over its heir to the French king. The child was brought back to London, and on 20 December he was sent off secretly with his mother to Gravesend to embark. At three o'clock next morning the king himself left his palace in disguise and made off to a waiting vessel at Sheerness.

James had done the one thing which in times of disorder leads most certainly to the overthrow of a government: he had run away from his responsibilities. It was useless to remain loyal to him when he was not there, when he was in fact no king but a useless fugitive; and somewhere a government must be found without delay. A group of peers met at Guildhall under the presidency of Halifax. On 21 December twenty-nine of them signed a declaration, announcing that they united themselves with the prince of Orange, and would undertake to keep order until he should arrive. London was on the verge of anarchy. On the night after the king fled rioters sacked and burned the popish buildings, and even attacked the houses of foreign diplomatists. Barillon's was guarded by soldiers, but that of the Spanish ambassador Ronquillo and two others were destroyed. The papal nuncio made his escape, but the mob caught lord chancellor Jeffreys at Wapping, and he was lucky to get into the Tower alive. Panic and false rumours shook the City. The train-bands were under arms, but they could not long be equal to their task, and outside London there was no force to take control. One of the last and most foolish acts of James had been to give orders to disband the army, and to disband it unpaid. It was nothing less than a necessity that William should take charge of the administration. He took steps to reassemble the army, with the exception of the Irish troops, and to bring it under his own command.

The course of events in revolutionary days leaves a lasting imprint on the settled governments which follow them. An accident added to the perplexity of this situation over which theorists were to argue and men of action were to fight for two generations. Some Kentish fishermen boarded the king's vessel as it lay waiting for the tide, brought him ashore, and then discovered who he was. The provisional government had him brought back with military protection to Whitehall. This ignominious return was disconcerting to all parties. James could do no good by staying, but if he were to go again, some would think he had been driven out and so had not cancelled their loyalty by a voluntary desertion. To their high notions of prerogative a forced abdication was no abdication, and it seemed that without force he could not now be made to renounce his kingdom. James proposed a conference, but William refused it and detained the messenger. At Windsor, where the prince now held his court, a meeting of peers under the presidency of Halifax decided that James must leave London. William sent forward his troops, and the king ordered his Coldstream Guards to give way without fighting and to allow the Dutch guards to take over their posts at Whitehall. So for one night they guarded him in his palace, and next morning he openly left by water for Rochester, where nothing was done to detain him. Six days later he was on board a smack, and when the English were celebrating Christmas Day he heard the mass at Ambleteuse.

VII

THE REVOLUTION SETTLEMENT
AND THE FRENCH WAR

ONCE James was gone, the constitutional settlement was reached quickly. An election was held and a body assembled which, since in the absence of a royal summons it was not technically a parliament, was called a convention.[1] Like the different convention of 1660 it laid down the main lines of a settlement to be reaffirmed by a regular parliament at a later date. It met on 1 February 1689 and finished this work on 23 February. It had to decide what arrangements were to be made for the future and what theory was to be adopted to make these arrangements and the past transactions square with the law. As to the practical question only two courses had any considerable body of support. James was so discredited and so unrepentant that it was the old choice over again between exclusion and a regency. Exclusion was the whig policy: it had the attraction of affirming the right of resistance, the dependence of government on consent, the subordination of the succession and the Crown itself to parliamentary authority. The success and solidity of the Revolution had been due, however, not to the whigs but to the tories, to those who, even in their complicity in revolution, had never ceased to believe that kings have a divine indefeasible right to hold if not to exercise their sacred office. This theory might be preserved intact if James were still nominally king, but with his powers transferred to other hands. The elections had, however, returned a considerable majority in the house of commons who would not be satisfied with this. They were not all whigs. Some of them had in mind merely the practical argument that if James were nominally king he and his son, with or without French armies behind them, would always be able to rally their supporters to overthrow the regents. The peers were more evenly divided; but they threw out the regency proposal by a majority of two, and in conferences

[1] For details see J. H. Plumb in *Cambridge Hist. Journal*, v (1937), 235 ff. An unusually large number of the members had not sat in previous parliaments, and 'moderates' were unimportant.

between the houses, the tories scored no successes except in showing that the theories of the commons involved a number of contradictions.

These theories were indeed thrown together with no regard for consistency in a resolution of which the conclusion was to declare the throne vacant. The grounds on which this conclusion was based were that James had endeavoured, by the assistance of evil counsellors, judges, and ministers, to subvert and extirpate the protestant religion and the laws and liberties of the kingdom, and having withdrawn himself out of the kingdom had abdicated the government. Plainly the mention of evil counsellors interpreted in the light of the legal doctrine that the king can do no wrong, pointed to them and not the king as the culprits. The first part of the resolution might have justified the forfeiture of the Crown, but forfeiture was something very different from abdication, which was the point of the second part, and the alleged abdication was stated to be the same thing as desertion, or a necessary consequence of it, which plainly it was not. But these faults of logic were forgiven since they served to unite the various groups who agreed on the conclusion.

If the throne was vacant the next question was how it was to be filled, and first of all whether conditions should be imposed on William or William and his wife. There was no time to overhaul the whole constitution before finally empowering William to act, so a compromise was made. The Declaration of Rights was drawn up, a document formally declaring illegal all those acts and practices of James II against which the Revolution was directed. Here again there were some theoretical flaws. It was declared illegal to maintain a standing army in time of peace; but there was no old law against that. This was merely making a law out of the complaints of the last twenty years. It was added that 'the subjects which are Protestants, may have arms for their Defence, suitable to their condition and as allowed by law'. The suspending power was condemned altogether, and the dispensing power 'as it hath been exercised of late'; in the subsequent Bill of Rights this was defined as the abolition of all *non obstantes* except such as were expressly authorized by Acts of Parliament. The Bill of Rights appeared to promise in the same session a bill to legalize further exceptions, which, however, were never made. While the document was being prepared various grievances were mentioned which would have taken months to discuss. There was the burdensome hearth-tax, the public revenue in general, the law of treason, the tenure of judges, extravagant bail and fines, the corporations. All these, however, could safely be left over. The control of supply was a sufficient lever for bringing them to discussion in due time. So it was too with the freedom of elections and frequent parliaments, which were mentioned in the Declaration.

The one remaining task of immediate urgency was the filling of the throne. Although it was agreed that William must be the effective head of the government, there were various ways in which this could be brought about. If James was no longer king and if the prince of Wales was not his true son and heir, then it might be maintained that, by the law of succession, some third person must have succeeded already. Before the lords accepted the theory of vacancy, Danby was for recognizing Mary as queen regnant, with her consort in some position which would have to be specially defined. The whigs had legal arguments against this: the succession had never been limited to her. But at this stage legal arguments did not matter: what decided the point was that William, after three months of silence, at last declared himself.[1] He said that he had no right or wish to dictate to the convention, but he claimed the right to decline any office which he felt that he could not hold with honour to himself and with benefit to the public. He would not be regent. He would not, with or without the royal title, accept a subordinate place by the side of his wife. If the estates offered him the Crown for life he would accept it; otherwise he would return without regret to his native country. He thought it reasonable that the princess Anne and her descendants should succeed before any children he might have by another wife than Mary. There was nothing to do but to comply with this decision. The princess of Orange came over from Holland to join her master. On 23 February they formally accepted the offer of the throne made to them jointly, and with it the Declaration of Rights.

These transactions and the document in which they resulted, full of the spirit of compromise and even evading some of the more thorny questions, have a very different complexion from the doctrine of the Revolution which was accepted as orthodox in the eighteenth century. The Revolution was in

[1] Privately he told Halifax on 30 December 1688 that he would not be regent and had not come over to establish a commonwealth (Foxcroft, ii. 201).

form conservative: it professed to restore and to preserve, not to innovate. The fact that it was revolutionary, that the convention was an assembly without legal precedent, was soon forgotten, but it was also forgotten that its real architects had included tories as well as whigs. The doctrine which came to be accepted included in the Revolution a number of reforms which were only obtained by parliament, sometimes after a tough defence of the prerogatives of the Crown, in the course of the next six years. But from the beginning the tories were unable to explain away in terms intelligible to the common man the contrast between their acts and their theory of non-resistance, while the whig interpretation of what had happened was ready to hand. It was stated clearly but moderately and cautiously by John Locke, the exile now returned, in his *Essay of Civil Government*, which he wrote 'to justify to the world the people of England'. Government, he said, is based on a contract or agreement, by which men come together to form an ordered society. Having done so they entrust the executive government to one or more persons. The executive, by violating the terms of its trust, may forfeit its rights; but society remains in existence, and is entitled to take the necessary steps to ensure that the work of government, the preservation of property, shall go on. Revolution, on this theory, is the ultimate safeguard of law.

The Revolution as interpreted by Locke was regarded by the majority of the governing class, until the break-down of the old régime in the early nineteenth century, as a masterpiece of political wisdom. The tablets and obelisks which commemorate it in English parks and market-places show how it was accepted as the basis of the prosperity and order in which the squires and tradesmen flourished. It was the Glorious Revolution and it became the object of almost superstitious reverence. It was indeed open to two opposite criticisms, the one conservative and the other radical. The conservative criticism was that of the Jacobites, whom no argument of expediency would dislodge from their personal loyalty to the Stuart house. The radical criticism was that of the writers who showed in chance allusions and incidental paragraphs that the ruling class was not entitled to speak of itself as the people of England. Locke himself was aware of the defects of the electoral machine, and a series of English and foreign observers commented on its anomalies; but parliamentary reform was in the distant future. So long as the danger·

of a Stuart restoration existed, the radical criticism could not gather effective force. The two criticisms cancelled one another out. The present need was to save what had been gained, and that would have been imperilled by a revival of party strife over the social foundations of parliamentary power.

The settlement of 1689 was enough for the moment, but there were many problems about the future of the constitution which could only be decided by the experience of its working in the new reign. Its development was bound to have two sides, the one consisting of changes in the law, the other of changes in conventions or working understandings supplementary to the law. It was ultimately by these understandings that the great problem left over from the Civil war, the problem of parliamentary control over the administration and administrative guidance of parliament, was to receive its solution in the system of cabinet government. That system has never been fixed and stereotyped in a set of rules, but has constantly responded to the changing conditions of the times. Even the changes in law have been dictated not by the logic of political theories, but by the tasks of the hour, so that it is impossible to disentangle constitutional history from political, personal, and party history. The Revolution was a great event. It established the British type of constitutional monarchy. The allocation of powers between the king and his subjects depended, however, on the next phase of the work of William III. The constitutional history of his reign and the next turns on the fact that his service was first of all military service. The aspect of his intervention in England which had all along been the most important to him had hardly occupied the attention of the English for a moment. There is no mention of foreign affairs in the invitation of the seven. It was of his own motion that William, before the meeting of the convention, ordered Barillon to leave the country within twenty-four hours. But, although it was not demanded by the English, it was well understood that a decisive change in foreign policy was a necessary, and to many a welcome, result of the Revolution. After a period of uncertainty which extended all through the times of division, England now stood amongst the opponents of France. She had entered on her classical foreign policy of alliance with the Dutch and the imperialists which lasted, with only one serious interruption, for sixty years. She had committed herself to a long period of European war.

The first domestic result of the war was that it prevented both sides from pushing disputes about prerogative to extremes. William viewed the position of the Crown much as Charles II had viewed it. Except for the specific points already settled he wished to preserve the prerogative. He made remarks to the effect that, while monarchies and republics each had their advantages, there was no government so bad as a monarchy without the necessary powers. The policy of the extreme whigs was to limit the powers of the Crown severely: in William's circle they were spoken of as republicans. They, however, equally with the king were committed to the war: the necessity of avoiding defeat outweighed all other considerations. The French fought for the restoration of James as well as for their own national ends, and that would have meant ruin for the whigs. William, on the other hand, was dependent on parliament for grants of money, and this, besides making him amenable to parliamentary pressure on all seriously disputed questions, directly solved without any discussion the first great open question about the future of parliament. Henceforth it met every year. The prerogative of summoning parliaments lost all importance. When William's war was over it left behind it such an expensive debt, and so many rooted habits of obtaining parliamentary sanction for the work of the executive, that there has continued to be, without interruption ever since, a meeting of parliament every year.

William put up a stout resistance to an enactment which was meant to end another of the Stuart devices for managing parliaments. It will be remembered that the Triennial Act of Charles II had left the king the power of keeping the same parliament for an indefinite period of time. As early as 1689 a bill was introduced to limit the duration of each parliament to three years. A second bill in 1693 was passed by both houses, but William refused his consent. A third, identical with the last, was thrown out in the next session by the commons; but the whigs pressed strongly for it, the earl of Shrewsbury even refusing to take office until it was passed. In the next year, 1694, when the war was at its second serious crisis, William at last gave his assent; and from then until 1714 the excitement of politics was kept alive by general elections at intervals which were never longer than three years.

The parliamentary history of the triennial bills was closely involved with that of three place bills, which aimed at ending the power of the Crown to control parliament by appointing members to paid offices and securing the election of office-holders. Only one minor provision from these bills became law during the war-period,[1] and they do not indicate whether their supporters fully understood what their consequences would have been. They might, indeed, have led to either of two contrasting results. One would have been a system like that which was later developed in America, with a strong executive standing entirely outside a legislative and money-voting assembly.[2] What the new country party aimed at, however, was not this but something directly in the tradition of the great rebellion, something closely allied to full parliamentary sovereignty. As a first step they wanted to keep sharp the weapon of impeachment. They wanted also a method of keeping the government dependent on the houses in its regular routine, and for this two alternatives were available. The first was that of forcing legislation by tacking controverted measures to those which were necessary for carrying on the government. The second was the expedient of parliamentary committees, derived from those of the commonwealth. A series of inquiries into the conduct of the war began in 1689 and went regularly on: they suffered, however, from the inability of the commons to administer an oath to witnesses. There was a tendency to push the system to much greater lengths than would have suited the Crown. In 1691 the commissioners of accounts interpreted their function of auditing very widely and there was a plan to make a surprise attack on the prerogative by giving direct control of the war to a committee.[3] In 1692 it was proposed that there should be a committee of both houses to advise on the state of the nation.[4] In 1696 a committee of trade was proposed, which was to take evidence from merchants and others and advise about the provision of convoys. The government, as we have seen, took the matter out of the hands of parliament by appointing the lords commissioners

[1] 5 & 6 W. and M., c. 7, forbids collectors of excise to sit in parliament. Other revenue officers were excluded by 11 & 12 W. III, c. 2, s. 150, and 12 & 13 W. III, c. 10, s. 89.

[2] It must, however, be remembered that ministers would have been able to sit in the house of lords, and this might have altered the relations of the two houses profoundly.

[3] Sir Robert Howard to William, 31 July 1691, in Dalrymple, App. C, pt. ii, bk. vi.

[4] Cobbett, Parl. Hist. v. 741; Lords' Protest, 7 December 1692.

of trade and plantations, the board of trade, a regular government department which continued to deal with all commercial and colonial business until the loss of the American colonies. The one great instrument of parliamentary control which the reign of William III finally established was the appropriation of supply.[1]

If the state of war led to the consolidation of the position of parliament, it also set limits to the growth of parliamentary power. It afforded a justification for what was in any case the inevitable result of William's temper and abilities, the fact that he was his own prime minister and that he kept military and foreign affairs tightly under his own control. None of his subjects had half his knowledge of European affairs. Foreign policy requires a rapidity of decision and not infrequently a secrecy which are impossible to parliaments, especially to parliaments which sit only in the winter months. Thus Locke recognizes that the 'federative power', that which deals with foreign relations, is distinct from the executive; but all through William's reign there were demands from the opposition parties, if not for parliamentary control, at least for parliamentary cognizance of foreign policy.[2] It was claimed that since the Norman Conquest no important foreign transaction had been done without the consent of parliament; but William was not moved by such arguments. He laid other treaties before parliament at its request, but not the treaty which contained the inmost secrets of his policy, the grand alliance treaty with the Dutch and the emperor.[3] So long as the war lasted this concealment led to no trouble: it was to be a more serious matter in peace.

The mere existence of a large army through nine years had a profound effect on the constitution. It was not in any way

[1] See above, p. 67. Mr. R. M. Lees has drawn attention to an interesting incident which shows in little the defects of direct executive action by an independent authority. The commissioners for wool appointed by an act of 1689 began work in 1698 after the peace. Their officers seized two French ships which had passed the customs, thus causing an international incident embarrassing to the secretaries of state. All the powers of the commission were 'concurrent' with those of other bodies; they were not exercised wisely, and there was no proper provision for finance. It lapsed in 1701. (*Economica*, nos. 40–41, 1933.) Another executive authority created by statute was the trustees for Irish recusant estates (11 and 12 W. III, c. 2). The commons treated the trustees, who acted from 1700 to 1703, as their agents.

[2] The essay of 1701 reprinted in C. Davenant, *Works* (1771), pp. 363 ff., gives the best arguments. For the whole subject see E. R. Turner in *Eng. Hist. Rev.* xxxiv. 172.

[3] Klopp, App. xii to bk. xiii.

contrary to the principle of the Declaration of Rights about standing armies, since that concerned only times of peace; but even in war it was made to depend as it had never done before on parliamentary authority. The right to enforce military discipline was granted by Mutiny Acts lasting for one year or occasionally for two, and the necessity of passing these has generally been mentioned as a further reason for annual parliaments. There were, however, certain years (1698–1701) in which no Mutiny Act was in force, but the military machine moved on without them; nor had the Crown abandoned its right to raise armies by its own authority. And, whatever the authority, the army stood like the navy in a close relation to the Crown and to the king as a person. Its officers, and the hundreds of officials who were needed in the ordnance-office and in the other parts of the military administration, formed an 'interest'. They were valuable material for a body of king's friends in parliament, more devoted than the ordinary country gentleman and less likely to become unmanageable through political ambition.

The executive had still by no means taken the shape of a parliamentary government of the modern type, and the earlier cabinets of William's reign could do little to control the business of the houses. The earl of Nottingham, for instance, when he took office as secretary of state, is said to have bargained with the king that he would follow his own sense of things in parliament though he would be guided by the king's sense out of it.[1] Godolphin was for carrying out the principle of a balance of parties both in the ministry and in the houses.[2] As the war went on this had to be given up, and, as we shall see, things moved in the direction of ministerial unanimity; but there was still no satisfactory plan even for conveying information from the government to the houses: in 1694 some members could not tell whether Wharton spoke for the court or not.[3] There was no certainty that ministers would be unanimous, and it was a matter of importance to know how a speaker stood with the king. William did not give up appearing at times, as Charles II and James II had done, in the house of lords. He sometimes sent messages to direct the course of debates, and once he got himself into a difficulty by taking up in a speech from the throne a position from which he had afterwards to withdraw. More than

---

[1] Burnet in Foxcroft, *Supplement*, p. 315. [2] Dalrymple, II. i. 38.
[3] Bonnet in Ranke, vi. 256.

once he used prorogations to end differences with parliament. Had there been a working party-system this might have been avoided, and the king would probably not have needed to use his veto on so many as three occasions. As it was, the means of controlling parliament were unsatisfactory and partly experimental: that in which the most progress was made was the creation of a body of members united to the Crown by ties of loyalty, interest, or cash.

The ecclesiastical settlement, like the constitutional, left disappointed extremists on both wings; but the lack of bitterness and disturbance over it shows clearly that old animosities were weakening and genuine tolerance growing. The Declaration of Rights had put an end to the possibility of a toleration granted by prerogative; it also announced that it had been found by experience inconsistent with the safety and welfare of this protestant kingdom that it should be governed by a popish sovereign or by any sovereign married to a papist: this was therefore made illegal by the Bill of Rights which enacted the provisions of the Declaration. Two acts were passed, which were no doubt unnecessary, to provide against conspiracies and insurrections of the Roman catholics. One was comparatively harmless: none of them was to possess arms or any horse worth more than five pounds. The other made permanent one of the measures which had been taken in times of panic: they were to be excluded from London and Westminster. Beyond that, however, nothing was done to increase the disabilities of catholics.[1] The law indeed was already so severe on paper that they could scarcely have been increased; but the Spanish ambassador was able to report that in fact the Revolution improved their lot. By ending the reckless provocations of James, it ended the protestant exasperation. The administration of the law was indulgent, and the Roman catholics, though effectively excluded from public offices and from the naval and military professions, became again what they had been under the Protectorate and in the earlier days of Charles II, a quiet body, not actively persecuted.

The protestant nonconformists were more fortunate. The great body of them had joined with the Anglicans in opposing

---

[1] Acts were passed in 1695 restricting their access to the professions and in 1700 restricting their right to own land and imposing severe penalties for saying Mass. They do not appear to have been enforced.

James. This earned them gratitude; but it was made more active by the fact that a considerable minority had stood aloof. James had indeed been misled by organized addresses of thanks into thinking that his attempts at toleration were more welcome to the nonconformists than was actually the case; but the greatest individual among them, William Penn, the quaker, was his friend and supporter, many of the quakers both in England and in Ireland were wholly with him, and not only quakers but a considerable number of independents. It was clearly necessary for parliament to reward the faithful and at the same time to win over those who had been convinced that the real enemies of toleration were the Anglican clergy and squires. The idea was sponsored by Nottingham himself, and welcomed by the clergy of whiggish and latitudinarian tendencies, of enlarging the boundaries of the church of England to include the more reconcilable nonconformists, in particular the presbyterians. A royal commission of bishops and other divines recommended a number of changes in the Prayer Book which, as some good authorities thought, would have made it acceptable to two-thirds of the nonconformists. But it is doubtful how much effective good will there was in any quarter. Even the friends of nonconformity feared that such a law would merely draw away a large body of people from it, leaving the remnant too weak to be sure of toleration. The nonconformist sects were unable to effect any reconciliation among themselves. Negotiations for this purpose in the 1690s failed,[1] and this in itself shows that the Anglicans are not to be blamed for the failure of the attempt at comprehension. The plan was, in any case, not tactfully brought forward. Before any clerical authority had been consulted, the houses of parliament were engaged in discussions about kneeling at the sacrament. Convocation was summoned and the lower house made ready to resist the proposals. The bill failed to pass the commons.

The nonconformists had to be content with another act, unofficially called the Toleration Act. This allowed protestant nonconformists who believed in the Trinity to have their own places of worship, provided they met with unlocked doors and certified the place of meeting to the bishop, the archdeacon, or quarter-sessions. They were allowed to have their own teachers and preachers, if these took certain oaths and declarations to

[1] See above, p. 23, n. 3.

which none of them had in fact any objection. The fear of non-conformist republicanism was still not extinct, but by this time it was really behind the times. The act, although it maintained the Restoration system of excluding the nonconformists from public affairs, may be taken as marking the point from which nonconformist life and thought were free to develop without interference by authority. A judicial decision towards the end of William's reign put limits to the power of the bishops to compel schoolmasters to take out licences, and the restrictions of the Clarendon Code on education were largely inoperative before that. Though bishops occasionally tried to hamper the nonconformist academies in the eighteenth century, they did not succeed. There was another step towards toleration which has sometimes been given too much prominence in histories of freedom of thought. The Licensing Act of the Restoration, which had already been in abeyance for one short period in Charles II's time,[1] ran out in 1695 and was not renewed. There was no strong desire to renew it: parliamentary opinion had ceased to regard ecclesiastical and administrative censorship as a guarantee for the public peace.[2] Henceforth the authors and publishers of offensive matter had nothing to fear from the censor before publication; but after publication, when they could not retreat, they were exposed to an oppressive law of libel. In religious literature this no longer mattered, but political writers were still to find that they were at the mercy of the government and the judges, without much hope of protection by juries. There were still to come some new, if minor, restrictions on the liberty of expression. In 1698 a new law, never yet repealed, was made against all who should by writing or advised speech deny the divinity of Christ. Not long afterwards, for political reasons, fresh restrictions were placed on journalists, though not on the writers of books.[3]

This modest instalment of toleration fulfilled its purpose, and no further act of parliament of importance carried the process farther until the nineteenth century. The only changes in the law were, as we shall see,[4] in the other direction: the Jacobite danger served as a reason or excuse for not enlarging the liberty

---

[1] See above, p. 28. There was a last renewal for two years in 1693.
[2] For four abortive press-bills between 1697 and 1704 see L. Hanson, *Government and the Press, 1695–1763* (1936).
[3] See below, p. 239.　　　　　　　　　　　[4] See below, pp. 232, 247.

of the lethargic descendants of the puritans, and the high churchmen withdrew something of their new tolerance after the first
shock of the Revolution. It was indeed in the history of the
church of England, not in that of the dissenters, that the Revolution marked the sharpest break. That church was the most
closely involved in it because, by virtue of their position, her
prelates were politicians. They had done their best to act
according to their principle of non-resistance, but by the time of
the crisis, they were sharply divided. Sancroft was the highest
dignitary among those who had scrupulously avoided going
beyond passivity in their opposition to James, and who now
held that they would not be justified in taking the oaths to
William and Mary which parliament prescribed. Deprived of
their offices, they formed a little community of their own,
numbering at first five of the seven bishops with one other
bishop who had not been of their number, and about four
hundred of the lower clergy. Their secession had not the historical importance of the secession of St. Bartholomew's Day
1662. The little flock held together, soon divided within itself
and always dwindling, until the early nineteenth century; and
some of its number were men of distinction, like the scholars,
George Hickes, Thomas Hearne, and Richard Rawlinson,
whom any writer on English history should remember with
gratitude. But the world was filled with men of less sensitive
conscience, to whom the nonjurors seemed merely to protest
against what could no longer be altered; and even the Jacobite movements drew but little strength from their obstinate
fidelity.

Their departure led to the preferment of supporters of the
new order. In the time of William III ecclesiastical promotions
were much influenced by Queen Mary, who did nothing un-
worthy of a grand-daughter of Clarendon, and the new bishops
included a number of robust and notable men. If Gilbert
Burnet, who became bishop of Salisbury, was lacking in tact
and taste, he was a good historian and a warm-hearted man.
Tillotson, the new archbishop of Canterbury, was a powerful
preacher and his character deserved respect. They and the
others lacked, however, a really deep sympathy for the body of
clergy of whom they were appointed leaders, either on their less
worthy or their better side. Most, if not all of them were whigs,
and they held the balance in the house of lords. So there grew

up, widening with each fresh appointment to a deanery or a see, a breach between the higher and the lower clergy. This disharmony had little effect on national affairs until the last years of William's reign, but there was a foretaste of it in 1689. In that year there was a 'sitting convocation'. The convocations of the clergy of the two provinces of Canterbury and York had been summoned regularly whenever parliament was summoned, but they had not sat for a good many years. They had done no business of importance since 1664 when Clarendon and Archbishop Sheldon, by a private and unwritten agreement, had transferred to parliament the taxation of the clergy, which was the only business in convocation of any interest to the state. In 1689 the assembly was revived in connexion with the comprehension plan; but the only result was a decided negative from the lower house, so that the experiment was not repeated until 1701, when it again turned out badly.

The religious life of England in the reigns of William III and Anne was better than its ecclesiastical history. It did not produce a single martyr, nor a saint, nor a devotional classic; but it was fruitful in all those charitable and humane activities which are the religious aspect of English practical sense. The forces which were bringing into being the great humanitarian movement of the eighteenth century were deeper and wider than the disputes of sects, as wide as the desire for reasonableness which was appeasing the wranglings about creeds. One of them was the sense of responsibility which grew on the English as they found themselves taking control of heathen populations overseas. The missionary spirit had been growing for a good many years when the Society for the Propagation of the Gospel in Foreign Parts was founded in 1701.[1] That society, which still lives, was an offshoot from the Society for Promoting Christian Knowledge, founded three years earlier and also still active, which did the like work in all its phases at home. The act of 1710 which established a commission for building new churches in London was the first Anglican attempt to bring civilization to the miserable thousands who swarmed in the areas over which London had spread in the Stuart period. The religious motive was at work in

[1] In 1662 Charles II granted a charter of incorporation to the New England Company, which still exists for the propagation of the Gospel in North America, but the Company was founded and collected its first endowment under an Act of the Long Parliament dated 27 July 1649.

a number of educational movements. The nonconformist schools and academies were not merely born of separateness and exclusion; on their positive side they stood for godly training of the young. There were charity schools of different confessions: the Jesuits at the Savoy under James II belonged to a movement which soon spread to the protestants and was the chief concern of the Society for Promoting Christian Knowledge. In the draft scheme of William III's time from which this and the Society for the Propagation of the Gospel arose, Dr. Thomas Bray wrote of his project as a 'Congregation pro Propaganda Fide', the Roman name.[1] Besides schools there were libraries. The society took over the provision of parochial libraries both in England and in the colonies, which had been begun, with other missionary and educational work, by Dr. Bray. The parochial libraries were recognized by an act of parliament of 1709, and on a small scale prepared the way for the local public libraries of the future. The rich nonconformist minister Dr. Daniel Williams, in a will made in 1711-12, left much to education and to the library which still perpetuates his name.

The tendency to good works was widening its scope. There were new protests against the cruelties of the prison system,[2] and the first searchings of heart about the slave-trade and plantation slavery may be traced in the English and American books of the last thirty years of the seventeenth century. The quaker workhouses and the half-philanthropic, half-economic, plans of individual quakers and others for relieving the poor point forward to the days of social reform.[3] There does not indeed seem to be much ground for the suggestion that 'a vigorous moral reaction within accompanied the external dynastic revolution':[4] the moral movement began earlier and was much longer in coming to completion. It was certainly influenced by foreign examples. As was to be expected at that time it had also a negative and

---

[1] J. W. Lydekker, in *Hist. Magazine of the Protestant Episcopal Church*, xii (1943), 13. See below, p. 416.

[2] Legislation for the relief of insolvent persons imprisoned for debts they could not pay began 1670-1 (22 & 23 Car. II, c. 20), with the revival of an act of the interregnum. The Elizabethan poor law had made some provision for it.

[3] See above, p. 53.

[4] Mark Pattison, 'Philanthropic Societies in the Reign of Queen Anne' in *Essays*, ii. 311. This essay, written in 1860, was based on Secretan's *Nelson* and therefore ascribes to Anne's reign much that was true at an earlier date. For more modern accounts see B. K. Gray, *Hist. of English Philanthropy* (1905), and G. V. Portus, *Caritas Anglicana* (1912).

repressive side, which found expression in the Societies for the Reformation of Manners. From about 1691 to about 1740 these societies, to which both Anglicans and dissenters belonged, in spite of much criticism were active up and down the country in prosecuting poor persons for moral offences. They, and the more definitely religious societies which began within the church of England about 1678 with the German preacher Anthony Horneck and William Beveridge, are signs of a tendency to voluntary association of a free and simple type for religious and social ends. On the one hand, they resulted from the restriction of the moral and social activities of the established church, the desuetude of ecclesiastical jurisdiction over the laity, and the withdrawal of the clergy from interference in the affairs of daily life. On the other hand, they show how society adapted its typical forms of association to new ends. The charitable and missionary societies had much in common with joint-stock companies. Their trustees included men who sat on boards of directors. English religion could press the business-like spirit into its service.

Religious life and institutions must have been influenced, like constitutional and economic development, by the long war; but the connexions are harder to trace. Here and there they may be indicated. A government that was fighting for its life looked at church matters from a more political point of view, regarding the bishops as peers and leaders of opinion rather than as fathers in God. The opponents of government were glad to ingratiate themselves with the largest organized body capable of controlling votes, the parochial clergy. The conviction that the cause of protestantism must be maintained by bombs and bayonets blunted many of the gentler religious feelings. The war weighed heavily on England. It was the longest foreign war she had waged since Queen Elizabeth; it was the bloodiest and the most costly. It was the first war of what may be called the modern type, the first of a series of wars lasting down to our own time, in which Britain has fought not only at sea but also on the frontiers of her colonies and as one member in a European coalition waging land war on the greatest scale. There were, indeed, parts of the world where Britain had economic interests but to which the war did not extend. Turkey was involved not in it but in the other war which continued alongside of it, in which the emperor and the Venetians were her main opponents. The

Baltic region was neutral. The Far East was untouched, and, though their Indian trade suffered from the war, both the English and the Dutch were able to draw from it some of the wealth they needed to finance their fleets and armies. With these exceptions it was a war in which the Europeans carried their hostilities to all parts of the world.

The diplomacy which grouped the nations for the struggle was almost completed before William III brought the might of England to bear against France. The powers had shown their inclinations, and there remained only the task of pinning them down by formal alliances. The Dutch had no choice but to engage in the war, and they had nothing to offer the English except what they were bound to give in their own defence. They hoped, however, that England would do more than merely fulfil the letter of the treaty of 1678: some relaxation of the anti-Dutch commercial policy seemed possible. This, however, the English would not concede. They agreed in a series of treaties in 1689 to come into the war with all their resources, but they drew the Dutch into exceptionally strong measures against French commerce, and stipulated that neither power should make peace without the concurrence of the other. The emperor intended to use his main resources for continuing his victorious advance down the Danube; but he was anxious to have subsidies to help him there and also to take a share of any gains which the Dutch and the English might make without his help. William urged him to make peace with the Turks, and be content with the extensive conquests he had already made: a favourable moment was to come early in the war, but, as we shall see, it was missed. And there were overwhelming reasons for giving way to the emperor on other points. The treaty of the Grand Alliance which was signed at Vienna on 12 May 1689 by the Dutch and the imperialists, and afterwards joined by William as king of England, had as its object the restoration of the settlements of Westphalia and the Pyrenees, or more precisely the undoing of the reunions and the restoration of the duke of Lorraine; but it had a secret article of greater moment. Behind all the European quarrels of the last thirty years there had always been the prospects of the death of the childless king of Spain and of the emperor, whose elective throne was one of the objects of the ambition of Louis XIV. The 'maritime powers', the Dutch and the English, wished the emperor to cling to his claims in both these directions and not to barter any part of them for French concurrence. By this means they could make sure not only of his alliance in the general struggle over the balance of power, but also of the preservation in the Spanish empire of the lax, conservative Habsburg rule. This would be more favourable to their commerce than any partition between the Habsburgs and such rival traders as the French. The secret article therefore promised Dutch and English influence with the electors to choose as king of the Romans, or designated successor to the empire, the emperor's son the archduke Joseph. It also promised that in the event of the death of Charles II of Spain without heirs, the two powers would use all their forces to support against the French the rightful claims of the imperial house to the Spanish dominions.

Spain was to be invited to adhere to the remainder of the treaty but this clause was not communicated to her, for it was to be expected that Spain would interpret the rights of the succession differently from the emperor. She had indeed no real alternative but to join in the war: the Spanish court wavered, but Louis declared war on Spain in April 1689. If he was to fight not only the emperor and a number of German states but the English and the Dutch as well, if in fact his German war could not be isolated but must be merely one side of a general war, then it was to his advantage to have Spain against him. She could put hardly any troops in the field, and at sea the most she could do was to convoy her galleons from America, but she offered both in the Netherlands and in Catalonia tempting countries to invade. Among the German princes the most important that joined the coalition was Brandenburg. The new elector, Frederick III, took a main part in keeping Fürstenberg out of Münster and Hildesheim, and, although his support could never be absolutely reckoned on, he was closely in William's interest. Saxony, the next strongest state of north Germany, came into the alliance readily once the siege of Philippsburg was begun. Bavaria, Hanover, and the minor principalities also preferred to stand up for the line of the Rhine rather than to permit a piece-meal devouring of Germany. There was a nearer approach to national German resistance than Louis XIV had ever encountered before.

There was one more ally, the mountain-duchy of Savoy, which

had its capital at Turin in the north Italian plain, and its western frontier on the other side of the Alps, with easy access to the plains of Provence. Placed between the French and the Spaniards of the Milanese, the dukes of Savoy had preserved their independence during the Franco-Spanish wars of the past century not by neutrality, but by taking a side and by accurately judging the best moment for changing it. Latterly they had been much under French domination, to which they were held by marriage alliances, and by the French garrisons in Pinerolo and Casale. Under French influence the Savoyards had lately renewed the persecution of the Vaudois, the protestants of the Alpine valleys; but it was an easy matter to call off the hunt and restore the dispossessed in order to make friends with the maritime powers. They had definite objects in their war: to free Pinerolo and Casale, to gain full sovereignty over certain imperial lands in Savoy, and to secure treatment as a sovereign state by the emperors. In return their adhesion opened high hopes to the allies: an army marching from the Milanese through a friendly Savoy might strike a blow against the heart of French naval power in Toulon and might penetrate far into southern France. Savoy, however, did not join the alliance until 1690: her defection was accomplished at the seemingly safe moment when France had her hands full already, and it came as a crowning and unexpected success for the allied diplomacy, at a time when in some directions, such as his relations with the pope, the position of Louis was improving.

A quarter in which William was less successful than he hoped was the north. Sweden in the sixteen-eighties had been alienated from France, especially by conflicts of interest in Germany. In spite of the danger to the Swedish provinces in Germany from Denmark and Brandenburg, Charles XI of Sweden had joined the league of Augsburg in 1686. In that year a usurpation in Holstein-Gottorp by King Christian V of Denmark ranged France and Denmark against Holland and Sweden, a combination which seemed to threaten Britain's freedom to trade with the Baltic. Charles II and James II of England had both refused to make an alliance with Sweden in exchange for commercial concessions and in 1683 the Princess Anne had married Prince George of Denmark, but England and Sweden were friendly. Charles XI offered William 6,000 troops in 1688, but the French party in Stockholm prevented their dispatch. Denmark actually hired out a contingent of troops which served in William III's campaigns in Ireland and Flanders, but such hirings in that period of cosmopolitan armies did not involve the abandonment of neutrality. In 1689 William helped to bring about the convention of Altona which settled the Holstein-Gottorp dispute for the next eighteen years or so and set free 20,000 Brandenburg troops for the war; but he did not succeed in persuading either power to join him. Their jealousies still made each reluctant to engage in war while the other was neutral and in a position to attack it; moreover they were both poor. During the war the interference of the maritime powers with French trade caused more than the usual difficulties with these neutrals, and they even talked of joint action to assert their rights. But the English and Dutch were dependent on the Baltic trade for their supplies of naval materials. Matters therefore did not go to extremities, and both powers were appeased by compensation and partial admissions of their claims. They exerted little influence on the diplomacy of the war-period. Sweden made repeated offers of mediation and was the mediator when peace ultimately came. At one time, in 1691, there seemed to be a chance of a 'third party' for peace, consisting of Sweden, Denmark, and some of the north German states, but in the end it was the course of the fighting and the affairs of the belligerent powers which decided when and how the peace was to be made.

For England the character of the war was decided by these diplomatic arrangements and by her own revolution.[1] Besides the sea and the five European theatres of war, the Danube, the Rhine, the Netherlands, north Italy, and Catalonia, she had to deal with two theatres nearer home, in Scotland and Ireland. For the first two years she was not much more than a spectator of the continental warfare, nor did many Englishmen understand how the fortunes of all these wars were linked together.

To see the war from the English point of view it is best to leave aside for the moment the operations of those years on the mainland, and to watch the events nearer home. In consequence of Colbert's efforts to build up all maritime resources, the naval strength of France when the war began, though not immediately available in the Channel, was relatively much greater than

[1] For its colonial aspects see below, pp. 329–32.

in 1672. James II had pulled up the British navy after the neglect of 1678–84, but the Dutch navy had declined. The French fleet, divided between Brest and Toulon, numbered some ninety ships of the line of all rates, the British and the Dutch more than a hundred. The maritime powers, indeed, began with high hopes of what they might do by naval pressure against France. They bound themselves by treaty to cut off all trade with French ports, whether of their own subjects or of allies or neutrals, a presumptuous measure which they did not succeed in enforcing, but which implied that they expected to be masters of the sea. In a sense they did actually achieve that position from the summer of the year 1692, but the preceding three campaigns gave no clear presage of such an event, and during those years invasion was a serious danger as it had never been during the Dutch wars. In 1689 the principal operations at sea were subsidiary to the fighting in Ireland.[1] Troops were landed there by both sides, but the preponderance in Ireland was at the beginning very heavily on the side of James II, so that the English depended for success there entirely on keeping the sea open for their transports. Notwithstanding this opening for a damaging blow by the French, neither side made any powerful concentration of ships. The English ferried over their army and carried out the relief of Londonderry without serious interference. The only engagement of any importance was a fight in Bantry Bay, where twenty-four French ships, which had been convoying troops, were met by Admiral Herbert with a squadron of nineteen, much stronger in guns. This action won Herbert the title of earl of Torrington, but it can scarcely be accounted a victory.

In 1690 the French Toulon fleet was at Brest, and this pointed out the direction in which the allies could make the most effective use of their ships; but the admiralty, yielding to the merchant's clamour for commerce-protection, failed to keep its forces together and to use them where they were needed. The united French fleet, the greatest France had ever equipped, put out to sea in June, when there were still two British squadrons away from the grand fleet on relatively unimportant service. When Torrington, off the Isle of Wight, had news that the French were approaching, he and the Dutch were thus numerically inferior. The ships of the line were fifty-six against sixty-eight, the

[1] See below, pp. 306 ff.

disparity in guns being somewhat less. The risks of an English defeat seemed infinite: the king was away fighting in Ireland, the queen, at the head of the administration at home, was surrounded by treachery and discontent. Torrington was a brave man, but he judged that it would be best not to join battle. He afterwards defended himself in a sentence which has been the text for volumes of naval controversy: 'Most men were in fear that the French would invade, but I was always of another opinion, for I always said that, whilst we had a fleet in being, they would not dare to make an attempt.' The doubtful point was whether the enemy would consider a fleet merely in being as equivalent to a fleet that could do them any harm. An admiral who really believed in the combat would not have been satisfied with such an uncertainty. He would have engaged, and even if he had been worsted, he would almost certainly have done the French so much injury that they not merely would not have dared, but would not have been physically able to invade. Torrington called a council of war, which reported to the government that the fleet was too weak to fight. He then fell back up the Channel; but the government in London refused to accept his view and ordered him to close with the enemy. Off Beachy Head on 10 July the battle was fought. Torrington was not in the frame of mind in which victories are won. His own squadron held off from the enemy while the Dutch had the hardest fighting. The French did not lose a single ship, and the allied losses were not heavy when they drew off and made for the Thames. Including ships which they destroyed on their retreat in order to save them from capture, the English lost one and the Dutch four. Their fleet anchored at the Nore.

This was very bad. The Dutch were angry: King William sent an ambassador to assure them that he would punish the guilty parties. Torrington was court-martialled, and though he was acquitted, he was never employed again. Happily the defeat had no great consequences. Its moral effect was mitigated by the king's victory at the Boyne on the very next day. The French did not invade. They may have felt some respect for the fleet in being, but in any case they had no army and no transports ready for a descent. They merely cruised about in the Channel and made a useless landing at the fishing-village of Teignmouth.

The next year but one saw a decisive naval battle. The

French this time made ready for an invasion. An army was collected in the Cotentin Peninsula. James II joined it, ready to embark, and the French fleet set out to clear the Channel. Now, however, they were numerically far inferior to the allies: ninety-nine of the line, Dutch and English, were on the way to meet their forty-four. The English commander was Edward Russell, afterwards earl of Orford, the admiral who signed the invitation to William in 1688. Orders not to fight were on their way to the French admiral, but he never received them, and he had a desire to retrieve the reputation which he had impaired in the previous year. He fought in a disadvantageous position, close in to his own shore, and though he fought well, his fleet was ruined. In operations which lasted for six days along the coast to Barfleur he lost fifteen ships of the line, most of them destroyed in the deep bay of La Hogue. It was a blow from which the French navy did not recover in that war. It did not again put a battle-fleet to sea. There was now little question of invading England or breaking the British communications with the army in Flanders. The allies had gained that command of the sea which was to be the first British objective in the long series of French wars now beginning. The battle of Barfleur or La Hogue was not a brilliant tactical feat like Trafalgar, nor were its results nearly so complete, but it was the first of a series of battles of similar strategic significance in which Trafalgar was the greatest and last.

Its results were incomplete because the British and Dutch did not follow it up by effective combined operations, and the French, although they renounced all major operations, were still able to use their naval resources to good purpose in the minor warfare of commerce-destroying. This is always the resource remaining to the weaker party in naval war. The English and Dutch, with their rich seaborne commerce, were vulnerable to it, and the French had great advantages from their geographical position in carrying it on. Privateering, an old-established industry in Dunkirk, Dieppe, St. Malo, and other ports, enjoyed during this and still more during the following war its greatest era of prosperity. Since French seaborne trade was almost at a standstill and there was no naval recruiting, it had an unlimited supply of seamen. The government gave it every encouragement and assistance. Naval vessels were let out on easy terms to firms which manned and sailed them as corsairs. More than once squadrons of considerable force cruised in the Atlantic to make prize of merchant vessels. Such hostilities could have only a limited effect. England was not then dependent on imported food-supplies, and, though the Dutch were already in that position, their supplies were not in fact interrupted. But, within its limits, the pressure was very effective. It caused grave discontent among merchants, which was loudly expressed in parliament and added to the widespread dissatisfaction of the English nation with the conduct of the war.

That dissatisfaction was mainly due to the fact that this was for them a new kind of war, a land-war. Whatever the English might think, the decisive theatre was Flanders, where the French were making their main effort, for as long as they were unbeaten there nothing could be gained elsewhere which might not have to be surrendered in the peace negotiations. The French had been fighting in this region for centuries, and it was still to be one of the usual scenes of warfare until our own time. Its geography had two main features, one natural, the river system, the other artificial, the line of French fortresses. Both made movement difficult, defence and evasion easy. The rivers were the arteries of military transport, but along them stood fortresses which could deny their use to an enemy; and for those who wished to cross them the rivers themselves were barriers. It was almost impossible to force a battle on an enemy who did not wish to fight. The French might have had the initiative throughout most of the war: in most of the campaigns they were first in the field, and in the earlier years they were superior in numbers and also had a larger proportion of cavalry and artillery. But they aimed only at improving their frontier-line by conquering one fortress after another, never at destroying the enemy's army and organization by blows driven home. They were not dissatisfied with a campaign if it enabled their army, without actual victory, to maintain itself at the enemy's expense, and their armies, whether from the sluggishness of the commanders or from the cumbrous march formations and methods of supply, seldom moved fast or far. Hence it was a war of trenches and sieges. Sometimes when many of the troops of one side were tied up in garrisons, the other would tempt the weakened field-army to an engagement. The French used a strategy of diversions, and William sometimes allowed himself too easily to fight at a disadvantage. The battles were pitched battles: the armies spent hours in drawing themselves up in order, and, once they engaged, their drill and discipline permitted only very simple changes of formation.

It was thirty years since any continental army had seen the red coats of the English; but the British forces which William led were not raw levies without a tradition of discipline and professional training. There had been gradual growth and improvement ever since Charles II had begun the history of the standing army with the First Foot Guards, Monck's Coldstream Guards, and the two regiments of Life Guards. It is easier to trace the growth of the army by units than by numbers, for one battalion or troop might at a given moment be double the strength of another, and there were numerous independent or non-regimented companies and troops. There were temporary additions in years of tension, like 1678, as well as in the wars, so that the growth of the army was by no means steady and regular. Its general course may, however, be roughly summed up. The militia, which was almost entirely untrained and played no part in any serious fighting, numbered throughout the period some 6,000 horse and more than 70,000 foot. Under Charles II the standing army in England and Ireland grew to about 19,000. James II brought it up to some 35,000. William III's entire pay-rolls reached their maximum in 1694 at more than 90,000, of which less than half were in Flanders. Of the forces there about a third of the foot and half the mounted troops were foreign hirelings, and there were some foreign troops in England and Ireland. The first official English drill-book for infantry dates from 1678,[1] and from the later years of Charles II there was a considerable number of military handbooks of all kinds, some translated from French or Dutch, others put together by unofficial writers, and apparently used in the practical training of troops. The standing army of James II had many experienced officers. In all the arms, infantry, cavalry, artillery, and the still civilian engineers, it could easily be made ready to meet European troops. The weakest part of the military machine was the administration. This was inefficient and corrupt, and during the war, when the army expanded but the finances were always inadequate, it went from bad to worse, so that transport, supply,

---

[1] *An Abridgement of the English Military Discipline, printed by Special Command for the Use of his Majesty's Forces.* Only one copy of the first edition, printed in Dublin, is known, and only one of the second, of 1682. The third came in 1685.

and pay were always badly managed. William III never had the opportunity, even if he had had the gifts, for making a thorough reorganization of the ordnance office. Bad organization, however, was usual at that time. There was so much waste and inefficiency even in the French armies, that it would be hazardous to say they were better in this respect than their opponents.

The second year of the continental war was not unfavourable to the allies. When it opened the French were in possession not only of Philippsburg but also of a number of other fortresses in the Palatinate and on the Rhine. In order to economize their forces and to relieve themselves of the necessity of holding the river from Philippsburg to Rheinberg, they took a step which aroused strong indignation in Germany, devastating every place of which their enemies could make any use there, including Heidelberg and Mainz. They put three armies in the field, one in Germany, a second in Flanders, and a third in Spain. William III, instead of concentrating on Ireland as the English wished him to do, sent 8,000 men under Marlborough to serve in Flanders. With their help the prince of Waldeck, who commanded the Dutch army in the absence of William, won a battle in the field, and the French lost Mainz and Bonn, two very important points on the Rhine. In 1690, however, things went badly. The neglected Irish situation demanded William's own presence and took away 40,000 good troops. The French had more than 70,000 men in Belgium; the allies considerably fewer. Waldeck was defeated at Fleurus. The hopes which had been founded on the adhesion of Savoy were dashed when the French marshal Catinat routed the duke at Staffarda, south of Pinerolo.

In the same summer the Turks, under a new and capable grand vizier, ceased to negotiate and took advantage of their enemy's western war. They retook Belgrade, and the emperor, having missed his chance of a favourable peace, had to give up his dreams of partitioning the Ottoman empire and settle down to hard fighting which outlasted the western war. The year of Beachy Head was one of bad news from every quarter except the Boyne.

In 1691 there were further defeats. A French diversion against their duchy of Cleves on the lower Rhine detached the Brandenburgers, and before William could bring his army south from Brussels the great fortress of Mons fell. After that there was desultory fighting in Flanders, with another reverse for Waldeck. Away in the south Catinat was still victorious: he conquered Nice and part of Piedmont. Barcelona was bombarded by the French, and there was nothing to set against all this except a check to the Turks and, if that were an advantage, the death of the minister Louvois, to whom the French army owed much of its efficiency and French policy much of its overbearing roughness.

The year of La Hogue opened a new phase of the war for England, but it saw no great change in the course of events on land. An attempt to make use of the new control of the sea by attacking Dunkirk was unsuccessful. Another great fortress fell, Namur, at the junction of the Sambre and the Meuse, so that Louis gained the whole line of the Sambre. The French commander, the marshal duc de Luxembourg, then threatened Brussels, so that William had to follow him down the opposite bank of the Senne. At Steenkirk William fought an offensive battle, but his attack was not well done. The prince-regent of Württemberg wasted time in a formal artillery duel. Count Solms, contrary to orders, halted the Dutch foot and moved the horse forward where they were useless. The ground had not been well reconnoitred, and the French put up a deadly musketry fire from under cover. Before the army fell into its retreat, the English had lost Mackay[1] and another general, two peers, and seven colonels. Their countrymen complained bitterly of the foreign generals. Nor did the year bring successes elsewhere. Victor Amadeus of Savoy invaded France, only to be held up in the narrow valleys and compelled to retreat. The prince of Württemberg was beaten and taken prisoner by marshal de Lorges. After the fighting of this year William gave up the idea of invading France, and told his confidential friends that nothing remained except to obtain peace. The original aims of the alliance were unattainable. There was no longer any chance of restoring the conditions of 1659 or 1678. But the war was still not half-way through.

The fifth year of the war, 1693, was another year of reverses almost everywhere. Some of the Hudson's Bay Company's forts were recovered, and the Dutch captured Pondicherry; but hardly any one in Europe knew where these places were, and these events had no effect whatever on the course of the main

[1] See below, p. 277.

war. On the Danube there was a dull campaign; the imperial army, insufficiently provided, withdrew from before Belgrade. Victor Amadeus fruitlessly besieged Pinerolo, and at Marsaglia met a defeat in which the second duke of Schomberg was mortally wounded. In Spain the marshal de Noailles captured Rosas, a small Catalan port. Lorges took Heidelberg, the capital of the Palatinate. An English raid on the port of St. Malo, a nest of privateers, was a failure, and off Cadiz the outward-bound Smyrna fleet of English and Dutch merchantmen fell into the hands of a French squadron, the worst shipping disaster of the war. In the Netherlands the campaign opened badly and finished worse. A minor fortress, Furnes, near the coast, fell, and Luxembourg moved against Liége, an important position on the Meuse, and the capital of a bishopric held by the prince-bishop of Cologne. William was able to frustrate this move by taking up an impregnable position at the abbey of Park. Württemberg ended the deadlock there by a successful diversion on the river Lys, after which Luxembourg struck against Huy and captured it, thus extending his hold on the Meuse. William then took up a defensive position by the villages of Landen and Neerwinden, but it was badly chosen. In the hope of keeping out the French cavalry he had so placed himself that his own cavalry had not room enough, and when the French attacked his front, he was unable to extricate his troops, so the battle of Landen too was a defeat. The king's army retired to Brussels, and the French took Charleroi; but long afterwards, when they remembered his bearing at Landen, his old soldiers would cry 'Brave! brave, by heaven!—he deserves a crown.'[1]

Only in the sixth year of the war did the allies begin to hold their own on the main front. Financial and administrative improvements at home were beginning to tell. Until the previous year the French armies had increased in size: this year they counted only about 100,000 men in Belgium, and for the first time they were decidedly outnumbered by the allies. A skilful march of Luxembourg upset William's plans of crossing the Scheldt from east to west and operating against some point on the coast, but Huy was recaptured. Another great event of this year was the dispatch of a British fleet to the Mediterranean. The voyage of Blake in the time of the Protectorate had been the first warning that Britain could become a Mediterranean

[1] The authority of Laurence Sterne's *Tristram Shandy* is that of good tradition.

power. She had no base of her own now that Tangier had been thrown away, but Spain was an ally, British ships could do something to hearten the Savoyard, and the Levant trade was one of the vulnerable points of France even more than of England. In 1692 the corsairs of Tripoli declared war on France and they assisted British naval forces. The time had now come for stronger measures. Orford appeared on the Catalan coast and saved Barcelona from the advance of Noailles. In spite of his grumblings, William made him stay in the port of Cadiz through the winter, a demonstration of power which prevented any new invasion of Spain by way of Catalonia, and made a great impression on both allies and enemies. It involved a strain on the organization of the admiralty, and expenditure which England could ill afford. She was frittering away some of her resources on minor enterprises which her command of the sea suggested. There was a deplorable failure against the great naval arsenal of Brest. Dunkirk and Calais were bombarded; but this was a great year for Jean Bart, the most famous of French privateer-captains.

On the whole, however, that year had been less discouraging than any of the others, and the next saw a further change for the better. True, Noailles was superseded by a much abler man, the marshal duke de Vendôme; more shells were expended to no great advantage in a bombardment of St. Malo. But there was a memorable success on land. The French had suffered a great loss in the death of Luxembourg. When the campaign opened, the French army was unduly weakened by being stretched along lines from Namur to the sea. William made a feint to-wards the west and came within about twenty-five miles of the coast; then he doubled back and, uniting his army with the Brandenburgers and the elector of Bavaria, laid siege to Namur. It was a great undertaking, and in previous years England would not have been equal to it; but there had been an event in England which greatly increased her strength in the field, the founding of the Bank of England. Free from financial embarrass-ment, the English were able to make an unprecedented effort. The siege was carried on with equal skill and courage. Away to the west the French vainly tried to call off the attackers by winning minor engagements and by bombarding the undefended capital, Brussels. The allied engineers and storming parties crept forward. The effort succeeded. After nearly three months of siege Namur surrendered. William had won the one great victory of his sixteen campaigns. It was not one of those victories which sweep away the opposing forces; but its news came like a thunderclap in London and Versailles. It was something new in the history of the age for a marshal of France to hoist the white flag on one of the greatest fortresses in Europe.

By 1695 the opposing pressures of the war had at last brought peace within sight. William by tireless diplomacy had held his alliance together, but every one of the combatants was feeling the economic and military strain, and it began to be a question whether there was enough inducement for any of the powers to continue to fight. The first real change affected Savoy. In 1695 the French with a view to peace surrendered Casale, and one of the duke's war-aims was satisfied. The English could not afford to keep their fleet in the Mediterranean for a second winter, and thus were no longer able to offer him effective support in his own neighbourhood. They could not stand in his way if he looked to his own safety, and in the treaty of Turin of 1696 he obtained from the French terms which were amply satisfactory to him. Pinerolo was to be handed over, and all Italian territory was to be neutral for the remainder of the war. The last of William's allies to come was thus the first to go, and the French troops in Italy were set free for the main theatre of war. They did not, however, turn the scales. The campaign of 1696 was feebly conducted. An attempt at the invasion of England in conjunction with a plot to assassinate its king was frustrated.[1] The English bombarded Calais again; but there were no events of greater importance. It was a difficult year for English finance and politics, and by no means easy in France. There was a general war-weariness, and a reason external to the war caused Louis XIV at this point to change the aim of his diplomacy from dividing his enemies to bringing about a general peace. The great Spanish question was looming nearer. France could not settle it to her greatest advantage if she had a war on her hands, and that a war in which Spain was one of her opponents. The serious illness of King Charles II therefore influenced Louis's course. In secret negotiations in the winter between Dijkveld and François de Callières, the preliminaries of peace were settled. All the French conquests since 1678 were to be restored, including Luxemburg and Strasbourg. William was to be recognized as king of England. No French support was to be given to his enemies, among whom James II was silently included.

In spite of this secret arrangement, hostilities were begun again in 1697 when April brought round the campaigning season. The French won an initial success by capturing Ath on the Dender. The official negotiations began at Ryswick near The Hague in a country-house of William's, and all that had to be done was to fill in the details of the settlement and persuade the allies to agree to it. The Dutch were to be allowed to strengthen their defences by placing garrisons in some of the fortresses of the Spanish Netherlands, and were to have large concessions in the tariff and other commercial matters.[1] They were satisfied. The emperor and the Spaniards, though they had contributed little to the common cause, were slow to accept; but the events of the campaign hastened the work. The French took Alost, lower down the river from Ath, and, more alarming, Cartagena, the great port of the Caribbean, and, worst of all, Barcelona itself. Emboldened by these successes they hardened their terms and withdrew the offer of Strasbourg. There was an anxious moment, but in September all the powers except the emperor signed, and he came in in October.

The peace was to last only four years; but at the time when it was made there seemed a good prospect of its lasting longer, and this prospect even seemed to improve somewhat as the months went on. The English had secured the one primary interest of their own for which they had entered the war, the establishment of the new dynasty and the settlement, which the opportunity of the war had enabled the ruling class to define so much to their own advantage. That was a real turning-point in the development of the nation, one which resulted from the expression of the will of the governing elements in 1688. In another respect the war also marked a real turning-point, though this was not deliberately willed and very few either foresaw it or appreciated its importance. It was the beginning of a new era in public finance. The war necessitated a great increase in expenditure. The net annual public income was above four

[1] The British plenipotentiaries took with them a draft treaty of commerce prepared by the board of trade, but made no serious attempt to secure agreement upon it.

millions in the last three years of real fighting. The debt at the
end of the war exceeded fourteen millions, and the annual
charge was equal to the whole ordinary permanent revenue
granted to Charles II at the Restoration. The war altogether
cost something in the region of forty millions. To raise these
sums the state, after straining the old methods to breaking-
point, called to its aid new devices which had a double effect.
They hastened the capitalistic development of the country's
economic resources, while at the same time they virtually ended
the long-drawn antagonism between the Crown and the commons over questions of taxation.

The financial problem at the beginning of William's reign
was in some ways like that at the beginning of Charles II's, and
the constitutional arrangements for solving it were no better.
The most pressing difficulties were dealt with by raising the
customs before they were voted, as James II had done, and by
a loan from the city of London. The commons settled down to
estimate the ordinary revenue in the same rough and ready way
as in 1660, and even thought at first of keeping it down to the old
figure of £1,200,000. When this was seen to be too low, they
increased the amount; but in order to keep control of the
government even this ordinary revenue, the king's 'own', was
voted for one year only, and afterwards year by year throughout
the reign. The cost of the war was all additional to this, and
even apart from that there were great difficulties. The administration at the beginning of the reign was very corrupt: improvement began with the setting-up of commissioners of public
accounts in 1691. They were a temporary body, but it became
the regular practice to set up such commissioners from time to
time with strong powers of inquiry, to ensure that expenditure
went into its proper channels. On the side of income much
needed to be done. Through bad administration and economic
depression the yield of the old taxes sank. One source of revenue
was given up because of its unpopularity, the hearth-tax, the
only existing direct tax, but only this one. A number of new
taxes were devised, both direct and indirect, including considerable burdens on foreign trade. The most important of them
was the land-tax, which remained through most of the eighteenth
century the stand-by of war finance. It was, in technical language, a rate: the land of the country was re-assessed in
William's reign so that a tax of four shillings in the pound

yielded a set sum. It is said that the repartition was unfair to the eastern counties; but it was never altered, and although many properties have had their land-tax redeemed under acts of the younger Pitt, on the rest it still survives, the oldest British direct tax.

No reform of the revenue could raise the sums that were needed for the war, and the war expenditure was met out of loans. Inexperience and the financial straits of the government led to many improvident arrangements. The rates of interest, in the early period of weak government credit, went as high as 14 per cent. and even so, in order to get the money subscribed it was necessary to resort to devices like the lottery loan of 1694, in which 2,500 tickets were given prizes in addition to the interest.[1] The debt-system was still primitive in the sense that there was no sinking-fund, and the system of borrowing direct from the public had hardly begun, while the floating debt was still imperfectly organized. But the magnitude of the public debt and the fact that it had come to stay and to grow made it from that time onwards one of the cardinal factors in public and private finance. Investors were now able to place their money not only in private loans and businesses and with joint-stock companies, but also with the government. The investment of money was being separated from its management, and the amount of money which was dealt in by financiers who were not traders was growing. The government, however, could command neither the ability nor the integrity which were needed to develop this system. It had to depend on associations of business men, and the eighteenth-century system grew up under which the state was financed by privileged companies.

Of these the most important from the moment of its foundation was the Bank of England. The agitation for a national bank of some sort had begun in the middle of the century, and many projectors, inspired both by Dutch and Italian examples and by the promising growth of private banking, had put forward schemes for banks under government auspices or with government monopolies for deposit business, for issuing paper money, or, more generally, for steadying and reducing rates of interest by providing a broad market for loans. The bank actually founded in 1694 did not exactly conform to any of the older

---

[1] This was the first of a number of such lotteries. The profits went to the subscribers, and it was only much later that lotteries were organized from which the state took the profits. See R. D. Richards in *Economic History*, iii. 57.

precedents or plans. It arose from the government's immediate
need for money, and it was a finance company with rather fewer
than 1,300 shareholders, under whig auspices from the start,
which undertook to raise £1,200,000 for the purpose of lending
it to the government at 8 per cent. In return for this service it
was incorporated as the first English joint-stock bank, and
allowed to issue notes, to discount bills, and to do other kinds of
banking business. It had as yet no monopoly. Its notes were not
legal tender, and there was no arrangement for converting them.
It had to take its chance in an unstable and competitive world.

The bank had to face both political and commercial opposition. On political grounds it was opposed by the tories, because
it would pledge the moneyed interest to support the Revolution
settlement, and by the extreme whigs, because they feared that
the power of borrowing from it might make the monarchy
absolute. This danger was forestalled by a clause in the act of
foundation which made it illegal for the bank to lend money to
the Crown without consent of parliament. The commercial
opposition came from several sources. The existing bankers were
business rivals. Some of the merchants feared that the bank
might discriminate in favour of some customers against others,
and might centralize the money market so as to make every
one depend on it for credit, and make every one's solvency
depend on its own. There were landlords who feared both an
increase in the political power of financiers, and a rise in the rate
of mortgage-interest if the bank came to control all the money
and the landlords as borrowers had to compete against the
merchants. To this line of criticism the government hearkened
to the extent of setting up in 1696 a formidable rival, the Land
Bank, which offered money at 7 per cent. instead of the Bank
of England's 8. This was one of four land-banks actually started
in 1695–6, differing in plan and scale but alike in raising money
on the least liquid of securities, the land of the subscribers, and
alike in being completely unsuccessful.

In spite of all this the Bank of England succeeded. Its immediate results were brilliant: it was the bank's loan that paid for
the recapture of Namur. Michael Godfrey, one of the deputy
governors, and a nephew of Sir Edmund Berry Godfrey, who
went there as a spectator from the bank's temporary branch
at Antwerp, was killed in the trenches. The bank was partly to
blame for a severe financial and monetary crisis which came in

the following year. In order to maintain the flow of remittances to the army it had to borrow £300,000 from the states of Holland in 1695 on stiff terms. It was the first English institution to issue notes in excess of its total deposits, and this coincided with the drain of war-payments to the Continent and with the expensive and difficult operation of reforming the silver coinage, which the government undertook in the same summer. The rate of exchange on Amsterdam became impossible, there was a pamphlet-controversy on the principles of money, and King William had to intervene to get the machinery of international payments restarted. The other bankers organized a run on the Bank of England, but the government saved it by a moratorium of a fortnight.

After the peace was signed it got a merited reward for its hardships in the form of an act enlarging its capital, increasing its privileges, and consequently placing its credit on a foundation which held firm. From this time the bank more than any other single factor was responsible for some characteristic features of the organization of English politics and business. The credit of the government improved; it was able to get money on easier terms and without earmarking revenue to pay the interest on it. The money-market became steadier and the security of deposits facilitated the growth of capital. Financiers as a body felt that their security depended on the bank and on the government which stood behind it: the Revolution settlement became the greatest of vested interests.

In general economic life the war changed the course of business in two ways. The demand for the supplies specially needed for the war stimulated certain industries, such as the West of England and West Riding clothing business, horse-breeding, lead and copper mining, and the munition manufactures. As it was for the most part a demand for large quantities of identical articles, it encouraged large-scale organization. It did not, indeed, lead to anything like a general boom. In many respects the war caused grave depression. It almost coincided with the worst run of harvests ever recorded, and agriculture was still so much the predominant occupation that this meant poverty all round. The woollen industry in other parts of England, where there were no army contracts, was obstinately bad. The shortage of corn, acutely felt in France from 1692, was one of the contributary causes of the peace. It was accentuated by the British and Dutch command of the sea, for the maritime powers in 1693 added special measures against corn to their warfare against French commerce.

It was, indeed, in the stopping and diverting of maritime trade that the war had its greatest economic results. The allies were unable, to the relief of the Dutch, to carry out their full programme of prohibiting the whole trade of French ports; but the English, by direct prohibitions and by tariff measures, made the most of the war as an opportunity for protectionism. It marked a step farther on the road by which war has come normally to involve a cessation of economic intercourse between belligerents and a limiting of the expansion of neutral trade into the resulting vacuum. It enabled a group of industries newly established in England by the huguenot refugees to take root; though their artificial growth had to be protected against French competition by all the energies of the mercantilist state. They were miscellaneous manufactures, mostly of consumption goods, in which hitherto the English had been with difficulty trying to emulate French skill. That which probably employed the greatest number of hands was the silk industry. Others were paper-making, cutlery, and the manufacture of plate glass for coaches, mirrors, and windows. The linen industry might have been another, but it failed to acclimatize itself satisfactorily, and in those which did settle down progress was unequal. The period of the huguenot settlement and the war saw, however, in England, as in some other countries, a distinct advance in the variety and excellence of home manufactures. Being new these manufactures grew up free from the old-fashioned restrictions of guilds and corporations. In some of them there were privileged joint-stock companies. All, compared with many of the older manufactures, were organized on capitalistic lines; that is to say that the control of the moneyed man over production was stronger and less subject to restraint. The tendency which was at work in the world of finance had its not unrelated counterpart in the world of industry. England was becoming not only a business nation, but a nation with a growing capitalist class and a growing class of wage-earners who owned nothing except their labour-power.

Like all revolutions that of 1688 implied a change in the positions of parties. The small inner group of James II's men for the most part vanished from public life. Jeffreys died in the Tower. Petre reached France before his master. Preston stayed in England to plot for a restoration, and was three times committed to the Tower before he finally lost all credit with his own party and retired to end his days in the country. Among those who changed sides at the last respectable moment Godolphin had the financier's privilege of being treated as a non-party man, and stayed in office. Sunderland returned for a brief spell of exile to wait in his big house at Althorp for better weather, but against him there was no impeachment. It is characteristic of the whole nature of the Revolution that scarcely any new men came forward to fill the vacancies. The new actors who had appeared on the stage of English life were foreigners, and though the king stinted no suitable reward in money and lands or military commissions or places in the household, he could not give them political offices, for which they were in no sense qualified. His closest friend, the soldier-statesman Hans Willem Bentinck, became earl of Portland and groom of the stole. His mistress, Elizabeth Villiers, the sister of Bentinck's wife, received large grants of land.[1] Schomberg was given the only dignity suitable to his exalted rank, a dukedom, and was made master of the ordnance.

For the administrative offices there were too many experienced men to choose from: the national unanimity had the result that almost every one thought his services deserved a reward. Three important offices were entrusted to commissioners, not individuals. There was no obvious man for lord chancellor, so the Great Seal went to three not very eminent lawyers who were succeeded after a year by another three of not much greater weight. At the treasury board Godolphin sat on, but his four colleagues made way for Lord Mordaunt (now earl of Monmouth) and Lord Delamere, two of the makers of the Revolution, Sir Henry Capel and Richard Hampden, the son of a famous father. The admiralty had six commissioners, Admiral Herbert and five politicians. The highest office in precedence granted to an individual was that of lord president of the council: this fell to the most appropriate man, Danby, who was the principal minister until 1695. The next greatest figure of the

---

[1] After Queen Mary's death her connexion with the king was severed and she married her cousin Brigadier-General Lord George Hamilton, who was created earl of Orkney.

later years of Charles II also came back into office: Halifax was lord privy seal. The two secretaries of state represented two very different elements. The rich and gifted, but strangely unstable, earl of Shrewsbury was a whig, and new to office, while the earl of Nottingham was a steady churchman and tory with some years of administrative experience. The other appointments followed the same plan of combining both of the old parties, giving rather more of the spoils to the whigs than to the tories. There were indeed tories of weight and influence who could not be included. Clarendon and his brother Rochester, formerly Laurence Hyde, had no sympathy with the new order. The elder brother retired from politics for good; the younger, still a privy councillor, became the most influential of the churchmen who held no office. The tory party was transformed. It accepted the new sovereign, but it could not transfer to a Dutch Calvinist all the old reverence for kingship. Before many years had passed its members accepted the utilitarian view of the constitution which Locke had expounded; there was no great division of opinion in England for two generations after 1689 on the philosophical theory of the state or on the relations of Crown and parliament. Of a political theory the tories were almost destitute. Where they differed from the whigs was in their sympathies and inclinations, especially in ecclesiastical matters. They were the church party, unfavourable to catholic and protestant dissenters alike. Although they accepted the new settlement of the succession, there were some among them who, in varying degrees, were for the present less hostile than the whigs to the Stuart family, and if there were in the future to be a new choice as to the further succession, it was clear that many of them would be easily satisfied on other points, so long as the new heirs were protestants.

The difficulties encountered by the governments of William were not caused by organized parliamentary opposition in the modern sense. In its modern senses the word 'opposition' was not yet used:[1] those senses are in fact correlative to the idea of a party government. In King William's time the current antithesis was between 'court' and 'country', and of these groupings the country party was always the less stable. It consisted of those who, for the time being, voted against the measures of the

---

[1] The *Oxford English Dictionary* has a reference from a tory writer of 1704 to 'those who make oppositions', but no example of 'the opposition' until well on in the eighteenth century.

administration. Some of its members did this with a hope of changing the administration, but ministers did not lose office if they failed to carry legislative measures. These were not tests of confidence in ministers. Parliament could obstruct such measures and harass the ministers individually, but it could not turn them out. The confidence they needed to retain was that of the king; so none of the changes of ministry in this or the following reign resulted from a parliamentary defeat. None of them was a wholesale party change, but they were all of the nature of what would now be called reconstructions of the ministry, and none of those in William's time resulted from general elections. In a general election it was indeed the common experience that the government automatically got a majority.

The first ministry had to cope with a whiggish majority in the commons. This began attacks on those of the ministers who had held office under the last two kings. It also promoted a new corporation bill declaring that borough charters could not be forfeited and excluding from municipal office all those who had been concerned in the recent surrenders. The king avoided this renewal of the party struggle for control of the electoral machine by dissolving the convention,[1] but he had to let Halifax resign his office, and Godolphin left the treasury board, though only to return again after eight months. The wavering Shrewsbury ceased to be secretary of state, and his place was taken by another good whig, Henry Sidney, Lord Romney, William's friend in Holland, and like Shrewsbury one of the seven who had signed the invitation. Shrewsbury's resignation was the first instance of a difficulty which beset William throughout his reign. There was scarcely any Englishman in high place whom he could trust. The few really upright characters like Nottingham were not the easiest men to work with, and the rest, whether from a weakness like Shrewsbury's or a calculating boldness like Churchill's, kept open by word of mouth rather than in written messages relations with the exiled court of St. Germain.[2] Some of them retained traces of a genuine loyalty to the Stuarts, others merely wished to be able to reconcile them-

---

[1] The treatment of municipal charters after the Revolution seems to require investigation: that of Abergavenny was forfeited in the reign of William III, and there may be similar instances elsewhere.

[2] It is possible that neither of these statesmen gave the Jacobites any real encouragement: see T. C. Nicholson and A. S. Turberville, *Charles Talbot, Duke of Shrewsbury* (1930), pp. 50 ff.; W. S. Churchill, *Marlborough*, i. 365 ff.

selves if there should be a counter-revolution: in neither case
was it easy to know how much rope to give them. Churchill's
military and administrative abilities were useful, and his close
relations with the Princess Anne earned him indulgence; but
in 1692 it was withdrawn. In both military and political circles
he had made himself prominent by voicing the grievances of the
English officers who, like himself, were excluded from the highest
commands. He made the Princess Anne's household a centre
of discontent. He may or may not have offended in some other
way. He was dismissed from all his offices, but without any
public statement of the reason, and he remained throughout the
remainder of the war without employment under the Crown.
In spite of the bitter anger of the queen, Anne with true courage
stuck to her friends, whose position for a short time in the spring
of 1692 became positively dangerous. On the strength of a clever
forgery the queen was led to suspect Marlborough of downright
treason, and, before his innocence was proved, he had to spend
six weeks in the Tower.[1]

It was inevitable that plots and rumours of plots should keep
up the intensity of political strife, and the governments, in the
desire to make opposition appear murderous and socially dangerous, had good reason for making the most of them. The real
Jacobites did not, in fact, include many men of ability or substance, but they had personal links, especially through the non-
jurors, with many of the moderate churchmen. The first serious
discoveries, which were made early in 1690, implicated Clarendon and Shrewsbury's resignation was connected with them,
though in exactly what way is not clear. A more definite plan
was detected in the last months of the same year. Lord Preston,
who had been secretary of state under James, was arrested on
his way to France with letters containing plans for the restoration of James with French help if he should become a protestant.
Once again Clarendon was involved, but he had merely to
undergo a brief imprisonment in the Tower. The nonjuring
bishop of Ely, Francis Turner, and the great William Penn
were also accused, but they were never even arrested and both
emerged from hiding after a few months. Preston was pardoned,
and only one accomplice executed. This clemency was due in

[1] The king, who was with the army abroad, wrote of this arrest that without
a full knowledge of the facts it was impossible to judge 'si l'on a bien ou mal fait'.
Correspondentie, i. 171.

part to the good sense of William himself. His ministers did not always understand these things so well. In 1694 one of the secretaries of state was Sir John Trenchard, a strong whig who had been concerned in treasonable activities in the time of Charles II and owed his pardon by James to the intercession of William Penn. Trenchard set out to harry the Jacobites, and instituted wholesale prosecutions in Lancashire on the strength of evidence from informers who were no better than those of the Popish Plot. The prosecutions failed and the government was laughed at.

There was no real police force and no means of information except what came from the magistrates and such persons as the secretaries' office could employ or reward, persons who in the nature of the case were open to all the temptations which turn the detective into the *agent provocateur*. In 1696 a change in the law of treason made the task of the government even harder. The state trials of Charles II, and especially the condemnation of Algernon Sidney, had made the whigs intent on weakening the powers of the prosecution. Bills for this purpose had been introduced in 1689 and more than once in subsequent years; in January 1696 William gave his assent to an act which ensured proper facilities for defence and required that no person should be convicted of treason except upon the evidence of at least two persons for each treason. A few days later the most dangerous of all the plots against William was set in motion. The death of Queen Mary in 1695 had isolated William as an object of Jacobite hatred. The motive for making away with him was strengthened since his death would no longer leave her in occupation of the throne. In February James II moved to Calais and there was activity in all the underworld of Jacobite agents and the more cautious upper strata of sympathetic politicians. The time and the place were chosen. As William drove home to Kensington Palace from his weekly hunting in Richmond Park he had to pass through a narrow and muddy lane between the river and Turnham Green. Here he was to be surrounded and murdered. The men were ready, but they talked, and on 24 February King William himself announced in parliament the plans of the assassination plot and the invasion from France.

The commons rallied to William's side with an association to defend the king's person and take vengeance on any who should bring about his death. Like that proposed by the whigs at the time of the Popish Plot it was modelled on the association in defence of Queen Elizabeth which had been formed after the murder of William the Silent. The whig majority in the commons were not allowed to have their wish of making adhesion to it a test of eligibility for parliament and for all naval, military, or civil offices. The Habeas Corpus Act was suspended, and it was provided that the existing parliament should be prolonged for six months after the king's death, which would otherwise have brought it to an end. After this display of national firmness for maintaining the revolution, William gave another example of his skill in dividing his enemies by well-timed mercy. Few of the conspirators were punished. Five were tried under the old procedure and executed. The new act then came into force and its procedure was followed in the trials of three more, who were also put to death. The result would have been the same if all eight had had the benefit of the new law. In the summer a conspirator was captured who stood far higher in rank and influence than any of the eight, Sir John Fenwick, who had held a general's commission under James II and whose wife was the sister of the earl of Carlisle. Fenwick, in the hope of saving himself, made a confession which revealed much of what the great men had been doing. The king already knew more of this than Fenwick disclosed, but his allegations made a stir in parliament. He mentioned Shrewsbury's name, and Shrewsbury offered to resign the office which he had resumed two years before. The king retained him, but Godolphin, who was also named, had to go. But Fenwick did not save himself either by his confession or by his other plan, which was to smuggle out of the country one of the two witnesses required by the law. The confession had aroused the hatred of the whigs, for its political effect had been more damaging to them than to the tories. When it became known that the witness had absconded a bill of attainder was brought in. It was the last time in English history that the legislature passed such a retrospective act, condemning an individual to death. There are emergencies in which such action is right, but this instance is less a proof that the reign of William III required the strong measures of an earlier age than an indication that parliament was capable of measures as tyrannical as those it had once resisted.[1]

---

[1] Major John Bernardi, with other minor Jacobites, was imprisoned after his capture at the battle of the Boyne under the authority of an Act renewed in 1702 and 1714. He died in Newgate Prison in 1736.

Even if William had not been a masterful man, preferring subordinates to advisers, the mixture of treachery and faction among the leaders of the English nation would have been enough to explain why he was his own prime minister, and why no Englishman had any influence in foreign affairs or much in anything except what was departmental. Many of the ministerial changes were made in the attempt to get efficiency in the conduct of the war. The admiralty board, always much criticized along with the secretaries' office whenever there were maritime losses, was changed in every war year except 1695: in the later years the professional naval element was strengthened, and there was added a business man skilled in admiralty contracts. The treasury board was remodelled equally often, and also became more expert as time went on. When considerations of party were taken into account, it was sometimes because individuals made themselves impossible; but at other times in order that the necessary business in parliament might be competently put through. From the earliest months of the reign the whigs were a party in a sense in which the tories did not become a political party until well on in the reign of Queen Anne: they aspired to a monopoly of office. This might have been easier to attain if they had not also had a programme of constitutional change; but they made some progress towards it, especially at the time of the return of Shrewsbury to office in 1694 in succession to Nottingham. The Great Seal had already been entrusted to a whig, Sir John Somers, though at first as lord keeper and only later with the full rank of lord chancellor. In 1697 Charles Montagu succeeded Godolphin as first lord of the treasury, and the key of the lord chamberlain went in that year to Sunderland, who had been much consulted by the king even in his retirement and who, though himself not bound by party ties, was in favour of governing through the party.

The men in office, whoever they were, had frequent occasions for noticing that the king gave them little of his confidence. Some of his favourite instruments were comparatively colourless underlings, like the hard-working William Blathwayt, who in a number of minor offices acted as an administrative factotum;[1] but there were others who could not but excite jealousy. Of these the chief was Portland, the only man with whom William was intimate during most of their lives. He had already

[1] See his *Life* by Gertrude A. Jacobsen (1932).

been richly rewarded for his services, when in 1695 the king gave orders for a grant to him of the honour of Denbigh, which was said to be worth a hundred thousand pounds. The gentry in that part of Wales thought it very much to their advantage to have the Crown as their landlord, and they applied both to the ministers and to members of parliament. In 1696, the year of crises, the commons protested against the grant and the king reluctantly stopped it. This was one among a number of signs that the English, without much distinction of party, distrusted the king's foreign friends and his European point of view. When the peace relaxed the sense of common danger this distrust had freer play, and the cohesion of the new settlement was tested. After the signature of the treaty of Ryswick William still reigned for four years and a half, and the interest of these years is that after disputes and agreements which more than once seemed to be leading in quite another direction, they saw the constitutional changes of the reign completed, the dynastic arrangements consolidated, and the decisive change in foreign policy confirmed. This resulted, like the former changes themselves, from the interaction of foreign and domestic forces.

VIII

AFTER KING WILLIAM'S WAR

ENGLISH politicians, not for the last time in history, once the peace was made, dismissed the Continent from their minds. In the Bill of Rights it had been agreed that it was illegal to maintain a standing army in time of peace. Now that peace had come it seemed a matter of course to reduce the army to the very small numbers needed for police purposes at home. The king told his parliament plainly that he thought England could not be safe without an army; but the commons paid no attention, and on the motion of the moderate tory leader Robert Harley, formerly a presbyterian and an ally of the whigs, they voted to disband all troops raised since September 1680. At that date, after the paying-off of the regiments raised in 1678 for the war that never happened and before the return of the garrison of Tangier, there had been only about 6,500 men under arms in England. Such a drastic reduction was most unwelcome to the king, but its effect was not immediate, for parliament had not yet provided the money which was needed to carry it out. The debates continued in 1698. In the new parliament of that year the 'patriots', the opposition, were stronger than before. Harley's new country party strengthened its parliamentary influence and worked effectively with the followers of Rochester and Nottingham. Able and ambitious young men like Henry St. John were attracted to it. Parliament was not appeased by the resignation of Sunderland or by the now more tactful advances of the king. It voted for a force of only 7,000 in England and 12,000 in Ireland. This decision was rendered the more unpalatable by the provision that all these troops were to be native English. The reduction of the fleet was comparably drastic.

It was at this point that William talked, to more than one person who could be trusted to pass on the threat, of retiring from his unmanageable kingdom to Holland. He cannot have intended seriously to take a step which would have imperilled all the work of his life, and he remained to suffer further humiliations. The house of lords saved him from a proposal to remove the militia from his authority and put it under that of parliament; but in the years 1699 and 1700 his political system was so much shaken by the attacks of parliament that the tory leaders were for a time able to dictate whatever measures they pleased. The lord chancellor, Somers, had to resign. The whigs were divided and undisciplined, and the tories in their opposition to the Crown became the heirs of a large part of the policy urged by the whigs against Charles II. The first great question was that of the Irish land grants. William had promised in 1690 that parliament (meaning, apparently, the parliament then sitting) should decide on the disposal of the million or so acres of land which had been forfeited by those who had fought for King James in Ireland. As time went on and parliament took no action, he had, however, fallen back on the traditional method of granting these lands by the exercise of his prerogative. We shall deal in another chapter with these grants as events in the history of Ireland.[1] In English history they were important because, in the first place, they were made to the inner circle of William's adherents, the foreign generals, Portland, Galway, Athlone, and favourites like Keppel, now earl of Albemarle, and Lady Orkney. They thus tended to consolidate the wealth and power of his political supporters. It was also represented by the rancorous partisans who now took the matter up that they had squandered great sums which might have been used for paying the expenses of the war. The sums were exaggerated, but the angry nationalist feeling of the commons was not satisfied by a request to the king to remove all foreigners from his councils. After a long parliamentary struggle, in which he was threatened with a refusal of supplies, he assented to a bill for reviewing all the grants.

When events had reached this stage there came a reminder that danger from outside was still near: the succession question was suddenly reopened. When Queen Mary died it might have been possible for William to marry again. His health and his inclination were both against this, but his servants at least drew up a list of eligible ladies.[2] The matter was, however, allowed to sleep, for the need was not urgent: the Princess Anne, although her family history had been full of calamities, had still a child remaining to her, William, duke of Gloucester, one year younger than the 'pretended' prince of Wales. On 30 July 1700,

[1] See below, p. 316.
[2] It is printed in *Correspondentie*, vol. ii, no. 89, and probably dates from 1696.

a few days after his eleventh birthday, this frail boy died.[1] Danger had suddenly come near again. Every schemer and intriguer woke up. It seemed that there was a new chance for the Stuarts, not perhaps for James but then for his son, who was only a child, and might perhaps become a protestant. The Princess Anne sometimes showed signs of an uneasy conscience and had exchanged messages of doubtful import with her father.[2] William himself, in conformity with his political approximation to France after the peace, had considered the possibility of some such plan. There were indeed other possibilities which promised to shut out more effectively the prospects of reaction or a republican revival. The cunning Victor Amadeus of Savoy had married the daughter of Charles II's ill-fated sister Madame, and while Savoy had been an ally it had seemed as if one of their sons might ultimately succeed in England. By going a step farther back in the Stuart pedigree it was, however, possible to find a far more promising cousin. The exiled queen of Bohemia, the daughter of James I, had left a daughter, now advanced in years, the Electress Sophia, whose son George Lewis was not only a protestant, but a man of energetic character, a capable general, and the ruler of Hanover, one of the staunch opponents of France among the German states.[3] The choice of the English king and nation could not but fall that way. By the Act of Settlement of 1701 the succession, after the Princess Anne and her descendants and William's if such there should still be, was limited to the electress and her descendants. Once again, however, in providing against danger the parliament exacted its price. The act dealt not only with the succession: it was also an act for 'better securing the rights and liberties of the subject'. It enacted a final large instalment of the programme of constitutional opposition.

Every future sovereign was to join, as William had done, in communion with the church of England. Should the sovereign be foreign born, this nation was not to be obliged to engage in any war for the defence of his continental territories without

---

[1] A pathetic curiosity of literature is the *Memoirs of Prince William Henry, Duke of Gloucester* (1789) written by J. Lewis, his manservant, and reprinted ed. by W. J. Loftie (1881).

[2] See the Roxburghe Club's *Papers of Devotion of King James II*, ed. G. Davies (1925), p. 166.

[3] Hanover had chosen the imperial side and strengthened its own position in 1691–2.

the consent of parliament. He was not to go out of the dominions of England, Scotland, and Ireland without the consent of parliament. This guarding against foreign interests was pushed even farther by the provision that no person born out of these kingdoms and not of English parents should be capable of sitting in parliament, or in the privy council, or of holding any civil or military office or of receiving any grant of land from the Crown. This provision, referring so plainly to the recent debates, was not to come into force until the Hanoverians should succeed, but it did then take effect and it remained the law until after Queen Victoria's accession brought the connexion with Hanover to an end. Another clause was intended to take effect at the same time: that all matters and things relating to the well governing of the kingdom which were properly cognizable by the privy council should be transacted there and that all resolutions should be signed by the privy councillors who advised and consented to them. This was due to the dissatisfaction of the commons with the informal system of cabinets, which was believed to make it harder to bring home the responsibility for advice given to the king. That system, however, had now become so firmly established that in Queen Anne's time the clause was repealed before it ever came into force.[1] At the same time, as we shall see, another clause of the act was materially modified, a clause disqualifying for the house of commons any person who held an office of profit under the Crown or received a pension. Two other clauses were, however, to stand. No pardon under the Great Seal was to be pleadable, as had been done by Danby in 1679, to an impeachment by the commons. The judges were to have fixed salaries, but they were to be removable by the Crown upon the address of both houses of parliament. This last clause reproduced the substance of a bill to which William had refused his assent in 1692; but he had never influenced the judges in their work, and it should be regarded simply as the formal termination of that control of judges by the executive which had died with the Stuart system. It removed the possibility of a new attempt to subject the judges to royal control: judicial independence has been a central fact of the constitution from the fall of James II. Although parliament showed itself tyrannical in the next century, it has never removed a judge for political reasons.

[1] See below, p. 255.

The fact that some of its clauses remained dead letters illustrates clearly the relation of the Act of Settlement to the emergency in which it was passed. If all had been safe outside, the
anti-monarchial tendency might have been pushed still farther,
and not only the commons but even the peers might have pro-
fited. Some of them, during the debates, talked of linking their
peerages with inalienable landed properties, and of limiting the
freedom of peeresses in their own right to marry beneath their
rank, hints of that desire for a closed aristocracy which was
again to be expressed in Stanhope's Peerage Bill in 1719. The
common sense born of danger prevailed, and it was not only
from the danger to the succession that it sprang. In the speech
in which he laid that question before the new parliament of
1701, William asked it to authorize him to enter upon negotiations which had been rendered necessary by another death,
long expected with various emotions, that of King Charles of
Spain. So much had been done to prepare for it by diplomacy,
and its results were still so hard to foresee that, although parliament made no difficulty about giving William the authority
he asked, in England the first consequence of the foreign crisis
was a heightening of party strife.

After the conclusion of the peace of Ryswick many factors had
combined to incline both William and Louis XIV to agree upon
some expedient for avoiding a new European war over the
Spanish succession. Louis was conscious of a decline in his
power. He failed to bring about the election of a French candidate to the throne of Poland, which had become vacant by
the death of John Sobieski in 1696. The new king was the elector
of Saxony, who had been serving as an imperial general against
the Turks. His successor in that capacity, Prince Eugene, a kinsman of the duke of Savoy but a Frenchman by upbringing, won
a victory at Zenta on the river Tisza, which was followed in 1699
by the first definitely victorious peace ever wrested from the
Turks by Christian powers. This brought a great increase of
territory to the emperor. Not only was Austria-Hungary
strengthened, with its centre of gravity outside Germany to the
east, but the French system of alliances in eastern Europe was
seriously impaired. There seemed little prospect of rebuilding
the group of French allies in Germany. Savoy was not to be
trusted, the less so since the duke was himself directly interested
in the Spanish question, both as a family connexion, and as a

neighbour of the Spanish province of Milan. It seemed, therefore, inadvisable to hope for the succession to the whole Spanish
monarchy. On the other hand, it seemed that the English and
the Dutch might well consent to let the French have some of it.
They were no longer bound by their promise in the treaty of
1689[1] to support the claim of the Austrian Habsburgs to the
whole inheritance. They were working up their trade and
manufactures under the favourable conditions of peace, and
they wanted a respite from war taxation. In the Ryswick
negotiations, to say nothing of earlier occasions, they had shown
themselves willing to make agreements with France for the
disposal of the territory of third parties.

Without serious difficulty, therefore, the three powers had
made a secret treaty in 1698 for the eventual partition of the
Spanish possessions, but this document has little historical importance because one of the three princes who were intended to
benefit under it, the heir to the elector of Bavaria, died, a child
of six, in the following year. A new treaty had to be made, and
under less satisfactory conditions, since the partition must now
be simply between a Bourbon and a Habsburg, with no member
of a less powerful family to take Spain itself and keep it independent. The second partition treaty of 1699 assigned Spain,
the Netherlands, and the colonies to the archduke Charles, the
second son of the emperor, but promised to France all the
Italian possessions of Spain, though with the condition that
France was to give the Milanese to the duke of Lorraine, taking
his duchy in exchange. It was easy to see that this plan had
grave defects. The possessions of Spain completely dominated
Italy, and even without the Milanese there was enough left in
Sicily, Naples, and the Spanish ports on the Tuscan coast to
alarm the Dutch for their Mediterranean trade. The emperor
obstinately refused to agree. He hoped that the treaty would be
so disappointing to the Spaniards that they would offer the
whole inheritance to his family. One part of his calculation was
sound. Their national pride resented the presumption of the
powers which tried to decide the matter over their heads, and
the whole weight of conservative interests was on the side of
keeping the monarchy together. But there were reasons why
they should think the French more fit to be entrusted with this
task than the Austrians. The French knew how to make the

[1] See above, p. 161.

most of their case by skilled diplomacy. They had now the support, which the emperor had forfeited by ill-timed self-assertiveness about ecclesiastical rights in Italy, of the Holy See. Above all, their power lay nearer to the heart of the Spanish empire, and, by themselves, they were stronger. The dying king was induced to sign a will in which all his possessions were bequeathed to Philip, duke of Anjou, the second son of the heir to the throne of France. Spain, enfeebled as it was, could not be deprived of this share in the control of its destiny. When the news came to Versailles it opened up glittering ambitions for world-wide power, and at the same time dismal apprehensions of new wars and sufferings; but, however great the conflict between hopes and fears, there was no real room for indecision. Refusal would have settled nothing except that it would have alienated Spain. Louis XIV accepted the will on behalf of his grandson.

So far was he, up to this point, from having taken a false step that the Dutch recognized Philip as king of Spain. William was against this policy, but he sent an English diplomatist, though without an official 'character', to his court, and the English parliament, accepting what had happened with positive relief, made a general attack on the authors of the Partition treaty. It was intelligible that they should prefer the will to the treaty, for the will stipulated that the Spanish Crown should never be united to any other, while the treaty had promised Spanish Italy not to a French prince but to France. There was as yet nothing to prove that Philip's accession would make a penny's difference to the English traders at Cadiz or in the Mediterranean or in the colonies. William was promised support in the necessary measures for the interest and safety of England, the protestant religion and the peace of Europe; and the request of the Dutch for the fulfilment of the treaty of 13 March 1678 was at once granted by parliament; but a month later, when the Partition treaties had been produced in response to its request, the conflict with the Crown broke loose again. It was not only that parliament, and apparently even the privy council, had not been consulted. There had been graver irregularities, and the principal person involved in them was Somers, the ablest of the whigs and the most hated by the tories. Somers had not broken any law or convention then recognized in affixing the Great Seal to the second treaty, although personally he did not approve of its contents: negotiation with foreign powers was still, according to the best opinions, the king's province. He had, however, laid himself open to serious criticism on the occasion of the first treaty by setting the seal to a commission in which the names of the negotiators were left blank. The tories in the commons took up these points with personal and party animus. Letting alone the tories like Lord Jersey who had been implicated as much as the whigs, they set about impeaching Somers, Portland, Orford, and Halifax.[1] The house of lords was favourable to these whig statesmen, and succeeded in obstructing the proceedings. Up and down the country, whether spontaneously or because Somers as lord chancellor had used his powers over the commission of the peace in the party interest, there arose expressions of sympathy for them.

What saved them, however, and damped down the hue and cry of faction was the increasing gravity of the European situation: protests against the action of the commons came in from the country, but they took the form of appeals for a firm stand against France. The justices and grand jury of the quarter sessions of Kent, a responsible and weighty body, with other freeholders, petitioned the commons to lay aside their differences and to vote supplies in order to put the king in a position to help his allies before it was too late. The petition threw the less moderate tories, such as Seymour, into a rage like that of James II when he was petitioned by the seven bishops. An Act against tumultuous petitioning had been passed in 1664. The Kentish members who presented the representation were arrested, along with others concerned in getting it up. The petitioners retorted by having the sergeant-at-arms arrested for irregularities in their own arrest. The commons begged the king to take measures to prevent a disturbance. Among the pamphlets written at this time was one by the first great English political journalist, Daniel Defoe, called *Legion's Petition*, which is significant because it claims that the people have a right to control the proceedings of parliament. It revives the view of parliamentary representation implicit in Shaftesbury's acts of twenty years before.[2] It states forcibly, in answer to parliamentary

---

[1] This is not the great marquis, who died in 1695. On his successor's death in 1700 a new Halifax peerage was created for Charles Montagu, born 1661, a lord of the treasury 1692, first lord 1697–9. In 1714 he again became first lord and was made an earl, but died in 1715.   [2] See above, p. 101.

tyranny, the radical criticism of the revolution settlement, anticipating the essential arguments of the radicals of the time of George III. It combines this constitutional criticism with strong support of the king's European policy. In his *True-Born Englishman* Defoe had exposed the absurdity of the paltry nationalism which made the tories wish to disfranchise huguenot refugees and exclude all men of foreign birth from office; but he was all for a stand against French aggression. Once the country gentlemen made up their minds to this, the parliamentary and oligarchic constitution would settle down firmly enough, and little would be heard of popular rights until the long external conflicts were no longer defensive in appearance. The old compromise of William III, liberty at home as the price for support in a foreign war, would be restored; and in this direction events were rapidly moving. As the prospect of war came nearer, excitement died down. In July 1701 the session came to an end. The impeachments were discharged; all the prisoners were released; the king once more had to leave for Holland.

When the commons agreed to give the Dutch the succour of 10,000 men which was due to them under the treaty of 1678 they had not contemplated more than participation in war as auxiliaries of the Dutch, which need not have involved England to the extent of all her resources. There had not even been an absolute necessity for the Dutch to defend themselves: if Louis had assured them that he would not interfere with their rights in the Spanish empire, they might have stood aside. These rights were twofold. First, there were the trading rights which they enjoyed, and amplified by smuggling, equally with the English. Secondly, there was the special right granted them after the peace of Ryswick, by which they maintained garrisons in seven fortresses of the Spanish Netherlands, called barrier-fortresses, thus ensuring for their own frontier a better defence than the decrepit Spanish army could give. This, too, in an indirect way was a British interest. For Louis, however, these two questions did not appear to be separable from the Spanish question as a whole. He was certain, in accepting the will, to bring on a war with the emperor, unless the court of Vienna felt itself too weak to fight for its claims, which proved not to be the case. He decided that the best way to meet this danger was to make sure of military preponderance all over Europe before the emperor and his old allies were ready. It was a miscalculation. Louis did not see that this was the way to call the alliance against him into life again, just as it was the way to resuscitate the union of parties in England. But at the time it was an error into which the ablest politician might have fallen. From the merely military point of view it succeeded immediately. The governor-general of the Spanish Netherlands was the elector of Bavaria, the next neighbour of Austria, who in the preceding years had been drifting towards a French alliance. He made no difficulty about admitting French garrisons and expelling the Dutch. In the first week of February 1701 that was done. Worse still, the elector of Cologne, the brother of the elector of Bavaria, took the same side, and in his territory a number of towns threatening the Dutch were occupied by the French. They also entered the Milanese. The pretence that the Spanish monarchy was to be independent of France was at an end even before the meeting of parliament in that year.

This was the situation with which William dealt in his negotiations at The Hague in the summer, and he dealt with it, as his lifelong opposition to France and his single-minded belief in the balance of power dictated, by setting up the framework of a new European coalition. He was helped by a brilliant campaign of Prince Eugene against the French in Italy. On 7 September the representatives of England, Holland, and the emperor signed the treaty of the grand alliance. By this they agreed that the French and Spanish thrones must never be united; but the sea-powers did not acknowledge the emperor's full right to the Spanish throne. They promised him compensation for it and retained the right to negotiate with France on this matter for two months more, after which they were to join in the war. The French were to have no share in the Spanish colonial trade. Nothing was yet decided as to the ultimate disposal of the Netherlands, or the colonies, or the Mediterranean: neither the Dutch nor the English forgot their own interests. The whole treaty was contingent, and further negotiation in the spirit of the partition treaties, though without much prospect of success, was still to be expected.

By an extraordinary coincidence there followed close together, and before Louis knew of the contents of this treaty, two French moves which completely changed the attitude of political England. Both became known in London in the same week in September. There had been disquieting news of French commercial designs in Spanish America.[1] Now it became clear that French commercial rivalry was as active as ever, for Louis prohibited all imports from England, Scotland, and Ireland. It was reported that he had sent orders to his grandson to do the same in Spain. This time there had been no long-drawn tariff war, but one sudden act of hostility. It was probably intended merely to frighten commercial England by giving it a foretaste of what war would mean; but, whatever its intention, it roused the business nation against France. The other piece of news blew away the marsh-lights of party ambition and showed up once more the realities of constitutional England's position. In these critical days King James II died. There was grave deliberation in the council of the French king. Only the princes of the blood were for upholding the dynastic principle in the face of expediency; but Louis was committed to that principle by all his past life. He caused James's son to be proclaimed king of England. Once more he counted on the divisions of England to nullify her power in arms, but this time he counted wrong. For France to try to impose a catholic king on her was the one thing needed to unite England for war. The tories, who had been glad enough to weaken William so long as his good understanding with Louis rendered the Jacobites harmless, were now all for saving the Revolution settlement. They vied with the whigs in loyal addresses. The British ambassador was recalled from Paris.

William was a clear-headed politician with a long memory, and he did not feel all the gratitude for this sudden conversion which the converts expected.[2] He had to prepare for war, and he wanted a parliament that could be trusted to support him; so he took the advice of the realist Sunderland and the party-leader Somers and dissolved the parliament. In the elections the whigs were well organized and determined. When the new parliament met at the end of December the king was well satisfied with the votes for troops. Party feeling, however, still ran high, and the tories found much to complain of in the fact that many

---

[1] The most important point was the *asiento* treaty of 14 September 1701. For the reports and their significance see Jean McLachlan (afterwards Lindsay) *Trade and Peace with Old Spain 1667–1750* (1941), especially pp. 30–45.

[2] His decision shows that he did not rate the services of Robert Harley to national unity so highly as Dr. Feiling, *History of the Tory Party*, cap. xii, or Professor G. M. Trevelyan, *Blenheim*, p. 116.

constituencies had bound their members by strict instructions to vote with the whigs. Here the tories were resisting the radical view of parliament as subordinate to the electors, and anticipating the position the whigs were to occupy when the question arose again in a more serious form two generations later. The present discussions and a quarrel between lords and commons over the events of the last sessions ended in a number of inconsistent resolutions which provided settlement enough for the time being. As the spring approached all minds were turned to the preparations for the war into which England was now certain to be drawn. In this moment of expectation, as King William rode in the park at Hampton Court, his horse stumbled and fell. The accident, trivial in itself, was more than his worn-out body could stand, and on 19 March 1702 he died.

His career illustrates the paradox that the strong men of history often achieve the opposite of what they intend. He had no intention of abating the prerogatives of the English Crown, but his elevation made the king constitutionally something like the first paid official of the state. William, indeed, never relinquished the dynastic view of monarchy, and he completed the long ascent of the house of Orange to royal rank; but his Revolution and his resistance to Louis XIV were two steps towards the downfall of the French monarchy and of dynasticism in and after the French Revolution. But in his central endeavour he succeeded. He devoted himself to the liberties of Europe, and his greatest work was in persuading the states of Europe to co-operate for these ends. For a whole generation he withstood the greatest military and political power in the world, never despairing. He enjoyed neither the thrill of victory nor the comfort of popularity, but he averted defeat.

IX

MARLBOROUGH'S WAR

O N the Continent fighting had already begun when Queen Anne came to the throne. In less than two months England and her allies formally declared war, and when the queen died twelve years later, although England had been at peace for more than a year, the last of the continental treaties of peace was not yet two months old. The reign thus coincides almost exactly with the war of the Spanish Succession and the subsequent settlement. It was a war of the same modern type which the last war had inaugurated: the maritime powers and the emperor, with a number of minor allies, were opposed to the French on land and sea, in Europe and the colonies.[1] There were indeed changes in the alliances and in the theatres of war. The Spanish empire was on the French side, and the French also had as allies Savoy and the elector of Bavaria and his brother, who had become prince-bishop of Cologne instead of Fürstenberg[2] and was also prince-bishop of Liége. The emperor was at peace with the Turks. The Dutch and English diplomatists in Constantinople succeeded in frustrating all the French attempts to revive the war on the Danube, partly no doubt because they had behind them a visible naval superiority in the Mediterranean; and the Austrians were troubled in their rear not by a Turkish war but by the best substitute the French could work up, a national revolt of the newly subjected Hungarians. In spite of these changes, however, the war in its first phase seemed to be almost a continuation of the last; it was not until after the first campaign that it showed itself as quite different for the English, novel in its aims, different in its geographical centre of gravity, different in the strength and interests of the allies.

The northern powers were once again neutral, and once again neither side induced them to abandon their neutrality. The condition of the north was, however, completely changed, for there had begun in 1699 the Great Northern War which dragged

---

[1] For the colonial aspects of the war see below, pp. 330 ff.
[2] See above, p. 130.

on long after the conclusion of the greater war to the south of it, but always remained distinct. The Danes hired out a few thousand troops to the sea-powers; but, as before, this did not draw Denmark into war with France. That these two wars could continue side by side without becoming involved together is an illustration of the way in which Europe was still not a single political system: the states of northern Germany were indeed affected by both wars, but each of them succeeded in keeping out of one, and confining itself to the other. In 1699 the young Swedish king, Charles XII, was attacked by a coalition of the Danes, the Poles, and the Russians, and he was at war with one or more of these powers for the rest of his life. His own German possessions and the Saxon electorate which belonged to the elective king of Poland were thus at war, at least until 1710 when the other powers concerned made a convention by which northern Germany was to be neutral. His marches in this region more than once created very lively alarms for some of the powers to the south and equally lively hopes for others, and for years it seemed as if the heroic king might intervene like another Gustavus Adolphus between France and the empire. His reasons for not doing so were much misunderstood at the time. Whatever they were, they were his own reasons, and little was contributed to them by the French or English or German diplomatists who courted him. For their countries the main importance of the northern war lay in subsidiary factors. The maritime powers had used force in trying to end it in 1700. It made the whole period still more warlike: it added to the demand all over Europe for munitions and military and naval stores of all kinds, and to the other economic consequences of a state of war. It added to the general distrust and nervousness which made allies half-hearted and treacherous, easily diverted by fears in a new direction from pursuing settled aims to which they were committed. It disturbed the trade of the maritime powers with the Baltic. The English and the Dutch, being neutrals in the northern war, had to put up with the usual interferences with neutral trade. In order to make their supply of naval stores less dependent on the Baltic countries, the English did all they could to develop the supply of timber, pitch, and tar from their colonies on the mainland of North America. These efforts met with greater success than before; but the Baltic supplies were still needed. Since every naval power was both a belligerent and a neutral at the same time, there was much less trouble over neutral rights than in the former war.

A journey across half Europe to humour King Charles XII was one of the innumerable minor services of the great Englishman who succeeded, so far as any Englishman could succeed, to the immense burden of duties which had been carried by King William. The king had been accompanied on his last journey to Holland by this man, a few months older than himself whom he had made ambassador to Holland, and commander-in-chief of his forces there, John Churchill, earl of Marlborough. Marlborough had perfect courage, faultless manners, and 'a good, plain understanding'. He had worked his way up through more than thirty years of military, political, and social experience. Beginning as the handsome son of a minor politician who was also a very minor historian, he had married a famous beauty, Sarah Jennings, the passionate friend of the new queen. He had acquired, and was still acquiring, wealth and powerful political connexions. From his first service under the duke of York at sea in 1672 and under Turenne against the Dutch in 1673, until the reduction of Ireland, he had given ample proofs of his military gifts. As a politician he had steered his way through the quicksands of the Revolution, but in 1692 the king had dismissed him from all his offices, to spend three years in disgrace.[1] Gradually events had turned in his favour. The death of Queen Mary had brought a reconciliation between the king and the Princess Anne. The approach of a new war had made him the man of the future, and already, before the great rewards and honours gained by his victories, he stood higher in favour and power than any other subject.

A subject could not exactly take the place of the king, and an Englishman could not become what William had been in Holland; but the Dutch did what was possible to preserve the old co-operation. Marlborough was not only ambassador to them: they gave him the command of their land-forces as deputy captain-general. They had now no stad holder, but Antonie Heinsius, the successor of John de Witt and Fagel as pensionary, carried on the tradition of William in diplomacy. Friction between the Dutch and English, especially over military and naval matters, could not be avoided. The states-general were in the habit of appointing 'field deputies' to exercise some degree

<hr />

[1] See above, p. 183.

of control over the commanders of their armies, a custom which
had been harmless in the time of William since he saw to it that
the deputies appointed were men who would give no trouble.
Marlborough, being unable to do this, had to undergo, at least
in his earlier campaigns, some obstructive interference from
these amateurs. This was the more noticeable because Marlborough shared to the full and helped to stimulate a change in
the spirit in which the war was conducted. It was not only bigger
and bloodier than the previous war; it was also more mobile.
Armies operated farther from their bases. Generals thought
more of battles and less of trenches. They wanted to move, to
strike, to pursue. The Dutch had good reasons for showing less
of this spirit than the French or the English. They were fighting
in defence of their own territory, and they had always before
them the fear of another 1672. They were conscious of a relative
weakening of their resources. Their quotas were fixed at the
beginning of the war in the old proportions of three to two at sea
and five to three on land; but throughout the war, and increasingly as it went on, in spite of the utmost exertions of which their
clumsy machine was capable, they fell short of this requirement.
In extending the scope of hostilities they also went more slowly
than the English. After a year's experiment in 1703–4 made in
common with their chief allies, they found they could not stand
the economic loss brought on by the English policy of prohibiting all trade and correspondence with the enemy. They were
conscious of an inferiority to their partner which was to have
memorable results.

The war began officially in the spring of 1702, though the
Italian fighting had been in progress since the previous autumn.
By August there was a standstill in that quarter: Eugene could
do no more than hold up the numerically superior forces of
Vendôme. In the Netherlands Marlborough conducted a satisfactory campaign against the main French army. The chief
event was the capture of Liége; but his real success was that he
established his reputation with the allies. In Germany the allies
lost ground. They occupied Kaiserswert on the lower Rhine;
but in south Germany the Bavarians declared openly for France
and were joined by a French army under Marshal Villars.

This brought danger nearer to the central block of Habsburg
dominions than at any time in the last war. The danger did not
materialize until the next year, but already the allies had reason

enough for anxiety about its effects on the emperor. The emperor for his part derived no satisfaction from a success of the sea-powers which was, in fact, more striking than valuable. Without clearing up the confused diplomatic position in the Peninsula, where the Portuguese had made an alliance with the Bourbons but seemed likely to behave as neutrals, they undertook a combined naval and military expedition in that direction. The objective had been decided by William III in consultation with Prince George of Hesse-Darmstadt, who had been governor of Catalonia under the late king. It was to be Cadiz, the great port of the Spanish American trade, and after Cadiz the admiral, Sir George Rooke, was instructed to send a force to the West Indies, to defend the colonies and intercept the Spanish bullion. This was not merely a return to the Elizabethan strategy against Spain; it was much more a result of the experience of Russell's fleet in the Mediterranean in the last war. The purpose was to obtain a naval base from which the Levant trade might be protected and the Mediterranean states supported or coerced. The expedition was, however, neither adequate in strength nor well led, and after a month of plunder and sacrilege in the villages of Cadiz Bay, it set sail for home. On this inglorious voyage Rooke chanced to hear that the annual treasure-fleet, homeward bound from Vera Cruz in Mexico, had arrived under French escort in Vigo Bay. The commander of the Dutch contingent insisted on an attack, and, well supported by the troops on land, the fleet broke the boom, sailed deep into the bay and destroyed the fleet. Only seven of the galleons were captured, but the booty was worth a million pounds, £95,000 of which was added to the English metallic currency. The victory had all the qualities which impress popular opinion, and it made the naval operations of the year seem successful, in spite of the failure at Cadiz and a minor failure in the West Indies.[1]

Next year in the Netherlands Marlborough's army was increased and outnumbered the French, but he was hampered by the Dutch again and could do no more than carry out the first stages of several plans without completing any of them. Bonn was captured, as in 1674, and Huy, which added to the value of holding Liége. Later in the year Limburg and Spanish Gelderland were occupied; but the Dutch met a defeat in battle,

[1] See below, p. 330.

and the French army was unshaken. Meanwhile in southern Germany things were going badly. The French and Bavarians had their difficulties, but they took the initiative throughout the campaign, and when they failed in one direction they were still able to succeed in another and to shake the determination of their opponents. Their first plan was to invade the Tyrol, to join hands across the Brenner Pass with the French army in northern Italy, and to advance against Vienna. It failed, because the Tyrolese mountaineers met it with a fierce, popular resistance; but when the invaders turned back to strike north and west, they pushed away the forces of the emperor and the South German princes. Augsburg, Altbreisach, and Landau fell. The Austrians were distracted by the swelling of the Hungarian rebellion, and it was fortunate for them that in this same summer their failures frightened them into adopting some urgent reforms which were advocated by Eugene. He became president of the council of war, and saw to it that a capable finance minister was at last appointed.

In this year the aims of the alliance were transformed by a clearing-up of the ambiguities of the diplomatic position in southern Europe. Two states joined the alliance each of which, though in wealth and population of minor rank, held some of the strategic and economic keys of power, Savoy and Portugal. Victor Amadeus of Savoy once more saw his opportunity in quitting the French side. He had gained nothing but hard knocks and hard words from his share in the Italian fighting, and he was negotiating with the emperor for some time before Vendôme brought matters to a head by arresting his generals and disbanding some of his troops. The emperor's main interest in the war was to acquire the Spanish possessions in Italy for his house, so that he had been slow to make terms with a neighbour whose ambitions crossed his own; but the English hurried matters on. They saw more clearly each year that they could not operate effectively in the Mediterranean without a base, and the active help of Savoy seemed to offer the chance of the best base of all, the great French arsenal of Toulon itself. The chance seemed easier and better worth seizing because the persecuted protestants of the Cevennes were in revolt, and support from the coast might spread civil war into the heart of France. A naval expedition of this year under Sir Clowdisley Shovell reinforced all these ideas. With thirty-five English and seventeen Dutch ships Shovell hurried round the African, Italian, and French coasts of the Mediterranean, but he accomplished nothing more than a political demonstration. The plan against Toulon was not, indeed, sound. Civil war seldom helps foreign invaders as much as they hope; their presence usually reconciles the parties and unites them in a national cause. To hold Toulon against France would have proved as difficult as it proved at the end of the century when it actually fell into British hands. For an invasion of France Provence was the most difficult of the possible approaches. All these objections are, however, easier to see now than they were then, and on 25 October 1703 a treaty of alliance was signed with Savoy.

Portugal, like Savoy, was nominally in alliance with France; and, although she had no intention of actively helping the Bourbon king of Spain, she closed her harbours to the allies. The sea-powers, however, could cut her off from her colonies, and if she remained nominally an enemy they would be justified in taking them from her altogether. Very little threatening was needed therefore to bring her over; but, if she was to be once more at war with Spain, she very properly wanted to have the purpose of the war made clear. She wanted, in fact, a rival candidate to King Philip. The landing at Cadiz had been made in the name of the emperor, who still claimed the whole Spanish monarchy for his house; but a candidate who would go to Spain in person would have a far better chance of local support. The emperor was slow to agree to this, since it amounted to falling back on the plan of partition which the maritime powers had always favoured; but he was not asked to contribute men or money, and before the end of the year 1703 the necessary steps were taken. His elder son, the Archduke Joseph, was to succeed to the Austrian territories and to Milan; the younger, Charles, was to go to Spain. The treaty of alliance with Portugal enabled the maritime powers to use Lisbon as their base for the Mediterranean, an invaluable benefit until Port Mahon took its place in 1708. Portugal was to supply 28,000 troops of whom the English and Dutch were to pay and provide for nearly half, in addition to sending 12,000 of their own men and a naval detachment to serve under Portuguese orders. The treaty was supplemented before the end of the year by a commercial treaty with the English alone which showed that in defining their attitude to the dynastic quarrel they had not allowed their attention to be diverted from economic interests.

This was the Methuen Treaty, named after its negotiator John Methuen. Methuen had been lord chancellor of Ireland, and his connexion with diplomacy in Portugal went back to 1691, but it is more relevant to notice that he had sat at the board of trade, had represented in parliament as a whig the clothing town of Devizes, and was the son of a man reputed to be the greatest clothier of his time. His treaty was not finally abrogated until 1836, and until Pitt's French treaty of 1786 it was one of the corner-stones of British commercial policy. It fell in with the prevailing ideas of the time by obtaining privileges for the favourite English exporting manufacture, wool, in exchange for admitting a commodity, Portuguese wine, which England could not produce for herself and which the Portuguese could send only in such quantities that they had to make up the balance by sending considerable sums in gold. Its terms were that Portuguese wines were to be admitted at a third less duty than those of France, while English woollens were to be admitted into Portugal as they had been before the late prohibition. There has been much controversy about the effects of the treaty, but it appears that the advantage gained by England was in a short time open to other states through the 'most favoured nation' clause in treaties. At the time when it was concluded it did not mean any direct sacrifice by the English, since the tariff on French wines was already virtually prohibitive, and it did open the Portuguese and Brazilian markets which had been closed. It is doubtful whether the Portuguese woollen industry could have attained real prosperity, and the Portuguese wine-trade certainly gained by the increase of port-drinking in England.[1]

During the winter of 1703–4 every one could see that the Grand Alliance could be kept together only by relieving the threatening situation in Germany, and most of the leading allied statesmen agreed that this could only be done if the western allies imitated the boldness of the French and dispatched considerable forces from Flanders into Germany. The first suggestion naturally came from the Austrians,[2] but Heinsius promptly

---

[1] It appears from M. A. Hedwig Fitzler, *Die Handelsgesellschaft Oldenburg* (1931), that Portuguese archives may furnish materials for revising this opinion. The best study is by H. Schorer in *Zeitschrift für die gesammte Staatswissenschaft*, lix. 434.

[2] This point is fully discussed in G. M. Trevelyan, *England under Queen Anne*, i. 323 ff.

agreed and the states-general accepted the plan in a very few
days. The political credit for the great plan must be distributed
evenly among all the participants. For its diplomatic and
military execution Marlborough deserves the greatest credit,
and second only to him Eugene. Marlborough's task was to
make the long march from the Netherlands to Bavaria, almost
as far as from Edinburgh to London, and then in conjunction
with the German troops to give battle. The length of the march
cannot have appeared very remarkable to the Austrians who had
fought in Piedmont and before Belgrade, but there was a formidable enemy on the right flank. Such a march was something
entirely new for the English and almost as much so for the
Dutch. It was admirably carried out. By the end of June the
position was that Eugene with 28,000 troops was holding a line
of trenches to keep back the French army of the upper Rhine
under Marshal Tallard, while the main allied army, commanded
by Marlborough in conjunction with the margrave of Baden,
was moving from the neighbourhood of Ulm towards the next
important crossing of the Danube at Donauwörth. This army
numbered some 26,000 Germans and Dutch and 9,000 British.
Against it, at Ulm, were 27,000 Bavarians and 36,000 French
troops under Marshal Marsin. A detachment of this force
numbering some 10,000 occupied the Schellenberg, a hill rising
between two and three hundred feet above the river near
Donauwörth, and in a fierce battle Marlborough beat them
from this position so soundly that Marsin and the elector retired
to Augsburg. Here they were joined by Tallard on 3 August,
for Tallard had eluded Eugene, and to judge merely by their
positions on the map the divided armies of the allies were now
in danger from this united force. The troops were still more than
a day's march apart when the commanders met and agreed
upon a plan, but it succeeded, and they made their junction.
On the morning of 13 August, starting from about five miles
away, they moved forward from their camp to attack the enemy.
It was a pitched battle in the grand style: Marlborough spent
five hours in deploying before he could engage. The French and
Bavarians had a defensive position such as the textbooks
recommended, with their right flank on the Danube and their
left against wooded hills. They were somewhat stronger in
numbers, 54,000 against 52,000, and much stronger in artillery,
but weaker in cavalry. For three hours of fierce firing and

charging they held their own, but they had against them a commander whose skill was equal to every turn of the battle and troops who did everything that was asked of them. In the afternoon their army was breaking and by nightfall it was broken. Tallard was a prisoner. More than half his men were casualties and nearly all his guns were taken. The remnant were partly retreating and partly in demoralized flight.

Such was the battle of Blenheim, the first great French defeat in battle since Louis XIV was king, the first resounding victory of an English general since the middle ages. Its immediate consequences were more than any one had hoped for. Southern Germany was soon cleared of the French. Vienna was no longer in danger. The emperor now had control of Bavaria and was sure of the support of the German princes. The English had tasted military glory, and they were not less susceptible than other nations to its intoxication. If we consider what might have been the results of a French victory, we must recognize in Blenheim the event which saved all central Europe from a long domination of French policy and French culture; but it took years of war and policy to make sure of the results of this day. Even while it was being fought the events in another theatre of war were advancing towards less simple conclusions.

The war in the Peninsula began soon after the landing of the Habsburg claimant King Charles III in the spring of 1704. It was much less well regulated than the war in Germany and the Netherlands: the Spanish and Portuguese armies were ill-found and ill-disciplined, and their morale fluctuated with the course of political as well as of military events. Among the foreigners on both sides who linked the Peninsular with the general European war were some of outstanding ability. On the French side there was James, duke of Berwick and afterwards a marshal of France, a figure symbolic of much in the history of the time. He was a natural son of King James II of England. His mother, now Mrs. Godfrey, the wife of a minor placeman in London, was the elder sister of Marlborough himself. On the other side Prince George of Hesse-Darmstadt was the wisest and most energetic leader, and it was on his advice that the campaign of 1704, otherwise marked by a good deal of movement but no decisive action, saw one great event. Curiously enough, although it solved a problem which many people in England knew to be urgent, its importance did not dawn on the

government until some time after it happened,[1] though Marlborough did not hesitate for a moment to treat it as one of the
cardinal points of the war. It was the capture of Gibraltar. The
rock and its harbour gave England the much-desired naval base,
the first of those strategic points from which the navy has been
able to support her trade and empire. The narrow strait was one
of the crowded highways of the world's sea-traffic, almost as narrow as the Sound or the Dardanelles, much narrower and easier
to control than the Straits of Dover. The actual capture in the
first week of August was easy enough and it was only by accident
that it caused more than 300 casualties: the garrison numbered
only 470 men, and the new fortifications, designed by French
engineers, had scarcely been begun. It was carried out by a
combined English and Dutch fleet in the name of King Charles
of Spain; but the garrison left on shore was mainly English.
On 24 August in a severe action off Malaga Rooke beat the
French Toulon and Brest fleets, but in the autumn a Spanish
force sat down to besiege Gibraltar from the mainland and a
smaller French squadron came to interrupt the communications
of the defenders. British naval reinforcements dispelled the
immediate danger; but when the winter came on the fate of
Gibraltar was still uncertain. Their exertions in holding it had
prevented the allies from carrying out any of their further plans
in the Mediterranean in that year. The duke of Savoy had to
hold on with no more help than that of a small Austrian corps,
and his position was far from happy.

Blenheim alone, however, was enough to make the allies look
forward to the campaign of 1705 with high hopes. Marlborough
planned a combined invasion of France along the line of the
Moselle. This was not such a good line as that which he
attempted in later years from the Spanish Netherlands. It was
a longer march to Paris, and instead of having the sea on his
right and little French territory on his left, he would have had
most of France on his left and great open areas of it on his
right. Still, if the imperial forces had come in good time the
allies would have had such a numerical superiority as to make
the plan well worth attempting. Partly through the fault of the
ill-conditioned margrave of Baden they did not come in time.
Another German general surrendered the great magazine of

---

[1] It was twenty-five years, for instance, before the dockyard was properly
organized.

Trier to the French, and the plan had to be abandoned. Marlborough returned disappointed to the Netherlands, where the
campaign did no more than show how much might have been
done with more effective co-operation. The famous defensive
'lines of Brabant' were carried, but, happily for the French, this
victory was not followed up. Bad news came from other theatres
of war. The revolt in the Cevennes had been handled with
timely conciliation and now Berwick stamped out its last embers.
Its worthy leader, Jean Cavalier, had been reconciled with
Louis XIV, but he fought against France in various parts of
Europe and died an English major-general and lieutenant-
governor of Jersey. The duke of Savoy was not rescued from his
alarming situation: Eugene failed to break through to join him,
and was only able to gain him a respite by diverting Vendôme's
attention to himself. Later in the year the duke felt himself
aggrieved because the English fleet, though in a position to do
so, did not come to his aid. It had been set free from its pressing
duty by the complete success of the defence of Gibraltar against
the besiegers. In March a fleet of twenty-six British and nine
allied ships had defeated the French squadron there and landed
reinforcements. In April the attacking army on land broke up
its camp and retired to Madrid. But the Spanish enterprise was
more and more attracting to itself the energies of the British.
They paid little attention to the other possible fields of service in
the Mediterranean. They saw a rising enthusiasm for the Habsburg cause in Spain which they could immediately turn to good
account. With all the available forces they attacked Barcelona,
the greatest trading town of Spain and the capital of the always
discontented Catalonia. In October it surrendered. The siege
cost the life of Prince George of Hesse-Darmstadt and the reputation of the victory, though according to some authorities it
really belonged to the navy, was snatched by a muddle-headed
busybody and braggart, the earl of Peterborough. King Charles
established himself in Catalonia, and a Portuguese and allied
army simultaneously advancing in the south brought King
Philip's throne into peril.

These successes, however, so far from curing the ill feeling
which the failures in other fields had engendered between the
allies, served to make it worse. Since the capture of Gibraltar the
Dutch had been unable to take more than a nominal share in
the Spanish operations, and they saw with alarm that the English

intended to use them in the interests of their own power and trade. The English were thinking of keeping Gibraltar for themselves, and not only Gibraltar but, if they could get them, other points in Spain and the Mediterranean as well. They had given up the attempt to cut off all the trade of the allies with France and Spain; but now they were seeking their own advantage in another way which implied direct rivalry with the Dutch. The war had hit their exports, and they were talking of compensating themselves not only in Portugal, Brazil, and the Levant but in Spain and the Spanish colonies. Those commercial interests in Holland which were always favourable to peace with France began to gain strength, and the British complaints of Dutch half-heartedness in the Netherlands war increased the tension between the allies. In Austria, to be sure, there was a favourable change. After a reign of forty-eight years the old Emperor Leopold died in May 1705 to be succeeded by Joseph, not a devout conservative like himself but a man of action and a reformer. Joseph put down a rebellion which broke out in Bavaria, but neither military success nor political reasonableness enabled him as yet to get the better of the Hungarian insurgents. Until they were disposed of the full strength of the Austrians was not available for the war.

Starting from this uneasy position, the fighting of 1706 brought sweeping changes. In the Netherlands Marlborough at last fought a campaign as glorious as that of Blenheim. It was not what he had wanted to do. He would have preferred to try the Moselle again, or, even more boldly, to have joined Eugene in Italy; but events there and in Germany ruled this out. The French concentrated the greatest part of their effort on a double advance on the upper Rhine and in the Netherlands. On the Rhine they made good progress. In the Netherlands, without waiting for an army from Metz which was on the point of joining them, they marched straight up to Marlborough, intending to fight. On 23 May they met him at Ramillies, a few miles from Namur. Once again the French had leisure to take up a defensive position which was as good as they could wish; once again Marlborough deliberately deployed to deliver an attack in due form. Once again the fight was long and hard, and once again Marlborough's cool judgement saved it and made it an overwhelming victory. The disordered remnants of the French and Bavarians were driven westwards by a close pursuit. Marl-

borough entered Brussels and the great fortress of Antwerp surrendered. During the rest of the summer the remaining fortresses
were attacked one after another. At Ostend the fleet helped
by bombardment from the sea. Louis called his best general,
Vendôme, from Italy; but, in spite of all he could do, by the
end of the year nothing was left to France in the Netherlands
except Mons, Charleroi, Namur, and Luxemburg.

The war in the Netherlands was won, and the same summer
saw the war in northern Italy won too. There the campaign
began badly. The duke of Savoy lost Nice. In spite of liberal
supplies of money and men from the sea-powers, the emperor
had great difficulties in getting his contingents into the field.
His high-handed methods offended the German princes, some of
whom were also made nervous by the nearing of the northern
war. In April an Austrian army was defeated, and it seemed in
the summer as if Turin, the capital of Victor Amadeus, must
fall to its besiegers. Not until September did Eugene arrive in
the nick of time to relieve it. He flung back the French army,
and Louis XIV gave up his hopes of Italian conquests.

For a moment it seemed as if the allies had won not only the
war which the Dutch had at heart in the Netherlands, and
the emperor's war in Italy, but even the third war on which the
English were set, the war in Spain. Early in the year Peterborough occupied most of Valencia without serious difficulty.
King Charles in person defended Barcelona against a siege by
sea and land at which his rival King Philip was also present, and
in May, when prospects looked black, he was relieved by a
British squadron. All Aragon rose against the French and Philip
had to withdraw to the safety of France. Scarcely was he gone
when the allied army under the Portuguese Las Minas and the
huguenot Ruvigny, now earl of Galway,[1] entered Madrid. It
was a chance which a resolute man would have seized without
delay, but King Charles delayed, and time soon showed that it
was only a chance and not a certainty. He entered Madrid and
was crowned, but that was all. The allies lacked money, and
their armies were not good. The support of Aragon only contributed to strengthen the hostility of Castile, the proud heart
of Spain. Philip, fugitive as he was, was an anointed king, and
soon he was returning with a new army of Berwick's. The allied
army, degenerating in quality and ill-led, failed to meet Berwick

[1] See above, p. 89, n. 1.

before he was too strong for it, and in August the French re-occupied Madrid. Fighting went on far into the winter, but, if its lesson had been understood, the allies would have known what they unhappily failed to learn, that they had lost Spain for good.

Where the allies succeeded they were faced by the problem of disposing of their conquests, and they all knew that their arrangements for the immediate future would very largely pre-judge what was done when it came to settling a general peace. In Italy the emperor took the decision into his own hands. By a treaty of 13 March 1707 he permitted Louis XIV to withdraw all his remaining troops, but he did nothing to obtain Nice and Savoy proper for the duke, nor did he gratify Victor Amadeus by making him viceroy of Milan, which he now treated as an Austrian province. All this was unpleasing to the maritime powers. They held that Milan ought to belong to Charles of Spain. They set store by the alliance of Savoy, and the release of French troops for service in Spain and Flanders was highly unwelcome to them. None the less they had to acquiesce, the more so because their attitude nearer home over the question of the Netherlands came near to estranging them from Austria altogether. Here it was they who would not hand over the ter-ritory to Charles. They could not deny his nominal right to it, but it was they who had conquered it, its defence would fall to them, and as its future concerned both of them vitally they wanted to make sure of a government under which their interests should be safe. Charles had given the emperor the right to appoint a governor there when the time came, and the emperor took the only step which could have divided the sea-powers on this question: he offered the governorship to Marlborough. Marlborough wanted to accept it. He had already been loaded with wealth and honours in England, a dukedom, an estate, a palace. In Germany he had gained the illustrious title of a prince of the Holy Roman Empire.[1] He was ambitious for the great emoluments and almost royal dignity of this great governorship of which the last holder had been an elector, next in rank to kings. It was at once made clear to him, however, that the Dutch would not tolerate the appointment of him or any other imperial or Spanish nominee. He kept some favour with the

---

[1] It turned out in the end to be an empty title when, at the peace, the lands annexed to it were restored to the elector of Bavaria.

Habsburgs and some hopes for himself by declining only for the present, but although these hopes were still alive three years later he never again came so near to his prize. A joint government of the English and Dutch was established which administered the Spanish Netherlands for the remainder of the war. Their future remained unsettled.

Two more campaigns ensued before the allies cleared up the growing divergence of their aims. In Spain the year 1707 dismally emphasized the lesson of 1706. Reinforced by some of their troops from Italy, the French were stronger than before. The allies also had some fresh troops, but their counsels were divided and they scattered their forces. On 25 April, at Almanza, on the road from the Mediterranean coast towards Madrid, their main army under Galway was hopelessly beaten by Berwick. Little was left to King Charles except Catalonia; and by capturing Lerida the French made ready to attack him there as well. In the following year, although they pushed on less rapidly than might have been expected, they ended with nothing left to conquer except two places on the coast, Alicante and Barcelona. Meanwhile the English, though they had done little to retrieve the position in Spain, had been active in other parts of the Mediterranean. In 1707 they had begun with a diplomatic dispute with the Austrians. Each power put forward a project which failed to appeal to the other as a contribution to the common cause. The emperor wanted to attack the Spanish kingdom of Naples and the English revived their design of attacking Toulon, which would also serve to relieve the pressure on Spain. As they could not agree on either plan they made the bad compromise of attempting both. The Austrians secured the whole kingdom of Naples at the cost of only a single siege; but, with little help from them and little or less than none from Savoy, the Toulon expedition failed. The land army under Victor Amadeus and Eugene was too weak, and the fleet could not help it except by frightening the French into scuttling their own ships of the line in the harbour. That indeed meant that the French could no longer oppose the English in the Mediterranean, and in the next summer another English fleet accordingly made two great conquests there. First it took Sardinia, with its rich agricultural land, for King Charles. Then it landed a small force on Minorca, which garrisoned Port Mahon. For the next forty-eight years this admirable harbour remained in British hands, a perfect naval station for summer or winter within the straits. Not subject like Gibraltar to attack by land, it was less than half as far from Toulon or Naples or Sicily. From this base the English were able to prevent any of the Mediterranean powers, and France in particular, from establishing an empire like that of the Romans, founded on the command of the inland sea.

In the Netherlands 1707 was a year of no important events, but 1708 brought a new success. The initial plan of the allies was for a triple attack on France by the Netherlands, the Moselle, and Alsace, under Marlborough, Eugene, and the elector of Hanover, the next heir but one to the English throne, who had succeeded to the command of the margrave of Baden. This plan, however, was thrown out of gear by an insurrection in the southern Netherlands. The inhabitants, exasperated by the minor oppressions of the Anglo-Dutch provisional administration, admitted French troops to the Flemish towns of Ghent and Bruges, and were about to do the same at Ostend. Vendôme, to take advantage of this turn of fortune, tried to seize Oudenarde, a fortified town where the Scheldt above Ghent is crossed by the road from Brussels to Courtrai and southern Flanders. Marlborough this time took the French by surprise, and, attacking before his army had finished crossing the river in the face of the enemy, gained another crushing victory. The French field army was scattered. Marlborough was for pressing forward and marching on Paris, but Eugene refused to leave Lille, the greatest fortress of France, intact on the flank of their communications. In August it was invested. In September a convoy from Ostend fought its way through to the besiegers in the nick of time,[1] and contrary to all the principles of fortification the town capitulated in October. The citadel still held out, and the elector of Bavaria made a futile attempt to relieve it. In December it surrendered. This was the worst blow Louis XIV had suffered. It meant not merely the recovery of the Netherlands by the allies, since Ghent and Bruges soon gave up their resistance; but, although the winter stopped campaigning for the time, it meant also that the first barricade on the best road to Paris was broken.

This was the crisis of the war. For a second time the sea-powers

---

[1] At this battle of Wynendael, where the English were commanded by Major-General John Richmond Webb, Marlborough's political opponents falsely accused him of not giving Webb the credit due to him, a slander which is repeated in Thackeray's *Esmond*: see F. Taylor, *The Wars of Marlborough*, ii. 214–15.

were masters of the Netherlands, and their position was even stronger than after Ramillies. The emperor was master not only of northern Italy but also of Naples, and at last he had the upper hand of the Hungarians. France had been humbled, and in this year famine had been added to her other miseries, but her resources were still great, and the longer the war continued, even if it continued victoriously, the harder it was to hold the Grand Alliance together. When, therefore, in the autumn of 1708 the French made overtures for peace there was every reason for taking them seriously. They were not the first such approaches. There had been feelers after Ramillies, but now there seemed to be the first prospect of agreement. It has indeed been doubted whether Louis's offers were quite sincere. An offer of peace is one way of weakening an enemy, and especially it is a good way of splitting a coalition. Whether he wanted peace or not, it was to Louis's interest to estrange the Dutch from the English. It was a game which his diplomatists had played more than once before, and this time they had good materials to their hand. They were able to provide the Dutch with a copy of a secret treaty by which the English had extorted from King Charles of Spain the promise of wide and exclusive commercial privileges in the Spanish empire. Even if the negotiations for a general peace were to fail, France could not lose from adding one more proof that the Spanish part of the war was an English affair by means of which the English were prosecuting their ancient rivalry with the Dutch. But the question whether Louis's offers were sincere is not very important. It is scarcely different from the question whether he had thought out the course his diplomacy should take in the event of a rejection of his advances. The advances themselves gave an opening for a serious negotiation.

That the allies had no desire for this was made clear by a document of May 1709, handed over jointly by English, Dutch, and imperial plenipotentiaries to the French minister Torcy, nephew of the great Colbert. It was a list of forty-two articles set out as preliminaries to a general peace. Besides including most of the territorial and commercial concessions which the three powers desired, it reserved the right to bring forward at a peace conference further demands on behalf of themselves and their minor allies. There were clauses which showed that it was a statement not of their conditions for peace, but of the aims for which they were determined to go on with the war. France was to secure the surrender of the Spanish monarchy to Charles III within two months of 1 June 1709. If Philip refused to abdicate she was to give the allies military assistance in turning him out of Spain.

The allies had thus agreed, when everything else was as good as won, to go on with the war until that one aim had been accomplished which had hitherto been a peculiarly English concern. There was to be, in the English phrase, no peace without Spain. In this decision, as events were to prove, even the English had been blinded by their successes on sea and land to the hopelessness of the Spanish enterprise, but the allies had reasons of their own for agreeing to second the English. The emperor had put forward a demand of his own which was equally unobtainable without the complete overthrow of France. He asked for Strasbourg, though he had not conquered it, and the French yielded. He asked for Alsace and that they refused. The Austrians were not alone in their obstinacy. The duke of Savoy asked for frontier cessions which the French were absolutely unwilling to give. The Dutch were negotiating with the English for an object of their own. They wanted the recognition of a pretention which was in its full extent somewhat disadvantageous to British interests. In dealing with the English they were the weaker party,[1] but the English plan required their co-operation and in the course of 1709 a further revelation of British secret diplomacy made it necessary to pay their price. They discovered that the British had obtained the possession of Minorca from Charles III as a pledge for their expenses in the war. Their ruffled feelings were soothed by the Barrier Treaty of 29 October 1709 which promised the Dutch all they wanted in regard to the future of the southern Netherlands. For a number of years their policy for that region had been the policy of the barrier. Except for the small inland province of Spanish Gelderland they did not want to annex it: to have done so would have excited English jealousy, would have given them an awkward catholic population to govern, and would have made it difficult to uphold that closing of the port of Antwerp which relieved their own seaports from the most dangerous competition. Without the responsibilities and burdens of annexation they thought that the possession of fortresses and of sufficient

[1] There is a convenient summary of the naval contingents of the two powers and the growing deficiencies of the Dutch in *Common's Journals*, 28 January 1711.

local revenues to maintain them would give military security. It was a system which they followed on a smaller scale on their eastern frontier, and to the south they desired only to renew it with safeguards against a new collapse like that of 1701. The English, always jealous of a strong power in those parts and now solicitous for the future of their trade with and through the Netherlands, were reluctant to accept all these Dutch demands. Their representative Lord Townshend yielded more than his principals intended. He agreed to a number of minor points, including that of Spanish Gelderland, which was also coveted by Prussia, and to a barrier of so many fortresses and on such conditions that it implied the virtual military and economic control of the whole territory.[1]

While these negotiations were in progress, the war went on, and, unfortunately for the allies, none of the remaining campaigns was so disastrous for France as 1704 or 1706 or 1708. The French in the Netherlands, though outnumbered, were now commanded by the best leader they found in the war, Hector de Villars. He was unable to save the magnificent fortress of Tournai, but when the allies advanced against Mons he met them in the field. The battle of Malplaquet (11 September 1709) added one more to the list of Malborough's victories, but it was gained at a cost of losses far greater than those of the French. It was followed by the taking of Mons, another stage on the road to Paris, but its moral was that the French had more fight in them than any one had supposed. Elsewhere nothing went well. In Spain the British fleet was too late to prevent the fall of Alicante, and the French won military successes both in the north and in the south. A repetition of the plan of invading southern France, this time from Germany and Franche-Comté, ended in an Austrian defeat, and Victor Amadeus kept his troops from taking part in it. Before the end of the year the Portuguese were tired of the war and began to negotiate with France. As soon as they heard the terms of the Barrier Treaty the Prussians did the same.

There were indeed official negotiations for a general peace in the earlier months of 1710 in regular conferences at the Dutch town of Geertruidenberg; but they only made clearer the impossibility of agreement with France. The demands and refusals were essentially the same as before. The French undoubtedly wanted peace if they could be sure that the allies meant to give

[1] See Map 7 f.

it, and they went rather farther than before in concession; but
the allies could hold together only by asking too much all round.
This collective stiffness was to go on while each power by itself
became more anxious to get a share of the Spanish inheritance
and be done with the war. If the French could carry on the war
at all, they would be able to choose which of their opponents it
would pay them best to satisfy separately and so detach. In 1710
they were able to keep the war going and, with one exception,
the theatres of war all saw tedious and indecisive fighting. In
south Germany very little happened at all. In the Netherlands,
the allies with considerable losses captured Douai, Béthune,
Aire, and St. Venant: the only fortresses now left close to their
road to Paris were Bouchain, Cambrai, and Arras, but there was
at least another year of fighting to look forward to. In Spain
during the greater part of the year they had surprising successes.
Strengthened by reinforcements they resumed the offensive and
won two battles which opened their way to Madrid. For the
second time Philip had to leave his capital; but the people of
Castile remained true to him as before. Charles took possession
of the city, but his position was made intolerable by guerrilla
warfare, and as a new French army approached he in turn had
to withdraw. The English lost a battle, and, though their allies
won another, the retreat had to continue, and in January 1711
a new French victory left Charles master of nothing but a part of
Catalonia. By that time the French ministers had chosen their
method for bringing about a peace. Among their opponents
they had selected the one whose secession was most likely to
serve their purpose. A new turn of events enabled them to make
a remarkable choice,[1] not in line with the traditions of their
diplomacy. They addressed themselves to the strongest of the
allies, the only one which had appeared as irreconcilable as the
emperor. They turned to England. In order to understand this
momentous step and the subsequent course of the war and the
settlement we must turn back to trace the history of English
parties from the beginning of Queen Anne's reign.

Queen Anne was neither a very intelligent nor a commanding
woman. She never failed to receive the respect due to her birth

---

[1] That at the decisive moment it was their choice and not that of the English
is proved by the document called the First French Memorandum cited by O.
Weber, *Der Friede von Utrecht*, pp. 22–23.

and her great position, but a good speaking voice was almost her only personal attraction, and she was seldom free for long from the fear of being bullied. Nevertheless her accession gave a decided turn to the course of party history. Her homely figure, still familiar in the statuary of provincial market squares, though not very queenly was an excellent rallying-point for that prejudiced but sound and sober England to which she belonged. She regarded the church of England as became Clarendon's grand-daughter. She appropriated all her revenue from the first-fruits and tenths of ecclesiastical benefices to the augmentation of poor livings, and this benefaction was separately administered until 1948 under the name of Queen Anne's Bounty. She shared the abhorrence of the country party for the memory of William III and the events of his reign. Thus in her first speech from the throne she said, 'I know my own heart to be entirely English.' Both then and in answer to nonconformist deputations she promised to stand by the Toleration Act; but these promises were cold and formal. She used her influence on the Anglican side, letting her preferences be known at election times as freely as her predecessors and soliciting the votes of individual members of parliament on party issues.[1] Her likes and dislikes always influenced the choice and dismissal of ministers. Sometimes they sprang from more personal emotions, but they always bore a relation to the success or uselessness of the men concerned. When she came to the throne there were changes which reflected not a change of policy but the change of sovereign persons. The man of the moment was Marlborough. He received the Garter and the highest military offices, including that of master-general of the ordnance, while his wife became the chief office-holder at court. The white staff of lord treasurer was conferred on the invaluable Godolphin, who not only shared Marlborough's views but was also allied to him by the marriage of his only son to Marlborough's eldest daughter. Marlborough and Godolphin had belonged to the new queen's little court when her friends had been out of power, but they were willing to work with any one who supported their main purpose of carrying on the war, and neither of them had that special loyalty which makes the

[1] See, for instance, her letter of 23 October 1705 asking Lady Bathurst's interest to induce her son to vote for Smith as speaker, which he did not do (Bathurst, *Letters of Two Queens*, pp. 262–3), and A. S. Turberville, *The House of Lords in the Eighteenth Century* (1927), pp. 34–35.

good party man. The whigs in fact were prepared to work with them both, and Marlborough had his link with the whigs, for his second daughter was the recently married wife of Lord Spencer, the only son of the inextinguishable Sunderland. It was at Marlborough's request that the queen continued Sunderland's substantial pension, and Spencer was a whig extremist. It was not to be expected that many of the politicians of the period would be so free from the spirit of faction as Marlborough and Godolphin, and, partly because of the influence of the queen's high tory uncle Rochester, who kept his place as lord-lieutenant of Ireland, most of the chief offices went to decided church of England men. Sir Edward Seymour, the typical 'country' leader, and useful in the control of parliamentary seats, became comptroller of the household. One of the secretaries of state was the conscientious but not very effective Nottingham; the other was Sir Charles Hedges, an admiralty lawyer.

The general election of 1702, resulting automatically from the demise of the Crown, brought in a house of commons in which about two hundred members belonged to no recognizable groups accustomed to act together, but the remainder, more than two-thirds of the whole, were in some sense leaders or followers. There were about thirty government members, men who voted with the ministers as a matter of course, such as admiralty officials, military governors, serving officers, the lord warden's nominees who sat for the Cinque Ports, customs officers from various seaports, post-office servants who represented Harwich, and officials of the duchy of Lancaster who were returned from Preston. There were larger or smaller groups of members who followed the court peers: Churchill and Godolphin commanded one of the smaller of these, numbering about a dozen. Harley, who as speaker helped to manage the house of commons, with his allies, could rely on eight or ten. The combined strength of the Rochester and Nottingham connexions accounted for about sixty. The fortunes of the political game turned largely on the personal and family junctions and separations of these teams; but there was much more in politics than the management of votes and the competition for power. About fifty members of parliament were engaged in commerce or banking. The dozen or so business men who sat for the outports were normally nonconformists and opponents of the court; but the bigger men were not whigs: they had links with the treasury and promoted their economic interests by taking part in the manipulation of votes.[1] Few of the members were destitute of public spirit; their agreements and differences depended at least sometimes on principles; they all knew that there was a war to win, and many of them could respond on occasion to leadership which rose above their squalid party routine.

From the beginning the composition of the ministry underwent a series of changes, for the most part gradual and never simple, which by 1710 brought a reversal of the British attitude to the war. Until then the conduct of the war was not seriously affected by party strife at home, although that strife was always bitter and always to some extent busied with naval and military issues. The narrower tories lost no opportunity of preaching the doctrine, which had become theirs in the last war, that England's best sphere of action was the sea, that the real advantages she must seek were maritime and colonial, that land war, besides being ruinously expensive, benefited no one except the greedy continental allies. They did not, however, once succeed in inducing parliament to refuse supplies for continental expeditions or subsidies. Nor had they a practical programme for greater activity at sea: it was evident that British naval power was being fully exerted, even if there were small failures and no colonial conquests. As party feeling so often will, the feeling on this question ran into a mean personal mould, and its most telling expressions were the praises and censures dispensed by parliament to generals and admirals. Rooke was no whig; Peterborough was a tory, and even if they blundered into their victories, to celebrate these was a way of spiting Marlborough, especially since Marlborough by the time of Malaga and Barcelona was working round to a whig alliance. First the Rochester tories and then Nottingham and his followers were turned out. This was, no doubt, partly due to the half-heartedness of the tories for the strategy of the war as he conceived it. Nottingham and Hedges might have stayed in office much longer if they had done more towards winning the war. Their successors were a moderate tory and an extreme whig, Robert Harley and the younger Sunderland himself (lately Spencer), but they were

---

[1] Here I follow the analysis of the parliament given by Mr. R. Walcott, Jr., in his essay 'English Party Politics (1688–1714)' in *Essays in Modern English History in Honour of W. C. Abbot* (1941). His book *English Politics in the Early Eighteenth Century* (1956), was published later than the present work.

alike in seeming warmer for the war. It was not mainly this, however, but the irreconcilable behaviour of the party men on other questions which decided ministerial changes.

These questions were many, but the most vital, because they sprang from the deepest division among Englishmen and were at the same time connected with the contest for office, were church questions. The chief, which came to the fore almost from the beginning of the reign, was that of occasional conformity. This was the practice of certain protestant dissenters who on exceptional occasions received the communion in Anglican churches. There are instances in which by local usage small bodies of nonconformists have long maintained this slight connexion with their parish churches. It was a kind of minor substitute for comprehension, and before it became a political question, moderate men on both sides regarded it as a means of promoting mutual understanding. Richard Baxter called it a 'healing custom'. In our own time it is countenanced by high ecclesiastical authority, at least for occasions when the holders of municipal or legal or academic offices attend celebrations of communion in their official characters. Many respectable people did so in Queen Anne's reign, from her own husband downwards, for Prince George was a Danish Lutheran. But this gave offence to the high churchmen, partly because by it they escaped from the operation of the Test Acts. So long as they were allowed this evasion, nonconformists could qualify to serve in municipal offices, in parliament, as officers in the army or navy, or in the civil administration. In 1702 therefore a bill was introduced imposing fines and disqualifications on all who, after taking the sacrament and the test, should attend nonconformist religious meetings.

The tolerant whig bishops were against the bill, and the house of lords, by amendments some of which raised a constitutional dispute, succeeded in defeating it. In the next year, hopeful that their chances had been improved by a slight increase of the number of tory peers through new creations, the tories introduced a new bill to the same effect, but the lords threw it out by a majority of twelve. The conduct of Marlborough and Godolphin, who disapproved of it but voted for both bills in order to retain the queen's favour, shows how difficult they found it to set their course through these cross-currents.

Their greatest advantages for retaining power and associating with them in office those who would accept their policy were the queen's confidence and the lack of alternative leaders for the war. During the victorious period down to Oudenarde, although they were often anxious about parliamentary affairs, these two advantages did not fail them. Of the two parties the tories were the more discontented, but the whigs had more to offer. The ablest of them formed a compact group popularly known as the 'junto' (from the Spanish word 'junta', a council). This was now composed of Lords Orford, Somers, Wharton, Halifax, and Sunderland, a formidable combination. Orford, the victor of La Hogue, had much experience of naval administration; Somers was a man of broad intellectual power and weighty in the law; Wharton, a great political manager especially in the county of Buckingham; Halifax, a financier equal to Godolphin in reputation; the young Sunderland, though dangerously indiscreet, was all intelligence and vigour. They lost no opportunity of pressing each other's claims to office, and one by one they gained it. Sunderland, helped by his mother-in-law the duchess of Marlborough, was the first. He became secretary of state in 1706. Two years later Wharton became lord-lieutenant of Ireland, and Somers lord president. In 1709 Orford was made first lord of the admiralty. Halifax, indeed, though employed in other capacities, held no ministerial office; but from the early part of 1708 the tories of every complexion were out of office and the ministry was, to all intents and purposes, a whig ministry supporting Marlborough and Godolphin.

By that time its two essential advantages were beginning to give way. The weary series of campaigns, bringing no visible prospect of peace, turned criticism of the accepted strategy into dissatisfaction with the war itself. The queen's personal distaste for the ministers who had been forced upon her, some of them irreverent about religion and some half republicans, was joined to an estrangement from the duchess of Marlborough. The duchess now had a rival. Mrs. Masham, her own cousin, had a small place at court and was related also to a politician who never failed to keep in touch with his relations, for their advantage and his own. This was Robert Harley, long ago a puritan, for some years now a moderate tory, wealthy, fond of the bottle, and lucid neither in thought nor in speech, but a reconciler and a maker of combinations, the very man to bring together all the disjointed forces of those who were tired of the war and the ministers. When he resigned the secretaryship of state in 1708 his prospects seemed dull: the heads of the ministry had detected him in intriguing for their dismissal, and a disagreeable discovery of the treasonable conduct of one of his clerks proved him to have been no vigilant master in his office. He went on assiduously undermining the ministry, with increasing support from the queen. He knew how to get good men about him, and he did better than the whigs in working up the means of influencing public opinion. They had Addison and Steele; he had Defoe[1] and, later, gained Swift. Gradually he placed himself and his party in a position from which they could spring forward as soon as the ministry took a false step. The ministry took two false steps. It bound itself to the foredoomed cause of no peace without Spain, and it impeached the Rev. Dr. Sacheverell.

Henry Sacheverell was a poor parson's son, and the grandson of one of the ejected nonconformists of 1662. He had become an undergraduate of Magdalen College soon after it was restored after its oppression by James II, and he was now one of its fellows. No good judge thought highly of his brains or character, but he looked impressive and he had a gift for inflammatory preaching. This he had exercised in the high church cause for several years with increasing fame, denouncing whigs, dissenters, latitudinarians, and low churchmen. In 1709 he preached before the lord mayor and aldermen of London a violent sermon[2] in which he repeated his familiar topics. He affirmed the doctrine of non-resistance, and said that the Revolution of 1688 had not been an act of resistance. He pointed to the ministers, and Godolphin in particular, as enemies of the church. What followed is hard to understand unless we remember that, although a full generation had gone by since the Popish Plot, the nation was still liable to frantic bursts of excitement on church questions. Perhaps the seven years of war, although the fighting was in the distance, had told on people's nerves. The government, in foolish exasperation, and against the advice of Somers, decided to turn against Sacheverell the portentous procedure of impeachment. There was a storm of pamphlets. The London mob went wild with enthusiasm for the victim. There were riots. Dissenting meeting-houses were wrecked and troops were called out. The day came

---

[1] How the author of *Legion's Petition* came to work for Harley is clearly explained by T. Bateson in *Eng. Hist. Rev.* xv. 238 ff.

[2] *The Perils of False Bretheren, both in Church and State* (1709).

for the decision of the peers: sixty-nine, including seven bishops, voted for conviction, fifty-two, of whom six were bishops, for acquittal. Such a minority, and a sentence merely that the sermon should be burnt and the preacher silenced for three years, were as good as a victory for the doctor and his supporters.

Three weeks later, when parliament had risen and Marlborough was overseas, Harley edged into office an enigmatic nobleman who was clearly not intended to strengthen his new colleagues. This was the duke of Shrewsbury, twice secretary of state, who had returned from a long idleness in Rome. His appointment was a first step towards disintegrating the ministry. The next, which came only a month later, was the dismissal of Sunderland. The Bank of England represented to the queen the danger of altering her ministers and dissolving parliament, but, mainly on Harley's advice, skilful measures were taken for dividing the ministers and maintaining something of continuity. The decisive step of dismissing Godolphin was taken on 19 August 1710, but Somers was persuaded to stay, Halifax gave his support, and Marlborough, though there had been years of exhausting friction, ending in an absolute breach, between his duchess and the queen, consented to retain his command. The treasury was put into commission with Harley as second lord and chancellor of the exchequer. His plans were always fluid, and at this time he wanted, or at least would probably have preferred, a coalition of moderate men under his own control, though his aim abroad was an honourable and safe peace, not a strong prosecution of the war. A few weeks, however, sufficed to show that this compromise was unattainable. Somers, Orford, and the rest of the whigs went out, and Harley found himself at the head of an almost purely tory ministry. He clinched his success by dissolving parliament. The general election which took place in the autumn of 1710 was the fourth of Queen Anne's reign. The others in 1702, 1705, and 1708 had rather reflected than caused the ministerial changes. The first had given the tories a majority of nearly two to one. The second had brought in a whig majority. The third resulted in the most whiggish parliament that there had been since the Revolution. In this fourth the tories supplemented the considerable electioneering power of the Crown by good party organization. Some lord-lieutenants and a number of justices of the peace were removed. The clergy used their great influence to the full; but Harley stood for moderation, and by means of Defoe and others he gave the dissenters private assurances of continued toleration which were not without effect. The new ministry gained a very large majority, something like three to one.[1]

[1] This included the Rochester tories, but most of Nottingham's followers did not support the ministry.

X

THE TORY PEACE

BESIDES its large majority in the commons, the new government had the same two advantages which had been so important hitherto, the queen's favour and a foreign policy to which there was no real alternative, this time the policy of making peace. It is therefore a memorable example of the instability of political power and greatness that four years later, though the peace had been made, the tory party was broken to fragments, and not merely out of office but destined to stay out for many years. There were tactical mistakes and faults of personal character which contributed to this, but there are always these even in a winning cause, and the failure was inherent in the nature of the victory. It is not that party success is always too narrow a foundation for a national policy; to that rule there are exceptions. At this time, however, English affairs were still as closely involved with foreign as in the time of Charles II, and the tories, compelled to seek support abroad, sought it from those whose alliance could not unite but only divided the nation. The story of the war and the peace in the last four years of Queen Anne is the story of how the tories became entangled in Jacobitism. It may be made more exciting by assuming that Jacobitism was an admirable romantic loyalty, or, alternatively, that it was a black treason; but in fact these party leaders were led into it by the necessities of their situation, and for this they deserve neither praise nor any blame except what must be shared by their antagonists.

As early as July 1710 the ministry was secretly in touch with Torcy through the medium of the Abbé Gaultier, a French priest with some experience as a secret agent, who was living in London as chaplain to the imperial ambassador. There have, however, been many such communications in time of war which have led to nothing, and this did not become serious until the bad news from Spain came in at the end of the year. For the next campaign the war was carried on, but in a new spirit. Having complained for so long that naval and colonial opportunities were neglected, the tories undertook an expedition to show how they could be

turned to account. In the previous year General Francis Nicholson, commanding English and colonial troops, had occupied
Nova Scotia. He was an advocate of an invasion of Canada, and
it was now decided to support him in this with a fleet and 5,000
men. The preparations were inadequate, and the force returned
from the mouth of the St. Lawrence without having effected
a landing. This misdirected effort had given the ministry an
opening for one of those pin-pricks by which it was now trying
to neutralize the influence of Marlborough without giving itself
the odium which was to be expected abroad, and even at home,
if he were dismissed. The military command for Canada was
given to General Hill, an officer whose principal merit was that
he was the brother of Mrs. Masham. Affronts like this, which
were multiplied, together with the uncertainty of the future and
failing health, for he was over sixty, interfered with Marlborough's action in the Netherlands, where he had to operate alone,
since Eugene was summoned to the Rhine. Nevertheless he did
well. He broke the lines in which Villars had entrenched his
army, the *ne plus ultra* lines. This was done by a night march of
amazing distance which exhausted his troops; but it has been
called Marlborough's greatest feat. He completed his campaign
by a victory which was his last, the capture of Bouchain. There
still remained other fortresses to master on the way to Paris, and
he still hoped to carry out the invasion. He had won the only
successes of the year. In the Peninsula the tories carried out the
inglorious dictates of common sense, of which they had seen the
necessity when the whigs were blind to it. Most of the British
troops in Catalonia and Portugal were taken to Port Mahon and
Gibraltar.

By this time the government had agreed to preliminaries of
peace with France. They had taken a short cut. Disregarding
the clause of the Grand Alliance against a separate peace, they
had sent Matthew Prior, an experienced diplomatist, to Paris,
and after a brief negotiation in London they had arranged terms
which were communicated in part to the allies. There was to be
a general peace conference, for which the place was soon fixed as
Utrecht. The Dutch and the emperor, seeing no hope of getting
a satisfactory peace for themselves except in conjunction with
the English, reluctantly and apprehensively consented to take
part in it. They were not aware of the long catalogue of concessions on which the French had already agreed with the

English, thus virtually securing English support in a policy of leaving their allies comparatively poorly provided for. These concessions covered the whole field of British interests, except the imaginary interest of establishing Charles in Spain. There Philip was to remain. The Spanish succession question, however, still presented difficulties. There would have to be some provision in the final treaty, for instance, to prevent the union of the French and Spanish Crowns. In this preliminary agreement, however, nothing was said about this, since the English feared that a startling event of the spring might rob them of their chance of making separate terms. The young emperor Joseph had suddenly died of smallpox, and his successor, who was elected to the empire without trouble in October 1711, was Charles himself. The new emperor not only spoke for Austria but had the remains of his Spanish claim to bargain with. His new dignity made ordinary opinion in England even less anxious than before to see him king of Spain, but it disposed the government to hurry on to a settlement of the purely English demands.

These, as the French conceded them, gave, like the whole course of the war, emphatic proof of the influence of British sea-power. Not only was there a list of territorial acquisitions which added Nova Scotia and Newfoundland to the colonies and provided Gibraltar and Port Mahon as bases for naval strategy. There was more. The fortifications of Dunkirk, the nest of privateers on the flank of the Channel trade, were to be destroyed. The Spaniards were to give the English equal trading privileges with the French, and, in addition, one privilege estimated to be worth millions a year which had been enjoyed since 1702 by the French and earlier by the Dutch, the *asiento* or contract for supplying African negro slaves to the American colonies. There was another commercial clause in which there lurked possibilities of trouble: a treaty of commerce was to be negotiated between England and France. Queen Anne's title to the throne, denied at the beginning of the war, was to be acknowledged, and with it the succession as regulated by parliament.

The English war-party, as the survivors of the late ministry and their followers must still be called, were ill-advised enough to join with their continental friends in an endeavour to overthrow this agreement. The Dutch were in close touch with the whigs in London. The emperor and the German princes had a dozen channels for using influence. The elector of Hanover, a serving general and one of the leaders of the continental war-party, encouraged Marlborough to use his influence with the queen against the preliminaries and kept in touch with English parliamentary combinations. The combinations were surprising: the whigs found an ally, with supporters in both houses, in Nottingham. In spite of his churchmanship and his long experience of office, the tories had done nothing for Nottingham since his resignation in 1704, and in his views of foreign policy he had now quite honestly more in common with the whigs. For this surprising alliance they, however, were to pay an equally surprising price: they were to accept an occasional conformity bill. Marlborough and Godolphin had once already voted for such a bill for reasons of expediency.[1] That the whigs should do so shows perhaps that in an extremity they preferred party interests to toleration, perhaps that they hoped to evade the electoral consequences of the enactment, perhaps that their judgement had deserted them. Their promise was made good: in the session of 1711 the bill immediately became law, and it was not repealed until 1719.[2] The new combination led to a vote of the house of lords against any peace which should leave any part of Spain or the Indies to the house of Bourbon. In the commons a similar motion failed. Nothing was neglected to work up political opinion against the preliminaries. Prince Eugene in person came to London on a special mission for the emperor, but when he arrived he learnt that Marlborough had fallen. The government had counter-attacked. From the records of the war they had raked up material for charges of peculation and accepting bribes which Marlborough was in a position to answer but which served well enough as a pretext for his dismissal from all his offices. He never again took a leading part in affairs. In the autumn of 1712 Godolphin died on a visit to him, and soon afterwards the duke, isolated and neglected though not in actual danger, withdrew to the Continent, not to land again in England until the day of Queen Anne's death. He lived on until 1722, very rich, honoured as he deserved, but old for his advancing years and not concerned to influence political events.

---

[1] See above, p. 224.

[2] It does not appear to have led to the intended results. The Hanoverian resident and other persons of distinction used their influence to keep the dissenting mayors and magistrates in the offices where they might be useful. The majority seem to have ceased to attend their places of worship and confined themselves to private services. See Edmund Calamy, *Historical Accounts of my own Life*, ii. 245–6.

The counter-attack of the government in the end of 1711 was made not only against him but also against the stalwart and extremely able young whig secretary-at-war Robert Walpole, the future head of the whigs when they reached their highest point of power. Walpole, on similar charges, to which he had an equally good reply, was impeached and sent to the Tower: the level of party acrimony was rising high. The government, however, had the queen and the commons with it, and it made sure of carrying its main point by a necessary if extreme constitutional expedient. The queen added twelve tory votes to the house of lords, by 'calling up' three eldest sons of peers and creating nine new peerages. In the meantime the congress at Utrecht was assembling, and there was another campaign to think of. The allied armies in the Netherlands were larger and better equipped than the French. Eugene was there. The duke's successor in the English command was the duke of Ormonde, who had commanded at Cadiz and Vigo. He set out with orders to fight, but in supplementary instructions of a fortnight later he was told not to hazard a battle or a siege. It took the allies only a few days to discover that he was in this false position, though it was left to an English parliamentary inquiry some years later to discover that the secretary of state had not merely given these treacherous orders to Ormonde but, without Harley's knowledge, had notified them to the court of France. What the allies learnt was enough in itself to cause deep anger and distrust. The Dutch protested to the British representatives at the congress, and received the unvarnished answer 'that considering the conduct of the states towards her majesty, she thought herself disengaged from all alliances and engagements with their high mightinesses'. Harley, a few days later, was still asserting that the government was not aiming at a separate peace, though the queen in June announced the English peace-terms as agreed, while those of the allies were to be settled at Utrecht. In July the English were acting in the field as a third party, or, in effect, as allies of the French. By the orders of the French king Dunkirk was surrendered to them. Ghent they already held and they occupied Bruges. Ormonde announced that his government had arranged an armistice for two months, in which he invited the allies to join. They refused and stood up for themselves as best they could, though with the ill-success that could not be avoided. A lost encounter at Denain was followed by the fall of three fortresses, Douai, Le Quesnoy, and Marlborough's last conquest, Bouchain.

With things going so well the French were in no hurry to come to a conclusion at Utrecht. The armistice was prolonged, and the congress lasted throughout the year. Its course was dominated by the agreement of England and France. When England had recognized Philip as king in exchange for a solemn if unreliable assurance that the French and Spanish Crowns should never be united, there was nothing for Charles to do but to quit Spain, which he did in March 1713. Much indignation was expressed at the desertion of the Catalans by the English, and it would certainly have been more decent to make some stipulation on their behalf instead of leaving them to shift for themselves. In the outcome their lot was hard. With French aid Philip's troops captured Barcelona in 1714. There were no executions, and only a few leaders were imprisoned, but the Catalans were deprived of their political privileges. Thus, like Aragon more than a century before, they were absorbed into the Spanish state under Castilian domination, to nourish their separatist feelings and ambitions down to our own time. The Emperor Charles gave up not merely his Spanish claim. He declared his willingness to allow the elector to be restored to Bavaria, and also to see Sicily given to Victor Amadeus of Savoy. He was even willing to let Max Emmanuel of Bavaria take Sardinia and to withdraw his demand for the restoration of Strasbourg. All this, however, was not enough to satisfy the French. According to their wont they raised their demands in proportion to their successes in the field. When they asked for still further concessions to Max Emmanuel, and for a guarantee that the Austrians would not extend their rule in northern Italy to Mantua and Mirandola, it was too much. The emperor broke off negotiations in April 1713 and resolved to go on with the war.

The Dutch were not so tough. They were at the end of their resources. Their public finances were in collapse. Nor, in spite of the almost hostile attitude of England, were their diplomatists able to act except in subordination to the English. It was not merely that they were now more than ever conscious of being the weaker partners; behind this was the more solid reason that their traditional policy had been not to resist France except with English support. At all times and not merely at this time the combination of those two great powers, of which they had felt the full strength in 1672, was patently too much for them. They had to be content therefore with what England would allow them to ask, and, in considering their demands, England showed the same unfriendliness which she had shown in her manner of breaking loose from her treaty obligations. This unfriendliness requires some explanation. It must indeed be attributed in part to the maladroit persistence of the Dutch statesmen in continuing to act with the English whigs. They might at least have tried to come to an understanding with the new government. They ought to have been prepared for the event of its becoming firmly established. And the economic rivalry had never died: there was no lack of Englishmen, whether politicians or pamphleteers, who, once the word went round that the Dutch were to be humiliated, repeated the old grievances and the suspicions of the previous generation. Most of these, however, were underlings who could have been silenced from above. They were not silenced because they had above them a man who really believed it politic to revive the old hatred and to risk throwing away the alliance of the Dutch in that critical time and in the critical future. This was the secretary of state, Henry St. John.[1] He was a man of headlong vehemence, a born partisan, whose gifts were all for fighting, and to whom it came naturally to seek reconciliation with an enemy by injuring a friend; but it would be unjust to think that he regarded the Dutch as friends. He thought of them not only as exorbitantly ambitious in the war, but as rivals in trade. The conduct by which the English justified their reproaches was the constant falling short in military and naval quotas and the remissness in other war measures;[2] but that related only to the past. In the present, St. John honestly believed 'our trade sinks and several channels of it, for want of the usual flux become choked, and will in time be lost; whilst in the meanwhile, the commerce of Holland extends itself, and flourishes to a great degree'.[3] This belief was mistaken in both its articles. British trade was flourishing; from its depression in 1705 it rose until in 1712 'our navigation and traffic had gained a manifest superiority over any former period of peace'.[4] The Dutch, who

---

[1] Born 1678; sat in parliament from 1701; secretary at war 1704-8; secretary of state 1710; created Viscount Bolingbroke 1712; impeached and fled to France 1714; in the service of the Pretender 1714-16; pardoned and returned to England; died 1751.   [2] See above, pp. 203, 218.

[3] To Drummond, 28 November 1710, in *Letters*, ed. Parke, i. 17.

[4] G. Chalmers, *Estimate of the Comparative Strength of Great Britain* (1794), pp. 89-90.

were harder hit by the northern war as well as by the French war, had no share in this prosperity. Their trade was, on the contrary, depressed. Its supposed condition and the fear of what it might become did them undeserved harm.

The terms which they secured were disappointing in the chief matter. The French treaty laid it down that their barrier in the Netherlands was to be such as they could arrange with the Austrians, if and when by making peace the Austrians should become sovereigns there. It was, however, not France or the emperor with whom they had to reckon here but England; and a new barrier treaty of 30 January 1713 with England fixed the diminished number of fortresses they were to receive, and withdrew some of the commercial privileges promised in 1709.[1] In other directions the Dutch did not fail to get solid advantages. France gave them a commercial treaty which included the abolition of the duty on salted herrings and other duties, and a narrow definition of contraband, the whole creating a position much like that of the treaty of Ryswick. There was also to be a commercial treaty with Spain. In Spanish Gelderland, which was to go to Prussia, the Dutch were to have a continuation of their barrier, the fortresses of Venloo, Roermond, and Stevensweerd.

The minor allies in southern Europe had their treaties settled at the same time. The duke of Savoy, who was to become king of Sicily, gained also a strip of territory on his Italian frontier: his power altogether was much enhanced, though his dominions were now divided by the sea and consequently open to naval pressure. Portugal had to be content with the resignation of French claims[2] to territory on the frontiers of Brazil and to the right of navigating on the Amazon. These treaties, and the Spanish treaties which were their complement, were not obtained without a renewal of English pressure on France. After the breakdown of the negotiations with the emperor the congress at Utrecht was unable to do anything. The British government became suspicious of what the French might intend, and in February 1713 sent an ultimatum threatening the renewal of the war in the spring unless the outstanding questions were settled. The negotiations were resumed and in April the treaties were signed. In England the church bells rang, there were bonfires in

---

[1] For the terms of the two treaties and the ultimate settlement with the emperor made in the treaty of 15 November 1715 see Maps 7 g and 7 h.

[2] The district of Cap du Nord between French Guiana and the Amazon.

the streets and illuminations by candles in the windows. The great national task of establishing the peace was done. It was done so well that the country was not engaged in a serious war again for a generation. There were perpetual fears and alarms. The diplomatic relations of the powers revolved round the chances of new wars. There were even great wars in Europe and lesser hostilities in which England was involved; but the peace-making had been expert enough to coin the exhaustion of the moment into a thirty years' exemption from war on the grand scale.

The commercial treaty negotiated at Utrecht was intended to end the economic war which had begun in Colbert's time or before. The French tariff was to revert to the level of 1664 and Great Britain was to give France the treatment of the most favoured nation. There were, however, four species of goods in which the French were not to relax their protective measures without a separate negotiation which was still to come. All four were very important in the economic rivalry of the two countries, woollen manufactured goods, sugar, salted fish, and the products of the whale-fishery. In addition British woollen goods were to enter France only through three staple-ports, Saint-Valéry-sur-Somme, Rouen, and Bordeaux, where they were to be subjected to the system of inspection which the French applied to those of their own manufacture. This might well be administered vexatiously. The British customs were imposed by parliamentary authority, so a bill was necessary to give effect to these articles. In parliament the whigs had for long been closely associated with protectionism in general, but there were others besides whigs who were friends to the vested interests which had grown up behind the high tariff. The distillers of brandy, the silk weavers of Spitalfields, and the French refugees in other industries dreaded a renewal of French competition. The great wool industry itself was supposed to be threatened. The dropping of the burdens on French wines would upset the system of exchange with Portugal which had given such satisfaction since the Methuen Treaty. A pamphlet controversy broke out which has great interest in the history of economic thought. The immediate issue was discussed in the light of theory: industrial protection, the balance of trade, the benefits of freedom of exchange were all elucidated, and the journalists used the statistics which had now been methodically accumulated at the Custom

House from the year 1696. In parliament the alignment on this question was mixed up with a political issue, and by a majority of nine votes the tariff clauses of the treaty were thrown out. The French agreed to let the remaining clauses take effect, but these mainly concerned the regulation of trade in a state of war, and curiously enough, when long afterwards the time arose for putting them into operation, British lawyers and statesmen had some difficulty in discovering whether they were in force or not.[1] At any rate, the chance of resuscitating Anglo-French trade was lost. Throughout almost all the eighteenth century the two nations competed in every open market, closed every market they could control, refused one another's goods, even some of those which they could not produce for themselves, and contributed scarcely anything to one another's prosperity. Had they carried out their bargain, each must have sacrificed some of the trade or industries which protection had fostered. The sacrifice would probably have been much more than repaid, but it would have accorded ill with the prevailing habits of commercial regulation.[2]

The political considerations which strengthened the will of a certain number of tories to vote against the clauses were connected with a grave division of their party. The extremists belonged to the October club, a body in existence since King William's time, which is said to have been named from its strong October ale. After the general election of 1710 it numbered 150 members of parliament, a good many of whom were known Jacobites, and its link with the ministry was St. John. The October club wanted measures for identifying the state with the church and landed interest. A bill was brought in to repeal the act of 1708 which permitted the naturalization of all foreign protestants. This act, always unpopular with high churchmen, had been rendered more objectionable by a considerable influx of refugees from the Palatinate whose settlement had occupied the government and the charitable in 1709 and 1710.[3] The immigrants, though deserving compassion, were destitute, and the act seems to have brought them over. The repealing bill

---

[1] See G. Bubb Dodington, Lord Melcombe, *Diary* (1784), pp. 130–2.

[2] For accounts of the incident see H. Schorer, *Der englisch-französische Handelsvertrag von 1713* (1900), and D. E. A. Harkness, 'The Opposition to the 8th and 9th Articles of the Commercial Treaty of Utrecht' in *Scottish Hist. Rev.* xxi. 219–26.

[3] See W. Cunningham, *Alien Immigrants to England* (1897), pp. 249 ff., and below, p. 344. For the occasion of their coming see above, pp. 122–4.

failed to pass the lords, but they passed another which imposed a landed property qualification on members of parliament.[1] In 1712 a new bill against foreign protestants was carried, and also a new press law which it was intended to administer in the party interest. This taxed paper, except that used for printing learned books, and required a stamp costing a penny to be placed on every paper which the government decided to be a newspaper, and a duty of two shillings a sheet on every pamphlet of more than half a sheet.[2] Although they were meant as party measures each of these three acts remained in force for many years: they became part of the oligarchical system of the eighteenth century even when that system became identical with whig rule. For the moment their effect was to please but by no means to satisfy the tory extremists. An instance of how far these were prepared to go was given in 1714, when feeling had indeed become exacerbated. Richard Steele, one of the highest in standing of the whig writers, was expelled from parliament on charges which could scarcely be justified except on the principle openly avowed by St. John that opposition to the government was opposition to the queen.

Harley was no enthusiast for St. John's extreme measures. The temperamental differences between the two raised difficulties between them from the early days of the ministry, but, if the younger man fretted at Harley's lack of a bold policy or of clear antipathies, he was at first in no position to set up as a rival. Chances, like an attempt on the life of Harley by a disappointed adventurer, preserved the leader's popularity, but confidence in his own thwarted ability drove St. John into a state of ambitious jealousy. He resented it when Harley was raised to the peerage as earl of Oxford while he had to be content with an inferior rank as Viscount Bolingbroke. He resented it again when Oxford and not he became a knight of the Garter. The rivalry of the two had not, however, become dangerous to the unity of the party at the time of the peace. In the summer after the signature of the treaties, taking advantage of the jubilations, the government anticipated by a few weeks the operation of the triennial act and dissolved parliament. The elections reduced their majority somewhat, but not enough to give the opposition much advantage.

[1] See above, p. 14.
[2] For the administration and evasions of this law see Mr. Hanson's book referred to above, p. 155, n. 2.

Among the tories, however, there was now a larger proportion of St. John's supporters. What made all this a serious matter was that little by little the gravest of all domestic problems had again been intruding itself on people's minds. The succession question was coming to life again.

When war began in 1702, so far as we can tell, the bulk of the English nation were roused against the attempt of the French to upset the regulation which parliament had confirmed and elaborated in the previous year. It was a question of defending Queen Anne against the pretender. A larger proportion of the leading politicians, indeed, exchanged civilities with the court of Saint-Germain. It was seldom that they committed themselves to anything, and few of them desired a Stuart restoration. They merely wanted to keep an opening for themselves if a restoration should come about. Their aim was 'insurance'. That they should have corresponded at all, however, shows that their confidence in the existing settlement was not absolute, and it shows further that they had good reason for qualifying it, since they themselves and the rest of their kind were capable of this measure of double-dealing. Marlborough and Godolphin both acted in this way, and even a man so deeply engaged in the whig cause as Somers. At this time, indeed, when there was any division of opinion connected with the succession, the whigs were no more but rather less the custodians of the Act of Settlement than the tories. The act, like the Revolution, had originated in a national policy embraced by both parties, and the tories, being in office, had no motive for making friends with the pretender. In 1705 they even supported a motion of Lord Haversham, an impetuous man who had come over from whiggism, to invite the Electress Sophia to make her residence in England. That would have forestalled any attempt of the pretender to dash across to England if anything were to happen to the queen, but the proposal was tactless in the extreme. Queen Anne had had much experience of adversity. It would be hard if, now she was at last on the throne, she should have this clever old German dowager installed close to her as a perpetual reminder of her own approaching death. She was indignant with the tories, and grateful to the whigs who defeated the resolution and consequently lost favour with the electress.

The long suspense over the Scottish union brought every

possible aspect of Jacobitism to notice.[1] As the pretender neared manhood he became a more important factor in the question. His character was not the best suited for his political prospects: he was very devout, not very healthy, and by no means an inspiring leader. Still he amounted to something and might amount to more. The story of his being a changeling was dropped. The whigs were not wedded to it, for if it were true it implied that his exclusion was due to his birth and not only to an act of parliament. The speculations, in which even William III had indulged, as to whether he might not give up his religion, were revived. His greatest disability was his dependence on the French. In 1708 he did himself a signal disservice by a descent on Scotland. In Scotland the moment was propitious: all the discontents with the union were at their hottest. But as a military plan the invasion was hopeless from the start. It was to consist of about 4,000 troops, sailing with a small naval escort from Dunkirk. The British fleet and its intelligence service were not asleep. At the very moment when James Edward alighted from his coach at the door of the *intendant* at Dunkirk, a strong British squadron took up its station unmolested in the offing.[2] Bad weather enabled him to slip past it, but everything went wrong. As the expedition lay at anchor waiting for the tide to take it into the Firth of Forth, the pursuers came up, and it made off northwards losing one ship captured in the stormy weather. The French admiral refused to set the prince and his followers on shore, and the survivors returned to Dunkirk to report an utter failure. The loss of ship and troops was small in comparison with the political setback. In London there had been a few days of panic, political and financial, but the nation rallied to the queen. And the queen rallied to the nation. Before this she had had feelings of sentimental regret and compunction about her treatment of her family, but now, in a speech from the throne, she called her half-brother a popish pretender, bred up in the principles of the most arbitrary government.[3]

These events, coming at almost the same time as Harley's dismissal and soon followed by the battle of Oudenarde, where the pretender was present with the French army, drew the whig government closer to the Hanoverian interest. Simultaneously

---

[1] See below, pp. 275 ff.
[2] H. Malo, *La grande guerre des corsaires* (1925), p. 89.
[3] *Lords' Journals*, xviii. 567.

George Lewis, the reigning elector and the Electress Sophia's heir, was becoming, both in virtue of his electorate and as the new imperial general, one of the leading men in the policy of fighting France to a finish. He maintained an attitude of perfect correctness in English internal affairs, but he joined with the Dutch and imperialists in doing everything he could to support the whigs in their war policy. He did not respond to the advances of Harley's ministry, nor was he impressed by an act of 1711 which accorded precedence to his mother and himself. Co nt Bothmar, the Hanoverian resident in London, was deep in the counsels of the whigs from the formation of Harley's government all through the parliamentary struggle over the preliminaries of peace. The tories knew that the whigs would lose no chance of injuring them with the elector; they were justified in fearing that if George became king of England he would at the least exclude them from office. As their short cuts to peace became more objectionable to the allies and their dangerous secrets multiplied, their fears increased.

In party conflicts just as in military operations there is such a thing as the fog of war, and both sides were misled by their ignorance of the real position of their opponents. The tories did not understand how indifferent the elector of Hanover was to English parties: they regarded him primarily as a person who might in the future have the disposal of ministerial offices, and they failed to see that for him it was British policy and not personal questions that mattered. The whigs were nearly as blind to this, and quite blind to the impossibility of the combination from which they feared a Jacobite restoration. That was the combination of the English tories with France and the pretender. It could only exist on paper: there were two unalterable impossibilities in it. The first was the steadfastness of James Edward in his religion. He would not renounce the cause which had ruined his father, and the irreligious English intriguers moved on a plane where such constancy could not be understood. The second was that, even if Louis XIV could ignore the British fleet, so long as the emperor was still at war against him he could not spare an army to help the pretender. With their eyes turned inwards on their own concerns both the English factions failed to appreciate this fact. The peace of Rastadt, which settled accounts between Louis and the emperor, as sovereign of his hereditary dominions, was not made until 6 March 1714. After that there was still a

delay before the peace of Baden, by which the empire wound up
its war in September 1714. This second interval is of no importance; but before the first treaty was made, the prospects of
English Jacobitism were already extinguished.

By the time when the treaties of Utrecht were signed the tory
ministers had good reason to fear that if the Hanoverian came to
the throne they would be impeached for high treason. During
the summer the events on the Continent made their prospects
seem worse: the French were gaining ground, capturing Landau
and Freiburg, and these reverses increased German resentment
against the tories. The tories were not indeed a Jacobite party.
There was much activity of Jacobite agents among them, and
from an early date in the peace negotiations attempts were made
to knot together the cause of peace with that of the Stuarts.
Gaultier had been in touch with the earl of Jersey, a former
diplomatist and secretary of state whose wife was a Roman
catholic. At the other end he had relations with Berwick. The
ministers went farther than before in their messages to the
exiled court. By means of the French ambassador, Oxford sent
to the pretender a draft declaration in which he was to renounce
the Roman church. There was so little secrecy that Bolingbroke
discussed the pretender's answer at a meeting of members of
parliament. The answer, however, was hopelessly unfavourable.
It promised nothing more than 'reasonable security' for protestantism, and thus it alienated practically all parliamentary
support. From that time there was no real chance of a restoration: the communications which the ministers continued to
send to the pretender represented only a desire to keep open any
possibility, however distant, of escape from their increasing
difficulties.

All along there had been Hanover tories, men whom nothing
could deflect from the lasting considerations of national interest
that had dictated the Act of Settlement. At the time of the peace
they numbered some fifty members in the house of commons;
and it was their defection which upset the commercial treaty.
So far as they were influenced by direct political considerations
their action may be explained by their growing suspicions of the
government: their leader, Sir Thomas Hanmer, on a visit to
Flanders and France in 1712 was courted by the French and
the Jacobites with the result that he became fixed in his opposition to them. But there was more behind this. That a high

churchman like Hanmer, a wealthy landowner of aristocratic
connexions, should act in this way did not mean that he regarded
the commercial treaty simply as an opportunity for obstructing
the designs of the government. It meant that for him the treaty
and Francophil Jacobitism both tended the same way: those
who wanted to restore the Stuarts were working against the
vested interests of the business nation. One of those interests in
particular was important for Hanmer. He was member for the
clothing county of Suffolk, where he had one of his estates. The
Hanover tories were the tories who supported the woollen and
silk manufacturers and the port wine trade, the established protective system as a whole. Nor can it be seriously doubted that
they opposed the treaty because they objected to it for its own
sake. They were protectionists, and partly for that reason they
were Hanoverians. Jacobitism was impossible not only for the
majority of churchmen but also for the strongest business
interests.

    The drift of events had split the tories but united the whigs.
Their determination contributed to keeping Jacobitism alive
among their opponents, but it is difficult to say how far they
went, and how far it was due to them that the situation became
strained to the point of crisis. The Hanoverian minister, the
huguenots, and the more active dissenters were all alert. The
whigs did not idly await the course of events. In order not to be
surprised by a *coup d'état*, they began to organize as they had
done in the time of Charles II and James II, to organize, if
necessary, for civil war. They made ready to act on their principle
of resistance. Once more they formed an association. They
collected arms. They enrolled troops. It was said that they had
some thousands of brass badges made which would serve for
uniform. There is nothing inherently unlikely in this; but there
are some difficulties in the way of accepting it all. From the
whig point of view such activities would have been creditable,
but no leading whig subsequently claimed credit for them. From
the government point of view they would have given an excellent
ground for arresting the whig leaders and breaking up their
organization; but the government, although its intelligence
service was good, arrested no one and accused no one. Not
one of the brass fusees appears to survive, and there is
nothing to show that, if they ever existed, their purpose was
that alleged. Much of the story rests on the statements made

long afterwards by witnesses who had few facilities for knowing the truth.[1]

At Christmas-time in 1713 the queen fell dangerously ill, and the nervous tension about the court was like that which precedes a revolution. During the remaining seven months of her reign her strength was visibly failing, and the politicians plunged from one crisis to another. In parliament the whigs and the Hanover tories now acted in concert. In March they carried in the lords a unanimous address that the queen might continue her inter-position in the most pressing manner in the Catalans' behalf. The government could not disown its obligations to them; but such intervention could form no part of the foreign policy which Bolingbroke, with his constant love of paper combinations, was hoping to construct on a basis of alliance with France, Spain, Savoy, and Sweden. Next the opposition moved in both houses that the succession was in danger. They had some facts to point to. The treaty of Utrecht had stipulated that the pretender should leave France, and before the treaty was signed he had betaken himself to Lorraine; but the whigs thought that even there he was uncomfortably near. When peace was concluded the army was, quite properly, reduced to a peace-footing of about 30,000 men; but instead of doing this in the fair and cus-tomary way by disbanding the regiments most recently raised, the government picked and chose. It even disbanded a regiment so senior as the sixth foot. There was no doubt that the regiments kept in being were selected for their fidelity to the government party. It was evident also that military commands of important places were being given to known or suspected Jacobites. Money from the treasury was being distributed in the Highlands; for Jacobite purposes, it was said. After a debate in which these charges were ventilated, the government had a majority of only twelve in the house of lords. They were losing supporters daily.

This brought the quarrel between Oxford and Bolingbroke to a head. There was no clear-cut difference between them on questions of principle: neither was fundamentally more a Jacob-ite than the other. Harley, with all his moderation and common sense, had never ranged himself with the Hanover tories. His dilatoriness and indecision were growing on him, and he never

[1] See Basil Williams, *Stanhope* (1932), Appendix E; *The Diary of Dudley Rider*, ed. W. Matthews (1939), pp. 47–48; Tindal's *Continuation of Rapin's History of England* xviii (1745), 167.

ceased to have some hopes on both sides. He talked about beginning secret official negotiations with James, but he never did it.
In the last stages of the quarrel he still tried to resume his old
relations with the whigs; but Bolingbroke too, immediately
before his fall, made similar advances. The difference between
them was that Bolingbroke was always impatient of half-
measures. There is no reason to think that he set out, after the
queen's illness, on a policy of Jacobite revolution. The pretender
had no better reason for trusting his intentions than before. But
he insisted on reconquering parliamentary support for the
ministry and on seizing real power in the country. Whatever
was to happen to the succession he thought he could save himself best by acting, not waiting. If the Hanoverian was to come,
it was best to have something to offer him, to be strong, to be
able to speak for political England, to be indispensable, even to
be dangerous. And so long as Oxford was at the head of affairs
all this was impossible. Bolingbroke, at the end of his patience,
asked the queen to dismiss Oxford.

For the time the queen reconciled them and kept them both.
Oxford saved himself by agreeing that the purging of the army
should continue, but now came a fresh incident which divided
them afresh. In April 1714 the Hanoverian envoy Schütz demanded for his master's heir the electoral prince, who had been
made duke of Cambridge in 1711 and was afterwards King
George II, a writ of summons to the house of lords. It could not
legally be refused, but the mere mention of it threw the queen
into pitiable distress. She dissuaded the elector from allowing
the prince to take his seat. Bolingbroke wrote another letter
to the same effect, the language of which gave great offence. The
plan was allowed to drop. The Electress Sophia was eighty-
four years old, and now she died. The elector, her son, was heir
presumptive to England. For the last time Oxford veered round
to the Hanoverian side. He once more exerted his remaining
influence with the queen, and the queen wrote to the duke of
Lorraine requesting him to expel the pretender. A proclamation
was issued offering a reward for his capture if he should land
in England. A last resource remained to Bolingbroke. Disappointed of the queen he had already turned to parliament.
He put himself at the head of the high church party, to which
Oxford, himself of presbyterian origin and supported by presbyterian electors, had never been more than a moderating influ-

ence. Bolingbroke himself was a deist, as emancipated in thought as he was in morals; but he had something to offer which squared well with his earlier domestic measures. His Schism Bill forbade any nonconformist to keep a school. It was meant not merely to wipe out the educational system which the nonconformists had built up for themselves, but, by giving the church an educational monopoly, to extirpate nonconformity in the liberal professions and in every part of the nation except the humblest. It extended to Ireland. In the commons it had a majority of more than a hundred. In the lords there were five bishops against it. Oxford could not make up his mind to oppose it, though he knew it would undermine his position. It was carried by seventy-seven votes to seventy-two. The queen died before it came into force. Although it was a dead letter and did not lead to the closing of more than two or three schools, it remained on the statute book for five years.[1]

Seeing his rival supplanting him in the party, Oxford worked against him behind the scenes. He did not resist, but rather encouraged an inquiry which was demanded by Nottingham and the whigs into the Spanish treaty of commerce, a matter in which it was believed the secretary's hands were not clean.[2] The first steps of the inquiry showed that there was something wrong, but next day it was cut short. The queen was carried down to prorogue parliament. The duel for power was transferred to the council board. It was hard for the queen to make up her mind. On the one hand there was Oxford, unintelligible, irresolute, shifty, and frequently drunk. In June he offered to resign. The alternative was Bolingbroke, a bad, dangerous man, faced by unanswered charges of corruption. One of them had to go, and she must decide which. All the politicians were intriguing, quarrelling, waiting. On Tuesday, 7 August, the queen in council at Kensington Palace gave Oxford his dismissal. He grumbled

[1] Two amendments were carried which are characteristic of the age. The act was not to extend to the tutors of noblemen's families, nor to teachers who, using the English language only, taught reading, writing, and arithmetic or mathematics 'so far as such mathematical learning relates to navigation or any mechanical art only'.

[2] Bolingbroke had been advised by Arthur Moore, a merchant and a commissioner for trade. We know now that in the provision of stores for the war in the Peninsula his relations with Moore had been indiscreet or even corrupt: see his letters to James Brydges in *Huntington Library Bulletin*, nos. 2, 8, 9. Harley made a similar charge in relation to the Quebec expedition of 1710: *Hist. MSS. Commission, Portland Papers*, v. 465.

and wrangled, and then went out. The queen was very ill, but she sat on in the council-room hour after hour, reconstructing the ministry. Oxford was beaten but Bolingbroke had not won. He had still to clear up the matter of the Spanish treaty. He was perhaps the chief minister, but he was still to be only secretary of state. The treasury should be put in commission: at any rate it was impossible then to name a new lord treasurer. Many names were mentioned for many offices, names of high churchmen, names of Jacobites. Nothing was really settled, and when the queen was carried to her bedchamber it was two o'clock on Wednesday morning.

She lay in bed. She was not asleep: this lethargy was mortal. On Thursday she spoke, but on Friday there seemed to be no hope. The council met, Shrewsbury presided, the baffling duke, whose futility no one could understand but who always knew his mind in an emergency. Two other dukes were there, Somerset, whose views on the succession had never wavered since he was in arms in 1688, and Argyle, whom Bolingbroke had cashiered from the army.[1] Bolingbroke did not know what to do. Something must be decided. There was the treasury: he proposed that they should recommend Shrewsbury for the treasury. The queen was able to receive the whole council by her deathbed. She handed Shrewsbury the treasurer's white staff. General James Stanhope wrote that day to his old Spanish comrade-in-arms, the emperor, that she could not live twelve hours and that the Hanoverian succession was saved.[2] On Saturday the council met again to take measures for the safety of the kingdom. On Sunday it met and heard that the queen had died in the morning.

[1] The traditional view that their presence was in some way irregular and represented a check for the ministers is mistaken. Shrewsbury was in office; Argyle had attended councils in March and May. That the ministerial crisis should have taken place in the privy council, not the cabinet, is constitutionally interesting; but we do not know exactly why it was so. (See H. W. V. Temperley in *Eng. Hist. Rev.* xxvii. 686.)

[2] Basil Williams, *Stanhope* (1932), p. 146.

XI

ECONOMIC AND CONSTITUTIONAL DEVELOPMENT UNDER QUEEN ANNE

ONCE they were over it became evident that the crises of Queen Anne's last years had been in a sense unnecessary. The Hanoverian king took possession of his throne without the smallest disturbance: he did not even hurry to the scene, but left regents in possession for several weeks. Bolingbroke fled to the Continent, and Oxford, after due parliamentary deliberation, was impeached and had to spend some time in the Tower; but the solid fabric of English political life was unshaken. While party leaders had been living in an atmosphere of drama, indeed of melodrama, their followers and the country at large had been settling down towards an unresponsive equanimity. The four and fifty years since the Restoration had made England less liable to civil war than she had ever been before. Even the war of the Spanish succession, though foreign war so often begets civil war, had been of such a character as to further this damping down of internal divisions.

The war of the Spanish succession was bigger, longer, bloodier, costlier than the nine years' war, but it made less abrupt transitions in economic and social life. It was a sequel, not an independent story, and so it saw merely the fulfilment of changes already well begun. The scale of national finance rose in proportion to that of the war. When it began the debt had been reduced from the fourteen millions of 1697 to twelve, but at the peace it had been nearly trebled. The annual charge for the debt had risen from £1,200,000 to three millions. There were no changes of great importance in the principles on which it was managed. The state was still largely financed by privileged companies: the Bank of England and the East India Company both added considerably to their loans, and another was created which operated on a still greater scale. This was the South Sea Company of 1711, a body different in origin and prospects from any previous English joint-stock company. Like the Bank of England it arose in time of war and primarily to deal with part of the public debt:

this was not, however, new debt. The company undertook a funding or conversion operation dealing with the great sum of nine millions. It was to enjoy, like the East India Company, a tra ling monopoly in distant seas. Its sphere was to be the South Sea or Pacific Ocean, in other words, Spanish America: it was to exploit the opportunities which were to be granted in the peace by the Spanish government. The moment at which it was made was one when, although the new British government intended to give up the struggle for Spain, there yet seemed a prospect of developing a great trade with the Spanish colonies. The Spaniards did not seem likely to admit tl.e French to a permanent share in that trade, nor able to maintain the exclusion of all foreigners from it. These hopes were not, however, justified by the event. The company did not start trading until after the peace and then found nothing to do except the comparatively trifling work of the *asiento*. Like the Darien Company and the French Pacific Company it exemplified the misleading effect of the Spanish empire on the imaginations of statesmen and capitalists. Its historical importance was to come a few years later, and not on the ocean but on the stock exchange.

The public revenue in Queen Anne's reign varied from year to year within narrower limits than before, never rising to six millions, but never falling below five. It was levied in the same ways, with considerable increases in indirect taxation. The rates of customs and excise were raised, and new additional duties were laid on coffee, spices, and some other articles. There were also new taxes on such manufactured articles as candles, leather, soap, paper, printed calico, starch, gold and silver wire. The system of taxing was not elastic enough to prevent the necessity for new borrowing, but it was not strained to its utmost limits. When the treasury had a difficulty in making both ends meet, it was because the city was disinclined to lend. The most serious financial crisis of this kind was in 1710, and it appears to have been made more serious by the dislike of the moneyed men, especially those connected with the Bank of England, for the new government and its policy. Thus it was to overcome a difficulty which was partly political in its origin that the South Sea Company was founded; but the new foundation was only a supplement, not a rival, to the Bank. The whole of the financial system of the last reign stood the strain of the new war well, and the Bank in particular consolidated its position. Its privileges were renewed in 1705 and 1709. In the latter year its capital was doubled and its monopoly was completed: it was to be the sole joint-stock company issuing bank-notes in England. A still more important change went through its decisive stages about this time, that by which the Bank became the regular banker of the government, taking over its cash from the receivers of taxes and investing its balances like those of private depositors. In the history of British currency and banking in general the reign of Anne is notably free from disturbances and controversy.

That is one of the many signs that this war was economically very different from the last. From the autumn of 1704 until the opening months of 1708 trade was depressed. The merchants complained loudly of the inefficiency of the provision of convoys for shipping. The number of ships of all sizes captured by the enemy up to that time may be put at about eleven hundred. The French, having accepted a position of inferiority in fighting ships, devoted greater energy and resources than at any other time before or after to privateering. In 1708 the dissatisfaction with the counter-measures of the admiralty led to a minor party crisis and an attempt to change the personnel of the admiralty board. Hitherto the board had been nominally the council of the queen's consort, Prince George of Denmark, as lord high admiral. In fact, however, it did its work in the same way as the normal admiralty boards, and was dominated by Marlborough's autocratic and unpopular elder brother George Churchill. The movement for a change was probably justified. It failed, but it may have done good; at all events, merchants' complaints began to grow less and shortly ceased altogether. The general course of trade was indeed quite unlike that in the former war. So far as the statistics of imports and exports reveal it, the lowest stage of depression was reached as early as 1705, and after that the totals gradually rose until, as we have seen, they exceeded in 1712 any figures previously reached in times of peace.[1] Their interpretation is a matter of some difficulty, but the general nature of this phenomenon may be stated confidently. British sea-power and political circumstances reduced to an extremely low point the interference of the war with shipping trade. The special demand created by the war, especially by our continental allies, stimulated British production at a time when the machinery of

[1] See above, p. 235.

capitalism was easily capable of expanding to satisfy the new requirements. Both French and Dutch competition were lamed by the land-war and by financial strain. British trade in the east had just at this time independently ripened to a very profitable condition. The increase of trade with Germany, Holland, and Portugal outweighed the shrinkage in trade with the enemy countries and with Africa, and the losses caused in the Baltic trade by the Great Northern war. At last the British merchants had done what they had so often attempted in vain: they had enriched themselves by war. Whether the nation as a whole was richer for it may well be doubted: the war had enriched the few probably without alleviating the poverty of the many, and perhaps by making it worse.

In constitutional development the reign takes somewhat the same place as in economic: it is marked by consolidation rather than by new beginnings. This resulted from the war and the growing wealth of the governing class. Against that class one traditional counterpoise had been the Crown. Queen Anne cared little for court splendour but she did not forget the religious aspect of her office. She 'touched', like her father and her uncle, for the king's evil. Long afterwards Dr. Johnson remembered the lady in diamonds and a long black hood whose hand was to cure him; and though it succeeded in other cases no better than in his, the miracle still found believers as it had done in the middle ages. But the queen's majesty was now circumscribed by law and expediency. Anne's own influence on affairs was considerable.[1] In ecclesiastical appointments she often decided for herself. In the choice of ministers and of ambassadors and officials it was always necessary to defer to her, and at times she asserted herself so strongly that her preferences were decisive. This influence, however, was intermittent. She had neither the knowledge nor the ability to understand and direct high politics. She usually presided in the cabinet and she was, like her predecessor, occasionally present at debates in the house of lords; but in business she was not much more than a figure-head. Her authority did not suffice to restrain the spirit of faction, much as she disliked it,

---

[1] On one occasion, in 1708, she refused her assent to a parliamentary bill. This was a bill for setting the militia of Scotland on the same footing as that of England: the text is in *House of Lords Papers*, new ser., vii, 21 March 1708. The incident has no constitutional importance except that it was the last exercise of the royal 'veto'.

and in her reign government by party struck its roots deeper. The way was prepared for the system in which the Crown was to govern by co-operating with the aristocracy and for the most part on terms which the aristocracy prescribed. Already in one important respect the limits of the royal discretion were clearly marked: from the beginning of her reign the household was supported by a special parliamentary grant, known not long afterwards and to the present day as the 'civil list', which could not be supplemented by drawing on the general revenue. From the strictly financial point of view the sovereign had become the greatest of the paid servants of the state.

Since at the same time the state was undertaking a great war in which rapid decisions and exhausting efforts were needed, progress was made in solving the problem which the Revolution had left unfinished, that of organizing the relations of the executive with the legislature.[1] The Act of Settlement had laid it down that as soon as the Hanoverian succession should come about, all placemen should be excluded from the house of commons. Party leaders, whether in office or merely aspiring to it, were soon dissatisfied with this principle: they wanted to increase their parliamentary power by the exercise or the promise of patronage. In 1705 after the ill-starred tory attempt to invite the Electress Sophia to England, the government brought in a bill to provide for a regency which, in the event of Queen Anne's death, should take charge until the Hanoverian succession should be safely consummated. The whig minority in the commons took this opportunity of adding a clause to exclude placemen from their house immediately. The tories, who were in a minority in the lords, were opposed on party grounds to confining the parliamentary action of ministers to that house, and generally to diminishing the relative weight of the commons. They therefore carried an amendment by which only certain specified officers were to be excluded. After disputes between the parties and between the two houses as to the offices to be specified, a compromise was reached. An act of 1705 repealed the clause of the Act of Settlement, but another act of 1707 excluded the holders of all offices not in existence before 25 October 1705. Thus parliament asserted its right to control the number of placemen who should sit in the commons.[2] Much complicated legislation

---

[1] See above, pp. 152-3.
[2] In 1709/10 the commons passed a place bill, but a very full house of lords

was necessary before this principle was worked out in its modern form, but its general tendency was clearly towards mutual control by parliament and the executive. In the first parliament of George I there were still 271 placemen.[1]

The war and the increase in the scale of all government work which it implied had thus, before 1705, confirmed the result of the war of William III. It had also contributed in other ways to strengthening the control of ministers over the commons. The leading ministers were peers and the house of lords had the better of several conflicts with the commons. The device of tacking was employed for the first Occasional Conformity Bill, but there was sharp controversy as to whether it was admissible. It failed in this instance, and it has never since been successfully used. The pretensions of the commons had, in fact, reached a point where other authorities were able to resist them. They had an undoubted right to the sole decision of disputed returns in elections to their house. The cases of *Ashby* v. *White* and *The Aylesbury Men* arose from the election of 1702 in the borough of Aylesbury, where some of Lord Wharton's whig protégés had not been allowed to vote. It was held by some of the judges and a majority of the peers that the commons had only a right to decide who had been chosen and not who might choose a representative. Legal obscurities were complicated by party interests, but the commons maintained that the lords had no right to hear appeals on this matter and that it was their own affair. The dispute was cut short by a prorogation of parliament, and the points at issue remain undecided to this day; but at least the commons did not win. It is indeed true that the lords never afterwards raised the issues, and that if they had done so in more recent times they would probably have been beaten; but for the time being the outcome of this dispute, and of others in the same parliament, was to establish their position as the more important house except for the control of finance.

It must be largely ascribed to the pressure of the war that no such disputes attended the progress which was made towards the modern system of cabinet government. The clause of the Act of Settlement dealing with the privy council[2] was due to an

in the presence of the queen threw it out after half an hour's discussion and without dividing (N. Luttrell, *Brief Historical Relation*, vi. 544). In the autumn of 1710 another place bill was passed by the commons and thrown out by the lords.
[1] Hatscheck, *Englische Verfassungsgeschichte*, p. 651.
[2] See above, p. 191.

old complaint freshened by the annoyance of the moment at the proceedings of Somers and others in making the Partition treaties. It was so drafted that it could not have much effect: a great legal historian remarked that 'it seems to say no more than that things which by law ought to come before the council ought to come before the council'.[1] What seems to have been objected to, however, was the pendant that every councillor must put his signature to all the advice he gave. That would have provided unanswerable evidence for the prosecution in political impeachments, and apparently for this reason[2] the provision was repealed by the same act of 1705 which repealed the clause about placemen. Queen Anne gave up the custom of removing from the privy council the names of those who were dismissed from office or who lost the favour of the sovereign. The numbers of the council rose to more than eighty, though the attendance even on important occasions was less than thirty. Clearly it was now essentially a formal body, part of the dignified rather than of the efficiently working element of the constitution. It was still, as it is now, the regular channel for certain kinds of official business, and the place for certain acts of the sovereign; but there were no real debates in it, and, even in the crisis at Anne's death, no decisions of policy were taken there. Throughout the reign there was a cabinet. It met regularly every Sunday, except when the foreign mails were delayed, and more often during the sessions of parliament. Its membership was decided by the queen, who usually presided. Besides the great ministers, she was in the habit of summoning the archbishop of Canterbury, and, when he was in England, the duke of Marlborough. The speaker of the house of commons also attended, but he was not yet above party; he was in fact one of the men who controlled the commons for the government, and for a short time Harley was both speaker and secretary of state. Besides the cabinet there was a more or less regular inner cabinet, or at least there were frequent discussions of the few leading ministers in which important decisions were taken without formality and without the presence of the queen. The cabinets of Queen Anne differed from those of William III mainly in being rather more settled and continuous. During the

---

[1] F. W. Maitland, *Constitutional History of England* (1909), p. 390.

[2] Burnet, folio ed., ii. 434, says 'it was visible that no man would be a privy councillor on those terms', which must apply to the latter rather than the former part. Political impeachment was, however, an obsolete weapon now that ministers were in effect responsible to parliament.

king's absences on the Continent after the death of Mary the place of the cabinet was taken by not very dissimilar meetings of lords justices. The cabinets differed from those of the present day in their composition and in the fact that they were never identical with the acknowledged leaders of a party or a coalition of organized parties. Allowing for the changes which have since come about in the work of government, we cannot say that they differed materially in their function. Whether they differed in having no prime minister is not much more than a question of words. There was indeed no prime minister who derived his office from a parliamentary majority alone, just as there was no ministry which lost office because it lost a parliamentary majority. The name of 'prime minister' came from the French *premier ministre* which had nothing to do with parliamentary majorities and was known in England in the time of Charles II. Under William III we hear of 'prime ministers' in the plural, the secretaries of state,[1] and under Anne though the plural still occurs, meaning the leading ministers,[2] the expression was sometimes used in the singular for the lord treasurer, first Godolphin and then Harley. It was not the usual name for that office. It was still sometimes used in other senses, and it cannot be said that there was yet an office of prime minister, but in Queen Anne's time almost as much as now there was ordinarily one leading minister in the cabinet. This was a necessity of the position while the country was at war and the sovereign a woman. The doctrine was indeed not unknown that a prime minister was foreign to the constitution; but the needs of the time were enough to prevent any revival of the doctrine that the sovereign should be the single head, the one point of unity for the manifold and so easily divergent purposes of the state.

After the Civil war and its sequel of acute party divisions, the constitution had now settled down. For a remarkably long period it was to undergo no fundamental change and even few considerable modifications. The Jacobite cause was lamed by the refusal of the pretender to identify himself, or to satisfy Englishmen that he really identified himself, with the religious and political compromise. The radical criticism was scarcely heard. A great majority of the political nation accepted what

---

[1] R. Molesworth, *Account of Denmark* (1694), p. 166.
[2] Swift, *Journal to Stella*, 5 May 1711. For an early approach to the singular use see Clarendon, *Continuation* (1849), pp. 85–90.

had been done, and it was becoming common for 'our constitution' to be spoken of as something which must be defended, and even as a product of exceptional political wisdom. The revolution principles of Locke which had been really revolutionary in his young days had become, when he died in the year of Blenheim, almost an accepted orthodoxy. The Sacheverell incident was the last public appearance of the doctrine of non-resistance which gained any applause. The best brains on the tory side accepted the utilitarian views of the whigs. Dean Swift, who, it is true, came over to toryism from the other side, did not find it necessary to change his theory of politics when he did so. Except Locke there were, in fact, no eminent writers who can be called in the strict sense of the term political philosophers. His influence produced a calm in the region, formerly so stormy, of the theory of political obligation. The area of disturbance was now the problem of the relations between the state and the church or churches. In the later years of William III and the early years of Anne there was a controversy, which produced some trenchant writing on both sides, over the rights of convocation. From 1701 there were sometimes actual sessions; in 1710 and some subsequent years convocation did some real business. The Jacobites and high churchmen claimed for it authority independent of the state, which the clergy on the government side denied. This was only a paper controversy. On its civil side the constitution was accepted, complete and secure.

The quality for which it was praised by contemporaries was freedom. There was a fair degree of religious toleration which, however much Dr. Sacheverell's friends disliked it, was congenial to a large proportion of Englishmen. They still saw religious refugees arriving destitute from the Continent. The Palatines of 1709–10 were the last body of the kind, but no one could foresee that what had been so common for nearly two centuries would not continue indefinitely. The mere fact that France was intolerant and absolutist and also the chief enemy in the long wars tended to make Englishmen proud of their own liberty. Every true report and every baseless rumour of arbitrary government in France showed them what they had escaped. As the name of the Bastille grew familiar, the Habeas Corpus Act came to be valued. Singularly little was said or known in England about the good side of French administration. Long years of isolation from the Continent combined with satisfaction in the victorious course of the war to make France, which in the time of Charles II had been taken as a model, now seem unsuccessful and misgoverned. Its characteristics were popularly supposed to be popery, slavery, and wooden shoes. Roast beef was our national boast. John Bull, invented in the brilliant pamphlet of that name by Arbuthnot in 1712, became the symbol of the Englishman as he liked to think of himself, honest, plain-spoken, and robust. Boxing, the 'science of self-defence', was national too. The individual was expected to stand up for himself, and on occasion he could rely on the support of a number of his fellow individualists collected together as a jury or an election crowd or a house of commons.

English life was very disorderly. Although Monmouth's rising was the last rebellion, there was scarcely a year in which London or the provincial towns did not see aggrieved people breaking out into riots. In the reign of William III there were political and economic disturbances, and others which sprang up from local anger against individual swindlers or bullies. In 1689 Norwich and Suffolk were disturbed;[1] in 1693 Worcester, Weymouth, Shrewsbury, and Colchester, while it was feared that the London ribbon-weavers would get out of hand.[2] Next year it was Peterborough, Northampton, Stamford, and other places in Lincolnshire.[3] In April 1695 there were riots in London against one Tooley, who kept a debtors' prison in Holborn and was suspected of kidnapping recruits for the army.[4] In the autumn riotous crowds were stealing corn in Suffolk.[5] In December there were three clothing places in Essex and three in Suffolk for which the privy council had to take measures.[6] In 1696 the recoinage caused riotous outbreaks in various quarters. In 1697 the London weavers were demonstrating outside the house of commons and the East India House in January against the importation of raw silks by the East India Company,[7] and in March they attacked a house in the city belonging to a gentleman of the company.[8] Other instances could easily be

---

[1] *Portledge Papers*, ed. R. J. Kerr and I. C. Duncan (1928), pp. 56–57.
[2] Ibid., p. 163; Privy Council Register, 4 May.
[3] Ibid., 21 June. For the suspicion of a political element in the Northamptonshire disturbances see William's letter of 15 July 1694 in Coxe, *Shrewsbury Correspondence*, p. 52, and Shrewsbury's reply, p. 54, that it was a mere corn-riot.
[4] *Portledge Papers*, pp. 199–200.
[5] S. and B. Webb, *The Parish and the County*, p. 488, n. 4.
[6] Privy Council Register, 19 December.
[7] *Portledge Papers*, p. 249.
[8] Ibid., pp. 254–5.

collected.[1] In Queen Anne's reign the word 'mob', first heard of not long before, came into general use.

One reason why public order was so defective was the absence of a police force. The parish constables were annually elected by their neighbours, and whether they served with more or less reluctance for one term or went on year after year, they were not very effective in the parish and did nothing outside it. In London and some of the larger towns local governing authorities kept a few night-watchmen and other paid officers; but for the most part the work of police was left to the magistrates and their private servants or tenants. When there was serious trouble the militia or the London train-bands were called out, or regular troops sent to the spot. Repression was possible, but commonplace detection and arrest were very difficult. Not only rioters but all ordinary criminals had every opportunity. The period from the Restoration to the death of Queen Anne was, for instance, the great period of highwaymen. Some of them are known to have been disbanded soldiers and even officers of the civil and French wars: no doubt the warlike character of the age multiplied crimes of violence. But what favoured them most was lack of governance. Most of the highwaymen held up travellers and took their money. Some had channels by which they could dispose of bills of exchange. There was at least one who had a 'racket' on the road-transport of an extensive district. The carriers regularly paid him a ransom to go unmolested. He had been condemned to death and then reprieved on condition of abjuring the realm; but, although he was generally known, he could lead his horse in broad daylight through the high street of Wakefield.[2]

Highwaymen, rioters, smugglers, and a whole dangerous underworld defied the government, and government itself, from the pensioned peer to the bribed elector, was corrupt. By modern standards it was clumsy and inefficient. There were scandals, more often exposed than corrected, in every executive department. There was scarcely a man in high place who was above suspicion, nor a subordinate who was strictly controlled. Yet, in spite of everything, the liberty, good and bad, was less remarkable

[1] For the whole subject see M. Beloff, *Public Order and Popular Disturbances, 1660–1714* (1938).
[2] Oliver Heywood, *Diary*, ed. Horsfall Turner, iv. 57; see also *Dict. of Nat. Biog.*, s.v. 'Nevison, John'.

than the success, the tremendous achievements, of the British state. There was misery and confusion; but there was victory. Contemporaries did not give themselves the trouble of inquiring into this paradox. They explained it by the courage of British soldiers and sailors, the 'conduct' of British generals and admirals, and the general superiority of everything that was British to everything that was foreign, and particularly of freemen to slaves. They saw that the long constitutional struggle had given them freedom, the freedom which they had demanded, the sum of hundreds of parliamentary resolutions which their kings had withstood. They did not reflect that they had paid for their liberties by turning the commonwealth into a fighting machine. There was a standing army. There was a fleet which cost nearly as much as the army. Public finance was so organized that it could support these great forces for years together, and at the same time pour out millions in subsidies to foreign allies. Behind it the private organization of the city, closely linked to it by the Bank, could raise supplementary foreign loans. The clothing industry, the lead and copper mines, the foundries and forges, the shipyards and the colonial forests could equip and supply the fighting forces of half Europe. A century of great wars had begun, and the nation was organized to face it.

In this organization the keystone was constitutional. In France and Prussia and almost everywhere militarism and autocracy went hand in hand, but what enabled Britain to deploy its strength by land and sea was the Revolution settlement. The main lines of policy were laid down by a small gathering of ministers who had at their disposal full departmental information about foreign affairs, finance, military and naval preparations, and trade. By means of parliament the ministers brought into the service of that policy the wealth and man-power of the nation. From 1713, by standing order of the house of commons, the government has had the sole right of initiating financial business there; but parliament with its high claims and privileges, was not an easy body to manage. The ministers got into difficulties and even into dangers if they failed to keep the two houses and the two parties in order. The parliamentary machine was liable to jam, but when it was working it had the merit that its decisions appeared to its own members to be spontaneous. The cabinet governed parliament and parliament governed the country, but parliament and even the country believed that they were free. William Penn expressed the consequence in a general rule: 'Let the people think they govern and they will be governed.'[1] They might be turbulent and ill-policed, but they had not their equals in the world for paying taxes and submitting to the drains of war. There were, to be sure, limits beyond which they would not be led. In Queen Anne's reign these limits were approached so near as to stand clearly out. There was a limit to what policy might compass: 'no peace without Spain' was too much. There was a limit to the demands the army might make on the nation: it was touched when the principle of compulsory service was brought in. In 1703–4 all able-bodied men without visible employment or means of subsistence were made liable to serve. There were grumblings about the abuses to which this led, but not about the principle itself. It is said that a bill was introduced to compel each parish and corporation to furnish a certain number of recruits; this was thought to be imitating France and not to be borne in a free country. But neither of these limits was narrow enough to cramp the aggressive tendency for many years to come. Policy remained ambitious of new markets and new colonies. The military and naval forces expanded enough to keep that policy fed. The British constitution was as successful as any other in mobilizing the national resources.

To understand fully the way in which this was done, it would be necessary to analyse the political structure of the country, and especially the representative machinery. It would be necessary to collect and tabulate thousands of facts about the genealogy, property, antecedents, connexions, investments, and ambitions of the thousands of men who sat in the house of commons. In time this will perhaps be done, as it is now being done for the period of George II and George III; but at present although many of the relevant facts are known, they are dumb from lack of correlation.[2] We do not know, for instance, precisely what numbers of members were controlled at different times by governments, by party clubs, by borough owners, or by influential peers and others who did not 'own' boroughs. We do not know whether the act of 1711 for a property qualification caused

[1] *Some Fruits of Solitude* (1693), no. 337.
[2] Although a number of useful contributions to this task have now been made, such as Mr. Walcott's essay mentioned on p. 223 above, I leave this sentence as it was originally written, if only to pay a tribute to the masterly work of Sir Lewis Namier, the first in this field.

any change in the social character of the house of commons. We do not even know how the earliest parliaments of the period compare in that respect with the latest. All these things are ascertainable and worth ascertaining; but even in our ignorance of them, we have ample evidence of one great fact about the representative system. Parliament was not the organ of a landed aristocracy divided on ecclesiastical, European, dynastic, and constitutional questions but united in its economic interests, On the contrary, it was a meeting-place where divergent economic interests were reconciled and combined so as to provide an adequate body of support for the government of the day.

The secret of British external power in the war of the Spanish succession is thus far from simple. One element in it was the comparative solidarity of the commercial and financial interests in supporting the war policy. Another was the common sense and grasp of the possibilities of the situation which caused the Scottish union to succeed and both the extreme war-policy and the Jacobite reaction to fail. This was the most valuable product of the now long experience of frequent parliaments.

XII

RELATIONS WITH SCOTLAND

THE period which begins with the Restoration has been called the most pitiful in the history of Scotland.[1] The evils from which England suffered, intolerance, oppression, bloodshed, turbulence, were worse there, and were not relieved by the compensating health of literature and intellectual life. Although the Scottish aristocracy was on the whole better educated and less insular than the English, few of its members contributed much to letters. Sir Robert Sibbald and the Edinburgh Philosophical Society, which met from 1705, had their part in the scientific movement, but it was a modest part. Economically Scotland was a poorer country. Edinburgh, the largest city, had some 20,000 inhabitants; Glasgow, the next largest, about 13,000. Aberdeen, Dundee, and St. Andrews had about 4,000 each; Perth, with slightly more, may be called the only other town. There was no body of merchants and manufacturers with the wealth and leisure which brought English trade and industry into fruitful contact with the movement of ideas. The only department in which the Scottish culture of the time left behind it work that is still alive was remote from affairs and from organized thought: there were, especially at the end of the period, some writers of songs. The conditions which were poisoning the lyrical impulse in England were not present here, and, though they depended on England for their best tunes, the Scottish writers were still able to sing about heroism and love without insuring themselves against being laughed at. None of them, however, wrote very much altogether or more than a little that was very good: it was just after the period ended that Allan Ramsay started the tradition of popular poetry which led on to Burns.

It would be untrue to say that Scotland gave nothing to English civilization. Two countries of such different historic traditions could not have lived side by side without mutual interchange, and in some things it was Scotland that gave and England that received. The Scottish universities, for instance,

[1] P. Hume Brown, *History of Scotland*, ii (1905), 379.

supported the growth of learning and education among the English nonconformists. Their sons, shut out from Oxford and Cambridge, were able to study at Glasgow. Their leaders were given honorary degrees, and this intercourse did something to save the English nonconformists from losing their hold on intellectual standards.[1] More generally the strength of the Scottish kirk was an encouragement to English presbyterians and other nonconformists. There were other things in which England learnt from Scotland. Already Scottish gardeners were drifting southwards. The regular army, from the first, owed much, as it has always owed much, to the inherited discipline and ability of Scottish professional soldiers. The medical school of Edinburgh began to lay the foundations of its great influence. But Scotland gave little to the main stream of English life. There was nothing to indicate the approach of a great school of philosophy and a great movement of imaginative literature. She seemed passively to undergo foreign influences, and if her lawyers went to learn in the Dutch universities and some of her noblemen drew more from French than from English manners, the strongest influence, filtering in through a thousand little openings, was that of England.

The English influence was most noticeable where it contrasted most with the old habits of Scotland and coincided with the modern tendencies of Europe in general. It helped secular interests to take the place of ecclesiastical as the first concern of the nation. It pointed out the direction in which Scotland was to seek emancipation from the material poverty to which so many of her difficulties were due. This was of course the direction taken by all mercantile states, that of encouraging manufactures and commerce by protective legislation. The poverty of Scotland was partly due to the lack of those resources which were most valuable at that time; but it was partly due to backwardness in ideas and methods. Although the lands suitable for corn were tolerably well developed, primitive systems prevailed in the much greater areas where only pasture could be profitable. The systems of tenure discouraged the cultivators from making improvements, and few of the landlords had the capital, though some had the will, to undertake clearing and planting and draining.

The parliament and privy council did little or nothing for

---

[1] Oldfield, Calamy, and Williams received degrees at Edinburgh in 1709 after the union, and Calamy also at St. Andrews and Aberdeen.

agriculture but they made many laws for industry. The exclusive privileges of corporations were stronger in Scotland than in England, and foreign trade was, in theory at least, much cramped by the monopoly of the convention of royal burghs and the system of the staple. Both the legislature and the judiciary did something to clear these restrictions;[1] but most of their constructive efforts failed. It appears to be the fact that Scottish shipping, like English, increased considerably in the period, in spite of the exclusion of Scotland from the English navigation system; and this may be partly due to the effects of protective laws. As a whole, however, the legislation seems to have imitated that of England without allowing for the great differences between the two countries. It is improbable that the whole population of Scotland at any time in the period reached one million. Most likely it was about 800,000 and if it increased, the increase was not great. The country was too small for the drastic restriction of imports and exports attempted in successive tariff laws, especially in that of 1663 which aimed at freeing Scotland from England's economic domination. There was so little capital available that only a small number of monopolistic trading companies could be established: the one great success of this kind was the Bank of Scotland, founded in 1695, one year after the Bank of England, as a private banking concern with capital of only £100,000 sterling. When a council of trade was set up in 1661 with extensive powers, it was given a task in which only a limited success was possible and no success worth mentioning was actually achieved.

The termination of the union with England which had existed under the Protectorate had a detrimental economic effect, well understood at the time, and this was one reason why so much energy was devoted to economic legislation. After thirty years of experience, this energy was directed more and more against England and commercial enterprises became more and more mixed up with political questions. An attempt in 1667 to negotiate a commercial treaty was a failure; in 1670 commissioners of the two countries, England being the less willing party, negotiated in London but failed to agree on terms for a constitutional union. In the end a legislative union of the two countries became an economic necessity for Scotland. The same

[1] See Miss Theodora Keith in *Eng. Hist. Rev.* xxviii. 678, and J. Davidson and A. Gray, *The Scottish Staple at Vere* (1909).

K

period of friction and conflict made it a political necessity for England. For a century wise men in both kingdoms had seen that the union of the two crowns in one person would not be enough. They had tried to solve the problem of reconciling good political organization with diversity of race and traditions. Hitherto they had not succeeded. Perhaps there was altogether too little intercourse between the two countries. Scotland had a narrow frontier and a mountainous interior. England had never been free for long from foreign or civil war. The civil wars had cut across the national division, giving each party in England a body of friends in the north and each Scottish party a body of English friends. Consequently, although armies had marched from each country across the border, there had not been a collision of the whole of one nation with the whole of the other. There was not such a national enmity as the Hungarians felt for the Austrians or the Catalans for Castile. Although the journey towards the union seemed to be one of growing mutual exasperation, the clearest eyes always saw that only a common policy could give England safety or Scotland prosperity.

The principle of the Stuart Restoration was that loyalty to the king was a sufficient basis for political co-operation whether between individuals or between the two kingdoms. Charles II's initial arrangements showed no such leanings to compromise as those for England. He chose his privy council without consulting parliament, and he caused the great marquis of Argyle, the chief of the covenanters, to be arrested. Argyle was acquitted on the main charge of being accessory to the death of Charles I. On the evidence of letters compromising enough, but communicated by George Monck of all people, he was condemned to death for complying with the usurping government. There could not have been a plainer case of condemning a man not for his crimes but for what it was feared he might do if he lived. The Restoration was, however, marked by clemency no less in Scotland than in England. Besides Argyle there were only three other victims. Nor was the constitutional settlement such as to give serious offence. The parliament which met in 1661 annulled the proceedings of all parliaments since 1639.[1] It provided for a militia which, although the full establishment was never made

---

[1] Mr. Godfrey Davies has drawn my attention to the texts of the two relevant statutes in *Acts of the Parliament of Scotland*, vii (1820), 86–88. They show discrepancies which have caused confusion as to their exact effects.

up, was meant to number 20,000 foot and 2,000 horse. The same parliament voted an annual grant of the excessive sum of £40,000. This remained as a standing burden on the country and relieved the king from the necessity of summoning further parliaments. After the dissolution of the first in 1663 the country was governed by the privy council, and parliaments seldom met in the remainder of Charles's reign. But parliaments in Scotland had no such standing as in England. Constitutional life ran so thin that they were hardly missed. There was no popular agitation for summoning them, and the attention of the people was fixed on the rivalries of political noblemen and, above all, on religious affairs.

The ecclesiastical settlement of 1661 was more than reactionary. It was a return to the episcopalian arrangements of James VI and Charles I, but during the long interval in which that state of things had been upset, a larger proportion of the aristocracy had become alienated from the presbyterian cause, and there was now a far better prospect than under Charles I of enforcing the royal will. The bishops were restored to parliament as in England. All ministers who had received their charges direct from their congregations and presbyteries, without presentation by patrons and collation by bishops, were to seek the authority of these persons. Between two and three hundred of them, or about a third of the whole body, a larger proportion than in England, preferred ejection. Most of these and of their adherents remained irreconcilable, as did their children and their grandchildren, until episcopacy ceased to be established and until the kirk was permitted to hold free general assemblies. The seeds of trouble were thus present from the beginning, and there were personal factors which embittered the inevitable resentment. The new archbishop of St. Andrews and primate of Scotland was James Sharp, a man hated by the presbyterians as a turncoat. He had helped to bring about the Restoration, and he had perhaps never been deeply attached to presbyterianism; but his change of sides was disastrous to his old associates and profitable to himself.

Sharp was a distant relation of the earl of Rothes, who was high in office during the earlier years of the reign and had to take the blame for the first serious disturbances which resulted from the ecclesiastical policy. Most of the ejections of ministers had been in the south-western counties, Ayr, Lanark, Dumfries, and

Galloway, which had a long record of religious opposition. There the devotion of the people to their old ministers and the insults and occasional violence offered to the new now led to a series of repressive measures which made matters worse. In 1663 heavy fines were imposed for non-attendance at church. By an act of the privy council even more severe than the English Five Mile Act the ejected ministers were forbidden to live within twenty miles of their parishes, within six miles of any cathedral church, or within three miles of any royal borough. Troops were quartered in the discontented counties to assist in levying the recusancy fines. For two years from 1664 a new court of high commission, founded at the suggestion of Archbishop Sharp, inflicted penalties which were irritating without being effective. By the time of the Dutch war the government was afraid of rebellion, the more so since rebellion might be combined with invasion. The council issued orders for disarming the disaffected districts and securing the persons of some twenty of their leading gentry. They had against them, however, the mass of the people in those parts. These were now gathering for worship in the only way left open to them, in field-meetings on remote moors and hillsides, with watchers on the heights around to give the alarm if the soldiery were seen. Of the officers who hunted them one of the most zealous was Sir James Turner, more honourably remembered as a writer on the military art. On 25 November 1666 he was in Dumfries on duty, when a party of men from Galloway made him their prisoner and marched him off with them into Ayrshire. This was the beginning of the Pentland Rising. It gathered perhaps three thousand men, poorly armed, undisciplined, and without a plan. They decided to march on Edinburgh, where they believed they would be well received, and in spite of the misery of a march in winter rain they refused vague offers of pardon if they would surrender to the royal commander, Sir Thomas Dalziel, who was following them up. The whole affair did not last a fortnight. The insurgent force dwindled fast. Coming within three miles of Edinburgh the rebels found that they had not the smallest hopes from the city. They headed straight for their own country across the bleak Pentland Hills, and on 8 December Dalziel closed with them on the ridge above Rullion Green. They lost only about a hundred killed and taken, but their resistance was broken and under cover of darkness they scattered in flight.

It was inevitable that the council should deal severely with this first outbreak, equally inevitable that every detail of the repression, the firmness of the martyrs under torture, the brutality of Rothes and the archbishop, should stiffen the spirit of the vanquished. Fifteen victims were hanged in the capital, four in Glasgow, some others in Ayr; but the rising had shaken the credit of the government and it led to a change of control which was meant to bring in a policy of reconciliation. Rothes and Sharp, though still in office, now definitely gave way to the influence of John Maitland, earl of Lauderdale, the leading figure in Scottish history for the next twelve years. Lauderdale's initial supplied the last letter in the name of the Cabal, and his rise was the Scottish counterpart of the fall of Clarendon. He, like Ashley, had begun as a presbyterian, and his correspondence with Richard Baxter in the years 1657–9 shows that his complex character was not without religion.[1] He had opposed a number of the more extreme measures of recent years, and his policy was at least more intelligent than that of mere suppression. He wanted to keep Scottish affairs in Scottish hands, and he was strongly against the proposals for a legislative union which were raised shortly after this time.[2] His method was to strengthen the royal prerogative, the English ministers taking no part in Scottish business. He was something of a scholar, and a realist through and through, nor did his heavy debaucheries harm his reputation as much as might have been expected. He began by proclaiming an indemnity, disbanding the army and dismissing Sir James Turner and others like him. In 1669 the First Letter of Indulgence was issued. This permitted such of the ejected ministers as had lived 'peaceably and orderly' to return to their livings if they happened to be vacant, accepting, of course, the episcopal establishment. About forty of the ejected took advantage of this, but the rest were naturally only further embittered. Shortly afterwards Lauderdale procured an Act of Supremacy which declared the king's authority to be supreme over all persons and in all ecclesiastical causes. This provoked a last

---

[1] It was published by Dr. F. J. Powicke in *Bulletin of the John Rylands Library*, vii (1922).

[2] In 1669 the matter was opened in both parliaments, and in 1670 it was discussed by commissioners at Westminster, but they failed to agree whether all or only some of the Scottish members should be joined to the English parliament. They were adjourned and never met again. The Scots suggested as an alternative occasional joint meetings of the two parliaments for business of special importance.

remonstrance from some of the episcopalians themselves, led by Alexander Burnet, archbishop of Glasgow, one of the worst persecutors of presbytery; but Lauderdale forced him to resign his see.

Five years later, probably in deference to the views of the English bishops, Burnet came back. On that side, and indeed on all sides, Lauderdale's policy could not achieve more than a temporary success. He was using the arts of the politician, the mixture of severity and conciliation which divides and undermines, not against men who could be bribed and persuaded, but against religious fanatics who would rather die and kill than forswear their beliefs. The Indulgences led to an increase of conventicles, and the worshippers now came armed. As early as 1670 a new act against conventicles was passed, and in 1673 the rise of parliamentary opposition on other matters, chiefly economic, pushed Lauderdale in the direction of fresh measures to prevent rebellion. He began to use against the presbyterians methods which had been used in Scotland against Roman catholics. Landlords and employers were declared responsible for the religious conformity of their tenants and workpeople. 'Letters of Intercommuning' were issued against individuals, that is letters ordering by the authority of the state a complete boycott of their persons. More than a hundred of these were issued in 1675. In 1677 a step was taken which alienated many substantial and reasonable people who had hitherto been quiet. Landowners were required to give bonds for the good behaviour of all persons residing on their lands. That was to make them responsible for men they could not control; and when many in the disaffected counties refused, this was taken as proof that there was immediate danger of a new rebellion. In 1678 therefore a new army was sent down with orders to take up quarters wherever it might be found convenient except in the houses of loyal persons indicated by the privy council. It consisted of 3,000 Lowland militia and 6,000 Highlanders. History knows it as the 'Highland host'. The Highlanders were the terror of the Lowlands, predatory clansmen whom good government kept in awe. To appeal to them was to appeal to lawlessness itself; but even this appeal failed, and after a month the host dispersed to its valleys, leaving fresh bitterness behind it.

The explosion came in 1679, when England was distracted by the Popish Plot. Of all the persecutors the most hated was Archbishop Sharp. He had insisted on the unjust condemnation of one James Mitchell for an attempt made on his life ten years before. There was not, however, any other premeditated attempt made against him. On 13 May 1679 twelve desperate men, outlaws for religion, were hunting among the lanes of Fife for the sheriff-substitute who was the chief agent of persecution there. They missed their quarry, but in the evening on Magis Muir, four miles above St. Andrews town, they saw coming from the direction of Edinburgh an unguarded coach and six. It was the archbishop, returning with his daughter from a council day. Believing that God had delivered him into their hands, they fired and missed him. He had a magical charm against bullets, they guessed. They had no silver bullet to break it with, so they dragged him out and hacked with their swords. It was a horrible revenge, and it was a signal for extremities on both sides. Before the end of the month armed men were demonstrating in a village near Glasgow. Others hastened to join them and on Sunday, 21 June, it came to a fight. Sending away the women and children who had come to worship with them, the covenanters took up a position on a boggy slope. They were a few hundred foot armed with muskets and pitchforks and a few score horse: they heavily outnumbered the troop of horse confidently led up against them by Captain James Graham of Claverhouse, an experienced officer home from the continental wars. Claverhouse was too confident. The ground was against him, and his men ran.

Such was the 'battle' of Drumclog. It was not, as Claverhouse thought, the first act of a planned rebellion: that was proved by events in the next few days. The insurgents gathered force and the government troops fell back before them, but they had no plans and no organization. They could not agree on a declaration of their grievances: they were divided as to whether the Indulgences were such or not. What the 'battle' and its consequences did prove was that Lauderdale's system of government had broken down, and the king acted wisely in sending his son Monmouth to Scotland to command the militia of the loyal counties. Monmouth was a soldier, personally attractive, and his marriage had given him position and interests in Scotland. As early as 2 July the two armies were facing one another across the Clyde where the road from Hamilton to Glasgow crosses Bothwell Brig. The rebels sent a deputation offering to surrender if they were promised a free parliament and a free general assembly of the kirk; but that was to ask for the undoing of the whole ecclesiastical settlement, and Monmouth refused. He moved against the bridge, and the rebel commander mismanaged its defence so miserably that nothing could have been worse. His men lost about four hundred killed and three times as many prisoners. This too does not deserve the name of a battle. It was merely the first hour of another season of punishment.

The number of executions was less than after the Pentland Rising: there were only seven. The crowds of prisoners from the rank and file were barbarously misused, and two hundred of them were drowned in a shipwreck on their way to servitude in the Barbados. Monmouth, however, in accordance with his instructions,[1] stood for clemency and understanding, and before the year was out he procured an Act of Indemnity and a third futile Act of Indulgence. Lauderdale was attacked by powerful enemies both in England and in Scotland. Even before the rising a petition for his removal on account of his friendship with the duke of York had been rejected by the English house of commons by a majority of only one. The king stood by him, but his active career was over and he never saw Scotland again. In 1680 he had a stroke, and he lingered only for two more years. In Scotland the king's next representative was the duke of York himself. His appointment, as we have already seen, enabled him to be near England and at the same time away from the disturbances of which he was the centre. It marked the decline of the influence of Monmouth and Shaftesbury. At the same time it put Scotland in strong hands, and it enabled James to take measures there to secure his own future. In a parliament in 1681 he obtained two acts which ensured his safe succession to that crown, whatever might happen in the southern kingdom. The first declared that no difference in religion could disqualify a rightful successor. The second imposed a test on all persons holding office in church or state and all members of parliament and electors. It originated with a motion that all such persons should take an oath to adhere firmly to the protestant religion; but the court party added further clauses condemning all resistance, renouncing the covenant, obliging the takers to defend all the king's rights and prerogatives, without meeting to treat of any matter, civil or ecclesiastical, but by the king's permission, and never to endeavour any alteration of the government in

[1] These were printed by Dr. C. Sanford Terry in *Eng. Hist. Rev.* xx. 127.

church or state. The protestant religion was defined as that of
the forgotten confession of faith of 1567. The extraordinary
logical confusion of the resulting oath, with a mixture of presbyterian and episcopalian elements and an unlimited submission
to prerogative, made it intellectually contemptible, but it served
its purpose. The head of the judiciary resigned his office rather
than take it. About eighty of the clergy gave up their livings.
The earl of Argyle, the son of the great marquis, agreed to take
the oath 'as far as it was consistent with itself'. For making this
reservation he was found guilty of high treason, but he had the
good fortune, after sentence of death, to escape from Edinburgh
Castle in disguise and to make his way to Holland. When James
returned to England in the spring of 1682 he had brought the
political machinery of Scotland into a subservience equal to
that which his brother was exacting in England.

He had not, however, made any progress in subduing the
extremists of the south-west. There was not, in the nature of
things, any new policy that he could devise for them, and none
of the small variations of which the old policy was capable could
have any effect except to harden their determination. James
has indeed been denounced by historians for taking part in the
persecution of one sect while he himself belonged to a persecuted
church for which he desired toleration. Many persecutors of all
confessions in the sixteenth and seventeenth centuries lie open
to that charge; but James has the justification that his opponents
were rebels in arms against the law, who would have over-
thrown what he believed to be the sacred rights of the Crown.
There is no evidence that he delighted in his work. In his personal dealings he appears to have been not less conciliatory than
Monmouth; but he had to reckon with men whom he never
met, and whom nothing could have conciliated.

In 1680 their history entered on a new stage: they formed themselves into a sect, known to themselves as 'the Society People' and
to others, after one of their leaders, Richard Cameron, as the
'Cameronians', a name best known now as that of the regiment
of infantry which was formed from them in happier times. They
publicly disavowed their allegiance to King Charles. A month
later Cameron was killed in a desperate fight, and in the next
year a second leader Donald Cargill was hanged with five others.
No longer keeping to self-defence they ambushed the agents of
the government, and the government retorted by giving the

soldiers power to shoot without trial any one who refused to re-
pudiate their 'Apologetical Declaration'. The cruel scenes of this
warfare are still living chapters in the martyrology of Scotland.

The accession of James as king made the struggle more savage
on both sides. Military executions continued, Claverhouse being
the most prominent officer engaged in them, and hundreds of
minor offenders were shipped to the American colonies after
having one ear cut off. Yet in spite of the guerrilla warfare in the
south-west James succeeded as quietly as in England. A parliament met and gave every expression of devotion to his person.
It granted him the excise for life, though Charles had had it only
for terms of years, and it passed an act to inflict the penalty of
death on all persons, preachers, or hearers who should merely
be present at conventicles. While this parliament was sitting
there came the attempted rebellion of Argyle, the northern
movement linked with that of Monmouth, and its moral was
that in spite of everything the king was master of Scotland.
Argyle and a group of Scottish exiles had concerted their measures
with Monmouth and his friends in Holland. Argyle sailed first
with arms and about three hundred men in three small ships. It
was a hopeless enterprise. Argyle was not the man to lead it and
had only a divided command. He came too slowly and the
government, warned beforehand, quartered troops among his
own highlanders to prevent their rising. Memories of former rebellions helped to deter all but a few hundreds from joining his
standard. The south-west was too cowed for an open rising. An
ill-advised attempt was made to land in Ayrshire, and after that
the united forces of the rebels attempted to march from the
western highlands on Glasgow. They were followed by a much
stronger royal force, and when they reached the Clyde at Kilpatrick they could no longer hold together. On 18 June Argyle
was caught by the militia. He was not brought to trial but
executed under his unjust sentence of four years before.

In Scotland, however, as in England, King James failed to
keep his adherents together. He did not alienate the whole
nation, but his system broke down and there was a Scottish
revolution, partly consequent on the English but altogether
different in character and even partly independent in its actual
occurrence. In 1686 trouble began over religion. The lord
chancellor (the earl of Perth) and the two secretaries of state,
one of whom was his brother, became Roman catholics. This

brother, Lord Melfort, was given the place of high commissioner
to the parliament when its holder, the duke of Queensberry, refused to make the change. Roman catholic services were held
openly, and at the beginning of the year there was a riot against
them in Edinburgh. In a letter to the parliament James announced that he was doing his utmost to bring about free trade
with England; but he also recommended the repeal of the penal
laws against Roman catholics. The parliament replied politely
but without promising anything, and James without hesitation
turned to the prerogative. He wrote to the privy council requir-
ing it to rescind the penal laws, and stating that his request to
parliament had been a mere act of courtesy. In order to give
effect to his wishes he removed eleven protestant privy councillors and put catholics in their places. The great part of the
beneficed clergy were alarmed by these measures, and their
expressions of concern led to results even more alarming. The
archbishop of Glasgow and the bishop of Dunkeld were deprived. James, however, did not fail to extend his toleration to
both sides. In 1687, at the time of his English Declaration of
Indulgence, he issued successive Letters of Indulgence, the latest
of which was framed to include all but the most obdurate presbyterians. It permitted all his subjects to worship God after their
own manner, provided they taught nothing to alienate the
hearts of the subjects from their prince.

   The policy of toleration almost succeeded. The persecution of
the Cameronians continued, and they had a last martyr in
James Renwick, who refused to purchase his life by recognizing
the government; but the majority of the presbyterians accepted
what was offered with relief. Catholic propaganda was carried
on by means of the press and of education and there was under-
ground discontent; but in Scotland there was no movement of
resistance. Preparations were made in 1687 for a new parliament
which was to be thoroughly packed by the use of prerogative,
and if it had ever met it would no doubt have carried out the
king's will. When the crisis came in England, however, James
had to let Scotland take care of itself. In September 1688 the
eastern counties were put in a state of defence, but in October
the troops were ordered to march to England.[1] When William
landed the Scottish government had no effective force at its
command. His supporters openly gathered in Edinburgh,

   [1] Colin, third earl of Balcarres in *Somers Tracts*, ed. Scott, xi. 495.

whence the lord chancellor tried in vain to make his escape. The catholic chapel in Holyrood was wrecked by the mob. In the south-western counties the presbyterians took the law into their own hands. At Christmas they 'rabbled' the two hundred intruding ministers, killing none, but turning them and their families out of doors among a hostile people.

The main decisions about the future of Scotland were taken in London. William summoned a meeting of the Scottish estates, which, without special pressure, contained a majority of his supporters; and, although Edinburgh Castle was still held for James by the duke of Gordon, no attempt was made to interfere with their work. Claverhouse, now Viscount Dundee, 'Bonny Dundee', after trying for a few days to work for James's interests in the convention, looked to his safety and rode out of the West Port at the head of his troops of horse. On 11 April, the day of the coronation at Westminster, the convention declared William and Mary king and queen, thus carrying out rather late in the day what the English events had made inevitable. The offer was accompanied by a Claim of Right which went much farther than the corresponding English declaration. It declared that the estates had the constitutional right to depose a king who had violated the laws, and it enumerated a long list of violations by which James had forfeited the crown. There was thus no attempt to mix the strict doctrine of the accountability of princes with the idea of abdication. Another clause was inserted which had no bearing on the issues immediately raised by James's proceedings: it said that the reformation in Scotland having been begun by a parity of the clergy, all prelacy in that church was a great and insupportable grievance to that kingdom. The practical effect of this was that the re-establishment of the presbyterian kirk in some form or another was made a condition of the calling of William and Mary to the throne. There were also a number of constitutional principles implied in the counts against James, and these included not only the denial of such prerogatives as that of levying custom duties without parliamentary sanction, but one of far greater moment. This was the illegality of the committee of the lords of the articles, the significance of which we shall notice later.

These main lines of the settlement had been laid down, but its detailed application had not been worked out, when it was put to the test of military force. The Lowlands were, outwardly at

least, as much William's as England. Edinburgh Castle surrendered in June 1689. In the Highlands, however, the fallen
king had many loyal friends. While he was in Scotland James
had maintained good relations with many of the chiefs. The old
religion was strong among them. Those who held the vast estates
forfeited by Argyle had reason to fear that they would be displaced by his son, who had sailed with William's expedition and,
in spite of his legal disqualification, had taken his seat in the convention. There was a leader at hand who had all the qualities
needed for making the best military use of the clansmen. After
his withdrawal from Edinburgh Claverhouse had been followed
by the well-founded suspicions of the government, and when
summoned to return to the sittings of the convention, he disappeared into the country of the Gordons. While he was collecting his irregular army, he was watched by Major-General Hugh
Mackay, a capable and experienced officer. When the two forces
met, Mackay had with him about three thousand foot, four
troops of cavalry, and four of dragoons or mounted infantry,
many of them untrained. Dundee was weaker in numbers.
Mackay set out to march up from Perth through Dunkeld to
take possession of the marquis of Atholl's castle of Blair, which
was being held for James. Blair Atholl overlooks the main route
by the river Garry through the heart of the mountains to Inverness. Less than four miles below it the river rushes through the
deep gorge of Killiecrankie. Mackay's force made its way
through the gorge and took up a position in the more open
valley above, but before its dispositions were complete the
enemy appeared on the higher slope. The fight was like one
stroke of lightning. Half an hour before sunset the highlanders
ran down the hill. The waiting infantry fired, but while they
were still fumbling with their bayonets, the old plug bayonets
which shut up the muzzles of their muskets, the claymores were
cutting at them and they broke. Mackay kept his head. For all
the confusion his casualties were the less, and with the remnant
that kept together he retreated in good order. Three days later
he was at Stirling, gathering reinforcements, and he promptly
marched northwards again. The Highlands were alive with preparations, but they had lost their leader. Claverhouse had fallen
in the charge at Killiecrankie, killed it was thought by a silver
bullet.

His successor, Colonel Cannon, did badly, and the one other

important action of the campaign showed that there were heroic qualities engaged against the Stuart cause. The government had taken into its service a regiment of the Cameronians, and they served with all their unequalled determination. Contrary to the advice of Mackay they were allowed to take up an isolated position in Dunkeld, where all the surrounding country was hostile and they were attacked by a much more numerous body of highlanders under Cannon. They fought like heroes. Their commander, William Cleland, was killed but the enemy fell back in disorder. The highlanders had dash without discipline or staying power, and from that time they did not threaten or disturb the Lowlands for another twenty-six years. Scotland had in fact, in freedom from actual fighting, as good peace during that period as England. There was a Highland problem, but it was the problem of governing the highlanders in their own homes, not that of keeping back their armies from the passes. They did not indeed give up the practice of cattle-lifting from their lowland neighbours, and the districts near the Highland line were constantly understocked and often pillaged. Nothing could be done to undermine the social system which made the clansmen such uncomfortable neighbours. However power fluctuated between the Campbells and their enemies, there remained the devotion of the clansmen and the heritable jurisdictions of their chiefs. The task of assimilation had to wait until loyalty to the Stuarts was only a romantic memory. What could be done was to prevent disorder from gathering into organized interference with the government, and the means for this were military. Mackay retained his command until late in the year 1690, suppressing an attempted rising and founding Fort William at the most important strategic point of the north-west.

In Edinburgh the Revolution settlement took its course. In church matters a settlement was reached which satisfied the overwhelming majority. The Claim of Right roundly declared episcopacy illegal. The parliament of 1690 abolished the royal supremacy and everything that could fairly be called Erastianism. The kirk was re-established as a separate authority independent of the state within its own sphere, and its moral authority was such that it really achieved and kept independence. Private patronage was abolished. A free general assembly was allowed to meet in 1690, and its democratic system of election made it a far truer and more authoritative representative of the nation

than any Scots parliament ever was. Happily the spirit of compromise was strong at that time, and the general assembly did
not revive those extreme pretensions which might have divided
the nation afresh. It never again claimed, as it had done under
Charles I, a right to nullify acts of parliament and forbid the
faithful to obey them. In 1693 a conflict over the right of the
assembly to determine its own meeting and dissolution was
avoided by a masterly procedure which is still used. Its elected
moderator and the royal commissioner both independently
announce the date, and by a pre-established harmony each
chooses the same day. The irreconcilable minority were bitterly
disappointed by the settlement. They were no longer persecuted,
but they saw an uncovenanted king, an uncovenanted parliament, and a kirk established by acts of state. Even their ministers
deserted them, but they continued as a separate body, refusing
to take oaths of allegiance and perpetuating their tradition. The
episcopalians fared ill. After the first 'rabbling' of episcopalian
ministers there was a clearance of those who refused the oaths to
William and Mary, and the work was methodically carried on
by commissions appointed by the general assembly. The clergy
then deprived were so harshly treated that the government
interfered to check the inquisition. In spite of this harshness the
settlement was far more solid than that of the church of England.
No effective support was given to their Scottish brethren by the
English bishops. The national church was allowed to resume its
polity without interference from outside. From that time Scotland was not politically shaken by religious disputes. The minorities were too weak to disturb the power of the ministers, and that
power became something like a social tyranny. But their very
success in their own sphere led them to be concerned less with
that of politics, where the secular tendency steadily gained
ground.

All this made the relations of Scotland with England simpler.
It eliminated religious questions from them. There was no longer
any inducement for either country to interfere with the church
polity of the other.[1] In two other ways the Revolution radically
altered their relations. The dynastic change affected them
differently. Scotland counted a much larger proportion of Jacobites than England, and in Scotland they had what they had
not in England, whole areas which they controlled and where

[1] For the exceptions to this statement see below, p. 291.

they could offer a welcome to an invasion. In the period of foreign wars which now began this went far to undo the unity in foreign policy which had resulted from the union of the crowns. Since 1603 Scotland had had no separate foreign policy. In diplomacy the king had been rightly referred to as *sa majesté britannique*. Now, however, Scotland might easily become as much a separate unit in the calculations of foreign statesmen as it had been in the time of Mary Queen of Scots. This possibility was reinforced by the other change of the time, the change in the constitutional position of the Scots parliament. Hitherto the parliament had been, in the modern phrase, a non-sovereign legislature. Through the committee of the lords of the articles it had been amenable to royal control, and, though it had some- times had an opposition party among its members, it had never been, like the English parliament, the chief centre of public life. Now that the lords of the articles were abolished, the parliament had the full power of initiating legislation and controlling all its stages up to the royal assent. It was thus able to lead opposition to England and to the Crown as it had never done before, and it did in fact do so until the legislative union.

William III saw clearly that legislative union would reduce the dangers of the dynastic situation, but unhappily his reign was marked by much friction between the two countries, and in two outstanding incidents he personally incurred odium in Scotland. The first arose out of the Highland problem. In the spring and summer of 1691 there were signs of unrest among the clans of the north-west, who had hopes of a French invasion; and the govern- ment distributed several thousands of pounds in bribes to keep them quiet, at the same time ordering the suspected chiefs to take an oath of allegiance before the fixed date of New Year's Day of 1692. In anticipation of widespread refusals 'letters of fire and sword' were drawn up in the long accustomed form, order- ing wholesale ravaging and slaughter. But this severity was not needed. The chieftains came in to take the oath. A single Jaco- bite chieftain, Macdonald of Glencoe, by accident presented himself too late for the appointed day. He had fought at Killie- crankie and his men were reputed to be as troublesome as any in the Highlands. Sir John Dalrymple, the master of Stair, who as under-secretary of state was the king's adviser in London on Scottish affairs, little thinking that such a step would cause any outcry, decided that an example should be made of these Macdonalds. He laid before the king an order for their extirpation. It is probable that the king did not read it: we know that he often signed papers so hurriedly that he did not know their contents.[1] At any rate his signature is still to be seen on the paper. The cruel order was treacherously carried out. Rather more than a hundred soldiers from Fort William, most of them highlanders of Argyle's regiment, were quartered on the valley. After living amicably with their hosts for more than a week they set about the work of massacre. Many of their intended victims escaped, but they butchered the chief himself, and with him thirty-three men, two women, and two children.

Jealousy of Dalrymple and hostility to the government of William led to an agitation which had never been aroused by the many similar affairs of earlier years. The news of it was industriously spread by Jacobite pamphleteers, and, however much allowance we make for party feeling, we must recognize that the details of the massacre were such as to outrage decent opinion. In 1693 the king instructed some Scottish statesmen to inquire into the matter, but they failed to make any report and the protests grew louder. In 1695 a Scots parliament was to meet, and it was expected to take the matter up. William anticipated its action by appointing a regular commission of inquiry. As a result of its excellent report Dalrymple had to resign and spend the remainder of the reign in private life. The earl of Breadalbane, who had acted with him, was charged with high treason, but never brought to trial. That was all that was done to punish the offenders. The general execration of the deed helped to build up the British sense of justice and humanity. There were still to be scenes of cruelty in the Highlands as long as the Stuarts called their friends to arms; but never again were the worst methods of frontier warfare combined with the worst methods of secret police.

The same parliament of 1695 passed an act for the Encouragement of Trade which led to the second untoward incident of the reign, the incident of the Darien scheme. Considerable numbers of Scotsmen had settled in the English colonies in America,[2] and

---

[1] See the valuable *Journaal* (1689–96) of his secretary Constantijn Huygens the younger (2 vols., 1876–7), many entries in which amply confirm Burnet's statement that William 'was apt to suffer things to run on till there was a great heap of papers laid before him, so then he signed them a little too precipitately' (folio ed., ii. 89).

[2] The most important separate settlements were those of the covenanters at Stuart's Town in South Carolina (1684) and the quakers in West New Jersey (see below, p. 340), both under the English flag.

even those who had been deported for political offences or common crimes had made good colonists. Scotland had, however, no colony of her own. Nor had she any company for oceanic trade. Various projects for colonies and companies had come near to success, and it was in harmony with the general tendency of economic legislation that they should be encouraged. In 1693 an act was passed which declared that Scottish merchants were at liberty to form companies for trading in all kinds of commodities in all parts of the world with which his Majesty was not at war. This act, however, was not a simple product of economic nationalism. If it had been that, it would have been no more than a paper project, for Scotland could not afford to engage in mercantilism on any great scale. The act was in fact partly promoted, like other Scottish enterprises of the time, by London merchants some, but not all, of whom were Scots. They saw in Scotland's legislative independence an opening for their own capital. It provided a base for operating against the monopoly of the English African and East India Companies. It would save them from the dubious status of the interloper and make them lawful competitors under another flag. The native Scottish impulse was strong, but it was the wealth and experience of the London group which now gave it its direction. After discussions between the interested persons in London and Edinburgh the act of 1693 was followed up by that of 1695, which constituted the Company of Scotland Trading to Africa and the Indies.

This Company was to have a monopoly of trade with Asia and Africa for all time and of trade with America for thirty-one years. Its monopoly was to be supported by valuable exemptions from customs duties and by other legal privileges. It was to have the right to found colonies in any part of Asia, Africa, or America not already in the occupation of a European sovereign. The relations between the London and the Scottish directors were never perfectly harmonious. The capital was fixed by the London promoters at £600,000 sterling, half to be subscribed in England and half in Scotland, a much larger sum than was contemplated in Edinburgh or by William Paterson, the principal organizer after the initial steps had been taken. Paterson was a man of more imagination than judgement who, like so many other 'projectors' or company-promoters, had enough knowledge and energy to take a hand in great schemes, but not enough common sense to make him a business man. He had been in the West

Indies, and, after making money in the city of London had
been in at the foundation of the Bank of England; but, after
serving as a director for the first year, he had quarrelled with his
colleagues and sold out. He was responsible for many of the mistakes of the Scottish company, but not for the flaw in its original
conception which revealed itself almost exactly at the moment
when the London half of the capital was declared to be duly
subscribed.

On that day, 2 December 1695, the English parliament met,
and the subject was at once raised in the house of lords. The
stock of the East India Company had been falling since August,
when it reached 91, and in one week of October it had dropped
from 72 to 50.[1] It was natural that the company should seek to
defend its monopoly by all means. There had been irregularities
in the giving of the royal assent to the Scottish Act: the king's
commissioner had neglected to submit it to the king, and its
contents probably went farther than the king anticipated. For
whatever reason the king replied to an address of both houses:
'I have been ill served in Scotland, but I hope some remedy may
yet be found to meet the inconvenience that may arise from that
Act.' The commissioner and the secretary of state concerned in
it were dismissed. The English house of commons, detecting
technical illegalities in the proceedings of the promoters, appointed a committee to draw up articles of impeachment against
no fewer than twenty-three persons. An essential witness against
them disappeared, and a royal proclamation failed to bring
about his surrender, so the impeachments were dropped; but
enough had been done to crush the English participation in the
scheme. The English shareholders got out of it, and left the
Scots to their own devices.

Scotland responded with an extraordinary national effort to
support the company. Since English money was not to be had,
the amount to be raised in Scotland was increased to £400,000,
and between February and August 1696 this great sum was
promised, though less than half of it was ever paid. More than
1,300 persons of every rank had signed their names, many of
them risking all they had, and their extravagant hopes of gain
were fanned by real national enthusiasm. The directors were un-
worthy of their trust. They showed from first to last an airy
disregard of difficulties which they ought to have faced. They

[1] Rogers, *Hist. of Agriculture and Prices*, vi (1887), 721.

infringed the monopoly of the Bank of Scotland, but the Bank was shrewd enough to wait without complaining. The emissaries whom they sent, quite legitimately, to buy ships in Hamburg and Amsterdam, were given wider and impossible commissions. They were to negotiate for a free port in the Hanse Towns, without authority from King William, whose diplomatic representative stopped the plan by a simple disavowal. They were to open trading relations and even raise subscriptions there and in Amsterdam, as if the merchants there would take less umbrage at their competition than those of London. These fantastic hopes did no harm because they led to nothing, but a decision was taken while the subscriptions were coming in which led to utter disaster. On the advice of Paterson it was decided to establish a colony on the Isthmus of Darien.

The place they chose was on the Atlantic coast, 150 miles nearer to South America than the point where the Panama Canal now joins the oceans. It needed no special knowledge or ingenuity to see that somewhere in that region one of the world's great highways was destined to run: for generations the Spanish mule-trains had carried the silver of Peru across the isthmus to Puerto Bello. Every one knew of the exploits of the buccaneers in those waters: it was not thirty years since Sir Henry Morgan took Panama, and now there was in Edinburgh as adviser Lionel Wafer, who had crossed the isthmus with the buccaneers in 1680.[1] But the directors were misinformed about everything they ought to have known. They were wrong about the climate of their site, about its resources, about the political conditions. They ought to have known that the good days of buccaneering were over. When they took their decision the Spaniards were in alliance with King William in the war against France; when it was put into effect the peace of Ryswick had made all the European powers favourable to combined efforts to establish peace beyond the line. The delicate negotiations over the Spanish succession had begun; and in London the Spanish ambassador protested against the violation of Spanish territory. From the Scottish point of view it seemed an outrage, but from the king's European point of view he was merely fulfilling his duty to international law when in January 1699 he sent a circular letter to the governors of English colonies ordering them to refuse all aid or countenance to the colonists. They were engaged on a lawless

[1] See below, pp. 328-9.

enterprise which could not have been recognized then as it might have been recognized in the days of Drake. Nor was it carried out with any of the efficiency which was needed even in rougher times if lawlessness was to be condoned.

The first of three tragic expeditions to Darien sailed in July 1698, with three vessels. Short of supplies and threatened with a Spanish attack it gave up the attempt to found a settlement within a year. A second expedition of two ships and three hundred settlers arrived to find the place deserted. Shipwreck and fever added to the miseries of these two unsuccessful ventures. The third, which sailed in September 1699, renewed the attempt and even beat off a Spanish attack, but on the arrival of stronger enemy forces accepted honourable terms and evacuated the colony. Even from this last voyage, however, not one of the four ships returned to Scotland. With a single exception all the enterprises of the Company were disastrous. The ship *African Merchant* returned in July 1700 from a trading voyage on the west coast of Africa which yielded a net profit of £46,668 Scots, or about £3,800 sterling. That was all there was to set against the loss of the whole of the Company's paid-up capital, with hundreds of lives, and humiliation which could not be computed. The national feeling which had blinded the subscribers now turned against England. Even before the last and worst news King William had written to Heinsius that the Scots, who were pressing for a reassembling of their parliament to discuss the affairs of the Company, were like raging madmen.[1] Fortunately he was not alone in drawing the right conclusion from this calamitous work of Scottish legislative independence. In his last message to the English parliament, he urged it to take steps to bring about a union.

Several years of friction and misunderstanding were still to pass before the great project could be carried out. The Darien scheme had a horrible sequel in the execution of Captain Green and two of his shipmates, of the English East Indiaman *Worcester*, on a false charge, which his judges knew to be false, of committing acts of piracy against the Company. But the cause of union was furthered by everything which showed the existing position to be intolerable. When Anne came to the throne this instability was shown by the revival of the dynastic question, by the new great war in the making of which Scottish statesmen had taken

[1] *Archives de la maison d'Orange-Nassau*, 3rd Ser., iii. 167.

no part, and by the growing violence of party divisions in the Scottish parliament. Both parliaments therefore addressed the queen with requests to appoint commissioners to negotiate for a legislative union. The position was not altogether favourable. The Scots parliament had been elected as long ago as 1689, and had sat by repeated adjournments ever since: the election of the new parliament took place while the commissioners were sitting, and it was uncertain how the new members would regard the great question. The English commissioners made this a pretext for allowing the discussions to drag; but their real reason probably was the old unwillingness to admit the Scots to equal privileges in trade and the colonies. On the two main issues there was agreement: there should be a common legislature and Scotland should accept the Hanoverian succession as it was laid down in the Act of Settlement. But when in February 1703 the commissioners adjourned until October they had failed. The Scots did not believe the English were in earnest and revoked the powers of their commissioners.

Their new parliament had a solid majority in favour of presbyterianism, fears for which had been increased by the tory attacks on dissenters in England. It was divided on everything else, and the divisions were rendered more violent and more confused by the personal rivalries of the leaders; but in the mood of the moment it was easier to combine in measures against England than for any other purpose. So much did the whig country party act with the episcopalians and Jacobites for this purpose, that it had been doubted whether some of its members were not aiming at reducing the policy to absurdity. By an act for the importation of foreign wines and liquors they dissociated Scotland from the English endeavours to support the French war by commercial pressure. Still more explicit was the challenge of the Act anent Peace and War, by which no future sovereign was to declare war on behalf of Scotland without the consent of the estates. The same consent was to be required for all treaties: thus foreign policy was no longer to lie in the king's hands. In the direction of limiting the prerogative no party was willing to go farther than this: there were few if any to follow the republican doctrinaire Fletcher of Saltoun, who proposed that national independence should be based on a strict limitation of monarchy. The lever which came nearest to their hands was dynastic policy, the only means by which they could at once add to their legal separateness and engage national feeling on their side. There were only two bonds of union between the two kingdoms. One, comparatively unimportant, was the common nationality enjoyed by all the queen's subjects. The other, from which this first one arose, was the personal union of the crowns,[1] and it was resolved to make the continuance of this union depend on the will of the Scottish parliament.

This was to be done by an Act of Security, according to which on the death of Queen Anne without issue, the estates were to name a successor from the protestant descendants of the royal line of Scotland, but this was not to be the same person as the admitted successor to the Crown of England unless 'there be such conditions of government settled and enacted as may secure the honour and sovereignty of this Crown and kingdom, the freedom, frequency, and power of parliaments, the religion, freedom, and trade of the nation, from English or any foreign influence'. There were other clauses to ensure the execution of the act, one of which was for the mustering of the whole able-bodied population as a militia. In 1703 the act was passed, but the queen refused her assent. This only redoubled the angry feeling of the Scots, and, in the next year, by refusing supply for the first time in their history, they secured its passing into law.

It was no longer possible for the English to postpone the settlement of constitutional relations with Scotland, as they had done in 1670, in 1690, and in 1703, by doing nothing. And, however strong their instinctive desire to resort to reprisals, they were restrained by an overruling consideration from beginning a real trial of strength. Whatever they did must not play into the hands of the French enemy. Their reply was therefore neither weak nor such as to admit of no withdrawal. By the Aliens Act of 1705 they first authorized the queen once more to appoint commissioners to negotiate with similar commissioners if such should be appointed from the Scottish side. They also provided that in the negotiations England should have something more to bargain with than before: they added a threat on their side to balance the threat of the Act of Security. From Christmas Day 1705 until the Scottish parliament should have passed an act

---

[1] For the international consequences of this see above, p. 280. The name 'Great Britain' was a reminder of King James I, as was the holding of Scottish peerages by Englishmen like the Fairfaxes and Falklands, and of English peerages by Scotsmen like James Hay, earl of Carlisle.

settling the Crown of Scotland upon the admitted successor to the Crown of England, every native of Scotland, with some few exceptions, should be taken as an alien, and, again with certain exceptions, trade between England and Scotland should be prohibited. Thus the unfavourable consequences of the policy of separation were clearly placed before the Scots, and at the same time they were given a last opportunity of withdrawing from it.

The subsequent debates in the parliament in Edinburgh were thus crucial: on them it depended whether union was to come now, or whether a new era of conflict and opposing foreign alliances was to begin. In Scotland it was a time of confused excitement. Captain Green was hanged a few days after the Aliens Act received the royal assent. There was a wild popular agitation against union. The parliamentary manœuvres were intricate and unexpected. But common sense won the battle. On 1 September the Scottish parliament resolved that commissioners should be nominated not by itself but by the queen. Since the queen and her ministers were all for union, it followed that the commissioners would meet with a desire to overcome the difficulties, and they were difficulties which could be overcome. On 27 November, two days after it met, the English parliament repealed the minatory clauses of the Aliens Act. As it turned out, with the exception of a single Scottish Jacobite, the commissioners worked with real good will. On both sides they included men of the highest legal and political ability and they did their work well. A failure of intelligence or temper might easily have made it extremely difficult; but in sittings which lasted only three months, in the middle of all the absorbing business of the war, they completed and signed their treaty. In the early months of 1707 the two parliaments passed acts to give it effect, and in May the union, the legislative union, was an accomplished fact.

It was a very great feat of constructive statesmanship, the more wonderful because it was the work of men nearly all of whom at other times had been led astray by selfish ambition or party passion. For both countries it was a free and advantageous contract: each was to benefit but each surrendered something. Each subordinated lesser but cherished interests to the over-riding interest of co-operation and order. The English gave up without reserve their commercial exclusiveness. According to

the economic ideas to which the English whigs, who then pre-
dominated in parliament and among the commissioners, were
specially addicted, this was a great sacrifice. So much did they
believe prosperity to be an artificial product of policy that they
did not foresee the great gain England was to draw from the
increase of its free-trade area. They also gave up the exclusive
control of England and Wales over their own political affairs:
forty-five Scottish commoners and sixteen representatives of the
Scottish peers[1] were included in the new parliament of Great
Britain and were free to vote on all matters even if they were local
English or Welsh concerns. This was one-eleventh of the whole
strength of parliament, and, though disappointing to the Scots
and allowing them a smaller proportion than that of the populations, it meant a great unsettling of the balance of forces in
England. In the house of lords very small numbers had decided
great issues in Queen Anne's earlier years, and in her later years
the Scottish element influenced the course of policy in both
the houses. When, a century later, the parliamentary union
with Ireland was added, it became possible and it sometimes
happened in fact that parliament enacted laws for England
against the votes of the majority of the English members.

In one other thing the English were generous in 1706, namely
in finance. Scotland had been very lightly taxed even in proportion to her much smaller resources. Her public debt was only
£160,000; in other words she had contributed scarcely anything
to the expense of the great wars. The Scots accepted the principle that the taxation and trade regulations of the two countries
should in future be uniform; but the English made it acceptable
by large concessions. For seven years after the union salt made
in Scotland was to be free of excise, though it was not to be
imported into England and the Scottish tax on it was to be
permanently lighter. Scotland was to be exempted from the
English stamp duties, the window-tax, and some of the taxes on
coal. The land-tax in Scotland was to yield only one-fortieth of
the English assessment. Finally, a sum of £398,085 was to be paid
over from the English to the Scottish exchequer as an 'equivalent'
for the share of the national debt which Scotland was to shoulder.
This provision, needless to say, was even more politic than liberal.

[1] No new Scots peerages were to be created after the union, another instance of
the tendency we have noticed in England to make the peerage a closed caste. See
above, p. 192.

£219,094. 8s. 7½d. from the equivalent went to pay off the shareholders and creditors of the Darien Company: so far as money
could do it that account between the two nations was closed.
All the English money distributed in Scotland helped to make
the recipients think better of their neighbours. Nor need any one
blush to remember that, as was bound to happen in those days,
a good many members of the Scottish parliament pocketed
private refreshers to their sense of proportion.

What England gained in exchange for her sacrifices was of
inestimable value. Scotland accepted the Hanoverian succession
and gave up her power of threatening England's military security
and complicating her commercial relations. Although there were
still to be two serious Jacobite risings in Scotland, in 1715 and
1745, and the latter of them came in the middle of Britain's next
great European war, they were only the last eruptions of a dying
volcano. It cannot be doubted that the sweeping successes of
the eighteenth-century wars owed much to the new unity of the
two nations. In so far as there was a common interest of Great
Britain it was obviously furthered. For the separate interests of
Scotland the chief gain was freedom of trade with England and
the colonies, a great expansion of markets. It may be reckoned
also as an advantage to both sides that the currency was unified.
What the Scottish commissioners had to watch in the negotiations was the safeguarding of their church and laws. No lasting
harmony would have been possible if either nation had claimed
the least right to interfere with the religious concerns of the other.
By the acts appointing them the commissioners were expressly
forbidden to treat of any alteration in the worship, discipline,
or government of either the church of England or the church of
Scotland. The high churchmen in England had some fears from
the union, but with little justification; the Scots had grounds
enough in their recent experiences for desiring strong guarantees.
One great danger to the kirk would be removed by the protestant
succession to the throne; but the necessary support of the general
assembly could not have been gained without a legal stipulation.
An act for the security of the Scottish church was therefore made
an integral part of the settlement. The Act of Union provides
that the 'Act for securing the protestant religion and presbyterian church government with the establishment in the said
Act contained' is to be a 'fundamental condition of the union'
and 'to continue in all times coming'.

The continuance of Scots law and of the separate judicial machinery of the country was not a matter of such primary importance; but it went deeper than mere expediency. Scots law had grown up under different social conditions and under a strong Roman influence, so that the law of marriage and inheritance, to name the chief instance, was radically unlike that of England. To have assimilated either to the other would have disturbed engrained social habits, and, strangely enough, the persistence of these two systems side by side has not led to any serious confusion. Moreover, it was good for Scottish self-esteem and in Edinburgh it kept up something of the status of a capital city to leave the courts of justice exactly as they had been. In this matter, however, no explicit guarantees were given. It was assumed that Scots law and the Scottish courts would be unchanged, and the Act of Union merely safeguarded their independence from encroachment by any of the ordinary English courts of law, to which no appeal was to be permitted. Curiously enough, nothing was said as to whether any appeal was to be permitted to the house of lords of the new parliament of Great Britain. The commissioners knew that this was a ticklish subject. Not only was the house of lords suspect to many Scotsmen because it included bishops, there was a further difficulty in the obscure and unresolved legal question whether any appeal lay from the Scottish courts to the Scottish parliament. Though the act evaded these difficulties, its silence left the way open for appeals to the house of lords, and within a very few years such appeals began to be made, apparently without exciting much attention or any popular discontent in Scotland. In 1709 such an appeal actually raised a question of the highest political and ecclesiastical importance: whether an episcopalian clergyman who had taken the required oaths to the state could be imprisoned for violating the uniformity of worship established by the law of Scotland. The house of lords, by a decision in favour of the appellant, gave or saved toleration for the episcopal branch in Scotland. The Scottish feeling for ecclesiastical independence was gravely offended by this decision, and even more by the Act of Toleration of 1712, which prescribed unacceptable oaths for the clergy. Legally both were compatible with the Act of Union, but they implied a disregard of the deep-seated convictions of the majority of Scotsmen. In subsequent times the appellate jurisdiction of the house of lords has done much to prevent inconvenient divergence between the developments of law in the two countries, and the influence of English thought and practice has been such that Scots law has not grown in anything like isolation.

This is only one illustration of the fact that the union had wider consequences in fostering unity than any one foresaw. Proximity and economic union became more potent influences with every increase in wealth and intercourse. The legislative union was not only the removal of a tangle in the fabric of government: it was the expression of a permanent identity of interests in common concerns. It is true that it was not always carried out in so wise and forbearing a spirit as that of its founders. On the Scottish side there were the Jacobite troubles. On the English side there was at least one direct infraction of the Act of Union.[1] In 1712 the tory parliament passed an act restoring the lay patronage of ecclesiastical livings in Scotland, and thus created a division in the kirk which lasted until our own day. There was much dissatisfaction in Scotland in the early years of the union over questions of taxation, and especially over the malt tax of 1713, which was materially inequitable and technically contrary to the act. In that year a motion for the repeal of the union was lost in the house of lords by a majority of only four. But the settlement survived these shocks. It became so much the accepted basis of political life that there is little meaning in the question whether it was justified by success. There never was at any time in the eighteenth or nineteenth centuries anything remotely resembling a practical alternative. The union was no more good or bad than the law of gravitation.

At the time when it was inaugurated it was, none the less, an act of will. It distinguishes the following from the preceding period, and it is not meaningless to ask whether it was the basis only of the later development of the life of the state or whether its results extended into social life, into literature and learning and individual character. The foundations of Scotland's future greatness in these things were laid long before, at least as far back as the Reformation, and they were strengthened in this very period by the passing of good laws for the establishment of schools, by the growth of tolerance, and by the gradual reduction of the forces of disorder. But the Scotland of Hume, of

---

[1] On the question whether or in what sense the parliament of the United Kingdom is 'sovereign' legal authorities appear to disagree.

Robertson, of Adam Smith, of Burns, and of Sir Walter Scott was the contented partner of England. In many indirect and unnoticed ways the union smoothed the way for the interchange of men between the two countries, for intermarriage, and especially for the southward drift of able and ambitious men from which England has gained in every sphere of life. In retrospect the old enmities at last gained a romantic glamour for imaginations which could be indulged in the new safety. The tartan, once dreaded and despised in the Lowlands, became the fancy dress of thousands of Englishmen with faint claims to Scottish descent. The two nations learned to laugh at one another and at themselves. Conditions may come about in which their political relations may need to be modified once more; but only an insane retrogression could bring back the nationalism which sought the honour and advantage of each in the injury of the other.

XIII

RELATIONS WITH IRELAND

IN the history of Ireland during the period there was nothing
to which the name of constructive statesmanship can be
given. It would have been remarkable if there had been, for
not only were the problems of government themselves extremely difficult, but the chances of solving them were reduced
almost to nothing by the cleavage between the English settlers
and the older inhabitants. We need not regard this as a conflict
of races. There was much mixed blood all over Ireland except
in the west, and along with differences of racial descent, there
were two of the most powerful causes of social disruption. Religious conflict was there, as we shall see, in the harsh forms which
it assumes when the persecutors are in a minority. Another
conflict, like the religious strife, had already a long history, the
struggle for the land, that is for home and livelihood. But what
made these contentions insoluble at this time was the recent
memory of the catholic rebellion of 1641 and the Cromwellian
repression which began eight years later. The history of the
rebellion, as it was written by and for the protestants, was largely
fabulous; but it was the events more than the propaganda that
embittered the two sides. Whichever had the upper hand,
neither justice nor lenity could well be expected.

The return of Charles II necessitated a new constitutional
settlement and a new land settlement. The constitutional settlement was naturally a return to the old Tudor and Stuart system.
The union of the three kingdoms was terminated and the Irish
parliament restored, but with its old subordination to the
English state. The English parliament could legislate for Ireland,
though for some time this power was little used. By Poynings'
Law of 1494 and an act of Philip and Mary the Irish parliament
was strictly subordinate to the English Crown. It could not
initiate legislation without the approval of the English privy
council, and its acts did not become law until they had been
returned to Ireland with similar approval. It had indeed something of the weight which must accompany even the most imperfect system of national representation, but it represented only

the protestant minority. The religious code of Queen Elizabeth remained in operation. It was, however, so little enforced in the reign of Charles II that there was a much nearer approach to toleration in Ireland than in England. The right to hold benefices was regulated in 1666 by an Act of Uniformity on the lines of the English act. Out of seventy presbyterian incumbents in Ulster, sixty-two were deprived.[1] Protestant dissenters, of whom the most important were the Quakers and the Scottish presbyterians of Ulster, were not very numerous and in practice suffered no disabilities except exclusion from the guilds and corporations of the towns. Catholics were also excluded from these in theory, though not at all rigidly in practice, and the laws about church attendance were not enforced.

The parliament was, however, entirely protestant and there were other circumstances which weakened it. The revenue was settled at the restoration on such a basis that the parliament had no occasion to assert itself in matters of finance. There was a hereditary revenue from rents and other dues and from customs, and this was supplemented by subsidies on land and movable property. In 1663-4 the revenue seems to have been £153,000, but after 1673 Ireland shared in the improvement of trade for the same reasons as England, and the revenue in the later years of Charles II was about double this amount. The expenses of government were well provided for, and in several years the exchequer had a large surplus. Further, there was no triennial act for Ireland; so there was only one general election in Charles's reign, that of 1661, and parliament never met after its dissolution in 1666. None of its acts were very important except those which dealt with the land.

The land problem was far larger and far more complicated than that of England. When the rebellion broke out in 1641 there were about eight thousand catholic landowners, large and small, in Ireland, and of these practically all were dispossessed in the Cromwellian settlement. Many went into exile. About a quarter of the number received compensation in the form of holdings in the counties of Mayo, Galway, and Clare equivalent to two-thirds or one-third of what they had formerly held. Nearly all the protestant landowners were similarly treated. Thus from all the counties to the east of the Shannon and from Sligo and

---

[1] From 1670 the Crown paid £600 a year to the Presbyterians for the support of their ministers, and in 1691 the sum was increased to £1,200, the *regium donum*.

Roscommon to the west, the old landowning class was expelled. It included the proprietors and their families, mortgagees and others with a pecuniary interest in the land; but not the tenantry and labourers except such as had fought against the English parliamentary armies. The agricultural poor were to remain as a subject population. Into the void created by the expulsion of their masters and leaders there were thrust two classes of English settlers. Some 35,000 soldiers who had taken part in the conquest of Ireland had their arrears of pay liquidated by grants of land at so many shillings an acre, the rates being different in the different provinces, Ulster, Munster, and Leinster. In addition to the soldiers and their officers there were some 1,200 capitalists, who had lent money to finance the invading armies. These received land at the same rates. Many of the common soldiers, however, needing ready money and not wishing to settle, sold their allotments to their officers or others; so that in the end the settlement did not establish a great body of small proprietors. It was indeed somewhat like the Norman conquest of England. This vast expropriation and re-appropriation was 'the foundation of that deep and lasting division between the proprietary and the tenants' which remained for two hundred and fifty years 'the chief cause of the political and social evils of Ireland'.[1]

The catholics indeed had good hopes at the time of the Restoration that it would be radically altered in their favour. The king and his advisers could not be expected to condone the rebellion of 1641, which had been a rebellion against Charles I; but the new proprietors included the soldiers and the financial backers not only of its repression but also of the subsequent and more successful Puritan rebellion against the king, and many of the dispossessed had been undone not by resisting him but by resisting these English rebels. Unfortunately, however, those who spoke for the Irish catholics in London, where the main decisions were taken, made the mistake of insisting too much on their equitable rights. They did not see that the government had to consider not only special cases like those of purchasers who had paid good money to the new settlers for their lands, but also the effect on opinion if the settlement were again put into the melting pot. In capitalist London it was the 'adventurers', the financiers of the settlement, who knew how to get what they wanted, and so the revision was partial in both senses of the

[1] W. E. H. Lecky, *Hist. of Ireland in the Eighteenth Century*, i. 106.

word. It began from principles laid down in a Declaration of November 1660 and applied by the Irish parliament in the Act of Settlement of 1661. In the immense complexity of the claims and disabilities there were necessarily exceptions at every point, but the general lines were these. The adventurers and soldiers already in possession were to keep what they had got: 1,769 such titles were confirmed. Officers who had served before the final reconciliation of the catholic rebels with the loyalists (that is before 5 June 1649, from which they were called 'the forty-nine men'), if they had not yet received lands, were to have rather more than half what was due to them: in the end there were not more than a hundred of these. Dispossessed protestants, if they had accepted compensation in Connaught or Clare, were to abide by their choice; if not they were to be restored to their old possessions. 'Innocent papists' if they had taken western lands were to have them again, but on hard terms and with serious exceptions; and to be considered innocent a papist had to prove not merely that he had been loyal, but that he had suffered at the hands of the rebels. In the result about seven hundred persons appear to have got through the meshes of this definition. When everybody else concerned had been compensated elsewhere, restoration of one sort or another was also promised to those papists who had been out in the first phase of the rebellion but had afterwards made their peace with the king.

This scheme might have been excusable as a rough and ready attempt to do justice within the limits allowed by the prejudices of the hour, if it had not been for one incurable defect. There was not enough land in all Ireland to carry it out. The areas could and should have been worked out from the start. The Cromwellian settlement had been based on a survey by the versatile Sir William Petty, called the Down Survey, because it was down on paper in the form of measured maps. The survey was now used in matters of detail but there was no proper calculation of the great totals. To make matters worse wide grants of land were made to the duke of York, the duke of Ormonde, and others. Disputes over individual estates led to growing exasperation on all sides. It was feared that the unsatisfied protestants might rebel and there actually was a plot to kidnap the lord-lieutenant, Ormonde. In 1665 the Irish parliament cut through the difficulties by the Act of Explanation. This provided that the adventurers and soldiers and purchasers in Connaught should give up one-third of their lands in order to increase the amount available for compensation; but that in all cases disputed between catholics and protestants every ambiguity should be decided in favour of the latter, and that, with a poor twenty exceptions, all other catholics whose claims had hitherto not been decided (for want of time) should have nothing. This pitiless decision shut out some three thousand catholics of native and English descent from the lands of their fathers. The net result of all these transactions cannot be stated exactly, but it is probable that the protestants owned in 1641 about one-third, and after 1665 about two-thirds of the good cultivable land.[1] In 1689 it was believed that two-thirds of the protestant landowners held under the Act of Settlement.[2]

Thus the land of Ireland was given mainly to the protestant ascendancy class, and by means which left a terrible legacy of bitterness. The economic effects of the changes are much harder to distinguish. There was, of course, incalculable hardship and injustice for individuals, and there was for a time the instability which must go with a social revolution: in 1661 land in Ireland was worth only seven years' purchase. But the period of upheaval did not last long, and before the end of Charles's reign land was selling for good prices. A considerable number of the new landowners were men of energy, and many of the others were probably compelled to sell their holdings within a few years. There was no change for the worse in the status of the tenantry: the tenant right allowed by the custom of the country was not interfered with by law until 1695. In spite of the difference of religion there was, as there had always been after previous settlements, some intermarriage between the new-comers and the older population. The settlers were not numerous enough to retain all that had been assigned to them, and, except for the Scots who continued to pass over to Ulster, they were not strengthened by much immigration. It is likely, though the question does not seem to have been adequately investigated, that on the whole and especially in the west the proportion of small to large landowners was increased, and this, in the circumstances of the time, probably tended to improve cultivation. Ireland was a poor country, and its agricultural methods, at their best and their worst, were behind the best and the worst of

[1] Sir W. Petty, *Political Anatomy of Ireland* (1691), pp. 1–3.
[2] Archbishop W. King, *State of the Protestants in Ireland* (1691), p. 161.

England. In fencing, draining, manuring, everything was to be done, and the wandering groups of half-nomadic herdsmen in the west were perhaps the most primitive people of the British Isles. Since there was not enough capital available for development on a large scale, the most promising method was the patient industry of the small man.

Whether for this reason or for others, the period of Charles II seems to have been one of agricultural progress.[1] It was certainly one of remarkable political quiet: the oppressed majority created no general disturbance. The protestants were never free from the fear of rebellion, and the severity of the late repression seems hardly enough in itself to explain why no rebellion broke out; it is not unreasonable to think that, although there were some years of famine as there were everywhere else at times, the political calm was assisted by economic recuperation. From contemporaries, however, this was disguised by the prevailing economic ideas and by disputes about the policy which resulted from them. Ireland was very deficient in those economic activities which the mercantile system specially favoured. Money-economy was but little advanced: the farmers farmed for subsistence and most payments were made in kind. There were few manufacturers, and there was very little foreign trade. Three-quarters of the foreign trade was with England, and the whole foreign trade was largely controlled by English merchants. The chief export was livestock, and of the cattle exported few were fattened. Of imports the most important was tobacco, but there were also sugar, various textiles, fruit, and corn. Ireland in relation to England was a poor pastoral country, with few natural resources suited to industry, with little chance of developing industries except by the help of English capital, and therefore condemned, in the absence of special measures, to export animals and their products in exchange for English manufactured goods and re-exports.

The English, however, unless their own interests forbade it, were willing to take special measures to change this. They were not yet jealous of Irish producers, and in the Restoration period there lingered the ghost of Strafford's policy of gaining strength for the Crown in Ireland so as to use it at need on the other side

---

[1] The best figures for Irish economic history in this period are given in the comparison of trade returns for 1641, 1665, and 1669 by the late Robert Dunlop in *Eng. Hist. Rev.* xxii (1907), 754.

of St. George's Channel. The duke of Ormonde, who was lord-lieutenant from 1661 to 1669 and again from 1677 to 1682, acted in this sense both in his public capacity and in administering his vast estates. He tried to build up manufactures by protective laws and by the importation of foreign workmen. At Chapel Izod and Carrick he set up the linen manufacture, which Strafford had wished to encourage, with the help of workers from France and Jersey. Unlike Strafford, who did not wish Irish woollen cloth to compete with English, he also encouraged the woollen manufacture: at Clonmel he set up Walloon weavers and in Dublin Dutch. These ventures were not successful. In 1675 some London merchants restarted that at Clonmel, but again without success. Whatever may have been the reason for the failure there is no proof that it arose from English policy. It is true that an English act of 1660 laid heavy duties on some classes of Irish textiles and that the Navigation Act of 1663 denied the Irish access to the colonial markets; but the venture of 1675 was made long after these acts, and there is nothing to show that the earlier attempts could have resulted in successful competition in the English and colonial markets if they had been left open.

Where the English parliament in the reign of Charles II did strike a blow, in spite of Ormonde's protests, at an existing Irish export business was in the cattle-trade itself. In 1663 the cattle-breeders and the landowners of England and Wales were not satisfied with the state of their business and were afraid of competition from Scotland and Ireland, where conditions were favourable and the standard of living was low. An act was therefore passed which prohibited the importation of live cattle into England between 1 July and 20 December (Old Style) in each year, that is through the period in which grass-fed cattle were in good condition.

From Scotland the movement of cattle was restricted, but less severely. The Irish were, however, allowed to trade with enemy countries during the Dutch war, and this seems to have mitigated the effects of the act. The English breeders, especially those of the north, were still not satisfied, and they continued to press for further protection until, in 1666, after disputes between the two houses of parliament, they obtained a complete prohibition of the importation of Irish cattle. During the next fourteen years this was extended to mutton, lamb, butter, and cheese. Scotland also forbade the importation of Irish cattle; and though the Irish parliament was allowed to retaliate against the Scots, this act remained in force until the union of England and Scotland. The English and Scots granted some licences of exemption from their acts, and there was much smuggling; but the important English market was practically lost. The heavy freight to Rotterdam made it impossible to compete with other importers in Holland, and the Irish export trade in store cattle sank low.

All this shows a narrow and illiberal policy in England and there were other instances of this at the same time, such as the exclusion of the Irish from the 'Greenland' whale fishery and the fisheries of Newfoundland. But, instead of being disastrous, the effects of the cattle acts on Ireland were beneficial. Unable to sell them lean, the Irish took to fattening more of their cattle and they set about improving the quality of their beef and butter. These trades were much more lucrative; indeed, as it is impossible to prove that their development was directly and mainly caused by the English protectionism, we must remember that this was the direction pointed out by nature and common sense for improvement, so that the positive energies of the able men of the country were on this side. The exclusion of the catholics from corporations did not keep them out of the provision trade. Numbers of the new settlers understood cattle: it is believed that their coming led to a decline of tillage, that is of subsistence farming. With the advantages of cheap land and labour and products which could stand longer voyages than cattle, the Irish were now able to undersell the English in the foreign and colonial markets. They also built up a good trade in victualling British and foreign ships of all kinds, which put in at Cork or other Irish ports for the purpose as the first call of their voyages. At the same time sheep-breeding was on the increase and cheap wool was exported to England. Even the woollen textile manufacture went ahead: there was some exporting, especially of coarse friezes, which were not made in England. Ireland could not in any case have rapidly taken up trade all over the world, and there is nothing to show that her trade really suffered from the English exclusions in this reign. The East India Company's monopoly kept Irishmen out of that great commerce; and in 1670 an act was passed which further restricted their potential trade with the colonies. The enumerated commodities[1] were not to be carried to Ireland unless they had first been landed in England.

[1] See above, p. 45.

Here the purpose was not to check Irish competition but to build up the entrepôt trade of London. But it was here again a possible, not an actual, trade from which the Irish were excluded, and it seems clear that in the later years of Charles II their capital and labour had adequate room for employment and expansion in the trades left open to them. There was real economic recovery.

Ireland did not indeed escape from the political upheavals of the Popish Plot. At the time of the Test Act in England the Irish government had enforced the law against Roman catholics more strictly: they were turned out of the corporations, and their bishops and regular clergy were ordered to leave the kingdom and did in fact go into hiding for a time. When Oates made his lying depositions, some of his imitators swore to false charges against Oliver Plunket, archbishop of Armagh. Shaftesbury did not scruple to fan the English panic by adding to it the fear of another Irish insurrection, and Plunket, as we have seen, was martyred.[1] Still Ireland remained calm, and there was nothing in the local position to make it necessary for Charles II to extend there the reactionary policy of his last years. He did, however, begin the remodelling of the municipal corporations by the use of the writ *quo warranto* as in England. This was continued and made general by James II. His accession necessarily led to a great change in the status of the catholics. The change, however, came in stages. James's first lord-lieutenant was his brother-in-law, the second earl of Clarendon, who, being as rigid an Anglican as his father, wished to maintain the protestant ascendancy and regarded it as the rule of the English over a different and irreconcilable nation. His authority was limited from the outset by that of the commander-in-chief of the Irish forces, Richard Talbot, earl of Tyrconnel. Tyrconnel was a fighting man, truculent and ambitious, the brother of a former Roman catholic archbishop of Dublin. His countess was a sister of Lady Marlborough. He worked whole-heartedly, as Strafford had done, to build up the royal power in Ireland; but on a catholic basis. He disbanded the protestant militia and disarmed individual protestants. Clarendon went along with him in admitting catholics to military commissions, to civil and judicial offices, and to the corporations; but with many misgivings and gradually losing all control. In January 1687 his place was given to Tyrconnel and the catholic reaction went forward unimpeded. The remodelling of the boroughs was completed. Catholic fellows were intruded into Trinity College. The whole machinery of the state was in catholic hands.

To the catholics political power meant something more than the emoluments and prestige of office. It meant the chance of turning the tables on those who had taken away their land. Before Tyrconnel became viceroy he and his intimates, especially the men of law, were making ready to attack the Act of Settlement. For the time they did not succeed. The king was getting what he wanted from Ireland. Three thousand Irish troops were sent to England in 1688. In Ireland prerogative had triumphed everywhere and there was religious liberty. But the protestants were alarmed and discontented. Only the quakers welcomed the religious changes. James had absorbed enough of Clarendon's warnings to shrink from embarking on a new social revolution.

To him, as to his forefathers, Ireland was a conquered and colonized kingdom; and if he had kept his thrones in England and Scotland, he would still have regarded it as it always had been regarded by Englishmen and Scots. When he lost those thrones, his relation to Ireland suddenly changed, and with it the relation of Ireland to England and to Europe. There was a short period of uncertainty. William of Orange also thought of Ireland as a dependency and not as a political unit with a will of its own. While he was administrator of England and not yet king, he sent an emissary to win over Tyrconnel, but the mission failed and the emissary deserted. Tyrconnel held Ireland for James, and William's enemies were quick to see that Ireland was the point of greatest immediate promise for them. It was long since it had been in the eyes even of continental diplomatists more than an appendage of England. During the first Dutch war of Charles II, when the French were allied with the Dutch, the idea had indeed been mooted that it might become a dependency of France: some Irish catholics had made this suggestion, which had also passed through the mind of John de Witt.[1] Quite recently Tyrconnel had played with the same idea. The French, however, could serve their purposes better without involving themselves so far. It was sufficient for them to transfer to Ireland the traditional policy which they could no longer carry on in

---

[1] Sir Charles Firth, in *Cambridge Modern Hist.* v. 110, presumably follows A. Lefèvre-Pontalis, *Jean de Witt* (1884), i. 375.

England, the policy of weakening England by civil division. James's flight to France gave them their opportunity. Within three months of his arrival he was packed off again, and on 22 March he landed at Kinsale.

His aims still diverged from those of the Irish. He wanted to return to Britain, merely taking Ireland on his way, and once he had got back to England or Scotland, he would no doubt have looked on Ireland as before. Even while he was there he was anxious not to throw away his chance of a reconciliation with the ascendancy class: he wanted to combine the strength of both elements for the work of government. To the Irish majority it was something that they had their king amongst them for the first time in three centuries, and that king of their own religion. They were loyal, but it was not with a loyalty like that of the English and Scottish Jacobites, rooted in age-long continuities. For them everything was overshadowed by the opportunity for a revolution at home. They were supported by the French soldiers and diplomatists, who wished well to James and to the catholic cause but whose overriding purpose was to divide England within itself, to divide Ireland, to divide Ireland from England. So from the beginning there were disputes about innumerable points in the political and social and military problems. The military problem was the most pressing, though it did not seem difficult. James had an army and the protestants had not; but they were in arms for William, and they controlled a part of the country where an army might land from England. After the landing of William of Orange in England, Tyrconnel had moved troops towards Ulster with the intention of quartering them in the most solidly protestant places and so preventing any movement in sympathy with the English revolution. The protestants, in alarm, had betaken themselves to defensible towns, and the stoutest men among them had become the leaders in organizing resistance. They proclaimed William and Mary king and queen. They now held Enniskillen, the one crossing between the lakes which separate Connaught from Ulster. They held Londonderry, then the chief port of northern Ireland. Their irregular troops were able to collect cattle and stores over most of the province and in the spring of 1689 raided to within thirty miles of Dublin.

There the counsellors were disputing whether James should go against them in person or not. If he went, he would be with his English advisers and would think of his English plans; if he stayed, the French and Irish would have his ear. He decided to go, but only to find that the military situation could not be cleared up quickly. Tyrconnel had some 40,000 men; but they were sadly short of arms and clothing, and the French had not sent either the money or the stores for which he had begged. There was no siege-train, and the operations against London-derry showed that the defence would be tough. It was therefore blockaded. A boom was thrown across the river Foyle below the town to prevent relief from the sea, and the army settled down to starve the townsmen out.

James could do no good by staying to watch this process, so he returned to Dublin. His absence had not appreciably affected the course of affairs in the capital: the remarkable events which now took place there could hardly have been prevented from the time when, shortly after his landing, he summoned a parliament. When it met on 7 May this parliament at once showed that the Irish were going to take matters into their own hands. It was technically a revolutionary and irregular assembly, like the con-vention in England: James, from the necessities of his position, could not summon it with the formalities which had been re-quired when Irish parliaments were subordinated to the English Crown. By its own act, however, it brushed aside the old subor-dination: it declared Poynings' Law void and abolished all judicial appeals from Ireland to England. It was revolutionary not merely in form but in its composition and spirit. Its members were in overwhelming proportion catholics: the protestants in the house of commons were at most fourteen. There were a fair number of men of position, but there was a woeful lack of experi-ence and political sense. The legislation was hurried, confused, and replete with the fallacies of nationalist and party spirit. An act was passed for the encouragement of trade, which pro-fessed to admit the Irish to trade with the English plantations. By the same act bounties were promised to ships of Irish build. By another the importation of British coal was forbidden, and, with singular optimism, a maximum price was set on coal pro-duced in Ireland. Toleration was nominally preserved, but tithe was to be paid in future by members of each confession to their own clergy. That would have left practically none for most of the Anglican clergy. And the whole foundation of the protestant ascendancy was to be dug away by the repeal of the Act of

Settlement and by a sweeping measure of proscription. This was called an Act of Attainder, and it condemned unheard to the penalties of treason about 2,000 persons.[1] It condemned them, that is, not only to death, but to a penalty easier to enforce and less likely to be remitted, the confiscation of their estates.

Everything in Irish history is controversial, and the patriot parliament of 1689 has had more than its share of invective and justification. The facts are obscure, because the authentic records do not exist: they were destroyed when the parliament was subsequently treated as illegal. The apologies are of little interest, because they rest on the principle, too often accepted in discussing Anglo-Irish relations, that two blacks make a white. The historical importance of the parliament is in its result, not in the purport of enactments which were never put into effect. Its result was that King James lost all chance of reconciliation with the ascendancy class. He had surrendered to the French and the dispossessed Irish. These Irish cannot be blamed for failing to give him the strength to hold his own. They had neither the money, nor the power of acting together, nor the military capacity, nor the leadership of the population which were needed to turn their national programme into reality. There were heroic exceptions, but as a body they did little for the king and thought first of their own revolution. An officer in James's army complained that instead of serving there or in Dublin they scattered to take possession of their recovered estates;[2] but it may be doubted whether many of them were qualified, after their long exclusion from responsibility, to do good service in the king's cause or their own.

Meanwhile the military problem was closing in and before the end of the year James was on the defensive. Londonderry held out against assault and starvation until, after needless delays, Colonel Kirke sent up a frigate and three ships with provisions. They cut through the boom and brought relief. The siege ended on 10 August. It had lasted a hundred and five days, with heavy losses on both sides; and its moral effect lasts till our own day. On the previous day, the third after the boom was opened, the men of Enniskillen won an engagement at Newtown Butler.

[1] That is mainly protestant landowners, most of whom had fled to England. It did not apply if the persons named surrendered.

[2] *Journal of Captain John Stevens*, ed. R. H. Murray (1912), p. 70. For the poor state of his army and for the numbers of troops see Tyrconnel's letters in *Analecta Hibernica*, vol. iv (1932).

They were moving, between 2,000 and 3,000 strong, to relieve the outlying protestant garrison in the castle of Crom on Lough Erne, when they met a superior force of the enemy. They attacked and drove off their opponents, capturing seven guns. This battle too has its place in the history of the spirit of the Ulstermen; but the stakes of the war in Ireland were too high for the decision to be left to local forces. King William had at first been disposed to regard it as altogether subsidiary to the continental war, and he did not yield to the English statesmen who urged him to lead an army against James in person. It was even with reluctance that he sent over his general, Schomberg, with a force which should have amounted to 20,000 men, or more than double the contingent sent in that year to the Low Countries. Schomberg landed on 23 August on the coast of County Down near Bangor. His army was far below its nominal strength, ill-provided and, except for the foreign regiments, untrained and badly officered. He had everything to complain of in the conduct of the supply departments. None the less he made a good start, capturing Carrickfergus and moving forward in September to Dundalk. Here, however, he had to halt. Rain and very heavy losses from disease were added to his troubles. The difficulty of the country impressed him and he was unwilling to force a battle. James was equally unwilling with equally good reason; so there was no decision and the two armies faced one another throughout a miserable winter. Schomberg was seventy-four. If he had been younger he might have acted more vigorously, but King William, the man most entitled to judge, was convinced by the reasons he put forward. In the meantime the impatience of the English parliament was rising. On 24 June 1690 William himself landed at Carrickfergus.

Schomberg had already moved, and had taken Charlemont, the last place in Ulster still held by the enemy. The protestant army numbered something less than 40,000 men, including six Dutch, eight Danish, and three huguenot battalions, so that the greater part of the infantry were foreign. Against them James had a somewhat smaller force, of which seven battalions were Frenchmen who had come over in the winter under the command of the romantic and incompetent duc de Lauzun. James had no more mind to take the offensive than in the previous year, and decided to hold the line of the Boyne, which runs into the sea at Drogheda, a long day's march north of Dublin. William's task was simply to march up to the river and attack the enemy: if he could cross, the capital was at his mercy. He found James in an entrenched position seven or eight miles above Drogheda, and without delay delivered his attack on 11 July. It was not a model operation, but in its main lines it was well planned. The main attack was frontal, but a smaller force crossed by a bridge and a ford up stream, and came in on James's left flank. James's casualties, 1,500 or so, were perhaps three times his opponent's. His army was driven from its position, but retreated in good order towards the Shannon. He himself, despairing too soon, spent only one night in Dublin, made off to Waterford and Kinsale, and landed in France before the end of the month.

The battle of the Boyne had thus given William possession of Dublin and rid him of the presence of his rival on Irish soil. After the delays of the winter and spring this had a great effect on opinion: the Jacobite revolution was over, and the beaten army suffered more than ever from divided counsels. The war, however, was not over. William had to carry on the campaign in a country where supplies were scanty and communications bad, with an army which was still far from good. He had to detach two battalions of infantry and three regiments of horse to England, where revolt and invasion might have followed the defeat of Beachy Head. He marched to Waterford, secured it as an additional base for his communications with England, and then turned westwards to attack Limerick, the lowest crossing of the Shannon. Lauzun and Tyrconnel, who was acting wholly with the French, had believed Limerick to be indefensible and had shipped the French contingent home from Galway, but the brave and patriotic Irishman Patrick Sarsfield inspired his countrymen to defend the threatened city. The rain held up the English as it had done in the previous year. Sarsfield successfully raided William's siege-train on the march. An attempted assault on Limerick was beaten off, and at the end of August William raised the siege. He returned to England. Schomberg had been killed at the Boyne and the command was given to William's German relative, Count Solms. The only other important military event of the campaign was a well-managed enterprise of Marlborough, who took possession of Cork and Kinsale, two ports valuable for communications with France or England.

In 1691 the English had to subdue the country west of the Shannon, of which the chief places were Athlone, Limerick, and

Galway. If they could take these, resistance could no doubt still be continued, but only by way of guerrilla warfare. There would still be a frontier-problem, half a military and half a police affair; but as long as these fortresses held it was war, a costly diversion from the continental campaign, tying up some 40,000 troops. The Irish were inferior in numbers, and there was friction between Tyrconnel, who had come back as James's lord-lieutenant, and St. Ruth, a French officer to whom James had given the military command. The attacking army was led by Godard, baron van Reede-Ginkel, one of the best officers in the Dutch service, an upright and generous man.[1] Ginkel moved forward in May and began well by crossing the Shannon at Athlone and carrying the town in July. He immediately went on towards Galway, and St. Ruth stood and fought at Aughrim, where he was killed and his army defeated. After a siege of two days Galway surrendered on favourable terms. At this stage it is possible that Ginkel might have ended the war by swift action; but he was certain of success in the long run and he closed in without hurry on Limerick, the last remaining refuge of the Irish. He hoped that it would surrender without fighting, but found it necessary to mount a siege; and, although Tyrconnel died on the day when the siege began, and a British squadron cut off the town by sea, it held out for half of August and all September. Its surrender was only a question of time, but a relieving squadron was on its way from France, and there was every reason for finishing off the campaign before the winter. Ginkel had already been acting in King William's spirit by offering pardon to the Irish who surrendered. In conjunction with the lords justices who were the king's representatives in Ireland he therefore negotiated for the surrender of the town.

The terms were meant to include all the Irish still under arms and to cover the questions over which they were fighting. There were two sets of articles, military and civil.[2] The military articles were easy to settle and were faithfully observed. It was agreed that those Irish soldiers who wished to enter the French service

---

[1] Born 1644; lieutenant-general in the Dutch service 1683; accompanied William on his English expedition; earl of Athlone 1691; second in Dutch command to Marlborough 1702; died 1703. The date of his birth and some facts of his earlier career are wrongly given in the *Dict. of Nat. Biog.*, which should be corrected from *Nieuw Ned. Biog. Woordenboek*, iii. 1017.

[2] For the full text see Appendix xvi to *A Jacobite Narrative of the War in Ireland*, ed. [Sir] J. T. Gilbert (1892).

should be transported to France, and in due time some 14,000 of them passed into this tragic but honourable exile. The treaty of Limerick is, however, remembered for the shameful history of the civil articles. On 3 October the Irish leaders had presented articles which explicitly asked for full toleration of catholics, and for complete indemnity and restoration of their estates. Ginkel refused these terms. Those which were signed by him and by the lords justices on 13 October contained thirteen articles. They were hastily and badly drafted, but their general effect was clear and in honour they were absolutely binding. The Roman catholics of the kingdom were to enjoy 'such privileges as are consistent with the laws of Ireland, or as they did enjoy in the reign of King Charles II, and their Majesties, as soon as their affairs will permit them to summon a parliament in this kingdom, will endeavour to procure the said Roman catholics such further security in that particular as may preserve them from any disturbance upon the account of the said religion'. Further, 'The lords justices and general do undertake that their Majesties will ratify these articles within the space of eight months or sooner, and will use their utmost endeavours that the same shall be ratified and confirmed in parliament'. It will be observed that there were ambiguities here: there was no definite promise to repeal the Elizabethan penal code, or to leave it in abeyance as it had been left in the time of Charles II. There was the same leaving of the settlement to parliament which had led to such unexpected results for the English nonconformists when it occurred in the Declaration of Breda. And there were those among the conquerors who needed no verbal loophole to break away from their duty to the conquered. On the Sunday after the treaty was signed the lords justices went to service in Christ Church Cathedral in Dublin, and heard a sermon from Anthony Dopping, bishop of Meath. This preacher maintained that with such faithless people no faith need be kept. King William removed him from the privy council, but in the end it was not the king's spirit but Dopping's which prevailed.

There was, indeed, a reason for this. The policy of colonization had failed and was abandoned. The influx from Great Britain ceased. The protestants had to be content with the position of a minority constantly on the watch against attempts to unseat them. Therefore the principal result of the revolutionary war in Ireland was the infliction of a new penal code on the catholics.

It began with some enactments of William III, and it was in the main completed under Anne, though supplementary severities were added under the first two Georges. It has been pointed out that a black parallel is available to turn this into a white: the legislation was modelled on that of Louis XIV against the huguenots. This argument is doubly bad in this instance, because these laws for Ireland were meant not to extinguish a minority but to degrade a majority. Since it was impossible to put an end to the catholic faith and worship, the catholics were to be discouraged from attaining wealth, advancement in the professions, or education. They were excluded from parliament. They were not to vote, nor to sit on juries, nor to be constables, nor to serve as soldiers or sailors, nor to be schoolmasters or private tutors. They were once more excluded from the corporations and from certain trades, while in others they were not allowed to have as many apprentices as were permitted to protestants. Special care was taken to undermine their position as landowners. They were not to buy land, nor to inherit it from protestants. Their own lands were not to descend like those of protestants intact but to be compulsorily divided among all the sons, if they were papists, when a papist landowner died. There were many provisions to prevent evasions of these laws, and there were other vexatious laws too numerous to mention. In the reign of Anne the priests were first brought into a system of registration, and then ordered to take an oath abjuring the pretender in terms which were known to be against their conscience.

It is, to be sure, true of these laws as of the previous penal laws, that they were not rigidly and consistently enforced. They were never equally enforced in all parts of the country, and except on occasions of political excitement or danger, there was laxity which increased as time went on. No one suffered death for his religion. Some catholic landlords, with the help of protestant friends or relations, continued to enjoy the estates they could no longer legally own. Though sometimes driven to concealment and always liable to minor hardships, a body of more than a thousand priests carried on its work in spite of the letter of the law. There were more than four thousand monks and nuns. The protestants regarded the code not as laying down the exact condition to which they would reduce the catholics; but as giving them a reserve of power, an armoury of weapons to which they might resort at need. There was, however, sufficient enforcement to effect the main purpose of the laws, and the existence of the reserve of power continually aided in this. The catholic population acquired the qualities of a subject population. It was orderly, at least in the political sense. The Irish Jacobites gave less trouble after the Revolution than those of either England or Scotland: the absence of a new movement of rebellion was as remarkable then as it was after the Restoration. But, if they were cowed, they were leaderless and lawless: when they had grievances they could not set in motion any machinery of organized opinion. For instance their remedy against the injustices of 'improving' farmers was cattle-maiming. Edmund Burke wrote some terrible sentences about the penal laws which have the more value as evidence because his mother was a catholic born while the code was being made. He wrote that 'all the penal laws of that unparalleled code of repression were manifestly the effects of national hatred and scorn towards a conquered people whom the victors delighted to trample upon and were not at all afraid to provoke. They were not the effect of their fears, but of their security.'[1] But he was writing more than a hundred years after the treaty of Limerick. There is no question that the Irish protestants were genuinely afraid of catholic Jacobitism. In 1708 some of the Irish catholics made preparations to move, for instance by seizing Galway, if the Pretender should succeed in his Scottish descent. There were known cases in which priests were concerned in smuggling off recruits to France. It was the fact, though it seems only to have leaked out in one particular case, that all the catholic bishops in Ireland were nominated by the pretender. And if the protestants had discovered nothing, no more would be needed to explain their action beyond the two civil wars within living memory, the second of which had been a French war as well.

Some further explanation is needed of the share of the English government. Under Poynings' Law it had ample power to stop any of this legislation, but it did not exercise that power. The Irish parliament under William III was not entirely satisfied with its constitutional position. It claimed the sole right to initiate money bills, but it failed to make the claim good. The real power of the Irish governing class lay, however, not in its own parliament but in the English parliament. It had so many links

[1] *Letter to Sir Hercules Langrishe* (1792).

with England, its maintenance was so much an interest of the ruling class in England, that it was able to circumvent the resistance of the king. There was more than his own tolerant principles to make William wish to treat the Irish catholics fairly. When Limerick capitulated, he wrote to the emperor that this gave him the chance of proving the falsity of the French insinuations that he was waging a war of religion. When, shortly afterwards, a complaint came from the papal *curia* by way of his great catholic ally that the treaty was being disregarded, William assured the emperor that it was false and emphatically promised that no one who obeyed his laws should suffer merely for religion. He does not indeed appear to have objected to the English Act of 1691 which excluded catholics from the Irish parliament. It was amended by the lords in such a way as to be, on a strict interpretation, consistent with the treaty of Limerick, and it did not disable the catholics any further than they were already disabled by the laws of England or of Holland. On another occasion, however, his pledges to the Irish and to the emperor brought him into disagreement with both the parliaments. In 1692 that of Ireland passed a bill of indemnity with so many exceptions that it was more a bill of proscription. The imperial and Spanish ambassadors asked him to refuse his consent and he refused it. The lord-lieutenant, unable to control the parliament, dissolved it. The indignant members addressed themselves to their friends in the English parliament, with the result that in 1693 the English house of commons addressed the king against an article added to the treaty, under which some of the papists had recovered their estates. 'These', they said, 'carry in them a very strong encouragement for the Irish papists and an abasement of the English interest there.' His answer was polite, but so general that it amounted to a refusal to reopen the question.[1]

Once again, in 1696, the imperial ambassador protested against acts which had been passed by the Irish parliament, this time for the expulsion of the religious orders. On this occasion William refused his consent, and the emperor saw to it that the

---

[1] Chandler's *Commons' Debates*, ii (1742), 414: the dates are 10–14 March 1692/3. The clause was in the draft originally agreed to at Limerick: how it came to be omitted is not absolutely clear. It was restored by letters patent of 24 February 1691/2. The text is in F. P. Plowden, *Hist. View of the State of Ireland* (1803), Appendix. In 1697 William finally gave way but apparently with little effect on property. See J. G. Simms, *The Williamite Confiscation in Ireland, 1690–1703* (1956).

heads of the orders warned their communities against engaging in any action against the government. In the next year, however, the king did not wholly comply with a similar request of the emperor's, and it appears that he was influenced by an extraneous consideration, and answered one intolerance by another. The Irish parliament passed laws forbidding regular priests and higher clergy to live in Ireland, excluding from public office protestants who married catholic wives, and confiscating half the property of catholic women who married protestant husbands. The imperial ambassadors in London and The Hague protested to the ministers and to the king, who was then in Holland. Before they had ceased to argue the matter, a new act for the Security of the king's person was passed in Ireland, more or less in consequence of the assassination plot in England in the previous year. This condemned to imprisonment for life and the confiscation of property, all who refused the oath of supremacy. No catholic could take this oath, and the imperial diplomatists urged the king to refuse his assent. The lords justices in London[1] were disposed to make some concession. Just at that time, however, in the negotiations at Ryswick the emperor was about to agree to a clause which deeply angered William. In the territories which Louis was about to restore to Germany the catholic religion was to be maintained as it was at that time, that is in the position Louis had given it after the revocation of the Edict of Nantes. At the surrender of Namur, William had agreed to allow Roman catholicism to be the sole religion of the town; but now he suspected collusion between the French and the emperor in a movement against the German protestants. This ruined the chance of inducing him to refuse his consent to the Irish act. He agreed to an important amendment: the act was only to be enforced at the king's pleasure. But, since his successors might well be less tolerant than he was himself, the act threatened danger to the catholics in the future.

Most of the penal statutes were enacted in Queen Anne's reign, and the religious policy of that reign reflected the changes of English government. The emperors attempted to influence it, but with little or no result. Joseph I, who was elected in 1705, and his successor Charles VI were less attentive to ecclesiastical interests than their father Leopold and more dependent on English support. Spain was no longer an ally. Thus Lord Wharton, who

---

[1] See above, p. 256.

was lord-lieutenant from 1708 to 1710, as a whig favoured the dissenters, but he passed the worst of the acts against catholic property. And in 1704, in the first tory phase of the reign, an act had been passed which showed that Anglicanism in Ireland was not willing to include even the protestant dissenters in the dominant class. This, by a clause which the English government inserted, imposed the sacramental test on all holders of public offices. This Act had a bad effect on the Ulster militia: in the Jacobite emergency of 1715 it was disregarded. It was much resented by the refractory Ulster presbyterians.[1] At a later time their discontent had important political consequences, and from the first it seems to have set going a movement of emigration from the north. The Ulster emigrants of this time went largely to America. Most of them appear to have been farmers. How important the emigration from Ireland was in the later seventeenth and eighteenth century it seems impossible to judge at least numerically. The attempts that have been made to calculate the population of the island in the period have little value: it is scarcely possible to say anything more definite than that it was more than one million and less than two. Whether it was naturally increasing or declining is not known, and no figures can be hazarded for the losses due to war. The numbers of emigrants were probably not large. The flights of the 'wild geese' who followed the 14,000 Jacobites to serve in the armies of France and other catholic powers went steadily on, but they were not to be numbered in tens of thousands in any one year. Apart from numbers, however, emigration was an impressive and melancholy fact. It meant that the mass of the Irish people was being drained of its best and strongest men, because no hardship was so bad as remaining in their homes. And for this the blame lies mainly on the penal laws.

Economic prosperity might indeed have prevented it, and conversely it is no doubt true that it was partly caused by economic evils; but these economic evils are not easy to estimate. In agrarian life the period introduced some new evils and accentuated some old ones. Absenteeism was already a serious matter at the Restoration, and it grew worse throughout the following half-century. It meant not only that absentee landlords consumed goods out of the country, but that to the owners of many thousands of acres their land was not an object of personal care

[1] See J. C. Beckett, *Protestant Dissent in Ireland, 1687–1780* (1948).

and interest but a rent-producing property to be handed over
to agents who were too often extortionate, inefficient, careless,
and disreputable. There were changes of ownership after the
revolutionary war, less in extent than those of the Caroline
settlement, but still very great. The enormous grants made by
William III to the countess of Orkney, Bentinck, and others of
his military and political circle were made from the lands of
James II, Tyrconnel, and the Jacobites excepted from the
benefits of the treaty of Limerick. They amounted to about a
million Irish acres.[1] They were resumed by parliament. About a
third of them was given back to the old owners, and two-thirds
put up for sale to protestants only, yielding £724,501. These
transferences must in all probability have had some effect in unsettling the conditions of life and work on these estates and elsewhere. The most serious agrarian measure, however, was an act
of 1695 which altered the conditions of tenancies. Hitherto in
many parts of the country customs had been in force which gave
the tenants some degree of security and therefore some incentive
to make the best of their farms by putting work and even money
into improvements. This new law declared that all unwritten
agreements to hold land, except short leases at rents of not less
than two-thirds of the annual value, were tenancies at will. It
thus gave landlords a much increased power of raising rents and
turning out their tenants. It removed some of the legal protection which had enabled the cultivators to keep something of the
character of a free peasantry.

How production and the standard of living were affected by
all this we cannot tell. Even in dealing with Irish industry after
the Revolution we can speak much more exactly about policy
than about its results. In English policy the Revolution wrought
a change to the disadvantage of Ireland. The heightened protectionism of the English parliament during the period of war with
France, and perhaps the greater power and continuity of parliamentary action, led to new restrictions on Ireland's economic
growth. Hitherto there had been limitations on Irish trade with
England and the colonies. They were now extended to Ireland's
trade with foreign countries. English politicians and pamphleteers began to regard Ireland itself as a colony, in the sense
of an economically subordinate community whose trade and
industry were to be directed into the channels most profitable to

[1] 121 Irish acres made 196 English statute acres.

the ruling power. Such an attitude led sometimes to wider opportunities for the subject country: in 1695, for instance, in consequence of the need of metal for the munition industries, the English duties on Irish bar iron were taken off. The iron industry, however, was small and was not one about which the Irish parliament was enthusiastic. Like other European legislatures, not all of which had any good reason for the fear, they were afraid that its consumption of fuel would unduly deplete their timber. In 1703 therefore they laid new duties on all iron exported except to England. And there is not any incontrovertible example of an English concession to Ireland's economic welfare in this period beyond such trifles as the admission of Irishmen to the 'Greenland' and Newfoundland fisheries in 1702. Nor were these disinterested: the reason for them was that the war caused a shortage of seamen.

On the other side of the account there stand severe restrictions on the trade in salt and beer, and there is commonly placed the much larger matter of the Irish woollen industry. The woollen industry, as we have seen, was the greatest and the most jealously protected of all England's lines of business, and in the 1680s it was clamouring for more protection. Ireland also was a sheep-breeding country and had a growing woollen industry, which its parliament was trying to encourage by protective and regulative measures. It was exporting less wool and using more at home. In addition to their own coarse friezes the Irish were beginning to imitate the finer English cloths called the old and new draperies. It was already provided by an English act of 1660 that Irish raw wool was not to be exported elsewhere than to England; but now the English clothiers began to be afraid of Irish competition in their markets. Their fears were unreasonable. The greatest export of Irish woollen manufactured goods was in 1687. It amounted to no more than £70,521 in value, and of that amount four-fifths stood for friezes.[1] During the French war of William III the export was very depressed, and when it rose in 1698 to rather more than half the level of 1687 in the quantity of friezes and rather more than double in the less important classes of goods, this must represent the release of accumulated stocks in the post-war replacement boom. But in that year the English

---

[1] Lord Sheffield, *Observations on the Manufactures, Trade and Present State of Ireland* (1785), pp. 153–4. For a modern statement of the English case, somewhat too favourable to it, see W. Cunningham in *Eng. Hist. Rev.* i. 277.

parliament, in accordance with the advice of the board of trade, imposed duties on the export of old and new draperies from Ireland which were in effect prohibitive. In the following year it prohibited the exportation of such Irish woollens except to England. It did not, however, interfere with the trade in friezes.

It was not intended that Ireland should be deprived of her foreign export market for woollens, a market then of no more than hypothetical value, without compensation. Ever since the time of Strafford the idea had been in the air that Ireland might have her woollen industry restrained in the interests of England, and have the injury made good by encouragement of her linen industry. In England linen was comparatively unimportant. It was, however, one of the industries which in England, as elsewhere, had occupied the attention of governments and projectors. The company which had set out earlier in the reign of William III to conduct it on a large scale had not been successful, and by this time was confining itself to trade rather than manufacture. If the English had wished to impoverish Ireland they would not have lacked an excuse for restricting the Irish linen trade as they restricted the Irish woollen trade. So far from doing this they promised to encourage it by all possible means, as an equivalent for the lost opportunities for the woollen manufacture. They kept their promise. They admitted plain Irish linen free of duty into England.[1] William III interested himself in the negotiations with Louis Crommelin, an able and experienced huguenot refugee capitalist who had been a linen manufacturer in a large way in France. Crommelin received all the facilities that the state could give him, and he used them well. If the fortunes of industries had depended, as almost every one then believed them to depend, on the policy of the states, the English would have had colourable reasons for thinking that they were treating the Irish with consideration.

In point of fact both they and the Irish overrated the power of the states in these matters. The Irish linen industry did very well, but not mainly by reason of government assistance. Governments on other occasions did as much or more without any success at all. In this instance they had on their side enterprising

---

[1] In Queen Anne's reign, import duties were laid on Irish checked, striped, printed, or dyed linens; but these, like the cotton duties, were equivalents of the English excise. In 1704 Irish linen in English bottoms was admitted to the West Indies.

men and real advantages, which may be summarized in the authoritative words of a modern writer:

The country was closely connected with England and Holland, the two great distributing centres; it was not troubled with local restrictions on trade; the climate was suited to manufacture; there was a good water-supply for bleaching; the peasantry could supply themselves with a certain amount of flax, and could carry on spinning and weaving as subsidiary occupations at a very small cost. The conditions of success were satisfied by Scotland and Ireland, better perhaps than by any other country; and in both Scotland and Ireland the linen trade became firmly established during the first quarter of the eighteenth century.[1]

There is little use in discussing what would have been the prospects of the Irish woollen manufacture if it had not been deprived of the foreign export market. It may be laid down confidently that mere inclusion in the English protective system would not have sufficed for it: when the East Anglian industry was losing ground to Yorkshire, Ireland could hardly have made headway. If the Irish parliament had been allowed to pursue a high protective policy of its own, it is difficult to believe that it could have created an export industry except at the expense of the prosperity of the country as a whole. But these hypothetical speculations can never be conclusive. Nor, when they are expressed in figures, is there any reason to attach importance to the emigrations of Irish weavers to England's competitors, France, Holland, Spain, and Portugal. It is thought that there was no decrease in the amount of wool grown in Ireland, so that the detrimental effects of the prohibition did not extend to the agricultural population except in so far as spinning was one of its subsidiary occupations. Nor is it known how many weavers lost employment and how long it was before they were reabsorbed into other occupations. The economic case for and against the woollen prohibition rests on conjecture. In all probability both sides were wrong. The real importance of the act is political: it illustrated the power which the British parliament possessed of dictating the economic laws of Ireland without regard to the parliament in Dublin.

This power had been exercised from time to time for many years without raising any practical difficulty, but a constitutional argument had been worked out on paper to the effect that new

[1] C. Gill, *Rise of the Irish Linen Industry* (1925), p. 15.

English statutes ought not to be considered legally binding on Ireland unless they were explicitly accepted by the Irish parliament. This argument was revived and brought into public notice in 1698 by a pamphlet entitled *The Case of Ireland's being Bound by Acts of Parliament in England stated*. It was the work of William Molyneux, a distinguished philosopher, mathematician, and engineer who sat in parliament as one of the members for Dublin University. Molyneux, besides the question of legislation, discussed the right of the English house of lords to hear appeals from the Irish courts, to the exclusion of the Irish lords; and this smaller matter was decided against his view shortly after, and perhaps partly in consequence of, the publication of his pamphlet. On the larger issue he put forward a variety of arguments of varying effectiveness, legal, historical, and political; but the essence of his reasoning is that government rests upon consent. He was, in fact, an admirer, and in this matter a disciple, of Locke. He wrote eloquently and with a wide view about the position of representative institutions in Europe at that time.

The rights of parliament should be preserved sacred and inviolable, wherever they are found. This kind of government, once so universal all over Europe, is now almost vanished from amongst the nations thereof. Our king's dominions are the only supporters of this noble Gothic constitution, save only what little remains may be found thereof in Poland.

It was the constitutional question about appeals and his misgivings about the economic laws which led him to write, but his point of view was that of a student of government as a whole. He did not indeed speak for the principle of nationality. He was a member of the English 'interest' in Ireland, and he used no argument that could be directly applied to broadening the basis of representation. In later times it was easy for others to make that adjustment of his arguments, and he thus counts as one of the precursors of Irish nationalism. The English house of commons, influenced no doubt by the idea that constitutional control was the best guarantee against Jacobitism, resolved unanimously that his book was 'of dangerous consequence to the Crown and parliament of England'.

Molyneux, however, did not believe that the only way to settle the constitutional relations of the two kingdoms was to give Ireland legislative independence. He held that if Ireland was to be bound by English statutes, Irish members should sit at Westminster, 'and this', he wrote, 'I believe we should be willing enough to embrace; but this is a happiness we can hardly hope for'. The Irish problem was indeed sufficiently similar to the Scottish problem for the idea of a union to occur to some Englishmen and some Irishmen for independent reasons. Ireland's autonomy, limited though it was, sometimes made Englishmen uneasy for their security. In 1703, when the Scottish union appeared to be coming, the Irish house of commons presented an address to the queen in which, after enumerating the economic grievances of the English interest in Ireland, it petitioned for either the 'full enjoyment' of the constitution or a union. In 1707, in congratulating the queen on the Scottish union, it asked the same for Ireland without the alternative. The Irish house of lords was not yet of the same mind; but the experience of Wharton's lord-lieutenancy convinced the bishops that even their church might suffer from the existing system, and the house of lords expressed the same hope. These petitions, and a number of pamphlets which expressed the same ideas, made no impression in England. The dominant business interests there were perfectly satisfied with the commercial regulations, and there was no immediate threat to English security from the side of Ireland. If a short answer has to be given to the question why the Scottish union came about in this period and an Irish did not, it must consist of two statements. The Irish parliament was in more effective subordination to the English government,[1] and Ireland was so quiet that English statesmen were not afraid of what might happen there. Nor was it to be otherwise until two generations had passed by.

Without looking forward to the end of this calm, we may say that the condition of Ireland at the end of this period was unhealthy. The division of classes resembled that in the poor agricultural countries of the Continent, but it was accentuated by a difference of religion and by evil memories. The English interest was not a homogeneous oligarchy. It included the trading class of the towns, except in the western towns like Galway and Limerick, where even severe special laws were unable to maintain protestants in a monopoly of economic and civic life.

[1] This did not include full control of Irish elections. In the general election of 1713 the Tories did badly, and it has been suggested that this may have provided Bolingbroke with an added motive for his precipitate action.

It included numerous dependants of the landlords, and middle-men who came between them and their tenants. It even compre-hended a less privileged element in the dissenters, of whom the Ulster presbyterians were discontented. But, with this exception, it had a strong sense of common interest and especially of com-mon grievance against England and common superiority to the catholic subject population. It had the qualities which are usual among dominant settlers. The gentry were given to sport and hospitality. On the large estates the mansions were often poor in comparison with those of England, both in spaciousness and in architectural style. The great days of Irish building and improv-ing set in under the Georges. But the Irish landowners lived with a slapdash splendour. Visitors from England were astonished to see how they duelled and drank. Their retainers imitated them as their means allowed, gaming and fighting at markets and fairs. Few of the landowners or those closely connected with them made active efforts to encourage industry, or entered into close relations with the towns. There were few to imitate Petty and Ormonde. Commerce was not dominant as in England.

The more important of the provincial towns were indeed com-parable in size with those of England. Cork, the largest, was flourishing by its provision trade, and two of the bridges over the river Lee were handsomely rebuilt in 1712 and 1713. Limerick and Waterford were next in importance, and the most populous inland town was Kilkenny, which had neighbouring coal-mines, a good road to Dublin, a woollen manufacture, and four annual fairs. But the only large town in Ireland was Dublin, the second city in the queen's dominions, which probably had somewhere about a hundred thousand inhabitants. It had the atmosphere of a capital. The legislature, the law courts, and the social life attracted much of the best ability of the country. The university was small, numbering two or three hundred students; but it was in touch with the intellectual movements of the time. In 1710 it obtained a laboratory, and in 1711 an anatomical theatre. The Dublin Philosophical Society, founded in 1684 with Petty as its president and Molyneux as secretary, was modelled on the Royal Society, with which it corresponded. It established a botanical garden and a museum, and published scientific papers. The revolutionary war only interrupted its existence. From this soil of intellectual activity there grew a number of writers as metropolitan in style and outlook as any in the world. Two, who were schoolfellows at Kilkenny and contemporaries at Trinity College, were Congreve and Swift. A younger man, also educated at Trinity College, was George Berkeley, one of the greatest thinkers and one of the best men of the age. Both Swift and Berkeley have their places in the Irish history of the next generation; but the greatest period of all three had more to do with England than with Ireland.

In the history of the Irish language it may be seen that the enlightenment of the age gathered itself for a few years in an attempt to help and educate the general population, but was overcome by the leaden prejudice of the English interest. Many of the Irish gentry understood the language and some even spoke it in London; but English was gaining ground. The status of the Gaelic poets had sunk low, and their tradition was far gone in decay.[1] Irish, indeed, was still the language of the great bulk of the population except in some of the maritime counties; but there were no schools where it was taught or where it was the vehicle of instruction. Queen Elizabeth had sent out a set of Irish types to Dublin, but only four books were ever printed with them, and those in small editions. The last was in 1652, after which the types were taken to Douai by the Jesuits. There and at Louvain and in Rome religious books were printed in the reign of Charles II, and the Irish catholic colleges abroad were the only centres of Irish scholarship. It happened that the great Robert Boyle was an Irishman. He took an interest in missionary work all over the world, and he helped to promote the translation of the Bible or other Christian books into the languages of the American Indians, the Turks, into Arabic and Malay. He became the moving spirit in an attempt to serve Ireland in the same way. He had a new fount of Irish type cast in 1680. Seven hundred and fifty copies of the New Testament in Irish were printed, and then for the first time the Old Testament, in five hundred copies.[2] The authorities of Trinity College were friendly to Boyle's ideas and provided some teaching of the language. This might have been the first step towards an Irish-speaking clergy. Their chief incentive would have been the attempt to make converts to protestantism, and that attempt was hopeless, but it would have meant a more useful clergy and one better

---

[1] E. Mac Lysaght, *Irish Life in the Seventeenth Century* (1939), pp. 308 ff.
[2] These books were also for circulation in the Highlands of Scotland: see below, p. 410.

able to understand the people. For a time the movement seemed to gather strength. Further copies of the Scriptures were printed in London under William and Mary. In Queen Anne's reign, when Boyle was no longer alive, the Irish parliament and convocation passed resolutions in favour of publishing books and instructing the clergy in Irish. The queen herself expressed approval. Six thousand copies of the liturgy and a catechism in Irish were printed. Yet at the moment when real success seemed to be in sight, the movement was stifled. There had always been opposition. When Boyle began his efforts there had been some of the clergy who desired the suppression of the language, and in 1711 there was a revival of the idea of undermining it by teaching only English. From that time no Irish bibles were printed and no Irish schools were opened until the nineteenth century.[1]

[1] This subject is treated by Christopher Anderson in his anonymous *Memorial on behalf of the Native Irish* (1815), and more fully in his *Historical Sketches of the Ancient Native Irish* (1828). I am indebted to the late Eoin MacNeill and Mrs. M. P. O'Sullivan for my acquaintance with this interesting author. For Boyle's interest in the Irish language see his *Works* (ed. Birch), i (1744), 109, v. 602 ff. In 1711 the nonconformist divine Dr. Daniel Williams provided in his will (editions of which were published in 1717 and 1804) for the translation of one of his books into Welsh and for an itinerant preacher in the Irish language.

XIV

OVERSEAS POSSESSIONS

THE wars and treaties of European powers were connected with colonial questions in every part of the world, in America, Africa, and the East; but in no region were so many of the great powers so continuously active as in the West Indies. At the time of the Restoration the situation there was very confused. The Spaniards held the greater part of the mainland coasts and most of the larger islands. They still claimed that the Caribbean Sea was *mare clausum*, not free for the navigation of foreigners except as they might permit. They claimed sovereignty over the whole of the land in virtue of being its first discoverers, and they rejected the English doctrine that effective occupation was needed to complete a valid title. But these Spanish claims no longer bore any clear relation to the facts. The English were firmly established in Barbados and in five of the little Leeward Islands. The conquest of Jamaica was now completed: the brave Spanish governor, Christoval Arnaldo de Ysassi, gave up the fight and took ship for Cuba some time between May and August 1660.[1] The English now had a base in the heart of the Caribbean. On its western shores there were English settlements, under no regular government, cutting logwood for dyeing, both in the Bay of Honduras and on the Mosquito Coast. More than two thousand miles east of Honduras, at the other extremity of this region, a new English sugar-colony was growing up on the South American coast about the river Surinam. Like the English, the French had their settlements, Martinique and others of the Windward Islands, with several of the Leeward Islands, including Guadeloupe, the largest of the group. The Dutch were also settled on the northern coast of South America, but they were less anxious to acquire territory. Their chief concern was trade and for this reason they held St. Eustatius and Curaçao and some smaller islands as entrepôts for trade with the neighbouring dominions of all the other powers. Their business was organized as skilfully as the staple-trades of Holland itself, and, in spite of all monopolistic regulations, they

[1] F. Cundall and J. L. Pietersz, *Jamaica under the Spaniards* (1919), p. 100.

controlled the supply of African slaves to both the Spaniards and the English.

One after another these intruders had gained a footing because the Spaniards had been too weak to keep them out, but they were not themselves under effective control from Europe. Until about 1688 the governments were not strong enough, and did not consistently attempt, to suppress the buccaneers. The name was originally applied to lawless men who lived by hunting the wild cattle in Hispaniola: *boucan* is meat dried in Indian fashion. Afterwards the same name was used for the filibusters or free-booters[1] who were sea-rovers. They were like the less chivalrous of the Elizabethan sea-dogs, except that they had permanent bases in the West Indies. Sometimes they held more or less regular commissions as privateers, and they always preyed upon the Spaniards; but often they became mere pirates and plundered any nation. The first result of official colonization by the northern powers was to strengthen them; both because it brought a rabble of seamen and emigrants, and because the governors of the colonies, lacking support from home, enlisted them to serve in the wars. Their principal station was the island of Tortuga, but from time to time they seized other strongholds, like Providence, and they were welcomed with their booty in ports like Port Royal in Jamaica. At first they were international. In 1663 it was estimated that there were fifteen of their ships with nearly a thousand men, English, French, and Dutch, belonging to Jamaica and Tortuga.[2] As time went on and the European governments asserted their authority, the buccaneers first became separated by nationalities and then in time were suppressed altogether, leaving behind only dispersed bands of pirates. The planters and merchants were in the end glad to see them put down: experience showed the advantages of legitimate trading.

While the buccaneers were powerful it was not only hostility to Spain, but also lack of authority, that prevented the other states from ending the old state of affairs in which, even when they were at peace with Spain and Portugal in Europe, there was 'no peace beyond the line'. The West Indies were beyond the range of the European international system. Sometimes this was for their advantage, as when the English and French agreed

---

[1] For the obscure etymology of these words see *Oxford Eng. Dict.*, s.vv.
[2] C. H. Haring, *Buccaneers in the West Indies* (1910), p. 273.

that their war of 1627 should not extend to these waters. On the whole, however, with the intermingled possessions, trade rivalries, and disputes about territorial rights, the local conditions led to conflicts. The West Indies continued to be one of the centres of international strife throughout the eighteenth century though by that time it was regulated in the same way as in Europe, and had become inseparable from the European wars.

One stage was marked by the second Dutch war. In 1665 de Ruyter attacked Barbados with a strong squadron, and the English had no choice but to base their defence on the buccaneers whom the governor of Jamaica had previously been trying to suppress. They were unmanageable and destroyed where they conquered, but they mastered the Dutch colonies of St. Eustatius and Tobago. In 1666, however, when the French joined the Dutch in the war the weakness of this policy was proved. The English hoped to capture the French plantations of St. Kitts (St. Christopher), where there were settlers of both nations, and so they declined to make a new agreement for neutrality. They made what was intended to be a surprise attack, but was an ignominious failure, and the English settlers in the island had to surrender unconditionally. More than 8,000 of them were shipped away, and their property was seized by the French. Lord Willoughby, the able governor of Barbados, got together an expedition for a counter-stroke, but his fleet was broken up by a hurricane in which he perished. The French captured one island after another. In 1667 naval ships from England regained the command of the sea and made various conquests, but the peace of Breda re-established the *status quo* of March of that year.[1] Although it came about in this almost fortuitous way, this redistribution of West Indian territory between the three powers lasted with little change until the middle of the eighteenth century. The Dutch kept Surinam, but the planters of Barbados, who had been jealous of its competition, were not sorry to see it go. France returned the English part of St. Kitts, taking Acadia (Nova Scotia) as an equivalent, but she kept Tobago and St. Eustatius. The French colonies, trade with which was soon thrown open to all French subjects, became very prosperous. The Dutch, however, never recovered their dominant position in West Indian trade, and this war therefore mitigated Anglo-Dutch rivalry in this quarter.

[1] See above, p. 68.

It also contributed to a change in British relations with Spain. The inferiority of the buccaneers as a factor in naval warfare and the strength of the French in the West Indies had been shown at the time when the French threat to Spain in Europe was beginning to cause alarm: all these factors tended to draw the English over towards co-operation with Spain. Charles II had already made attempts to get the contract for the supply of slaves which was not granted to the English until the treaty of Utrecht. During the war he made new advances to the Spaniards, but these led to no definite result until 1670. By that time a series of outrages had convinced the Spaniards that they could not cope with the buccaneers, and had led them for the first time to appeal to the English government against them. These exploits were carried out with the connivance of the governor of Jamaica. In 1665 three British captains, one of whom was Henry Morgan, made their way up the river and sacked Granada, the capital city of the province of Nicaragua. In the next year another party again looted and largely destroyed it and spent six months pillaging as far as the Pacific coast. In 1668 Morgan with some 400 men seized Puerto Bello, the port from which the Spanish silver fleets sailed to Europe. His men committed every sort of cruelty and brought back to Port Royal a quarter of a million pieces of eight.[1] In 1669 he was again at his work, and though Spanish protests led to a proclamation of peace by the governor of Jamaica, there was one more raid, the greatest of them all, before the news of the final treaty arrived from Madrid. In the winter of 1670–1 Morgan with a force which grew to about 36 ships and 1,800 men, English and French, after taking Granada and Providence Island, again captured Puerto Bello. He then marched across the isthmus and after a pitched battle took Panama. Old Panama was never rebuilt after this destruction. The Spaniards never received any compensation for these losses. The treaty of 1670 consigned them to oblivion, and at last recognized the sovereignty of Britain in her West Indian colonies. This was the first treaty in which the Spaniards definitely ceded colonial territory.

In the interval before the third Anglo-Dutch war relations

---

[1] This coin, familiar in romance, and also known as the Spanish dollar, or patacone, was worth 8 reals. At par about 38 reals went to the pound sterling, so that totals always sound better when given in Spanish currency.

between the English and the French were not good. The French restored the English portion of St. Kitts, but only after undue delays and in a devastated condition. The lack of cordial feeling between the two nations and other reasons, such as the weakening of the English by the administrative separation of the Leeward Islands from Barbados in 1671, prevented the English from taking any effective part in the war of 1672–4. In the main they busied themselves with trade while the French fought the Dutch, a state of things which continued until the general peace of 1678. By that time the Dutch held only a minor position in the West Indies, and the chief competitors for power were the English and French. Until the outbreak of the first Anglo-French war the buccaneers were not suppressed: the English reconciliation with Spain in Europe was still only uncertain and occasional. Henry Morgan was knighted and became lieutenant-governor of Jamaica. In the late 1670s there was a succession of raids on Spanish ports. In 1680 a party made its way across the Isthmus of Panama and, sailing in captured Spanish ships, pillaged the coasts and commerce of the Pacific. They had not been long on their journey when the Anglo-Spanish treaty of 1680 was signed, which at last stipulated for a real peace beyond the line and indirectly recognized the right of the English to trade in West Indian waters. When the buccaneers returned by way of Cape Horn in 1682, the survivors found themselves treated as pirates. The French, within a very few years, also controlled their buccaneers, and in the Anglo-French wars they were no longer an important factor.

Although in 1686 James II had made a fresh neutrality treaty with France for the whole of America, it was disregarded by both sides when war broke out. The English were now in full alliance with the Spaniards. In 1689 they were still sufficiently jealous of the Dutch to refuse to undertake joint naval operations in these waters; and they did not regularly send out naval squadrons thither from Europe. The fighting was therefore mainly defensive. St. Kitts fell, partly because the Irish and other Jacobite elements there went over to the French. It was recovered in 1690, but in the next year an attack on the French islands undertaken with the local forces of the Leeward Islands failed badly. In 1693 the squadron in the West Indies was reinforced by a larger force under Sir Francis Wheler. Fifteen hundred sailors, an equal number of soldiers, and eight hundred

M

Barbadian militia were landed on Martinique, but their preparations were inadequate and after some desultory attacks
they withdrew. The smaller islands were quite exhausted by the
war and took little further part in it. In 1695 a French force
spent six weeks ashore in Jamaica. They were ejected by the
settlers. The home government sent an expedition to Jamaica
in the same year with two regiments of foot; but disease and
mismanagement rendered it useless. A last naval force in 1697
failed to prevent the French from inflicting serious losses on the
Spanish towns and trade. The war ended with no transfers of
territory, but with widespread impoverishment and depopulation. It was followed by an outburst of piracy by the seafaring
men, whom the peace deprived of their employment as
privateers. The home government's first attempt to suppress
them was made by granting a commission to Captain William
Kidd in command of a privateer, the *Adventure Galley*, in which
some of the leading whig politicians were shareholders. Kidd
turned pirate himself and, before he was hanged, the incident
made much noise in party politics at home.

In the war of the Spanish Succession the French began by
sending forty ships of the line to the West Indies, to secure to
themselves the advantages of their new Spanish alliance. In
1702 the main part of this force returned to Europe convoying
the silver-fleet. Vice-Admiral John Benbow, with seven English
ships, had a good opportunity of attacking a weaker French
squadron which remained to operate against English and Dutch
commerce. Unfortunately four of his captains failed to join in
the fight, and it was a failure. Benbow was mortally wounded.
Two of the captains were court martialled and shot. There is a
still popular folk-song about this dramatic but unimportant
affair. In 1708 Vice-Admiral Charles Wager, commanding at
Jamaica, with three ships, attacked the Spanish silver-fleet. He
sank a great part of the treasure but his success was incomplete,
and two of his captains were afterwards cashiered. During the
remainder of the war he became very rich from his share of the
prizes taken from the French and Spaniards, but there was no
other notable encounter. The treaty of Utrecht gave the English
the whole of St. Kitts, but made no other change in the West
Indies. The main stress of Anglo-French rivalry had in fact
shifted to the mainland of North America.

The wars were not the only causes of disaster to the English colonists. There were earthquakes: Jamaica suffered much from an exceptionally severe one in 1692. In some of the smaller islands the seafaring Carib tribes were dangerous enough to set limits to European conquests. Nevertheless there was some territorial expansion. The Bahamas, in the Atlantic outside the line of the greater islands, were settled early in the reign of Charles II. Salt-rakers from the Bermudas began to make use of the Turks Islands from 1678, and there were other trifling acquisitions. The only important impulse to expansion came from the growth of wealth and population in the West Indian colonies themselves. It is indeed improbable that there were more white men in the colonies at the end of the period than at the beginning. The immigration from Europe was no more than sufficient to counterbalance the high mortality from the bad climates. The numbers probably fluctuated somewhere about 50,000.[1] In Jamaica they increased with the progress of settlement, but in other islands they diminished as the cultivation of sugar spread and became the predominant occupation. The subsidiary crops, such as indigo, tobacco, and cotton sank in importance, and only Jamaica produced most of its own food-supplies. The sugar-plantations were worked by slave-labour, and the white men, especially in Barbados, which remained the richest island, ceased to include a numerous class of small landowners. Only slave-owners and their dependants remained. The slave-population increased very considerably, from somewhere about 35,000 to somewhere about 150,000. These are small numbers, but the West Indies seemed to European economists and statesmen of the time the most valuable of all colonial possessions. Their products did not compete with those of Europe. They were paid for with manufactured articles exported from Europe, and these exports were so large that there was a balance in favour of the old countries.

The settlements on the west coast of Africa, though they had a not unimportant trade of their own in gold and ivory, existed chiefly for the supply of slaves and therefore were in the main an economic appendage of the West Indies and America. Strategically also they belonged to the same system: the fleets in the Anglo-Dutch wars operated on both sides of the Atlantic in the

[1] This is the estimate of Dr. J. A. Williamson in *Cambridge Hist. of the British Empire*, i. 266–7. It includes the population of the healthy Bermudas, stationary at about 9,000.

same expeditions. On the west coast the Europeans lived in their factories, which were fortified, but they had no sovereignty over the land or its natives. The coast-tribes acted as intermediaries between them and the slave-hunters of the interior. There was little incentive for white men to explore up the rivers, and few of them did it. If it had not been for European rivalries the atmosphere might have been one of quiet routine, but these rivalries were acute, and the Europeans, especially the Dutch, made use of native allies against their rivals. Before the Restoration the Dutch had been the main suppliers of slaves to the English West Indian plantations, but it was part of the policy of the navigation laws to oust them from this lucrative trade. This was the purpose of the African Company of 1662, the 'Royal Adventurers Trading into Africa'.

This was the third English African Company, but it made a fresh start in the slave-trade and there was only one factory of importance for it to take over from the East India Company, which had leased it as a calling-place on the sea-route round the Cape. This was Cormantine, a few miles east of the Dutch station of Cabo Corso or Cape Coast Castle. In 1663, as we have seen, Captain Holmes's expedition, as a prelude to the Dutch war, captured or destroyed all the Dutch settlements on the coast, and in 1664 Fort James was founded on an island about twenty miles up the Gambia, as a new centre for English trade and power. This, however, was only the beginning of a confusing series of captures and recaptures. In the same year de Ruyter won back all the Dutch forts except Cape Coast Castle and also took Cormantine. The treaty of Breda confirmed Cape Coast Castle to the English. The African Company was ruined by its losses and surrendered its charter in 1672, to be followed by the still more ambitious Royal African Company of England. Until 1687 this company was very prosperous. It set up six forts on the Gold Coast, and another post at Whydah, farther east, on the Slave Coast which became its principal centre for this trade. Cape Coast Castle was strengthened and rose to be second in importance only to the Dutch factory at Elmina. Anglo-Dutch rivalry was, however, henceforward unimportant in this region. In the war of 1672 the Dutch were not strong enough to take any aggressive measures here. They suffered serious losses at the hands of the French, who expelled them for good from the neighbourhood of Cape Verde, so that in the future they were mainly confined to the Gold Coast, while the French built up their power north of the Gambia in Senegal. There was indeed a dispute between the English and the Dutch of which the history is still obscure: as late as 1692 the English were asking for the restitution of Cape Coast Castle, which the Dutch seem to have taken and restored at unknown dates.[1]

This dispute, however, did not seriously injure good relations, since the two powers were then hard put to it to hold their own as allies against the French. In this war the English fought the French in Senegambia. They took two French forts and lost them again, after which the French destroyed Fort James. Here again the course of events is not clear, but the place appears to have been soon regained and in the war of the Spanish Succession to have been twice retaken by the French. In the treaty of Utrecht it remained English. The French wars had caused considerable losses to the company, and in 1697 parliament put an end to its monopoly, though securing to it certain dues from other traders as contributions to the upkeep of its forts. It was unable to withstand competition on these terms, and in 1708 became insolvent, surviving until 1750 in a state of much reduced activity. The slave-trade, however, flourished, and contributed to the prosperity not only of the West Indies but also of New England, which was largely concerned in it and in various forms of contraband and permitted trade with the West Indian islands of all nations.

The strengthening of European control over the colonies, exemplified in the suppression of buccaneering and the increased action of naval squadrons, had also a constitutional expression. This may be described in general terms which apply, in spite of the great social differences between them, to the West Indian colonies and also to those of the North American continent. At the beginning of the period all of them were chartered colonies. They were of two types. Some, which have been called 'corporate' colonies, had no imperial executive, but made their own arrangements for their internal government. These were the New England colonies, Massachusetts, Plymouth, Connecticut, and Rhode Island. The other type was that of the proprietary colony, in which an individual or a syndicate held

---

[1] See R. F[erguson], *Brief Account of Some of the Later Incroachments and Depredations of the Dutch* (1695), p. 55, and Dursley's dispatches of 7/17 October, 29 November/9 December 1692 in S.P. 84/220 in the Public Record Office.

under the Crown a sort of feudal overlordship. Besides the West Indian colonies, Virginia and Maryland were held in this way before the Restoration, and there were new proprietary grants of Carolina in 1663, New York and New Jersey when, or rather before, they were conquered from the Dutch, the Bahamas in 1670, Pennsylvania and Delaware in 1681–2. It was, however, impossible for the Crown to carry out its navigation policy or to co-ordinate defensive measures or intercolonial relations and the general maintenance of order without encroaching on this system, and by the end of the period it was obsolescent. All the colonies except Rhode Island, Connecticut, Pennsylvania, and Maryland had become royal provinces, with governors nominated by the Crown. Even in these there were royal customs officers, and vice-admiralty courts had been set up in the time of William III. On a number of occasions the home government had interfered with the internal affairs of the colonies.

The tendency towards central control was a result of the growing strength and stability of the English state: it was in some ways parallel to the strengthening of the control of the French crown over its colonial possessions, and is thus a part of the general European development of the age. In the British colonies it has a peculiar importance because of its consequences in the development of the constitutions of the colonies. The colonies tended to conform to a type of constitution derived, so far as colonial conditions permitted, from the English parliamentary system of the time. The governor represented the king. From the time of Charles II care was taken to choose as governors men of sense and character. Some were colonials, but more were members of the English governing class. From 1676, when Colonel Jeffreys was appointed to Virginia, some of the best of them were regular officers of the army and navy. In the earlier days some of them did not stand above the level of the rough contests of the settlers for wealth and power. Henry Morgan did not break with his past when he became lieutenant-governor of Jamaica. Others tried to rule with a high hand, when it would have been better to humour the colonists. Such was Lieutenant-General Parke, the governor of the Leeward Islands, who was murdered in 1710 by a mob. But the majority were men of ability who conscientiously carried out their duties in spite of constant difficulties. They were often ill-supported from England: their salaries, for instance, were apt to be years in arrear. Many subordinate offices were granted by letters patent to Englishmen who did not reside in the colonies but consigned their functions to deputies over whom the governors had no adequate control.[1] The colonists were almost all compelled to work so hard for a meagre livelihood, and were so much shut off from knowledge of affairs at a distance, that they seldom appreciated the urgency of the general interests which the governors specially personified. The cases of serious friction between them and the governors were, however, as yet exceptional and they were nothing worse than passing incidents.

Each governor had a council, in which he himself presided. It had anything from ten to twenty-eight members, leading inhabitants of the colony nominated by the Crown on the advice of the board of trade or committee of council. It advised the governor on his executive work, and thus resembled the privy council as it had been before the rise of cabinets; but it was also the upper house of the legislature. The lower house was the assembly. These assemblies became by the end of the period the chief distinctive institutions of the British colonies. Historically they originated in different ways. In the proprietary colonies they began as rudimentary groups representing the settlers for limited purposes prescribed by the proprietors. In New England they were much more important, because the communities were from the first self-governing. In New York, which in its Dutch days had no such body, the assembly was conceded by William III after the episode of Leisler's rebellion. Jacob Leisler, a German brewer, had come forward in the time of James II as the leader of the protestant and anti-French elements, and had set up a democratic dictatorship. He failed to obtain recognition from the new government in England, but, after his trial and execution, the usual amount of self-government was granted. It arose, in fact, sooner or later, inevitably from the conditions of these vigorous but distant and necessarily self-centred communities. As these grew in wealth and population, the assemblies ceased to be merely subordinate bodies for purposes of local government and became, both in procedure and in their powers, analogous to the English house of commons.

The relations of the colonial legislatures to the Crown were not allowed to grow up without attempts at regulation. To some extent these attempts reflect the constitutional changes at home,

[1] See J. H. Parry in *English Historical Review*, lxix (1954), 177 ff.

but the policy of the various committees and boards for the plantations had a cont'nuity of 'is own which was not much affected by political changes. It was worked out by the departmental experts, and it was seldom discussed in parliament. Throughout the period parliament left the larger colonial matters almost altogether to the Crown. From about 1675, when the 'lords of trade' were given their separately organized office,[1] constitutional matters were carefully watched. In 1677-9 an attempt was made to bring Jamaica and Virginia under the same system which was used for Ireland, the system of Poynings' Law.[2] Virginia had just come through a rebellion and for the moment accepted a batch of acts drawn up in England, though it appears the governor did not disclose the proposed change of system. Jamaica rejected it outright, and it was allowed to drop. The system was indeed too tight to be enforced at a distance of 3,000 miles by a government which was often imperfectly informed. After it had dropped, there was a phase of renewed interference corresponding with the reaction in the later years of Charles II. It was more than mere formal coincidence that the writ of *quo warranto*, used against the English corporations, was also turned against the Somers Islands Company in the proceedings, begun in 1682, which led to its dissolution.[3] The writ was the appropriate instrument for the purpose, and the proceedings belonged to the same general class as those in which the proprietors of the Barbados had forfeited the greater part of their rights at the beginning of the reign. The conflicts of claims between rival grantees and between grantees and settlers could only be disentangled by the law-courts. But when in 1683 the same writ was launched against the charter of Massachusetts, this resulted from the policy of enlarging royal power. The wholesale evasions of the trade-laws there had been backed up by the assembly. After trying the inadequate normal means at its disposal, the government secured the forfeiture of the colony's charter.

This was followed by an endeavour in the last years of Charles II and the reign of James II to unify the states of New England

---

[1] See above, p. 44.   [2] See above, p. 294.

[3] On 12 February 1688/9 in the proceedings on the Claim of Right the lawyer Treby reported 'that cities, universities and the plantations ought to be secured against *quo warrantos* and surrenders, and their ancient rights restored' (*Commons' Journals*, x. 17) but colonial administration is not mentioned in the Declaration of Rights.

under a single government with no popular element. Such a union would have been advantageous for military organization as well as for the enforcement of the laws of trade, and it suited the views and aims of the Stuarts. It collapsed with their fall, but the conditions were so unfavourable to its success that the failure is not to be regarded as essentially a result of the English revolution. The home government was not strong enough to enforce real imperial control. The colonial population could not for long have been governed without popular assemblies. The pressure of external danger was not yet strong enough to bring about a lasting union of even neighbouring colonies.

There were other attempts at such union over larger or smaller areas. Leisler summoned representatives from the colonies to concert an attack on the French in Canada. The southern colonies were too far away to be interested, but in May 1690 there met in New York representatives of that state and of Massachusetts, Plymouth, Connecticut, and Maryland. This has been called the first-American Congress: it planned a small expedition, which ended disastrously. William III renewed the charter of Massachusetts in 1691, incorporating with it Plymouth and Maine and the regions claimed by the English in Acadia and what was afterwards New Brunswick. William Penn in 1697 and 1700 made various proposals for a common organization of all the mainland colonies. He proposed an annual congress of two representatives from each colony, under the presidency of a royal commissioner, to regulate disputes between the colonies and contributions for defence. He also made plans for unifying currency and various branches of the administration of the law. These ideas are the more interesting because Penn was on the one hand a friend of James II, and on the other, the author of a plan for a federation of the states of Europe;[1] but they came to nothing. In only one place did a scheme of federation attain a certain measure of practical usefulness, and that was in a remote group of unimportant islands. In 1690, for the purposes of the French war, the Leeward Islands began a series of general assemblies, and in the early years of the war of the Spanish Succession these were given what was meant to be a permanent constitution; but as the pressure of war relaxed they fell into desuetude.

[1] See below, p. 422.

For English history, as distinguished from the local history of the colonies, these plans of regional federation and the constitutional questions in general were not important at the time. Their significance is that they foreshadow developments which could not come to maturity until far on in the eighteenth century. Until then, except for the wars, the one part of colonial affairs that really concerned the English at home was the underlying growth from which a constitutional revolution was in due time to break out, the great and surprising growth in population and material wealth. There was, first of all, territorial expansion. We have already dealt with this in the West Indies. In North America at the beginning of the period the English were established in three regions. In the south-east corner of Newfoundland, the nearest American land to Europe, there were a few hundred settlers with no towns and not even a village of as many as a hundred inhabitants. For the English, as for the French, the importance of Newfoundland lay in its great sea-fisheries. These were valued not only for their cod but as training-grounds of seamen for the navies. The fishermen came annually from Europe, cured their catch on shore and carried it home. Newfoundland was more than 700 miles from the New England colonies, but, when the navigation laws came in, it began to be used as a depot for contraband trade with them. They included some 33,000 inhabitants. Boston, the capital of Massachusetts, was the most important English-speaking town in America. The New England settlements were mostly within 30 miles of the coast. Only in the south-western corner did they reach farther: the valley of the Connecticut was settled for nearly 80 miles, and inland from Boston the farmers and pioneers had pushed more than half-way across towards it. The settlers were far from being in contact with the French of the St. Lawrence valley, but the French held the fort of Penobscot, at the mouth of the river of that name,[1] and Acadia (or Nova Scotia) with its two neighbouring islands. To the south-west, New England was bounded by the Dutch settlements of New Netherland. The other English colonies on the coast, Maryland and Virginia, were reached by a coasting voyage of several days which few had any occasion to undertake. They were narrow belts of settlements round the deep estuaries and inlets of the sea, communicating with one another mainly by

[1] This fort was captured by the British colonists in 1704.

water and numbering some 30,000 inhabitants including some negroes.

The first addition was made by the colonization of Carolina. The purpose of this was commercial. It was not intended that the new colony should compete with those already established by growing tobacco or sugar, but it was hoped that it would be suitable for the products which were then obtained from the Mediterranean, silks, fruits, and oils. The proprietors included Clarendon, Albemarle, and Ashley, besides the governor of Virginia and a Barbados planter: these names show that the enterprise was part of the economic expansion of the Restoration period. It had indeed been anticipated by sporadic settlers, and the new settlers came largely from the existing colonies, such as Barbados, where there was a redundant population; but it was a creation of central planning, and as such it was not a success. It grew up in two separate colonies, only one of which, South Carolina, had a town worth mentioning, the port of Charles Town. The chief lawful occupation was the growing of food for export to the West Indies, but the few thousands of settlers were also engaged in every form of forbidden trade, from smuggling to piracy.

The next acquisition, New Netherland, which was won in the Dutch war while the Carolinas were only beginning to be settled, was of very different character and value. That it made the English territory continuous from north to south was not in itself of much immediate importance except for administrative purposes, because the few dealings between the groups of colonies were still conducted by sailing along the coast. Its commercial importance even then was, however, very great and for the future it was the chief gateway of North America. New York was already second only to Boston. It was the outlet for the furs which came down the Mohawk and the Hudson from the Great Lakes, and its position on this route made it as important strategically, in relation to the French in Canada, as it was in commerce. The French *intendant* in Canada vainly urged his government at home to insist on the return of New Netherland in the Breda negotiations, in order that the French might afterwards purchase it from the Dutch. The Dutch territory across the Hudson river from New York, which became known as New Jersey, ultimately formed a separate province. In the early days it was subject to proprietary rights which had a confused history, and one of the people concerned in them was William Penn. He was interested in America for various reasons, amongst which were his wealth and his parentage. He had money to invest. His father was the admiral who commanded in Oliver Cromwell's 'western design', and his mother was a Dutch-woman. Some years after his dealings with New Jersey he formed a much larger project on his own account. In 1681–2, to discharge a Crown debt to his father, Charles II granted him proprietary rights over what became Pennsylvania. This was cut off from the coast-line by New Jersey and Maryland, but access was gained to it by the river Delaware, on which its capital, Philadelphia, was placed.[1] The land was so suitable for settlement and the colony so wisely managed that it grew rapidly and Philadelphia took its place beside Boston and New York.

Rivalry between the English and the French in North America had its small beginnings in the reign of Charles II. The Hudson's Bay Company was incorporated in 1670. Amongst its purposes was the search for a 'north-west passage', a route to the far east round the north of America; but it did little to find this. It was almost entirely engaged in the fur-trade, buying furs from the Indian trappers and shipping them from Hudson Bay. This northern route was far away from the French route down the St. Lawrence, but the French did not admit the English claim to this region in virtue of prior discovery. The company established trading-posts and by 1682 it had a line of them round the southern and south-eastern shores of the Bay. The oldest was on Rupert's River. There was one on Charlton Island in James Bay. The others, going northwards, were Forts Albany, Severn, York and Churchill, and Port Nelson. In 1682 a French inter-loping expedition appeared in the bay. Its adventurous leader, Pierre Esprit Radisson, was temporarily estranged from the English Company, which he had helped to establish, and now he had a grandiose plan for opening up the fur-forest from this northern outpost. The French attacked and captured Port Nelson, but it was restored, partly in consequence of the friend-ship between Charles II and Louis XIV. In spite of that friend-ship, however, local rivalry was growing, as at an earlier date Anglo-Dutch colonial rivalry had grown notwithstanding alli-ance in Europe. In Newfoundland there was another sign that

[1] The colony of Delaware was given a separate government in 1703.

it was hardening. There the regular English policy had been to discourage settlement, partly in the interests of the navigation system and more especially in order to keep the fisheries in the hands of the large armed vessels from the west of England. If a local fishing population were allowed to grow up, the English would drop out of the catching and curing industries, and with comparatively few ships would merely transport the fish across the Atlantic. The naval officers who convoyed the fishing fleets were instructed to enforce strict rules against coast settlers, but some of them urged a contrary course. The French from 1662 had their own settlements with their centre seventy miles away from the principal English village, St. John's. To the naval eye it was plain that if the English evacuated their places, the French would step in. In 1680 the board of trade came over to this view and decided to maintain the colony. A governor was appointed, and Newfoundland became a potential theatre of war.

Before the French wars began there was another collision on the Hudson Bay coast. In 1686 a French force marched overland and captured all the company's forts except Port Nelson. Once again Louis XIV restored them, with one exception. Neither party, however, had finally quelled the other, nor were the disputed claims settled, and it is partly for this reason that in the French wars these northern coasts were the scenes of more continuous fighting than the West Indies. Under William III there was fighting at several points, but it served to prove that the temporary successes gained by the colonials could be reversed by regular forces from Europe. The colonists on both sides had neither the resources nor the discipline and cohesion which would have been necessary for success in ambitious operations over large distances. The Comte de Frontenac, formerly a conspicuously successful governor of Canada, had a plan for attacking New York by sea and simultaneously by the Hudson valley with the aid of the Indians. Sir William Phipps, of Boston, who had begun life as a ship's carpenter, captured Port Royal in Acadia, but it was recovered by a single French warship. Phipps failed badly in what was meant to be an attack on Montreal by a naval force on the St. Lawrence converging with an overland march of the militia. In Newfoundland there were local raids and in the last two years of the war French squadrons from Europe did much damage to the English settlers, but an English expedition restored the fortifications.

The only American question left for discussion in the Ryswick negotiations was that of the Hudson Bay forts. One of the British plenipotentiaries at the peace conference wrote a letter to the secretary of state which shows that this was still regarded as an outlying question hardly belonging to high politics:

We are now arguing with the French about the rest of our articles, in which nothing appears of much difficulty, only as to that of Hudson's Bay business (which, at the bottom, is a branch of private interest of trading companies), we are left without the necessary informations of fact, much more without able and full proofs of what is said, as to the original right upon which all will turn.[1]

The forts had changed hands several times during the war. By the middle of 1695 the French had taken them all. In 1696 the English recovered them once more, but in 1697 the French expedition which overran Newfoundland went on to capture Port Nelson. This was only a few days before the signing of the peace of Ryswick, and the news had not reached the conference; but under the treaty the French were given all the forts except Fort Albany.[2]

The colonial results of the war of the Spanish Succession were quite unlike those of this war. Instead of vicissitudes there were decisive changes. Instead of a single subordinate provision in the terms of peace there was a whole series of territorial transfers. This was due not to local events but to the British victories in Europe. The local forces as before were ineffective. In 1704 and 1707 there were unsuccessful expeditions against Port Royal. In 1708 another combined expedition against Canada failed: Colonel Francis Nicholson advanced towards Lake Champlain and had to retreat, and the English naval force which was to have co-operated with him was diverted to Portugal. In 1710 an English squadron enabled Nicholson to take Port Royal; but the ambitious attack up the St. Lawrence in 1711 failed ignominiously.[3] In Newfoundland the French three times raided St. John's. Yet the treaty of Utrecht restored the Hudson Bay forts and promised compensation to the company for its losses. It gave the whole of Acadia to Great Britain, and the whole of Newfoundland, reserving to the French only the right to carry on

---

[1] Sir Joseph Williamson to Shrewsbury 6/16 August 1697 in W. Coxe, *Shrewsbury Correspondence*, p. 362.

[2] Under art. vii of the treaty the *status quo ante bellum* was to be restored in all other colonial possessions, and under art. viii commissioners were to settle the claims in Hudson Bay.   [3] See above, p. 230.

fishing and curing on the 'treaty shore' from Cape Bona Vista round the northern point of the island to Point Rich. This did not amount to a final clearing-up of the North American situation. It would be nearer the truth to say that it definitely committed both powers to a final struggle for power in those parts. The British were now established both north and south of Canada and able, once they could bring efficient forces to the spot, to attack it by both land and sea. The French, on the other hand, had a naval base for defence in Cape Breton Island, and they in turn were established north, south, and west of the British mainland colonies. It was already possible to travel from one French post to another from the St. Lawrence to the Gulf of Mexico. These enormous distances were, however, a weakness in the French position. The strength of the British lay in the compactness and tenacity of their little settlements. They were destined never to surrender the North American places ceded to them at Utrecht. They intended to exert in these waters the sea-power of which Gibraltar and Minorca were more conspicuous prizes.

Although they were won by campaigns in Europe, the gains of the wars were made durable by the expansive forces which built up the colonies. These were nearly all growing in population, and by the time of the treaty of Utrecht the numbers were roughly 110,000 in New England, 73,000 in the middle colonies, 157,000 (including negroes) in the southern mainland colonies, or 350,000 altogether on the mainland of America.[1] There were not so many as 400,000 white men under the British flag in the whole western hemisphere, not so many as the population of London then was. Their economic importance was out of all proportion to their numbers. It was out of proportion even to the money value of their products, because what they sent to Europe was new wealth, and the markets they provided for European exports were new markets. Their importance was that they brought about change in the balance of European economy, and as a transforming force their rate of growth was more significant than their absolute size. The conditions of colonial life, with endless undeveloped land, favoured the natural multiplication of the settlers. The old sources of recruitment from Europe had

[1] G. Chalmers, *Introduction to the History of the American Colonies*, ed. of 1845, ii. 7, gives 434,000, including 58,850 negroes, for the mainland colonies in 1715.

not dried up, but the average annual immigration was smaller in this period than in the preceding thirty years and in some ways its character altered. There were still religious exiles who came over. One of the leading ideas of William Penn in his colonizing work was toleration, and the record of Pennsylvania in this was better than that of any other American colony. It is said that in 1680–2 the small population of South Carolina was doubled by refugees from religious intolerance; but the liberty of religion offered by the laws of Carolina in the time of Shaftesbury and Locke did not attract the numbers of settlers who were expected. The only numerous body who came over for religious reasons after the time of Charles II were not Englishmen but the Palatines.[1] Several thousand of these were brought over in English ships, after their flight to England in 1708–9, and settled in New York, the Carolinas, and most of all in Pennsylvania.

This was the origin of the excellent German-speaking element in Pennsylvania, to which there were new-comers throughout most of the eighteenth century. Other parts of Europe sent emigrants to the English colonies: there were, for instance, French and Swiss protestants in South Carolina, but their numbers were small. In the southern colonies there was in fact a shortage of labour, and this period was marked by the failure of certain bad methods of adding to the white working class there and in the West Indies. The life of sub-tropical plantations had no attractions for the European labourer who was free to go elsewhere. A free white man had such opportunities of earning a livelihood where men were few and land was cheap that he would not remain as a mere agricultural wage-earner. The majority of those who went out to the plantation-colonies were therefore men who went against their will or in ignorance of what awaited them, and were kept for a longer or shorter time after their arrival in a servile status. The deportations of political prisoners to Barbados in the interregnum had set an example, and we have seen that it was followed by the Stuarts both in England and in Scotland. From the reign of Charles II statutes permitted persons convicted of certain crimes to choose transportation as an alternative to the death penalty. Private enterprise provided the colonies with indentured labourers. Persons who could not afford to pay for a passage entered into a contract with the master of a ship by which, in return for being carried to

[1] See above, p. 238.

America, they allowed themselves to be sold for a term of years
after their arrival. No doubt some of these white 'servants' did
well after they had earned their liberty, and many were well
treated while they were still bound. They were more highly
valued than the negroes. But the system necessarily opened the
way for deception by the shipper and cruelty by the employer.
In 1670 Shaftesbury carried through an act of parliament
against 'spiriting', forcible kidnapping for the purpose of carrying the victims off to colonial slavery. The penalties were small,
but it appears that by the time of the English Revolution this
evil had been stamped out. The other abuses, however, continued. The system was radically bad and therefore incapable
of solving the labour-problem. As the slave-trade grew this was
increasingly met by the use of negro labour. Before 1660 Barbados was the only colony which used negroes in considerable
numbers. By 1714 it was clear that they were to become the
working class of all the colonies from Maryland southwards.

Only in North Carolina did the number of native Red Indians
who were reduced to slavery run to even a few hundreds. They
were not docile like the Africans, and they were not, like the
Africans, separated by the width of the ocean from their friends
and their own customs. In North Carolina the proprietors
resisted the enslavement of Indians, and it led to chronic warfare with the native tribes. The natives everywhere set limits
to the pace of expansion. There was no region where they were
not useful to the white men in one way or another. In the more
southerly colonies they supplied food, and they taught the
colonists methods of cultivation suitable to the soil and climate.
In the north they were an indispensable link in the chain of
trade, especially in the fur-trade. Like all the trade which white
men carried on in all parts of the world with backward races,
this was conducted by exchanging manufactured articles of
trifling cost for the hard-won native wares; but amongst the
European goods there were some which created trouble. There
were alcoholic liquors. There were fire-arms and ammunition,
sold to the natives in the first instance for hunting. The governments of the colonies tried to regulate trade generally and these
two trades in particular, but with only limited success. The
colonists would not give up a profitable traffic, and while there
were other European nations as their neighbours it was useless

for the English to act alone. The Dutch, as long as they held New Netherland, supplied arms in large quantities.

If it was impossible to check these dangerous trades, it was difficult to regulate the vital question of the ownership of the land. Some of the governments, especially in New England, prohibited private purchases of land from the natives. Their policy, which they were able to a large extent to enforce, was that new settlement should be in organized communities and on land bought with express public authorization. Even so there were endless opportunities for misunderstandings about boundaries and conditions. The prices with which the Indians were satisfied were derisory even when the new-comers did not defraud them, but there often was fraud. William Penn set a high standard of honest dealing with the Indians and his colony was rewarded with friendliness on their side; but in general the colonists failed to solve the problem. It was hoped that Christian missions would be of use. They were carried on with real enthusiasm, especially in New England, where John Eliot, the Apostle of the Indians, was supported by the home government and by Boyle and other philanthropists. Eliot aimed at educating the natives as well as converting them, and he established townships of 'praying Indians' which were native reservations. The faithful Mohawks still preserve the handsome set of communion-plate presented to them by Queen Anne. The colonial governments were compelled, however, by the necessities of the case to build up step by step a virtual protectorate over all the Indians within the areas of settlement, and the Indians saw that, whenever the white men wanted more land, they meant to take it.

The first Indian rising in the English colonies had been as early as 1622 in Virginia, but the serious fighting of the latter part of the century came after a comparatively genial period. In 1675 King Philip, a chief who had been made to acknowledge himself a subject of the king of England, began to fight on the New England frontier. It was hard for the colonies to organize the defence of the isolated farms and villages, and the fighting on both sides was cruel. It ended the missionary impulse: the ethnological theory that the Indians were the lost ten tribes of Israel gave way before the alternative theories that they were Hamites, divinely condemned to be hewers of wood and drawers of water, or even that they were incarnate devils. Peace did not come till 1678, two years after the death of Philip; but the war greatly strengthened the control of the English over the natives. While it was in progress Indian war began, in 1676, in Virginia. This grew out of petty thefts by the Indians, followed by reprisals and the murder of six Indian chiefs at a conference. The elderly governor, Lord Berkeley, would do nothing, so the settlers took matters into their own hands, and under the leadership of Nathaniel Bacon soon found themselves in the position of rebels. They were put down with needless severity: there were forty executions. At no time after this was there any grave danger to English colonists from unassisted native risings; but the French wars inaugurated a new and more terrible phase of Indian warfare. The five nations of the Iroquois were neighbours and friends of the English, their ancient enemies, the Hurons, Algonquins, and others, allies of the French. In the fighting for frontier forts the French used Indian auxiliaries, who scalped their prisoners. The treaty of Utrecht has a clause promising that these tribes shall all be free from molestation on one side or the other, and also that the sovereignty of the Europeans over the natives is to be exactly delimited. The Indians could hold up the European advance only momentarily unless they had European aid.

The wild conditions of the frontier, the illegal sea-trading, the hardships from which none of the colonists were altogether exempt, the widespread slave-owning, and the great empty distances made American life radically unlike life in Europe. Nevertheless, these colonies were English, and they contributed something more than trade to the life of the English people. Education was slowly spreading. Harvard College, founded in 1636, provided New England with a body of well-trained ministers of religion. There was much theological writing, and there were poets, one or two of whom had real technical skill, though they lagged behind the changes of fashion in Europe. The best literary work was on the history of the colonies and most of them had something to show in this department. A considerable proportion of the works of American authors were published in England, but the more solid of the productions of American presses were also known here. At the beginning of the period the only such press in English territory was at Cambridge, Massachusetts. Boston had one in 1675. They were subject to a close censorship, which extinguished the first attempt at an American newspaper in 1690; but in 1704 the *Boston Newsletter* began a long life. Philadelphia had a printing-office in 1687 and New York in 1693. The southern colonies, mainly because their towns were smaller, were less advanced. William and Mary College at Williamsburg in Virginia was intended for higher education, but for the time did not become more than a school. The cultivated and munificent General Christopher Codrington, born in the Barbados, where he succeeded his father as governor, but educated in Oxford, made in his will the first provision for higher education in the West Indies. He died in 1710, but Codrington College, which never exactly fulfilled his somewhat curious plan, was not begun until 1714.

The influence of the American colonies on the English mind thus did not lie in any intellectual current. It was conveyed partly by individuals who brought back to the mother country the energy, not always beneficent, of the colonists. Such were Sir George Downing and Codrington, and in another way William Penn. Again, the religious diversity of the colonies was, like the presbyterianism of Scotland, a reassurance to the English nonconformists. Most important of all, the consciousness of expansion strengthened the confidence of British statesmen in their relations with the European powers.

We have seen that towards the end of the period statesmen did not all regard the affairs of colonial trading companies as an integral part of the interests of the state. In Asia the English were represented only by two trading companies, the Levant Company and the East India Company. The trade of the former was one of the inducements for the occupation of Tangier and afterwards of Gibraltar and Minorca. The latter was itself destined to become an imperial power, and in this period Englishmen began to foresee that they were to enter upon this career in the East. It was also made plain that it was to be undertaken by the Company and not by the Crown. At the Restoration the English did not own an inch of Indian territory. The Company held its factories as a tenant of the native rulers, and its masters had no desire to alter their status. In northern India the mogul power, ruling from Delhi, was still sufficiently strong to give traders the peace they needed, and the principal English station was at Surat, where they carried on their business side by side with the Dutch. From 1668 the French also had a factory there. It was the principal city of the west coast of India.

On the eastern coast the chief English factory was Fort St. George, at Madras. Subordinate to it were factories at Masulipatam and three other places on the Coromandel Coast, and also those far away to the north-east. These were at Balasore, in Orissa, and Hughli, in the Ganges delta. There was a factory at Basra on the Persian Gulf, but it was on the point of being abandoned. At Mokha on the Red Sea, the centre of the coffee-trade, the life of the factory had more than one such interruption. In 1661 the Company withdrew from the port-to-port trade in Asia and so reduced the number of its factories. It also had establishments in the Malay Archipelago. Of these the head was Bantam in Java. Another was at Bencoolen in Sumatra. The Company claimed the island of Pulo-Run under the Swiss award consequent on the peace-treaty of 1654, but was not in possession. Lastly, as we have seen, the Company at this time leased some factories on the west coast of Africa as calling-places on the voyage round the Cape.

The cession of Bombay by Portugal as part of the dowry of Catharine of Braganza in 1661 was something new in kind. Bombay came to the king, not the Company, and it was held in full territorial sovereignty. When the English acquired it they succeeded to the position of the Portuguese, who had come to India as conquerors. The Portuguese governor was extremely unwilling to surrender it, and, when the earl of Marlborough arrived with five men-of-war to take possession, he met with obstructions which were not overcome until 1665. Charles II, however, soon found that the expense of maintaining the place brought him no direct benefit, and in 1668, after considering its complete abandonment, he handed it over, on payment of a quit-rent, to the Company. It rapidly grew in wealth and importance, and in 1687 the 'presidency' of the west coast was transferred to it from Surat. By this time the Company's position was fundamentally changing. The Dutch wars were comparatively uneventful in its sphere, but each of them did something to simplify the relations of the two countries. In the treaty of Breda, by the surrender of their claim to Pulo-Run, the English took a step towards leaving the Dutch a free hand in the Malay Archipelago.[1] In the later war the English lost some ships, but the

[1] Before the treaty of Breda came into operation, the king of Macassar, by arrangement with the Dutch, broke up the English factory there, which was never re-established.

Dutch used most of their energy against the French, so that the English suffered less than either of their two rivals. It was during this war that the English finally possessed themselves of St. Helena, which was granted to the Company by the Crown and used as a place of call on the Cape route. In 1682, in time of peace, the native princes, instigated by the Dutch, expelled the English from their factory at Bantam, and, in spite of frequent complaints, it was never restored. This was a blessing in disguise. There was little to hope from competing with the Dutch in Indonesia, where they were strongest, and any such attempt diverted men and money from more effective employment in Hither India. The presidency at Bencoolen dragged on its existence until the nineteenth century, but it was ill-managed and its commercial importance was small. The Company traded also with China, but only intermittently before 1698, and, except in 1701–4, not on a large scale. It was able to concentrate almost all its efforts where they were most needed and best rewarded.

The first great local change to be faced was the enfeeblement of the mogul empire in the last years of Aurungzeb, who reigned from 1658 to 1707. In 1664 a Maratha raid on Surat, when the town was sacked but the English factory withstood the attack, gave the first indication that the Company might have to protect itself by changing its status. In 1670 Surat was again in danger from the same Maratha chief, Shivaji, and in 1677 he was in the neighbourhood of Madras. In Bengal the English were oppressed by the local nabob. All over India there was disorder, but the resolute Englishmen on the spot knew from experience that if they were allowed to take strong measures they could protect themselves from it. In 1679 Richard Keigwin, who had retaken St. Helena, was commander of the garrison at Bombay. In command of the East India Company's ship *Revenge* and a few small craft, he fought Shivaji's fleet of forty or fifty sail, and scattered it. At the India House in Leadenhall Street, the directors were for economy and against ambitious commitments. Keigwin was recalled to England before his victory was known, and orders were sent to reduce the garrison. He returned to Bombay. In 1683 the garrison mutinied against the hesitating policy of the Company. Keigwin put himself at its head, took control of the government, and wrote to the king that he was holding Bombay for him. Charles referred the matter to the directors of the Company, and they sent out a new governor who was accompanied by a frigate of the navy besides the Company's ships. But they brought a general pardon and Keigwin submitted in a level-headed manner. From the beginning to the end of his rebellion, which lasted nearly a year, no blood had been shed. He retained his naval rank, and died bravely at the head of a landing-party in the West Indies in 1690.[1]

By then, however, the same directors who had put Keigwin down, and would have been glad to see him hanged, had come over to the forward policy for which he had stood. The events at Bombay probably contributed to their change of heart, but other troubles had a greater share in it, and the decisive turn seems to have been given by the loss of Bantam. The charters granted in 1661 and 1683 gave the Company the right to coin money, to exercise jurisdiction over English subjects, to make peace and war and to enter into alliances with Indian rulers. The new charter granted by James II was still wider. The Company was, as the directors themselves avowed, 'in the condition of a sovereign state in India'. They were determined to have their factories no longer at the mercy of the Indians, and they set about raising a large revenue from duties in order to maintain strong naval and military forces. In a dispatch of 1687 they urged the president of Surat, in words which are often quoted, to 'establish such a politie of civil and military power and create and secure such a large revenue . . . as may be the foundation of a large, well-grounded sure English dominion in India for all time to come'.

It was easier said than done. The great prosperity which the Company had enjoyed throughout practically the whole reign of Charles II was interrupted in the subsequent years. Profits were again diminished by the competition of interlopers, English merchants who traded independently in contravention of its monopoly. An expensive expedition with ten armed ships and a military force was sent out in 1686. Its instructions were to capture and fortify Chittagong, to make war on the king of Siam and to capture Salsette Island, near Bombay, from the Portuguese. Only the first of these ill-assorted projects was begun. The expedition reached Hughli, but hostilities began prematurely and the English had to retire down stream to a village on the site of the modern Calcutta. The Mogul emperor ordered a general attack on the factories. Those at Surat, Patna,

---

[1] Ray and O. Strachey, *Keigwin's Rebellion* (1916) tells the story well.

Casimbazar, Masulipatam, and Vizagapatam were lost, and Bombay was besieged. Reinforcements from England enabled the English to evacuate Bengal with all their goods. They appeared before Chittagong but found it too strong to attack. The policy of aggression had overleapt itself. The only effective retaliation open to the English was to stop the Indian pilgrims from going to Mecca by sea. This enabled them to obtain peace in 1690, but only on payment of a fine of £17,000 and with other humiliating conditions. A by-product of this disastrous affair was, however, the foundation of Calcutta, which, after twice being abandoned in consequence of the war, became a permanent settlement after the peace, and began the growth which has made it the first city of India.

The English Revolution, for reasons partly personal and partly constitutional and economic, weakened the influence of the Company at home. Until the later years of Charles II there had been whigs among the directors, but from that time it had worked in close co-operation with the Crown and the court party. Its trade was built up on the export of bullion, and after the Revolution there was a return to theories of the balance of trade which were adverse to this export. Trading monopolies in general were now attacked in parliament. The interlopers, who had been worsted in their attacks during the last Stuart decade, now rallied. They pressed their cause in parliament and formed an association. For some years they were kept at arm's length, and in 1693, not without heavy bribery of the ministers, the Company obtained a new charter from the Crown. This success undid itself. The house of commons, jealous of the prerogative, resolved in 1694 'that all the subjects of England have equal right to trade to the East Indies, unless prohibited by Act of Parliament'.[1] In 1695 some unpleasant incidents which had nothing to do with the Company or even with trade led to the dismissal of a number of public officials for corruption. The whigs took advantage of the general indignation to begin a parliamentary inquiry into the accounts of the city of London and the East India Company. The bribes of 1693 were discovered: the duke of Leeds, who had received 5,500 guineas, was impeached. The Company's reputation was hamstrung and this was the end of the duke's career. Some of the interlopers made the mistake at this time of going into the scheme for the

[1] *Commons' Journals*, 19 January 1693/4.

Scottish Company trading to the Indies; but the English element in this was so soon extinguished that the mistake did them as a body no permanent harm. In 1698 they won a real victory when they made a loan of two millions to the government, and were incorporated under the name of the General Society. This was a regulated company, in which the members were to trade individually, and its privileges did not override the vested interest of private traders already engaged in East Indian business; but, in accordance with arrangements in the charter, the bulk of the interlopers then formed a joint stock company, and for ten years the two East India Companies, the Old and the New, existed side by side.

The directors of the Old Company met this situation with common sense and self-restraint. They had their forts and factories, and their experienced servants in London and in the East. Although their privileges were held on a precarious tenure, they had not been forfeited. The directors acquired a financial interest in the New Company. In the East the rivalry between the two companies was intense. It was a strange thing that a European nation had allowed two powerfully organized corporations of its merchants to compete against one another in a distant trade. It inevitably meant that each would try to outbid the other in buying in India and to undercut in selling in Europe: it pared away profits at both ends. The New Company stood for the principle of establishing friendly relations with the moguls and the Indian princes in general, and abandoning the imperialistic policy. However much there was to be said for this, its agents lacked the necessary diplomatic skill, and they were obstructed by those of the Old Company. In trading operations they failed to weaken the Old Company in its presidencies of Bengal and Madras. In the third, Surat, they threw the business of their rivals into confusion by provoking a quarrel with the authorities which led to the closing of the factory; but they gained no trade for themselves. Their finances were crippled from the start by their loan to the government. By 1702 it was only a question whether the Old Company would consent to a fusion or insist on fighting to a finish. Fortunately for both parties King William III and his ministers and parliament wanted to end the contest, the more so since war with France was about to begin, and, if it supervened on this commercial civil war, might easily drive the English out of the Indian trade altogether. In April 1702 a preliminary agreement was made for the union of the two companies on the basis of a very reasonable valuation of their assets. It took some years for the friction between the two interests to die out, but in 1708, largely as a result of the wise mediation of Godolphin, the United East India Company was finally constituted. The short-sighted exclusiveness and the equally short-sighted individualism of the seventeenth century were transmuted into a compromise which rested on self-interest so enlightened that it resembled public spirit. The body then constituted acquired in time not only almost the whole seaborne trade of India but also the imperial inheritance of the moguls.

XV

LITERATURE AND THOUGHT

AUTHORS do not form such a well-defined community as painters or musicians. None the less there was a general life of literature by which all writers were touched to some greater or less degree. At its centre were the literary men in the narrower sense, the men who were most directly concerned with skill in expression, that is the imaginative authors, poets, story-tellers, all whose books had anything of poetry or humanity in them, and amongst these the critics. Even the most narrowly technical writers responded, according to their capacities, to the changes of literary fashion. Thus there are social changes in the conditions of authorship which lie at the centre of the manifold literary history of the time.

The first of these was the development of the reading public and of the organization by which it was supplied with books. Authors continued to be largely dependent on royal or noble patrons for their livelihood, and most of the important books of the time begin with fulsome dedications in which these bene-factors are thanked for their past or future favours. If the writer were a clergyman he might be made domestic chaplain, or tutor to the patron's sons at home or on their travels abroad; he might be presented to a living, or, if he served one of the great party-leaders, he might aspire to a deanery or even a bishopric. Thus the clergy wrote about many things besides theology: there were political pamphleteers like Swift, the greatest of all, and party historians like White Kennet, who became bishop of Peterborough. A layman might find in letters the path to diplo-matic and political office, like Locke and Addison and Prior, or simply to pensions and a maintenance, like Dryden. These were the great prizes of literature, and every writer did his best to win them. No one disdained the protection of the great. There were indeed humbler rewards, in the form of hard cash, from other quarters. Writing for the theatre brought its modest remunera-tion, but the theatre belonged to the world of fashion, and the prologues of the dramatists show that they too were sup-pliants for a collective patronage. Writing for the booksellers, who were also the publishers of the time, gave access to a wider public, but the booksellers could not afford to pay well, and the majority of those who wrote simply for them were no better than hacks.

The position of authors was strengthened by the system of publishing books by subscription, that is after circulating a prospectus and obtaining a sufficient number of promises to buy. This device was growing commoner throughout the period. The first great success was with Dryden's translation of Virgil, which brought him £1,200; but this was far surpassed by the translation of Homer, for which Pope issued his proposals in 1713, and even by the folio edition of Prior's poems which, like Pope's Homer, was published in the reign of George I. Minor authors benefited in proportion, and, though the system soon developed in unscrupulous hands into a means of fraud, it did a real service. There were still few large libraries except those which were frequented only by scholars, and there were no circulating libraries.[1] Only substantial men could buy folios, but the growth of London and the improvement of communications with the country put authors within reach of a great number of people who could afford to buy printed matter. Journalism thus made rapid strides. The *London Gazette*, which took that name in 1666, having begun in Oxford in the previous year, was official, an instrument of government. It followed a French model. The London newspapers were mainly political and, in their advertisements, like the *Gazette*, served practical purposes. They became more numerous and more specialized. The *Daily Courant*, the first daily newspaper in the world, began in 1702. The commercial press came into existence. So did the provincial press, though at first it was unimportant enough. In William III's time there were papers in Norwich and Worcester and one for Lincoln, Rutland, and Stamford. Under Queen Anne newspapers were published in York, Liverpool, Nottingham, Hereford, Bristol, and Exeter. But the most important change was the rise of literary journalism. The reviewing of books came in from the Continent, at first for learned books, but soon for books of all kinds. This facilitated the circulation of literary ideas: hitherto there had been no vehicle for written judgements on particular books except in books and pamphlets and in the correspondence of literary men. Scarcely had reviewing begun

[1] See above, pp. 15, 158.

when literary periodicals took on a still more attractive function: they became a means of selling good literature by instalments. In 1709 Captain Richard Steele, an Oxford man who was editor of the *Gazette*, started the *Tatler*, a miscellaneous periodical published three times a week, with a mixture of news, gossip, and criticism. He was helped by his Oxford contemporary and political ally Joseph Addison, and, as they went on with it, the *Tatler* became less miscellaneous and more ambitious. It approached the character of its more famous successor the *Spectator*, which the two friends began in 1711. The *Spectator* is still readable and popular; it is full of wise and graceful discussions of literature, manners, and public affairs. It has a didactic air, and it rather tamely avoids anything that could give offence except to political opponents; but it did much to educate taste in every sphere. Like the *Tatler* it paid well and was promptly reprinted in volumes.

In the *Spectator* commercial men and their affairs were treated with a respect which they had never before received from the polite literature of Stuart England. This is one sign among many that by the later years of Queen Anne literature was coming to be more the common possession of the nation, or of the better-educated classes, than it had been before. This is to some extent due to the fact that literary men were now enjoying more of a common social life and sharing it with men of business and affairs. If we compare the biographies of the dozen great writers of our period whose works are still a living part of the nation's reading, it will be clear that this was a new growth of the time. It is not a mere accident that of the two who survived from before the Restoration one was provincial and the other socially isolated. Sir Thomas Browne had travelled, and his *Religio Medici* was known in translations all over Europe; but he practised and wrote in Yorkshire and in Norwich. John Milton was a Londoner, but even if he had not been blind, and altogether out of sympathy with the spirit of Charles II's reign, it is hard to believe that he would have lived any life but that of dignified privacy. Of the younger generation, all the great writers mixed freely in a half-public club-life.

There was a tendency for this sort of life to develop all over England at this time. The fellows of colleges in Oxford and Cambridge had their common-rooms where they drank and smoked together in much the same informal way in which they met in taverns outside the college walls.[1] In London the new meeting-places were the coffee-houses. Coffee came from the Levant. When John Evelyn was an undergraduate at Balliol in 1637 he tells us there came to the college one Nathaniel Conopios out of Greece. 'He was the first I ever saw drink coffee, which custom came not into England till thirty years after.'[2] In 1664 Pepys went to a coffee-house to drink chocolate.[3] But liquors of all kinds were sold at these houses, and their clients consumed wine and spirits as copiously as the other convivial circles of the time. They were in fact clubs run for profit by their proprietors. It is said that in 1708 London had 3,000 of them. Many of them became centres for various kinds of business. Marine insurance had its home at Lloyd's Coffee-house. The name is still used for the great exchange which has grown out of it. Merchants, stock-jobbers, whig and tory politicians all had their places of resort, and likewise the literary men. There was the Grecian, where classical scholars consorted. At Button's Addison could be found. At Will's Dryden in his old age had a chair by the fire in winter and by the window in summer. There and in a score of other houses of the kind literary men mixed informally with one another, with city men, with men about town, and with politicians. The word 'club' was used in its other sense for bodies which had periodical meetings, and several of these have their places in literary history. There was the Kit-Cat Club, of which the secretary was the publisher Jacob Tonson. All the whig political noblemen belonged to it, as well as Addison, Steele, Congreve, and Vanbrugh. On the tory side there was the Brothers Club, where Swift brought together St. John, Prior, and others. The literary life of England was concentrated in London, and the literary life of London was club-life. It had the defects of club-life: there was more familiarity than intimacy; fashion counted for more than conviction; quickness in talk outshone depth of thought; it was worse to be laughed at than to be wrong. But club-life has its advantages. It brings out what men have in common; it helps them to set up common standards of judgement; it smoothes away the idiosyncrasies which hinder co-operation in common tasks.

[1] The oldest dining-club now surviving in England is said to be a secular priests' dining-club, which has met continuously since James I's reign, except during the excitement of the Popish Plot, when the members gathered in small groups in different taverns.

[2] *Diary*, 10 May.   [3] Ibid., 24 Nov.

Such, for better and worse, was the effect of the metropolitan coffee-house intercourse on letters. It came at a time when there were tendencies in literature which needed a sociable environment in order to develop to the full. There was a critical tendency, a keen interest in theoretical questions about the subjects and technique of letters generally and especially of poetry and the drama. The critical essays of the *Spectator* came late in a long series. For more than a generation there had been an active cosmopolitan discussion in which the English derived most of their ideas from France, on the proper arrangement and component parts of an heroic poem, on the relative merits of modern and ancient literature and learning, on the value of rhyme, on the imitation of nature. The criteria to which all these questions tended more and more to be referred were those of appropriateness and 'good sense'. Pedantry and obscurity became the dread of the polished writer. He aimed at being, like the best French writers, a man of the world addressing himself to men of the world. The French influence worked not only through the masterpieces of the writers of the period, all of which were read and many of them translated or adapted. It was also conveyed by persons. The poets Denham and Cowley shared the exile of Charles II in France. From an early date after the Restoration one of the literary oracles of London was Monsieur de Saint-Évremond, a political exile who had been a general in the French service. Charles II made him keeper of the ducks in St. James's Park, and he pottered about, giving literary advice, until he died in Queen Anne's reign at about 90 years old. John Locke knew France, though his friends there were foreigners and huguenots, none of whom frequented Versailles.[1]

Foreign influences fertilize soils that are ready for them, and in one great change the example of France may be seen to combine with half a dozen native tendencies working the same way. This was the transformation of prose style. Milton and Sir Thomas Browne had written the prose of their generation, sonorous and ornate, with curious conceits and long sentences, branching into clause after clause, but not braced together into tight grammatical periods. French prose had learned a luminous ease, and English prose copied from it. Addison and Swift, if rather more formally, wrote, not in vocabulary but in construction, as we write now. In France the critics saw that the change

[1] See C. Bastide, *John Locke* (1907), p. 58.

had been, at any rate partly, due to the new scientific spirit, the desire to think clearly without the scaffolding of scholastic formalism. In England too the scientists, with singularly few exceptions, worked at perfecting language as an instrument of thought. Hobbes had anticipated them in terseness and precision, though he still kept illustrative quotations and metaphors which were meant as much to adorn as to explain his arguments. The Royal Society exacted from its members a compact and unembellished way of speaking. Dr. Wilkins wrote a large volume on the possibility of a symbolic language which should be as precise as mathematical notation. Wallis wrote an English grammar. Evelyn and Petty worked on projects for dictionaries of various kinds. Locke in his *Essay* had much to say about the nature and functions of words. Newton, as a youth, studied phonetics and other aspects of the science of language.[1]

What these scientists were trying to do was good for many purposes besides those of science. The only pamphlet which Swift published over his own name was a proposal for the setting-up of an academy for correcting the English language. Swift did not understand the aims of the scientists. He jeered at them, but his genius too was for point and directness. His prose was much nearer to the spoken word than that of Charles I's time. So was Dryden's, clean, free, and informal, expressing his copious flow of thought without visible effort. With them the racy simplicity of colloquial English found its place in the art of writing. It had never been used only in speech. There had always been soldiers and travellers who wrote their narratives tersely. There had always been pamphleteers and other political and religious propagandists who, in order to convince, wrote simply.[2] From an early date in the seventeenth century, even from the sixteenth, there had been a familiar letter-writing manner. The Englishmen who published their letters had written more artificially, but in France it had become the fashion to print less laboured private letters. It is thought that some of the best English letter-writers, for instance King Charles II himself, were influenced by the French epistolary style, so that here, too, France played a part; but it was only in liberating a vigour which had been kept under.

Dryden in his later years corrected some of his earlier sentences, taking away the pendent clauses that trailed at the end of them, and giving them something more of the form of the Latin periods. In the eighteenth century, English prose was to carry this to the point of monotonous regularity, but that had not yet come about.[1] The greatest English classical scholar of the period, Richard Bentley, wrote like a man who knew the texture of Latin prose; but in him, too, grammatical coherence was combined with a homely pungency which came straight from his West Riding character. The new prose seemed to those who used it to be derived from, or to resemble, that of the ancient classics. Addison considered that he stood 'for the essential and inherent perfection of simplicity of thought above that which I call the Gothic manner in writing'.[2] This was to extend the term Gothic unfairly. Chaucer's prose, written when Gothic art was still alive, had not the faults that were now so distasteful, and simplicity had many attractions besides that of being classical. In more ways than one it fitted the needs of the age in religion. William Penn was one of those who wrote in the new manner. He had his French model: *Some Fruits of Solitude*, with all its Christian gravity, is written in the manner of the relentlessly worldly *Maximes* of La Rochefoucauld. But a greater influence on Penn's style was the plain speech of the quakers, the rejection of the vain and superfluous which made them always use 'thee' and 'thou', and express themselves with the utmost economy of words. If the quakers were singular in making this a rule for daily life, many other Puritans shared the same feeling. In 1666 John Bunyan wrote in the preface to his autobiography, *Grace Abounding to the Chief of Sinners*:

I could also have stepped into a style much higher than this in which I have here discoursed, and could have adorned all things more than here I have seemed to do, but I dare not. God did not play in convincing of me, the devil did not play in tempting of me, neither did I play when I sunk into a bottomless pit, when the pangs of hell caught hold upon me; wherefore I may not play in my relating of them, but be plain and simple, and lay down the thing as it was.[3]

---

[1] For an example of the insufferable pedantry of imitating Latin too closely see the book by Christopher Wase mentioned below, p. 413, n. 1.

[2] *Spectator*, No. 70.

[3] In *Grace Abounding* Bunyan's style is less colloquial than his story-telling manner, as in *The Life and Death of Mr. Badman*.

Remote as Bunyan's mind and audiences were from those of
the divines of the church of England, they too arrived by their
different road at something like the same conclusion. In the
earlier part of the century sermons, both in quantity and influence one of the most important branches of literature, had
two characteristics which, after the Restoration, they could no
longer keep. They were consciously authoritative: they were
the pronouncements of divinely commissioned expositors. Consequently they had more than their share of all the admired kinds
of obscurity, intricate conceits, and pretentious parades of learning, quotations from Latin, Greek, and Hebrew. Now the clergy
had to change their note. In comparison with the Jacobeans
they seem to be on the defensive. Their purpose is to explain and
to convince. The practical aim of edification dictated, just as the
aims of science dictated, simplicity of means. Here again there
were great French preachers who led the way. From the time
of Charles II a number of writers on the art of preaching, amongst
them Dr. Wilkins, laid down rules of which the first was that the
preacher's manner must be plain. Archbishop Tillotson, another
West Riding man, was the great master in this new style. Dryden,
who, if it had not been for this testimony, might have been supposed to have learnt everything from France, frequently owned
'with pleasure that if he had any talent for English prose, it was
owing to his having often read the writings of the great Archbishop Tillotson'.[1]

Even with this we have not come to the last of the reasons for
the change in prose. It was, on another side, the result of England's becoming a business nation. Simplicity and clearness are
very near to utilitarianism, and the new prose was the prose of
every sort of utility. The writer who typifies this side of it is
Daniel Defoe. We have already met him as a powerful pam-
phleteer. He was a protestant dissenter. His education at a
dissenting academy is not likely to have included all the subjects
he said he learned there, but it was miscellaneous and he seems
to have known scarcely anything about the classics. At one time
he was a hosiery-factor in London, at another he was concerned

[1] Congreve, Dedication to Dryden's *Dramatick Works*, 6 vols. (1735). The literary
history of preaching is exhaustively treated in W. F. Mitchell, *English Pulpit Oratory
from Andrews to Tillotson* (1932). Dryden, like the divines, came to eschew emblems
and indirect representation. The new fashion was to say one thing at a time. In an
essay reprinted in *The Cultural Revolution of the Seventeenth Century* (1951) Mr. S. L.
Bethell relates this to the treatment of faith and reason in Anglican theology.

in the manufacture of tiles at Tilbury. He was not a success as a business man, but he had an active mind and he accumulated an extensive, if inaccurate, knowledge of all kinds of business operations. This and his power of observing men he put at the service of governments. He was employed to explore and influence opinion in England and Scotland. He had adventures, some of them unpleasant. The worst was in 1703, when he was condemned to the pillory for his pamphlet *The Shortest Way with the Dissenters*, in which he ironically recommended that nonconformity should be rooted out with the utmost severity. The details of his life are, however, very hard to make out because, although he made a great many statements about it, none of them seem to have been altogether true. He seems to have been unable to distinguish truth from fiction. His curious French name was his own invention: his father was a butcher called James Foe. At the end of our period Defoe was only beginning to discover that he could do better at writing convincing fiction than at any of the other things he had attempted. He had written *The Apparition of Mrs. Veale*, and may even have thought it a true story; *Robinson Crusoe* and his other novels, along with his bogus histories, were still to come. But he was already in his place as the first of the great popular journalists. Neither scholarly nor truthful nor dignified, he had a genius for writing to suit the ordinary man. He always had a story to tell and a plan to explain, and he was always full of what looked like robust common sense. There was nothing graceful or romantic, let alone noble, about him and much that was vulgar; but he proved that a plain man writing for plain men may have more readers than any other sort of author.

Since poetry and prose are not absolutely separate compartments, and each always influences the other, similar tendencies were at work in poetry. The French influence, the critical study of forms, the imitation of classical models had the effect here too of ending the tortuous solemnities of the baroque and making all the poets aim at lucidity. Of the writers of the older tradition we need not discuss any except Milton, incomparably the greatest poet of our period. When it began he was known as the one English writer who had written really good original Latin poems. In this he was alone not merely among his contemporaries: he had had no predecessor, and it is almost true to say that he has had no successor. England has been poorer in original

Latin poetry since the Renaissance than either Italy or France or Holland. When in 1663 Louis XIV asked his ambassador, Cominges, a military man, for information about the state of literature in England, the only report he got on poetry was that *un nommé Miltonius* had written good verses in Latin.[1] This has been regarded as funny, but it was adequate to the facts. The other living poets, Cowley and Denham, Waller and Marvell, were of no interest to Europe; even now they are, apart from a few lines here and there, notable only for the steps they built for the ascent of poetry. Milton had already done much better than any of them in English: he had written *Comus* and *Lycidas*. But the whole of his English verse written before the Restoration may be read in little more than an hour. He had shown himself a great master of the music of English words. He had brought back from Italy the serious beauty of the late Renaissance. But he was best known to the few as a Latin poet and to the many as the terrible controversialist of the puritan revolution.

Not so much because he had held office under the Protectorate, for it was a subordinate office, as because he had ruthlessly defended the execution of Charles I, the Restoration brought him into danger. To Cominges he was Miltonius *qui s'est rendu plus infâme par ses dangereux écrits que ces bourreaux et les assassins du roi*. It is not certain whose intercession saved him. There were several men of influence who appreciated poetry and some who knew him. However it came about, he was spared. Already, in 1658, he had begun the epic poem which had been his ambition before the civil war. He had considered various other subjects, such as King Arthur, which would have suited his pride in the English soil and name. His final choice was the fall of man, to the mind of his time the greatest of all themes. Thus *Paradise Lost* gave to England what Italy and Holland had already, a long poem, following the accepted rules, and narrating the rebellion of the angels and the history of Adam and Eve. It was like the painted ceilings of Italian palaces, with their clouds and deities, except that it was vaster and sombre and, in spite of all its mythology, real. Moreover, it was individual. Its ideas were Milton's own. There was the belief in 'rational liberty' which was his central passion, true liberty

> which always with right reason dwells
> Twinn'd, and from her hath no dividual being.

[1] J. Jusserand, *A French Ambassador at the Court of Charles II* (1892), p. 205.

There was enough about tyranny and the office of a king, about spiritual liberty and temporal power, to make the censor hesitate before he gave his licence. There were allusions to astronomy which showed that Milton was not willing to let the new scientific knowledge disturb his convictions about God and man. But the poem accorded neither with commonplace republicanism nor with commonplace puritanism. It had a glorious invocation to wedded love defamed by hypocrites as impure. And all through, from beginning to end, speaking for himself alone as only the greatest artists can, Milton spoke for half mankind.

In spite of everything the poem had a respectable circulation from the first. One after another the arbiters of taste spoke well of it, Dryden more generously than any, and as the old divisions were smoothed away Milton's poem became a part of the national inheritance. A series of critical articles by Addison in the *Spectator* marked its general acceptance: the *Spectator* was the more ready to appreciate Milton because it was on the whig side, but it offended no one in this. His later poems are shorter and have less of what used to be called the sublime. *Paradise Regained* is in form an epic poem on the temptation in the wilderness. It justifies the deep confidence which Milton retained after his disappointments at the hands of the people, 'a miscellaneous rabble', and of human philosophies:

> Who therefore seeks in these
> True wisdom, finds her not, or by delusion
> Far worse, her false resemblance only meets,
> An empty cloud.

In *Samson Agonistes*, adapting the form of Athenian tragedy, he wrote another unapproachable masterpiece of golden language and solemn wisdom. Its final chorus is worthy to stand as the last word of Milton's work and of his age.

For his world, the world to which he had belonged although at so many points he had transcended it, no longer lived with the life that can be expressed in great poetry. Puritan England had its literature. John Bunyan wrote *The Pilgrim's Progress* in prison, probably in the year after Milton died, and that too is a work of genius; but it is a book of the people; its genius is untutored. The nonconformists were coming to live in their own circle of knowledge and pursuits, far enough away from Latin poetry and Italian cultivation. Their representative authors in the next age did not contribute to the national literature, and the only famous writer from among them who became a national possession was Defoe, who was destitute of both poetry and religion. Where poetry and cultivation were still maintained was in the club-life of London, and there, however the heroic and the sublime might be held in respect, they were out of reach. The great man in those literary circles was John Dryden, and the contrast between his personal fortunes and Milton's is like the contrast between their works. Dryden was a schoolfellow of Locke's at Westminster, and like Milton he was at Cambridge. He inherited a small estate, but depended most of his life on his writings. He was only twenty-seven when he wrote very laudatory 'Heroic Stanzas' on the death of Oliver Cromwell, an indiscretion which did him no great harm after the Restoration; he was fifty-five when he became a Roman catholic under James II. He was no turncoat: all his life he respected order and authority, disliking fanaticism and faction. He was a born writer, with a spontaneous felicity in both verse and prose. He responded to the changes of the literary atmosphere. His *Annus Mirabilis* is a poem about the wonders of the year 1666, the plague, the fire, the Dutch war. It is completely baroque. There are classical similes, nautical terminology, speeches by the admirals, a prayer by the king, affecting passages which ring false:

> The wanting orphans saw with watery eyes
> Their founder's charity in dust laid low,
> And sent to God their ever-answered cries,
> For he protects the poor who made them so.

But in 1681, in *Absalom and Achitophel*, a satire on Monmouth and Shaftesbury, Dryden has thrown away all this obsolete apparatus. He closes with his prey as cleanly as a hawk bringing down its bird. There is no moralizing or apostrophizing, simply a story with each of the characters drawn in epigrammatic words that have become proverbial. Neither Dryden nor any one else ever equalled this in political satire. There was, in fact, no other opportunity for such straightforward scorn and indignation as loyal and reasonable men felt at the time of the Popish Plot. And it may be remarked about the political verse of the period generally that it was limited to the ideas and emotions of the ordinary political man. It is clearly the work of poets who were either themselves politicians, like Marvell, or hacks and dependants of politicians. The quantity of political verse is very great and much of it shows finished workmanship, but it is all written either for or against some leader or some party. Butler's *Hudibras*, indeed, which we have already noticed,[1] versified the mood of most of the nation, but it did not bring its author the rewards he had expected. The later satirists had more *savoir-faire*, but the result was that their derision and invective, however sincere and however witty, were intellectually as empty as the odes in which they celebrated victories or royal birthdays. Literature could not seize the greatness of the tragic issues which were being decided in war and policy, because it had no sure footing of its own outside the mêlée. Between Milton and Wordsworth no poet saw deeper into the life of the state than the statesmen themselves could see.

Dryden was the supreme satirist, but his satires were few and, of course, short. The greatest part of his great output consisted of plays, and here again he showed his adaptability. He was indeed so great a believer in adaptability that he did some surprising feats of adaptation. There were new methods in the technique of verse and in dramatic construction on some sides corresponding in origin and effect with the new prose. In verse the main change was that longer poems were now written in self-contained rhymed couplets, known as heroic couplets. Dryden learned from Denham how to run these smoothly together and improved on the lesson. In the making of a play it was now considered necessary to observe the unities of time, place, and action, to make a play the working-out of a single situation in one place and within the limits of a single day. Dryden rewrote Shakespeare's *Troilus and Cressida* according to these formulae. He helped to recondition *The Tempest* in the same way; but when he set to work on *Antony and Cleopatra* he turned back to blank verse. The result, *All for Love*, is often regarded as his greatest work; but it reveals strange limitations in his appreciation of Shakespeare, whole-hearted though it was. Still more curious is his opera *The State of Innocence*, which is founded on *Paradise Lost*. It is said that he asked Milton if he might do it, and that Milton answered by giving him leave to tag his verses. This writing for the stage was like journalism, hurried, superficial, and meant to catch the popular taste. All was grist that came to its mill, and adaptation was the quick way to provide

[1] See above, p. 18.

what was wanted. So Dryden, like his contemporaries, poured out versions of French plays as well as original pieces of all kinds; but he recognized himself that several of his contemporaries surpassed him in comedy, and in tragedy he never felt at home.

The Restoration drama, as it is called, is a great body of plays written not in the period of the Restoration proper but from that time until well on in the reign of Queen Anne. Down to the end of William III's time its general character underwent no great change, and though its sentiments varied with the course of political and social events, its writers formed a single school. The closing of the theatres by the Long Parliament put an end to the marvellous dramatic poetry which had begun under Queen Elizabeth, and not too soon, for it was working itself out. After some small preliminary ventures under the late Protectorate, the stage made a fresh start when Charles II returned. Two theatres were opened in London, the King's and the Duke's. The king's company, after several moves, settled in 1663 at the Theatre Royal in Drury Lane. The licencees and the companies engaged from the first in the quarrels and jealousies which seem to be inevitable in theatrical management; but the upshot was that in London there was always at least one licensed theatre and never more than three. In the provinces there were no fixed theatres, and the touring companies were few and bad. In the arrangement of the stage the French model was now followed, with a drop curtain and painted scenery. Another innovation was made which may or may not have had some effect on dramatic art: the women's parts were played, as in France, by actresses and not, as in the older English theatres, by boys.

The theatre was closely connected with the court; it belonged to 'the town' in the narrow sense, and its main business was with fashion and amusement. Tragedy was a regular part of its province; but its tragedy was literary and artificial, far less vigorous than its comedy. Among the tragic writers Thomas Otway stood highest, but the best that can be said for his *Venice Preserved* is that it approached the level of tragedies written in other times and other countries. The comic writers were more in contact with life. Wit and manners, the play of intrigue and conversation, were what they wrote and what they spent their time in. Their characters ran into types, the wild gallant, the provoked husband, the country wife. None of them did it as well as Molière was doing it in France, but several of them did it to admiration, and the form was flexible enough to fit various personalities. William Wycherley was a coarse, powerful, downright portrayer of folly, affection, and vice. William Congreve was the best English master of polished wit, so dexterous that its exactly sustained artificiality makes it even better. His men and women, with their descriptive names like Millamant and Fondlewife, are perfectly made. They are not portraits of living men and women, but living embodiments of the standards by which men and women were forming themselves and estimating one another.

The best-known fact about the Restoration drama is that it is immoral. The dramatists did not criticize the accepted morality about gambling, drink, love, and pleasure generally, or try, like the dramatists of our own time, to work out their own view of character and conduct. What they did was, according to their respective inclinations, to mock at all restraints. Some were gross, others delicately improper. It used to be said that this was due to the lascivious court of Charles II, and that the courtiers brought it back with them from France. The last suggestion is false, for the French drama of the time was on the side of both virtue and decency. Nor is the first part quite right. Charles II himself was licentious, and his courtiers behaved as might be expected of a herd of young men and women whose chief business was amusement. A good many stories of them were noted down by diarists like Pepys, and a whole book on the subject, in a vein suitable for a prying footman, was written by one of the courtiers in his old age.[1] But court immorality did not go out with the Stuarts, and it never led to complete freedom in literature. Publishers of pornographic books were prosecuted in the reign of Charles II. The dramatists did not merely say anything they liked: they also intended to glory in it and to shock those who did not like it. They were aware of a disapproving public opinion out of doors. At first, in the reaction against puritanism, they were in high spirits, though King Charles himself was said to have taken care to purge the stage from all vice and obscenity.[2] Very soon it was clear from their apologies in prologues and prefaces that their naughtiness was self-conscious. Wits joined the moralists in condemning it, and in 1698 a non-juring divine, Jeremy Collier, published *A*

---

[1] Anthony Hamilton, *Mémoires du comte de Grammont* (1713).
[2] R. Flecknoe, 'Short Discourse of the English Stage' in *Love's Kingdom* (1664).

Short View of the Immorality and Profaneness of the English Stage which frightened them all. He had no difficulty in proving that the dramatists allowed vice to triumph over virtue and used shocking language. His knowledge of their offences was so minute that, as Dryden justly wrote, 'it might be possibly supposed that he read them not without some pleasure'. But it was time for Dryden to comply. He very honourably pleaded guilty.

In 1704, when Vanbrugh was about to become manager of the new opera-house in the Haymarket, the Society for the Reformation of Manners wrote a letter of protest to the archbishop of Canterbury, describing the dramatist, with illustrative quotations, as 'a man who had debauched the stage beyond the looseness of all former times'. The protest was no longer needed. Taste had changed. The youngest of the great dramatists of the school, the Irishman George Farquhar, wrote with a natural freshness that was new. He gave up 'the town' as a subject, and drew people as he had seen them in knocking about as an actor and a soldier. His careless, good-hearted character comes out in his plays; but they also pleased because they fitted the changed mood of the public. The drama was coming to be more a national possession. Addison's *Cato* of 1713 rounds off the change with impeccable respectability. In one respect, indeed, the drama had all along served a public wider than that of theatregoers: the songs from the plays and operas were the best of all it could show. Some of them have been made immortal by Purcell's settings; but many others have not only grace and finish, but real lyric charm.

Dryden died in the last year of the seventeenth century, when Alexander Pope, the next of the great names in English poetry, was twelve years old. Pope was a precocious genius, an exceptional being, more tormented than gratified by the social life into which his ambition early carried him. He was born to a position rather below it; his physique was poor; in religion he was a Roman catholic. He jarred on other men and they jarred on him. But he surpassed every one else in technical command of the instrument Dryden transmitted to him, and during Queen Anne's reign he published three poems which showed all its possibilities. His *Essay on Criticism* was a perfectly managed argument, reproducing, with constant reminiscences of the French and Latin critics, the rules of polished appropriateness after which this is called the Augustan age of English literature.

The Rape of the Lock is a mock heroic poem in five cantos. It was occasioned by the wrath of a young lady of Pope's acquaintance when Lord Petre, one of her admirers, without her permission, cut off a lock of her hair. *Windsor Forest* is an example of what is supposed to be an English invention, first made by Sir John Denham in his *Cooper's Hill* of 1642, the local poem, the poem about a particular place. Some of the greatest English poetry of later times belongs to this genre. The country tradition is one of the intimate continuities of our literature. Shakespeare was a great countryman, and he was not the first; but oddly enough the period of the invention of the local poem in the proper sense was one in which, for all the talk about nature, the feeling for places ran very thin. Pope's *Windsor Forest* begins with the muses, with Pan, Pomona, Flora, and Ceres, and ends with the commercial benefits expected from the coming peace with France. There are so many allusions and reflections; the language is so conventional; and there is such a lack of anything that might not have been said of any other place where there were trees and streams, that it is hard to remember Pope had walked and ridden in that forest every day for years.

This was not only because the poets belonged, wherever they went, to 'the town', it was also because their art was, like all the European literature of the time, seeking the generalized, and moving away from the particular. The new prose had the same quality, and so had the current tendencies of thought. Pope himself later in his life was to express this aspect of deism in his 'Universal Prayer':

> Father of all, in ev'ry age,
> In ev'ry clime ador'd,
> By saint, by savage, and by sage,
> Jehovah, Jove, or Lord.

To the Augustan writers 'earth' meant not the loam of the next field but the terrestrial globe, 'sky' not the changing clouds over the parish but the astronomical heavens. Their poetry was limited by this, but it was made more widely intelligible. 'Man' meant not the individual but the highest common factor of all individuals, mankind in the abstract, as Pope wrote of it (not him) in his *Essay on Man*. Such cosmopolitan writing was well suited for export, and it is a central fact of the history of literature and thought in this period that there was a free interchange of ideas and influences between the literatures of different countries and between the branches of literature. In poetry and criticism and imaginative literature England, as we have seen, owed much to foreign and especially French examples, and her own influence abroad was not important. French poetry and drama were radiating all over Europe; but in prose of all kinds England began to exercise abroad an influence comparable to that of France.[1] She took her place in enabling the thought of western Europe to attract first the curiosity and then the admiration of inquirers from other European countries and even from outside Christendom.

The fruits of this planting were gathered later, when literary forms like the periodical essay and ideas like political liberalism had become effectively worked into the literatures of foreign countries; but before the end of our period there were interesting signs that foreigners were coming to England to learn. England was now able to teach the foreigner. She had indeed shed the prejudices and the habits which could never be valuable except to her own people, the religious intolerance, the Anglican narrowness, and, because she was learning so fast, she had always something to impart. What chiefly brought the inquirers was in fact the scientific movement. In 1664 a Greek, Constantine Rhodocanakis, described himself on a title-page as 'one of His Majesty's chymists'. A Greek orthodox church was built in 1677 in Soho, where the name of Greek Street commemorates the colony. In 1701 Cambridge gave an honorary degree to Neophytus, archbishop of Philippopolis, and when Queen Anne passed through Oxford on her way to Bath in 1705, she was addressed by seven Greek students, probably all from Smyrna.[2] There were foreign correspondents of the Royal Society, some of whom came in person to visit it, like the Frenchman Le Fèvre, and the German Oldenburg, who was its first secretary. Christiaan Huygens, the greatest of Dutch mathematicians and physicists, visited London three times. He had personal links with English society through his father and brother, who were in the service of the princes of Orange; but science was already

---

[1] For this matter generally and for the French huguenot refugees and other translators of English books see P. Hazard, *La crise de la conscience européenne, 1680–1715* (1935), i. 83 ff.

[2] T. E. Dowling and E. W. Fletcher, *Hellenism in England* (1915), pp. 45–50. Students of the relations of religion and capitalism may make what they please of the fact that the land for the church was given by the economist Nicholas Barbon, who was concerned in building in Soho Fields.

fully cosmopolitan. Moreover, since the most specialized scientific studies still intersected with practical applications, it was not only scientists who came but men interested in the making and use of material things. The most famous of them was Peter the Great of Russia, who lived in England for some months in 1698 studying ship-building and navigation at Deptford, as he had studied them in Holland. He was the greatest among many. The new industrial knowledge was quickly disseminated by learned travellers, by business men, and by artisans.

It would not be easy to take stock of the progress made by the scientific movement at about the end of our period; but, without going into too much detail, some rough indications may be given. The departments of knowledge were becoming differentiated: 'natural knowledge' was falling into divisions with their distinctive boundaries and methods. The greatest progress was in mathematics, pure and applied, and here indisputably the greatest figure was Sir Isaac Newton.[1] It seemed indeed that Newton had settled the main principles of mathematics, physics, astronomy, and optics once and for all. Pope wrote an epitaph:

> Nature and Nature's Laws lay hid in Night.
> God said, Let Newton be! and all was Light.

Long afterwards Wordsworth in his old age wrote of Newton's statue in the ante-chapel of Trinity College, Cambridge, as

> The marble index of a mind for ever
> Voyaging through strange seas of Thought, alone.

Neither of these poets praised his supreme intellectual powers too highly, but his work was neither isolated nor final. As a boy he had read some of the chief English and foreign books on mathematics, and at Cambridge he had teachers who were well abreast of the general movement of science. He took up the subjects which were being actively examined everywhere, and he was well aware that his investigations had a bearing on practical life. Mathematics had a hundred applications to practice; astronomy, the mechanics of the heavens, was the theoretical basis of navigation and geography. From the recoinage of 1696 Newton was an official of the royal mint, and he applied his mind both to the technique of coin-manufacture and

---

[1] Born 1642; at Trinity College, Cambridge, 1661–5, Fellow 1667; F.R.S. 1672; M.P. for Cambridge University, 1689 and 1701–2; warden of the mint, 1696, master, 1699; knighted 1705; died 1727.

to the economics of the currency. He was not infallible: his theory of light especially was much controverted. But his great discoveries were central in the thought of his time. He had a great share in providing it with its greatest instrument, the calculus. He formulated for it the law of universal gravitation, the greatest single step that had ever been taken towards bringing a multitude of complex phenomena into a single system. He completed and rounded off the fundamental scientific work of the era that began with the Renaissance.

In his relations with other scientific workers Newton was touchy and difficult. Biographical writers who pay more attention to his psychological make-up than to the contents of his works have sometimes tried to rule out as oddities all those parts of his writings and correspondence which were not followed up by the scientists of the eighteenth and nineteenth centuries. In this they are mistaken. His influence on thought about the universe came from his work in mathematics and physics; but he also paid attention to two subjects which the educated opinion of his day believed to be equally relevant to this theme, namely chronology and prophecy. Newton's astronomy was the study of planetary and sidereal movements in measured time. There were also observed regularities, cycles, and correspondences in human affairs. For centuries the astrologers had tried to explain these as connected with the movements of the stars. The new astronomy superseded their work, and also the measuring of time came to be applied more scientifically to human history. Early in the seventeenth century, for the first time, the Hebrew, Greek, Roman, and other systems had been unified in a common scheme of dates. Newton went over this ground in his own circumspect way, isolating concrete data for which explanations could be sought. He summarized his results, for Biblical and ancient history, in a short treatise which was published after his death.[1] It is work of respectable quality, but few of Newton's original suggestions on this matter proved to be fruitful.

His work on prophecy is more interesting. He seems, indeed, to have thought that others were more competent than he was to deal with some of the applications of mathematics to theology. He encouraged his friend John Craig, a canon of Salisbury, to write an ambitious, though not valuable, book with a title modelled on Newton's own: *Theologiae Christianae Principia*

---

[1] *The Chronology of Ancient Kingdoms Amended* (1728).

Mathematica (1699). Robert Boyle endowed a famous series of lectures 'for proving the Christian religion against notorious infidels . . . not descending to any controversies that are among Christians themselves'; and Newton gave his advice and approval when the first lecturer, Richard Bentley, based his confutation of atheism on the Newtonian system. He himself, however, went no further in apologetics than to have an eye in his *Principia* 'upon such principles as might work with consider- ing men, for the belief of a Deity'.[1] He was indeed sceptical of the doctrine of the Trinity as he understood it.[2] But he did apply his method elaborately and minutely to the prophecies. That these in some sense came true was commonly accepted. Newton concluded from his researches that they do not prove it possible to foretell the future, but that their fulfilment is evidence of the working of Providence. He published nothing on this subject, and we cannot tell whether he was satisfied with his notes and arguments; but, whatever defects they may have, they are not, strictly speaking, unreasonable. The enlighten- ment of the eighteenth century narrowed its field of vision when it rejected the notion of Providence. It promoted to the rank of a universal science the Newtonian physics, which its own author regarded as a subordinate chapter in the explanation of the nature of things.

Among the other English scientists of the time one of the most famous was the Hon. Robert Boyle, whose name is carried on by 'Boyle's law' on the relation between the volume, density, and pressure of gases. This was a milestone on the road of investiga- tion into the physical properties of the atmosphere, a road followed in Italy, France, Holland, and Germany as well as in England, which was to lead before long to the cardinal invention of the steam-engine. Boyle, in the spirit of the time, had eyes for the practical value of what he was doing, though in this con- nexion it seems mistaken to lay much stress on the fact that he was at one time a director of the East India Company. Some of his most distinctive work was in chemistry, but here he was not able to do much except to clear away by discussion and experiment some inherited dogmas and the tradition of the alchemists, for whom the study of the composition of substance had been distorted by cloudy hopes of performing miracles.

[1] Letter to Bentley 10 December 1692 in *Opera*, iv (1782), 429.
[2] See below, p. 386.

Though his method was strictly scientific he did not despise the aim of transmuting metals. He did not intend to do it by magic, but he thought it worth while to procure the repeal in 1689 of the fifteenth-century statute against 'multiplying gold'. The fact is, however, that neither chemistry nor the other sciences less intimately connected with mathematics registered such decided advances as physics. Good work was done in them, but it was pioneer work, clearing obstructions and plotting out the fields, but as yet yielding no heavy crops.

Botanical studies were active, and two British botanists hold high positions in their European development at this time. The period was less notable than that which followed it, when the Swede Linnaeus was at work. Robert Morison, who was educated at the universities of Aberdeen and Angers and became professor of botany at Oxford, was one of Charles II's physicians and was also his botanist and keeper of his gardens. He took up again the study of systematic botany, which had been for some time neglected. It was pursued with more definite results by John Ray of Cambridge. Ray's collection of botanical specimens may still be seen in the Natural History Museum at South Kensington, and other museums have other collections of this period. Some of them include plants from abroad. The Royal Society had correspondents in America and the East Indies, and scientific travellers were beginning to contribute valuable knowledge. John Banister, a correspondent of Ray and Locke, travelled as a naturalist in the East Indies and in Virginia. William Sherard, the founder of the Oxford chair of botany, as consul of the Levant Company at Smyrna, made botanical and antiquarian journeys in Asia Minor. Geology also gained in this way, and some early collections of foreign minerals survive; but the backwardness of geological opinion is shown by wordy controversies as to whether fossils were works of nature or of man, and as to the interpretation of the cosmogony of the first chapter of Genesis.

Anatomy had made great strides in the sixteenth and seventeenth centuries. Harvey, the discoverer of the systemic circulation of the blood, had died in 1657, but his work was continued, especially with the aid of the microscope. Some of his greatest successors were foreigners, but modern research tends to raise to a high place in anatomy and still higher in physiology Richard Lower, who studied science in Oxford with Boyle and

Locke and was one of the Royal Society from 1667. In the English universities medical studies were not very fruitful. It has, however, been remarked that 'during the sixteenth and seventeenth centuries the surgeons' branch of the Barber-Surgeons Company, almost alone among the gilds showed signs of progress and not of fossilization'.[1] This progress, evidenced by the examination-system and the provision of instruction, went on during our period. Medical books were plentiful, but in England the most prominent contributions to medical knowledge lay in clinical observations, on the borderland between the science and the art of medicine. Here Thomas Sydenham became a celebrity. He was an Oxford man and a friend of Locke, but he owed little to university teaching and was a contemner of theory. He made observations of the epidemic diseases of London in successive years, and he improved the methods of studying diseases. He gave names to certain special diseases: we owe to him, for instance, the identification of hysteria. He also introduced some novel methods of treating patients, which were intended to cure or relieve them. Altogether he stood half in and half out of the scientific movement.

'Science' is a word of many meanings, and it was not used then at all as it is used now.[2] What we call the scientific spirit was not then so called, and the French writers of that time who wrote of the triumphs of *l'esprit géometrique* were thinking of something more special. If we regard it as implying not only precision and system but also dependence on the facts of observation, we may say that the scientific spirit left its impress on the study of human conduct and society. Some of those who studied it drew nothing more from this spirit than the new manner in prose and a greater or smaller share in the new breadth and openness of mind. One such man was the great marquis of Halifax, whose political writings provide an illuminating commentary on his career and times. He wrote as a believer in constitutional monarchy, in politic moderation, in toleration with precautions for the safety of the state, and in efficient naval defence. He traced the line to which English policy swung back from its aberrations to one side or the other.

---

[1] A. M. Carr-Saunders, *The Professions* (1933), p. 74.
[2] See the *Oxford English Dictionary* for this and cognate words: it will be noted that 'scientific' was newly coined by Whewell in 1840.

He wrote, as he appears to have spoken, with compelling eloquence and aphoristic wit, but he was not a theorist. In this respect Sir William Temple, who like Halifax was a practical statesman and a writer of fine prose, drank more deeply of the scientific stream. His memoirs and letters and other political pieces keep close to the facts, especially of international affairs; but he aimed at a scientific analysis of political life, holding, as he put it in his *Observations upon the United Provinces of the Nether-lands* of 1673, that 'most national customs are the effect of some unseen, or unobserved, natural causes or necessities', and that 'whilst human nature continues what it is, the same orders in state . . . will ever have the same effects upon the strength and greatness of all governments'.[1]

Attempts have been made in subsequent times to apply deter-minist ideas like these to the interpretation of history; but in our period the writers of history did not do this except incidentally and on a very small scale. Some of the writers of county histories, a branch of study which kept and increased its popularity, dealt not only with manorial and ecclesiastical antiquities, but also with industries and agriculture, and, in these connexions, with soils, with minerals, and with natural history generally.[2] They were applying the scientific ideas of causation to their limited subject-matter, and historians of wider scope now and again threw out explanations of laws and customs from climate or geo-graphy. There was not, however, any serious philosophy of history. In the course of an international controversy on the comparative merits of the ancients and the moderns, the way was being cleared for the conception of general progress which became the framework of much of the historical thought and narration of the eighteenth and nineteenth centuries, but his-torians did not yet regard each period of history as a part of a continuous process as long as time. It was in fact not uncom-mon to distinguish history from chronology.[3] The distinction implied that time was an empty framework on which separate histories were hung, in successive order but each forming a

[1] A reprint of this book, which was considered in its time the best English work on a foreign country, appeared in 1932 with a short introduction by the present writer.

[2] One of them, John Aubrey, whose descriptions of Stonehenge and Avebury are famous, was one of the founders or precursors of prehistoric archaeology.

[3] As, for instance, in Locke's 'Thoughts on Education' in *Works* (1823), ix. 174–5. Thomas Fuller, however, in *The Holy State* (1642), p. 74, wrote that the 'general artist' is 'well seen in Chronology, without which History is but an heap of tales'.

whole in itself. And this was true enough of the great majority
of the historical works then written in England. There was
nothing to fuse them with the chronological investigations by
which the reckonings of time in the ancient, medieval, modern,
European, and oriental worlds were being fixed in their mutual
relations. These were the concern of astronomers, philologists,
and other experts; but the ordinary historian merely wanted to
narrate or explain some self-contained story with a beginning
and an end, or at most to instruct and guide by the examples of
the past.

First there were those who dealt with the events of their own
times. Since the times were lively, they were many and various.
At the first remove from the newspaper-writers came annalists.
From 1678 for more than thirty years Narcissus Luttrell copied
down the principal items from the news-letters and public
sources of information, adding a few rumours that he picked up
in conversation and a few comments of his own. He did not work
over his materials, and the six volumes of his *Brief Historical
Relation of State Affairs* were not published until 1857, but he does
deserve to be classed among historians and not merely among
the makers of their raw materials So does the huguenot Abel
Boyer, who as a journalist has a place in the growth of parliamentary reporting, and who also published annual volumes on
the events of Queen Anne's reign which were afterwards combined in a substantial folio volume. There were a number of
other writers in this class, but none of them is useful now except
to the historian who wants exact information on small points
of fact. Above them in every way except this come the political
historians, of whom the best is Gilbert Burnet.

Burnet's *History of my own Times* was published after his
death; but it was intended to be read, and the author recast and
rewrote his manuscript from time to time as the events unrolled,
always making it more a survey of their whole course and less
a mere chronicle or a mere autobiography. The desire to tell his
own story was, to be sure, one of his motives. He had a naïve
sense of his own importance, and as he really was important,
though less so than he thought, he had ample opportunities of
writing about himself; but for the reader this is an advantage,
and makes his readable book run along even more easily. This
desire to write about oneself and one's own affairs was common
at this time in England as in France. We owe to it a number of

books that are still full of life. There is Pepys's *Diary*, the best of all, so well known that it is enough to refer to it as the complete account from the age of twenty-six to the age of thirty-six of a man who shared in the business and the alarms, the enjoyments, and the mental activity of Charles II's England. There is the graver and much shorter work of John Evelyn, which, though known as a diary, was much touched up before it reached its present form.[1] There were the jottings of Celia Fiennes, a non-conformist lady of quality who toured England on horseback. All of these, and more, show the prevalence of the desire to note down what concerns oneself. Not far removed from it is the desire to vindicate oneself, as Clarendon did in his *Life* which carries his story from the Restoration to his fall. There is the desire to vindicate those near to oneself, as two women, of very different outlook, did in the lives of their husbands who fought on opposite sides in the civil war, the duke of Newcastle and Colonel Hutchinson. Political biographies, like biographies generally, were becoming better and more frequent, and political history written with party sympathies might easily have been a sort of collective political biography. Burnet, however, made it much more. He was a vigorous partisan, an exile who came back with William III and was rewarded with the rich bishopric of Salisbury, and so he was not impartial. But he had learning and great experience; he had travelled; he had thought much about the functions of the historian. He had written, industriously amassing documents, a standard protestant *History of the Reformation*. His book therefore shows the events of his time as a connected whole. They are interpreted in the light of his comprehensive knowledge and good sense. Sometimes he was inaccurate, sometimes he was unfair, and sometimes he was credulous. Political opponents made the most of his lapses, but the more closely modern historians examine his work, the better they like it.[2]

Antiquarian lawyers had contributed so much to the great constitutional disputes of the earlier Stuart period that historical books, by a well-established tradition, were the heavy artillery of party controversy. The publication of Clarendon's *History of*

---

[1] The six-volume edition by Dr. E. S. de Beer is so richly annotated that it is a most useful book of reference for the period.

[2] As, for instance, Mr. Osmund Airy, whose two-volume edition of the History down to the end of Charles II's reign (1897 and 1900) is the only fully annotated modern edition.

the Great Rebellion in 1702–4 armed the Anglicanism of Queen Anne's time with a classic. There were also books, some of them now quite forgotten, through which tories or whigs discharged ammunition from all the other periods of English history. Each side cited documents against the other, and the criticism of the opponent's case led to an improvement in the knowledge and handling of these materials. Independently of party there was a growing sense of their value. Specialists of various kinds, it may be noted in illustration of this tendency, were testing their work by historical studies. John Wallis, one of the chief among the precursors of Newton, wrote a *Treatise of Algebra* which was historical as well as practical. William Fleetwood, a divine who was interested in political economy, inaugurated the special studies of economic history by his *Chronicon Preciosum* of 1707. Thus a genuinely scientific spirit was stimulating historical inquiry, and this spirit affected history in its political aspects. Mainly at the suggestion of Lord Somers, the government of William III commissioned Thomas Rymer, historiographer to the king, to search all the public repositories for treaties and agreements between the Crown of England and other kingdoms. Rymer was an interesting man in other ways: as a literary critic he seems to have been the first Englishman to base his study of poetry on the quotation and discussion of actual passages from the poets. He did his historical work well, and, thanks to the support of Charles Montagu, earl of Halifax, he published a great series of volumes, Rymer's *Foedera*, which are still among the indispensable authorities for English history. Another historian, Thomas Madox, who succeeded Rymer as historiographer royal and enjoyed the patronage of Somers, also wrote books which are still used by the learned. He was a clerk in the augmentation office, and his studies, especially his *History of the Exchequer* to the end of the reign of Edward II, published in 1711, laid new foundations for the study of medieval English administrative documents and methods.[1]

In the first half of the century some of the legal and ecclesiastical antiquarians had felt the need, as they pushed back to the origins of English institutions, for a better knowledge of the language of the Anglo-Saxon literature and laws and charters. There was already a lectureship in Anglo-Saxon at Cambridge,

---

[1] There began in 1707 informal meetings of a few scholars in London which led ten years later to the foundation of the Society of Antiquaries.

and in our period this study became much more active. Its principal centre was now Oxford, where George Hickes, once dean of Worcester and afterwards a non-juring bishop, published his great *Thesaurus* of the northern languages. He gathered about him a group of keen and able helpers. To review the studies of the Teutonic languages at this time it would be necessary to name about a dozen good scholars. There was even one woman, Elizabeth Elstob, the sister of one of the Oxford circle, who, though she was not very learned, was the first English-woman to work in this field, and deserves, if only for the discouragements she suffered, a place among the founders of women's education. Several of the strong currents of the time were helping to carry Teutonic studies forward. The growth of large libraries and of a class of librarian-scholars gave an impulse to exploring and cataloguing: Humfrey Wanley, a protégé of the earl of Oxford who managed and catalogued his great collection, the Harleian manuscripts, also made a catalogue of Anglo-Saxon manuscripts in England. The Oxford University Press did good service by procuring a set of Anglo-Saxon type, known as the Junian type from the name of Francis Junius, a scholar of German race and Dutch upbringing. Junius represented the European side of the movement. He was a comparative philologist, and did important work on the Gothic and other languages. English scholars joined him in this, and the English movement was part of a general revival of interest in northern antiquities in which, amongst others, Frederick III, the scholar-king of Denmark, played a part. The fact that Frederick's son was the consort of Queen Anne contributed its trickle to the stream: he accepted the dedication of Hickes's great work and gave a hundred guineas for it. All this quiet preparation was soon to have great results. It laid the foundations of English philology. It was related to a new appreciation of the medieval mind which also showed itself in the beginning of the revival of Gothic architecture. English literature before Chaucer was still neglected, but taste was being educated towards a new liking for it. When Addison in the *Spectator* found beauties in the ballad of Chevy Chase, he was turning his eyes that way. The romantic movement was soon to begin.

Philological studies were broadening out in other directions. In Oriental languages valuable work was done, especially by the professors of Hebrew and Arabic in Oxford and Cambridge.

Edward Pococke, the great English orientalist of his time, died in Oxford in 1691 at the age of eighty-six and his collection of Oriental manuscripts went to the Bodleian. Among those who continued his work were one of his sons, and his successor Thomas Hyde. They were gradually working away from the predominantly Biblical interest, though England's increasing contact with the east kept this alive. Oriental chronicles were studied and translated and Hyde's chief work was on ancient Persian religion. He also published the fifteenth-century astronomical tables of Ulugh Begh, the grandson of Tamerlane. John Spencer, master of Corpus Christi College, Cambridge, was the first to trace the connexion between the Jewish rites and those of kindred Semitic peoples, and so has been called the founder of the study of comparative religion. There were, however, wide fields of Oriental scholarship which Englishmen did not yet touch. None of them studied Sanskrit. They contributed little of importance to the study of the furthest east.

The best work in linguistic study, best in accuracy, literary judgement, and historical imagination, was done not in these preparatory studies of new fields, but in the classics, where the accumulated learning and the strict criteria of a long tradition were applied. The regular work of the university scholars who wrote for publication was the editing of classical texts, and there was a stream of editions in which the standard of knowledge and acuteness steadily rose. One Englishman, however, though there were always some to disparage him, stood head and shoulders above the rest and was the greatest classical scholar in Europe in his time. This was Richard Bentley of Cambridge, where he became master of Trinity in 1700 at the age of thirty-eight. The masters of Trinity are appointed by the Crown, and Bentley's greatness was better understood by the six distinguished prelates who advised King William III[1] than by many of the residents in the universities. He was the king's librarian, and his lodgings in St. James's Palace had been a regular meeting-place for some of the leading minds of the country; at one time Locke, Newton, Wren, and John Evelyn used to gather there twice a week. Bentley was worthy of his place in that company: we have seen how his Boyle lectures were an application of Newton's system to theology.[2] His original work, however, was mainly

---

[1] They were commissioned after the death of Mary to deal with ecclesiastical patronage. [2] See above, p. 375.

classical, and it had many sides. He showed an unrivalled, if sometimes excessive, ingenuity in emending corrupted texts. He discovered some of the principles of Greek metres. It was he who showed that the language of Homer originally contained a letter, the digamma, which afterwards dropped out of the alphabet. To the world in general he was best known for his *Dissertation on the Letters of Phalaris*, which appeared in its completed form in 1699.

This extraordinary book grew out of the controversy, which we have already mentioned,[1] about the comparison of the ancients and the moderns, round which much of the literary criticism of the period revolved. A good many writers with no real knowledge of the matter took part in it, the best-known Englishman among them being Swift, whose *Battle of the Books* was written during the course of the episode in which Bentley figured. Swift was at the time a literary assistant of Sir William Temple, in whose house he lived, and it was Temple who in 1690 had transferred the great controversy from France to England. In his *Essay upon the Ancient and Modern Learning* he bestowed high praises on the Letters of Phalaris, a Greek tyrant of about 600 B.C., with condescending sneers at the scholars who had quite rightly pronounced them to be a forgery. This unfortunately caused Dean Aldrich, the amateur of architecture and music, to put up a young Oxford man, the Hon. Charles Boyle, to publish an edition of the letters, and still more unfortunately the young man in his preface unjustly accused Bentley, as the king's librarian, of refusing him due opportunities for his work. Bentley did not hurry to reply, but after a couple of years he intimated, with sufficient proof, that he had not behaved badly, that the letters were spurious, and that Boyle's edition was very bad. Boyle with the assistance of several of the ablest members of his university produced a feeble and unmannerly reply. Then Bentley in an astonishingly short space of time annihilated them in the *Dissertation*. Nothing could surpass it for force and controversial point. Its style is alive with shrewdness and humour. But its importance far transcends the trivial occasion and the contemptible opponents: it is full of new and brilliant lights on the language and life of the ancient Greeks. It is one of the supreme examples of the constructive use of erudition.

This was not Bentley's longest battle. Soon after he became master his encroachments on their rights led to hostilities with

[1] See above, p. 359.

the fellows of Trinity which swayed to and fro in Cambridge and in the law-courts until his old age. His arrogance no doubt prevented him from doing as much as he could have done to make his college a centre of advanced study of every kind, from Greek to astronomy, but he did much. When Swift, and later Pope in the *Dunciad*, took him as a representative of pedantry, they condemned not him, but themselves. The horror of pedantry was indeed, as we have seen, part of the strength of the intellectual posture of the time. Modern writers sometimes complain that the greater part of the learned work then accomplished did not come up to the standards of exactness which have since been found necessary, forgetting that a pursuit of accuracy for its own sake may merely waste time without serving any purpose. Scholars kept a balance between the need to get results and the need to have them in a finished form. The quarryman must come before the sculptor. There were expert carvers like Bentley, but they were still few; the general character of the scholarship of the age was rougher, but it was not the less meritorious for that. Its yield of solid results was very large.

We have noticed that among the literary men there was one, of varied attainments and experience, who had come into contact with most of the newer currents of thought, John Locke. We have seen how his political doctrines, beginning as a creed for revolutionists, became at last through the march of events an orthodoxy which most of the parties accepted, and none rejected except eccentrics or extremists. The same thing happened, almost to the same degree, with Locke's opinions on most of the·many subjects he wrote about. He had a rare power of setting out the essentials of a subject in an orderly way. With all his candour and uprightness he was one of the matter-of-fact majority. He was content to leave a number of unresolved contradictions in his writings, so that on one side or the other they satisfied many men. Comparatively few could agree with the more severely logical thinkers who afterwards chose one of two alternatives where he had cloudily admitted both. Thus he succeeded in making a synthesis of the English thought of that active and creative period. In theology his book on *The Reasonableness of Christianity as delivered in the Scriptures* (1695) fixed the comfortable resting-point of the newer Anglicanism, short of deism, but beyond a mere acceptance of revelation. In philosophy his *Essay concerning Humane Understanding* (1690) also took rank as a classic. It renewed the attempt of the Cambridge Platonists to make terms between the scientific movement and the older Christian philosophies, but it did so in the opposite way to theirs. They were idealists: they thought the whole was what explained all the parts, and the all-inclusive whole was mind, the universal mind which lights the spirit of man, the candle of the Lord. Locke began at the other end. His method was 'plain historical', or as we should say 'psychological'. He surveyed the actual operations of the human mind, noted what it did, estimated the limits of what it could do, and then went on to consider what it was. His point of view was thus near to that of natural science and acceptable to the investigators who knew that they were finding new truths which could not be reached by the application of general principles conjured up by mere reflection. But he did not relinquish the belief in the validity of what is known by reflection. He tried to explain that reason finds its truth as the senses find theirs. So here too he averted, for the time being, a conflict of opinions.

The conflict was not entirely suppressed in any of the spheres of thought. The British moralists, who were active during Locke's lifetime and throughout the eighteenth century, though they showed little disagreement and even little curiosity about what acts are to be considered virtuous and what are not, were sharply divided on the question whether the essence of morality lay in a specific moral sentiment or in some compounding of non-moral elements into enlightened self-interest. In theology there were deists, who would not accept revelation, and the deistic controversy, begun by John Toland's *Christianity not Mysterious* in 1696, lasted long after it had reduced Toland almost to beggary. There were unitarians, who accepted revelation but were not convinced of the divinity of Christ: Newton secretly shared these ideas.[1] A ferocious Trinitarian controversy arose alongside that with the deists. At the other extreme there were believers in revelation and *a priori* knowledge who rejected Locke's reliance on experience. In 1705, the year after Locke's death, a circle of friends was gathering in Dublin, where his ideas had been introduced by Molyneux, to discuss the new philosophy, and one of them was already preparing fundamental criticisms of them on a new line of his own. This was

[1] See the selection of his *Theological Manuscripts*, ed. by H. McLachlan (1950).

George Berkeley, who, in three books published before the end of our period, carried English philosophical studies into a new phase of fundamental questioning. But Berkeley was still a young man waiting for his reputation. In philosophy, as in thought and letters generally, the later years of Anne saw a remarkably wide agreement between Englishmen of different tempers and antecedents. Locke was comprehensive, but his opponents confined themselves each to his own department. His inconsistencies were less important than the fact that, however loosely, he seemed to have brought all knowledge into one scheme. The looseness of the union helped to preserve it. From his time, as in Europe generally, philosophy, theology, and science each went its own way, troubling little about the others, assuming on the whole that they had no need to interfere with one another. It was long before any new synthesis satisfied more than one, or at most two of the three.

XVI

THE ARTS AND SOCIAL LIFE

TASTE, even that of the most sensitive connoisseurs, is so sure to ebb and flow from one generation to another that there is no use in discussing whether, or in what sense, the period from the Restoration to the death of Queen Anne was the greatest age of English architecture. That it was a great period of building is a mere matter of counting and measuring. All over the country many large and expensive structures were put up. The Civil war and the subsequent years of poverty and confusion had interrupted such work. When prosperity returned there were arrears to be made up, postponed intentions to be fulfilled, both in public and in private building. The colleges of Oxford and Cambridge, the great political noblemen and prosperous country squires, municipalities which had outgrown their town-halls, benefactors who established alms-houses, canons who wanted better residences in their closes, innkeepers who had to accommodate the growing traffic of the main roads, all these and many more were busily building. The fire of London necessitated a great rebuilding which broke with many traditions and opened the way for new practices, giving scope and livelihood to every one, from the architect to the brickmaker. It came at a time when there was already a tendency for buildings to become bigger. Many of the prevailing ideas of the time were favourable to ambitious building. Sir Christopher Wren wrote: 'Architecture has its political use; publick buildings being the ornament of a country; it establishes a nation, draws people and commerce; makes the people love their native country, which passion is the original of all great actions in a commonwealth.'[1]

As the period went on its political history expressed itself in stone and brick. The monarchy led the movement. Charles II was never able to carry on the great reconstruction of Whitehall Palace or to complete the palace which he began at Winchester. His financial difficulties quenched these hopes like others. The rise of the standing army was, however, the occasion for Wren's

[1] C. Wren, *Parentalia* (1750), p. 351.

building at Chelsea Hospital, begun in the later years of Charles's reign, and the less imposing Kilmainham Hospital, outside Dublin. Chelsea Hospital was modelled on Louis XIV's Hôtel des Invalides in Paris, and housed some hundreds of pensioners as it does to-day. The naval war of William III has its majestic monument in Greenwich Hospital. The architectural legacies of the wars against Louis XIV are curiously appropriate. The French palaces, the Louvre, Versailles, Saint-Germain, Marly, expressed the various phases of Louis's system of government, of his ambition, and of his personal life. Hundreds of miles away in foreign capitals new palaces recorded the friendship or the defiance of other princes, as does, for instance, the Schloss in Berlin. In England there was no edifice to challenge these, but there were modest palaces or palatial houses suited to the constitutional monarchs. William and Mary and Anne enlarged or rebuilt Kensington[1] and Hampton Court. The victory of Blenheim was celebrated by the palace built at the public expense on the old royal manor of Woodstock, and the victor was also given Marlborough House in the palace of St. James. But it is a sign of the duke's position in an aristocracy whose proudest members stood but little below their sovereigns that the architect of Blenheim built on much the same scale at Castle Howard in Yorkshire. The magnate who owned it was first lord of the treasury for six months, but owed all his grandeur to lands and consequence inherited from his ancestors.

Since there were so many great commissions to execute, and since the noble and royal patrons took an enlightened interest in the work on both its practical and its artistic side, the status of the architect underwent a change. For a long time there had been architects, men who did the work which architects do now and did not spend much of their time in other ways. Inigo Jones, although he was also a designer of scenery and dresses for masques, was as much an architect in this sense as any of his successors, and there is no complete breach of continuity between his period and the next. The great majority of architects were, however, still men who spent most of their time about the buildings and little at their desks, combining some or all of the functions of architect, master-mason, clerk of the works, and contractor. Men of this type and of unpretentious social standing were still doing expensive and beautiful work in the last

[1] William bought the old house at Kensington from Nottingham in 1689.

years of the seventeenth century, like the bridge at Clare College, Cambridge, which was built by such a man, the son of the builder of the college itself. Considerable buildings were still not uncommonly produced in this way until far into the eighteenth century, as small houses and cottages have been down to the present time. But for the large works the architect was now separated from the master-builder. His artistic individuality disengaged itself from close association with what now became the subordinate crafts, and he worked in the light of scientific and mathematical knowledge on the one side, artistic and antiquarian scholarship on the other, both of which were embodied in books and formed a part of a conscious culture, even a cult. Critical standards were formulated, or rather imported, which the educated noblemen could understand, and, to apply them, the architect did well to be a man of some liberal education.

There was still no system of professional training for architects in England other than apprenticeship: architecture was not taught in any school or academy. The two greatest among the architects whose works have already been mentioned came into architecture from the world of power and fashion and intellectual interests and wit. Sir Christopher Wren was the nephew of an eminent and influential bishop. As an undergraduate he was one of the circle in Oxford which preceded the Royal Society, and he was known for his versatile ingenuity in the more practical applications of the physical sciences. He might have gone far as an astronomer or anatomist, though in either case it would have been on the experimental and inventive sides of the subject; but when he was about thirty he became assistant to the surveyor-general of works and his uncle and his university friends put him in the way of designing a chapel in Cambridge and a hall for university ceremonial in Oxford. He began very much as an amateur, and his only period of regular training was a sojourn of a few months in Paris after his first buildings were erected. Captain John Vanbrugh, who built Castle Howard and Blenheim when Wren was an old man, seems also to have had no formal training except during a stay in France from the age of nineteen to twenty-one, and he did not take to architecture seriously until he was well over thirty and had made a name as a playwright. It was an easy step from science to architecture. Robert Hooke was city surveyor in London after the fire and designed several important buildings. William Molyneux, whom we have noticed in connexion with Irish politics, was one of the chief engineers and surveyors-general or the king's buildings there, and built part of Dublin Castle. The same step might even be taken from polite learning, and Henry Aldrich, dean of Christ Church, was the first and best of a group of amateur architects who, probably with discreet assistance from more experienced friends, put up a number of meritorious buildings in Oxford. Another good minor architect of a quite different type, without any of the academic coldness, was Henry Bell, who was twice mayor of King's Lynn: he began as an engraver. Among the outstanding names there are only two who had the regular career of professional architects: Talman, Wren's personal opponent and the builder of Chatsworth, and Nicholas Hawksmoor, who was trained under both Wren and Vanbrugh.

The change in the position of the architect was very closely connected with a great change in architectural style. The Gothic tradition had long been enfeebled. It had been shaken by successive renaissance influences from abroad since the time of Henry VIII, and it had been frontally attacked by the entirely contrary Palladian system of Inigo Jones. It was still not extinguished. There was a conservative feeling which kept it alive, especially for ecclesiastical buildings. Inigo Jones himself had built a Gothic chapel in Lincoln's Inn. Gothic had gone on continuously in Oxford, though losing more and more its characteristic ornaments and details. At the Restoration Archbishop Juxon had the great hall of Lambeth Palace rebuilt in its main lines as a Gothic building. The great architects of the period had a feeling for Gothic which combined, in such a way that they cannot be sharply distinguished from one another, this conservatism and an appreciation of the good qualities of the old work, and the beginnings of a desire to revive and imitate it as something quaint and picturesque. Wren tinkered up some Gothic buildings, and put Gothic steeples on some of his city churches. Vanbrugh wanted to preserve the old manor-house at Woodstock. Hawksmoor screwed the transept of Beverley Minster back into the perpendicular, and, soon after Queen Anne died, advised the fellows of All Souls to preserve what was strong and durable in their fifteenth-century buildings. These architects cannot be blamed if their renderings only roughly resembled the original Gothic themes. They were not cramped, like the Gothic revivalists of the nineteenth century, by servile imitativeness. A long time was to elapse before there were slowly made available the collections of engraved drawings and plans and sections, with the letterpress in which students rediscovered the chronology, the constructive principles, and the aesthetics of Gothic. Engravings of medieval buildings began to be published as illustrations to books and in independent series, but, since we see clearly only what we understand, they were still almost all vague or incorrect in detail. Thus the medieval tradition, though it still survived in small buildings and in construction, left no trace in the ornamental details or the usual designs of fashionable architecture.

The new manner which took its place was the revived Roman style called Palladian from Palladio, the sixteenth-century Italian who had laid down its rules. Instead of pointed arches, traceries, and buttresses, it had pillars with flat entablatures and low pediments, regular façades, rectilinear outlines, square- or round-headed doors or windows, everything that we are familiar with in buildings which have no Gothic in them. It had a literature which soon grew large enough to have a marked influence on the great building enterprises of the time. Robert Hooke, scientist and architect, saw an English translation of Vitruvius about 1675. There were handsome folio volumes of plates, of which the first was Palladio's on Rome, republished at Oxford in 1709. There were translations of foreign manuals, of which John Evelyn made one. But the great architects were men of such a stamp that they did not allow themselves to be cramped, like their successors of the next period, by a dogmatic system of rules, and they were less subject to literary influences than to the example of the living schools of foreign architecture with which they came into contact. French influence was the strongest, and flowed in through many channels. The long wars had no appreciable effect in making Englishmen wish to shelter themselves from the French domination in the arts. National spirit had not begun to assert a claim over these things. During the desperate struggle of the Dutch against the French and English in 1673-4 the correspondence of Bentinck shows him ordering leather gloves for himself and William, his master, at the sign of the Cross Keys at the Royal Exchange in London, and suits of clothes for the prince in Paris, though not from the tailor there who, we are told, worked for most of the German princes, charging very reasonable prices, and giving credit when necessary. We have seen that Wren and Vanbrugh studied in France. Montague House, the great mansion on the site of which the British Museum stands, was built and burnt and rebuilt in our period: one of the successive houses was by a French architect, Pouget. The French influence did much good, and in a minor way some harm: it impoverished, for instance, the manner of internal plaster decoration.

Another foreign influence was the Dutch. Captain William Winde, an Englishman born in Holland, was at work on various great houses soon after the Restoration. The higher architecture learnt some of the Dutch ways which had for long been creeping into the ordinary house-building of the eastern counties. One of these was the skilful use of brick as a material. Brick came in the eighteenth century to be looked upon as unsuitable to be seen in correct Palladian compositions. Like other Dutch methods brickwork was used more freely after the Revolution, for William III himself and several of the nobles who came over with him were interested in building, and had taste enough to draw the attention of the English architects that way. Wren, in his later work, for instance in some of his London steeples, freely used Dutch motives; and there are some technical devices, such as the 'rubbing' of brick to fit in with stonework, which he seems to have taken over at that time. There was an interchange between the two countries: if the pulleys in sash-windows are a Dutch invention, the primitive form of the sash, held up by notches, in spite of its French name (from *chassis*) seems to be English.[1] Certainly the sash-window has never been so common in any continental country as it soon became here.

This matter of sash-windows is a trifle, but it shows that the English architecture of the period had its own distinct character and was not a mere compound of influences from outside. The distinctness of the English manner is, in fact, very remarkable, and it is evidently the outcome of specially English conditions and of the English character of the architects. In the whole of England it is difficult to find an example of what is called the baroque. Certainly not one of the great buildings of the time can be said to belong to that manner. The baroque, as it

---

[1] See *Oxford English Dict.*, s.v. 'sash-window'. *The Delights of Holland* (1696), p. 66.

flourished before and during this time in other European countries, is best described not as a style, but as a tendency which
may express itself in any style and which has overtaken most
styles in their later stages. It is the tendency to extravagance and
exuberance, to sweeping curves and swelling surfaces, loaded
with ornament and ignoring or concealing the limitations of
structure. In this sense English classical architecture escaped the
baroque in Wren's time as English Gothic had escaped it in the
fifteenth century. To some extent the material conditions determined the result. After the fire of London, for instance, the
rebuilding could only be undertaken if the cost was narrowly
watched: economy meant plainness, and the simplicity of the
streets and squares then built set a habit. Brick also became
commoner, and unhappily worse in quality, for the same reason.
The external use of plaster ornamentation died out about the
same time, probably partly under the stress of practical considerations. It is usually said that the exhaustion of the forests
was the cause of the discontinuance of half-timber building,
another form of building which easily lends itself to elaborate
ornament. Here, however, a change of taste and other considerations played a part. In London for reasons of safety only
brick and stone were allowed after the fire.[1] Elsewhere there
are many examples, even before this, of half-timbered houses
which were faced or encased with stone, whether for warmth
and convenience, or because stone had become easier to get, or
merely because it seemed a nobler material. And, however much
weight is to be allowed to these practical reasons, on the broad
matter of the absence of baroque from English architecture,
there is ample evidence that the main cause was that it did not
appeal to the English architect or his patron.

Moderation and common sense were, as we have seen, the
qualities to which the greatest successes of English statesmen
were due. Reasonableness was the criterion applied to religion
and morals. Literature was sober, and by the end of the period
it was for the most part respectable. The great architects shared
this spirit of the place and time.[2] Wren, so far as is known, never
gave himself airs as an imaginative artist. He was a fundamentally practical man. His statement of the requirements of a protestant church is a model of the exact adaptation of means to

[1] See T. F. Reddaway, *The Rebuilding of London after the Great Fire* (1940).
[2] Vanbrugh's exceptional position is explained in this chapter and the last.

definite ends. In order that the preacher may be heard, the pews
must all be within the range of an average voice, and so forth.[1]
His buildings excelled, like Vauban's fortresses, in their adaptation to their sites. He was capable of lapses of taste in various
directions, and he was not a great master of ornamentation; but
he had in his bones an aversion from the superfluous and the
fussy. He had it, and he communicated it to others; but he drew
it from the English air. Even Vanbrugh, who was partly of
Flemish descent, and had a vein of the baroque in him, was no
exception. He always worked for effect, akin to the stage-effects
he had known in his other career, and above all for the impression of strength and size. He sacrificed much convenience to his
grouped lateral blocks of building, and his detail was heavy and
coarse to match his monstrous scale. But even Vanbrugh's
buildings have their own austerity. They are solid and plain,
not in the least over-ornamented or fantastic. Taste, even that
of the most discerning, ebbs and flows, so that sometimes this
common quality of the English architecture of the time is
thought to be a merit, a disciplined purity; but sometimes it is
disapproved of as unimaginative and timid. However that may
be, it is English.

This does not only mean that to the inhabitants of every other
country it was foreign; it means that these buildings gave an
artistic expression to much of the life and character of the
country. One respect in which this was so was in the growing
effacement of local differences. We have noticed the disuse of
half-timber building and the spread of brick. It was some time
yet before the improvement of transport spread cheap materials
like brick and Welsh slates all over the country. There were still
districts like the Pennines and the Cotswolds where there was
nothing to compete with the local stone for either utility or
cheapness; but the levelling was beginning, and like most of the
other changes it worked its way downwards from the great
buildings to the smaller. By the middle of the eighteenth century
it was practically complete, and it is easier to locate one of the
large houses of the beginning of the century by the appearance
of the surrounding country than by the architecture of the house
itself. Another sign of the times, particularly in London, was the
development of public control over the planning of houses and

---

[1] C. Wren, *Parentalia* (1750), p. 318, repr. in *The Wren Society*, vol. ix (1932),
p. 15.

streets. The medieval municipalities had exercised certain powers in these matters, and the Tudor and Stuart sovereigns had vainly attempted to control or to check the expansion of London. They had found that there were limits to what they could achieve, and the experience after the fire showed clearly that these limitations could not be removed. Wren made a plan, which has been much admired, for reconstructing the whole of the burnt part of London and its approaches with splendid vistas and regularities, but he and the other architects who did the same were mistaken in thinking that the fire really afforded an opportunity for a clean sweep of the old tortuous and inconvenient streets. The superstructure had been destroyed, but the ground remained in the same ownership as before and there was no fund in existence from which even a few of the owners of sites could be bought out. Town-planning therefore had to be unambitious; but the task of rebuilding gave a stimulus to civic pride and enterprise, and the new regulations for the construction of houses, for the width of streets, and for sanitation generally are very creditable to the effectiveness of the parliamentary and municipal machine.

The rebuilding of London was Wren's great opportunity, and he proved himself more than worthy of it. In a very long life he completed a prodigious number of buildings there and elsewhere. His successor as architect at St. Paul's Cathedral commemorated him in the proverbial inscription, *Si monumentum requiris, circumspice*, and no more need be said about the qualities of his works than simply that nearly all of them are still standing and may be seen.[1] Of his relation to other architects it may be said, without disparaging him, that he was not an isolated man of genius, but the greatest figure of a great period. It was, indeed, greater in architecture proper than in the ancillary and decorative crafts, and these were less English. In them a greater proportion of the delightful and promising work was done by foreigners, and the traditional native crafts were withering in provincial seclusion. The formal garden, which was often the architect's concern, had its literature of translations like architecture, and its powerful foreign influences, French and Dutch. In the carving of stone and wood and in metal-work generally there were many foreigners at work, and it is difficult to point to many eminent native names or to distinctively English beauties.

[1] This sentence is no longer true after the war of 1939–45.

Among sculptors Edward Pierce or Pearce deserves mention. He worked under Wren, of whom he made a portrait bust, and he did well in various tasks, from fonts to monumental effigies. Some of his English contemporaries, however, were filling Westminster Abbey with affected and incongruous images, and the best remembered sculptors of the time were the Holsteiner Cibber, the father of Colley Cibber the actor and author, and Grinling Gibbons, born in Holland, who worked mainly in wood. Gibbons's work, in great quantity even without what is falsely ascribed to him, is familiar to sightseers in most of the important buildings of the time, and it set a long fashion; but in the beginning it too must be reckoned as foreign. Ornamental ironwork was of the simplest before this time, but it now attained great distinction, and this is said to be entirely due to a foreigner Jean Tijou, who designed magnificent iron gates and railings. Lead-work was more important than might be supposed, because many lead cisterns and garden figures have been taken away and melted down: here again the chief name is that of a Dutchman, John van Nost, who had a leadyard in Piccadilly.

In the minor decorative arts less closely associated with building the same foreign influences may be traced. The most esteemed silversmith of Queen Anne's time, for instance, was the Frenchman, Paul Lamery. In these arts also there came, as in France, the beginnings of that Oriental influence which was to become powerful in the next generation. Chinese porcelain had been imitated in Europe with some success fairly early in the seventeenth century: the fashion for collecting it was encouraged by Queen Mary.[1] Curiosity about China had been growing for some time. Books about it had been translated. In the time of James II a Chinaman was lionized in Oxford and had his portrait, now in the royal collection, painted by Kneller. Chinese ornamentation had been used in silversmith's work.[2] In 1688 two authors called Parker and Stalker published a *Treatise on Japanning*, or lacquering, with many designs. It was already taught as an accomplishment in schools for girls.[3] In 1691

---

[1] There are English allusions to it in the time of Charles II, as in Wycherley's *Love in a Wood* (1672), Act II, sc. 3, and earlier, as in Evelyn's *Diary*, 19 February 1652/3.

[2] C. J. Jackson, *Illustrated History of English Plate*, 2 vols. (1911), gives numerous instances. See also E. A. Jones, *Old English Gold Plate* (1907), plate xi; *King's College Plate* (1932), p. 49.

[3] *Verney Memoirs*, iv. 221; but it is not quite clear whether this should be dated c. 1675.

Japanese wall-papers were being imitated in London, and two years later there came the Patentees for Lacquering after the manner of Japan.[1] Screens and wall-papers from the Far East were used in houses. The knowledge of China among English artists was not profound. The fifth act of Purcell's opera *The Fairy Queen*, which was produced in 1692, had a Chinese scene. Unfortunately the drawings for it do not survive, but there is something suspiciously vague about the description 'a transparent prospect of a Chinese garden, the architecture, the trees, the plants, the fruit, the birds, the beasts quite different to what we have in this part of the world'. The Chinese men and women are represented in the inappropriate character of primitive innocence. This hesitating early *chinoiserie* thus illustrates not only growing intercourse with the East, but still more a feeling for the strange half-known. Below the steady tide of the ruling taste an undercurrent was pulling towards exotic gracefulness and caprice.

Household furniture, so far as the claims of utility permitted, came under the same influence. The rich, who had apartments for show and dignity, as well as for working and eating and sleeping, provided themselves with chairs and tables suitable to match their red or black and gilt lacquered cabinets and cupboards. Oak gave way before the elegant walnut, with its variegated surfaces. Foreign craftsmen taught the use of walnut as a veneer, and the construction of furniture changed accordingly. The fine French skill in inlaying brass or steel in the wood was not acquired by English craftsmen, and the English furniture kept its individuality, though some of the favourite pieces began from foreign models. Grandfather clocks were made possible by the improvements in clock-making. Their woodwork and the conventional ornaments of their faces followed Dutch patterns that came in with William III. The long-case clock is only a mechanism boxed in, with the dial at a convenient height for the eye, but its proportions, leaner than they afterwards became, suited the taste of the period. Chairs, after the Restoration, were made taller in the back; cane seats came into fashion. The old thick-set and squarely upholstered chairs died out, and the solid-backed chairs of the old shape lingered only in provincial farm-houses, while London patterns more and more came to be imitated in all parts of the country. In make as in materials

[1] Scott, *Joint-Stock Companies*, iii. 72, 119.

there was a new elegance. By the time of Queen Anne cabriole legs came in, and there were many small pieces of furniture for the needs of a sophisticated social life, card-tables, escritoires, screens. Many of them are still in use. They are still copied, and, except where physical comfort is wanted, the domestic *décor* of the Queen Anne period is still modern, a living and easily intelligible part of our own world.

With all the material survivals that have come down to us it is an easy matter to picture the outward appearance of England in that day. In London there are whole streets and squares that have scarcely altered, whole museums full of the furniture and clothes and trinkets of their inhabitants; and even a person whose imagination is almost completely atrophied must sometimes see the ladies step out of their sedan-chairs while the link-boys hold up torches. One aid to this, which we should have in some foreign countries, is lacking: little of what we can picture of the English outdoor scene in town or country comes from painting. There are few paintings of any artistic merit representing the streets of London, or even country landscape. From the works of Francis Barlow we know what shooting and hawking and hunting looked like. Once in a way there may be some angular figures of mowers and morris dancers in the big picture of his fields done to decorate the hall of a Gloucestershire squire, but popular life and even social life in general are not represented. There was no school of genre-painting in England: not for long after this time do we begin to see the life of the farmhouses and inns and village-greens through the painter's eyes. There was not even, as in the time of Hogarth, a homely school of satirical painting and caricature. There were scarcely any representations of daily life except the crude woodcuts of the chapbooks, efforts so artless that they do not even arrive at the excellence of literal copying. Painting, in fact, was aristocratic. It belonged to the cultivated and resplendent higher stratum of the governing class.

This was not, however far our modern taste may be carried by an occasional tidal wave of appreciation, a period in which painting flourished in England. There were a considerable number of capable painters at work, and their community deserves notice for its social relations at the time when the foundations were being laid for the subsequent building of a national school. At present there was no national school. There were special little accomplishments in which the leading London artists were Englishmen, such as miniature painting, where the great Samuel Cooper, who died in 1672, and his younger contemporary Flatman stood highest from the Restoration to the Revolution. The dominating painters were, however, foreigners. There was a succession of court painters who, following in the footsteps of Sir Anthony Van Dyck, moved in the highest circles and made great fortunes and collections of works of art. First was the Dutchman Sir Peter Lely, who, with his foreign assistants and pupils, recorded the features of the admirals of Charles II's fleet and the beauties of his Court.[1] Before they had faded he had a rival in the German Godfrey Kneller, and Kneller, knighted by William III and made a baronet by George I, had an almost endless array of sitters, among them ten reigning sovereigns. His successor in repute was the Swede Michael Dahl, who had been turning out dull commissioned portraits in increasing quantities since before the Revolution.

These highly successful men were surrounded by a few Frenchmen and a number of Dutchmen and Flemings, some of whom narrowly missed similar success and achieved really good work in their art, while others were mere hacks and assistants. There was a demand for hackwork of various kinds. The busy portrait-painter painted the head, and by special favour the hands, leaving the rest to his staff. In the absence of other methods of reproduction, copies of famous masterpieces and of portraits were wanted for houses, and the large decorative paintings of their ceilings and walls were often beyond the physical capacity of an unassisted painter. In this kind of painting, very little esteemed now, the two leaders were the Italian Verrio and, after him, the Frenchman Laguerre. It has no continuity at all with the English tradition of decorative painting, which was dead or dying with the traditional manner in building. The new work in historical, religious, and allegorical subjects came full grown from the continental renaissance in its later phases. The

---

[1] Charles II and James II also employed the excellent marine-painters Willem van de Velde (c. 1611–93) and his son of the same name (1633–1707). It is much easier to use their pictures as evidence for naval history than to use Lely's as evidence for the characters of his sitters, but it is at least clear that Lely has little of Van Dyck's romance, and that instead of the grace and nobility that his master ascribed to the men and women of Charles I's time, he made his men virile and his women contentedly sensual.

first Englishman to practise it was Robert Streeter, who was also a landscape-painter and died in 1680; James Thornhill, who was five years old when Streeter died, was the pupil of an English master and worked his way up as a 'history painter' so that in the time of Queen Anne's successor he earned a fortune and a knighthood.

Some of the Englishmen studied abroad, and others were taught by the immigrants; but the art was striking its roots in the soil. The painters were a good deal intermarried, and in some ways their little community was unlike English society in general. There were, for instance, in a time very barren of feminine accomplishments, some women painters, like the daughter of Remigius van Leemput, who was married to an English painter, or Mary Beale, the wife of a minor placeman with a scientific and pecuniary interest in artists' colours. The art spread outside the professional circle. Francis Place was an amateur who lived in York. Alexander Pope took lessons in the art, though he never followed it seriously. A more curious amateur was Simon Digby, who in the time of William III by his great skill in water-colours recommended himself to men in power and ladies and so was raised to the bishopric of Limerick.[1] There were lady amateurs, like Christiana Verney whom Kneller painted in the act of drawing. The widening interest in painting of which these are examples, with the growing demand for pictures,[2] led to an improvement in the status of the painters. Along with them the engravers went up in the world, and the proportion of Englishmen doing good reproductive work, especially in the newly imported mezzotint, increased. John Evelyn added an account of it to his history of engraving. He also translated a book on painting.[3] There were other translations, one of them by Dryden,[4] but no Englishman wrote an original book of any importance on the graphic arts, and the English school was not yet sufficiently distinct or established to be the subject of any book whatsoever. A milestone on the road towards a national school was marked by the foundation of an academy

---

[1] R. Mant, Hist. of the Church in Ireland, ii (1840), 366.

[2] In 1693 there was 'une Auction continuelle d'excellentes peintures' at Exeter Exchange in the Strand: F. Colsoni, Le Guide de Londres, ed. W. H. Godfrey (1951), p. 8.

[3] Sculptura or the History and Art of Chalcography (1662); Idea of the Perfection of Painting, from the French of Fréart de Chambray (1668).

[4] De Arte Graphica by C. A. Du Fresnoy (1695), prefaced by the 'Parallel of Poetry and Painting'.

of painting in 1711, with Kneller as its president. It did not accomplish great things, but it was a sign that great things might soon be within reach.

To turn to the history of music is to turn to an art with a well-established native tradition. The professional musicians, in the most inclusive sense, were not very numerous; but their position was secure and well defined, and there were enough stages of rank and remuneration among them to provide a real career for the talented. From the choristers of the outlying cathedrals to the king's composer, they formed a body, almost an organized body. Although religious and secular music were, to an extent which we shall notice in a moment, distinguished from one another, they were not produced by two distinct bodies of composers. The eminent musicians who were at the head of their profession were those who had charge of the music in the chapels royal, and they were also expected to provide for court occasions of every degree of solemnity or levity from a royal funeral to a masque. There was not one body of church organists and another of composers for the theatre, but a body of musicians. There was also a music-loving public. In this the Court was only the greatest and most splendid of households. The English were fond of domestic music. From the sixteenth century they had produced more freely than other nations music for the keyed instruments which well-to-do people kept in their houses. Many spinets were made soon after the Restoration: Samuel Pepys records that he bought one.[1] The gentry sang to the lute and danced to the accompaniment of stringed instruments. Part-singing was popular in town and country. Possibly the fact that Pepys was given to it makes it occupy too large a space in the popular conception of the period; but there can be no doubt that it was fixed in the national mode of life.

Among the humbler classes there was music for dancing and there were popular songs. On the village green the pipe and tabor were the ordinary instruments of the morris dancers. The fiddler was still uncommon except in cultivated circles. Not that folk-music was, as modern enthusiasts have supposed, an untutored expression of the mind of the people. Much of it was no doubt transmitted and spread abroad by being sung and heard and sung again. In that way it could go far and live long,

[1] *Diary*, 13 July 1664, 2 September 1666.

and be strangely corrupted, or even sometimes improved, as it passed from one singer to another. We know that some songs ran quickly through the kingdom. The most famous is *Lilliburlero*, a satirical song against the Irish and popery written by Lord Wharton and set to a quick-step by Purcell, which was sung by the whole army and half the people at the time of the Revolution. In this instance we know that there were printed copies of the words and music, and we know the names of the author and composer. In many other instances folk-songs can be traced, though not so easily, to originals which were the work of educated musicians, and sometimes it can be shown that printed copies of the words of a ballad and even printed copies of the tune helped to diffuse it. How much of folk-art is, in any period, degenerated culture must always be difficult to estimate, but even if the proportion is very large, as it seems to be here, that does not diminish the significance of the musical habits of the populace. If a great many people enjoy singing and playing and dancing, wherever they get their tunes, there will be the more chance for taste and talent to become trained and make their way upwards.

The puritan revolution interfered with the musical life of England both where it was grave and where it was gay. Organs and choirs in churches were prohibited, and a number of the organs were broken up: there was a check to the composing of ecclesiastical music. The theatres were closed, which meant that the songs in the plays were no longer performed in public. But there was no general attack on music. The tradition was so strong that it merely turned into other courses. Many solo songs were written suitable for the capacities of amateurs singing in their own homes. In the later years of the Protectorate the prohibition of stage-plays was evaded by the performance in great houses and in public of masques and a kind of opera. The stream of English music-publishing, much narrower before, began its broad and continuous flow from the time of the Commonwealth. John Playford, the first important music-publisher in London, went on working until James II's reign, and he introduced at least one improvement in musical typography which was adopted in foreign countries. With the Restoration all the restraints were suddenly ended. The reopened theatres made a greater use of music than before, and, as we shall see, opera took its place beside the drama. The cathedral choirs were restored and organ-building began. It is not altogether fanciful to say that organ-building shared in the general interest of the time in technology. Far more organs were built in our period than were needed to make good the losses of the inter-regnum and the fire of London. At least one important improve-ment was made by an Englishman: Abraham Jordan in 1712 invented the swell-box, a contrivance for varying the force of the sound. The two great organ-builders of the period were the German Bernard Schmidt or Smith and the possibly half-French Renatus Harris. They competed keenly against one another, and there were famous trials of their organs by experts, which were followed by their supporters as exciting sporting events. That is one sign of the importance of the musical public. Another, much more important, is the rise of public secular music in London. Music has never been centralized in London like literature, but no doubt it was the great size of the capital that made public concerts possible. At the same time the rapid improvement in the technique of vocal and instrumental execu-tion was marking off the standard of the professional from that of the amateur. In 1672 John Banister, lately master of the king's band, started in his house in Whitefriars the first regular series of public concerts in England or indeed in Europe. There was a concert every afternoon and the price for admission was a shilling. At the weekly concerts begun six years later in Clerken-well by Thomas Britton it seems to be uncertain whether there was any charge for tickets or for coffee. He was a working 'small-coal man', but his concert-room, with its little organ, although it was only a loft over his warehouse, was a resort for music-lovers of the highest social rank. Britton was also a bibliophile and had a good chemical laboratory. His career is the best proof of the genuineness of the aristocratic interest in music and intellectual pursuits. The most spectacular concerts were got up for great occasions. Purcell wrote a song for the Yorkshire Feast, a meeting of Yorkshiremen in the Merchant Taylors' Hall in 1690. He and most of the other good composers of the time con-tributed to the celebrations of St. Cecilia's day which were held annually with a few intervals from 1683 to 1703. They were organized by a committee which commissioned a poet to write an ode and a musician to set it: the two odes written by Dryden for these days are still familiar. One further point about the social environment of music may be mentioned. There were capable amateur composers, and one of the best was Dean Aldrich, whom we have already noticed as an architect.

This alteration of the exterior conditions of music was bound up, as cause and consequence, with profound changes in music itself. All over Europe the seventeenth century saw the rise of a new music. In the middle ages the development of music had been mainly ecclesiastical, and its final product had been a richly elaborated choral singing, conceived as a combination of voice-parts, subdued to a common devotional purpose. The beautiful secular music of the English madrigal school had been an outgrowth of this, and no new impulse of fundamental importance had made itself felt in England before the Civil war. The old tradition had, however, lost its power of creative development, and the interruption of puritanism, superficial as it was in some respects, opened the way for the tardy entry of a new spirit from abroad. In Italy at the beginning of the century there had begun experiments, some of them crude but some of them rich in promise, in making music the vehicle for the emotions of the individual soul. The religious gave way to the secular, counterpoint to melodic expressiveness, devotional harmonies to dramatic declamation. Opera was invented, with its high emotional effects, its tunefulness, its ornaments, and its connecting passages of recitative, intermediate between song and ordinary speech. This was quite different from the old English masques, which were episodic and not continuous, with mythological or symbolic characters and not human persons. It was coming into England in the last years of the interregnum, fitfully and uncertainly, and when Purcell wrote his charming *Dido and Aeneas* at the age of about thirty it was momentarily naturalized. By the time of Queen Anne it had taken its regular place among the higher amusements of London, and Lord Wharton as lord-lieutenant introduced it to Dublin; but it established itself under foreign influences, and from its first permanent settlement it had the character of an imported luxury. In fact the whole new musical outlook of which opera was one manifestation came in from abroad and kept much of its foreign manner and technique. There were signs now and again of a musical nationalism: Harris's English birth was one of the points in favour of his organs, and Banister had to give up the king's orchestra because he preferred English to French violinists. But the king and his England were on the side of the invaders.

For Charles II the new music was what he had known in France. He encouraged the French influence by sending the promising young Pelham Humfrey to study under the court musician of Louis XIV, Lulli, who had come from Italy and was making a great fortune and dominating the whole music of France. Some of the results of the French influence were almost ludicrous: the best English composers lent themselves to making anthems with orchestral introductions, and solos in the operatic manner, which are said to have suited the tastes of Charles II. Purcell in 1683 in the preface to his volume of sonatas said that it was his object to give a 'just imitation of the most fam'd Italian masters: principally, to bring the seriousness and gravity of that sort of musick into vogue and reputation among our countrymen, whose humor, 'tis time now, should begin to loath the levity, and balladry of our neighbours'. He had, however, been himself receptive of French influence, and it was probably by the king and his circle that he was brought into contact with the Italians. He was, in fact, typical of the English musicians of his time in responsiveness to new demands and new fashions. They were coming in from many sides: not only France and Italy sent their gifts, but also, growingly, Germany. There was, however, a distinctively English school, unlike any other, until a fairly definite point in the reign of Queen Anne, and its unequalled master, while his short life lasted, was Henry Purcell himself.

He was born a year or two before the Restoration and he died, aged thirty-seven, in 1695. His father, of the same name, was a gentleman of the Chapel Royal, and choirmaster at Westminster Abbey. Coming of a family of musicians he followed the regular professional career, acquiring a wide knowledge of everything concerning his art, and composing a great quantity of music for the church, for the stage, for concerts, for stringed instruments, for the harpsichord, and for private singing. No Englishman of his time attained in any other art to a facility, an expressiveness, or a grace like his. He was not alone: he was at the centre of a national art. But it was short-lived, and its separate history ended when, in the reign of Queen Anne, the music of England became merely an outlying part of that of the Continent. In so far as this was a personal achievement it was the work of Georg Friedrich Händel, who paid his first visit to London as a producer of Italian opera in 1706. The suitability of opera sung in Italian for the London stage was one of the subjects judiciously discussed in the *Spectator*. Its acceptance was one subsidiary aspect of the authority soon established by Handel, to write his name as he did after he settled here for good. He represented the music of the eighteenth century, which in his time was already a great power in Germany: Handel was twenty-five when he came to England, and he was one month older than Bach. There is a kinship between the massive harmonies of their age and its regularized architecture, its grand style in painting and its solid, confident rationality in thought. Handel's music became the standard music of Georgian England not through any personal or accidental attractiveness, but because they belonged to each other. The English music of the Restoration would have been called transitional if its experiments and its native qualities had been followed up; but they were not mature enough to hold attention when the full-grown continental style was brought in bodily.

The arts provide not only individuals, but also the communities to which they belong, with an ordered setting for their desires and their ideas. Like them the changes of manners and fashions in this period may all be brought into relation with the same great currents of life. There was, to begin with, the same interaction of metropolitan and provincial, of native and foreign, of habit and utilitarian adaptation. Change worked most slowly in the life of the countryside, but even there social customs were modified just as surely as agricultural methods. The clergy came down from the universities and the gentry went, more often than before, backwards and forwards between their manor-houses and London: like the furniture of their houses the furniture of their minds did not remain the same. Even country sports and pastimes followed the times. The modern game-laws began in the reign of Charles II. Their principle was to restrict the right of shooting game-birds to the landowners, but even yeomen were excluded if they were worth less than £100 a year. This is an expression of the privileged position of the governing class; but it also arises from more special causes. The regular fowling-piece was now a gun instead of a cross-bow, so game was easier to kill. Enclosure and disafforestation diminished the amount of cover. Thus game became scarcer, and, as in France in the same century, it was legally protected because the supply

was running short. Foreign influences are to be seen even in
sports. At least two pastimes came in from Holland. One was
yachting for pleasure, in which Charles II set an example rapidly
taken up by those who could afford it. The other was the use of
iron skates. Pepys in 1662, passing by the pond in St. James's
Park, for the first time in his life 'did see people sliding with their
skeates, which is a very pretty art'.[1] Horse-racing had been
known before this period: Cromwell's major-generals suppressed
race-meetings as dangerous assemblies. It suited the Restoration
well, and from that time Newmarket became the centre of the
sport. The history of the English thoroughbred horse begins in
the reign of Charles II, and like so many other English pedigrees
it begins with foreign immigrants. Charles II brought in six
Arab mares, or more probably barbs from Barbary, North
Africa. Of the famous stallions from which the chief strains of
English racehorses are derived, the first was the Byerly Turk,
Captain Byerly's charger in King William's war in Ireland. The
second, the Darley Arab, was imported by a Yorkshire squire
concerned in merchandise, and the third, 'the Godolphin horse',
was brought in after our period by the second earl of that name,
a great racing man like his father. The regular records of the
turf begin in 1709.[2]

The race-meetings at Newmarket and the more local meetings up and down the country were not the only concourses of
the wealthy and their hangers-on. At the proper seasons the
prosperous classes took advantage of improving roads and the
security of travel, such as they were, to flock to watering-places.
For about a century English medical writers had been advocating the internal and external application of the waters of Buxton,
Bath, and such-like places, as treatment for various diseases.
Benefactors, more or less disinterested, had been providing
amenities for visitors, and there were already a number of inland
spas, on the continental model, equipped for both cures and
amusement. The English had ceased to believe in the miracles
of holy wells, though St. Winifred's well at Holywell in Flint-
shire still attracted its pilgrims; but the scientific movement
gave rise to a superstition of its own, and this well was one of

---

[1] *Diary*, 1 December. Bone skates had been used since the middle ages, but
presumably they were not sharp enough for elegant skating.

[2] That is the records of races run, which are reprinted in the various *Racing
Registers*. The horses, of course, have their place in economic and military history
as well as in that of sport.

hundreds to which religious sceptics resorted for medicinal virtues which were largely imaginary. Even if they were sceptical about these too, the holiday life of the watering-places was delightful. From letters and the growing literature of guide-books we can see how parties drove out from their lodgings to see the wonders of the Peak or the Cheddar Gorge. Sea-bathing was already recommended, though not practised except, apparently, by men who liked to swim; but the distaste for water was beginning to fade. Some country mansions had bath-houses, and indoor baths in private houses came into use. In short, everything combined to favour the watering-places. Their number multiplied in the second half of the seventeenth century remarkably. Many are now forgotten. Sydenham perpetuates the memory of the great physician. Sadler's Wells has kept a little more than its name through all the overpowering growth of Islington. Hampstead still has its Well Walk. In many parts of the country there are physic wells which can only be found by studying the map. But many of those which were social centres in this age have lived and grown continuously. Bath, 'The Bath', was the greatest of all. Buxton, St. Winifred's, Har-rogate, Scarborough, Tunbridge Wells, all had their beginnings in the first half of the century or earlier; but amongst the newly discovered spas there were Malvern (from 1654), and after the Restoration, Leamington, Matlock, Ilkley, and perhaps Cheltenham.[1]

As transport improved and many kinds of social and com-mercial intercourse increased, local differences were gradually smoothed and softened all over the British Isles. It was still an adventure for an Englishman to visit the Highlands of Scotland or the west of Ireland; but the last wolf in Scotland was hunted down about 1690, and even in Ireland few survived.[2] We have already noticed the greater uniformity of architecture. Another sign of the accessibility of remote places was the weakening of the old Celtic languages. Of Welsh a contemporary observer wrote: 'it wears out more and more in South Wales, especially since the Civil Warres'. He notices also the decline of Cornish.[3] It is said that the last sermon in the Cornish language was

---

[1] For the whole subject see the admirable essay of Mr. R. Lennard in *Englishmen at Rest and Play* (1931).

[2] J. E. Harting, *British Animals Extinct within Historic Times* (1880), pp. 175, 198, 202-4.

[3] J. Aubrey, *Brief Lives*, ed. Clark, ii (1898), 329.

preached at Landewednak, near the Lizard, in 1678. Cornish had one disadvantage compared with Welsh: although it was beginning to excite the interest of scholars,[1] no books in it were printed. In Welsh there had long been printed books. In this period a good many thousands of copies of the Bible in Welsh were circulated, and the lapsing of the old restrictions on provincial printing, by enabling Welsh books to be printed nearer home, must have helped the language to keep its ground.[2] The first Manx book was printed in 1699. In about 1687–90 the number of Gaelic-speakers in Scotland was estimated at about 200,000, and it was stated that about half the preachers in the Highlands preached only in 'Irish', that of the women and children scarcely one in twenty could speak English, and that the Highlanders were very much in love with their language and jealous of all designs against it.[3] They could, of course, benefit from such copies of the Irish translation of the Scriptures as reached them. After some years of preparation the Shorter Catechism and fifty of the Psalms were printed in Gaelic by 1660. In 1694 there were apparently more than 2,000 copies of the Book of Psalms, and there were later editions in 1702 and 1707.[4] No English government made any deliberate attempt to crush these languages: it was not supposed that they kept out English ideas and impeded the unification of the state. On the contrary the languages were encouraged, or at least some encouragement was given to the publication of books written in them, because they were the languages not of the governing classes, but of the governed. It was by them that the governed could be educated in the useful arts and in the protestant religious ideas. National co-operation was to be promoted by using the existing diversity of language, not by putting it down. The decay of the old languages resulted from social changes which may also be seen at work in the various forms of English. The old Scots language sank in the middle of the seventeenth century to the status of a dialect: books published in Scotland

---

[1] See *Dict. of Nat. Biog.*, s.nn. 'John Keigwin' and 'Edward Lhuyd'.

[2] There was no printing-press in Wales until 1718; but in 1695 Thomas Jones, a printer of Welsh books, moved his press from London to Shrewsbury (I. Jones, *Hist. of Printing and Printers in Wales and Monmouthshire* (1925), pp. 9, 34). For the Irish language see above, p. 323.

[3] See the anonymous paper in Boyle, *Works*, i (1744), 121–3.

[4] *Minutes of the Synod of Argyll, 1652–61*, ed. D. C. Mactavish (1944) and the same writer's Introduction to *The Gaelic Psalms, 1694* (reprint of 1934).

from that time were written in the language of London. It is difficult to pick out landmarks in the long-drawn decadence of the local dialects of England; but one fact may be mentioned which shows that, as the public read more and travelled more, it became more sharply aware of the contrast between standard English and the provincial ways of speaking. Defoe is said to be the first leading English writer who introduces characters speaking in dialect which is not mere caricature but an attempt at correct reproduction: there is, for instance, some tolerably good broad Yorkshire in his *Memoirs of a Cavalier*.[1]

The speech of educated men, like the new tastes and manners diffused through the country, came from the capital, and the social life of the capital had its centre in the court. The rambling and irregular buildings known as the Palace of Whitehall, where the court had its usual abode, were less like a palace than a splendid village. The Houses of Parliament and Westminster Abbey were close at hand, with Westminster Hall where the common law judges held their courts. The offices of the secretaries of state and other ministers were in rooms or houses fitted into courtyards and passages among the royal apartments. On one side was the river, where state barges or humble hired pairs-of-oars came and went for business or pleasure or pageantry. On another was the park, the promenade of all fashionable people. Of the great projected rebuilding nothing was completed except the historic and beautiful banqueting hall, which still stands, and around it were buildings of various sizes, dates, and styles, made still more confused by patching after a destructive fire in 1697. The fire indeed put an end to Whitehall as a royal residence. William III had never cared for it: he thought the air of Kensington suited his health better, and he liked to go as often as possible to his rebuilt Hampton Court. For the rest of his reign, therefore, he had no house in Westminster except St. James's Palace across the Park, which was inconvenient and far from stately. It sufficed for his needs and those of the often invalid Queen Anne.

By their time the court was losing some of its attractions. Throughout our period it was, far more than a court can be in more modern times, the centre of the social life of the powerful and great. Its ceremonial was less rigid, more human and picturesque than it afterwards became. The court was also the

---

[1] Published in 1720: its authorship is not certain.

magnetic pole of the ambitions of artists and professional men of all kinds. Not only were there the lucrative household offices for great noblemen: the king's establishment included, as it does now, physicians and surgeons, a librarian, a poet laureate, and chaplains, but also painters, an historiographer, and, as we have seen, musicians, of whom one was the royal composer. Royalty stood at the head of the whole system of patronage of the arts and sciences. King Charles II established the office of astronomer royal, and it was by no accident that the association in which all the leading scientists met was the Royal Society. But the scientific movement needed no extraneous support: it subsisted by its own strength. It never resembled in England as it did in France the activity of an administrative department. Literature and the arts also did not need to lean on the favour of kings. Although, as we have seen, music and the theatre responded to the wishes of the court circle, especially in the time of Charles, even then the festivities of the court were losing their place as the scene of some of the best visual and audible artistic work of the country. Shakespeare, Ben Jonson, Inigo Jones had given of their best to Queen Elizabeth, James I, and Charles I; but the monarchy of the Restoration was less fortunate in the gifts that were brought to it except in music. After Dryden and Purcell the history of the arts and letters in England would suffer very little if all mention of kings and courts were omitted. The monarchy was able in fact to imitate Louis XIV only in externals and trivialities: its position in society was much like its constitutional position in the state. The weighted keel of the nation was the governing class.

The governing class owed none of its power and capability to any superiority in its educational institutions. Bishop Burnet, who was entitled to pronounce this opinion, wrote of the English gentry as 'for the most part the worst instructed, and the least knowing of any of their rank, I ever went amongst'.[1] The French wars and other disturbances restricted to a comparatively small number the custom of making the grand tour, or a shorter stay in foreign countries, and foreign travel at best is only a completion for a training of which the framework, to be stable, must be welded at home. Besides foreign travel, the only other distinctively aristocratic method of education was the keeping of

[1] *My Own Time*, Conclusion.

tutors, nearly always clerical, in the great houses. Although many men of learning and good character held such positions, it was hard for them to do well by their pupils. They were inferiors and dependants: there was always a danger that inconsiderate employers might push them down to a status like that of the ill-used governess of later times. Even in the universities, where their attainments were properly respected and they had behind them the prestige of great institutions, the college tutors often stood in a direct personal relation to the parents of their pupils and looked to them for preferment. The colleges and the universities themselves through the proctors did, however, enforce some sort of discipline. It was only after the Restoration that corporal punishment was given up in Oxford and Cambridge, and although it was easy for an undergraduate to be idle, dissipated, or intellectually neglected, there were rules which he had to obey and penalties by which they could be enforced. There were impositions and fines and, in the last resort, rustication for a time or complete expulsion. And as a member of a community of several hundred youths, mostly between seventeen and twenty-one, the young patrician mixed with his contemporaries.

They were carefully graded by rank, from the nobleman and the gentleman commoner to the servitor who paid for his education by more or less menial work, but even the nobleman, who dined at high-table with the dons, did not move in quite the same atmosphere of deference as he found at home. In so far as he got from teaching the capacity to fill his station in life and to enjoy his leisure, it was substantially from the same teaching as was provided for the other members of his own college. Of these very few belonged to the poorest class. There were not many who were entered as 'plebeians', that is the sons of yeomen or tradesmen (which probably includes artisans as well as small shop-keepers), and these often had allowances from their parents and were as comfortably off as those next above them.[1] The majority were the sons of landowners, clergymen, professional men or prosperous men of business. A number of writers of authority complained that the curriculum was little suited to their needs. Burnet, thinking perhaps more of schools than universities, 'thought it a great error to waste young gentlemen's years so long in learning Latin by so tedious a grammar'.

[1] C. Wase, *Considerations concerning Free Schools in England* (1678), p. 72.

He wanted to simplify and to modernize, and there were other educational reformers who proposed other changes for the same reason. John Locke in his *Thoughts on Education* of 1690,[1] one of the greatest of all books on the formation of character, recommended such Latin as the particular pupil was likely to need, and along with it drawing, arithmetic, astronomy, history, account-keeping, gardening, and shorthand, but not Greek, nor fencing, nor, for the ordinary gentleman, music. It was only through the influence of Locke himself that modern philosophy superseded the traditional scholasticism in the universities. Moreover, the old system of disputations and exercises qualifying for degrees had sunk into decadence. There was nothing quite so bad as the caricature of a degree-giving in Molière's *Malade imaginaire*, but the ceremonies were merely formal and provided neither a classification according to merit nor a real test of the candidate's acquirements.

On the other hand, it must not be supposed that the universities were altogether inefficient. The colleges offered, through those of their fellows who became tutors, teaching in small classes or by individual advice and influence, which made up for the shortcomings of the larger whole, and they kept an eye on the progress of the undergraduates. Still more important is the fact that, in spite of their political and ecclesiastical wranglings, the two universities were great seats of learning. We have abundantly seen how both the older and the newer studies flourished in them. They were the homes of the most erudite and enlightened theologians, classics, orientalists, philologists, mathematicians, and even of chemists, architects, and musicians. In Oxford there may still be seen as memorials of the period a museum built for the collections given by Elias Ashmole in 1683, with some remains of the collections themselves, and the observatory used by the great astronomer Edmund Halley when he was a professor in Queen Anne's time. Economics, indeed, was not yet a full university study, but the old libraries of Oxford and Cambridge show that there were men there who followed what was published on trade and government. Perhaps the most signal proof of their intellectual breadth and effectiveness is given by the university presses. Their privilege of printing gave the universities the opportunity of promoting publications, and of having them supervised and directed by great scholars. Oxford

---

[1] See also the *Correspondence of Locke and Clark*, ed. B. Rand (1927).

in particular, if it made some mistakes like that about Phalaris, made a noble use of the opportunity. From its reorganization by Dr. Fell in the reign of Charles II the Oxford University Press did a great work for good printing and good learning.[1] Bentley followed by reorganizing the press at Cambridge. And, although some of them wrote slightingly of their education, it must not be forgotten that almost all the Englishmen who achieved anything in learning or literature in the period were bred up at Oxford or Cambridge.

Towards the end of the period there were traces of growing laxity in the work of professors and tutors, but there were few signs of the torpor which spread over educational institutions in the eighteenth century. The most noteworthy instance of this was in the Inns of Court, which ceased to provide teaching for students and ceased to require them to reside during term, so that they lost their character of a legal university. The public teaching of law practically came to an end, and it was not revived in London until the nineteenth century. This, however, is to be explained rather from the history of the legal profession than as typical of the state of educational institutions. In spite of some other signs of approaching decadence the educational system was greatly strengthened. We have already noticed the non-conformist academies. There were also many additions to the number of free schools or grammar schools. These schools, all more or less Anglican and under clerical control, varied in size and character. Some were large and well endowed with exhibitions to the universities. In a growing number the head masters or other masters took in boarders from a distance. Others were by their constitution or narrow revenue 'only nurseries of piety and letters, as preparatory to trade'.[2] Their governing bodies were of many sorts, city companies, colleges in the universities, trustees recruited by co-optation, sometimes anomalous bodies in which some nobleman had the hereditary right to nominate the head master. The schools, however, were all mainly local and socially fairly comprehensive. The two colleges of Eton and Winchester stood outside the system, and Westminster, where a succession of able head masters trained up several of the most eminent men of the time, also had a position of its own; but with these exceptions, and a few others like Christ's Hospital and other orphanages, the free schools constituted a national

---

[1] See F. Madan, *Oxford Books*, iii (1931). [2] Wase, p. 53.

system for schooling after, and sometimes including, the elementary stages. Of the 475 which existed in England and Wales in the early nineteenth century, 40 or more were founded in this period, and in addition to the new foundations there were many handsome benefactions to existing schools.[1] Towards the end of the period there were unhealthy signs in some of the schools, for instance 'rebellions' of the boys against their masters, but there was no falling-off in the support given to education by the community.

Another important part of this support was the foundation of charity schools. This movement was closely related to religious philanthropy. Its central motive was the laudable desire to raise the children of the poor from their ignorance. It is a mistake to inquire too nicely into the reasons why this desire existed: any humane and educated person was distressed by the sight of extreme ignorance such as was possible then to a poor child in England. On the one hand this had a religious side: it was shocking to come across a boy of ten, a 'witty' boy, who knew nothing about Jesus Christ.[2] At the other extremity it had a utilitarian aspect: there were writers who pointed out that the idle and undisciplined children might be learning, or even practising, productive trades, and that even hedging and ditching could be done better by labourers who knew enough arithmetic to do simple measurements and sums. These were two motives, but between them was a genuine and spontaneous kindliness which made many people wish to help poor children by teaching them. It moved, of course, within the limits of the social imagination of the times. The philanthropists were anxious to avoid educating the poor above their station. Not infrequently, as in the poor-law schools, they made the handicraft-school into something scarcely distinguishable from a factory. But they began a great work. From the early days of the Society for Promoting Christian Knowledge, and mainly under its auspices, the schools were founded in remarkable

[1] Here I calculate from N. Carlisle, *Endowed Grammar Schools*, 2 vols. (1818). In some cases the actual foundation may have been earlier and forgotten in consequence of a reconstruction in this period; but this is rendered less likely by the fact that Carlisle used the materials collected by Christopher Wase, who circulated a questionnaire authorized by the vice-chancellor and the regius professor of civil law in Oxford: see *A Certificate in order to the Collecting and Reporting the State of the Present English Free-Schools* (1673).

[2] Oliver Heywood, *Diaries*, ed. J. Horsfall Turner, iv (188), 24: the date is 1681.

numbers both in London and in the provinces. They were
supported by voluntary contributions, and managed by local
committees of governors, drawn mainly from the middling
people, and including nonconformists as well as Anglicans. By
the end of Queen Anne's reign there were more than a thousand
schools, and they had placed out more than two thousand
children as apprentices. The charity of unpretentious people
had laid the foundations of a great movement of reform.[1]

The charity schools taught girls as well as boys, though the
boys were far more in number than the girls. In female education generally there were new ideas stirring. Some writers, both
theorists and teachers, continued the old tradition that women
were naturally unequal to men in intellect, or, as the new science
taught, in the physiology of the brain. The girls' boarding
schools and day schools still taught a miscellaneous curriculum
in which accomplishments had a leading place, especially for
the well-to-do. There were music, 'limning', shell-work, moss-
work, embroidery with gold and silver wire. 'Work' in general
meant needlework, as it still does in domestic language. A
travelling lady noted in Shrewsbury in 1698: 'Here is a very
good schoole for young gentlewomen for learning work and
behaviour and musick.'[2] Good girls' schools were still uncommon, and it was only exceptionally that they rose to such
heights as the school at Chelsea for which Purcell composed his
Dido and Aeneas. Some of them disseminated something of the
French culture of the time in letter-writing, the art of conversation and the reading of romances; but others were under suspicion for their morals, and it would be rash to say that there
was any general improvement. There was, however, a promise
of far-reaching change. Feminists were arising. In England there
was no original or powerful leader of this school, but there were
several women who took up the ideas of continental feminists
like the Dutchwoman Anna Maria van Schuurman or the
Frenchwoman Mademoiselle de Scudéry. An experienced
schoolmistress, Mrs. Hanna Woolley, in her *Gentlewoman's Companion* of 1675 wrote the following blunt and telling words:
'Vain man is apt to think we were meerly intended for the
world's propagation and to keep its humane inhabitants sweet
and clean; but, by their leaves, had we the same literature he

---

[1] See M. Gwladys Jones, *The Charity School Movement* (1938).
[2] Celia Fiennes, *Through England on a Side-Saddle*, ed. E. W. Griffiths (1888), p. 191.

would find our brains as fruitful as our bodies.'[1] And, as though to prove her right, a number of women authors made reputations in various kinds of writing. Margaret, duchess of Newcastle, was an eccentric and rather a bore. Mrs. Aphra Behn, the first Englishwoman to make her living by her pen, was an adventuress. Elizabeth Elstob was a scholar, but not a great scholar. They were only pioneers, but they found the trail.

The life of London, where there was less for the housewife to do than in the country, was favourable to the growth of social companionship between men and women, and this is seen in the part played by women in the world of Pope. It was aided by a growing refinement and liberality of manners: Steele and Addison did much to persuade their countrymen to treat women with respect. The same softening of human relations may be seen in other spheres. There is, for instance, the problem of witchcraft. Throughout western Europe this was one of the battle-grounds where rational humanity faced cruelty and prejudice. In England the civil war and the violence of the middle of the century intensified the nightmares of common people, and the sixteen-sixties saw a decided increase in the number of trials and in the number of executions of witches. As time went on the justices of the peace became much less willing to send accused witches for trial at the assizes. The judges, with some exceptions who were not amongst the unlearned or the unprincipled, became more rigorous in watching the evidence and bolder in withstanding public prejudice. Throughout the seventies and eighties the trials and convictions were falling off, and by the end of the eighties accounts of witchcraft were very rare.[2] The last English judicial execution for witchcraft came in 1712, and in the same year there was a public controversy in which for the last time educated Englishmen stood up for the old belief in sorcery as a crime. An ordinary village quarrel at Walkern in Hertfordshire ended in the prosecution of Jane Wenham for conversing with the devil in the form of a cat. Three clergymen testified against her, and she was condemned to death. The judge obtained her pardon from the queen. There was a war of pamphlets on both sides, and after it the belief sank to its proper place as a superstition. In 1736 the English laws

---

[1] Introduction, p. 1.
[2] W. Notestein, *Hist. of Witchcraft in England from 1558 to 1718* (1911), p. 283.

against witchcraft were repealed. In Scotland, as in New England, the record of the late seventeenth century was even worse than in England, but, not much later, the same changes in opinion and practice came about.

There are other directions in which we can trace the beginnings of a humanitarian movement in both its inseparable aspects of a healthier sympathy with suffering and a better understanding of its causes. The time had not come when there was either a social conscience or a machinery of social control capable of dealing with the fearful overcrowding, bad feeding, and disease which ate up human life, especially in London.[1] The growth of medical knowledge, however, led to a growth in the available number of useful medical men, and to improvements in the organization of the medical profession. These in time, when they came into alliance with the new scientific interest in statistics, were to create the great public health movement of the eighteenth and nineteenth centuries. In the earlier part of the period there was a long contest between the Royal College of Physicians and the Society of Apothecaries. The physicians wanted to keep the exclusive right of rendering medical services, but the apothecaries, who were satisfied with smaller fees, refused to confine themselves to making and selling medicines and pills. At the time of the great plague the apothecaries, like the nonconformist ministers, gained ground by staying at their posts and rendering help. In 1687 the College scored a point by making a rule that in certain conditions the members were to give their services free. A year later it established a free dispensary, or out-patient room, in London, the model for many such institutions in other towns. The apothecaries fought against this, and their opposition was not altogether disinterested; but in 1703 a judicial decision of the house of lords settled the relations of the two classes of practitioners for more than a century to come. The apothecaries were permitted to direct the remedies as well as to prepare them, and they existed as an inferior but numerous and, up to their lights, a useful body. Midwifery also made progress in this period, and to it belong the first English dentists who were anything more than primitive drawers of teeth.[2]

[1] The condition of London at the end of our period is described in M. Dorothy George (Mrs. Eric George), *London Life in the Eighteenth Century*, 2nd ed. (1930); but as yet there is no such excellent survey for earlier periods.

[2] A. M. Carr-Saunders and P. A. Wilson, *The Professions* (1933), pp. 72 ff., 107. See also above, p. 377.

When we turn to the abuses which aroused the great reformers of the next age, those of prisons, of asylums, of slavery, we find here and there protests, mainly in the name of religion, but we do not find investigation and organized plans for amelioration. The humanitarian spirit could move only within the limits set to it by rooted habits. It could not, for instance, stop the prevalence of duelling. All the best minds of the time could see, as the best minds had seen long before, that this custom was barbarous and foolish. Not only divines but soldiers and men of the world like Steele wrote against it. It was forbidden to military officers by the articles of war and to the rest of the world, as of old, by law and proclamations.[1] But men of the class which bore arms reserved the right to execute the laws of honour for themselves. Sometimes an exceptional duel aroused public indignation. The worst perhaps was that in 1668 between the duke of Buckingham, the minister of the Cabal, and the earl of Shrewsbury, the father of the duke of Shrewsbury. It is interesting to speculate whether the strange character of that statesman was influenced by this terrible event of his eighth year. His mother was Buckingham's mistress, and it was said that when the two men met at Barn Elms she held her lover's horses, disguised as a page. The seconds fought besides the principals, and Shrewsbury was run through the body. Before he died a few weeks later, both combatants, in spite of the proclamations, were given free pardon by the king. No scandal was bad enough to shake the system of defending 'honour' or answering an insult with the sword. William III said that if he had not been a king he would have called out Marlborough at the time when he was dismissed from office. Marlborough fought at least one duel. Wharton never gave but never refused a challenge, and twice he disarmed his opponent in duels fought over parliamentary elections.

If there was no effective opinion against duelling, it is not surprising that there was no movement against war. Writers on international law all held that there was such a thing as a just war. The Dutch wars of Charles II were aggressive, but they were thought to be amply justified by commercial rivalry and by a recital of particular injuries and affronts. In the great French wars, Louis XIV was believed to be the wanton disturber of

[1] In 1660 and 1679/80 (Steele and Crawford, *Tudor and Stuart Proclamations*, nos. 3245, 3710), for Ireland in 1685 and 1690/1 (ibid., nos. 957, 1194), for Scotland in 1674 (ibid., no. 2380).

European peace. The principle put forward in the declarations of war, in speeches from the throne and in treaties of peace, was that if the exorbitant power of France were checked, a balance of power in Europe could be restored. It was like an application of the newly discovered laws of mechanics: equilibrium would preserve peace by making it impossible for any one power to hope to prevail over the rest. Such hopes were false, and there must have been many who knew that they could not have borne a searching criticism; but there was no widely held and soundly constructed alternative doctrine. It was not that the wars of that period meant less in expense and suffering than those of later times. Armies and navies were smaller, and even smaller in proportion to the numbers of the peoples; but they were as large as the poorer and simpler societies of those days could afford. In every great war there was some state which fought until it came within sight of revolution at home. Nor were all observers so obtuse that they could not feel the misery and waste. When the early quakers maintained that no war was lawful for Christians, they used not only Biblical arguments, but objections of morality and common sense. Robert Barclay, their apologist, wrote not only against rendering evil for evil, but also against going 'a warring one against another, whom we never saw, and with whom we never had any contests, nor anything to do; being moreover altogether ignorant of the cause of the war, but only that the magistrates of the nations foment quarrels one against another, the causes whereof are for the most part unknown to the soldiers that fight, as well as upon whose side the right or wrong is'.[1]

How came it that, instead of being taken up by the churches, which were still powerful with princes and with the common people, or by the statesmen, who knew the dawning enlightenment of a scientific age, this remained, in England as abroad, the protest of unheeded sects? The answer would be long, but the history of England in this period contributes something to it. The machinery of the state was now so heavy, it held together so much of the wealth and authority by which men are governed, it rolled forward in its old courses with such momentum, that opinion could restrain or divert it only by being itself organized in a like way. Another quaker, who was also a great man of

---

[1] *Apology for the True Christian Divinity . . . preached by the People in Scorn called Quakers* (Latin, 1676; English, 1678), Proposition xv, xvi.

affairs, William Penn, sketched out, as others on the Continent
had done before him, a plan by which the united states of Europe
should meet in a parliament and settle their differences at peace.[1]
It was, however, a visionary scheme, quite out of contact with
realities. It had no practical influence, and it was long before it
even attracted attention as a curiosity. Only a programme could
give effect to the protest, and a programme buckled on at every
joint to the iron facts of political and economic society. Of this
there was not yet a beginning, and so, while many smaller evils
were dispelled by reason and humanity, war still held the collective courage and energy and intelligence of the nation in its
enchantment.

[1] *Essay towards the Present and Future Peace of Europe* (1693/4), reprinted in *Works*
(1726), ii. 838 ff., where the margin ascribes it to 1695.

BIBLIOGRAPHY

In the following list of authorities no title is given in more than one place, so that each section is to be supplemented from the others related to it. The books referred to above in footnotes or in the text are not all mentioned here, and critical observations already made in the volume are not here repeated. Only one edition of each book is mentioned. In a few cases a reason is given for the choice, but in others it is sometimes the best, often, where later editions are not materially better, the first, and in a few instances the only edition available in any of the chief English libraries.

GENERAL

BIBLIOGRAPHIES AND WORKS OF REFERENCE. The best general guide to the authorities is G. Davies, *Bibliography of British History, Stuart Period, 1603–1714* (1928). Another work of high quality is C. L. Grose, *Select Bibliography of British History, 1660–1760* (1939) and much material is included in the elaborate *Bibliography of British History, 1700–1715*, 5 vols. (1934–42) ed. by W. T. and Chloe S. Morgan. D. G. Wing, *Short Title Catalogue of Books printed . . . 1641–1700*, 3 vols. (1945–51), though not perfect is an invaluable book of reference. Bibliographical guides in the technical sense are less adequate than for the previous period. F. Madan, *Oxford Books*, vol. iii, 1931, goes down to 1680. *The Term Catalogues, 1688–1709 and 1711*, ed. E. Arber, 3 vols., 1903–6, are useful contemporary lists of new publications, admirably indexed. The *Transcript of the Registers of the Stationers' Company* is continued in 3 vols. from 1640 to 1708, ed. G. E. Briscoe Eyre, 1913–14, but has no index. For details of editions, authorship, &c., the best authority is the *British Museum Catalogue of Printed Books*. A new edition is in progress (1960–) but this does not contain, like the other, full subject-entries under the names of countries. G. K. Fortescue and others, *Subject-Index* (1902–) records the accessions of new books since the printing of the general Catalogue. The Royal Historical Society publishes a valuable series of lists of *Writings on British History*: the first volume (1937) dealt with publications of 1934.

Bibliographies of special subjects are mentioned below in the appropriate sections. The work of one eminent historian of the period is dealt with in *A Bibliography of the Writings of Sir Charles Firth*, 1928. There is no comprehensive catalogue of the pamphlets of the period, but the *Catalogue of the Pamphlets at Lincoln's Inn*, 1908, is useful. Many pamphlets are reprinted in collections of which the two most important are *The Harleian Miscellany*, 8 vols., 1744–6, and the *Somers Tracts*, 16 vols., 1748–52. Tables of the contents of both these are given in the *Catalogue of the London Library*, 2 vols., 1913–14 (and supplements): this and the *Subject Index* of the same library, 4 vols., 1909–54, are useful for many purposes. Some of the most influential pamphlets are reprinted in the collected works of their authors, amongst which may be named those of Sir William Temple, 2 vols., 1720; John Locke, 9vols., 1822; the marquis of Halifax, 1912 and in Miss H. C. Foxcroft's important *Life of Halifax*, 2 vols., 1898 (which is brought up to date in her shorter book *A Character of the Trimmer*, 1946); Jonathan Swift, *Prose Works*, ed. Temple Scott, 12 vols., 1897–1908; John Arbuthnot, *Life and Works*, ed. G. A. Aitken, 1892. The most complete collection of Defoe's works is, that of 1840 in 20 vols.

For the manuscript records the most comprehensive guide, though not well arranged, is H. Hall, *Repertory of British Archives*, pt. i, *England*, vol. i, 1920, not to be continued. Those in the Public Record Office are summarily described in M. S. Giuseppi, *Guide to the Manuscripts preserved in the Public Record Office*, 2 vols., 1923–4, and some of them in greater detail in the official series of 'Lists and Indexes'. The Stationery Office publishes from time to time a complete 'sectional list' of official record publications, known as 'List Q'. The British Museum and Bodleian libraries each have printed catalogues of different units of their collections; in the British Museum a subject-index to the whole is available in the manuscript room.

By far the most important book of reference for every aspect of English history is *The Dictionary of National Biography*. The reprint in 22 vols., 1908–9, has some corrections of the original edition of 1885–1901. It should be used with the corrections published from time to time in the *Bulletin of the Institute of Historical Research*. There are short lives of some Englishmen not noticed by the *Dictionary* in J. H. Hora Siccama, *Aanteekeningen op het register op de journalen van Huygens*, 1915, published by the Historisch Genootschap of Utrecht. Two important dictionaries of university men are J. Foster, *Alumni Oxonienses, 1500–1714,* 4 vols., 1891–2, and J. and J. A. Venn, *Alumni Cantabrigienses,* pt. i, *to 1751,* 4 vols., 1922–7, the latter a work of admirable research. For peers and their families G. E. C[okayne], *The Complete Peerage,* 8 vols., 1887–98, should be consulted: the excellent new edition begun by the Hon. Vicary Gibbs (1910–) has reached the letter T. *The Complete Baronetage* by G. E. C., 16 vols., 1900–9, is a companion series. W. A. Shaw, *The Knights of England,* 2 vols., 1906, is a list of dates of knighthoods.

For the dates of events the following are convenient: from 1660, S. Clarke, *The Historian's Guide,* 3rd ed., 1690; [1678–1714] N. Luttrell, *Brief Historical Relation of State Affairs,* 6 vols., 1857; [1703–14] A. Boyer, *History of the Reign of Queen Anne digested into Annals,* 11 vols., 1703–13, and *History of the Life and Reign of Queen Anne,* 1722. For the dates and personal relationships of rulers in all countries the best repertory is still *L'art de vérifier les dates,* 23 vols., 1818–19. Genealogical tables are given in H. B. George, *Genealogical Tables,* ed. J. R. H. Weaver, 1930, and in vol. xiii of *The Cambridge Modern History,* 1911.

No general encyclopaedia of the modern type was published in English during the period: the first edition of E. Chambers, *Cyclopaedia* belongs to 1728, but so far as it relates to mathematics and the sciences it is largely anticipated by J. Harris, *Lexicon Technicum,* 1704, 2nd ed., 2 vols., 1708–10, which is arranged alphabetically. For current information on all public matters, from weights and measures to the constitution and personnel of government offices, there is an excellent book of reference in E., and from 1704 J., Chamberlayne, *Angliae Notitia or the Present State of England.* For the dates of editions and other bibliographical details see the list by Muriel M. S. Arnett in *Bulletin of the Institute of Historical Research,* No. 43 (1937). After the union with Scotland the title was changed to *Magnae Britanniae Notitia,* and the editions were 1708 (22nd), 1710 (23rd). The last edition published was the 38th, of 1755. G. Miège, *The New State of England* (1691–1758) was a rival publication of the same type. Compendious lists of peers, office-holders, &c., are in R. Beatson, *Political Index,* 3rd ed., 3 vols., 1806, and *Handbook of British Chronology,* ed. F. M. Powicke (1939).

The chief periodicals are *The English Historical Review* (1886–), for which there are indexes to vols. i–xx, xxi–xxx, and xxxi–xl, and the *Transactions of the Royal Historical Society* (1871–): see

List and Index of the Publications of the R.H.S. and of the Camden Society, ed. H. Hall, 1925. The two societies are now merged: both have published original texts, of which some are mentioned below.

POLITICAL HISTORY

GENERAL AND DOMESTIC. Of the contemporary general histories the most important (see above, p. 379) is Gilbert Burnet, *History of my own Times*. The best edition of the whole is in 6 vols., 1833, the best edition of any part that on Charles II's reign by O. Airy, 2 vols., 1897. The growth of the history is traced and relevant material printed in Miss H. C. Foxcroft, *Supplement to Burnet's History*, 1902; the *Life of Gilbert Burnet*, 1907, by the same writer and T. E. S. Clarke, has a critical study of Burnet as an historian by Sir Charles Firth. P. Rapin de Thoyras, *History of England*, with a continuation by N. Tindal, 28 vols., 1726–47, has independent value, but like Burnet is on the whig side: Rapin sailed with William III in 1688. The other general historians who wrote before the opening of archives in the nineteenth century are now of less value. For a survey of them see Sir Charles Firth in *Transactions of the Royal Historical Society*, 3rd ser., vii, 1913.

Leopold von Ranke, *History of England*, 6 vols., 1875, is a clear survey of the action of British governments and parties written by a great master. After 1702 the scale is much reduced. In appendixes are valuable criticisms of the authorities with documents, especially reports of a Prussian agent, 1690–5. Ranke is better on foreign than on domestic affairs, in contrast with Lord Macaulay, whose whig and liberal point of view does not greatly differ from his own. Macaulay's *History of England from the Accession of James II* is a classic. It was originally published in 5 vols., 1849–61; the best edition is in 6 vols. with illustrations chosen by Sir Charles Firth, 1913–15. There is no adequate annotated edition, but the notes by T. F. Henderson in his edition of 1907, reprinted in 5 vols., 1931, are useful. Later historians frequently explain at each point why they differ from Macaulay: his account of the reign of William III is less satisfactory than the earlier portions. For a criticism of the whole work in the light of subsequent research down to 1914 see Sir Charles Firth, *Commentary on Macaulay's History* (1938).

Only one detailed work subsequent to Macaulay covers the

whole period from 1660 to 1714. This is Onno Klopp, *Der Fall des Hauses Stuart*, 14 vols., 1875–88, a political history giving the substance of the dispatches of Austrian diplomatists and especially valuable from about 1678. It is adverse to the Stuarts and, though dull, is important. David Ogg, *England in the Reign of Charles II*, 2 vols., 1934, is the fullest history of the reign and is continued for the next two reigns (1955). G. M. Trevelyan's *England under Queen Anne* is less purely political than what previously ranked as the standard work for the period, Lord Stanhope, *History of England comprising the Reign of Queen Anne*, 1870, but is mainly concerned with political, military, and naval affairs. The three volumes have separate titles: *Blenheim*, 1930; *Ramillies*, 1932; *The Peace and the Protestant Succession*, 1934. They include the results of the widespread research of recent years and of some new work on manuscripts. Though it has a certain continuity with the whig tradition the book cannot be called one-sided. It may, however, be remarked that there has been in recent years a movement of reaction among some historians away from the whig tradition and in favour either of the Stuarts or of the moderate tories. This has not produced any large work like those mentioned above but monographs and scattered studies. Of these the most important are named in later sections of this bibliography.

Some of the best written and some of the most useful books on the period are biographies and memoirs. Clarendon's *Life* of himself, 2 vols., 1857, must be named first, and for both reasons, though it has shortcomings. W. D. Christie, *Life of Shaftesbury*, 2 vols., 1871, is full of matter. *The Lives of the Norths* by the Hon. R. North, ed. A. Jessop, 3 vols., 1890, is one of the best authorities on the reaction under Charles II and James II. The author writes as a convinced tory about his notable brothers, three of whom were Lord Keeper Guilford, Dudley North, merchant and economist, and John North, master of Trinity. The *Memoirs* of Sir John Reresby, ed. A. Browning, 1936, were written by a Yorkshire tory who died in 1689. Those of Thomas Bruce, earl of Ailesbury, 2 vols., 1890, are vivid but unreliable: he wrote them in his old age as a Jacobite exile. *The Life of James II . . . collected out of Memoirs writ of his own Hand*, ed. J. S. Clarke, 2 vols., 1816, is of very unequal value. The best parts throw much light on his policy, but especially after the Revolution much is un-trustworthy. The original memoirs are lost: the relation of the printed book to these is discussed in the Rt. Hon. W. S. Churchill, *Marlborough, his Life and Times*, 4 vols., 1933–8. This powerful book is not academically faultless, but for all ordinary purposes, military and political, it supersedes the earlier lives, for which see below, p. 441. Queen Mary wrote some interesting autobiographical pieces on the period 1688–93, which are to be found in *Lettres et mémoires de Marie, reine d'Angleterre*, ed. Mechtilde, Comtesse Bentinck, 1880, and *Memoirs of Mary, Queen of England*, ed. R. Doebner, 1886. Hester W. Chapman, *Mary II, Queen of England*, 1953, is the most adequate biography. Bolingbroke has attracted many biographers and baffled them all: the best attempt is W. Sichel, *Bolingbroke and his Times*, 2 vols., 1901–2. An authoritative three-volume work on *Thomas Osborne, Earl of Danby* has been published by Professor A. Browning (1944–51); the second volume consists of letters and the third of documents.

Political and private correspondence has been published in great masses, but it has seldom been well edited. The motive for publication has often been family piety or interest in the picturesque and personal qualities of the letters. Some of the collections are selections made almost at random, and even the Historical Manuscripts Commission gives practically no explanatory notes. Of its publications the most important for this period, in addition to some mentioned in other sections below, are the *Portland Papers*, 9 vols., 1891–1923, which contain besides other materials a mass of Harley's correspondence, including Defoe's letters; the *Papers of the Marquess of Bath at Longleat*, 3 vols., 1904–8, which have more of Harley's papers and some of Prior's; *Ormonde Papers*, vol. iv, 1906, letters from Sir Robert Southwell, 1677–80, giving an account of English politics. The Commission's *Eighteenth Report*, 1917, contains tables of the contents of its publications down to that date, and it has also published other lists and guides. Among the collections published unofficially one of the most interesting for students of human nature is *Letters of two Queens*, ed. A. B. Bathurst, 1924: the queens are Mary and Anne and the greater part of the letters were written by Mary in *c.* 1673–88. *The Hatton Correspondence*, ed. E. M. Thompson, 2 vols., 1878, is useful for the political history of the last forty years of the seventeenth century. The correspondence in the *Poems and Letters of Andrew Marvell*, ed. H. M. Margoliouth, 2 vols., 1927, is mainly of political interest and runs from 1653 to 1678; the editing is of high quality. That of the two great whig writers of Queen Anne's reign has been published in *The Correspondence of Sir Richard Steele*, ed. R. Blanchard (1941), and Joseph Addison, *Letters*, ed. W. Graham (1941): the latter has much of Irish interest. *The Ellis Correspondence*, ed. G. J. W. Agar-Ellis, Lord Dover, 2 vols., 1829, consists of letters addressed to a public servant of some consequence in 1686–8. *The Wentworth Papers*, ed. J. J. Cartwright, 1883, begin in 1705 and are useful for the Utrecht negotiations, where Thomas Wentworth, Lord Raby and afterwards earl of Strafford, was one of the plenipotentiaries. They were, however, selected with an eye to the amusement of the general reader. Among them are some newsletters from Abel Boyer: this trade, half-way between confidential letter-writing and journalism, was plied all through the period and many newsletters have been published. There is a long series, from about 1660 to 1700, in the Historical Manuscripts Commission's *Le Fleming Papers*, 1890. With the newsletters as with the letters in general the difficulty of the historian who uses them as authorities is that there are so many of them and such inadequate charts through the confusion.

In using the modern monographs on special subjects or aspects of the period it is necessary to notice what materials have been accessible to each author, and for this purpose Mr. Davies's *Bibliography* (see above, p. 423), giving the publications in each section in the chronological order of their appearance, is very useful. K. G. Feiling, *History of the Tory Party, 1640–1714* (1924) is the fullest and best study of the interaction of personalities: while useful as a corrective to the whig tradition, it is avowedly sympathetic to a moderate toryism of which it somewhat over-emphasizes the continuity. J. Pollock, *The Popish Plot*, 1903, is a polemical work and does not prove its main contentions. W. T. Morgan, *English Political Parties and Leaders in the Reign of Queen Anne, 1702–10* (1920) and its continuation in an article on the ministerial change of 1710 in *Political Science Quarterly*, xxxvi, 1921, though based on much manuscript evidence and contributing some correct results, have many inaccuracies. F. Salomon, *Geschichte des letzten Ministeriums Königin Annas von England*, 1894, covers the period 1710–14 and gives new documents: it is a spirited and ably argued defence of the tories, unfortunately not equally fair to their opponents.

FOREIGN RELATIONS. Most of the treaties with foreign powers

are in J. du Mont, *Corps universal diplomatique*, 8 vols. in 15, 1726–31. Modern editions of some or all of the treaties with Austria, Denmark, Sweden are published in those countries: for titles see D. P. Myers, *Manual of Collections of Treaties*, 1922. The only up-to-date edition of the treaties in English is Frances G. Davenport's *European Treaties bearing on the History of the United States and its Dependencies*, vols. ii–iii, 1650–1715 (1929–34). C. Vast, *Les grands traités du règne de Louis XIV*, 3 vols., 1893–9, gives texts of the leading treaties with brief introductions and notes.

The Royal Historical Society has published a summary list of *British Diplomatic Representatives, 1689–1789*, ed. D. B. Horn, 1932, with references for their correspondence. For the earlier part of the period and for foreign representatives see the four parts of *Notes on the Diplomatic Relations of England*, ed. C. H. Firth, (1906–13). The *Repertorium der diplomatischen Vertreter aller Länder*, ed. L. Bittner and L. Gross, vol. i, *1648–1715* (1936) gives only the heads of missions. A study of the organization of British diplomacy and the forms used in its written communications is a desideratum. Miss Violet Barbour has dealt with 'Consular Service in the Reign of Charles II' in *American Historical Review*, xxxiii, 1928, and Miss Margery Lane has written on 'The Diplomatic Service under William III' in *Royal Historical Society Transactions*, 4th ser., x, 1927: the definite article in the title is scarcely justified. Quantities of diplomatic correspondence and similar materials have been published, but it is largely a matter of chance whether a particular negotiation has been dealt with in this way or not. There is not yet for this period any official calendar of the State Papers Foreign in the Public Record Office. Their bulk is so great, and such a large proportion of their contents is repeated in many dispatches, that for a calendar to be of manageable size it will be necessary to devise stricter methods of planning than have been practised for earlier periods. Little attention has been paid to this problem by those who have worked on the correspondence in other repositories. This consists of official papers retained by ministers and diplomatists instead of being returned to the custody of the old State Paper Office, and also of unofficial letters exchanged alongside of the official communications. Many letters of both classes have been published in biographies and in collections of papers edited, often badly, at the instance of the families of the writers or recipients. Many more are in the series of the Historical

Manuscripts Commission. There is a chronological list of the diplomatic correspondence in these and the British Museum Manuscript Department by Frances G. Davenport in the *18th Report* of the Commission, 1917. A fuller list of the materials on British relations with Holland only, by S. J. van den Bergh, is in *Bijdragen voor vaderlandsche geschiedenis*, 5th ser., vols. iii–iv, 1916–17. Since the publication of all the diplomatic correspondence *in extenso* is impossible, some of the secondary authorities which summarize it must be regarded as almost equivalent to original sources, e.g. Klopp's book mentioned above, p. 427. The Royal Historical Society has made an attempt to provide, in its series of *British Diplomatic Instructions*, a key to the history of foreign relations which shall be at once first-hand and short. The idea was derived from the French 'Recueil des instructions données aux ambassadeurs', of which the two volumes *Angleterre, 1648–90* (1929), were ed. by J. J. Jusserand. These give the elaborate instructions which explained to French representatives both French policy and the conditions of the countries where they served. The English instructions are much less informative on both sides, and the volumes of the series are filled out with somewhat arbitrarily selected dispatches. The volumes falling within our period are *France, 1689–1721*, ed. L. G. Wickham Legg, 1925; *Sweden, 1689–1727*, ed. J. F. Chance, 1922; *Denmark, 1689–1789*, ed. J. F. Chance, 1926.

Such being the complex relation of the primary and secondary printed authorities, we now name some of both classes together, taking first those which concern British relations with all or several of the continental powers, and then those more especially concerning relations with a single power. The best textbook for the relations of the European states is M. Immich, *Geschichte des europäischen Staatensystems*, 1905. Sir John Seeley, *The Growth of British Policy*, 2 vols., 1895, is still the most readable interpretation of the whole development; but it is now largely superseded. Sir J. Dalrymple, *Memoirs of Great Britain and Ireland*, has appendixes of documents on the period 1681–92 which are still of value: the first edition, 2 vols., 1771–3, is the best. For the policy of Charles II the following are valuable: K. G. Feiling, *British Foreign Policy, 1660–72*, 1930, a minute study; T. H. Lister, *Life and Administration of Clarendon*, 3 vols., 1838; Violet Barbour, *Henry Bennet, Earl of Arlington*, 1914 (see also Arlington's *Letters*, 3 vols., 1710); T. P. Courtenay, *Memoirs of the Life of Sir William*

Temple, 2 vols., 1836, and Temple's *Works*; Julia Cartwright (Mrs. Ady), *Madame, a Life of Henrietta, Duchess of Orleans*, 1900; W. Wynne, *Life of Sir Leoline Jenkins*, 2 vols., 1724. From the later years of Charles II the most important body of correspondence is that of William III. Portions of this have been published in a number of works, amongst which the two most important are *Archives de la Maison d'Orange-Nassau*, 2nd ser., *1584–1688*, ed. G. Groen van Prinsterer, 5 vols., 1857–62; 3rd ser., *1689–1702*, ed. F. J. L. Krämer, 3 vols., 1907–9; and *Correspondentie van Willem III en van Portland*, ed. N. Japikse, 6 vols., 1927–37. Dr. Japikse has also written a standard biography of *Willem III de stadhouder-koning*, 2 vols., 1930–3. Two publications of the Historical Manuscripts Commission give the correspondence of secretaries of state in William's reign: Nottingham's are in the *Papers of Mr. A. G. Finch*, 3 vols., 1913–57, and Sir William Trumbull's in the *Downshire Papers*, pts. i and ii, 1924. The *Shrewsbury Correspondence* was edited by W. Coxe in 1821[1] and the correspondence of James Vernon by G. P. R. James in 1841 with the title *Letters Illustrative of the Reign of William III . . . from 1696 to 1708*. The bulky work of the Marquise Campana de Cavelli, *Les derniers Stuarts à Saint-Germain-en-Laye*, 2 vols., 1871, contains many important documents. In Queen Anne's reign the diplomatic correspondence of Marlborough and Harley is printed with their general letters (pp. 441, 428). Bolingbroke's *Letters as Secretary of State* were published in 4 vols., 1798, by G. Parke. The intricacies of diplomacy in the reign must, however, be followed chiefly in the works of modern historians. C. von Noorden carried his *Europäische Geschichte im achtzehnten Jahrhundert*, 3 vols., 1870–82, based on archives, down to 1710. O. Weber, *Der Friede von Utrecht*, 1891, is the best survey of the pacification.

For relations with France the most important work down to 1679 is F. A. M. Mignet, *Négociations relatives à la succession d'Espagne*, 4 vols., 1835–42. This gives the chief documents, with connecting narrative, the best method of presenting the material if a first-rate historian is available to do it. J. J. Jusserand, *A French Ambassador at the Court of Charles II*, 1892, narrates the mission of Cominges in 1662–5. Ruth E. Clark, *Sir William Trumbull in Paris, 1685–88* is a useful monograph. A. Legrelle gives much detailed information, interpreted always in favour

---

[1] For a calendar of the collection see the Historical Manuscripts Commission's *Buccleuch Manuscripts at Montagu House*, vol. ii, 2 pts., 1903.

of Louis XIV, in *Notes et documents sur la paix de Ryswick*, 1894, and *La diplomatie française et la succession d'Espagne*, 2nd ed., 6 vols., 1895–1900. Torcy's *Mémoires* . . . *depuis le traité de Ryswick jusqu'à la paix d'Utrecht*, 3 vols., 1756, should be read with L. G. Wickham Legg, *Matthew Prior*, 1921.

For Holland original materials are abundant, such as the letters of John de Witt, later editions of which supplement the *Brieven*, 6 vols., 1723–5 (French translation, 4 vols., 1725), the *Dispatches of Thomas Plott and Thomas Chudleigh*, ed. F. A. Middlebush, 1926, the correspondence of John Drummond with Harley in the Historical Manuscripts Commission's *Portland Papers*, vols. iv–v, Strafford's correspondence in vol. ix, and many shorter publications. The most considerable of many modern studies are two essays (of 1864 and 1889) on William III before 1689 by the great Dutch historian, Robert Fruin, in his *Verspreide geschriften*, vols. iv–v; N. Japikse, *De verwikkelingen tusschen de republiek en Engeland, 1660–5* (1900). C. L. Grose, 'The Anglo-Dutch Alliance of 1678' in *English Historical Review*, xxxix, 1924; Gabryelle van den Haute, *Les relations anglo-hollandaises, 1700–6* (1932); R. Geikie and Isabel A. Montgomery, *The Dutch Barrier, 1705–19* (1930). G. N. Clark, *The Dutch Alliance and the War against French Trade, 1689–97* (1923) deals with economic relations, and is briefly continued in articles by the same author on the following war in *Economic History Review*, i. 262, and *British Year Book of International Law*, 1928, p. 69. The neglect of the diplomacy of the Spanish Succession War by Dutch historians has led to misunderstandings and to an unfair treatment of Dutch policy; these are discussed by P. Geyl in *Mededeelingen der Koninklijke Akademie, Afd. Letterkunde*, 1929. The Historisch Genootschap of Utrecht has published a valuable edition of *The Correspondence, 1701–1711, of Marlborough and Heinsius*, ed. B. van 't Hoff, 1951.

For Brandenburg-Prussia documents are more ample than for the other German courts: many are in the series *Urkunden und Aktenstücke zur Geschichte des Kurfürsten Friedrich Wilhelm*, 21 vols., 1864–1915, in addition to which the *Briefe aus England* of Otto von Schwerin, 1837, gives his reports of 1674–8. *The Letterbook of Sir George Etherege*, ed. S. Rosenfeld, 1928, is of more social and literary than diplomatic interest, though it belongs to Etherege's mission to the imperial diet at Ratisbon in 1685–8. The *Lexington Papers*, ed. H. Manners Sutton, 1851, are extracts from Lexington's Vienna correspondence of 1694–8. A. F. Přibram, *Franz Paul Freiherr von Lisola*, 1894, deals with the most individual of the imperial diplomatists. Two books by Sir A. W. Ward are the best English studies of British relations with Hanover: the lectures, *Great Britain and Hanover*, 1899, and the fuller study *The Electress Sophia and the Hanoverian Succession*, 2nd ed., 1909. For a clear account in German see W. Michael, *Englische Geschichte im achtzehnten Jahrhundert*, vol. i, 1895 (English c. 1936). Besides the article mentioned above, p. 64, n. 1, Professor Brinkmann wrote on 'The Relations of England and Germany, 1660–88' in *English Historical Review*, xxiv, 1909; and ibid. xxiii, 1908, the best account of relations with the Hanseatic towns under Charles II.

The contemporary works by or about British diplomatists in the Northern states and Russia are more valuable for the history and condition of those countries than for the negotiations. The best of them is J. Robinson, *Account of Sweden*, 1694. In the same year Robert, Lord Molesworth, published an *Account of Denmark* which is much inferior. A *Relation* of the earl of Carlisle's three embassies to Russia, Sweden, and Denmark in 1663–4 was published in 1669 by Guy Miège. An *Account of Russia as it was in 1710* by Charles, Lord Whitworth, dates from 1758. Molesworth's final report on his mission, published by J. F. Chance in *English Historical Review*, xxxix, 1924, is a specimen of a scarce type of document. All the other surviving examples from this period should be published. Three useful articles are: H. L. Schoolcraft, 'England and Denmark, 1660–7' in *English Historical Review*, xxv, 1910; Margery Lane, 'England and Denmark, 1689–97' in *Royal Historical Society Transactions*, 3rd ser., v, 1911; J. F. Chance, 'England and Sweden in the Time of William III and Anne' in *English Historical Review*, xvi, 1901.

For Spain the most important book is the *Original Letters and Negotiations of Fanshaw, Sandwich, Sunderland and Godolphin*, 2 vols., 1724, which covers 1663–78; but the Spanish archives still need examination and will probably disclose valuable evidence. E. Prestage, *The Diplomatic Relations of Portugal with France, England and Holland from 1640 to 1688* (1925) is a clear preliminary survey. Violet M. Shillington and Annie B. W. Chapman, *The Commercial Relations of England and Portugal*, 1907, is a brief study based partly on diplomatic correspondence. F. Kilchenmauer, in *Schweizen Studien zur Geschichtswissenschaft*, vi, pt. 1 (1914), dealt with the mission of Thomas Coxe to the protestant cantons in 1689–92. Except for the alliance of Savoy British dealings with Italy were not very important. The only substantial original material in print is the *Diplomatic Correspondence of the Rt. Hon. Richard Hill, 1703–6*, ed. W. Blackley, 2 vols., 1845; but for this period, as well as those preceding and following it, work on archives is badly needed. D. Carutti, *Storia del regno di Vittorio Amadeo II*, 1863, is not adequate for modern needs.

LEGAL AND CONSTITUTIONAL

The most authoritative general work is Sir William Holdsworth, *History of English Law*, 12 vols., and index vol., 1922–38 (not the first ed. in 3 vols.). This covers the whole ground from early times to the end of the seventeenth century, and in some sections proceeds beyond our period. It supersedes all former syntheses of research and gives systematic reviews of the authorities. The author expresses decided opinions on some political and economic matters with which specialists will disagree, but on legal and strictly constitutional points his judgements, frequently original, are to be accepted. For some purposes of reference Sir William Anson's systematically arranged *Law and Custom of the Constitution* is the best textbook: vol. i, *Parliament*, ed. Sir Maurice Gwyer, 1922, has some corrections in the light of recent research, as has the new edition of vol. ii (in two parts), *The Crown*, by A. B. Keith, 1935. A. Amos, *The English Constitution in the Reign of Charles II*, 1857, is still useful. The relevant portion of F. W. Maitland, *Constitutional History of England*, ed. H. A. L. Fisher, 1908, is only a sketch by a historian of genius. J. Hatscheck, *Englische Verfassungsgeschichte*, 1913, is a work of learning and originality, and, though it has the imperfections which a foreigner could scarcely have avoided, is very useful, as is J. W. Gough, *Fundamental Law in English Constitutional History*, 1955.

The work of the privy council and the development of cabinet government have been explored in the following articles, which do not exactly agree in their conclusions and should be compared: E. I. Carlyle, 'Clarendon and the Privy Council', in *English Historical Review*, xxvii, 1912; H. W. V. Temperley, 'Inner and Outer Cabinet, 1697–1783', ibid., and 'Documents illustrative of the Powers of the Privy Council in the Seventeenth Century', ibid. xxviii, 1913; Sir William Anson, 'The Cabinet in the Seventeenth and Eighteenth Centuries', ibid. xxix, 1914; E. R. Turner, 'The Privy Council of 1679', ibid. xxx, 1915, 'The Development of the Cabinet, 1688–1760', in *American Historical Review*, xviii–xix, 1913, 'The Lords of the Committee of Council', from 1688, ibid. xxii, 1916, 'Privy Council Committees, 1688–1760', *English Historical Review*, xxxi, 1916; G. Davies, 'Council and Cabinet, 1679–88', ibid. xxxvii, 1922. The ambitious work in which Professor E. R. Turner attempted to treat the whole subject definitively from 1603 to 1784—*The Privy Council of England*, 2 vols., 1927–8; *The Cabinet Council of England*, 2 vols., 1930—contains a mass of information, but the handling is hasty and imperfect, and the conclusions require thorough testing.

Trials which raised important constitutional points, as well as those of political interest such as prosecutions for treason, are recorded in various compilations of which the most convenient is the *State Trials*, ed. W. Cobbett, 34 vols., 1809–28.

PARLIAMENT. The best edition of the Acts of Parliament is *The Statutes of the Realm*, 9 vols. and Index, 1810–28. The numbering differs in other editions and it is sometimes impossible to know which is referred to: a table of these references in parallel columns is given in all editions subsequent to 1893 of the official *Chronological Index to the Statutes*, which is frequently reissued. The formal proceedings of the houses are in the *Journals of the House of Lords*, vols. xi–xix, and *Journals of the House of Commons*, vols. viii–xvii. The texts of bills are in the *Manuscripts of the House of Lords* which are calendared down to 1678 in the *3rd–9th Reports* of the Royal Commission on Historical Manuscripts, and from that date to 1712 in 13 vols. of which the first four are published by the Royal Commission and the remainder by the house of lords. They contain many other documents of great value. *The Protests of the House of Lords*, ed. J. E. Thorold Rogers, vol. i, 1875, are useful. For reports of debates the compilation of William Cobbett, *Parliamentary History of England*, vols. iv–vi, 1808–10, is almost as useful as the editions on which it is founded; but many reports have to be sought in diplomatic correspondence and elsewhere. Mr. L. F. Stock's *Proceedings and Debates of the British Parliaments respecting North America*, vols. i–ii, 1924–7, is the only edition satisfying modern critical requirements. The official *Return of the Names of every Member returned to serve in each Parliament*, 2 vols., 1878, may be supplemented from a number of works dealing with particular counties and boroughs. Two parliamentary diaries have been edited by American scholars, that of John Milward, 1666–8 by Caroline Robbins (1938) and that of Sir Edward Dering, 1670–3 by B. D. Henning (1940).

Among secondary works relating to parliament are three by A. S. Turberville: 'The House of Lords in the Reign of Charles II' in *English Historical Review*, xliv–xlv, 1929–30; *The House of Lords in the Reign of William III*, 1913; *The House of Lords in the Eighteenth Century*, 1927. It is hoped that the organized research of the History of Parliament Trust will throw much new light on the development of the house of commons in this period. There is a good deal of information, imperfectly organized, in E. and Annie G. Porritt, *The Unreformed House of Commons*, 2 vols., 1903–9.

THE CENTRAL GOVERNMENT. By far the most important series of volumes giving the acts of the various organs of state, usually in summarized form, are the Calendars prepared at the Public Record Office. The *Calendar of Treasury Papers*, ed. J. Redington, vols. i–iv, 1868–79, deals only with papers of minor interest addressed to the treasury; but the *Calendar of Treasury Books*, ed. W. A. Shaw (1904–), is the leading authority on financial history. It begins with 1660 and covers the period in twenty-eight volumes (several of them in more parts than one). The introductions to the volumes give valuable information on the financial system; but those on Charles II contain also polemics in vindication of his integrity and foreign policy. These have inspired most of Charles II's recent defenders, but they should not be followed without serious reservations: see the review of vols. ii–v by Sir Charles Firth in *English Historical Review*, xxvii, 1912. The *Calendar of State Papers Domestic* now covers the years 1660–84, 1689–1704. These papers are not only important for affairs in England but touch Irish and foreign affairs and are leading sources for naval and military history. The *Calendar of State Papers Venetian*, of which vols. xxxii–xxxvii, 1931–7, cover 1659–72, gives the reports of Venetian diplomatists, but these are less valuable in this than in earlier periods: their chief interest is in the accounts of English events. The *Calendar of State Papers Colonial, America and West Indies*, covers the whole of the period. From 1704 the *Journal of the Board of Trade and Plantations* forms a separate series, of which vol. ii goes down to 1715, while vols. i–ii of the *Acts of the Privy Council, Colonial Series*, form a supplementary series for the whole period.[1]

A most useful summary of the public accounts is given in the *Return of Public Income and Expenditure*, pt. i, 1869, which begins with the Revolution.

The excellent calendar of *Tudor and Stuart Proclamations* by R. Steele and the earl of Crawford, 2 vols., 1910, is not an official publication.

The most useful modern books on the organs of the central government are Florence M. Grier Evans (afterwards Higham), *The Principal Secretary of State to 1680* (1923), which is continued by M. A. Thomson, *The Secretaries of State*, 1932; and the following works dealing with the machinery of colonial government: C. M. Andrews, *British Commissions, Committees and Councils of Trade and Plantations, 1662–75* (1908); R. P. Bieber, *The Lords of Trade and Plantations, 1675–96*[2] (1919), and the same author's article in *English Historical Review*, xl, 1925; O. M. Dickerson, *American Colonial Government, 1696–1765* (1912), which is in fact almost a history of the board of trade. There is need for research into the other branches of administrative history. One of the special subjects which need investigation is taxation: S. Dowell, *History of Taxation and Taxes*, 4 vols., 1884–5, does not suffice. W. Kennedy, *English Taxation, 1640–1799* (1913) is a brief study of the social effects of taxes and their relation to public opinion. The excise, especially on salt, is dealt with in E. Hughes, *Studies in Administration and Finance*, 1934, and the customs in Elizabeth E. Hoon, *The Organization of the English Customs System, 1696–1786*, 1938.

For the post office J. C. Hemmeon, *History of the British Post Office*, 1912, is useful, and there is some further information in the sketchy work J. W. Hyde, *The Early History of the Post in Grant and Farm*, 1894, which goes down to 1685.

LOCAL GOVERNMENT. The standard work is S. and Beatrice Webb, *English Local Government from the Revolution to the Municipal Corporations Act*, vols. i–vii, 1906–27, which deals with many matters before 1688, where it nominally begins. The same authors' *History of Liquor Licensing in England*, 1903, is a pendant, as is E. Cannan, *History of Local Rating in England*, 1896. The

---

[1] For the dates of publication of separate volumes of these series see *List of Record Publications* issued by the Stationery Office.

[2] For this period see also W. T. Root in *American Historical Review*, xxiii, 1917.

most useful guides to the innumerable publications on separate
localities are C. Gross, *Bibliography of British Municipal History*,
1897; J. P. Anderson, *Book of British Topography*, 1881; A. L.
Humphreys, *Handbook to County Bibliography*, 1917; *Index of
Archaeological Papers*, ed. G. L. Gomme, 1907, and supplements.

ECCLESIASTICAL

No historian has yet written about English religion in this
period from a point of view independent of the differences of
creed, except historians of thought who are unsympathetic to all
religious dogma, for whom see below, p. 452. The nearest approach to a general history is the diffuse and antiquated *History
of Religion in England*, vols. iii–vi, 1870–8, by J. Stoughton, a congregationalist minister. For the Roman catholics there is no
adequate general history; the contemporary materials are mainly
devotional and controversial, and those subsequently published
predominantly biographical or concerned with particular orders
and institutions. The series of the Catholic Record Society
(1906–) is the chief collection, and for ordinary purposes of
reference *The Catholic Encyclopaedia*, 15 vols., 1907–14, should be
used. H. Foley, *Records of the English Province of the Society of Jesus*,
7 vols., 1877–82, is important. The principal documents for the
church of England are given in three works of E. Cardwell,
Documentary Annals of the Reformed Church of England, 2 vols., 1839;
*Synodalia, a Collection of Articles of Religion, Canons and Proceedings
of Convocations of Canterbury*, 2 vols., 1842; *History of Conferences and
other Proceedings connected with the Revision of the Book of Common
Prayer*, 1840. For the vast literature of sermons, theological
treatises, tracts, and biographies reference may be made to Mr.
Davies's *Bibliography* (see above, p. 424) with the remark that perhaps the best book for conveying an impression of the Anglo-
catholic point of view is E. H. Plumptre, *Life of Thomas Ken*, 2nd
ed., 2 vols., 1890. The most useful survey of the history of the
church of England in all its aspects is C. J. Abbey and J. H.
Overton, *The English Church in the Eighteenth Century*, 2 vols.,
1878. N. Sykes, *Church and State in the Eighteenth Century*, 1934, and
later writings by the same writer are valuable. F. Makower,
The Constitutional History of the Church of England, 1895, is the
best legal textbook. G. V. Portus, *Caritas Anglicana, or an Historical Inquiry into those Religious and Philanthropical Societies that*

flourished between 1678 and 1740 (1912) extends beyond the bounds of the church of England.

The literature of nonconformity is, from the nature of the case, less extensive than that of Anglicanism; but it is very voluminous and the work done upon it by historians varies much from one sect to another. For the clergy ejected in 1662 the eighteenth-century work of Edmund Calamy has been amplified under the title *Calamy Revised* by A. G. Matthews, 1933. C. E. Whiting, *Studies in English Puritanism, 1660–88* (1931), is a learned but unsympathetic work by an Anglican clergyman, and its interpretative value is small. For the baptists there is an excellent *Baptist Bibliography*, 2 vols., 1916–22, by W. T. Whitley, and the same author wrote a short *History of British Baptists*, 1923. The congregationalists have not been so well served: R. W. Dale, *History of English Congregationalism*, ed. Sir Alfred Dale, 1907, is not a work of profound research. The presbyterians, from the lack of direct successors, have attracted few modern students: A. H. Drysdale, *History of the Presbyterians in England*, 1889, is the most recent survey. For the quakers there is adequate bibliographical aid in Joseph Smith, *Descriptive Catalogue of Friends' Books*, 2 vols., 1867, and supplement, 1893; and *Bibliotheca Anti-Quakeriana*, 1873. The quakers have the best records of any nonconformist body, and they also have the best modern account of their history in W. C. Braithwaite, *The Beginnings of Quakerism*, 1912, and *The Second Period of Quakerism*, 1919: the dividing line between the two volumes is at about 1661. The three greatest writers among the dissenters of the period each wrote many books, but one work of each may be named. Richard Baxter's autobiography is called *Reliquiae Baxterianae*, ed. M. Sylvester, 1696: it may be supplemented from F. J. Powicke, *Life of Richard Baxter*, 2 vols., 1924–7. George Fox's *Journal* was current in a much edited version until 1911 when the original text was published in 2 vols., ed. N. Penney. John Bunyan's *Pilgrim's Progress* has circulated in innumerable editions: the best text is that ed. by J. B. Wharey, 1928.

C. Roth, *History of the Jews in England*, 1939, is a good textbook with references to authorities. *The Transactions of the Jewish Historical Society* (1894–) contain some valuable studies.

MILITARY

There is no general military bibliography for this period: recourse must be taken to library catalogues, particularly that of the British Museum, *s.v.* England, Army. Sir John Fortescue, *History of the British Army*, vol. i, 1899, goes down to 1713 and is on a smaller scale than the other volumes of the series. It is best for operations, but gives a brief account of administration, and is very readable, not less so because in places it is too positive. C. Walton, *History of the British Standing Army, 1660–1700* (1894) is a standard work, but less satisfactory in its accounts of operations than in other parts. A book on military organization in the period of Queen Anne is badly needed. C. Dalton, *English Army Lists and Commission Registers, 1661–1714*, 6 vols., 1892–4, is an indispensable guide for personal details. The professional military literature of the period in England, outside the drill-books, has little value: many of the books are treatises by would-be reformers or arid accounts of campaigns by subordinate officers or chaplains, who did not fully understand the movements. Modern historians have to work mainly from record-sources and from the correspondence of politicians and generals (see above, pp. 428–9). The most important bodies of printed military correspondence for the period, besides those of William III, are in W. Coxe, *Memoirs of the Duke of Marlborough*, 3 vols. and Atlas, 1818–19, and *Letters and Despatches of John Churchill, Duke of Marlborough*, ed. Sir G. Murray, 5 vols., 1845. The earlier biographies of Marlborough have been in the main superseded by Sir Winston Churchill's book (see above, p. 428), but for political affairs Coxe is still useful, and there are good accounts of the campaigns in F. Taylor, *The Wars of Marlborough*, 2 vols., 1921, which has very good maps, and C. T. Atkinson, *Marlborough and the Rise of the British Army*, 1921. For the main theatre of the war of the Spanish Succession the standard work is J. Pelet, *Mémoires militaires relatifs à la succession d'Espagne*, 11 vols. and Atlas, 1835–62; with which should be used *Feldzüge des Prinzen Eugen von Savoyen*, 20 vols., index vol. and Atlas, 1876–92. A. Parnell, *The War of the Succession in Spain*, 1888, is good, though in some respects controvertible, especially in relation to Peterborough. There are no such thorough modern books on the war of William III. For the campaigns of 1690–4 there is an imposing old book, J. de Beaurain, *Histoire militaire de Flandre*, 2 vols.,

1755, with good maps; but it does not state the numbers of the armies employed. Attention should be paid to the short critical summaries of William's campaigns in C. von Clausewitz, *Hinterlassene Werke*, 2nd ed., ix, 1862. The *Journal of the Society for Army Historical Research* (1923–) has some good articles on the period.

NAVAL

G. E. Manwaring, *Bibliography of British Naval History*, 1930, is useful though not first-rate. There is no satisfactory general history of the royal navy: Sir William Laird Clowes, *The Royal Navy*, vol. vi, 1897, lacks references to authorities and continuity of treatment. It is easier to follow the course of the wars in the standard foreign works, J. C. de Jonge, *Geschiedenis van het nederlandsche zeewezen*, 2nd ed., 5 vols., 1858–62, and C. de la Roncière, *Histoire de la marine française*, vols. iv–vi, 1920–32. For the place of naval events in general history the best book is A. T. Mahan, *The Influence of Sea Power on History, 1660–1783* (1896): this book had a remarkable effect on opinion, but its value is in the greater matters: for details of operations it should be used with caution. For the construction of ships J. Charnock, *History of Marine Architecture*, 3 vols., 1800–2, is still the best general book.

Much more has been done in naval than in military history to publish record materials, and the correspondence available is also valuable. For Charles II's Dutch wars the *Bescheiden uit vreemde archieven omtrent de groote nederlandsche zeeoorlogen, 1652–76*, ed. H. T. Colenbrander, 2 vols., 1919, are important and their contents are mainly in the English and French languages. There is additional material in *Journals and Narratives of the Third Dutch War*, ed. R. C. Anderson (Navy Records Society, 1947). Samuel Pepys was the greatest naval administrator of the period, and his papers form the basis of a number of publications. The Navy Record Society, whose admirable series includes several other works on the period, some of which are mentioned below, has published a *Descriptive Catalogue of the Pepysian Manuscripts at Magdalene College, Cambridge*, 4 vols., 1903–23, with an important general introduction by J. R. Tanner. Dr. Tanner's lectures on *Samuel Pepys and the Royal Navy*, 1920, and his editions of Pepys's *Naval Minutes*, 1926, and of the *Private Correspondence*, 2 vols.,

1926, and *Further Correspondence*, 1929, are also useful, and he made other studies of Pepys in periodicals and elsewhere. Pepy's famous *Diary*, ed. H. B. Wheatley, 10 vols., 1893-9 (see above, p. 380), is of less interest in this connexion, because it was written before he rose so high; but it should not be neglected. For the naval expedition of William III there are many authorities, the chief on the English side being the Historical Manuscripts Commission's *Dartmouth Papers*, vol. i, 1887 (vol. iii, 1896, is good for the Dutch war of 1672-4). A modern study based on a wide use of authorities is E. B. Powley, *The English Navy in the Revolution of 1688*, 1928. Much printed information has accumulated on the naval wars against France, for instance in the *Calendar of State Papers Domestic* (see above, p. 437), Sir George Rooke's *Journal* for 1700-2, ed. O. Browning (for which, however, see the review by J. F. Chance in *English Historical Review*, xiii, 1898), and S. Martin Leake, *Life of Sir John Leake*, ed. G. A. R. Callender, 2 vols., 1920. J. Ehrman, *The Navy in the War of William III*, 1953, deals with all sides of its subject. An important Dutch work is J. C. M. Warnsinck, *De vloot van den koning-stadhouder, 1689-90*, 1934. J. H. Owen, *War at Sea under Queen Anne, 1702-8*, 1938, is another work of research. A very good modern work on a special field is Sir Julian Corbett, *England in the Mediterranean*, 2 vols., 1904. For the more technical aspects of naval history and for selected subjects such as maritime law and privateering reference should be made to bibliographies. *The Mariner's Mirror* is a periodical which, although much concerned with nautical archaeology, publishes valuable articles on all aspects of naval history, including some on this period.

ECONOMIC

The most learned general account is to be found in E. Lipson, *The Economic History of England*, vols. ii–iii, 1931; but for the systematic arrangement of the material W. Cunningham, *The Growth of English Industry and Commerce*, pt. ii, *Modern Times* 6th ed., 1917–19, is still valuable. Both these books are based mainly on printed authorities. Cunningham's generalizations have been much undermined by subsequent writers: his work, like that of most recent writers, marks a transition in the methods of economic history. It began from the activities of the state and the opinions of theorists, both of which left masses of accessible materials behind them, and it tends to make greater use of the more direct but more scattered and less intelligible records of actual economic life. There is no full general survey of the authorities, but sectional bibliographies are published from time to time in the *Economic History Review* (1927–   ), the leading periodical. For many purposes of reference the *Encyclopaedia of the Social Sciences*, 15 vols., 1930–5 is useful.

For the action of the state and information arising from it, besides the authorities mentioned above, pp. 437ff., the following may be named. Sir C. Whitworth, *The State of the Trade of Great Britain*, 1776, is a series of official abstracts of annual returns of imports and exports from 1696. For an estimate of its value see G. N. Clark, *Guide to English Commercial Statistics, 1696–1782*, 1938. Sir Frederick Eden, *The State of the Poor, or a History of the Labouring Classes in England*, 3 vols., 1797, is by no means confined to the history of the poor law. A. E. Feavearyear, *The Pound Sterling*, 1931, is the best summary of monetary history; Sir Charles Oman, *The Coinage of England*, 1931, the most modern numismatic history; E. L. Hargreaves, *The National Debt*, 1930, a terse history by an economist. L. A. Harper, *The English Navigation Laws*, 1939, and D. G. Barnes, *History of the English Corn-Laws*, 1930, are useful monographs. R. G. Albion, *Forests and Sea-Power*, 1926, provides one of the links between economic and naval history. There is no adequate account of the history of economic thought. P. Mombert, *Geschichte der Nationalökonomie*, 1927, is perhaps the best, but it is necessary to use the works of the writers of the period and such monographs on them as Lord Fitzmaurice, *Life of Sir William Petty*, 1893, and E. F. Heckscher, *Mercantilism*, tr. M. Shapiro, 2 vols., 1935. R. Gonnard, *Histoire des doctrines économiques*, 2 vols., 1921–7, is clear and interesting, but not altogether reliable.

The best general work for agriculture is R. E. Prothero (Lord Ernle), *English Farming Past and Present*, 1912. Another useful book is A. H. Johnson, *The Disappearance of the Small Landowner*, 1909. E. C. K. Gonner, *Common Land and Inclosure*, 1912, is to be used with caution. The contemporary literature of agriculture is more hortatory than descriptive, and a knowledge of the actual methods and production can be gained only from a number of scattered recent articles. A general idea of the face of England at the end of the period may be gained from the first edition of Defoe's anonymous *Tour through the Whole Island of*

Britain, which, though published in 1724-7, was probably based on his recollections of journeys in the time of Queen Anne and earlier. A valuable modern work on the farmers' markets is N. S. B. Gras, *The English Cornmarket,* 1915. J. E. Thorold Rogers *History of Agriculture and Prices in England,* 7 vols., 1866-1902, is a great repertory of information on prices of all sorts; but unhappily it is inaccurate. Its value is examined in F. Simiand, *Recherches anciennes et nouvelles sur le mouvement général des prix,* 1932, and in two articles on earlier portions of it, E. F. Gay on 'The Inquisitions of Depopulation and the Domesday of Enclosures' in *Royal Historical Society, Transactions,* new ser., xiv, and H. L. Lutz, 'Inaccuracies in Rogers's History of Prices' in *Quarterly Journal of Economics,* xxiii, 1909. The purposes of economic specialists have determined the plan of Sir William [Lord] Beveridge, *Prices and Wages in England,* vol. i, *Price Tables: Mercantile Era* (1939). Sir W. Ashley, *The Bread of our Forefathers,* 1928, is almost the first step towards the much-needed history of English diet. Gladys Scott Thomson, *Life in a Noble Household* (1937) and *The Russells in Bloomsbury* (1940) give admirable pictures of one of the greatest English families in country and town.

For industry and commerce the most important single work is W. R. Scott, *English, Scottish, and Irish Joint-Stock Companies to 1720,* 3 vols., 1911-12. An original, though not definitive, study is G. Unwin, *Industrial Organization in the Sixteenth and Seventeenth Centuries,* 1904. Much of the best work on industry and commerce is in books on particular companies or localities, which cannot be enumerated here. There is a growing number of good books on special branches of activity, among which are J. U. Nef, *The Rise of the British Coal Industry,* 2 vols., 1932; G. R. Lewis, *The Stannaries,* 1908; H. Heaton, *The Yorkshire Woollen and Worsted Industries,* 1920; G. D. Ramsay, *The Wiltshire Woollen Industry in the Sixteenth and Seventeenth Centuries* (1943); A. P. Wadsworth and Julia de L. Mann, *Industrial Lancashire and the Cotton Industry,* 1931; H. Hamilton, *The English Copper and Brass Industries to 1800* (1926); R. B. Westerfield, *Middlemen in English Business,* 1915. Alice Clark, *The Working Life of Women in the Seventeenth Century,* 1919, is a useful study.

On banking and finance, besides monetary histories, and other books relating to state action, there are some useful books, but investigation is still needed. J. E. Thorold Rogers, *The First*

446 BIBLIOGRAPHY

Nine Years of the Bank of England, 1887, is in the main superseded by Sir John Clapham's excellent book *The Bank of England, a History*, vol. i, *1694–1797* (1944). R. D. Richards, *The Early History of English Banking*, 1929, makes use of important banking records.

RELATIONS WITH SCOTLAND

At the points where Scottish touch English affairs, they are recorded in many of the books mentioned in the earlier sections of this bibliography. Burnet was himself a Scotsman, and had more to do with Scotland than England till he was thirty. He was connected with some of the leading people in Scotland, and he is as good an authority on Scottish history as on English. Macaulay, though of Highland descent, was apt to write disparagingly about the country, but he dealt with its affairs fully and gave a description of its state at the end of the seventeenth century. The best textbook on Scottish history is P. Hume Brown, *History of Scotland*, 3 vols., 1911. There are several good guides to the records and materials: M. Livingstone, *Guide to the Public Records at the General Register House*, 1905; *Index to the Papers relating to Scotland in the Historical Manuscripts Commission's Reports*, ed. C. S. Terry, 1908, with supplement to 1927 by C. Matheson, 1928; *Catalogue of the Publications of Scottish Historical Clubs and Societies and of the Volumes relative to Scotland published by the Stationery Office*, ed. C. S. Terry, 1909. *The Scottish Historical Review*, a valuable periodical, lived from 1904 to 1928 and was revived in 1947. There is an Index to vols. i–xii and one for vols. xiii–xxv. It is not possible here to do more than mention some of the leading authorities bearing directly on the matters treated in the present volume. *The Acts of the Parliament of Scotland*, 12 vols., 1814–75, contains the proceedings as well as the Acts. *The Register of the Privy Council of Scotland*, 2nd ser., vol. ix and 3rd ser., 9 vols., to 1684 (1908–25), is the most important source for the administrative history of the period. *The Lauderdale Papers*, ed. O. Airy, 3 vols., 1884–5, may be supplemented by the same editor's set of papers addressed to Lauderdale in 1660–9 in *Camden Miscellany*, viii, 1883. For the period after Lauderdale there are the *Letters to George, Earl of Aberdeen*, 1851, and *Letters of James Graham of Claverhouse*, 1843. For the Revolution the chief authorities are the *Leven and Melville Papers, 1689–91*, 1843 and Lord Balcarres, *Memoirs touching the Revolution in Scotland*, 1841.

The volume of *State Papers and Letters addressed to William Carstares*, ed. J. McCormick, 1774, relate to one of the chief Scottish advisers of William III. A convenient summary of ecclesiastical affairs is given by Sir Thomas Raleigh, *Annals of the Church in Scotland*, 1921. The contemporary ecclesiastical literature is, of course, controversial. The most important ecclesiastical documents are quoted in R. Wodrow, *History of the Sufferings of the Church of Scotland from the Restoration*, 4 vols., 1836. There is some important matter in the *Acts of the General Assembly of the Kirk of Scotland, 1638–1842*, 1843.

The Darien incident has been carefully studied. It is treated in different parts of its context in Professor W. R. Scott's *Joint-Stock Companies* (see above, p. 445), in Theodora Keith, *Commercial Relations of England and Scotland, 1603–7*, 1910, and most fully in two books by G. P. Insh, *Scottish Colonial Schemes, 1620–86*, 1922, and *The Company of Scotland trading to Africa and the Indies*, 1932. Documents bearing on it are in Sir Paul Rycaut, *The Original Papers and Letters relating to the Scots Company*, 1700; *The Darien Papers*, ed. J. H. Burton, 1849; *The Darien Shipping Papers*, ed. G. P. Insh, 1924. For the minor printed authorities see the *Bibliography of Printed Documents and Books relating to the Scottish Company*, ed. J. Scott, 1904.

Three modern books on the union are important: W. L. Mathieson, *Scotland and the Union, 1695–1747*, 2 vols., 1905, a continuation of his *Politics and Religion in Scotland, 1550–1695*, 2 vols., 1902; P. Hume Brown, *The Legislative Union of England and Scotland*, 1914, which has an appendix of documents; A. V. Dicey and R. S. Rait, *Thoughts on the Union between England and Scotland*, 1920. An aid to the detailed study of the proceedings which led to the union may be found in C. S. Terry, *The Scottish Parliament, its Constitution and Procedure, 1603–1707* (1905). The Scottish parliament is also treated in vol. ii of Porritt's book (see above, p. 437).

RELATIONS WITH IRELAND

There is a short bibliographical guide in R. H. Murray, *Ireland, 1603–1714* (1920) and from 1938 there has been a very good periodical in *Irish Historical Studies*. H. Wood, *Guide to the Records deposited in the Public Record Office, Dublin*, 1919, is not rendered useless by the fact that most of the records in question were destroyed in the civil war in 1922. *The Statutes at Large*

passed in the Parliaments in Ireland, 20 vols., 1786–1801, do not include the acts of the parliament of 1689, for which see the
polemical work of T. Davis, *The Patriot Parliament of 1689*, ed. Sir
Charles Gavan Duffy, 1893. *The Journals of the House of Lords*,
8 vols., 1779–1800, and *The Journals of the House of Commons
of the Kingdom of Ireland*, 20 vols., 1796–1800, give the proceedings. The most important collections of documents and
correspondence are to be found in T. Carte, *History of the Life of
James, Duke of Ormond*, 6 vols., 1851, originally published in
1735–6; the Historical Manuscripts Commission's *Ormonde
Papers*, 10 vols., 1895–1920; the *Orrery State Letters*, ed. T.
Morice, 2 vols., 1743; *Essex Papers*, ed. O. Airy and C. E. Pike,
2 vols., 1890–1913; *Correspondence of Henry Hyde, Earl of Clarendon*,
ed. S. W. Singer, 2 vols., 1828; C. de Mesmes, comte d'Avaux,
Négociations en Irlande, 1689–90 (1844, reprinted 1934). Much of
the history of the Revolution and the war is derived from pamphlets and narrative sources which cannot be mentioned here.
There is a *Calendar of State Papers Ireland, Charles II*, in 4 vols.,
extending to 1670, after which these papers are calendared in
the Domestic series. The Irish Historical Manuscripts Commission has published in its *Analecta Hibernica* (1930–   ) some documents of this period and guides to manuscript materials: two of
its important publications are *A Census of Ireland, c.* 1659, ed.
S. Pender (1939) and the *Calendar of the Orrery Papers*, ed. E.
Mac Lysaght (1941).

A new standard of impartiality was set up by W. E. H. Lecky,
History of Ireland in the Eighteenth Century, of which the first volume,
first published in 1877, sketches this period. Lecky was not a very
persistent searcher for new facts, but he had sound judgement,
and he was as much interested in social conditions as in political
history. Neither his detachment nor his breadth of view is to be
found in the works of later writers. R. Bagwell, *Ireland under the
Stuarts*, 3 vols., 1909–16, is accurate and well arranged, and may
be called a standard work for the period down to 1690; but it is
predominantly political, and the reader will have no difficulty
in inferring that the author was a protestant landowner. R. H.
Murray, *Revolutionary Ireland and its Settlement*, 1911, is a history
of the times of James II and William III, valuable for its attention to European relations, but inexact in details. Historians
have unfortunately accepted too freely the contentions of some
modern writers who have dealt with economic matters. Alice E.

Murray, *Commercial and Financial Relations between England and Ireland from the Period of the Restoration*, 1903, is largely based on pamphlets and, although it makes use of record sources, lacks critical method. Its views are accepted in G. A. T. O'Brien, *The Economic History of Ireland in the Seventeenth Century*, 1919, and *The Economic History of Ireland in the Eighteenth Century*, 1918. M. J. Bonn, *Die englische Kolonisation in Irland*, 2 vols., 1906, is a very good book.

OVERSEAS POSSESSIONS

The literature of this subject, especially for America, is so large that no more can be attempted than to give a few titles of text-books, and standard works, omitting altogether the original authorities. Modern work on colonial history started comparatively late. This circumstance, together with the sharply defined limits of its sources and the high respect for methodical organization in the United States, has resulted in an unusually high standard of technical skill. In literary finish and attractiveness many of these books are, however, unequal to their wonderful subject-matter. For the central government in relation to the colonies see also above, p. 437.

A good textbook of the whole subject is J. A. Williamson, *Short History of British Expansion*, 1922; a larger work with bibliographies, *The Cambridge History of the British Empire*, vol. i, 1929. H. E. Egerton, *Short History of British Colonial Policy*, 5th ed., 1918, is the textbook for the intentions of the home government. Sir John Seeley, *The Expansion of England*, 1883, made a great impression when it appeared, but it is now out of date, and it was always the expression of an individual point of view: see the introductory essay by K. A. von Müller in the German translation, 1928. The best general series of textbooks on the separate colonies, though it does not include those now in the United States, is that called *The Historical Geography of the British Dominions*, ed. by Sir Charles Lucas, of which the volumes touching this period are H. E. Egerton, *The Origin and Growth of Greater Britain*, new ed., 1920; Sir C. Lucas, *The Mediterranean and Eastern Colonies*, 2nd ed., 1906; and *The West Indies*, 2nd ed., 1905; A. B. Keith, *West Africa*, 3rd ed., 1913; Sir C. Lucas, *Canada and Newfoundland*, 1921; P. E. Roberts, *India*, pt. i, 1916. For the colonies which afterwards became the United States one of the most comprehensive works is C. M. Andrews, *The Colonial Period of American History*, 4 vols., 1934–8. Rather above the rank of a textbook, though brief, is A. P. Newton, *The European Nations in the West Indies to 1688*, 1933. Unfortunately it has no footnotes, but it gives a very clear account of the international rivalries. A. B. Keith, *The First British Empire*, 1930, is the best short survey of the constitutional system. G. L. Beer, *The Old Colonial System*, 2 vols., 1912, superseded all previous works on economic relations. H. L. Osgood, *The American Colonies in the Seventeenth Century*, 3 vols., 1904–7, with its continuation *The American Colonies in the Eighteenth Century*, 4 vols., 1924, is a solid history of institutions. M. C. Tyler, *History of American Literature*, 2 vols., 1879–97, is the best survey of the authors of the colonial period. P. Miller, *The New England Mind, The Seventeenth Century*, 1939, and E. A. J. Johnson, *American Economic Thought in the Seventeenth Century*, 1932, are sound studies. The *American Historical Review* is the leading periodical. It is not confined to American history.

There is no adequate general history of the British West Indies as a whole during this period, no doubt because, strictly speaking, they were not a whole. Work on separate islands or groups has been active, and the following may be mentioned: J. A. Williamson, *English Colonies in Guiana and on the Amazon*, 1923, and *The Caribbee Islands under the Proprietary Patents*, 1926; V. T. Harlow, *History of Barbados, 1625–85* (1926), and *Christopher Codrington*, 1928; H. Wilkinson, *The Adventurers of Bermuda*, 1933; C. S. S. Higham, *The Development of the Leeward Islands under the Restoration*, 1921; C. H. Haring, *The Buccaneers in the West Indies in the Seventeenth Century*, 1910, and L. M. Penson, *The Colonial Agents of the British West Indies*, 1924; A. P. Thornton, *West-India Policy under the Restoration* (1956).

Louise F. Browne, *The First Earl of Shaftesbury* (1933) is useful for colonial policy under Charles II. Enid M. G. Routh, *Tangier* (1912) gives the best account of that episode.

The Publications of the Hudson's Bay Record Society have superseded all earlier histories of that region.

For the East India Company, Sir William Hunter, *History of British India*, 2 vols., 1899–1900, is a standard work. There has recently been much investigation on the economic side, but not always with happy results. W. H. Moreland, *From Akbar to Aurungzeb, a Study in Indian Economic History*, 1923, is an excellent book. H. B. Morse, *Chronicles of the East India Company trading to China*, vol. i, 1926, is full and accurate; but B. Krishna, *Commercial Relations between India and England, 1601–1757* (1924); S. A. Khan, *The East India Trade in the Seventeenth Century*, 1923, and P. J. Thomas, *Mercantilism and the East India Trade*, 1926, though containing both new information and some suggestive arguments, should be used with caution. Work on the period has been facilitated by the publication of two series of calendars of the records of the old India Office. That of the *Court Minutes of the East India Company* now reaches 1679, 6 vols. covering the period from 1660 (1922–38), and 6 vols. of *The English Factories in India*, 1921–52, cover 1655–77. The *Journal of Indian History* (1921–   ) though the articles in it are of unequal quality, has published some of high excellence, including guides to certain classes of materials. Of the modern school of Indian historians, the chief was Prof. Sir J. Sarkar, whose *History of Aurungzib*, 5 vols., 1912–24, and *Shivaji and his Times*, 1919, deal with leaders who came into contact with the English. It is to be hoped that the development of historical studies in India will deepen the understanding of the mutual influence of the two civilizations in this period.

For voyages and travels the principal series of publications is that of the Hakluyt Society (1847–   ), but its work is mainly to supplement the old collections, such as the *Collection of Voyages and Travels*, ed. A. and J. Churchill, 8 vols., 1744–7. Our period, however, is one in which exploration was of less importance to England than in the earlier seventeenth century or the later eighteenth.

LITERATURE, THOUGHT, AND SCIENCE

The authoritative *Review of English Studies* began publication in 1925. Although more like a collection of essays than a textbook, *The Cambridge History of English Literature* is the best general guide: vols. vii–ix, 1912, cover the period. *The Cambridge Bibliography of English Literature*, ii, *1660–1800* (1940) is convenient for reference. The period will in due course be covered by a volume of the *Oxford History of English Literature*. A useful annual review of *The Year's Work in English Studies* has been published by the English Association since 1919, a more elaborate annual *Bibliography of English Language and Literature* by the Modern Humanities Research Association since 1921. Bibliographies of special subjects, often very minute, are numerous. It would be out of place here to give lists of the works of the imaginative writers or of books mainly important for literary appreciation and criticism: it will suffice to name a few outstanding books which relate the imaginative literature to general history. Samuel Johnson's *Lives of the English Poets*, ed. G. Birkbeck Hill, 3 vols., 1905, is still the best of all such books. The lives were originally published in 1779–81 in a collective edition of the poets themselves. A. Nicoll, *History of Restoration Drama*, 1923, and *History of Early Eighteenth Century Drama*, 1925, are standard works. W. J. Courthope, *History of English Poetry*, 6 vols., 1895–1910, is the best single book on a subject on which no single book can be enough. Two very useful reprints of short pieces otherwise often inaccessible are *Seventeenth Century Critical Essays*, ed. J. E. Spingarn, 3 vols., 1908–9, and *Dryden's Essays*, ed. W. P. Ker, 2 vols., 1900.

On the newspaper press A. Andrews, *History of British Journalism*, 2 vols., 1859, is not altogether superseded by the more commonly used H. R. Fox-Bourne, *English Newspapers*, 2 vols., 1887. Mr. J. G. Muddiman (identical with Mr. J. B. Williams), besides some useful articles, published a *History of English Journalism to the Foundation of the Gazette*, 1908, and *The King's Journalist, 1659–89* (1923), which deals with Henry Muddiman. The best guide to the materials is R. S. Crane and F. B. Kaye, *Census of British Newspapers and Periodicals, 1620–1800* (1927). S. Morison, *The English Newspaper*, 1932, deals with printing and *format*.

For the history of thought in general there are no satisfactory surveys: none could be expected except from an accident of genius. Leslie Stephen, *History of English Thought in the Eighteenth Century*, 2 vols., 1876, begins with writers of the Restoration period, and has been much used by later historians. It is well written, but Stephen's mind was neither very acute nor capable of wide sympathies: he praises his authors in proportion as they approximate to a rather ingenuous Victorian agnosticism. A good textbook on the history of philosophy is W. R. Sorley, *History of English Philosophy*, 1920, based on the author's chapters in the *Cambridge History of English Literature*. For the place of English thought in the general European development E. Cassirer, *Das Erkenntnisproblem in der Philosophie und Wissenschaft der neueren Zeit*, vols. i–ii, 3rd ed., 1922, may be recommended. H. Sidgwick, *Outlines of the History of Ethics*, 1886, is now much out of date, but is still useful. The later part of J. Tulloch, *Rational Theology and Christian Philosophy in England in the Seventeenth Century*, 1872, was for a long time the best book on the Cambridge Platonists, but it is now superseded on the historical side by F. J. Powicke, *The Cambridge Platonists*, 1926, and on the philosophical by E. Cassirer, *Die platonische Renaissance in England und die Schule von Cambridge*, 1932. There are several good monographs on Locke such as J. Gibson, *Locke's Theory of Knowledge*, 1917, and J. W. Gough, *John Locke's Political Philosophy*, 1950. For Berkeley the *Life*, 1871, by A. C. Fraser, has been superseded by that of A. A. Luce, 1949. There is no adequate life of Locke. Those by Peter, Lord King, 1829, and H. R. Fox-Bourne, 2 vols., 1876, must be used, and H. O. Christophersen, *Bibliographical Introduction to the Study of Locke*, 1930. It is curious that the affiliations of political thought generally in the period have not been thoroughly studied. There are two good short textbooks in G. P. Gooch, *Political Thought from Bacon to Halifax*, 1914, and H. J. Laski, *Political Thought from Locke to Bentham*, 1920, and some useful *aperçus* in G. P. Gooch, *The History of English Democratic Ideas in the Seventeenth Century*, ed. H. J. Laski, 1927, J. N. Figgis, *The Theory of the Divine Right of Kings*, 2nd ed., 1914, H. F. Russell Smith, *The Theory of Religious Liberty in the Reigns of Charles II and James II*, 1911; but much more work, both detailed and comparative, is needed.

Two readable contributions to the history of the study of the past are D. C. Douglas, *English Scholars*, 1939, on work in England on English medieval history from about 1660 to about 1730, and Sir Thomas D. Kendrick, *British Antiquity*, 1950, on the study of prehistoric times.

The connexion between philosophy and the scientific movement is discussed in E. A. Burtt, *The Metaphysical Foundations of Modern Science*, 1925. Work on the scientific movement itself has been active in recent years, and besides studies of individual experimentalists, there have been editions of treatises and correspondence. L. T. More, *Isaac Newton, a Biography*, 1934, supersedes the previous lives; a full-scale edition of Newton's correspondence is being prepared for the Royal Society. *The Diary of Robert Hooke, 1672–80*, ed. H. W. Robinson and W. Adams, 1935, in spite of some imperfections, is important. C. E. Raven, *John Ray, Naturalist*, 1942, is excellent. M. Cantor, *Vorlesungen über Geschichte der Mathematik*, 4 vols., 1880–1908, is a standard work, and the following are useful: R. Grant, *History of Physical Astronomy*, 1852, W. W. Rouse Ball, *History of the Study of Mathematics at Cambridge*, 1889, W. W. Bryant, *History of Astronomy*, 1907, E. Mach, *The Science of Mechanics*, tr. from the German by T. J. McCormack, 1893. For other sciences there are J. von Sachs, *History of Botany, 1530–1860*, tr. by H. E. F. Garnsey, 1890; C. Singer, *Short History of Biology*, 1931, a popular work. The last-named author has also written a very readable *Short History of Medicine*, 1928. A valuable book of reference is *The Roll of the Royal College of Physicians*, 1861. Of the various histories of the Royal Society the fullest for this period is T. Birch, *History of the Royal Society of London*, 4 vols., 1756–7, which goes down to 1687 and should be supplemented by the Society's periodical *Notes and Records*.

There has been no universal history of technology since J. H. M. Poppe, *Geschichte der Technologie*, 3 vols., 1807–11, which is still useful, until the publication of the five-volume *History of Technology* edited by Charles Singer and others, 1954–8, of which vol. iii covers the period.

THE ARTS AND MUSIC

The chief original authorities on architecture and the arts are the buildings and other works of art themselves, while for purposes of comparison photographs or other reproductions of them are necessary. It is beyond our present scope to indicate where these are to be found. For the historian the main difficulty in using them is that the attribution to particular artists has in the past been done with a view either to commercial profit or to possessive vanity, or on grounds of supposed stylistic resemblances. There are still many writers on the history of the arts whose use of evidence is not strict enough. Except where, as in silversmiths' work, the hall-marks give proofs of date and authorship, the chronology and general correlation of the specimens is often obscure, and one artist hard to distinguish clearly from others. For architecture a new standard of completeness and accuracy has, however, been set by the publications of the Wren Society (1924–   ), the twenty volumes of which have done more than fulfil the society's initial programme of giving a complete view of Wren's work. H. M. Colvin, *Biographical Dictionary of English Architects*, 1954, though brief, gives the results of much accurate research. Sir Reginald Blomfield,

History of Renaissance Architecture in England, 2 vols., 1897, is a long essay rather than a full history, and many of its judgements are highly personal. J. A. Gotch, *The Growth of the English House*, 1909, and N. Lloyd, *The History of the English House*, 1931, are useful. Katharine A. Esdaile, *English Monumental Sculpture since the Renaissance*, 1927, and other works by the same writer have contributed much new knowledge. K. Clark, *The Gothic Revival*, 1928, is a most interesting and suggestive essay, but requires correction in detail. Two works dealing with London may be mentioned: G. H. Birch, *London Churches of the Seventeenth and Eighteenth Centuries*, 1896; W. G. Bell, *The Great Fire of London*, 1920, which is valuable for architecture besides superseding all former accounts of the fire. The county surveys published by the Royal Commission on Historical Monuments (1913–   ) are gradually providing a full *corpus* of materials.

For painting the contemporary literary authorities (see above, p. 401) are of little value. Horace Walpole, *Anecdotes of Painting in England*, 4 vols., 1762–71, was for long a standard authority, but it has been mostly superseded by work on documentary sources, the best of which is to be found in the publications of the Walpole Society (1911–   ). C. H. C. Baker, *Lely and the Stuart Portrait Painters*, 2 vols., 1912, is the best conspectus of its subject, though parts of it are conjectural. Much good work is to be found in catalogues of permanent or loan collections, of which the most useful to the historian is Rachael (Mrs. R. L.) Poole, *Catalogue of Portraits in Oxford*, 3 vols., 1912–25. B. S. Long, *British Miniaturists*, 1929, and A. M. Hind, *History of Engraving and Etching*, 1923, are the most convenient guides, both works of much learning. For the history of furniture, P. Macquoid and R. Edwards, *Dictionary of English Furniture*, 3 vols., 1924–7, is perhaps the most useful work; the various catalogues of the South Kensington Museum are valuable, and there are many illustrated books such as H. A. Tipping, *English Homes, 1066–1820* (1920–   ), F. Lenygon, *Decoration and Furniture in England, 1500–1820* (1914) and *Decoration in England, 1660–1770* (1914), R. W. Symonds, *English Furniture from Charles II to George II*, 1929, but an adequate general history does not exist. Ll. Jewitt, *The Ceramic Art of Great Britain*, 2 vols., 1878, is a good book; for books on goldsmiths' and silversmiths' work see above, p. 397, n. 2. M. A. Jourdain, *English Secular Embroidery* (1910) may be mentioned; for gardens it is best to use Marie Luise Gothein, *History of the,*

Garden Art, English tr., 2 vols., 1928, a work not limited to England.

There is a very good textbook of its subject in E. Walker, *History of Music in England*, 1907; and two successive volumes of *The Oxford History of Music*, though very different in plan and purpose, are valuable, vol. iii, *The Seventeenth Century*, by Sir Hubert Parry, 1907, and vol. iv, *The Age of Bach and Handel*, by J. A. Fuller-Maitland, 1902: they are not confined to England. For reference Sir George Grove's *Dictionary of Music and Musicians*, ed. H. C. Colles, 4th ed., 5 vols., 1940, is constantly useful. Among the editions of the musical works of the period the first place belongs to the series of the Purcell Society (1878–), which is collecting Purcell's works from the earlier editions and manuscripts. The best general guide is the *British Museum Catalogue of Printed Music, 1487–1800*, ed. W. Barclay Squire, 2 vols., 1912. R. North, *Memoirs of Musick*, ed. E. F. Rimbault, 1846, is an interesting book by the author of the *Lives of the Norths*; two other useful books are J. S. Bumpus, *History of English Cathedral Music*, vol. i, 1908, and *The Old Cheque-Book of the Chapel Royal*, ed. E. F. Rimbault, 1872.

SOCIAL LIFE

Our knowledge of manners and customs comes from all the more personal kinds of literature, letters, diaries, plays, romances, and biographies, and from scattered allusions in almost every kind of records, so that there is no possibility of systematically reviewing its sources. Contemporary books which seem to cover parts of the ground are not always what they seem. Thus a widely used book of etiquette, *The Rules of Civility*, 1671, is translated from a French original by Antoine de Courtin, and sets a new standard rather than describes manners as they were. The same may be true of cookery-books, which in this period seem to have been only for the well-to-do. A brief but useful sketch of most sides of this large residuary subject is given in the co-operative book *Social England*, ed. H. D. Traill, 2nd ed., vol. iv, 1903. The most important contemporary work on large parts of the subject is R. Blome, *The Gentleman's Recreation*, 1686. On special branches there are J. Strutt, *The Sports and Pastimes of the English People*, ed. J. C. Cox, 1903; J. P. Hore, *The History of Newmarket and the Annals of the Turf to the end of the Seventeenth*

Century, 3 vols., 1886; J. Ashton, *History of Gambling in England*, 1898; E. F. Robinson, *The Early History of Coffee Houses in England*, 1893; W. Notestein, *History of Witchcraft in England from 1558 to 1718* (1911). The accounts of foreign travellers in this period are not of much value. For French travellers see G. Ascoli, *La Grande Bretagne devant l'opinion française*, 2 vols., 1930. *The Travels of Cosmo III, Grand Duke of Tuscany*, 1821, describes a visit of 1669, but is chiefly interesting for the views which illustrate it. B. L. Muralt, a Swiss, visited England in the time of William III. His *Lettres sur les Anglais et les Français* were published in 1725 and in English as *Letters describing the Character and Customs of the English and French Nations* in 1726 with an English commentary. It is an amusing book, but Muralt really knew very little about England.

On education there are some excellent histories of particular institutions but few good general works. The relevant chapters of the *Cambridge History of English Literature* (see above, p. 451) supply the place of a textbook. F. Watson, *The Beginnings of Modern Subjects in England*, 1909; Katherine Lambley, *The Teaching and Cultivation of the French Language during Tudor and Stuart Times*, 1920; H. M. Maclachlan, *Education under the Clarendon Code*, 1931, are useful monographs. Dorothy Gardiner, *English Girlhood at School*, 1929, is a general account of female education. The history of the English universities in relation on the one hand to knowledge and on the other to national life remains to be written. There are rich materials, and from them have been made some scholarly special studies and some readable compilations, but that is all. During our period two strange characters kept diaries in Oxford, both of them valuable for the social life of the university and also for many other matters of wider interest, especially in the field of history. They may be read in *The Life and Times of Anthony Wood*, ed. A. Clark, 5 vols., 1891, which goes down to 1695, and *Remarks and Collections of Thomas Hearne*, 11 vols., 1885–1918. Personal materials are the basis of J. E. B. Mayor, *Cambridge under Queen Anne*, 1911. C. Wordsworth, *Scholae Academicae*, 1877, is still the best introduction to the university studies of the period. J. B. Mullinger, *The University of Cambridge*, vol. iii, 1911, which does not go beyond about 1670 is a much more solid work than Sir Charles Mallet, *History of the University of Oxford*, vol. ii, 1924. Sir J. E. Sandys, *History of Classical Scholarship*, vol. ii, 3rd ed., 1921, is a standard work, and

J. H. Monk, *Life of Bentley*, 2 vols., 1833, one of the best English biographies.

MAPS

The maps published during the period may be studied with the help of T. Chubb, *The Printed Maps in the Atlases of Great Britain and Ireland* (1927); Sir George Fordham, *Studies in Carto-Bibliography*, 1914, and *The Road-Books and Itineraries of Great Britain*, 1924.

LISTS OF THE HOLDERS OF CERTAIN OFFICES

Archbishops of Canterbury

1660   William Juxon.
1663   Gilbert Sheldon.
1677   William Sancroft.
1691   John Tillotson.
1694   Thomas Tenison.

Lord Chancellors and Keepers of the Great Seal

1658   Sir Edward Hyde, afterwards earl of Clarendon.
1667   Sir Orlando Bridgeman, lord keeper.
1672   Anthony, earl of Shaftesbury.
1673   Sir Heneage Finch, afterwards Lord Daventry, lord keeper.
1675   The same, now earl of Nottingham and lord chancellor.
1682   Sir Francis North, afterwards Lord Guilford, lord keeper.
1685   Sir George Jeffreys, afterwards Lord Jeffreys.
1689   Commissioners: Sir John Maynard, Sir Anthony Keck, Sir William Rawlinson.
1690   Sir John Trevor, Sir William Rawlinson, Sir George Hutchins.
1693   Sir John Somers, lord keeper.
1697   The same, now Lord Somers and lord chancellor.
1700   Sir Nathan Wright, lord keeper.
1705   William Cowper, afterwards Lord Cowper, lord keeper.
1707   The same, lord chancellor.
1710   Commissioners: Sir Thomas Trevor, Robert Tracy, John Scrope, Sir Simon Harcourt, afterwards Lord Harcourt, lord keeper.
1713   The same, lord chancellor.

Lord Treasurers

[Italics distinguish the names of the treasurers from those who held the office in commission.]

1660   Commissioners: Sir Edward Hyde; George Monck, afterwards duke of Albemarle; Thomas, earl of Southampton; John, Lord Robarts; Thomas, Lord Colepeper; General Edward Mountagu; Sir Edward Nicholas; Sir William Morice.
     Later, *Thomas, earl of Southampton.*
1667   Commissioners: George, duke of Albemarle; Anthony, Lord Ashley; Sir Thomas Clifford, Sir William Coventry, Sir John Duncombe.
1669   The same without Sir William Coventry.
1672   *Thomas, Lord Clifford.*
1673   *Thomas, Viscount Dunblane, afterwards earl of Danby.*

1679   Commissioners: Arthur, earl of Essex; Hon. Laurence Hyde, afterwards earl of Rochester; Sir John Ernley; Sir Edward Dering, Sidney Godolphin, afterwards Lord Godolphin.

Later, the same without the earl of Essex and with Sir Stephen Fox.

1684   The same without Sir Edward Dering and Sidney Godolphin.

Later, the same without Sir Stephen Fox but with Sir Dudley North and Henry Frederick Thynne.

Later, the same without the earl of Rochester, but with Lord Godolphin and Sir Stephen Fox.

1686   The same without Sir Dudley North and Thynne, but with John, Lord Belasyse and Henry, Lord Dover.

1689   Charles, earl of Monmouth; Henry, Lord Delamere; Sidney, Lord Godolphin; Sir Henry Capel; Richard Hampden.

1690   Sir John Lowther; Richard Hampden; Sir Stephen Fox; Thomas Pelham.

Later, the same with Lord Godolphin.

1691   The same without Sir John Lowther and Pelham, but with Charles Montague, afterwards earl of Halifax and Sir Edward Seymour.

1694   The same without Hampden and Sir Edward Seymour, but with Sir William Trumbull and John Smith.

1695   The same without Sir William Trumbull.

1696   The same with Sir Thomas Lyttelton.

1697   The same without Lord Godolphin but with Thomas Pelham.

1699   The same without Sir Thomas Lyttelton and Pelham, but with Ford, earl of Tankerville, and Hon. Henry Boyle, afterwards Lord Carleton.

Later, the same without Montague but with Richard Hill.

1700   The same without the earl of Tankerville but with Lord Godolphin.

1701   The same without Smith but with Thomas Pelham.

Later, the same without Lord Godolphin but with Charles, earl of Carlisle.

1702   *Sidney, Lord Godolphin, afterwards earl of Godolphin.*

1710   Commissioners: John, Earl Paulett; Robert Harley, afterwards earl of Oxford; Hon. Henry Paget; Sir Thomas Mansell; Robert Benson.

1711   *Robert, earl of Oxford.*

1714   *Charles, duke of Shrewsbury.*

Presidents of the Council

1679   Anthony, Lord Ashley.
1679   John, earl of Radnor.
1684   Laurence, earl of Rochester.
1685   George, marquis of Halifax.
1686   Robert, earl of Sunderland.
1689   Thomas, earl of Danby.
1699   Thomas, earl of Pembroke.
1701   Charles, duke of Somerset.
1702   Thomas, earl of Pembroke.

1708 John, Lord Somers.
1710 Laurence, earl of Rochester.
1711 John, duke of Buckinghamshire.

Lords Privy Seal

1660 William, Viscount Saye and Sele.
1661 John, Lord Robarts, afterwards earl of Radnor.
1669 Commissioners: Sir Edward Dering, Sir Thomas Strickland, Robert Milward.
1673 Arthur, earl of Anglesey.
1682 George, marquis of Halifax.
1685 Henry, earl of Clarendon.
      Later, commissioners: Robert, Viscount Teviot, Robert Philips, John Evelyn.
1686 Henry, Lord Arundel of Wardour.
1689 George, marquis of Halifax.
1690 Commissioners: William Cheney, Sir John Knatchbull, Sir William Pulteney.
1691 Thomas, earl of Pembroke.
1697 Commissioners: Sir Thomas Mompesson, Sir Charles Cotterell, James Tyrrell.
1699 John, Viscount Lonsdale.
1700 Ford, earl of Tankerville.
1701 Commissioners: Edward Southwell, Christopher Musgrave, James Vernon.
1702 John, marquis of Normanby, afterwards duke of Buckinghamshire.
1705 John, duke of Newcastle.
1711 John Robinson, bishop of Bristol, afterwards bishop of London.
1713 William, earl of Dartmouth.

Lord High Admirals

1660   James, duke of York.
1673–84   Various commissioners.
1685   King James II.
1689–1701 Various commissioners.
1702   Thomas, earl of Pembroke.
           Later, George, prince of Denmark.
1708   Thomas, earl of Pembroke.
1709–14   Various commissioners.

Secretaries of State

1660 Sir Edward Nicholas (south).   Sir William Morice (north).
1662 Sir Henry Bennet, afterwards
        Lord Arlington (south).
1668   Sir John Trevor (north).
1672   Henry Coventry (north till 1674,
                                          south 1674–80).

1674 Sir Joseph Williamson (north).
1679 Robert, earl of Sunderland (north till 1680, south 1680–1).
1680   Sir Leoline Jenkins (north till 1681, south 1681–4).
1681 Edward, Viscount Conway (north).
1683 Robert, earl of Sunderland (north till 1684, south 1684–8).
1684   Sidney Godolphin (north). Later, Charles, earl of Middleton (north till 1688; south 1688).
1688 Richard, Viscount Preston (north).
1689 Charles, earl of Shrewsbury (south).   Daniel, earl of Nottingham (north).
1690 Henry, Viscount Sidney, afterwards earl of Romney (north).
1692 Sir John Trenchard (north till 1693, south 1693–5).
1693   Charles, earl of Shrewsbury (north 1693–5, south 1695–8).
1695 Sir William Trumbull (north).
1697 James Vernon (north 1697–8; sole secretary 1698–9 and in 1700; south 1700–2).
1699   Edward, earl of Jersey (south).
1700 Sir Charles Hedges (north 1700–4, south 1704–6).
1701   Charles, earl of Manchester (south).
1072   Daniel, earl of Nottingham (south).
1704   Robert Harley, afterwards earl of Oxford (north).
1706 Charles, earl of Sunderland (south).
1707   Henry Boyle, afterwards Lord Carleton (north).
1710 William, Lord Dartmouth (south).   Henry St. John, afterwards Viscount Bolingbroke (north 1710–13, south 1713–14).
1713 William Bromley (north).

INDEX

Aberdeen, 263.
Abergavenny, 182 n.
Abingdon, James Bertie, 1st earl of, 139.
Absenteeism in Ireland, 315.
Acadia, see Nova Scotia.
Adda, papal nuncio, 54.
Addison, Joseph, 226, 355, 357–9, 361, 365, 370, 382, 408.
Administrative offices during the French war, 180.
Administrative system, 13–17.
Admiralty, the, 110, 186, 251.
Adventure Galley, privateer, 330.
Africa, west coast of, 331–3, 349.
African Company (Royal Adventurers Trading into Africa), 332.
African Merchant, ship, 285.
Agriculture, 37–39; in Scotland, 265; in Ireland, 299.
Aire, 220.
Albemarle, Arnold Joost van Keppel, 1st earl of, land grant to, 189.
Albemarle, George Monck, 1st duke of, 3–6, 64–67, 266, 339.
Aldrich, Henry, 384, 391, 405.
Alicante, 215, 219.
Aliens Act (1705), 287, 288.
Allin, adm. Sir Thomas, 64.
Almanza, battle of, 215.
Alost, 174.
Althorp, 180.
Altona, convention of, 163.
Amazon, the, 236.
America, North, Scots settlers in, 281–2.
America, South, 325.
American Colonies, North, 333–48.
Amsterdam, 84, 134.
Anatomy, 376.
Anderson, Robert, 42.
Anglesey, Arthur Annesley, 1st earl of, his library, 15.
Anglo-French commercial treaty (1713), 237–8.
Anglo-Saxon language, 381–2.
Anne, queen: as princess, 134, 139; and question of succession, 146, 190; and Marlborough, 183; account of, 220–2; queen Anne's bounty, 221; personal distaste for her ministers, 225; estrangement from duchess of Marlborough, 225; and electress Sophia, 240; and old pretender, 241; and Bolingbroke and Oxford, 246–7; her considerable influence, 252; 'touching for the evil', 252; and the cabinet council, 255–6; and Scotland,

285, 287; and Ireland, 311, 314; communion plate presented to Mohawks by, 346; at Oxford, 372; illness and death, 245, 248.
Annesley, Arthur, see Anglesey.
Antwerp, 70, 87, 213, 218.
Apothecaries, 419.
Arbuthnot, John, 258.
Architecture, 388–96.
Argyle, Archibald Campbell, 1st duke of, 277.
Argyle, Archibald Campbell, 9th earl of, 118, 120, 273, 274.
Argyle, Archibald Campbell, marq. of, 266.
Argyle, John Campbell, 2nd duke of, 248.
Arlington, Henry Bennet, 1st earl of, 56, 63, 71, 72, 75, 77, 80.
Army, the: pay due to Monck's army under Charles II, 4, 6; James II's (1688), 132; under James II, 122, 168; under William III, 138, 151–2, 168–9, 178; the Crown and parliament and, 152; growth of, 167–9; operations in the French war, 167–74; reduction after the peace, 188; compulsory service, 261; Scottish professional soldiers, 264; in Ireland, 305, 307; Irish soldiers transported to France, 309, 315.
Arras, 220.
Arundell, Henry, 3rd baron Arundell of Wardour, 123.
Ashby v. White, 254.
Ashley, Anthony Ashley Cooper, 1st baron, see Shaftesbury.
Ashmole, Elias, 414.
Asiento, the, 221, 250.
Astronomer royal, 412.
Astronomy, 373.
Ath, 174.
Athlone, 308, 309.
Athlone, earl of, see Ginkel.
Atholl, John Murray, 1st marq. of, 277.
Attainder, Act of, 306.
Aughrim, 309.
Augsburg, league of (1686), 128, 134 n.
Aurungzeb, 350.
Avaux, count d', 134.
Aylesbury Men, The, 254.

Bach, J. S., 407.
Bacon, Nathaniel, 347.
Baden, margrave of, 208.
Baden, peace of, 243.

GENEALOGICAL TABLES
AND MAPS

II. THE SPANISH SUCCESSION

[The names of some persons not mentioned in the present volume are omitted. Those of the claimants to the succession are in small capitals, the kings of Spain in heavy type.]

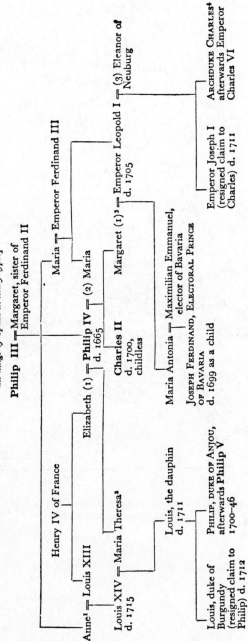

[1] Anne, on her marriage, renounced her claims, which thus passed to her sister, Maria.

[2] Maria Theresa, on her marriage, made a conditional renunciation, which Louis XIV held to be ineffective because the conditions were not fulfilled.

[3] Margaret was recognized in her father's will as heiress after Charles II and any descendants he might have. The claim of Joseph Ferdinand was derived from her.

[4] Charles's claim was derived, through his father, from Maria, the daughter of Philip III.

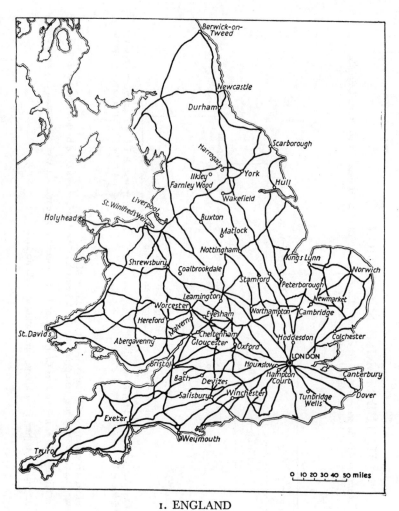

1. ENGLAND

Showing main roads and towns mentioned in the text

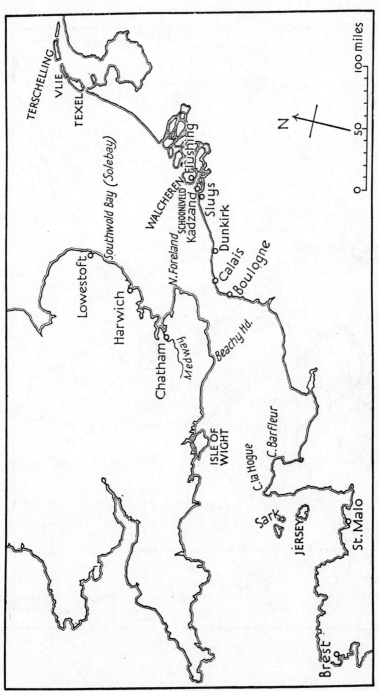

3b. NAVAL OPERATIONS OF THE DUTCH AND FRENCH WARS

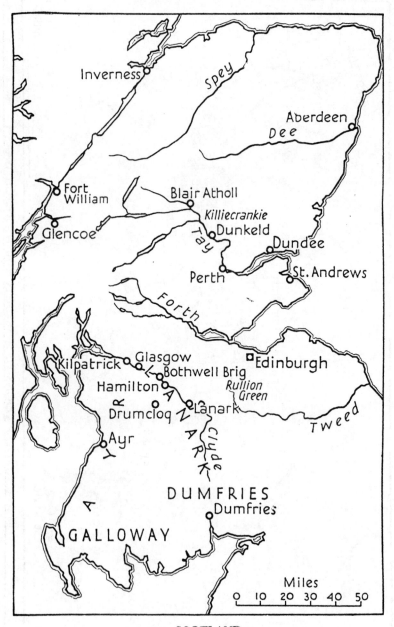

Inverness

Spey

Aberdeen
Dee

Fort
William

Blair Atholl

Killiecrankie
Dunkeld

Glencoe

Tay

Dundee

Perth

St. Andrews

Forth

Kilpatrick

Glasgow

Edinburgh

Bothwell Brig

Hamilton

*Rullion
Green*

Drumcloq

Lanark

Tweed

Ayr

L A N A R K

Clyde

D U M F R I E S

Dumfries

A Y R

GALLOWAY

Miles

0   10   20   30   40   50

4*a.* SCOTLAND

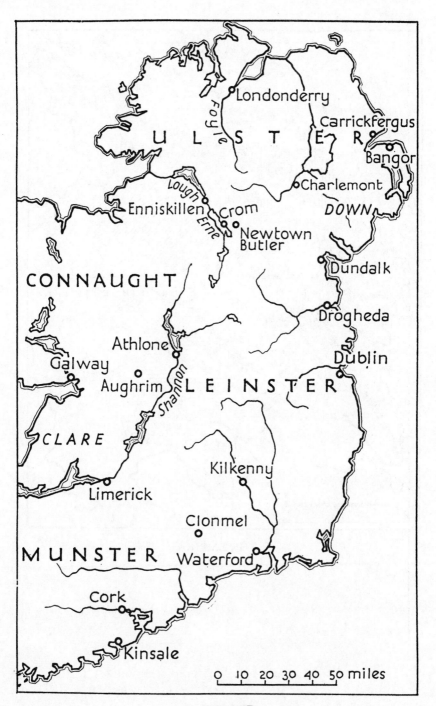

4b. IRELAND

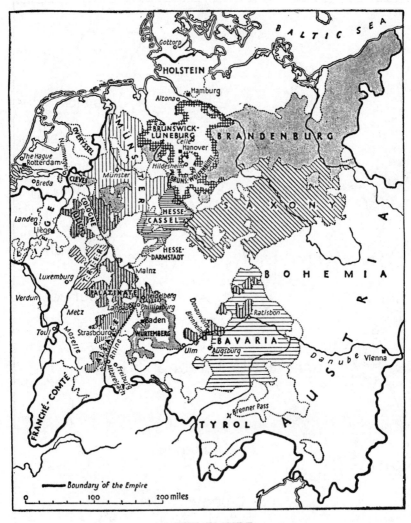

BALTIC SEA

Gottorp

HOLSTEIN

•Hamburg

Altona°

BRUNSWICK-
LUNEBURG
•*Celle*
•Hanover
Hildesheim
BRUNS-WOLFENBÜTTEL

BRANDENBURG

OVERYSSEL

MÜNSTER

The Hague•
Rotterdam•
Nymwegen

•*Breda*

CLEVES

Münster

COLOGNE

S A X O N Y

LIÈGE

Landeg•
Liège•

HESSE-
CASSEL

B O H E M I A

TRIER

HESSE-
DARMSTADT

Luxemburg•

•*Mainz*

A
U
S
T
R
I
A

Verdun•

PALATINATE

Heidelberg
Langhausen
Phillipsburg

Ratisbon•

Metz•

•Baden

Donauwörth
Blenheim

Rhine

WÜRTEMBERG

Toul•

Strasbourg•

Moselle

Freiburg
Hüningen

Ulm•
•*Augsburg*

BAVARIA

Danube Vienna•

FRANCHÉ-COMTÉ

✗ *Brenner Pass*

T Y R O L

A U S T R I A

———— Boundary of the Empire

0   100   200 miles

5. THE EMPIRE

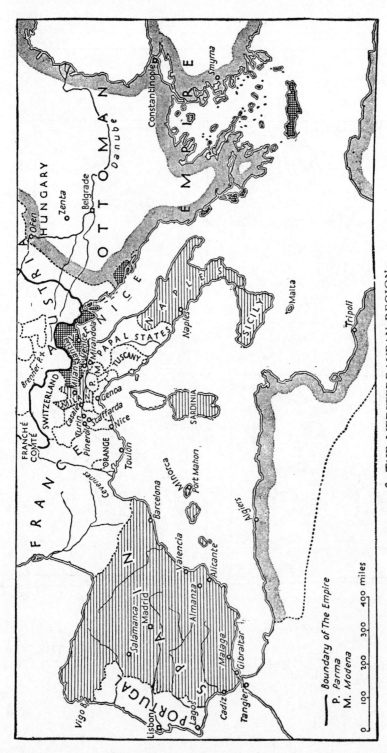

6. THE MEDITERRANEAN REGION

[The horizontal hatching indicates Spanish, and the cross hatching Venetian territory.]

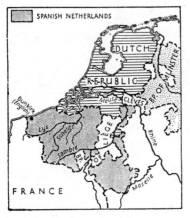

a. Frontiers in 1660

b. Frontiers of 1668—Treaty of Aachen (Aix-la-Chapelle)

e. Battles and Sieges, 1703-12

f. Barrier Treaty, 1709

7. THE LOW

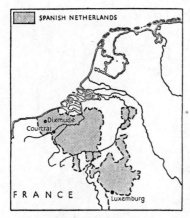

c. Frontiers of 1678—
Treaty of Nymwegen

d. Battles and Sieges, 1689-97

g. Barrier Treaty, 1713

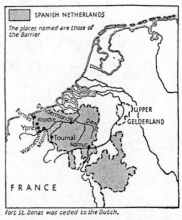

h. Frontiers of 1713 (Treaty of
Utrecht). Barrier Treaty, 1715

COUNTRIES

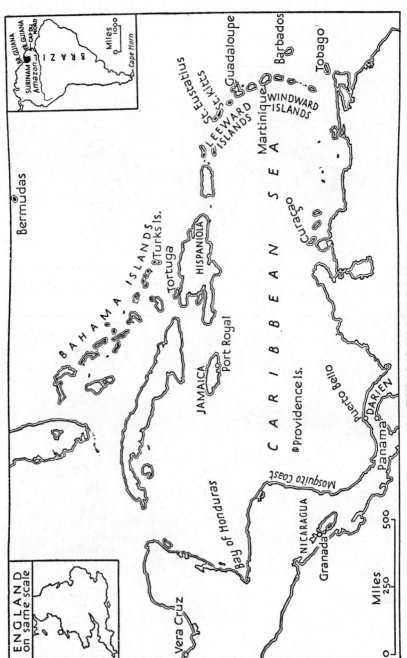

8a. THE CARIBBEAN REGION

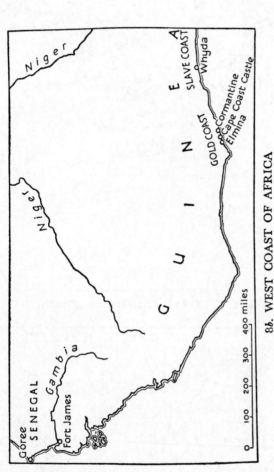

8b. WEST COAST OF AFRICA

9a. THE NORTH AMERICAN COLONIES

9b. THE EAST INDIES